The teaching of English

The teaching of English

FROM THE SIXTEENTH CENTURY TO 1870

Ian Michael

VISITING PROFESSOR, UNIVERSITY OF LONDON
INSTITUTE OF EDUCATION

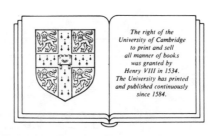

The right of the
University of Cambridge
to print and sell
all manner of books
was granted by
Henry VIII in 1534.
The University has printed
and published continuously
since 1584.

CAMBRIDGE UNIVERSITY PRESS

CAMBRIDGE

LONDON   NEW YORK   NEW ROCHELLE

MELBOURNE   SYDNEY

Published by the Press Syndicate of the University of Cambridge
The Pitt Building, Trumpington Street, Cambridge CB2 IRP
32 East 57th Street, New York, NY 10022, USA
10 Stamford Road, Oakleigh, Melbourne 3166, Australia

First published 1987

Printed in Great Britain by the University Press, Cambridge

British Library cataloguing in publication data
Michael, Ian
The teaching of English:
from the sixteenth century to 1870.
1. English language – Study and teaching – Great Britain – History
I. Title
420'.7'1041   LB1576

Library of Congress cataloguing in publication data
Michael, Ian, 1915-
The teaching of English.
Bibliography.
Includes index.
1. English philology – Study and teaching – History.
I. Title.
PE65.M5 1987   420'.7   86-20704

CU

ISBN 0 521 24196 0

SE

CONTENTS

TABLES

PREFACE

This book is an enquiry into the early history of the teaching of English, to English speakers, in Britain, with some reference to America. Its intention and limitations are stated in the first chapter.

It is a pleasure to express particular gratitude to the trustees of the Leverhulme Foundation for their assistance through the award of an Emeritus Fellowship.

Anyone whose work touches on the history of the English language owes a debt to Dr R.C. Alston. It is not too much to say that his industry and persistence in producing *A Bibliography of the English language* and the facsimile editions of early texts over the imprint of the Scolar Press have opened up important areas of study, the very possibility of which had scarcely been glimpsed before.

I am much indebted also to the staff of many public and university libraries for their tolerance in responding to enquiries of unavoidable but timetaking vagueness, and to many antiquarian booksellers, from whose catalogues I have acquired more information than they have received orders from me.

I am especially grateful to Professor L.C. Knights and to Mrs Knights for their constant support and to Dr A.K. Pugh and to Dr. Edwina Burness, who also have read part of the book in draft. I have received valuable help and advice from Vivian Salmon, Joyce Broomhall, Dr E. Jennifer Monaghan, Dr T. O'Raifearteagh, John P. Marmion and Kenneth Coram.

It would be interesting to study the ways in which authors express in public the gratitude they owe to their spouses. The attempt to express it is an honourable convention, and my debt and my gratitude are too great for me to wish to break it. But the purpose of the convention is not altogether clear. My wife does not need to read a preface in order to know how I feel, and the reader receives no useful information unless he knows us both – in which case he does not need it. Some authors conceal their feelings within an abbreviated Latin dedication of uncertain meaning and direction, but it is best, I think, to admit the inherent selfishness of all books of this kind (a selfishness that words alone cannot make good) and to say thank-you in a single English word.

IAN MICHAEL
Bristol

CHAPTER ONE

The enquiry:
scope, method, texts

The enquiry

The intentions and limitations of this enquiry are an essential part of it: they do not belong to a preface, even though they are expressed in personal terms. The enquiry has two sources. I have always been puzzled by statements that English is a relatively recent addition to the curriculum:

1983 '[It is surprising] how recently English has entered the curriculum . . . Our very notion of literacy – of a functional command of reading and writing – is a development of the nineteenth century.'[1]

1978 'English is a comparatively new subject.'[2]

1974 'A young subject, less than one hundred years old . . . It is not till the end of the nineteenth century that there was anything even approximating what we now roughly subsume under the heading "the study of English".'[3]

1919 'Of conscious and direct teaching of English the past affords little sign.'[4]

The second line of thought was also interrogative. I was surprised that historians of education, whose work on the institutional, social and legislative aspects of their subject was sometimes detailed and vivid, said so little about what happened in the classroom itself. It seemed unlikely that there was no evidence, and even more unlikely that such evidence could be dull. These two lines of thought coalesced into an intention to see what early evidence there was for the teaching of English in school. I am interested in what teachers did, in their intentions and in the methods by which they tried to realise them. My emphasis is bound to be on teaching more than on learning, because that is where, historically, the emphasis has been. This book is therefore the product of a singlehanded journey of exploration. I must stress its exploratory nature, not defensively, but because the type and quantity of the evidence could not be known

[1] Colin MacCabe, *The Guardian*, 28 February.
[2] Peter Gordon and Denis Lawton, *Curriculum change in the nineteenth and twentieth centuries*, p. 80.
[3] Arthur N. Applebee, *Tradition and reform in the teaching of English: a history*, pp. ix, 5.
[4] *The teaching of English in England* (Newbolt Report), para. 18, the first in a 'historical retrospect'.

beforehand. The results of the enquiry have been affected not only by limitations on time, money and competence but also by the necessarily raw condition of most of the evidence. The explorer returns after a long absence with bottles, boxes and bags. On arrival he exclaims, in a variety of modest phrases, 'Look what I've found!', but it takes him longer to sort out his findings than it did to collect them, and he needs the help of many specialists before it can be known whether he has brought anything useful. The more he analyses his material the more he feels that if only he could make the journey again in the light of the knowledge he now has his miscellaneous collection could be made orderly, coherent and complete.

The enquiry is restricted to the three centuries before 1870. It is not perverse to stop it just at the date when many people suppose English teaching to have begun. The year 1870 is a convenient mark for the culmination of what could be described as the first modern phase in the teaching of English, and Edwin A. Abbott and J.R. Seeley, in the dedication of their *English Lessons for English People* (1871), considered that 'the present seems to be a critical moment for English instruction'. To study the subject after 1870 would require a different approach and different methods, appropriate to the increasing quantity and diversity of evidence. Such a study needs to be made, in more detail than has yet been attempted. I have sought evidence mainly from textbooks and from a certain amount of general writing on education which bears directly on the teaching of English. The volume of evidence has turned out be so great that the textbooks, standing at first just at the centre of the area to be explored, have come to mark its limits, beyond which stand biographies, local and school histories, local newspapers, periodical literature, mid-nineteenth-century educational journalism and reports of government committees: all awaiting the comprehensive investigation for which I hope I am helping to prepare the way. I have chosen to cover the textbook material fairly thoroughly, over the whole period. To shorten the chronological range of the enquiry would spoil one of its main purposes. To have brought into it, as samples, a little evidence from all the relevant areas would have made it broader but too superficial. If all the relevant material were to have been covered thoroughly the enquiry would have collapsed.

A survey which includes the teaching of reading, spelling, rhetoric, logic, composition, grammar, elocution, poetry, fiction, drama, over a period of 300 years necessarily touches on important social and cultural issues. The teachers are figures in an enormous landscape, which I have not attempted even to sketch in. Neither the reader nor I would take any pleasure in a shuffle of abstractions and influences, named and then dropped. Even to outline – particularly to outline – with discrimination such an extensive background (not just a few trees in a park) for these very varied teachers would require a rare kind of scholarship and skill.

So little is known of the work of these early teachers that I have given a lot of detail, especially in direct quotation, but not, I hope, an oppressive amount. I have wanted the teachers to speak for themselves whenever possible. They are authentic and vivid. If they are longwinded I have cut them. Provided they are quoted fairly they present more accurately than could be done by any summary their intentions and their methods. I have also followed the teachers in discussing what they considered important and what they found difficult, even if sometimes we are impatient with their preoccupations. Their detailed and at times emotional concern with the functions of letters and syllables is an aspect of the history of pedagogics and of linguistics which has not yet been studied in detail, and even chapters 2 and 3 of the present work, which express some of this concern, are no more than an introduction.

During the eighteenth and nineteenth centuries there is a close relationship, sometimes supportive, sometimes crossgrained, between British and American textbook writers. *The New England Primer* was first published about 1690; the earliest American spelling-book, *An Epitome of English Orthography* in 1697; the earliest American grammar of English in 1773: Thomas Byerley's *A Plain and Easy Introduction* (Alston IV, 189; I, 315). But textbooks originating in America were rare until the 1790s. The majority were imported from Britain; many were reprinted in America. The earliest American printing of an English spelling-book seems to have been the 1716 Boston edition of William Thompson's *The Child's Guide to the English Tongue*, and of a grammar the 1775 Philadelphia edition of Lowth's *A Short Introduction* (Alston IV, 284; I, 228). The present enquiry draws on much of the known American material before 1800, but some unique copies have not been consulted because they are too frail even to photograph. After 1800 the number of relevant texts increases rapidly and it has not been possible to use their evidence in a way which is systematically representative. But as American material grows more abundant it also grows more distinctive. I have therefore drawn as fully as I can on accessible American works and on a few early nineteenth-century texts from American libraries. American texts are even less known in Britain than are early British texts in America. The small number which are mentioned here may encourage more detailed study: they are not an adequate base for generalisation.

The enquiry is an enquiry, not a tract. I am not seeking to show that what teachers of English do now has been thought of before; nor that our predecessors used methods which we ought to adopt. I comment often on particular methods and on the work of particular teachers, but I am concerned with change more than with estimates of progress. I am not looking at the past in order to rebuke, or to encourage, the present; but I believe that most of us find that our teaching has greater depth and more interest, for us and often for our pupils, if we have a picture of what earlier generations were trying to do, and some awareness of our professional roots and of the variety of soils through which these roots strike. Such considerations, however, are less important than the pleasure, which it is pointless to analyse, of entering imaginatively a little way into the mind of someone doing work which seems to resemble your own (though how close the resemblance it is not always easy to say) in circumstances which are very different (though how different it is, again, not easy to say). I like the mixture of surprise, recognition and sympathy with which I read about George Moore, a country schoolmaster in Massachusetts, who wrote in his school journal for 25 December 1828: 'Happened to think that today is Christmas, but saw no one taking any notice of it, and thought, if I did, I should appear rather off, and so let it pass. Informed scholars for the first time that *composition* would be required of them weekly.'[5]

Criteria: skills in English

The subject English is notoriously difficult to delimit even today, and before questions can be asked about its historical development certain problems of method have to be resolved. If questions about evidence relate solely to activities which in the twentieth century are considered to be components of English, for instance composition, it would seem (in that example) that this branch of English was first taught early in the nineteenth century, when the first textbooks appeared referring to composition by that name. Such a conclusion would be false. What we call composition was taught, in English, in seventeenth- and eighteenth-century schools as part of a subject called rhetoric and through the writing of themes. Obviously enough our search must be for relevant activities, whatever they are called. Activities which are components of twentieth-century English teaching can be identified without difficulty when they are found in the past, even if they have an unfamiliar name; but we cannot assume that twentieth-

---

[5] Quoted by William J. Gilmore, 'Elementary literacy on the eve of the industrial revolution: trends in rural New England, 1760–1830', *Proceedings of the American Antiquarian Society*, 92.1, April 1982, 109.

century activities are the only ones to have been components of the subject. There may well have been activities, perhaps called English, perhaps not, which were components of the subject but now are not. What the enquirer needs is criteria of relevance more general than specific activities and more permanent than their names. Such criteria are those often used nowadays in an attempt to set limits wide enough to encompass the range of activities within the present subject English, but not so wide that they cease to be limits. These criteria are the four skills which the activities are intended to develop: expressing yourself in speech and in writing, in your mother tongue; understanding (in a very broad sense of the term); and judging what you hear and read.[6]

These criteria enable us to decide, for example, the relevance of translation into and out of Latin; of logic and rhetoric, taught in English and Latin in seventeenth- and eighteenth-century schools; of textbooks of memory-training throughout most of the period. They do, however, still leave uncertain the status of the teaching of reading, spelling, pronunciation and handwriting. Although reading is a skill preliminary to almost all subjects, not just to English, it has always been so closely linked to the teaching of English that it would be strange to ignore it. It is in fact to the teaching of reading and spelling that *English*, as the name of a subject, is first applied: by Francis Clement in *The Petie Schole*, 1587, who includes in his preface 'a word or two with the english teacher'. The relevance of reading and spelling is further strengthened in two ways. The textbooks which are evidence for *how* children were taught to read are also evidence for much of *what* they were first given to read; and the teaching of children how to read was for a long time inseparable from, and sometimes identified with, teaching them to spell. One of the unexpected products of this enquiry is the abundant evidence relating to reading and spelling and to the complex difficulties with which the teachers were struggling. The teaching of pronunciation arises, usually indirectly, in efforts to teach the sounds of the letters and the division of syllables, in the organisation of spelling-lists by phonetic criteria and in the teaching of elocution. The teaching of handwriting, although by analogy with spelling it might be considered a basic component of English, is excluded from the enquiry except in so far as some copybooks provide small fragments of literary experience. In neither past nor present practice has handwriting had the quasi-linguistic status acquired by spelling through its methodological links with reading and its practical links with etymology.

[6] Cf. Department of Education and Science, *English 5 to 16*, HMSO, 1984.

Treating the subject historically under the two headings expression and understanding (or, as I prefer to call it, interpretation) fails, however, to accommodate grammar. Grammar and linguistic study generally are, like rhetoric, relevant both to interpretation and to expression. Grammar is largely concerned with structure. In seeking to understand what we read we need to perceive its structure; in expressing ourselves we are constantly using our knowledge of the structure of the language, especially when fluency falters and we need to exercise conscious control. But the teaching of grammar has been until recently so autonomous an aspect of English teaching that it would be misleading to divide the study of its development between expressive and interpretative skills, as is just possible in the study of rhetoric. This enquiry is therefore organised in terms of four skills: reading and spelling; interpretation; expression, including performance skills; linguistic control. These divisions and their names are not wholly satisfactory, but none would be. 'Interpretation' may seem a pretentious term in this connection, but it is a reminder, as 'comprehension' and 'understanding' are not, that the pupil's response to what he or she reads is not solely intellectual, and is very far from being mechanical; it is a selective response, influenced by the pupil's feelings, and it entails a measure, however small, of personal judgment.

Texts

The enquiry is based on a study of textbooks, but it is not always easy to say what a textbook is. The difficulty is important because I have undertaken a very tentative quantitative analysis of the material, and this is necessarily affected by marginal judgments about what is relevant. By a textbook I mean a book used by pupils in class; or a book read out of school in preparation for work to be done in class; or a book used by teacher or parent for practical guidance; or a manual of self-instruction. I have recorded all the British texts about which I have any information, even if no copies now exist, or if they exist but I have not seen them. I have attempted to categorise the texts, but it is impossible to do so satisfactorily. Many textbooks contain material relating to more than one of the four skills. A spelling-book may contain fables for the children to read and grammar for them to learn by heart; a grammar may contain lists of the figures of speech and exercises in composition. Nevertheless, if any analysis is to be attempted, some categorisation must be attempted. I have therefore allotted each British title to one of fourteen categories, showing the type to which it primarily, if not exclusively, belongs. Table 1 shows the distribution of these texts (in their categories, here conflated into ten groups) over six periods of fifty years between 1571 and 1870: periods which coincide as well as any would with phases in the development of English teaching. Table 1 records also a number of British texts dating from before 1571 or after 1870 which are included in the discussion but not in the analyses, and the small number of American texts that I have consulted. The enquiry is based on about 2700 texts, of which about 70 per cent have been consulted.

Tables 2–5 show in more detail the distribution, in five-year periods, of the texts recorded in groups 1, 2, 5 and 7. For the periods up to 1770 the texts recorded in group 4, nearly all of them rhetorics, have been included in both Table 3 and Table 5. This is an attempt to allow for the fact that rhetoric covered both interpretative and expressive skills.

With one exception these analyses, though rough, will permit some generalisation. There is, however, a particular difficulty over literary texts. Children's literature has been much studied, but neither the books themselves nor their modern critics give much guidance as to the extent, if any, to which an individual book might have been used in school. We do not at present know enough about classroom practice to distinguish on any general grounds children's books which are likely to have been used in school. We know that pupils were more likely to study poetry than prose: it was shorter, more difficult, and more rewarding to learn by heart. We think that in the classical schools it was a common assumption during the whole of the period that reading English literature was a proper, but private and domestic, part of a young gentleman's upbringing (and more so of a young lady's). But we know also that the 'English schools', in contrast to the grammar schools, gave considerable attention to the reading of English literature, even if there was little formal teaching of it until the second half of the eighteenth century. We suppose that as books became less expensive children would sometimes, perhaps often, bring to school some book to read on their own, to copy, to memorise, to be influenced by. I have therefore judged each literary text individually: from the implications of its title, from its preface, from what is known about the author, from other external evidence.

Over the period as a whole, teachers and the writers of textbooks paid more attention to linguistic training than to the teaching of interpretation. But we may not yet be able to see correctly the balance between these two activities. Textbooks dealing with language are self-evidently textbooks; grammars especially attract the attention of bibliographers and are easily identified. Works of literature, whether anthologies, selections from a

Table 1. *Chronological distribution of texts*

		1571–1620	1621–1670	1671–1720	1721–1770	1771–1820	1821–1870	Total recorded	Total consulted	% consulted
1 (S, RE)	T	15	25	83	69	185	339	716		
	C	9	21	55	48	74	192		399	
	%	60	84	67	70	40	57			57
2 (RA, RH, RS)	T	6	1	7	34	173	325	546		
	C	6	1	7	30	138	209		391	
	%	100	100	100	88	80	64			72
3 (P)	T	–	–	–	7	55	28	90		
	C	–	–	–	7	44	20		71	
	%				100	80	71			79
4 (B)	T	7	8	8	15	25	18	81		
	C	7	8	7	13	21	14		70	
	%	100	100	88	87	84	78			86
5 (G)	T	3	11	15	49	204	377	659		
	C	3	10	15	47	158	193		426	
	%	100	91	100	96	77	51			65
6 (La, D)	T	2	–	2	15	34	56	109		
	C	2	–	2	13	25	25		67	
	%	100		100	87	76	46			61
7 (Ex)	T	3	1	7	9	27	42	89		
	C	1	1	6	7	22	28		65	
	%	33	100	86	78	81	67			73
8 (C)	T	–	1	6	6	17	7	37	35	
9 (Ed)	T	3	9	12	19	33	44	120	120	
10 (Lo)	T	3	5	2	6	7	5	28	27	

	T	C	%
British total, 1571–1870	2475	1671	68
Texts before 1571	9	8	
Texts after 1870	41	18	
American texts	183	183	
Overall total	2708	1880	69

T Number of texts recorded
C Number of texts consulted
% Percentage of recorded texts consulted

Group	Category code	
1	S	Spelling, excluding orthographical reform; dictation; elementary punctuation; exercises in false spelling.
	RE	Elementary reading.
2	RA	Anthologies; single-author texts; readers not in series; copybooks.
	RH	Books primarily for home reading but perhaps used in school.
	RS	Readers in series
3	P	Performance; elocutionary and dramatic texts; pronunciation; memory.
4	B	*Belles lettres*; rhetoric; criticism; prosody; history of literature.
5	G	Grammar; exercises in false syntax; advanced punctuation.
6	La	Language; vocabulary; orthographical reform; etymology; history of the English language.
	D	Dictionaries used in school.
7	Ex	Written expression; oral expression when distinguished from performance; debate.
8	C	Compendia.
9	Ed	Educational texts relating to English teaching.
10	Lo	Logic: texts likely to have been used in school.

Table 2. *Texts recorded in group 1: spelling and elementary reading*[1]

[1] The vertical axis represents the number of new texts published in each of the five-year periods into which the horizontal axis is divided.

single writer, or individual novels or plays, are not necessarily textbooks. They become textbooks if they are used in school. They are not so readily identified by their titles and they do not show up in a bibliography as clearly as linguistic texts. Inspection is necessary, and not always sufficient, to establish their status. Many more works will have to be examined from this point of view before we can assess the volume of textbook material available for the teaching of interpretation. I have not seen enough of such books to be at all sure about the balance, especially during the nineteenth century, between the teaching of language and the teaching of interpretation. I have no doubt that the figures for group 2 (literary texts) are understated.

Textual conventions

The authors' spelling, punctuation, capitals and emphases have been kept throughout, except that long *s* and consonantal *i* and *u* have been

Table 3. *Texts recorded in group 2: literary texts (including rhetorics to 1770)*[1]

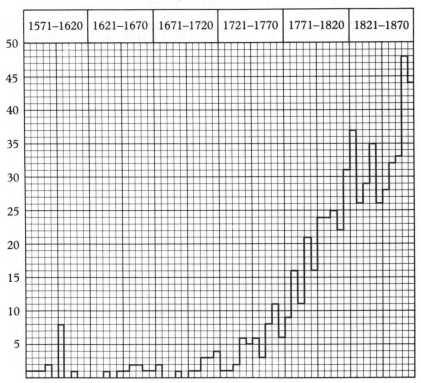

[1] The vertical axis represents the number of new texts published in each of the five-year periods into which the horizontal axis is divided.

modernised. Anonymous works are cited in the text by title and date; otherwise only the author's name and the date of the work are given. Bibliography 1 has been arranged accordingly, so that the author's name and the date of the earliest known edition are prominent. If a work is quoted from an edition later than the first, both dates are given in the text: the earlier one to direct the reader to the correct entry in the bibliography, the later one to show him which edition has been quoted. Short references have been incorporated within the text: I hope the reader's eye can pass as rapidly over a bracketed page reference as over an index number.

The representation of spelling and of the division of syllables has been standardised. The printers' practice varies in ways which are not important but add a complication to what already makes awkward reading. I have therefore in all cases separated letters by a hyphen, letters and syllables by a

Table 4. *Texts recorded in group 5: grammar*[1]

1571–1620	1621–1670	1671–1720	1721–1770	1771–1820	1821–1870

[1] The vertical axis represents the number of new texts published in each of the five-year periods into which the horizontal axis is divided.

comma, and syllables by a semi-colon, as: *m-a-n, man; d-a, da; r-i-n, rin: mandarin.*

Unless the context gives it another reference 'the period' means the period covered by this enquiry, and references to the 'first' appearance of some feature relate only to this body of texts.

Bibliographies 1-3 include a small number of works discovered after these tables had been compiled.

Table 5. *Texts recorded in group 7: written expression*
(including rhetorics to 1770)[1]

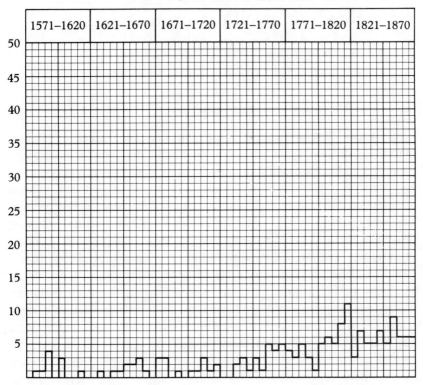

[1] The vertical axis represents the number of new texts published in each of the five-year periods into which the horizontal axis is divided.

CHAPTER TWO

Reading, spelling, pronunciation: the elements

Introduction

The historical development of the teaching of reading is usually described in terms of method: alphabetic, syllabic, phonetic, phonic, look-and-say. Even though the terms are imprecise, such an analysis may sometimes be appropriate for the end of the nineteenth century and for the first decades of the twentieth, but it is not relevant to the period discussed in this chapter. The early teachers, of course, had their methods, but they did not follow, or discuss, a Method. The evidence cited in this chapter shows, perhaps surprisingly, how varied their approaches were. Their central concern was the relation between the teaching of reading and the teaching of spelling. At no time was there complete agreement as to how the two skills should be related, and during much of the period there was little conception of them as separate skills. Until well into the nineteenth century the dominant view was that reading was learnt through spelling, which should therefore precede it; but in fact the early stages of both processes were taught in such close relationship that they cannot be distinguished. There were two main reasons for the dominance of the view that reading should be learnt through spelling. The first was the belief that complex material was most easily learnt if it had been broken down into its smallest parts, which were then learnt and recombined in order: letters were studied first, then syllables, then words, then sentences. There was great emphasis therefore on the individual letters (their names, their sounds) and on syllables, which were classified by the number of letters in them, by the sounds of their vowels, and by the position of their consonants. Words were listed, to be read and spelt, in a variety of ways but especially by the number of syllables in them. In both reading and spelling the attention of teacher and pupil was concentrated on the letters: their sounds, the order in which they occurred, and the ways in which they could properly be grouped in syllables.

Emphasis on the syllable is particularly marked (and to us particularly strange) in the practice of dividing a word into its component syllables in obedience to a number of rules. This practice, a stage in the teaching of reading but frequently identified with spelling, became a major concern of teachers about 1675. Its importance began to decline a hundred years later, and the technique had been abandoned by 1820. At the same time dictation, previously little used, became popular as a means of teaching spelling, and the lists of isolated syllables disappeared. Spelling and reading were becoming more separate, and the view, explicit at intervals since the middle of the seventeenth century, that reading should be taught without spelling, was now more frequently expressed.

The second reason for making reading dependent on spelling was the assumption, made by nearly all teachers, that short things were easier to learn than long ones. This too led teachers of reading to follow the sequence letter, syllable, word. It was only occasionally pointed out that a mono syllable like *cough* was more difficult to read and to spell than a word of five syllables like *examination*.

About 1800 the belief that reading was dependent on spelling weakened, but it never died. The few who questioned it did so on the grounds that complex things whose wholeness and distinctiveness were striking to the eye, such as a material object (especially a human being or an animal), a pictured object, an ideograph or a word, were apprehended as wholes and could be 'learnt' without being first analysed into their smallest components. Although this view was not then new, it was first expressed in relation to the teaching of reading by a few individuals during the middle of the seventeenth century. It slowly gained strength during the latter part of the eighteenth century, from the 1770s, and by the 1850s was generally familiar but not generally applied. Closely related to this emphasis on wholeness was the idea of context: words were more easily learnt if they were presented either in the context of other, related, words or in the setting of a picture. The two ideas had met, and had been almost indistinguishable, in the work of Comenius. One practical expression of the reliance on context was a change, about the middle of the eighteenth century, in the design of spelling-books. Hitherto the first part of a spelling-book, containing perhaps 10,000 words in graded lists, had usually been followed by simple reading-passages. The change was to alternate lists and passages, so that words of the same (it was supposed) degree of difficulty were met at the same time in spelling-lists and reading-passages. About 1820 the further step was taken of deriving the spelling-list from the vocabulary of a reading-passage.

Pronunciation, which naturally arose in the teaching of reading as a performance skill, arose also in connection with reading and spelling: in the attempts of sixteenth- and seventeenth-century spelling-reformers to achieve a phonetically rational alphabet; in the attempt (dutifully but unenthusiastically undertaken in the spelling-books) to give the sounds, as well as the names, of the letters of the alphabet; in the division of syllables; and in the categorisation of spelling-lists. At intervals during the whole period, a writer would admit that pronunciation could not be taught out of a textbook.

The structure and material of this chapter are derived from the texts, and therefore reflect the views and primary concerns of the teachers. Many of these seem familiar to us, others are strange. Much of the strangeness comes from the intensely analytical approach, which is almost universal. It concentrates the teacher's attention on *material*, which his pupil is to *remember*. One development during these 300 years is the gradual extension of this approach to one based on the concept of a *skill*, which the pupil has to *apply*.

Pupils and teachers at work

In order to put the teachers and their pupils in the centre of the picture it may be helpful to begin with the comments of a few teachers of reading about the organisation of their work. The textbooks refer often to the humble qualifications of teachers, to their low pay and to the difficulty of their work. This is too broad a theme to be more than illustrated here, but it is a vivid part of the background to the teaching of reading, which James Thomson, the poet, described as 'a low task'.

1581   Mulcaster complains that boys coming up to the grammar school are badly prepared in their elementary work, 'whose imperfection . . . doth marveilously trouble both maisters and scholers, so that we can . . . scantly tell how to place the too too raw boyes in any certaine forme' (chap. 41).

He proposes, however, that teachers of young children should be paid more than any other teachers.

1596   Coote is writing his spelling-book partly for 'such men and women of trades (as Taylors, Weavers, Shop-keepers, Seamsters, and such other) as have undertaken the charge of teaching others'. He tells his reader that once he is familiar with the book 'thou maiest sit on thy shop-bord, at thy loomes, or at thy needle, and never hinder thy worke, to hear thy scholers'.   (preface)

A century later to teach reading can still be described as a low task:

(1700) 1710   'It is commonly thought so tiresom an *Undertaking*, to teach *Children* to Spell and Read *English*, that a peevish *School-master* is not judged to have Patience enough to do it. And, therefore they are sent to a *Mistress* . . . where, partly thro' the *Ignorance* of many *such Teachers*, and partly *Neglect*, the *Children* often spend whole Years to *little Advantage*.' Parents say that the children are sent to school only 'to be rid of their Company at *Home*: So that their *Children*, if *Boys* are

left *afterall*, to be taught by a *Master*, and the *Girls* too often Untaught; or at least, are so imperfect in their *English*, that they do scarce ever attain to *write* or *read* intelligibly: And many of the *Boys*, tho' removed to a *Master*, fare little better; for most *Masters* are ambitious of having the Repute of a *Grammar-School*: And if they are qualified for it, and do undertake it, *that alone* will employ them.'

(John Urmston, preface)

Feeling can be just as strong in the following century:

1815 'To instruct children in the Rudiments of Reading is doubtless one of the most arduous, the most irksome, and perhaps the most unthankful offices in which any person can be engaged. Many children have naturally an aversion to books; and others are so dull and inattentive that it is scarcely possible to teach them anything; yet the parents of such . . . expect an equal progress with those whose talents and application are as opposite as light is to darkness.'

(John Hornsey, 1807, preface to 1815 edn)

The organisation of the pupils is frequently discussed:

1596 'Let every one of thy scholers . . . provide and use this booke: then divide thy scholers into 2, 3 or 4 sorts, as thy number is (for moe thou needest not, although thou hast a hundreth scholers) and place so many of them as are neerest of like forwardnes, in one lesson or forme, as in Grammar schooles, and so go through thy whole number, not making above foure companies at the most: so that thou shalt have but foure lectures to heare, though thou hast an hundreth scholers, whereas before thou haddest fortie lectures, though but fortie scholers. Then when thou wouldest heare any forme, call them forth all, bee they ten, twentie, or moe together: heare two or three that thou most suspectest to be most negligent, or of dullest conceit, and let all the other attend: or let one read one line, sentence or part, another the next, and so through: so that all do somewhat, and none know, when or what shall be required of him, encourage the most diligent and tenderest natures.'

(Edmund Coote, preface)

Quite the fullest picture is provided by John Brooksbank, who, although his books seem chaotic, had firm ideas about the organisation of his pupils' work and takes us close to it. After learning the letters in the lowest form Brooksbank's pupils move up a form and begin to read, going over the same material as before in units of increasing length:

1654a 'Your lowest form being thus perfected in spelling, you must now enter them in the next, which I call the *lower form*, wherein they are to learn to read, what they formerly spelled . . . When that form are to read their Lesson, call them all out together, and let them all stand with their *Books and feskews*[1] in order, as they did in spelling, then *bidding the highest, midlmost, or lowest, or whom you pleas*, read the *first syllabl* in the first Chapter, all the rest looking on, and pointing thereat with their feskews, be ready to read the *syllabl*, if bid, and when it is their turn; and thus let

[1] A pointer, usually held by pupil or teacher or attached to some kind of finger-stall or cap. Cf. Tuer, 1897, pp. 24–36.

them read every Scholar his *syllabl* by turn, till they have learned over the 7 *first Pages*: then let them read them over again, every one his *two, three, or four syllabls a piece*, til they have in the same manner read over the same 7 first Pages; after that beginning to read the same again every Scholar reading his line, in order, through the twenty two Chapters . . . til they are able to read all the said Chapters very readily, and perfectly.'   (p. 23)

The said chapters, in *An English Monosyllabary*, are composed of simple, if increasingly eccentric, sentences such as:

1651   Chap. 1   Ah! wee see an ox dy by an ax.
         Chap. 5   Oh God! his game is gon, as sure as a gun.
                 He that did ly on his bum, and ban, was his bane.
         Chap. 7   Hit the lads eye-lids with the rods or the ruds you see on the beds.
         Chap. 11 Let the welch belch in a halch, if they filch.
         Chap. 23 Those scrowls, were scraul'd with scrawls in the school.

George Snell, 1649, and, more fully, Richard Lloyd, give us a glimpse of children working in small groups; Owen Price organises the transition from spelling to reading; and Thomas Lye gives advice on the management of a whole class:

1654   'Of putting syllabizers to set forms. Schollars that can syllabize rightly, will be made therein more ready, if they be ranged into forms by couples, or rather by three or foure in company; that while one doth spell the Lesson, the rest giving good heed thereto, some may learn thereby to do the like: And others that have better skill may reform mistakes of him that is the Reader, untill all of them by turnes have spelled, and read their Lesson: And in conclusion, they may equally divide the Lesson into severall parts, for every couple whereof, each one in his turn reading word by word in his Book, the others part may require his Partner to spel the same accordingly without book: And the Reader that heedeth the same by Book, may reform all errours of the speller, swarving thence; which being used with care and diligence for a while, will for ever after make right spelling habitual to the company.'   (Lloyd, pp. 28–9)

1665   'As your boyes do grow up, you may both for your ease, and their advantage, muster them into three forms: The first shall be employ'd in Spelling; and because the Memory is more quick and retentive in the morning, they may then con the Rules they have spel'd the After-noon before. Then let them proceed to read the words under them in the After-noon, and some of the next Rules for their Lessons the Morning following. Let your second Form recite dayly some part of the Rules; and when perfect in them, of the difference of Words, then bid both Forms stand out: Examine and Pose them, and put them to Pose one another for priority of Places: Then in the After-noon guide them on to reading, first the easier part of the Bible, and parsing every Word according to the Rules . . . You may make a remove of those that are perfect in these things, once a Quarter to your third Form: yet still let them say their Parts with the rest, and spend the residue of the day in Arithmetick, Writing, Geographie, or Historie. And before you dismiss them at night, let them

pronounce clearly, in the audience of the School, the summe of what Histories they
have read that day.'   (Owen Price, pp. 7–8)

1673 'As soon as your Children can truly read their Letters, *cast them all into
distinct Forms-or Companies*: The grand reason, why you hear Children *so much*, and
yet teach them *so little*, is, because you hear them *so confusedly*. Put therefore as
many of them into one form, as you judg to be of an *equal* capacity, or *at least* no great
difference between them . . . When the whole Form comes to read their Lesson, *Let
it be your chief Care to make them all attentive*. To that end, charge them all to *look
intently* on their Books; To *hearken* diligently to Him that reads. To quicken their
Attention, ask those, whom you observe most heedless, *What is the last Word?*'
                                                              (Lye, 1677, A3)

By the middle of the eighteenth century the picture seems to have changed
little,[2] at any rate in Ireland, whence come two very full accounts of
teaching:

1740 'Whether the Children be in Number small or great, they may all be divided
into 3 Classes. 1. The lowest for learning Letters and Syllables off Book. 2. The
middle Class, in the little Play-Book [*A play-book for children*, 1694, by J.G.]. 3. The
highest, in *The Irish Spelling-Book*.' The Master 'may divide each Class into 2
Parts, as if they were of different Schools, and place a Head over each Division, who
is to take care of his Dividend, and see, that every Boy therein be well prepared in
each Lesson. When this is done, two or three out of each Division, weekly in their
Turns, may alternately instruct, and prepare the two lower Classes in their Lessons
. . . When any of the Classes come to say their Lessons to the Master, all may sit
down in Order by the Sides of a long Writing-Table (supposed to be in very School)
and then any two Opponents he calls out, may stand at the lower End of it, and each
carefully observe the Performance of his Adversary, and where he does amiss, be
ready to prompt him, but not without a Beck from the Master. The other is to do the
like with *him*, and so are the rest to do throughout the Class. The Mistakes of each
Division, may be prick'd by the Master with a Pin, in two small Lines or Columns
respectively, and the Excess for each Lesson be kept in a Register of the Week.'
                                     (*The Irish Spelling Book*, pp. 342, 343)

Samuel Edwards, a Dublin schoolmaster, wrote about 1735 *Proposals for
Educating Children*, which he published in 1765 in the form of a note
attached to the introduction to his *An Abstract of English Grammar*. The
long introduction, from which the following extract comes, is an expanded
version of the *Proposals*, written now after thirty years experience; it is all
full of interest:

1765 'In *general* they are all arranged in Classes, and have Lessons appointed
them at Night, which they are to repeat in the Morning; then they are to say two
labored [i.e. memorised or prepared] and two *reading* Lessons; and have besides

---

[2] Cf. the detailed description by 'a Pennsylvanian schoolmaster, 1730', quoted by Sol Cohen,
1974, I, 558–9.

about two Hours, which for three Days in the Week are employed in Writing, and
the other three Days (for such as are qualified) are spent in Ciphering. The Classes
are usually three, First, the spelling Class; then the Grammar and explaining Class;
and Thirdly, the Class of improved Boys.'   (Edwards, p. viii)

Even fuller is the account by David Manson, a Belfast teacher, in his *A New
Pocket Dictionary*, of the organisation of spelling and reading in three
classes, each divided into three companies. The method of work was both
hierarchical and co-operative. The children helped each other, but
proficiency led to the status, briefly held, of king, queen, vice-chancellor.
Manson is unusual in admitting to problems of discipline, which he refused
to control by corporal punishment:

1762 'Those who leave their seats, or neglect their business by idleness or foolish
tricks, are sent to the trifling club . . . Noise, being extremely disagreeable and
difficult to suppress, claims a distinct consideration. One person only can be heard
at once; the rest must therefore *speak, spell,* and *read* below their breath. Whoever
wants to speak to the teacher, must do it after one has done reading and before
another begins. The teacher calls *Noise,* whenever he knows the author; upon
which the offender marches to the trifling club: But if he neglect going till the
teacher call him by his name, this is a double catch: therefore all who are noisy,
generally march at the first call. Every scholar has the privilege of protecting those
who sit next him, by putting his hand on the noisy person's head, before the teacher
call *Noise,* and warning him to speak below his breath.'   (Manson, pp. 10–11)

In 1763 the governors of the Trades Maiden Hospital, Edinburgh, 'found
that the standard of reading was not satisfactory, and arranged the girls into
three classes, the lowest to study words of one syllable, the next words of
two syllables and easy passages from scripture, and the third to read words
up to seven syllables' (Law, 1965, p. 130). The linking of school
organisation to syllables was not unique. Charles Bryant, a schoolmaster in
Norwich, explains that Book I of his *A Key to Letters,* 1769, is a separate
publication of the elementary part of Book II, 'for the benefit of small
Schools, where perhaps there is seldom occasion for words of above two or
three syllables' (preface). John Binns, a Yorkshire teacher, describes the
progression from the alphabet to the monosyllables, to reading without
spelling, and then through two-syllable words to connected reading:

1788 'When Scholars well knew the Alphabet, they were immediately classed
with those who spelled in the Monosyllables. They all stood up together every
Lesson; the best Reader began first to spell, and the Rest plied the same Words after
him. When he had said over a Column another began to spell the next Column . . .
thro' the whole Class. This Method was used every Lesson till the Pupils could
easily read every Word in the Monosyllables without Spelling. But for Variety's
Sake, some of the first Scholars in the Class used to say alternately, three, or four

Times in a Week, in the reading Lessons of Words of one Syllable, without Spelling the Words, whilst the Rest plied after them. As soon as they could read all the Monosyllables, they were classed with those who spelled in Words of two Syllables: still continuing to say alternately, as before, till they came to the little Tables which are mostly taken out of the Lessons . . . Then besides Spelling, as before, they were set to read a Page every Day for their last Lesson; which served as a Proof of each Day's Improvement. When they could easily manage the Tables, then they were classed among those who said in the Scripture-Names; and as those Names are seldom used in Writing, except by Clergymen, it was judged best to let the Scholars read them alternately . . . without spelling them . . . By the above Method' the scholars 'repeat one for another, which also leaves the assiduous Teacher little more to do than guide the Pronunciation, and take Care that they ply diligently'.   (preface)

The difficulty of teaching reading to large classes of children as cheaply as possible reinforced those mechanical methods which were readily questioned by teachers better endowed with resources, if not also with sensitivity. The spirit informing these methods is illustrated by the report of a master in a Birmingham Lancasterian school:

1815 'The boys are exercised by telegraph. When the slates are cleaned, the dictator of the eighth class stands up, and dictates a word with its meaning . . . He then sits upon the desk and writes what he has dictated . . . and so on through all the classes . . . When the slates are full, which is known by the dictators all standing up, the exercising monitor exhibits SS for *show slates*. He then gives a gentle rap, which raises up an inspector at the end of each desk. A second rap sends them forward to inspect the slates, and they remain at the opposite end of the desk till they hear a third rap, when they all return, and write upon the backs of their slates the names of defaulters, adding a mark for each offence. The inspection is over in about two minutes; and being done at the same moment, by a boy seated at the end of each desk for the purpose, gives the school more the appearance of a machine, in which the boys superintend and instruct each other, than when the whole school was inspected by the monitors of classes, who have in that case the appearance and all the consequences of *eight little masters.*'

(Report of the British and Foreign School Society to the General Meeting, November 1815, pp. 37–38, quoted by Gordon and Lawton, 1978, p. 130)

This report is interesting not only for its illustration of well-known methods of mass instruction but for the pride with which the writer accepts the metaphor of a machine. He sees the machine not only as a means of mass production but also as a means of enabling pupils, even in large numbers, to take part in, and to have some responsibility for, their own education: it is better, he thinks, for the pupils to be functional members of a self-regulating organisation than for them to be little bosses. Such potentially humane use of mechanical methods was not common. More representative are the following instructions, for younger children, from the National Society's *Practical Manual*, for the use of script cards:

1833 'The class stand or sit in a square, the teacher and assistant occupying one side of it, (or in a circle). The teacher says, "shew cards". At the word "shew" each child puts the right hand to the card placed under the left arm; and at the word "cards" draws it forth . . . The teacher gives out, "the first word on the second line from the top". The cards are placed under the slates so as to see the word and line alluded to. The teacher points to a child to begin.'

The first child says 'l', the second 'a', the third 'la', the fourth 'comma', and so until the nineteenth child has said 'lu' and the twentieth 'full stop'.

'The children should be directed to drop the right hand from the slate to the side of the body after each letter is written. The readiness to catch the signal for this will soon discover the most proficient child in the class. The lesson appears on the slates thus:

     la, le, li, lo, lu

It must now be read, by each child taking part and the rest repeating. Let it be read several times over. Examine the slates and assign places.'   (pp. 6–7)

Reading- and spelling-skills

Because the teaching of reading is discussed by so many authors in terms that are applicable to what we would call spelling; because even to these authors the term 'spelling' had two meanings; and because much of this discussion is elliptical (few authors seeking to explain their methods systematically) it is difficult to keep in their historically correct relationship the two processes which we call spelling and reading and the other, different, processes which were at different times conducted under each of these labels. It is sometimes helpful to refer, without using the terms 'reading' and 'spelling', to the precise activities that, on the evidence of the texts, it can be assumed that pupils would have carried out. The following checklist sets out seven skills that pupils were expected to exercise in the early stages of learning to read words taken in isolation. What may at first seem a piece of overelaboration reflects a complexity that is real but has hitherto not been examined in detail. The chief cause of the complexity is the importance attached by seventeenth-century teachers to the letter and the syllable, and thus to the view that the word could be approached only through mastery of the syllable. In order to demonstrate the authenticity of the list of skills, each statement of a skill is followed by the substance, in our words, of the teacher's instruction that initiates it. 'Syllable' is taken, as it often was, to include one-syllable words, and 'word' is taken to mean words of two syllables or more.

In the seven skills listed here the pupil:

1. *Identifies:* *The pupil identifies a letter whose name he hears.*
   T. (pointing): Which of these letters is *B*?

2. *Names:*
   2.1   *The pupil names a letter that he sees.*
   T. (pointing to *B*): What is this letter called?

   2.2   *The pupil names a letter whose sound he hears.*
   T.: What letter(s) can make the sound . . . ?

   2.3   *The pupil names in sequence the letters of a syllable that he sees.*
   T. (pointing to *pop*): Name the letters in this syllable.

   2.4   *The pupil names in sequence the letters of a syllable that he hears.*
   T. (saying 'pop'): Name the letters that make this syllable.

   2.5   *The pupil names in sequence the letters of a word that he sees.*
   T. (pointing to *poppet*): Name the letters in this word.

   2.6   *The pupil names in sequence the letters of a word that he hears.*
   T. (saying 'poppet'): Name the letters that make this word.

3. *Sounds:*
   3.1   *The pupil sounds a letter that he sees.*
   T. (pointing to *B*): What sound does this letter make?

   3.2   *The pupil sounds a letter whose name he hears.*
   T.: What sounds are made by the letter *G*?

   3.3   *The pupil sounds in sequence the letters of a syllable that he sees.*
   T. (pointing to *pop*): Give the sounds of the letters in this syllable.

   3.4   *The pupil sounds in sequence the letters of a syllable that he hears.*
   T. (saying 'pop'): Give the sounds that make up this syllable.

The pupils would not be required to sound the letters of a word: a word would be sounded syllable by syllable.

4. *Says:*

    4.1   *The pupil says as a whole a syllable that he sees.*
                T. (pointing to *pop*): Say this syllable.

    4.2   *The pupil says as a whole a word that he sees.*
                T. (pointing to *poppet*): Say this word.

5. *Writes:*

    5.1   *The pupil writes a letter whose name he hears.*
                T.: Make (write) the letter *B*.

    5.2   *The pupil writes as a whole a syllable that he hears.*
                T. (Saying 'pop'): Write this syllable.

    5.3   *The pupil writes as a whole a word that he hears.*
                T.: Write 'poppet'.

    5.4   *The pupil writes as a whole a word that he has in mind.*

In 5, writing is the primary response. In 6.3, 6.4 and 7.4, it is a secondary one. In addition to the skills of 5 the pupil would be required to write, i.e. to copy, letters, syllables and words which he sees.

6. *Divides:*

    6.1   *The pupil divides orally into its syllables a word that he sees.*
                T. (pointing to *poppet*): Divide this word into its syllables.

    6.2   *The pupil divides orally into its syllables a word that he hears.*
                T. (saying 'poppet'): Divide this word into its syllables.

    6.3   *The pupil divides (in his mind or orally) into its syllables a word that he has in mind.*

    6.4   *As 6.1, but the pupil writes his response.*

    6.5   *As 6.2, but the pupil writes his response.*

    6.6   *As 6.3, but the pupil writes his response.*

7. *Puts together:*

    7.1   *The pupil puts together orally the letters of a syllable that have been named to him in sequence.*
                T.: What do *p-o-p* make?
                P.: *P-o-p* make *pop*.

The pupil would not normally be required to treat a word in this way: a word would be handled syllable by syllable.

    7.2   *The pupil puts together orally two syllables that he sees, and makes a word.*

T. (pointing to *pop* and *pet*): What do these syllables
make together?

P.: *Pop* and *pet* make *poppet*.

7.3   *The pupil puts together orally two syllables that he hears,*
and makes a word.

T. (saying 'pop' and 'pet'): What do these syllables
make together?

P. They make *'poppet'*.

7.4   *As 7.3 but the pupil writes his response.*

A written response (copying) is unlikely to be required when the pupil sees
the two syllables, as in 7.2, but an equivalent requirement might arise in a
game played with letter counters.

The letters of the alphabet

One might think that the alphabet in itself would have presented few
problems either to the teacher or to the learner. Certainly the most
elementary of the early spelling-books take for granted the constituent
letters, their order and their names. But for a long time there was some
uncertainty and occasional confusion about all these matters, which are
often discussed by teachers, especially those with an interest in
orthographical reform. Even in relatively modern times it seems that too
rapid exposure to the names of the letters could cause confusion in an
educated person. Horace Mann is quoted as telling how:

'A Mr Ottiwell Wood, at a late trial in Lancashire, England, giving his name to the
court, the judge said, "Pray, Mr Wood, how do you spell your name?" To which the
witness replied, "o double T, I double U, E double L, double U, double O, D." The
learned judge at first laid down his pen in astonishment; and then, after making two
or three unsuccessful attempts, declared he was unable to record it.'

(Dawes, (1848) 1849, p. xix)

Until the eighteenth century there was uncertainty even about what letters
constituted the alphabet: whether the pairs *i,j* and *u,v*, were to be regarded
as distinct letters; whether, if they were distinct letters, they should be
distinguished equally in upper- and in lower-case alphabets, and in
alphabets of differing typefaces; whether *i* was to precede *j*, and *u* to precede
v in alphabetical order, or vice versa. These matters affected the spelling-
books, which customarily displayed the alphabet in Roman, in italic, and
frequently in English (Gothic) type, both upper and lower case.

At the beginning of the seventeenth century the general practice in the spelling-books was that *j* did not appear in any form of the alphabet; both *u* and *v* appeared in lower-case Roman alphabets, less frequently in English ones; but in capital alphabets only one form was used for both vowel and consonant and this form might be either *U* or *V*. In the lower-case alphabets *v* preceded *u*. Throughout the seventeenth century the conso-nantal forms *j* and *v* were being given separate status more frequently, but there was still great variation. McKerrow, referring to English printers generally, says that modern practice became normal about 1630; but spelling-books seem to have been slow to change. By the early years of the eighteenth century the consonantal forms were normal in the spelling-books, although until late in the century *J* might be omitted from the upper-case alphabet, as in an edition of *The New England Primer* printed in Boston about 1790, and *v* might still precede *u*, as in *The Court Letter Writer*, 1773, and in William Scott's *An Introduction to Reading and Spelling*, first published in 1776, which lists *v* before *u* in both its alphabets. Even when *j* and *v* were included in the alphabet they were frequently, until the end of the century, referred to by their old names 'consonant *j*' or '*v* consonant', and Robert Ross, in *The New American Spelling Book*, 1785, gives *I,J* and *U,V*, as examples of letters whose names are 'often confounded' by the ignorant and ill-rewarded authors of spelling-books. By 1800 modern practice was usual in lower-case alphabets, but not in upper-case ones. Even so, many ABCs, produced as cheaply as possible from mixed typographical sources and for local distribution, show that old founts and old conventions persisted. Five ABCs, one of 1830, the others undated but later, are reprinted in Peter Stockham's *Chapbook ABC's* (1974). Three of the five list the alphabet as well as giving a pictorial text for it. Of the three alphabetical lists two are modern, and one gives *v* before *u*. In the five pictorial texts one is modern, two give *i* and *v* only, and two give *j* and *u* only. In three out of the five books the text is inconsistent with the list. Another picture alphabet, published in 1819, gives *i* (for *ink*) but no *j*, and *u* (for *uncle*) but no *v*; whereas a second alphabet, issued by the same publisher in the following year, gives *j* (for *joiner*) but no *i*, and *v* (for *vintner*) but no *u* (Opie, 1980, pp. 10–19).

Variations between different spelling-books, in the enumeration of the letters, would not be as confusing to the pupil as inconsistencies within a single text. Because many elementary textbooks drew on a variety of previous publications, inconsistencies arose such as are found (an extreme case) in Tobias Ellis' *The English School*, a work otherwise of some originality. The fifth edition, 1680, contains six separately engraved picture alphabets. One alphabet gives *j* and *i* in both upper- and lower-case form; two alphabets give *j* and *i* as capitals only; one gives *i* only as a consonant (for *Iew*); one gives *i* only as a vowel (for *Instrument*); one gives *j* only as a consonant (for *Jackdaw*). *V* and *u* are treated more regularly, although in one alphabet they are both omitted. In all cases where *j* and *i*, and *v* and *u* are given *j* precedes *i* and *v* precedes *u*.

The status of *j* and *v* is a minor matter, but it was felt by the teacher to be of practical importance, and there are many comments such as the following:

1695 In *The Writing Scholar's Companion* the first sentence makes special mention of 'the *j* Consonant with a turn'd tail, and the *v* consonant with a sharp bottom; which are most justly now allowed, to be different Letters'.

1700 Richard Browne shows that the consonantal forms are not yet taken for granted. He lists an alphabet of nineteen consonants and then says, 'Add to these the *j* and *v*, which are ever used as Consonants.' He also describes their shape, in a way he does not for other letters (pp. 2,4). Lane's *A Key to the Art of Letters*, on the other hand, published in the same year, includes *i,j* and *u,v* in their modern order without comment.

1721 Isaac Watts, less firmly: 'I have here followed the old and usual Custom of making Twenty-four Letters, and distinguishing the *u* and *i*, into Vowels and Consonants afterwards; tho it had been much more proper and natural, if our Fathers had made the *v* and *j* Consonants, two distinct Letters, and called them *ja* and *vee*, and thus made six-and-twenty.'   (p. 2)

1756 Daniel Fenning has a firmer recommendation: 'I advise all Masters and Mistresses never to let a Child know there are two *i*'s, or two *u*'s, but let them learn the Child to call the long *j* (*ja*) and the sharp *v* (*vee*).'   (p. 1)

The standing of the letter *h* is also questioned, but is usually treated with a sensible inconsistency. *H* is always included in the alphabet, but its status as a letter is frequently denied. Towards the middle of the eighteenth century the difficulty dies away.

1569 Hart: '*H* . . . whose propertie is to signifie onely the breath . . . as we use it before and after the sound of the vowel in laughing . . . hah, hah, hah . . . where the *h* hath no sounde but as you woulde blowe to warme your handes.'
                                                      (fol. 35, misnumbered)

1661 Thomas Hunt: '*H* is not properly a letter, but a *note of aspiration or breathing*, yet (for avoyding of multiplicity of rules) it shall be call'd a consonant.' (p. 19)

1676 George Robertson says of *h*, 'it is but a nicetie to deny it the name of a Letter'.
                                                                        (p. 12)

1711 Gildon, who is keeping close to Wallis, allows that, '*H*, tho' excluded the Number of Letters by Priscian and some of our Moderns on his Authority . . . is manifestly a Consonant.'   (p.41)

1712 Maittaire, a scholarly teacher of Greek as well as the author of an English grammar, disagrees: '*H* is not properly a Letter; and its use will be taught among those marks, which belong to Syllables . . .' (p. 7). 'There belong to syllables several Notes or marks of Pronunciation . . . The Spirit or breathing is twofold, either Soft and small, or Harsh and thick; the last is expressed by *h*.'   (p. 15)

1755 Sayer Rudd, on the other hand, says that *h* 'has a just claim to *the title* of A LETTER, at lest in our tongue'. His grounds are that aspiration in English is indicated by a distinct character, not just by a mark, as in Greek, and that it indicates 'a *power*, in the formation of syllables, *peculiar to that character*'.   (p. 45)

Most of the subsequent spelling-books accepted *h* without comment. In those grammars which classified the letters by their sounds, *h* was treated as a consonant; the more thoughtful of them admitted that it could not be classified as any *kind* of consonant. It remained an aspiration.

Double letters. Accompanying the alphabets in many spelling-books until the first quarter of the nineteenth century, were lists of 'double' or 'joined' letters. The application of the term 'double letter' varied widely. Most often it referred to typographical ligatures such as ct, ff, ſh; sometimes it referred to digraphs representing diphthongs; sometimes to combinations of two or three consonants that were considered to represent a single sound, as *ss, sh, ch, th*. The orthographical reformers often treated these combinations as alphabetical units with their own names. *Sh* is called *she(e)* (Bullokar; Lloyd, 1654; A. Lane) and *sha* (Gill); *wh* is called *whe* (Bullokar, Gill, A. Lane) or *why* (Lloyd, 1654); *th* is nearly always *thee*, and *ch* is *chee* (Bullokar). Rudd distinguishes several of these senses of the term *double letter* and distinguishes also between their initial and final sounds: *ch* at the beginning of a word is called *chee* (as in *child*) or *khee* (as in *chord*) but at the end of a word (as in *patch*) it is called *etch* (pp. 46–7).

    W was sometimes called a double letter because it was formed by two *U*'s; *x* because it was equivalent to *ks*, and *z* because it was equivalent to *ds*. The typographical double letters are merely listed for reference: the teachers hardly ever mention them. A more active approach to them is recorded from France. Michel Foucault quotes an early eighteenth-century suggestion that in a large school the first class, who are beginning to learn their letters, should be divided into four streams, one of which would be for pupils 'who are learning the double letters (*ff, ss, tt, st*)'.[3]

Superfluous letters. The reformers of orthography all sought to remedy two particular defects of the English alphabet; that one symbol could represent

---

[3] M. Foucault, *Discipline and punish*, Penguin, 1977, p. 160.

several different sounds, and that one sound could be represented by different symbols. The writers of spelling-books could do little about these defects, but they commented regularly on the difficulty caused to young pupils by what Hart had called 'superfluous letters' and by the variety of sounds represented by the vowels. The reformers differed over what letters were superfluous, according to the system of symbols that they were advocating. The ordinary teachers, however, who were making their comments on general grounds, might have been expected to agree with each other more than they did. They managed to agree that *c, x* and *q* were superfluous; most of them said that *j* was; many that *y* and *z* were. But this kind of discussion died away early in the nineteenth century, when the teachers were content to leave the matter with the standard comment that the alphabet was 'redundant and defective'.

The order of the letters. The relative positions in alphabetical order of *i,j* and *u,v* were referred to above. Considered alternatives to the traditional order were suggested by reformers of orthography, who believed that their proposals, because they were rational and systematic, would make teaching easier. Alternatives were later put forward by teachers on purely pedagogic grounds. John Hart, 1570, begins his alphabet with the vowels, followed by *l, m, n, r, h* and a new symbol, called *sheares*, for the sound of *sh*. These eleven letters are to be taught first. At some stage, but he does not specify it, the symbols for the diphthongs are to be learnt. The remaining fourteen letters, arranged in pairs, 'brother and sister', complete his alphabet. He stressed the need to teach the names of the letters in any order and apart from any meaningful context, as by spelling words backwards (pp. 239–46). Hart thought of his new alphabetical order as more than a teaching-aid: he hoped it would be generally adopted, and he arranged the index to his *Orthographie*, 1569, in accordance with it. Other orthographical reformers (Bullokar, Gill, C. Butler) used the traditional order, but Richard Hodges, 1644, whose reforms were limited to the addition of diacritical marks to the ordinary letters, put his alphabet in a new order, designed for teaching. First came the vowels, then the diphthongs, then (omitting some of his special letters) the consonants ordered phonetically: *l, m, n, r, f, v, s, z, j, g, c,* and *k* and *q, d, t, b, p, x, h, y, w*.

The emphasis on teaching is more explicit in *The Needful Attempt*, 1711, where the author, though advocating a reformed spelling, uses the traditional letters in a new order. The vowels come first ('tis best to place them first, and to teach them first'); then the consonants according to their shape. The author later, in his reformed spelling, lists the consonants 'furst, in dhair yusual aurder, faur dhe sak auf sutch az mai hav beegun to lairn um so . . . yet faur dhe beter and sooner lairning to rit um . . . i think it best to plas um odherwez too'. First come the nine consonants which do not rise above or fall below the line (the 'shaurt wonz') then the downward long ones, and the upward long ones: r n m v w t s x z   j y p q g   l b h k f d (pp. 4, 15, omitting diacritics). The author lists the alphabet in its traditional order only for those pupils who have already learnt it; he would wish others to learn the new order from the start. Thomas Crumpe, in *The Anatomy of Orthography*, 1712, gives the traditional order first but recommends that the letters should be taught in his reformed order: 'The 5 Vowels; the 8 Mutes; The 4 Liquids; The double Consonants' and *h*, *w* and *s*, which 'cannot properly be reckoned either Mutes or Liquids' (p. 5). Crumpe represents a transition: he belongs to the writers already discussed, who were primarily theoreticians and orthographical reformers, even if they were also teachers, but he belongs also with later writers, whose concern was solely with teaching-methods. They did not repudiate the old alphabet; they supplemented it with what may be called a 'learning order' of the letters, to be discarded once their pupils could read.

Naming the letters. Teachers were less concerned about variations in alphabetical order or status than with the names of the letters, which preoccupied them to an extent that may surprise us. The names were directly related to most of the methods of teaching spelling and reading that were current until well into the nineteenth century. The early ABCs, hornbooks and spelling-books did not name the letters: their makers assumed with Mulcaster that the names were 'familiar in our daielie use'. The practice of listing the names of the letters alongside the alphabet became popular during the second half of the seventeenth century, when it was adopted in nearly half the relevant texts. It was a little less popular during the first half of the eighteenth century, and between 1750 and 1830 the names appear in about a quarter of the texts. Thereafter the practice is much less common; the names of the letters are considered mainly by some reformers of the alphabet (Donald Walker, 1836) and indirectly by those giving special attention to teaching-methods (Gall, a. 1832; J.F. Denham, 1834; Favell Bevan, 1836; J.M. McCulloch, 1837). William Martin's *Intellectual Grammar*, 1852, is a late instance of an ordinary textbook listing the names.

In the sixteenth and seventeenth centuries it was universally assumed that a letter's name was derived from, and ideally should represent, its sound. It was also assumed, generally but not universally, that you could not read unless you could spell. To spell a word was to say its letters in order, *by name*; reading a word was achieved by putting together, in order, the *sounds* made by its letters. It was almost always assumed that before you could learn the sound or sounds made by a letter you had first to know its name. The relation between names and sounds was therefore important, but confusing. The confusion came sometimes from a failure to distinguish the two ideas, sometimes from an awkward but not uncommon use of *name* to mean the name of a sound; sometimes from both, as seems to be the case of John Warden:

1753 'I have denoted the names of the letters by figures . . . Wherever the same figure is annexed to the same letter . . . it is to have the same name . . . In those diphthongs where both the vowels are pronounced, the sound of each vowel is expressed by the figure denoting that sound. Thus, in *sŏǔnd o* is marked *ŏ*, being the same name it is expressed by in *sŏt*, and *u* is marked *ǔ*, being the name it is expressed by in *trǔe* . . . The teacher must be very nice in informing [his pupils] of those different names, and exercise them therein. This should not be left, till they can readily tell how many names each particular letter has, and when they are sounded by their different names.' (pp. xi, xii)

The nature of consonants caused teachers great difficulty. Consonants, by definition, made no sound by themselves; the exceptions, such as *m*, reduced the scale but not the strength of the difficulty. The name of a consonant could not therefore just be its sound, or one of its sounds, as was the case with the vowels. A vowel had to be added to the consonant (*e*, for example, added to *b*) so that the letter could have a pronounceable name (*be* or *bee*). This traditional convention worked satisfactorily in the teaching of spelling, but in the teaching of reading, because names and sounds were not clearly distinguished, the names of consonants were used in the sequence of *letter sounds* in almost the same way as they were in the sequence of *letter names* used in spelling. Hence came the 'absurdities' which received comment over the centuries, as by John Hart: '[The letters] are misnamed much from their offices and natures, whereby the desirous are much the more hindered from learning to reade, though they were never so willing' (1570, p. 234). Hart supposes that 'a reasonable man, ignorant of letters' would pronounce the first three letters of a word such as *three* or *throw* as 'teacher' because he would sound *t* by its name *tee*, *h* by its name *ache* (pronounced *aitch*) and *r* by its name *er*. Putting together the first three sounds would give *tee-ache-er* (*ibid.*). Such comment on the absurdities arising from the names of some of the letters persisted well into the nineteenth century.

The names of the consonants were puzzling. It seemed odd that some were formed with an *e* before the consonant (*el, em, en*) and others with an *e* after (*be, ce, de*). In order to make the alphabet more tidy, and more teachable, new names were suggested that followed one or other pattern throughout. If the consonant–vowel pattern (CV) was adopted *l*, *m*, *n* were called *le*, *me*, *ne*: if the vowel–consonant pattern (VC), *b*, *c*, *d* were called *eb*, *ec*, *ed*. The vowel that helped to make these names was held to be arbitrary: it did not have to be *e*. So alphabets were proposed in which other vowels, usually *i*, took the place of *e*, and the names of consonants following the VC pattern were, for example, *ib*, *id*, *ip*, and on the CV pattern *bi*, *di*, *pi*.

The nature of consonants was not, of course, as basic a cause of difficulty to the teachers as was their belief that reading was best taught by joining together the sounds of the letters taken individually. But for many teachers it was in the names of the consonants that the difficulties and the 'absurdities' seemed to lie. Two easements were proposed. The first was based on the assumption that, for pupils learning to read, the transition from vowel to vowel, within a word, was physically easier than the transition from vowel to consonant. In the word *tot*, for instance, the sequence of sounds would customarily be [tə-ɒ-tə]. By giving the letter *t* two names, one on the CV pattern (*te* or *ti*), the other on the VC pattern (*et* or *it*), it was possible to prescribe that the CV form of the name should be used at the beginning of a word or syllable, and the VC form at the end. *Tot* would then be read as [tə-ɒ-et]. An additional advantage of using names of both CV and VC patterns was that a final consonant was not followed by a shadowy vowel sound which the pupil was supposed to ignore.

The second, and more substantial, easement was a return to the ancient concept of force (*potestas*) or power. The force of a consonant was the effect it had when sounded as part of a word, an effect that could not, therefore, be produced by attempting to sound the consonant by itself. In a nineteenth century-example: the force of *d* in *dog* is what is left if you take away the sound of *-og*. This force came to be represented by some teachers, not by the form *de* (which was misleading because it imported the sound of *e*) but by the form *d'*. The force was known as 'incipient sound', and the pronunciation of the word *tot* would have been represented by *t'-o-t'*. But by this time the ideas of name and sound had been adequately separated and the names of the letters were not in themselves a source of difficulty to the teacher.

Name, sound and power

Name and sound

It is not surprising that there should have been uncertainty and inconsistency in discussing the names and sounds of the letters. The term 'letter' is itself ambiguous, as was the Latin *litera*. Usually both terms refer to the written character; sometimes, and not infrequently, they refer to the speech sound represented by the character. The less ambiguous term for speech sound was 'element' (*elementum*), but even this could be used to denote a part of the written word, a letter or a combination of letters. Priscian warns against the possibility of confusion: 'Abusive tamen et elementa pro literis et literae pro elementis vocantur' (Book I, para. 4); and Simon Daines, eleven centuries later, repeats the distinction of 'the antient Latinists' between letters ('Charactericall notes') and elements ('the first grounds or Principles of speech'). The distinction, however, 'is confounded in the generall acception, which promiscuously termes them Letters', (1640, p. 2). This ambiguity in the term 'letter' is further documented by David Abercrombie (1965b). Its significance here is that it illustrates, and helps to explain, the difficulties that the teachers met in handling the names of the letters as a preliminary to teaching children to read. The teachers confused name and sound not because they were stupid but because, like their predecessors in antiquity, they lacked an adequate terminology in which to control two interacting symbolic systems, one visual and one oral. In addition they experienced the difficulties met by all who try to write about speech sounds.

It is consequently hard at times to know just what method of teaching is being described. Brinsley, in 1612, is writing 'for the helping of the younger sort of Teachers', addressing a reader 'who tenderest the poore Country schooles'. He is anxious to make his methods plain, and in a long book he has room to do so. In describing the first step in teaching the alphabet he says,

'The childe is to be taught, how to call every letter, pronouncing each of them plainely, fully and distinctly; I mean in a distinct and differing sound, each from others, and also naturally . . . More specially to bee carefull, for the right pronouncing of the five vowels, in the first place . . . because these make a perfect sound, so that they may bee pronounced fully of themselves . . . After these vowels, to teach them to pronounce every other letter: which are therefore called Consonants, because they cannot make a perfect sound of themselves, without a vowell.'   (p. 15)

Brinsley goes on immediately to say that this stage of the teaching can, and he later says it should, be carried out orally, 'before the childe do knowe any letter on the booke'. In the margin he notes: 'Right calling the letters before the children doe know them'.

It seems that 'calling' and 'pronouncing' the letters mean that Brinsley's children repeat the sounds that the teacher makes but do not, at this stage, relate the sounds to a written character. What sounds does the teacher make when the pupils are learning the vowels? Does the teacher say something to the effect of: 'The first vowel is called *ay* and it can make the following sounds: *ay* as in *hay*, *ā* as in *cart*, *ă* as in *man*'? This would be to distinguish name and sound, to call and pronounce the vowels. But Brinsley's brief description does not suggest such an unprecedented approach:

'You must teach them . . . to call their five vowels, and to pronounce them right: Which they will presently learne, if you do but only cause them to repeat them oft over, after you, distinctly together thus: a, e, i, o, u, after the manner of five bels, or as we say; one, two, three, fowre, five.'   (p. 19)

What the children are saying must be the names of the vowels; but in saying the names they are also, of course, saying one of the sounds made by each vowel.[4] Name and sound overlap. The children are next, according to Brinsley, to learn to 'pronounce' the consonants. Although he does not say so explicitly it seems clear that Brinsley expected the consonants also to be 'called' by name, as the vowels had been. But he does explicitly say that the consonants cannot be 'pronounced' by themselves. The children are 'to put the consonants in order before every vowell, and to repeate them oft over together; as thus: to begin with *b* and to say *ba, be, bi, bo, bu* . . . Thus teach them to say all the rest, as it were singing them together' (*ibid.*). But we still do not know exactly what the children said. Did they combine the consonant with the name of the vowel (which they had just learnt) or did they, as seems likely, combine the consonant with one or more of the sounds of the vowel, which might or might not be the name of the vowel and to which Brinsley has so far made no unambiguous reference?

The children next have to put the vowel in front of the consonant, when they must be using vowel sounds different from the names of the vowels: *ab, eb, ib, ob, ub* not *ayb, eeb, ibe, obe, ube*. The names and the sounds of the letters are not fully distinguished in Brinsley's mind, partly because the key terms *letter* is itself ambiguous. A letter as a character can have a name. A letter as a sound has no name: the name of a sound is the sound itself.

An alphabetic approach to the teaching of reading necessarily led to the consideration, at an elementary level, of both the names and the sounds of the letters. Teacher and pupil used the names in order to refer to the letters. The pupil used the sounds when joining together the components of a word he was reading; when in oral spelling he referred to the characters that represented these components he customarily used the names. It was understandable that confusion could arise between name and sound, as in the practice censured by Buchanan, 1762:

[4] If 'teaching' of this kind seems improbable or exaggerated it should be noted that in 1817 the Ackworth School committee thought that too much time was being spent on 'learning the sound of the vowels' (Thompson, 1879, p. 145: see Bibliography 4).

'I cannot help taking Notice here of a very absurd Method, which tho' it derives its Origin from more illiterate Times, is still inadvertently practised; I mean that of sounding the Vowel *i* always long in Syllabication, though in Pronunciation it be short. For Example, in spelling the Word *Divisibility*, a Child is most ridiculously taught to sound the Syllables thus: *d-i* (*dI*) *v-i* (*vI*) that is (*dIvI*) *s-i* (*sI*) (*dIvIsI*) *b-i* (*bI*) (*dIvIsIbI*) *l-i* (*lI*) (*dIvIsIbIlI*) *t-y* (*tI*) (*dIvIsIbIlItI*): which gaping uncouth Utterance being quite foreign to the true Pronunciation of the Word must woefully deprave and vitiate the Ear.'   (p. 41)

Frequently, therefore, 'sound' was equated with 'name', but the practice was not universal. Richard Hodges in *The English Primrose*, 1644, ran counter to the general tendency and made an explicit separation between name and sound. His reformed alphabet of forty-four characters is listed in three columns headed respectively 'figures' (that is, the shapes of the letters), 'Names' and 'Forces' (that is, powers). *H* is named *hee* and its force is shown in the word *cates; w* is named *wee* and its force is shown in *wine* is shown in the word *cates; w* is named *wee* and its force is shown in *wine* (sigs. B1-B2). For Hodges *hee, kee* and *wee* are names of letters, distinct from their sounds. John Newton, 1669, however, who also makes an explicit distinction between name and sound, and also shows the alphabet in three columns headed 'Shape', 'Name' and 'Sound' (here equivalent to Hodges' 'Forces') gives *hee, kee* and *wee* as sounds; their names, according to Newton, are the traditional *ach, ka* and *double u* (p. 3).

The inconsistency between Hodges and Newton is caused not by confusion but by a difference of policy. Hodges wants the names of some letters to correspond more closely with their sounds; he makes no attempt to represent the sound of a letter standing by itself, but represents the sound in the context of a whole word. *Hee* is his new name for *h*. Newton keeps the traditional names, and tries to represent the sound of the letter standing by itself. In order to do this he, like Hodges, gets as near as he can to a separate representation of the sound. Hodges uses the representation (*hee, kee* etc.) for the name, Newton for the sound.

Edward Young also illustrates the difficulty of relating name and sound: 'Consonants without vowels will make no sound at all.' Therefore he says, 'The sound of Consonants is as followeth: *b* (*bee*)*c*(*cee*). . . . .*z* (*zed*)' ([1675] 1710, p. 2). It was natural for him to refer to the sound of the consonant *b* by the name of the letter; it was quite unnatural, however, to treat *z* in this way, and many teachers adopted the form *ze*, by analogy with *bee* and *cee*. Young was using names as the best means of referring to sounds.[5] At the end of the

[5] The same inconsistency of terminology is found in *The Child's Bible*, 1677, sig. A3; *The Irish Spelling Book*, 1740, pp. 25, 28, 316; Drummond, 1767, preface; Lawrie, 1779, p. 9; Moscrip, 1790, p. 8; Robinson, (1800) 1819, p. 1.

eighteenth century Richard Edgeworth was still making explicit the distinction that an unsettled terminology had obscured:

1798   'We should never name the consonants by their usual names; if it be required to point them out by sounds, let them resemble the real sounds or powers of the consonants: but in fact it will never be *necessary* to name the consonants separately, till their powers in combination with the different vowels be distinctly acquired. It will then be time enough to teach the common names of the letters ... It must appear strange that a child should be able to read before he knows the names of his letters; but it has been ascertained, that the names of the letters are an incumbrance in teaching a child to read.'   (p. 44)

In *A Rational Primer* the Edgeworths slightly weakened their main point, saying only that, 'it will be of no essential disadvantage to teach the names of the consonants, provided, that the child be made to distinguish the sounds of the letters from their names' (p. 29). It is the wording of the proviso in the last clause that is important here.

By the early part of the nineteenth century the relation between name and sound is seldom a source of trouble, but in 1817 Fulton and Knight describe a child who hesitates over reading the word *gone*. The teacher asked him to spell it:

' "*Gee o en e*." "Well, what do *Gee o en e* make?" "Jō'ne". "You're a dunce." So says the Tutor, but we say, "Sweet child! you have combined these sounds *most correctly*, and have shown what you are capable of under *rational* tuition." It is this use of the *common names* which we condemn – making them a guide to pronunciation; a use for which they are totally unqualified.' ([1811] 1817, p. 69)

Fifty years later J.S. Laurie sums up the cause of all the difficulty. He takes it for granted that the old method of teaching reading 'by means of spelling' is ineffectual because

'... it is impossible to distinguish the letters by names which shall at the same time adequately represent their sounds. Spelling a word should denote merely the statement of its alphabetic symbols in their proper order, but it practically involves also an apparent analysis of the composite sound of the word into its several elementary sounds.'   (Longman, 1862, preface)

Sound and power

The distinction between power, in its strict sense, and sound appears, sometimes at long intervals, throughout the whole period during which the names of the consonants cause difficulty. John Hart, the first of the English writers to discuss the difficulty, takes an unusual but emphatic view: 'The consonants may all be framed and uttered sensibly to the eare without the naming of any vowel or Diphthong' (1569, fol. 32b). Later he says that *l* should be named as if one was saying *lion* but omitting the *-ion* (1570, p. 242) and Bullokar similarly illustrates the name of one of his new characters by saying it has the sound of *th* in *thief*, 'the vowel of that syllable being left unsounded and leaving out *eef*' (*Short Introduction*, 1580, p. 2). In the same way the anonymous *Reading made most Easy*, 1821, wants *ch*, *ph*, *sh*, etc. to be treated as 'single characters', their names to be expressed by stopping the pronunciation of *chance, physic, shall*, before sounding the vowel (p. 4). This is the strict use of the idea of power. Hart repudiates the normal practice of naming the consonants by the addition of a vowel before or after (*be* or *eb*): such letters

'. . . are indifferent for all vowels and diphthongs, both before, and also after them, and therefore ought not to have the name stayde with any of them, for that is to the learners hinderance, as much as may be: and it is as reasonable to name the vowell with the helpe of any one or other Consonant, as the Consonant by the helpe of anye one or other vowell'. (*ibid.*)

The same thought is in Cooper's mind when he says, 'It would be . . . easiest to young beginners, if all the letters were named according to their proper power' (1687, p. 25).

Confusion was sometimes avoided by using the idea of power, but often, as with 'name', both 'power' and 'force' were used to include the idea of sound, so that all letters, vowels as well as consonants, were said to have power. Some teachers used 'name', 'sound' and 'power' as equivalent terms (as does the *Oxford English Dictionary*, s.v. *Power*, 3b). If some teachers were confused, their practice is in most cases clear once their individual use of the terms has been established. Many, through to the late nineteenth century, used 'power' or 'force' for 'sound'. Early instances include:

1625 'Sound, usually termed power, is . . . that whereby a word is pronounced.' (Hayward, fol. 8)

1674 'In the Letters are commonly considered three things, viz: The name, the figure, and the power: This power should be included in the name; and the difference both of figure and power together, should produce a different name. This name and power, so often thwarting one another, has given occasion to several endeavours of correction.' (Coles, p. 99)

In saying that the power should be included in the name Coles is thinking of letters like *h, w* and *z*, the names of which carry little if any reference to their sound and had been criticised by reformers of orthography. The need for different names refers also to *i* and *u*, the consonantal forms of which (*j* and *v* differ in both figure and power from *i* and *u*) should have distinct names, not just '*i* consonant' and '*u* consonant'.

During the seventeenth century and the first half of the eighteenth,

teachers tried to meet the difficulty of the consonants by adjusting their
names in the ways described later in this chapter. The strict idea of power
was not lost, but it was not used in this context. Simon Daines, 1640, uses it
in the closely related, and often discussed, question of how to teach the
pronunciation of the consonants in endings such as *-ble, -cle*: 'The manner
of pronouncing them is thus as followes. Frame your voice as if you would
sound all the letters, and withall the *e*; but so soon as you have pronounced
the two consonants, there stop, and omit the *e*' (p. 60). It is not until nearly
two centuries after Hart and Bullokar that the idea of power is again
explicitly and consistently applied to the names of the letters.

Sayer Rudd, 1755, states that names should be derived from powers. He
bases his opinion on two assumptions:

> 'As *every letter* is generally supposed to be *the mark* of some one simple sound; so *the
> name* of the letter, in strict propriety, ought likewise to be a simple sound in itself . . .
> [and] that ALL THE NAMES of the letters, if natural, be *such* as arise directly out of *the
> powers*, respectively belonging to *the several marks*, or *letters*, themselves.'
>
> (pp. 5–6)

His reformed alphabet is displayed in four columns, headed 'Figure',
'Name', 'Power' and 'Example', and he represents the powers of the letters,
throughout, just by the letter itself. This is, for the consonants, consistent
with the strict interpretation of power: he uses the ordinary name *bee* for *b*;
its power is represented as *b*, and is exemplified in the word *bed* (p. 7). So
also with the other letters. His hope is that: 'The learner's ear, however
young, will immediately catch *the true power* of every letter on the bare
caling-over *it's name*; by which means his speling will be instantly render'd
both *more easy* and *certain* to himself, and *more expeditious* and *pleasant* to
the master' (p. 48). In his alphabet he wishes to treat *-gh*, as in *cough* and
sigh, as a single character, which must therefore have a name and a power.
But the *gh* in *sigh* is silent; its function, as Rudd puts it, is 'to lengthen and
roughen the syllable'(p. 47n.). If *gh* has no power it can have no name, and
Rudd enters in the name column just the word 'silent'. To the *gh* in *cough* he
gives the name 'eff' and represents its power as *ff*. This unimportant
entanglement brings him, however, to an important conclusion:

> 'In words of this kind, *the names* by which we call the two letters, *gh*, whether in a
> separate state, as *g* and *h*, or whether as *initial* and *final* aspirated *letters* . . . are so
> entirely distant from *the actual power*, which the letters themselves bear in
> pronouncing those words . . . that they are absolutely of no use for conveying to us
> *the true force* of these letters in the affair of speling them. For which reason, I have
> been inclined to think, that the best way of making *the power* of these letters . . .
> familiar to youth, would be, to lay before them a . . . list, of all the words, in our

language, where they occur, . . . that so, they may . . . learn *their use* by *frequent inspection* (reading such words and getting them *by heart*, without attempting to spell them).' (p. 47n.)

Even such a tentative suggestion that some words might be learnt as wholes was, at the time, very rare.

For most teachers, however, such an adherence to the strict interpretation of power caused practical difficulties, and they compromised. Lenoir, 1800, maintained that his pupils must not use the names of the consonants; all letters were to be referred to by the names of the eighty-four pictorial emblems that his system provides: the letter *v* is called *glove*, and the word *glove* is to be pronounced by 'laying stress on the last letter or sound somewhat lengthened'. He is trying to represent the power of the consonant by reducing as far as possible the phonetic context in which it occurs. But this is just the ground on which he has already criticised the traditional names. The names *bee*, *dee*, he says, are equivalent to whole words, and therefore 'the superfluities of these must . . . be thrown off in syllabication: and thus an infant is required to make use of [a] metaphysical faculty, viz. that of abstraction' (p. xx). Lenoir therefore has to compromise, either by Sheridan's pattern of names. *eb*, *ec*, *ed*, etc. (below, p. 43) as he recommends on p. xx, or by adding to the consonant letter 'the *u* short as heard in *sun*' which 'ought to be preferred to any other vowel', making the names *ub*, *uc*, *ud*, etc. (p. xxxiii).

Lenoir's emblems were a dead end but his struggles with the idea of power seem to have been followed closely by J.F. Denham, 1834, who adopts the same kind of compromise but puts the supporting vowel before, not after, the consonant. To the consonant Denham attributes 'incipient sound'. His objection to a spelling-method of teaching reading is that the pupil 'has an additional habit to acquire, namely, that of rejecting *all* but the *incipient sound* of each letter, although in the first instance he pronounces much more'. Denham lists, as well as can be done in writing, the *sounds* of the consonants, saying of his representative example *b*: 'The only sound which should be uttered in pronouncing this letter, is that which peculiarly belongs to the consonant itself, suppressing the *vowel* associated with it *as much as possible* . . . As nearly as it can be *written*, however, it should be like the word *ŭb*, *ŭ* being suppressed' (pp. 8, 9). A similar procedure is suggested in *The Syllabic Reading Book*, 1869.

J.M. McCulloch, in his reading-books, repudiates the idea of incipient sound and advocates a strict form of power:

The letters should be pronounced as nearly as possible with *the sounds they possess in combination*; so that the pupil may be able to gather the sound of the word from the sound of the letters which compose it, instead of requiring to be taught the habit of dropping all but the initial sound of each letter.   (1837 (i) *Directions*)

The strict use of the notion of power was never popular. It appealed to the theorist, but in practice it usually took a weaker form, in which a vowel sound was added to the consonant, thus enabling the teacher to talk about the ineffable. Such a weakening is seen in the work of Honoria Williams, who in 1817 advised teachers not to call consonants by their alphabet names, but as if they were followed by French *e*, as *se, le, ne . . . ze*. Teachers who did not know French should pronounce the names *sur, lur, nur . . . zur*, 'taking great care not to sound the *r*, which is only written to shew that the *u* is short' (pp. 1–4). An Inspector of Schools, referring particularly to Mrs Williams' book, might well comment that this is 'a method which requires a good deal of care in applying' (Jelinger Symons, *School Economy*, 1852, p. 83n.). Favell Lee Bevan adopts the same method in two works: 'The Letters and Spelling *may* be taught according to the common Method: but the Pupil's progress will be *much* facilitated if the *consonants* are called by the names which best convey an idea of their *power*: if *s* is called as the French word *ce*' (*c.* 1836, sheet no. 1). Bevan's later work, *Reading without Tears*, 1857, in advocating the method, shows its resemblance to Denham's incipient sound: 'In spelling such a word as DOG – the first consonant would be called by its new name, D', and sounded like *de* unaccented in French' (p. xii). In the same way T.B. Smith, 1858, illustrates 'the phonic method' by explaining that *an* is composed of *ah* and *nuh* pronounced quickly. By this method the pupil can eventually 'sound the syllable at sight, without pronouncing the letters separately' (p. 113). The sounding of the conson- ants in isolation (an artificial problem) was still seen as something which needed a solution. The teacher, showing letter cards to a class, is expected to say:

1859 'These five letters are called vowels. On the next and following lines other letters are placed before them; these are consonants. Most of you, I dare say, know that the first is called B (*be*). That is its *name*, but its *sound* is only b' (*pronouncing the letter without any vowel-sound but a simple aspiration sufficient to make it heard*) as you hear it at the end of the world *slab*.'   (Thelwall, p. 1)

1876 Similarly William Robinson wants *b* to be 'pronounced' like the last syllable of *robber*, and to be represented in 'the truer phonic utterance' by *b*', although he recognises that to call it *be* is more practical.   (p. 11)

Naming consonants

The CV pattern

Even if the practice of naming the consonants by strict reference to their power was too ideal, the teachers believed that there was still a problem. A more acceptable easement of their difficulty was to extend to all, or nearly all, the consonants the patterns of name shown by, on the one hand, *b*, *c*, and *d* and, on the other, by *l*, *m*, *n*: the CV and VC patterns referred to above (p. 32). CV names had been suggested for particular letters, especially *he* for *h* (Gill, (1619) 1621; Butler, 1633), *je* for *j* (Hume, 1617; Butler; Brooksbank, 1654b), *we* for *w* (Hume; Gill; Butler) and *ze* for *z* (Butler), but the first teacher to apply the CV pattern thoroughly was Richard Lloyd, in *The Schoole-Masters Auxiliaries*, 1654. Lloyd established the pronunciation of each of his new names by means of a lively comment. He calls *f* '*fee*, the lawyers reward' (and Dublin schoolchildren gave it the same name in 1904; below, p. 71) and similarly:

h   '*hee*, that speaketh of a Male'
k   '*key*, that doth lock and unlock the doors'
l   '*lee*, that is used to drive Buck-cloths' (i.e. lye for use in the washtub)
m   '*mee*, whom all should favour'
r   '*ree*, the drivers word to put horses from him'
w   '*wee*, the Schollers'
x   '*xee*, that fetcht up knotty flegme'
y   '*yee*, the Teachers'
z   '*zee*, the noise of hot iron in water.'

In spite of his *tour de force* with *x*, Lloyd does not apply the CV pattern to five of the consonants; he gives no reason for the exclusions:

c   '*Cuco* that doth always sing the same ditty'
g [hard] '*Gagogu* the Ganders call' (he does not say which element is to represent the name)
g [soft] '*Gheegegi* the Carters charge'
j   '*Jay* that devoureth the garden fruit'
n   '*Ney*, the speech of Horses'
p   '*Pye*, both bred and meate'.

The vowels in his alphabet keep their ordinary names, but are also glossed:

a   'the deafe mans answer'
e   'the kids bleating'
i   'the best Scholler'
o   'the wonderers language'
u   'a note of courting doves'   (pp. 4–5)

In the same year as Lloyd, John Brooksbank uses both CV and VC patterns in what seems an entirely random way:

'You must not suffer your Scholars to call these six Letters *h, g, j, v, w, z,* as they are usually, but most ignorantly, and unfittingly called here in *England,* but to giv them names according to the Analogy of the names of the rest of our *Consonants,* and their own proper powers, as not to call *h ache,* but *eh, nor g jee,* but *guee;* nor to call *j i* but *jee;* nor *v u* but *ev;* nor *w doubl u* but *woo* nor *z zed,* nor *zad,* nor *ezet,* nor *uzet,* nor *uzzard,* but *ez.'*   (1654a, pp. 15–16)

In the breezy and staccato work *Magazine,* 1703, the author, G.W., seems prepared to accept either a CV or VC pattern:

'B is a Consonant hath no name-sake . . . For put a vowel before or after it, its all one for the name and value, for every value of a letter is according to its name, or ought to be, for the name is proper to the figure as call [*d*] *de* or *ed,* 'tis all one . . . Call *b be,* or *eb;* but use custom.'   (p. 21)

G.W. is an erratic reformer and sits lightly to the question of names; the only ones that he uses in his own text follow both patterns, *ev* for *v, we* for *w* and *ye* for *y.*

The CV pattern, using *a* for the vowel, is recommended after much hesitation in *the Needful Attempt,* 1711. The author wants a CV pattern, but he thinks at first it should be formed with *-ee.* His final recommendation refers to the twenty consonants in his reformed alphabet: 'If these be taught at first by the Names *ra, na, ma, va . . . ha, ka, fa, da,* they would so, perhaps, be more easily learnt' (p. 15 orthography normalised).

Compared with G.W., William Johnston is a moderate reformer. He sees clearly the difficulty of teaching the names of the consonants:

1764   'The sound of a consonant . . . is conveyed by that part of its name, in which its sound is heard; and not by the vowels of its name . . . as when *b* is called *bee,* it's sound is not in the *ee,* but in the *b* . . . The true sounds of *b* . . . [etc.] . . . are conveyed by their common names . . . The names of *h, w, y,* and *z,* are inconvenient, because they hinder the perception of their proper sounds in words.'   (p. 5)

The names which Johnston proposes for new letters nearly all follow a CV pattern. A 'hard' *c,* as in *care,* is called *chee;* a hard *g* is called *gay;* a hard *x,* as in *wax,* is called *ecs,* but the 'soft' *x,* as in *exalt,* is called *egz,* and the *x* of *complexion* is labouriously called *cshee.*

During most of the eighteenth century the CV pattern by itself seems to have had little support; its last proponents, the Edgeworths, 1798, merely listing the names of all the consonants as *ba, ca, da,* etc. without discussion (p. 45). The reformers advocated sometimes a VC pattern or, more frequently, a mixed pattern using both CV and VC. These mixed patterns are described below. It is not until 1803 that a practically pure CV pattern re-emerges, in George Nicholson's *The Juvenile Preceptor* and in *The Progressive Spelling-Book*, 1810, which Nicholson printed. The American, Richard W. Green, 1829, advocating *he*, *er*, *we*, *ye* and *ze*, says 'those teachers who have adopted these names have been much more successful in teaching the first principles of reading, than those who adhere to the old names' (p. 179). In *The Anti-Spelling Book*, 1833, the 'natural' names for the twenty-four consonants are also given, as in *ke* for *c*, *fe* for *f*, and *ze* for *z*, but these names are to be pronounced as if written *kuh, fuh, zuh* (p. 25). The names of the consonants according to this system correspond therefore to the names devised by Honoria Williams and F.L. Bevan. From a different point of view that of the spelling reformer, a pure CV system with *-e* was advocated by Donald Walker in 1836. He, like the author of the *Anti-Spelling Book*, was wholeheartedly consistent in forcing even *x* into the system, as *kse* (pp. 6, 10).

The VC pattern

The VC pattern of names (*eb*, *ec*, *ed*), first proposed in the mixed system of *The Writing Scholar's Companion*, 1695 (below, p. 45), is, as a single system, associated with Thomas Sheridan in the 1780s. But James Buchanan, who attached little importance to the names of the letters, had earlier supported the idea of such a system in his 'Observations concerning the Manner of expressing the natural or mute Sounds of the Consonants' (1762, pp. 20f). About *b* Buchanan says: 'Its mute or natural Sound . . . resembles the Syllable *ib*; to express it truly, first put the Lips together, and try with the Lips thus closed to pronounce *ib*; which is impossible, tho' by this Contact or Motion we hear the Sound of *b* exactly.' He treats all the consonants except *h* (*ha*) and *j* (*dsh*) in this way, which is only a step from using these VC forms as their names. Sheridan's pattern, with *-e*, first appears in the *Rhetorical Grammar* prefixed to his *General Dictionary*, 1780, and separately issued in 1781. In his reformed alphabet he lists 24 consonants, of which 21 are formed on the VC pattern with *-e*; these include *edge* (*j*), *eks* or *egz* (*x*) and *ez* (*z*). *H* (*ha*) and *q* (*qua*) are the only standard letters which he excludes from the system, of which he says: 'By sounding these . . . characters in this manner, their nature and powers will be expressed in their names. And I have placed a vowel before the . . . consonants . . . contrary to the usual practice' (1781, p. 7). In his *Elements of English*, Sheridan expresses the hope that this system of naming the consonants will make it easier for children to learn a pure pronunciation:

1786 'The reason for recommending this mode of sounding the alphabet is, that
when all the consonants are pronounced with a vowel before them, the exact
position of the organs in forming those consonants is made manifest, and children
may be taught mechanically to produce the sounds of those which they do not
readily catch by the ear: whereas, in pronouncing many of them, with the vowel
after, as *bee, cee, gee,* &c. the organs are left in the position of sounding the vowel *ee,*
and the formation of the consonant is lost.'   (p. 4)

Sheridan's system of names is taken over, along with much else, in a school
textbook printed in Edinburgh in 1784: *A General View of English
Pronunciation* (p. 3). George Fulton, 1817, described the system as he
and George Knight had long followed it in their school in Edinburgh. It
incorporated Sheridan's names into the 'regiment' of letters: 'To the
Common SOLDIERS (or Consonants) we give the names assigned them by Mr
Sheridan, annexing to each some word with which the Pupil is well
acquainted; thus: *eb – Bird, ec – Cat . . . es – Screw . . . ev – Veal.'* These names
were used by teacher and pupil. The pupil, faced with the letters *b, d, a, c,* is
expected to name them *eb, ed, a, ec*; the teacher names a letter at random: '*eg
– Gun*', which the pupil is expected to pick out from among the letters of a
'dissected Alphabet' (pp. 23–4).

Sheridan and those who followed him closely thought it one of the
advantages of his system that the names for the letters expressed also their
powers. But a weakened form of Sheridan's system achieved some
popularity in the 1820s and 1830s. It is first seen in Lennie's *The Child's
ABC, c.* 1820, where Sheridan's names, with one or two variations, are
listed in a column headed 'Powers', parallel with one headed 'Names', in
which are listed what we would call the customary names of the letters
(p. 5). The same intention seems to be expressed by Meston, 1823. He uses
Sheridan's names for the sounds of the letters but keeps the customary
names as well: 'After learning the vowels, the child may proceed to the
consonants. He begins with *b,* and is taught that *b* sounds *eb,* pronouncing
the *e* very short . . . thus, *eb-a* [makes] *ba; eb-e* [makes] *be* . . . He must,
moreover, learn to spell in the usual way; *be-a, ba; be-e, be'* (p. 192). The
author's examples obscure the point he is making. His first example relates
to pronouncing, to reading aloud (Skill 3.3): in teaching a child to read the
syllable *ba* its component sounds are broken down into *eb* and *a.* The second
example relates to spelling (Skill 2.3): in teaching a child to spell the syllable
ba the component sounds must be represented by their letters, which are
named, *b, a.* Sound and name are being distinguished; there is no confusion
on that point. But they are handled simultaneously, in a way which one
would expect to be muddling. Nevertheless the same practice is followed by
J. Lordan in a spelling book of 1827 (pp. 9, 17) and by James Gall in 1832.

Gall lists the alphabet first by powers in a VC pattern with *i-* (*ib, ic, id,* etc.) and then by name, *ay, bee, cee,* etc. It does not matter, he says, which system is used (p. 25).

The VC pattern with *i-*, first suggested by Buchanan in 1762, next appears in Archibald Douglas' spelling-book of 1770, where the consonants all have alternative designations, representing presumably their names and their powers. *B* is *bee* or *ib, C cee* or *ic,* and so throughout, including *Q, cu* or *ic,* and *X, ex* or *ix. H* is *aitch* or 'aspiration' (p. 9). William Scott, in the 1796 edition of his *An Introduction to Reading and Spelling,* first published in 1776, lists first the customary names but follows the list with: 'Or thus at first: *ai, ib, ic, id, ee, iff, ig, ih . . . iv, oo* [u], *oo* [w], *ix, eye, iz*'. He makes no comment about these alternative names, although they appear in just this form nowhere else. The only other writers to use this VC pattern are James Gall, mentioned above, and R. Kay, of Newcastle on Tyne. In his *The New Preceptor,* 1801, Kay lists the alphabet 'by the new method' (that is, Sheridan's) which he says he has used for twenty years. He is not entirely consistent, departing from the pattern not only with *w* and *y*, as was often done, but also with *h* (*hah*), *j* (*idge*), *k* (*kah*) and *q* (*queh*) (p. 8). William Woodbridge in America makes an isolated use of this form by recommending *iv* as an alternative to *vee* (1800b). Goold Brown, 1850, also in America, expressed at length his disapproval of many innovative names, including *he, er,* and *oo* for *w*; but his especial scorn is for the VC pattern with *i-*, the whole alphabet of which he quotes 'from a Scotch gentleman of good education' who, one suspects, had been taught from William Scott's textbook (Goold Brown, 1850, 1875 edn, p. 151).

The mixed pattern

Several of the teachers quoted have recommended both CV and VC patterns, either as alternatives or as part of a (not very clearly expressed) policy of distinguishing names from powers, or sounds. An earlier policy, however, had a deeper (but not at first a more clearly expressed) pedagogic purpose. It proposed both CV and VC patterns not as alternatives but to be used together in a mixed scheme (above, p. 32). This pattern first appears in *The Writing Scholar's Companion,* 1695, where both the CV and the VC patterns are offered. The author lists the consonants: *be – eb, ce – ec,* etc., including *re – ar,* and, as their only forms, *we, ex, ye.* His explanation does not make it clear how the two patterns are related. 'The Consonants . . . should be thus sounded and named, with an *e* before and after them; to impress upon the mind (as much as possible) the true sound, and force of

every Consonant as well at the end, as beginning of every word or Syllable.'
After listing the pairs the author goes on to say of the consonants: 'If you
sound them with *a, i, o,* or *u* before and after them frequently in your mind,
you will find it a most excellent way to fix the natural sound of the
Consonants in your Memory' (pp. 1–5). But the important point in the
Companion's arrangement is only hinted at in the author's explanation. If a
consonant, say *b*, has a name that ends in a vowel (the CV pattern) there will,
in a spelling method of reading, be a smoother transition from the initial
consonant of a syllable to the following vowel, *be-a-de, bad* than if the name
of the initial consonant is of the VC pattern, *eb-a-de, bad*. Conversely, at the
end of a syllable there is a smoother transition from the vowel of the syllable
to the final consonant of the syllable if the name of that final consonant
begins with a vowel, *be-a-ed, bad*. The method assumes that the transition
from vowel to vowel is easier for children to make, and leads more readily
into the sound of the complete syllable, than the transition from consonant
to vowel or vowel to consonant. The method therefore requires all
consonants to have two names, one on the CV pattern for naming the initial
letter of a syllable, one on the VC pattern for naming the final letter.

This combination of CV and VC is found, in exactly the same form but
without comment, in Gildon, 1711, and Harland, (a. 1714). Tuite, 1726,
adopts the same practice and comments: 'Consonants having two names,
according to their position, *l, m, n, r,* may be call'd *le, me, ne, re,* and do
sound so before a vowel' (p. 4). John Yeomans provides an odd variation.
He comments on the inconsistency of the names of the letters:

1759 'In former alphabets, no two authors ever yet agreed in naming, neither was
there any form at all in the names of the letters; for sometimes, in giving the
consonants names, the vowels would precede the consonants, and otherwise the
consonants preceded the vowels, as in spelling *bee dee* the consonant comes first, but
in *ell em* the vowel. It was never considered, that, in order to make the names of the
letters short and complete, the vowels must continually forego [always precede] the
consonants, or the consonants continually forego the vowels. There could not have
been given our *h w y* more inconsistent titles than those our Lexicographers and
Abecedarians at present permit.'   (p. 50)

Yeomans first lists the alphabet in a CV system with *y*, saying that *by, cy, dy,*
etc. are to be pronounced *bee, cee, dee,* etc. This is 'the old Alphabet, with
the proper Names of each Letter . . . accommodated to the New Method'
(p. 49). The new method is presumably his own method of phonetic
representation. Later in the work, however, he states his allegiance to a
mixed system. In 'the Syllableium' he gives all the consonants, in both CV
and VC forms, abandoning his use of *y* to represent the sound *ee*. *B* is named
bee or *eb*, *c* is *see* and *kee* or *ec*, *g* is *ghee* and *eg*, or *jee* and *edg*; *w, x* and *y* alone

have single forms, *hoo, eks* and *hee*. Yeomans makes it clear that he regards these innovations as names: 'Note, That to begin words, the first name, and in ending of words the other, will be approved the most expedient to be made use of' (p. 64). This comment puts him directly into the line of descent from the *Writing Scholar's Companion*.

Variations of this mixed system of naming the letters continue into the nineteenth century.

1773 Abraham Tucker combines the CV and VC patterns in the same way as does the *Companion*, but restricted to three consonants: 'I do not see the necessity of giving the names we do to all our letters, as "de, ef, atch, zed", for most of them may be sounded alone without the aid of any others . . . But there are three letters, *c, p, t*, which cannot be pronounced alone, and I have given them double names "ecce" or "ecca", "ippi" or "ippy", and "itti" or "itty"; in order that either branch may be taken as they are found to follow or precede a vowel, so that I would teach a learner to spell *crack* by "ca, r, a, ec".' (p. 6)

Tucker is, for these three letters, combining into one name, with a change of vowel, the VC and CV forms *ec/ce, ep/pe* and *et/te* which *The Writing Scholar's Companion* and a handful of later spelling-books had suggested for the consonants as a whole.

1776 William Perry, in *The only sure guide to the English tongue*, lists the names of the letters, giving the consonants alternative CV and VC forms: *c* is called *cee* or *ek*; *g* is called *jee* or *eg*; *h hee* or *aitch*. (p. 1)

1782 In *The Real Reading-made-Easy* Thomas Spence, like Kay at one time a teacher in Newcastle on Tyne, proposes a mixed system, but he makes the vowel *i*, as Kay had done in his VC system (above, p. 45). Spence's alphabet, which he first put forward in *The Grand Repository*, 1775, is described in his text by Mr Man, a Kruzone'in, that is, an inhabitant of Robinson Crusoe's island and the spokesman for the economic and orthographical reforms that Spence advocates in his fable. The CV forms *bi, di*, etc. are given for all letters, the VC forms *ib, id* etc. only for eight of the consonants (pp. 43–4). No reasons are given for adopting this system, but Spence was an admirer of Sheridan, whom he had quoted extensively in *The Grand Repository*. The Kruzone'in spokesman was only echoing Sheridan when he said to the English sea-captain, 'U mŭst nŏt ĕkspĕkt ŭs too spĕl so ăbsŭrdle ăz u doo.'

1793 Foster Waterman's *The Child's Instructor*, published in Boston, Massachusetts, names all the letters according to the mixed system. Waterman is consistent, from *be* or *eb* to *ze* or *ez*, and is probably following William Perry, whose dictionary he acknowledges.

1799 Enoch Hale, also in Massachusetts, follows the same practice as Waterman.

1807 Abner Kneeland, of New Hampshire, in his *A Brief Sketch of a New System of Orthography*, says that the letters *l, m, n, r, f, s* would be more correctly called *le, me, ne*, etc., but the change is not worth making because 'the names by which they are now called give the same sounds, and do not naturally give different ones'. Like the others he calls *h he*, *w we* and *y ye*. What is puzzling, and differs from other mixed systems, is his comment that *b, d, g, k, p, t* would properly be called *eb, ed,* etc. He does not explain why he suggests changing existing VC names (*el, em, en*) into CV ones while at the same time changing existing CV ones (*be, ce, de*) into VC ones. Of Kneeland it can, perhaps justly, be said that he was confused, and by his own account his contemporaries thought so. The *Brief Sketch* is a preliminary to his proposals for orthographical reform, which involve representing the sound of *e* as in *let* by the letter *a*, and the sound of *i* as in *fit* by the letter *e* (pp. 7–8). In his *A Key to the New System of Orthography*, 1832, Kneeland describes the development, and the frustrations, of his attempts at reform. They began in 1801, but his *The American Definition Spelling Book*, 1802, does not give the mixed system of names, which first appeared in the *Brief Sketch*, and was continued in *The American Pronouncing Spelling Book*, 1825, for which he could not get acceptance in schools, and in the *Key* of 1832.

Names of particular letters

The names of the vowels were thought to cause no difficulty: name and sound were securely and usefully united. John Walker, 1791, is the only writer who draws attention to the fact that as each of the vowels can represent several sounds there could be a choice of name. He asks whether the letter *a* is to be called 'aye' or 'ah' or 'aw' (p. 8). The context of his question is a comparison of English with Irish and Scottish pronunciation; he is not thinking about the teaching of reading.

C   was often thought, not only by reformers, to need two names: one for its 'hard' and one for its 'soft' sound. Hence *kee* or *es* (Hodges, 1644), *kee* or *cee* (Butler, 1633; Lane, 1700), *ka* or *see* (Cooper, 1687); *kee* and *see* (W.L. Robinson, 1862); in the VC pattern *ek* or *ess* (Sheridan).

G   received the same treatment. The name of 'soft' *g* was usually represented as *jee* or *ghe*; 'hard' *g* was named *ga* by Hart and A. Gill, *gee* by most others, with variants such as *ge* (Aickin, 1693), *guee* (Brooksbank, 1654b), *ghee* (Lane, 1700; W.L. Robinson, 1862), *guh* (Bayly, 1771). In the VC pattern hard *g* was usually *eg* or *ig*, with *edzh* (Sheridan) for soft *g*.

H   The familiar name is spelt in many ways: *ach, ache, atsh, aitsh, aytsh, haitch, each*, but there is regular support for a CV pattern, normally *he*, even amongst those who do not adopt the pattern generally, from Gill, 1619, to Salem Town (USA) and Hyde Clarke in 1853. Less frequently the name keeps the old Latin form *ha* (Tuite; Sheridan) or *hah* (Hart). Brooksbank alone calls the letter *heh* (p. 16). In 1603 Alexander Top is the first to comment on a puzzling aspect of the name for *h*. He disapproves of calling it *atch* because that name leads children to spell *heere*, for example, 'as if they should beginne *tcheer* . . . the children must [i.e. they are at present required to] learne to spell *ch, ee, r, heere*' (sig. D1). He is protesting against a practice that seems to require a word beginning with *h* to be spelt with a vowelless form of the name *atch*: not *atch* but *tch* or *ch*. Top's remedy is to name *h he*. The same point is made by Owen Price, 1668, in catechetical form: 'Q. Why do you call (ach) *h, he*? A. I call (ach) *h, he*, be-cause when the Teacher as-kes a child, what spell's (ach) *h-a*, he will be read-dy to an-swer, *cha*; whereas if he had as-ked him *he-a*, he would have said, *ha*' (p. 5). Some light is thrown on this by a passage in *The Child's Bible*, 1677, where the author states a general rule: that 'the names of Consonants always give the sound of that word, which they make when they are put together without the Vowels, which belong to their names. As for example, *ef, a, en*, spells *fan* . . . the Vowel *e* being put away, which belongs to the names of the Consonants *f, n*.' But if this rule is applied to *h*, the author says, an absurd result follows: 'So *ache, e* (by putting away the Vowels which belong to the usual name of the Letter *h*) spells *che*.' *H* should therefore be named in the same economical way as are the other consonants, by having a single vowel sound attached to it: *he*. As a separate question the author discusses double consonants such as *ch, ph, sh*. He thinks they should have names of their own; he calls *ch* 'che', and would spell *church*, therefore, not in the ordinary way, which he describes as '*se, ache, u, ar, se, ache*', but '*che, u, ar, che*' (A6b). A different treatment of the double consonants, but a similar illustration, occurs amongst the reforms obscurely put forward by G.W. in *Magazine*, 1703, to which David Abercrombie drew attention (1965a) *Magazine* is written in such a jerky style that it is difficult to interpret. The author has been saying that *c, t* and *h* 'do fool our ears' in words like *hatch*, as does *d* in words like *hedge*, and *h* in *Philip*. He then makes the obscure comment: 'Now if you had said HURH spells church, and GUG spells Judge, I could easily believe it' (p. 23). Abercrombie says that what G.W. is doing is 'to base the sounds of the letters *h* and *g* on their traditional names' instead of following the usual practice of reformers, to base the name on the sound. This is true as far as it goes, but it leaves unexplained the loss of the initial vowel in the name *atch*, of which there are now two earlier instances. The exclusion of the vowel seems to be an attempt to express the power of a consonant, by omitting the vowel sound of its name, and therefore belongs to the line of thought described above. All three writers, Top, the author of *The Child's Bible*, and G.W., touch on the idea. G.W. applies it to the double consonants in a way quite different from that in the *Child's Bible*; in the latter *ch* is called *che*, whereas for G.W. '*H* is vain, in *Ghost, Scholar*, not in *Churh* [sic], but *c* is, therefore it deserves to be turn'd out of doors' (p. 24). *C*, that is, is unnecessary in *church* because *h* already makes the sound of *ch*.

J is usually *jay* or *jea*, but is also called *je* or *jee*, not only by the reformers· but by other seventeenth-century teachers (Hume, Brooksbank, Preston, Young, Cooper). Price, in 1665, gives '*j* consonant' or 'tayl'd *j*' the name *jod*, and in 1668 he calls it *je*. The Hebrew name *jod* is used until the end of the eighteenth century (Hume; Coles, 1674; Care, 1687; Fogg, 1792), but its standing is insecure. Dyche, 1707, thinks the name useful, 'but because the Hebrew Names of Letters are not at all receiv'd into our Alphabet, I take the Liberty to call it *ja*, as best agreeing with the rest of our English Names of Letters' (p. 110). In the VC pattern the name is *ij* (W. Scott, (1776) 1796), *idge* (Kay, 1801) or *edge* (Kneeland (American), 1807; Fulton and Knight, 1817). An unidentified colonial spelling-book gives *j* the name *iazh* (C. Johnson (1904) 1963, p. 176) but this is probably a misprint or a misreading of *idzh*, a form that appears in *Watts's Compleat Spelling-Book*, 1737, but not in Watts' own book of 1721.

K   It is difficult to interpret the variants of the name for *k*. The traditional name is usually written *ka*, sometimes *ca*, and presumably both were pronounced 'kay'. Some writers who name *j* 'jay' (Gildon, Tuite) give *ka*, not *kay*, as the name of the following letter. The consistency of their own alphabet would require *ka* to be pronounced 'kah'. However consistency is less likely than a fairly uniform pronunciation as 'kay', however spelt. The first work in which a spelling with -*ay* appears is Dyche's *A Guide to the English Tongue*, 1707, where the name is *cay*.

Q   Over *q* there is the same uncertainty as over *k*. The name appears regularly as *cu* or *ku*, but also as *qu* (A. Gill; Newton, 1669; Maittaire, 1712; Bayly, 1771). These forms presumably represent the same pronunciation as the *cue* of Gildon (1711) and of the grammar prefixed to Johnson's *Dictionary* (1755) and of the version that P.W. Fogg offers fastidiously: 'Shall I omit or insert the full-length name of this grotesque character? – It is *kyoo*' (Fogg, 1796, p. 163). But the name is given at least once (by William Perry, a Scot) as *coo*, and some uncertainty remains about its customary pronunciation. Forms of the name that must have carried a different pronunciation are *que* (Lye, 1671), *quee* (Hodges, 1644; *The Child's Bible*, 1677; Lane, 1700); *qui* (R. Lloyd, 1654); *qua* (Sheridan) and *ke* (D. Walker, 1836). In the VC pattern *q* is excluded, save by Scott ([1776] 1796) who names it *ic*, as he had already named *c*.

R   when not having its modern name was fitted into either the CV pattern as *re* or into the VC pattern as *er*. As between *er* and *ar* there seems to have been for a long time a social or dialectal distinction, the signification of which is not fully brought out in Simon Daines' comment that the name of the letter is *er*, 'notwithstanding so many *Infantuli* produce *R, quasi ar*' (1640, p.17). Elphinston refers to the name of *r* as '*er* (vulgarly *ar*)' (1765, I, 9) and the same view is expressed more fully by the American Noah Webster in 1789:

'Another very common error, among the yeomanry of America, and particularly in New England, is the pronouncing of *e* before *r*, like *a*; as *marcy* for *mercy*. This mistake must have originated principally in the name of the letter *r*, which, in most of our school books, is called *ar*. This single mistake has spread a false pronunciation of several hundred words, among millions of people. To remedy the evil, in some degree, this letter is named *er*, in the *Institute*. In a few instances this pronunciation is become general among polite speakers, as *clerks, sergeant*, &c.'

(Webster, 1789, *Dissertation 2*, p. 105)

Webster goes on to say that 'the true sound of the short *e*, as in *let*, is the correct and elegant pronunciation of this letter in all words of this class' – that is, those like *mercy*, which he is discussing. The name of the letter spelt *er* must have been pronounced by him as in our *error* and not as in *ermine*.

V   like *j*, was often given its Hebrew name *vau* (Hume; *Thesaurium*, 1689; Browne, 1700; Owen, 1732; Lowe, 1755). Otherwise it followed the traditional CV pattern *ve* or, less often, *va* (Fisher, [1693] 1700; Gildon, 1711; Sproson, 1740; Samuel Johnson, 1755). The VC pattern *ev* appears as early as Hart, 1569, and Brooksbank, 1654b. The *Instructions for Beginners*, 1728, are emphatic: 'All good Masters call the long crooked *j*, *jay*, and the pointed *v*, *ev*' (p. iii).

W   like *h*, had a name unrelated to its sound. Nevertheless the traditional name was in regular and increasingly unquestioned use. The alternative was nearly always *we*, occasionally *woo* (Brookbank), *oo* (Yeomans, 1759; Sheridan; Titus Strong (USA), a. 1821), or *ou* (Perry, 1776a). Owen Price, 1668, again gives the reason: 'I call (dou-ble u) *w*, *we*, be-cause, if the Tea-cher askes, what spell's (double u) *w-a*, the learner will in rea-son an-swer dou-ble-u-a spell's dou-ble-u-a, but when he is asked, what spell's *we-a*, he will frame his mouth (as he seeth his tea-cher) to say, *wa*' (pp.5–6).

Y   The only alternative regularly proposed for *y*'s name, written *wi, wy* or *wye*, was *ye* (*yee* or *yi*). The form *ye* appears as early as Top (1603) and Hume, who offers the Hebrew *yod* as well, and as late as Salem Town

(1837). Archibald Douglas, 1770, gives an alternative, and puzzling, name 'I pronoun'.

Z   The naming of *z* was regularly commented on because of the variety of forms in which the traditional name occurred: *zad, tzad, zod* (Dixon, 1728; Dyke, *c.* 1746; Lawrie, 1779; [Primer] 1780), *zard, ezod, ezed, uzet, ezat, izzard, ezzard, uzzard, edsard* (Daines, 1640). George Fisher, 1700, amuses himself with the pronunciation of *Nebuchadnezzar* which, because *z* is called '*Zed*, or *Izord*, and may as well be termed *Buzzard*', he represents as '*Ne-bu-chad-ne-i-zord-i-zord-ar*' (p. 3). He would have sympathised, one hopes, with the teacher in an Irish country school 'who had never been able to compass the word *Nebuchadnezzar*' and used to ask her pupils 'to call it Nazareth, and let it pass' (M. and R.L. Edgeworth, 1798, p. 66). The Edgeworths' own name for *z* was *za*, because 'the sound of *z* [the child] cannot by any conjuration obtain from the name *zad*, the only name by which he has been taught to call it' (p. 41). Sometimes the comments about *z* refer to the difficulty of using the traditional name in the teaching of spelling, and it was this difficulty that encouraged the alternatives *ez* and *ze*. The name *ez* occurs first in Hart, and *ze* in Bullokar. *Ez* is advocated by Hodges, 1644; Brooksbank; Cooper, 1687, and Aickin; less frequently in the eighteenth century (*Irish Spelling Book*, 1740; Sheridan, 1786). The other VC form, *iz*, is advocated by Dun, a. 1766, and, in accordance with their overall pattern, W. Scott (1776) and Kay. The more popular alternative name was *ze* (Lloyd, 1654; Lye, 1671; Preston; *The Child's Bible*). It is often given as an alternative to, and not in place of, *zed* by those who keep otherwise to the traditional names (Clarke, 1853). American practice adopted *zee* or *ze* almost from the first (Webster, 1783; Caleb Alexander, 1797b; Babcock, 1798), but Robert Ross, 1785, gave both *zee* and *zed*; Woodbridge, 1800, gave only *zed*, Isaiah Thomas, 1785, only *zed* or *s hard*, and James Carrol (1795) only *ez*. In 1850 Goold Brown, who firmly supported traditional names because they were part of the culture, nevertheless named *z zee* without question (p. 151).

The sounds of the letters

As reading was for most pupils most of the time a process of joining together the sounds represented by a sequence of letters it seemed desirable to teach the sounds that each letter, or diphthong, could represent. But the difficulty of doing so was very great, for reasons that make it difficult also to describe the attempt briefly.

In each half century between 1600 and 1800 about half the relevant texts make some attempt to describe the sounds of all or most of the letters. In addition a small number of texts discuss only the sounds of the vowels. Between 1801 and 1850 the proportion drops, on average, to less than a quarter, and it falls steadily during that period. There was little disagreement concerning what might be taught about the sounds of the letters: the question was how much, if any, was appropriate to a particular writer's purposes. The principal matters that might be discussed were:

(i) A description of the speech organs and of the speech sounds related to each.
(ii) The sounds represented by the vowels.
(iii) Diphthongs and, occasionally, triphthongs.
(iv) Silent letters (a constant preoccupation).
(v) The classification and function of consonants.
(vi) Miscellaneous aspects of the function of particular letters, relating to pronunciation and correct usage.
(vii) What was generally called accent or accentuation, that is, stress.

The writers might treat this subject matter in detail, or in outline; it might be silently omitted; it might be explicitly rejected.

The speech organs would be entirely outside our present concern if it were not for the work of some seventeenth-century writers that belongs to, or was influential in, the schools. John Wallis' English grammar, 1653, although written in Latin and intended for adults, was used by textbook writers as, to a lesser extent, was Wilkins' *Essay* of 1668. Both describe the speech organs as part of their treatment of phonetics. Owen Price, in *The Vocal Organ*, 1665, and Christopher Cooper, in *The English Teacher*, 1687, both writing for school use, refer in some detail to the function of lips, tongue, teeth, palate and throat.

More elaborate than most, but still rather naive, is William Baker's emphasis in 1724 on 'the *various Sounds* of Letters, and the *Composition* of Syllables and Words'. He illustrates this emphasis by a laborious description of the formation of the sound of each syllable in, amongst other words, *excommunication*:

'Coming to *m*, I close my Lips, and express the *Power* thereof by a kind of *hum* – and forcing the Breath through the Nose. This *hum* – I continue with an easie Transition, 'till I come to the third *Syllable* . . .' thus, he says, we see 'how (in dividing Words into Syllables exactly) the *Powers* of Letters are compleated and framed, according to the different opening and shuting of the *Mouth*, or otherwise disposing of the *Organs* or *Instruments of Speech*, as *Vowels* and *Consonants* variously occur.'   (preface)

Later authors of school or elementary texts, even the elocutionists, did no more than occasionally and briefly refer to the influence of an organ on a particular speech sound (e.g. Sheridan, 1781, Section 2; W. Martin, 1851b, who classifies the letters of the alphabet 'according to the organs of speech'; W.L. Robinson, 1868).

Teachers regularly attempted, at varying levels of sophistication, to enumerate and describe the range of sounds represented by each of the five (or more) vowels and the variety of ways in which the same vowel sound could be represented by different letters or combinations of letters. The general practice was to say, for each vowel, how many different sounds it could represent, and to illustrate each. The number of different sounds for any vowel varied from writer to writer to such an extent that those who doubted the value of such an analysis had ample evidence on which to argue. To the letter *a*, for example, Ann Fisher assigns two different sounds ([1763] 1801); Ash, 1760, and many others, assign three; Johnston, 1764, and many others, assign four; Caleb Alexander (USA), 1797b, assigns four but gives five; James Pike (USA) 1808, assigns five. W. Perry, 1776a, assigns six; Peter Walkden Fogg, 1792, eight; in 1798 (p. 45) the Edgeworths say *a* has three sounds; in 1799 (p. 4) they say it has five. The length and quality of vowel sounds are described in varied terms: long, short, broad, narrow, mid, slender, small, shut, obscure, acute, clear, open, full. The most helpful and, in spite of regional and other variations, the most widely used, method of indicating pronunciation was, of course, to give illustrative examples of words that the pupils already knew how to pronounce.

There was no agreement, during the whole period, about what a diphthong was, about how many (if any) there were in English, and whether the customary classification into proper and improper diphthongs was valid or useful. A proper diphthong was traditionally defined as 'a Joyning of two vowels in the same syllable, wherein the power of both is kept' (Cooper, 1687, p. 14). Improper diphthongs were those where there was only one vowel sound although there were two vowels. Only the more thoughtful writers distinguished between diphthongs and digraphs. The number of diphthongs in English was regularly stated, with enormous variations according to the author's understanding of the term; especially whether he was classifying sounds or combinations of letters. A representative number would be Price's twelve proper and eight improper diphthongs. Not many writers recognised the triphthong. Ben Jonson had warned them: 'The *Triphthong* is of a complexion, rather to be fear'd then lov'd: and would fright the young *Grammarian* to see him. I therefore let him passe' (chap. 5). Examples, rather doubtful ones, sometimes given, as by Hayward, *c.* 1625, and Ash, 1760, are *beauty* and *lieutenant*.

Silent letters, in spite of the many different reasons there could be for their 'silence', were often treated as a group, in a distinct section of the textbook, even at an elementary level. The practice was popular with teachers because it provided the pleasures of collecting and categorising, but it is unlikely that it helped their pupils much. Henry Preston, 1674, for instance, writing a simple manual in rhyme, tells his readers in one paragraph that *c* is silent in *sick* and in a list of other words ending in *-ck*, and in the next paragraph that *c* is silent after *s* in *concupiscence* and *sciatica*. James Carrol, in *The American Criterion*, 1795, takes each letter of the alphabet in turn and describes when, if at all, it is silent: '*U* is silent in *buoy*, *buy*, *Guy*, *mantua*, and in the second syllable of *pursuivant*' (p. 55). He and many others give particular attention to *e*, and 'final *e*' is often treated as a separate category. Increasingly during the eighteenth century the teachers' emphasis changes: at first it is merely on the presence of what they perceive as silent letters; then the silent letters are treated as signs and causes of anomalous pronunciation and spelling; eventually, if they are discussed at all, it is in the context of etymology. A late but emphatic example of the older approach is the anonymous *The Principles of English Reading*, 1855, in which all the reading lessons are based on the open and shut sounds of the vowels, signalled by the presence or absence of final *e*. Silent letters were indicated by various typographical means, the commonest being italics and the rarest being the Edgeworths' 'mark of obliteration', a small angled stroke under each silent letter (1798, p. 43).

The classification of consonants was carried out at two levels. The phoneticians attempted a detailed treatment, but most teachers were content with a routine and traditional classification into two categories: mutes and semi-vowels; among the latter there was often made a sub-class of liquids. The constituents of these classes varied, but the basic classification remained unchanged. In 1594 Paul Greaves gives as mutes *b*, *c*, *d*, *f*, *g*, *k*, *p*, *t*, and as semi-vowels *l*, *m*, *n*, *r*, *s*, *x*, *z*. Edward Clark, 1680, gives the same mutes, without *k* or *f*, and the same semi-vowels, with the addition of *f*. In 1820 P.H. Pullen lists the same mutes as Greaves, without *f* and *q*; he separates *l*, *m*, *n*, *r* as liquids, and lists the semi-vowels as *s*, *x*, *z*, *f*, *v*, *g* soft, *j*. Pullen also gives the organic classification into labials, dentals, gutturals and nasals that, together with palatals or 'palatines', was regularly made.

The ordinary method of presenting, in a school textbook, the sounds of the letters was to offer a number, at best a sequence, of statements of varying degrees of fullness and generality. Of the letter *S* Dilworth says only, '*S* is frequently sounded like *z*; as in *present*, *presume*' (p. 87). John Jones, 1701, asks in effect what letters or combinations of letters are used to represent the sounds of *S*. In reply he gives thirty different representations, some requiring sub-classification, some, such as *uces* in *Gloucester*, of a desperate singularity. The most frequent comments or quasi-rules regarding *S*, until late in the eighteenth century, are:

1. *S* has two sounds, 'hard' or 'hissing' (*mist*) and 'soft' or 'buzzing' (*rose*). A few writers add the sound of *sh* (*passion*).
2. Initial *s* is hissing.
3. Final *s* is buzzing.
4. Final *ss* is hissing.
5. After semi-vowels *s* is buzzing.
6. Between vowels *s* is buzzing (*rose*).
7. *S* is silent in, e.g. *island*.

By the nineteenth century it had become apparent that it was futile to expect any one to learn anything of practical value from instruction of this kind. *S* always proved difficult in performance. Clara Hall's *The Poetic Primer*, about 1830, contained a poem *Fly Away, Ladybird*, written without an S in order to avoid 'the terrible hissing effect' and to provide 'a useful hint to those who are in the habit of composing hymns to be sung in public, by charity children'.

If efforts such as the foregoing were certain to be ineffective – and it is not just the exercise of hindsight to believe that they were – one must ask why they were maintained for so long in the spelling-books. There are many strands in a possible answer. When in the teaching of reading so much importance was attached to the function of individual letters and to the sounding of short syllables, it was natural that an attempt should be made to display the sounds of the letters and diphthongs. There was a long tradition, going back to the Roman and Greek grammarians, of such discussion. There was likewise a long tradition of applying analytical procedures to any material that had to be studied: it was intellectually and pedagogically proper to do so. Furthermore it was generally assumed that children who were capable of learning by heart even a long and complex rule were capable of applying it and learning from its application. These traditions and assumptions were reinforced from time to time by special interests: in phonetics and its application to orthographical reform and universal language; in socially acceptable pronunciation; in public speaking and reading; in the needs of foreign students of English. If such varied influences kept in the spelling-books a description of the sounds of the letters, why did the descriptions become so much less frequent after 1800, appearing in only 10 per cent of the texts by the middle of the nineteenth century? There are two related reasons. The educational level of teachers, even of those who wrote textbooks, was rising, as was their understanding of how children learned. In addition, teachers had increasingly realised, during the eighteenth century, that such knowledge of different sounds, especially vowel sounds, as was practicable from book-learning could best be achieved through the organisation of the spelling-lists themselves. A late attempt to teach the vowel sounds descriptively appears in Lordan's *The New London Pronouncing Spelling Book*, 1827, where he advocates what he calls 'parsing the sounds' or 'tuning the ears of the scholars'. He illustrates the method:

'Q. What is the sound of *a* in *band*? Should the answer be 'broad *a*' ... the word may be pronounced by the Teacher, with the broad *a*, as *bawnd*; on the second trial, the pupil may call it long Italian *a*; the word should then be pronounced *barnd*: on the third attempt, the pupil may call it long slender *a* [as in *paper*]; when, on the teacher's pronouncing it *bande*, the fourth and last trial will bring the correct answer [i.e. 'the short Italian *a*', as in *fat*].' (pp. 11–12)

But Lordan also arranges his spelling-lists by vowel sounds, and it is through the spelling-lists that the teaching of pronunciation was by now usually attempted.

Those writers who doubted the value of trying to describe pronunciation in print refrained from doing so, usually without comment. It is pointless to speculate about their motives, but it cannot be said that they were any less thoughtful, nor their books any less popular, than those making a contrary decision. Seventeenth-century books in which the sounds of the letters are not considered include Elisha Coles' *The Compleat English Schoolmaster*, 1674; John Newton's *The English Academy*, 1677; N.S.'s *The English Tutor*, 1677; Tobias Ellis' *The English School*, 1680, and *The New England Primer* [1690] 1727. All these works had at least one subsequent edition, some of them many more. Eighteenth-century works of similar standing that omitted the sounds of the letters are Daniel Fenning's *The Universal Spelling Book*, 1756; John Clarke's *The Rational Spelling Book*, 1772; Charles Vyse's *The New London Spelling Book*, 1776 and editions to 1864; Thomas Dyke's *Reading made perfectly Easy* [1746] 1776 and editions to 1815; Robert Ross' *The New American Spelling Book*, 1785, and Isaiah Thomas' work of the same title and the same year.

Expressions of doubt about the value of trying to describe pronunciation begin to appear early in the eighteenth century. Before that the traditional practice, even if observed in only about half the texts, had not been questioned in print; after that, the practice was a declining one, against which objections were no longer necessary:

1700 'As for Diphthongs, Triphthongs, Mutes, Liquids, Semivowels . . . being more of Curiosity, than Use, Here is little said of them.'

(George Fisher, 1700, p. 43, misprinted for 47)

1734 Henry Boad omits 'remarks upon the sounds of the letters, &c . . . which many spelling books are bothered with'. The sounds should be discussed in grammars, if anywhere. (The grammarians, of course, often said that the sounds should be discussed in spelling-books.)

1743 James Corbet: 'I own I am unwilling to say any Thing on this Head; because most of the Rules laid down for the sounding of Letters, admit of so great a number of Exceptions, that . . . they rather confound than improve the Scholar' (p. 45). Corbet nevertheless prescribed rules.

1753 John Warden says it is 'impossible to explain the principles in the pronunciation of the *English* tongue, but by the mouth of one well skilled therein'. Even if an explanation were attempted, the teacher using it would be 'in great need of superior qualifications' in order to correct all the mistakes made in the customary explanations.

(p. vii)

1755 Dr Johnson, although he follows custom in describing the sounds of the letters 'perhaps with more reverence then judgment', admits that it is useless 'because of sounds in general it may be observed, that words are unable to describe them'.

(Grammar in the *Dictionary*)

In the context of elementary spelling-books nothing more need have been said.

Teaching the alphabet

What may be called the obvious method of teaching the alphabet is the one about which the textbooks say least. It is 'obvious' that you begin at the beginning and teach the letters in their alphabetical order, by name, as quickly as possible. There is nothing to say about something so obvious. It is necessary to distinguish between knowing the letters and knowing them in alphabetical order. Robert Cawdrey, instructing the reader how to use his dictionary, must assume that he can read (know his letters) but nevertheless finds it necessary to advise him: 'Thou must learne the Alphabet, to wit, the order of the Letters as they stand . . . and where every Letter standeth: as *b* neere the beginning, *n* about the middest, and *t* toward the end' (1604, preface). Those teachers who do discuss methods of teaching the alphabet are those who are proposing alternatives to, or aids for, the obvious method. The alternatives and the aids show little change: most are discussed in sixteenth- and seventeenth-century texts; many are as old as the practice of teaching the letters in Latin and Greek. The one gradually developing practice that does seem to show a new understanding of language and of how children learn is that of teaching the letters not in isolation but in the context of a word. The obvious method could be slow. Hoole says it could take children 'of a slower apprehension', being taught the whole alphabet at once, up to a year to know six letters (*The Petty-School*, 1660, pp. 4–5). He therefore recommends teaching one letter at a time, as does the author of *Instructions for Beginners*, 1728, who also says that it takes up to a year to learn the alphabet by ordinary methods. His own practice, however, of teaching just one letter a day enables children to master the whole alphabet in twenty-six days. Speedier still was the technique followed by J. Sims, master of Cripplegate School, London, who reported to the SPCK in 1700 that 'he had discovered a secret method by which he could teach the alphabet in a day's time' (M.G. Jones, 1938, p. 106).

The writers of most spelling-books, even if they listed the alphabet, expected children to have learnt it at home, and to know the letters by their names. Henry Wotton, writing about 1672, described how his prodigious son William learnt the alphabet at the age of three from inscriptions on gravestones and from capital letters that the father wrote on walls (Henry Wotton, 1753, p. 33). Brooksbank is unusual in describing how a class of children can be taught to identify the letters:

1654a 'They of your *Lowest Form*, are all to be the first Learners to *know their Letters, and to spell* . . . Having all your Scholars in this form disciplin'd and marshall'd . . . let them all stand out, each *in his place and order*, with his book in his left hand, open, at the first Chapter, and his feskew *on the foremost finger of his right hand*, then bid sometimes the *highest*, sometimes the *midlmost*, and sometimes the *lowest* in that Form, or which you pleas, begin to name the first Letter (*a*) in a English Letter, he and all the rest in the Form pointing at the same with their feskews: then let the next name the next letter, which is also (*a*) in a Roman letter, all the rest likewise looking upon the same, and pointing thereat with their feskews . . . but if your Scholars be very *young*, or dull, then let some Boy of the Form next abov, stand behind each such, teaching them how to hold their books, and feskews, and how therein direct their eyes and feskews, whereby in few dayes they will know what to do.'

(pp. 14–15)

Trying to teach the alphabet all at once caused difficulty. Repeated attention to the letters was obviously necessary, but only one spelling-book, *The Illuminated London Primer*, 1845, repeats each letter several times in the same typeface: 'The teacher, pointing to a line of *a* should say what are all these . . . and so on. By this means the child, having a number of each letter presented to its view, will retain the recollection of the different forms.' A more thoughtful alternative was to divide the letters into groups, while still keeping them in alphabetical order. Such a step is perhaps too obvious to have been mentioned. It is referred to only by Hoole, 1660 (*Petty School*, p. 10), before the end of the eighteenth century. Abner Reed, of Connecticut, 1800, keeps the alphabet in order but divides it into six uneven groups. Fulton and Knight, 1817, suggest breaking it into five groups according to the incidence of the vowels: *abcd*; *efgh*; *ijklmn*; *opqrst*; *uvwxyz* (p. 22). Exactly the same grouping is recommended in *The Proton*, 1828, where the alphabet is arranged without 'puzzling a child's sight with words, or names, before he can make out the letters (as in the generality of Spelling-Books)'. The author disapproves also of random lists and of a perpendicular alphabet list (p. iv). Andrew Thomson, before 1827, is quoted by Diack, 1965, p. 16, as teaching first the letters *o, m, i, s, x, b, y*, but it seems that these were chosen because they easily formed two- and three-letter words. In a spelling-book published about 1840, but dating from the 1770s, the alphabetical order is maintained, but it is recommended that the letters are first taught in groups of not more than six (J. Green, 1780, 1840 preface). William Hill, in the second edition of his *The Educational Monitor*, 1848, recommends groups of three, and in a Glasgow school about 1860 four letters had to be learnt each week and the whole alphabet known before a pupil might begin to read words (Scotland, 1969, p. 201).

The more common practice was to treat the vowels first, in one group, and then the consonants, which might or might not be further grouped: in the doggerel of William Scoffin, 1690, 'Let Children first, their Vowels learn to know: / Then Consonants; and so they'l forward go' (p. 2). An unusual exercise, distinguishing vowels and consonants, is prescribed by John Moscrip, of Berwick-on-Tweed:

1790 'Before beginning to teach dissyllables, the scholars should be put to perform the following *Exercise*, viz. to name the vowels and consonants in this Rhapsody thus, *b* a consonant, *a* a vowel, *e* a vowel, *x* a consonant, &c. till they can name the vowels and consonants very quickly.'   (p. 64)

The rhapsody begins: *baexcellentparticularlywonderfulimpertinentsolemnity* . . . but the exercise is linked by Moscrip not so much to learning the letters as to making his pupils 'quick-sighted' in distinguishing them. This type of exercise, also called a rhapsody and meant to develop quicksightedness, is found in Kay, 1801, and in *Reading most Easy*, 1821, where the teacher is warned: 'It is not saying there are five Vowels which will render the Scholar quick-sighted to divide by the most easy rules' (p. 6). In *Easy Lessons*, *c.* 1830, the two-letter syllable lists are conflated in a rhapsodic form, but it is not clear what the pupil was supposed to do. If each syllable in the following example was to be pronounced, how was the exercise better than using real words, and what was the point of stringing the syllables in this terrifying form: *Legijuhogafedycubaviturisapynomiquo?* Methods were combined. Hannah Kilham (1818a) recommended five groups: the vowels, three groups of six consonants, in alphabetical order, and a fifth group comprising *x* and *z* (p. 5). W. Draper, 1822, also takes the vowels first, in three groups of two (counting *y* as a vowel) followed by the consonants, in order, in pairs, *y* in its consonantal form joining the final pair (pp. 11–14). These procedures were put forward because they made for improved teaching; they were not part of a scheme of orthographical reform, as were the earlier proposals already described. The change of concern, from orthographical reform to teaching-methods, is illustrated by a comparison of the work of James Ellis in *The Perfect Schoolmaster*, 1719, with the very similar proposals made in *The Needful Attempt*, 1711 (above, p. 30). Ellis takes first the vowels, then the consonants, 'those that are most alike in their Shape . . . are set together, that the Child may see how one differs from another'. But Ellis' arrangement of the consonants, in an unbroken line with many letters repeated, makes it difficult to see which shapes his pupils found confusing. The list begins, as one might expect, with *bd*, *pq*, *hb*; long *s* and *f*, *s* and *z*, *g* and *y*, are adjacent but the sequence *xklvyc* does not suggest any obvious resemblance of shape (p. 2).

In *A Practical Treatise on Day-Schools* the author grumbles:

1816 'There appears to be very little method adopted in teaching the letters . . . In general, the child is made to repeat from A to Z, and from Z to A, till, by dint of continual repetition, he begins to distinguish them. Those which are widely dissimilar in their forms, he probably really knows in a few months; but *b* and *d*, *p* and *q*, long *s* and *f*, are often a source of confusion to him for years.' (p. 12)

The writer's positive suggestion is that the child 'should be provided with one letter, or at most two, according to his age and capacity', each on a card, which he learns 'with the assistance of the boy who sits by him'. When the learner successfully identifies these letters he receives the others by ones or twos, and makes them also on a slate. In Meston's *A Practical Essay*, which on this topic closely follows the *Practical Treatise*, it is recognised that 'the task of teaching and learning the alphabet is irksome' and is best done at home. The vowels are taken first:

1823 'Instead of giving a child the whole alphabet to learn at once, the teacher should have the letters painted upon slips of wood or strong card. When a child begins to learn the letters, the master should give it the slips with *i* and *o*, the two vowels simplest in form, and set beside him a boy just beginning to read. They are to be provided with a slate and pencil, or rather, a shallow box filled with dry sand. The elder boy is to teach the younger to trace these vowels . . . on the sand or slate, and then to point them out in a page of large print.' (p. 191)

The other vowels follow, in the order *e, u, a*; then the consonants, but nothing is said about the order in which they are to be taken.

Hart had seen his grouping of fourteen consonants into phonetically related pairs as part of a teaching sequence. Alexander Gill and the later orthoepists were, as theorists, unconcerned with teaching-methods, and as teachers they were concerned not with the alphabet itself but with analysing the range of sounds represented by the letters in a way that would help the teaching of correct pronunciation. It is not until Thomas Sheridan that phonetic considerations are again applied to learning the alphabet:

1786 'Children ought not to be taught to sound the consonants in the promiscuous manner in which they are found in the alphabet. The natural order is first to begin with the labials, as those are the first sounds uttered by all the children in all parts of the globe [because the lips grow strong from sucking] . . . To these succeed the dentals; and the next sounds uttered by children are *da* and *ta* . . . this arises from the tongue's being constantly exercised about the gums, to alleviate the pain while they are cutting their teeth. The last and hardest sounds are the palatines, which requiring that the tongue should be drawn back, an action to which it had not been accustomed, are the most difficult to attain.'   (p. 5)

Sheridan's three successive groups of consonants are therefore (i) *b, p, m*; (ii) *d, t, z, s*; (iii) *g, k, l, r*. He classes *n* as nasal and partly palatine, *f* and *v* as partly labial and partly dental. The first syllable exercises that he provides conform to this sequence.

A phonetic grouping of the letters was not uncommon, but it is not always possible to say how far it was related to the teaching of the alphabet and how far to an analysis of sounds, meant for subsequent study. In William Angus' 'pronouncing alphabet' the vowels are discussed first, and the consonants are listed in groups that are phonetically related, e.g. *bpm, vf, dt*, but on the evidence of Angus' books generally it is far from certain that he expected the alphabet itself to be learnt in this order (Angus [1809] 1827 and 1815). The same holds true of *The Rhyming and Pronouncing Primer*, of the same period, where it is not clear whether the letters are first learnt in phonetic groupings and later in alphabetical order, or the other way round. Such desire as there may have been to teach the alphabet in a new order determined by phonetic criteria cannot have been very powerful. The general practice continued to be what W.B. Hodgson later objected to: 'The letters are taught by their names, not by their sounds; in the arbitrary order of the alphabet, instead of in the natural order of the organs by which they are pronounced' (1868, p. 10). There is, however, evidence to support Hodgson. James Pillans, 1827, is quoted by Hunter Diack (1965, p. 15) as grouping the letters into 'brotherhoods' formed by the same organ, and William Martin, 1852, had grouped them 'according to the organs of speech': vowels, aspirate, labial, nasal, dental, guttural, palatal. This grouping was not a new alphabetical order. Martin assumed that the alphabet was already known, that the letters had been previously studied in quite a different grouping, by shape (below, p. 65) and were immediately to be met in a further classification: those lower-case letters which resembled the capitals (fifteen letters) and those which did not (11 letters). His aids to learning the alphabet were rather elaborate. Another elementary book, *Watson's Second Book of Reading*, 1859, also groups the letters first by shape and then 'according to sound . . . of the lips, gums, palate, teeth, tongue and nose'. John Cassell's *The Child's Educator*, 1855, gives an order 'according to the simplicity of sound', omitting without explanation *cjqr* (p. 31).

It was the arbitrariness of alphabetical order that led some teachers to regroup the letters into a learning-order based on their sounds. A more frequent response was to teach, but not necessarily to reorder, the letters in groups based on their shapes. Joseph Aickin, 1693, had calculated that, allowing for the differences between lower-case and capital letters, and between roman, italic and English typefaces, 'the several characters, or shapes, used . . . amounted to one hundred and fifty-eight' (p. 14). There was ancient precedent:

1569 'Quintilian says it is not good to teach the names and order of the letters, before the shapes . . . wherefore the teacher should change and vary their order diversely, that the learner might print in his memory their shapes, and so by seeing them to be able to name them: even as the best way to know a man, is by the sight of his favour and proportion, whereby his name is the better retained.'

(Hart, fol. 58; orthography modernised)

Mnemonic descriptions of the letters are rare in the textbooks, because a picture was more effective, but it would be surprising if they were not common in actual teaching. Richard Lloyd, 1654, whose mnemonic descriptions of his CV names were quoted above, p. 41, was equally ingenious in describing the shapes of all the letters: *b* is 'the new Moon stuck at the bottom of a Stake'; *m* is 'the great Rakes head with the teeth downward' (pp. 2–3). In 1748 James Todd refers to such methods, borrowed from the teaching of Hebrew, as things of the past: it used to be customary to teach 'the Characters of the Language symbolically . . . *c* is like a Half-moon, *o* like an Hand-ball, *e* has a crooked Back' (p. 65). The picture alphabets, now much improved, tended to make such descriptions unnecessary, although William Hill, 1865, combines both. Hill's descriptions of his method, in an earlier work, is as terrifying as anything in *Hard Times*, which it precedes by two years:

(1847) 1852 'Before the pupils are fatigued the teacher may turn to the black board and vary the exercise, by writing upon it the word *arm* in *capital letters*, and pointing to the letter A, he may say – *what is A like?* The pupils will answer, A is like a pair of fire tongs. The teacher pointing to the letter R may say – *what is R like?* The pupils will answer, R is like the step of a coach . . . The teacher may then request the pupils to spell the word *arm* six times in this manner, a-r-m, arm, one; a-r-m, arm, two; a-r-m, arm, three; a-r-m, arm, four; a-r-m, arm, five; a-r-m, arm, six . . . Request the pupils to enunciate the whole sentence in connection with each letter, as B is like a pair of spectacles; A is like a pair of fire tongs; R is like the step of a coach. Pupils disciplined under the influence of this exercise will have no time to gape, or to talk, or to lug each other, or to tread on each others toes, or to bite the corners of their books into pulp.'   (William Hill, p. 18)

The practical question that kept references to shape in the textbooks was how to prevent children from confusing certain letters. The unquestioned method, from about 1700 until the 1820s, was to bring together the letters whose shapes were confusingly similar, usually about seven or eight pairs. This pedagogically reasonable (if misguided) practice was, during the eighteenth century, sometimes extended, unreasonably, to the whole alphabet: all the letters were grouped according to some criterion of shape. A final stage, introduced in 1830, was to group all the letters according to the kind of lines that composed them. Of the first method, applied to lower-case letters, there are twenty-one instances, beginning with George Fisher's *New Spelling Book*, 1700, first published in 1693 under another title, and ending with *Reading made most Easy*, 1821. The most frequently confused letters, on this evidence, were *b* and *d* (in all twenty-one texts), *p* and *q* (in eighteen) and *r* and *t* (in sixteen); but *c* and *e*, *h* and *k*, *f* and long *s*, are paired many times. Only six of these texts make a similar pairing of capitals, of which *EF*, *CG* and *BR* are the most frequent. The extension of this method to include all the letters occurs in texts between 1740 and 1850. The groups are very varied, reflecting not only the subjectivity of such judgments but also a surprising independence amongst the authors of a type of book usually considered to be blatantly derivative. *The Primmer*, 1786, lists the capitals in two rows of thirteen, headed 'similar letters', although few of the letters juxtaposed seem to resemble each other; the incomplete list of lower-case letters begins: *b d p q g c e* . . . but ends merely with '&c.'. The other groupings are selections of pairs of various degrees of similarity, some, such as *yr*, rather strained. An influential application of the method, generally attributed to the influence of Pestalozzi, was developed by Andrew Bell. He taught first the two vowels, *i* and *o*, and the two consonants, *l* and *t*, whose capitals were simplest in shape: *ILTO*, which became the name of the method, represented not only a classification of the letters by shape but, more weightily, the principle of teaching them through writing, in sand or on slate, from the very first. (Cf. Iremonger, 1818, 1825 edn, p. 14; *Practical Manual*, 1833, p. 6.) A. Scott, 1822, praises both Pestalozzi and Bell but prefers his own system whereby the capitals *I* and *O* are learnt first; then *L, V* and *H, K*; then *C, G*; then *P*. The most interesting method is that introduced by Bartholomew Dillon in 1830. He says that the alphabet is to be learnt neither letter by letter nor all at once, but in five groups according to shape; and shape is defined by the nature of the lines from which capital Roman letters are formed:[6]

1. By straight lines	*I L T F E H*
2. By oblique lines	*X V A W*
3. By straight and oblique lines	*Z K Y N M*
4. By curves	*O Q C G S*
5. By lines and curves	*J U D P B R*

Dillon's lower-case letters are similarly arranged by 'simplicity of form', but necessarily by less objective criteria: 1. *i r t f l j*; 2. *k h u n m*; 3. *v y w x z*; 4. *o c e a g*; 5. *b p d q s*.

James Gall, 1832, also advocates teaching the letters in groups according to their shape, supported by descriptions such as 'two-wedged *w*' and 'short-legged *h*' (p. 25), and James Brown (USA), (1826) 1834, quotes extensively from Dillon and adopts his scheme, with acknowledgement. A similar plan, but with different results, is followed by Walter McLeod, 1848, whose six groups of lower-case letters arranged 'according to the *lines* which enter into their construction' (p. 16) are:

1. *o c g q*
2. *b d p r k*
3. *i f l h t j e*
4. *a v w x y z*
5. *m n*
6. *s*

William Martin, a. 1852, grouped only the capitals in this way, using four out of Dillon's five classes, again with different results:

1. Horizontal lines	*I E F L T H*
2. Perpendicular and inclined	*A K M N V W X Y Z*
3. Perpendicular and curved	*B P R D*
4. Curved	*C G O Q S U J*

[6] Cf. C.C. Fries' division of capitals into fifteen 'stroke', five 'circle' and six 'stroke and circle' letters (1963, p. 125).

Martin put Dillon's 'oblique' group 2 into his own 'perpendicular and inclined' group, and treated *U* and *J* as curved, whereas Dillon had seen them as formed by lines and curves (Martin, p. 7). This grouping by line and curve is applied in *Watson's First Book*, 1859, to lower-case letters with results that are scarcely memorable:

1. Circular	*o c e*
2. Angular	*v y w x z*
3. Waved	*s a g*
4. Perpendicular and circular	*b p d q*
5. Perpendicular and curved	*l i r t j f h k n m u*

Although alphabetical order is not in itself relevant to the early stages of reading, its eventual practical importance is so great that it was natural for even the elementary texts to follow the traditional practice of hornbook and catechism: to display the letters in order. If the letters were listed in alphabetical order it could be assumed that children would learn them in that order. If, when the letters had been learnt *only* in alphabetical order, the children were shown them in that order and asked to name them, they might very well name a letter without being able to identify it outside the sequence of the alphabet. Lady Fenn, 1787, uses this common experience to explain her presentation of the alphabet in a variety of styles and sizes of type intended to 'imprint' the letters on a child's attention: 'A child who has a retentive memory, and much vivacity, will often repeat the letter by rote, and never look at, nay, scarcely *know* one character' (preface). If words or syllables were used as the material from which children were asked to identify individual letters it was thought that the context might enable them to guess the letter correctly. Two teaching-procedures were therefore advocated. The first, requiring no special material, was to spell words backwards (Hart, 1570, p. 246). The second procedure was to require the pupils to identify letters printed in random order. From this second procedure developed the regular practice of printing one or more 'promiscuous' alphabets in the preliminary pages of a spelling-book. The promiscuous lists always contained all the letters, and were usually, but unnecessarily, confined to one instance of each: a jumbled alphabet rather than the series of random letters that the teaching method required. Authority for the method went back to Quintilian, and the technique is no doubt as old as any ordered alphabet. It was common from the end of the sixteenth century until the middle of the nineteenth. At least 120 instances, more than half of them in the nineteenth century, are known, but it was discussed hardly at all. The promiscuous alphabet may have been more of a conventional aid than a real help. Even Aickin, who lists the consonants in a jumbled order, seems to rely on the randomness of syllables and words:

1693 'For the better inculcating of the names and shapes of the Letters into childrens memories, and understandings, instead of keeping them half year in the *A, b c*, teach them the Letters not in Alphabetical order altogether, but as they are mixed in Syllables, words and Sentences: for many children can say the Letters by rote, who in the mean time know not one of the Letters by their shapes: therefore you must take particular notice of the difference of the shapes of the Letters: for many of the Letters are almost alike.' (p. 16)

The most thorough treatment of the promiscuous alphabet is that by John Warden, 1753. He gives ten jumbled alphabets: two lower-case sequences (roman and italic) of letters alike in shape; four instances (lower-case and capital, roman and italic) in which the vowels and the consonants alternate but both keep their alphabetical order; four instances (lower-case and capital, roman and italic) of a third sequence that he describes as 'two consonants betwixt two vowels, throughout the alphabet' (p. x). What the child saw, in this last instance was: *bacceddiffoggujjakkellimmonuppy-qqarreſsittovvuxxyzza* (p. 3). Order is imposed even on randomness.

The promiscuous technique is applied to words by James Porterfield of Edinburgh in the 'proofs' he regularly introduces into his two books of 1694 and 1695. The proofs are exercises for practice in reading. The words are random, but have an evocative quality that sometimes suggests a more secular narrative source than their ostensible provenance in the Bible or the Shorter Catechism. The pupils are required to read, for example: 'Partiality burial entangle carpenter approved abhorred magistrate accomplish beguiled consulted instructers inventers . . .' (1695, sig. 13). Joseph Aickin, in the passage already quoted, recommended that children should learn the letters 'not in Alphabetical order altogether, but as they are mixed in Syllables, words and Sentences'. This recommendation expresses a view of learning that ran counter to the then almost-universal assumption that small items should be learnt before the larger items of which they were constituents. This minority view will occasionally be met in the larger context of learning to read; Aickin and a few writers in the nineteenth century are unusual in applying it to the learning of the names of the letters:

1824 Edward Quin, of New Jersey: 'We should . . . give the child such words as are familiar to him; he will then, soon learn the names of the letters, and in a few days perceive their full use.' Quin's method would make obsolete 'the mode of instruction, by the repetition of the detached letters of the alphabet'. (preface)

1834 J. Orville Taylor described how children in New York State District schools learned the alphabet in a week, being taught through whole words.
(J. Orville Taylor, *The District School*, N.Y. 1834, pp. 142f. Quoted by Mathews, 1966, pp. 57–8)

1837a J.M. McCulloch recommends, instead of learning first the whole alphabet, 'the simpler and better method of teaching them first one series of letters and then another, with the accompanying exercises on syllables and words'. (Directions)

1848 In *Winks' Spelling and Reading Book* the letters are to be learnt not through the alphabet but through two-letter words: 'By the following Lessons Children may be taught the names and sounds of Letters much easier than by the usual way: *by my go do | no lo to so | he if ye up . . .*'   (p. 2)

1856 *The Child's Book to begin with*: The author suggests 'an easy method of teaching the alphabet', which is to learn to read, as whole words, the following, which contain all the letters of the alphabet, in a context of words, if not of meaning: '*if do have or we tub it me . . . zone lo queen*'.   (p. 4)

1866 Edward N. Marks: 'The schemes [for teaching the ABC] – it is a misuse of the word to call them "systems" – . . . have all been tried, and of course, they have all been more or less successful.' It may be a waste of time to teach the alphabet but 'the alphabet should be *learnt* . . . It is sheer waste of time . . . to teach the alphabet in order that children may "know all their letters" before they begin to *read*, and then to promote them to the "*a-b, ab*" class or columns.' The alphabet should be learnt in its order. 'Let the child learn the alphabet "by heart" in the way most pleasant to him. The abstract form of it is not attractive as a mental exercise . . . The learning of the alphabet should not – need not – be imposed as a task. Let the children begin with short *words*, and read them at sight *without spelling them*.'   (Introduction)

Brinsley, 1612, was quoted above, p. 33, as recommending that children should learn to name the letters before they could identify their shapes. Brinsley was so influential that it is surprising no reference is made to the method except by Hoole, who says that he has 'known some' who have followed it (*Petty School*, p. 5). It is likely that the value of the method was weakened by the discrepancies between name and sound, and it is perhaps significant that the only later book to propose the method continues to confuse the two:

1827 'It is recommended . . . to commence teaching children the alphabet *without* printed letters. By making a child repeat the names of the letters, the sound of them (which is the *original*) is conveyed to the EAR; and in *due time*, the letters, which are *copies* of the sound, may be presented to the EYE.'   (Lordan, p. 9)

The opposite recommendation, that the shapes should be learnt before the names, was quoted from the Edgeworths, above, p. 36, but seems to have been equally disregarded until spelling-methods of teaching reading were being more widely questioned, in the second half of the nineteenth century:

'The *names* and *order* of the letters . . . should not be taught at all in the Infant School . . . the child . . . does not need them in learning to read' (William Robinson, 1876, p. 7).

The aids, such as drawing letters in sand, by which these methods could be supported are older than spelling-books, are well known and are mostly still in use. Amongst those which now have little support is the lavish practice of Herodes Atticus, a wealthy sophist and Roman senator in the second century A.D., who is said to have bought for a stupid son twenty-four slaves, each given the name of one of the letters of the alphabet (Reeder, 1900, p. 64). The usual intention, and certainly the usual effect, of alphabet pictures was just to add some pleasure and interest to what was assumed to be a dull task. Occasionally a writer might suggest that the association between picture and letter would help the pupil to learn the letter, but it was never explained how, for example, a picture of a monkey in one position made the letter *M* memorable and an adjacent picture of a monkey in another position made memorable *A* for Ape (Lye, 1671), nor by what process learning *R* was made easier by the accompanying picture of a 'Rose-col-or-ed Ou-zel' (Houston, 1826). Perhaps the best that could be said was that pictures made 'the strongest impression on their [the pupil's] brain, notwithstanding its extreme softness' (Lenoir, 1800, p. xxiv). The association was thought to be helpful even when there was no picture and the pupil had to rely on memory, as in James Hutchinson's *Modern Spelling Book*, 1852 (1859 preface): 'The pupil is instructed to say A, aunt; B, ball; C, cat . . . When the letters are pretty well known, both forward and backward in this way, the child is to be taken into the promiscuous reading, still only naming the letters with the words attached, and not forming them into words.'

To say that the vast number of delightful picture alphabets, the naive and the sophisticated, the shoddy and the witty, are pedagogically unimportant may seem perverse, but it is not a modern comment. J. Cook, 1792 (preface) and the author of *The Anti-Spelling Book*, 1833 (p. 15), reject picture alphabets because the children look at the pictures, not at the letters. The picture alphabets were at first thought to instruct children directly, fixing the names and shapes of the letters. Later the instruction was thought to be only indirect, in that the pictures increased the children's pleasure and willingness to learn. The picture alphabet became a convention, a means by which adults could amuse each other; their pleasure was reinforced by the pleasure that the children also took in the pictures. The pictures created a mood in which learning could take place; they played no part in the learning itself. It could be maintained that by focusing attention not on the letter but on the picture, which could usually be taken to represent a number of things and could suggest a number of irrelevant words, the alphabets tended to increase the difficulty of learning the letters. Fortunately for them, children have always shown a welcome ability to sidestep the force of such theoretical considerations. In addition to picture alphabets, the letters were also carved on dice or on blocks made from ivory, bone or wood; separate letters were made from the same materials or even from sugar (Coles, 1674, p. 102), and were also printed on cards. One of these card collections, of great ingenuity but little known, is J.B.'s *Ludus Literarum*, 1674. The book contains instructions for playing thirty-four games with one or two packs of letter cards, and a box of counters. The book cost a shilling; a pack of letters cost fourpence alone, sixpence with the counters. The letter cards could be in English, Greek or Hebrew. The English, that is Roman, pack, like our Scrabble, was arranged in harshly regulated proportions: four cards of *E*; three cards each of *A, C, I, M, N, O, R*; two each of *B, D, F, G, H, L, P, S, T U*, and one each of *K, Q, SS, W, X, Y, Z*. These proportions kept the number of cards to the familiar total of fifty-two. Most of the games are intended to teach spelling, to adults as well as to children, but the first two are 'fitted chiefly for Abcdarians'. The first game 'is chiefly intended for young ones to have the Letters exactly perfect, according to the method of them; and by looking thus upon them often it will imprint or impress them most readily, easily and lively in their minds and phansies'. Even those who already know their letters well 'may not be asham'd to play this Game awhile . . . till they have the naming of the Letters backwards as readily and perfectly as forwards'. The first game which, as often in such books, is not described with the fullness one would wish, is 'to play the Alphabet forwards and backwards'. The players, in turn, play the cards, if they can, in alphabetical order; any player who holds two or more consecutive cards in his hand collects all the cards previously played, leaving only the latest in the sequence, on which play continues. The second game, 'the lowest Game as to troubling or employing the brain of any I shall mention', is played in the same way but with vowel cards only (pp. 2 and 3 of the first numeration).

Most of the games and toys were designed to focus the child's attention on the shape of a single letter. A 'perforated screen . . . designed to confine the child's eye to any letter, syllable, or word which you wish' is used in Lady Fenn's box of toys for home use (1785, p. 24). A similar purpose is achieved by Wallis' Revolving Wheel, *c.* 1830, which is described in the catalogue of the Norfolk Museums Service (David Jones, 1980) and by the Revolving Alphabet, a toy of 1820 illustrated in Clifton Johnson, (1904) 1963, p. 28.

The alphabet wheel was used also in the classroom. The British and Foreign School Society Manual describes one wheel, 4 feet in diameter, containing one alphabet of capital letters and in an inner circle a lower-case alphabet. In the capital alphabet *EF* and *MW*, and in the lower-case *bd* and *pq*, are repeated because they are so easily confused (*Manual*, 1816, p. 6). The same need to fix the pupil's attention is met in an unusual way in *A New Lottery Book*, 1819, where the letters are printed, two to a page, on one side of the leaf, on the other side of which are two related pictures. The child is invited to stick a pin through a picture and then turn the leaf to see how successful he has been in piercing the corresponding letter (Whalley, 1974, p. 33). The names and order of the letters were fixed also by chanting and singing, more effectively if at the same time the letters were being pointed to on a board. In 1904 Mr Leopold Bloom, in Dublin 'passed Saint Joseph's, National School. Brats' clamour. Windows open. Fresh air helps memory. Or a lilt. Ahbeesee defeegee kelomen opeecue rustyouvee ...' (James Joyce, *Ulysses*, 1937 edn, p. 51). More than a lilt had often been attached to the alphabet. Thomas Morley had set the hornbook to music in 1597 (the words are quoted in full in *OED*, s.v. *Christ-cross*, 3) and in *The Pretty Play Thing*, c. 1790, the letters are sung in turn to a chorus when members are admitted to 'the Society of Cuzes. The Order of Cuzship is of more ancient and honourable date than the Lumber-Troopers, Gregorians, Ubiquarians, Hurlothrumbos'. The chorus, 'which we are assured is the Foundation and Rudiments of all their Learning' runs (although it is difficult to fit the words to it) thus:

BA - - - ba, BE - - - be, BI - - - bi - - - bi--bi; BO - - - bo,
Ba - - - be - - - bi - - - bo; BU - - - bu, Ba - - - be-- bi - - - bo - - - bu.

(pp. 53–58)

James Rodgers in 1825 marches the infants of Cheltenham to their reading-places while they sing 'some appropriate verses, say the alphabet, to a tune called "In my cottage near a wood",' while J.R. Brown taught the infants of Spitalfields to sing *Auld Lang Syne* to alphabetical words;

ABCDEFH
IJKLMN
OPQRSTUV
WXYZ
a e i o u y are vowels
The rest are consonants
And no word can be spelt without
a e i o u y   (1837, p. 22)

Auld Lang Syne is also the tune used in the American *Union Spelling Book*, 1838, where the verse is sung to the capital letters and the chorus to the lower-case ones – a distinction it would seem difficult to make vocally (Nietz, 1961, p. 28).

Syllables

The author of *A New Booke of Spelling with Syllables*, (1567) 1610, ends the work with these words: 'Therefore let the Scholler, being thus traded [i.e. schooled] from letters to syllables of one Consonant: from syllables of one Consonant, to syllables of many Consonants: from syllables of many Consonants, to words of many syllables; proceede to sentences' (p. 27). He was expressing the customary view: 'Letters compose Syllables: Syllables, words: words, Sentences: and Sentences make Orations or Books. Wherefore you must first learn the Letters' (Joseph Aickin, 1693, p. 2). The visual discreteness of the letter made it the natural starting-point for the teaching of reading, just as the visual discreteness of the word made it, until the middle of the eighteenth century and for all but the most reflective teachers, the finishing-point: if you could read words, you could read. The component letters of a word were found by breaking the word down, by spelling. The word could then be reconstituted by building it up from its component letters, in reading. In both processes the syllable was the central feature, midway in the analytical sequence: words – syllables – letters; midway in the synthetic sequence: letters – syllables – words. The teachers stress the point:

1621 'The difficultie of reading chiefly consisteth in the ill sorting of their sillables.'
(Evans, A7b)

1687 'The ground-work of reading and writing . . . depends upon the knowledge of syllables.'
(Cooper, p. 29)

'It is very necessary both for *True Writing* and *Reading*, to understand the Nature and proper Division of *Syllables*.'
(Henry Care, p. 8)

(1708) 1710 'Thou canst spell Syllables, and read whole Sentences.'
(Kennet, p. 8)

Even towards the end of the eighteenth century the author of *The Primmer*, 1786, stressing in his preface the connection between his elementary reading-book and 'the Assembly's excellent Catechism' on to which it is intended to lead, says that every 'syllable' in the Catechism is to be found in the primer. He is not just being emphatic; he is thinking of the contents of his book in terms of syllables rather than of words.

A syllable, in English as in Latin, was traditionally defined but with even less practical effect than such definitions usually achieved. The criterion, largely an arbitrary one, was that of completeness or separateness:

1616 'A full, and perfect sound in a word.'
(Thomas Granger, *Syntagma Grammaticum*, c4)

1687 'The sound of one or more Letters in a distinct measure of breathing.'
(Cooper, p. 27)

[1745] 1750 'A compleat Sound uttered in one Breath.'   (Ann Fisher, p. 31)

1755 'As much of a word as is uttered by the help of one vowel, or one articulation.'
(Samuel Johnson, *Dictionary*)

A frequent rule was that a word comprised as many syllables as it contained vowels or diphthongs; but the exceptions were too numerous for the rule to be very helpful. A further rule, also taken from Latin, was that in a word of more than one syllable any syllable except the last should end in a vowel. To this rule also there were many exceptions, mostly created by contradictory rules for the division of syllables. The syllable was regarded as the unit out of which all words except monosyllables were constructed; not only reading but also correct pronunciation depended on the proper formation of syllables, and hence on the correct division of words into syllables. Because reading depended on the correct division of syllables, and because reading was so often considered to be a process dependent on, or parallel with, spelling, the division of syllables came to be equated with spelling itself. The syllabic structure of words was emphasised at every stage, with long words and with short ones:

(1576?) 1587 'If there fall a doubt of spellyng any word to the writer, let him devide it into syllabes. That done, he shall very easily perceive what to write. Example: this word *communication*, hath six syllabes, which beyng thus distinctly devided *Com-mu-ni-ca-ti-on*, write it so orderly syllabe after syllabe. Likewise do with all other words, which would otherwise trouble you.'
(Francis Clement, pp. 17–18)

(1673) 1677   Qu.   What sounds *a-n*?   [Skill 7.1]
        Ans.   *An.*
        Qu.   What sounds *g-e-l*?
        Ans.   *gel.*
        Qu.   Put it together.   [Skill 7.3]
        Ans.   *Angel.*   (Lye, preface)

(1784) 1788   Robert Ross in America gives with understandable interest 'an Indian Word, consisting of fifteen Syllables. Accented on the 2d, 5th, 10th, and 13th Syllables:
      Noo-wo-man-num-mau-che-kod-tan-ta-moo-on-gan-nun-nun-nash.'
(B7 verso)

Syllables are divided as part of two distinct processes. On the one hand dividing a word into its syllables is a technique that can be used when you are uncertain how to pronounce a word that you meet in reading. When dividing syllables in reading you must look at a sequence of printed letters and group them according to the rules.

You must either pronounce each group as you come to it or, having formed all the groups first, you hold them in your mind's eye and pronounce them in sequence. When writing, on the other hand (as in the example from Clement), or in oral spelling, you pronounce the word to yourself and divide it by ear into its syllables, moderating the resulting divisions by the appropriate rules. The rules are more helpful when applied to reading than when they are applied to writing. In reading, the letters are already present, and the rules, which refer always to letters, can be applied easily to material that is visibly in front of you. In writing, you have to provide the letters yourself, mentally, before you can apply the rules; but providing the right letters is precisely the task that the rules are meant to assist. Several teachers, therefore, including many who state the rules, advise the learner just to spell as he pronounces. They are not being inconsistent: they are providing precise rules for the reading-technique and general advice for the writing-technique. The distinction between the two techniques is obscured by the use of the term 'spelling' for both, and by the fact that in both the learner *is* dividing the words into syllables. The distinction lies in the difference between the two sequences of operations. When the learner was reading it was supposed that he carried out three operations on material already in his view. He had to group the letters of the word by rule; to pronounce each group; to pronounce the whole word. When the learner was writing it was supposed that he carried out three operations also, but not the same ones. He had first to pronounce the word that he was to write; then divide it by ear into its syllables; then check these groups against the rules. This last step would be necessary only if he was to write or say the word syllable by syllable, as he often had to. In the teachers' own words:

> *1674*   For spelling right, the syllables you'l find,
>   By parting them in sound within your mind.
>
> (Henry Preston, p.2)

1695 'To write English any thing tolerably well, the distinct sound of each Syllable is most carefully to be attended. Therefore you must be sure to repeat every long word syllabically in your mind . . . before you write it down . . . pausing . . . at every Syllable.'   (*Writing Scholar's Companion*, p. 22)

This distinction between two uses of the division of syllables is, of course, here made explicit in a way that was not in the minds of seventeenth-century teachers; but it is implicit in their practice. Two writers from the end of the seventeenth century illustrate the dominant position of the syllable and show the application of two of the rules for the division of syllables:

1668 'If the learner is puzled in spelling a word of many syllables, let the teacher put him to tell on his fingers how many syllables are in it; how to part, and join the letters in each syllable; how to bring them together one after another; and let him be perfected in this exercise before he read's without spelling: thus, *e-x, ex; t-r-a, tra; extra; o-r, or; extraor; d-i, di; extraordi; n-a, na; extraordina; r-y, ry; extraordinary*...
Q. What if there be a consonant between two vowels in one word?
A. A consonant between two vowels must be joined to the latter, as *r-e, re; p-a, pa; repa; r-a ra ; repara; t-i, si; reparati; o-n, on; reparation;* not *rep-ar-at-i-on.*'

(Owen Price, p. 6)

Joseph Aickin describes the stage when the pupils can read any syllable on its own but are uncertain how to identify the syllables in a word; the rules tell him:

1693 'Now to teach them to spell or divide Polysyllables, you must do thus: since they can sound any syllable without naming the Letters: take your pointer or pen, & place it on the last letter of the [first] syllable in a word of two syllables, and make him sound that Syllable and so the last syllable likewise, and tell him the Rule by word of mouth for dividing of the syllables: as for example in the word *Kingdom*: put your pointer to *g* and tell them, when two Consonants are in the middle of a word, the first consonant belongs to the first syllable and the other to the last syllable.'

(Aickin, A6b)

Proper beginnings and endings

Some rules for the division of syllables relied on the fact that certain combinations of two or three consonants could begin a word, whereas others could not. Many words begin with *bl-* but none with *bt-*, many with *scr-* but none with *scp-*. Similarly certain groups of consonants are found at the ends of words: *-tch, -ld*. Attention was focused on these 'beginning' consonants, especially, because a knowledge of them was required by the most frequently invoked rule for the division of syllables. This rule said that a word such as *master* was to be divided *ma-ster*, and not *mas-ter*, because *st* was a combination that could begin a word, whereas *martyr* was to be divided *mar-tyr* because no word could begin, and therefore it was not correct for a syllable to begin, with *rt*. In the language of the time *st* was a combination 'proper to begin a word' and *rt* was not. 'Proper' in this connection implies not so much a standard of correctness as the 'property' of being a combination of consonants found at the beginning of a word. The application of the rule is the same process as that by which we identify the components of an ambiguous compound. On the back of a lorry appears the single word STARTHRUST. If you read it as START . . . you are faced with the segment . . . HRUST, which is rejected because HR is not accepted as a possible beginning to a syllable. This rejection precedes the further recognition that HRUST does not form a word or suffix.

Edmund Coote, 1596, lists thirty beginning combinations of two consonants, of which the first ten are: *bl-, br-, ch-, cl-, cr-, dr-, dw-, fl-, fr-, gl-* (p. 5). Many teachers required their pupils to learn these lists by heart. Coote's advice to his fellow teachers is: 'Here examine your Scholer, what consonants wil follow *b* and let him answer *l* or *r* and so practise him in al the rest. For the more perfect he is in them, the more ease and benefite you shall finde, when you come to the rules of division' (*ibid.*). The lists of beginning consonants are common during the seventeenth century and occur throughout the eighteenth. One of the last to follow the practice is the SPCK's *A Spelling Book upon a New Plan, 1796.* John Wood, (1828) 1829, in describing how syllables and combinations of two consonants had been dropped from teaching in his Edinburgh school, shows that such lists were customarily read aloud. In what he calls the old methods *bl* was pronounced 'bil' and *bla* 'bil-a' (p. 184). Beginning combinations were more often needed, and more often given in the texts, than ending ones. Between thirty and thirty-five beginning combinations of two consonants were usual, but the number depended on the author's definition of a consonant and on his interest in rare words. Lye, 1671, makes forty-two by including Greek forms (*ps-, mn-, cn-*), which others usually disregarded, by distinguishing two sounds each for *ch-* and *th-*, and by including, as did many enthusiasts, *bd-* for *bdellium* (p. 6). Initial combinations of three consonants were treated in the same way; writers listed between six (Cooper) and fourteen (Lye). Combinations proper to end a word were more numerous. Christopher Symes, about 1681, lists more than seventy-five 'gradations subjunctive' for final combinations. *The British Instructor,* 1763, lists sixteen single letters that may end a word, forty-one double (of which the first five are *-bb, -ch, -ck, -dd, -ff*) and thirteen three-letter combinations (of which the first five are *-dth, -ght, -hth, -lch, -lph*). One of the most elaborate presentations is Daniel Farro's 'Scale', which he introduced in his *Royal Universal British Grammar,* 1754. The Scale is a table divided into three columns. The centre column contains vowels and diphthongs; the lefthand column contains combinations of consonants that can begin a word, and the righthand column combinations that can end a word. 'By committing these to Memory the tender Pupil is qualified to divide the long Words into proper Syllables' (1776, p. 4). The tender pupil is expected to cover over the outside columns and add to the vowels, from memory, each of the thirty-three two-letter and twelve three-letter initial combinations, and each of the forty-eight two-letter and fourteen three-letter final combinations (1754, p. 16; 1776, p. 5).

At their worst these lists, like many of the exercises of collection and classification, were in danger of being indiscriminate; but they had a clear purpose in relation to the rules for the division of syllables.

The division of syllables

The rules that governed the division of syllables were meant to help pupils with the reading, spelling and pronunciation of words in which particular features frequently caused them, and their teachers, to stumble:

1688 'I have likewise observed, that in long Words of Three, Four, Five, or Six Syllables, though some Petty School-Masters have sometimes luckily stumbled upon the right Sound of the Word, giving it its proper Name in the Lump, (more by Luck than Learning) but when for their Scholars better Instruction and Satisfaction, they were to take the long Word asunder, and particularly Pronounce each Syllable, apart by itself, they have been sadly puzled both in the proper Division, and true pronounciation of them, to their Scholars manifest detriment and discouragement, and their own expressless prejudice and disparagement.'
(*The Compendious School-master*, preface)

Young William Wotton, however, in more favourable circumstances, had a father who would 'without a Book, teach him *to know and join a syllable*, first of two Letters, then of three', so that at the age of four years and six weeks, in 1672, 'at first sight, he knew how to divide Words of two or three Letters in a Syllable; and the Tediousness of Spelling . . . was quite taken away from him' (Henry Wotton, 1753, p. 36).

One of the two most frequently stated rules for the division of syllables applied to words in the middle of which there was a cluster of consonants. The rule is here abbreviated CC. How are the consonants to be distributed between the vowels on each side of them? This was seen as a problem because it was assumed that a syllable ought to end in a vowel (above, p. 73). On that assumption, words in which vowels and consonants alternated were easily pronounced and easily divided: *Ba-by-lo-ni-an*.[7] The assumption was expressed in the other frequent rule (here abbreviated VCV) that a single consonant coming between two vowels should go with the second vowel: *honest* was to be divided *ho-nest*, not *hon-est*. But where there were two or more consonants the question of distribution arose: *adulteresses*. If the division made each syllable end in a vowel the result was

---

[7] The unattributed examples in this section are all from Ellis, [a. 1670] 1680.

unpronounceable: *a-du-lte-re-sse-s*. The problem was still more obvious with words containing three or four consonants: *demonstration*.

To meet the difficulty caused by such a cluster of consonants a number of rules, applied previously to Latin, were widely used. These rules were based on the idea already described of consonantal groupings 'proper' to begin a word. The CC rule said that if the consonants were proper, as in *afraid*, they were kept together as the beginning of the second syllable, *a-fraid*. If they were not proper they had to be divided: *ta-ber-nacle*. Coote illustrates the use of both CC and VCV in a dialogue between two pupils, Robert and John. Coote, addressing the teacher, says, 'Make your scholer reade over the dialogue so often, untill he can do it as readily & pronounce it as naturally, as if he spake without book':

1596 'Robert   How many syllables are in this word *rewarded*?
      John   Three.
      R.   How prove you that?
      J.   Because it hath three vowels . . .
      R.   How divide you them?
      J.   *Re-war-ded.*
      R.   Why put you *w* to *a*?
      J.   Because it is one consonant betweene two vowels.
      R.   And why divide you *r* and *d*?
      J.   Because they cannot begin a syllable.
      R.   What is the best way to spell a long word, as this, *admonition*?
      J.   I must marke how many syllables it hath, which I find to be five, then take the first, *a-d*, *ad*, then take the next, *m-o*, *mo*, then put them together, *admo*, so spell and put to the third, *admoni*, and so untill you come unto the end.'   (Coote, p. 34)

A special case of CC, which was often prescribed, was that if a word contained two instances of the same consonant between vowels, as *potter*, the consonants had to be separated: *pot-ter*. This rule is here abbreviated C = C. The same principle applied if there were three consonants (CCC) of which the last two were proper, as *wor-ship*, and even if there were four, as *trans-gress*, although in the latter case a further rule, described below, supervened. In a word like *wrestling*, which contained a cluster of three consonants but no proper beginning, the division was made according to a proper ending. As *-est* could end a word the regular division was *wrest-ling*. The CC rules vary in the detail with which they are expressed, not in substance:

1644 'When either two or three diverse consonants come together betwixt two vowels, if they bee such as wil begin a word, they must begin a syllable in any part of the word, as in *sur-prise* . . . But al compound words are excepted.'

(Hodges, N2)

1701 'When there are several different Consonants between the Vowels, as many of the next to the later Vowel go along with it in Division, as will begin an English Word or Syllable; and the rest (if any) go with the former Vowel; as in *a-stray . . . con-stable . . . part-ner*, &c. Except the overruling Compounds alter the Case, as it often happens; as in *fast-ing, wast-er, ob-lation*.'

(John Jones of Llandaff, p. 130)

1747 *The English Tutor* illustrates four ways in which a word containing three consonants between two vowels may be divided: as (i) *o-strich*, (ii) *crotch-et*, (iii) *bol-ster*, (iv) *oint-ment* (p. 25). *Ostrich* is so divided because *str* are a proper beginning; *crotchet* because *tch* are a proper ending; *bolster* because *st* is a proper beginning and therefore begins the second syllable but *l* cannot stay with *st* (*lst* not being a proper beginning or ending) and must be attached to the preceding vowel; *ointment* because *nt* is a proper ending, from which *m* has to be separated.

1771 'Two consonants proper to *begin a word*, must never be seperated; as *fable*; divided thus *fa-ble* . . . Three consonants that *end any word* must be joined to the former vowel; as *lighten*, divided into its two syllables thus, *light-en*.'

(Meilan, pp. 295–30)

The supervening rule to which both Hodges and Jones refer relates to compound and derivative forms (CD). Two illustrations, both from unpretentious manuals, are representative:

1732 'Derivatives are generally spelt like their Primitives; as, *tempt, tempt-ed*; *covet, co-vet-ous* . . . Compound words are spellt as their Simples; thus, *crafts-man . . . trans-act*.' (Owen, pp. 4–5).

1798 'Let words formed and derived be divided according to their original or primitive; and the consequence of this rule is, that these terminations; *-age, -ed, -en* . . . ought to go by themselves in spelling; as *herb-age, boast-ed, gold-en* . . . . A preposition, as *ad-, un- . . . per* . . . must be pronounced by itself, as *ad-e-quate, un-equal . . . per-ad-ven-ture* . . . yet we say *pe-ruse*, instead of *per-use*.'

(*The Complete Young Man's Companion*, pp. 8–9)

Both the foregoing quotations illustrate the equation of spelling with the division of syllables, and the second one illustrates the close relation between the division of syllables and the teaching of pronunciation, an aspect of the spelling-lists. The CD rule overrode all others, but this is not always apparent. The rules overlap. *Tempt-ed* and *trans-act* in the quotation from Owen, and *herb-age* and *gold-en* in the second quotation, would in any case have been divided this way, according to CC. In *co-vet-ous* CD is genuinely overriding VCV, because by VCV the division would be *co-ve-tous*, and in *boast-ed* it is overriding CC, according to which the division would be *boa-sted*. It was realised sometimes that 'a mere English scholar' might not recognise that *adorn*, for example, was a compound and should be divided *ad-orn*; if he does not see that the word is a compound he must divide it according to VCV: *a-dorn* (Gordon, [1755] 1765, p. 8).

Thomas Hunt's schoolboys, opposing each other, treat CD more fully than do many texts, and give us in however stylised a form a glimpse of seventeenth-century classroom life:

1661 'Lewis   But may not the syllables of some compounded-words *thwart* some of these rules?

Martin   Yea, that they may.

L.   Your reason for it.

M.   My reason is; because the simple-word when it is compounded, will (for all that) keep the same letters, as when it was simple.

L.   Pray instance in some compound-words, that thwart these rules.

M.   I will, *un-apt*, where the former syllable endeth with a consonant, against this rule 'The former syllable cannot end with a consonant, except the latter syllable begin with a consonant.' *Dis-like*, where *sl* are divided, though they will begin a word, as *slo-ven*.

L.   Do not these and the like derivatives, *speak-ing, strength-en-ing*, cross your rules?

M.   Indeed they do, but because it would be troublesome to make *new* rules for them, we will reckon them (at present) amongst the compounded ones, and so these (like the others) being found in a kind of composition, every word must have it's own letters, not mingled with others.'   (p. 108)

A further rule, relating to the separation of adjacent vowels, is frequently illustrated by the word *triumph*. There would seem to be no alternative to the obvious division *tri-umph*, but the rule (VV) that two vowels not forming a diphthong should be separated arose because both pupils and teachers were sometimes uncertain what a diphthong was, and were thought to need guidance in dividing the syllables of apparently similar words like *reaper* (*rea-per*) and *creator* (*cre-ator*). Richard Browne, 1700, faces this rule with what even his devout pupils must have thought rather a rare problem:

'Q.   Suppose, as in *Elioenai*, I have several Vowels together; How must I divide them exactly into Syllables?

A.   Let a Word have as many Vowels as possible, yet this Rule is infallible, viz. As many of them as are distinctly sounded, so many Syllables there are, and accordingly they must be divided.

Q.   Then, How spell you *Elioenai*?

A.   It must be divided thus, *E-li-o-e-nai*, where both the *o* and the *e* are proper syllables, because they are distinctly sounded.'   (p.13)

John Walker, 1791, is unusual in giving a considered explanation and defence of the rules, distinguishing their different functions: 'The object of syllabication may be, either to enable children to discover the sound of words they are unacquainted with, or to show the etymology of a word, or to exhibit the exact pronunciation of it.' All that children need at first is VCV and CC in its simplest form; they cannot be expected to know about proper beginnings. This he calls the synthetic method. The analytic method is to show the etymology of a word: *ortho-graphy, theo-logy*. To show pronunciation you must 'adopt the analytic method, by dividing it [the word] into such partial sounds as, when put together again, will exactly form the whole, as *or-thog-ra-phy*' (I, p. 70).

The rules were still active in the middle of the nineteenth century, but less widely used. In 1812 Thomas Roome, quoting Walker's explanation verbatim, breaks them up into nine separate rules of 'syllabication', but they are no longer connected primarily with spelling. Thomas Arnold, 1844b, in a book whose object is 'to enable even a village schoolmaster to train his pupils to a considerable knowledge of words', gives three of the rules, VCV, CC and CD, with the caution, 'the words are not always divided properly for spelling, but for the purpose of showing their formation' (preface). In much the same spirit Morell [1857] (1865) gives CC, VV and CD, stressing the last: 'The rules for dividing syllables must be regarded as *subordinate* to Etymological propriety' (p. 5).

By no means all the writers and critics of textbooks approved of the rules. Some did not mention them; some gave the rules but cast doubt on their usefulness; some repudiated them. The almost unanimous reason for doubting the rules was that they too often ran counter to the way in which words were actually pronounced. As early as 1633 Charles Butler gives the rules but at the same time dismisses them: 'The Directions therefore, being thus uncertain for the English, leave we them to the Latin, whose they are: & let this one rule serve us for all. Syllables are so to be divided in spelling, as they are in speaking: and so consequently in writing at the line's end' (p. 31). Wallis similarly says that if syllables in English have to be divided we should go by what we hear, 'aurium judicio', and the same advice is given by Wharton (repeating Butler's second sentence) for those who find the rules 'too many and too intricate'. Later seventeenth-century writers making the same recommendation are Cooper, 1687; Care, 1687; and the author of *The Best and Plainest English Spelling Book, c.* 1700. The two most emphatic are George Robertson and Elisha Coles. Robertson, 'schoolmaster between the two North-doors of Paul's, in the new Buildings', sees the rules as an obstacle to spelling, and will have none of them. His book, *Learning's Foundation Firmly Laid*, 1651, is eccentric and obscure. Apart from an interesting preface and two pages of 'brief directions' there are no instructions or rubrics describing how the book is to be used: lists of syllables and words, in English, roman and italic type, fill the pages according to a plan that can only be guessed at. The arrangement is deliberate. In his preface Robertson says that anyone who can himself read can teach a person 'of ordinary capacity' to read within a month, if he follows the author's directions: 'which directions are here altogether omitted, because the principall of them cannot be imparted but by word of mouth'. He himself, however, is 'willing to impart' them, in the new buildings, presumably.[8] His brief directions include: 'In spelling of a long word let them go on to the end, without stop or division into syllables: and instantly go it over again once or twice, every time faster, untill they have the right pronunciation of it' (A4b).

This is another of those early and rare indications of a method that, if it does not go so far as an approach through the 'whole word', at least eschews the customary atomism. Robertson seems to have been an unusual teacher, in his attitude to children as well as in his methods. In his preface he answers a critic who objects that his methods are not suitable for dull children:

1651 'To whom I answer, I know nor do acknowledg no such thing as a dull person, either young or old; but (though there be degrees in that as in other things) all are capable . . . those that be called block-heads or dul, are much injured, because the reasons do not proceed from themselves, but either from the carelessness of parents, who do not keep their children close to Schoole; or their too much indulgency, that will not commit them wholly to the Tutor; or from the rigor of a rigid cruell teacher; or from an irregular endless Method of teaching, of many years practise, and in the end no perfection; impossible to be comprehended of a tender-brained-childe.'   (preface)

Elisha Coles, quoting Wallis, attacks the rules for the division of syllables on the grounds that they were originally applied to Latin and are not suitable for English; in fact Coles goes on the offensive and says that 'if Latin had been naturally pronounc'd as we pronounce it now, those Rules had been as improper for that language, as they are for ours'. He attacks the 'grand and fundamental Rule' that 'whatsoever letters may begin a word, must also begin a syllable'. Why then do the authorities write *Gyp-sy, Jas-per*? There are, he says, almost two thousand English words 'which, if they were so spel'd would quite lose their English pronunciation'. He then attacks the VCV rule:

1674 'A single consonant (say they) between two vowels must needs be joyned to the following vowel. Shew me the ground of this necessity: I say there are no such English words as *a-ni-mate, e-ve-ry, de-li-ver*, &c. and it needs no other proof than

---

[8] Compare the ironic offer by the author of *The Anti-Spelling Book*, 1833: 'Any person . . . entertaining the least doubt as to the sounds designated by the Author, may, on application at the Publishers', hear the several letters pronounced' (preface).

the having on a pair of English (not *Arcadian*) ears ... The true Rule of spelling (in all languages whatsoever) is this; Words are so to be spelt, as they are afterwards to be pronounc'd.' (pp. 105-7)

Elisha Coles is likely to be one of those attacked by the author of *Thesaurium Trilingue Publicum*, who defends the rules:

1689 'I have followed the old and true Method of *Spelling* and *Dividing*; for the better keeping up the Credit of Good Education, which would soon grow into Contempt, if (after the Opinion of some careless Men) we should spell every word according to the Pronunciation that time by Corruption has given them: For if so, an Age would so alter any Tongue, and especially the *English* and *French*, that we should scarce know the Original of ten words in five hundred; nay all Learning in general would thereby lose the good esteem it has ... Orthography being the right Port thereto.' (preface)

One of the most obvious cases where the rule was at odds with pronunciation was a word like *honest*, quoted above (p. 77) where a short stressed vowel was followed by a single consonant. It seems to have been the practice amongst many seventeenth-century teachers to apply the VCV rule to spelling but not to pronunciation. In pronunciation the single consonant was treated as if it were double. The earliest textbook to refer to this resolution of the difficulty was *A New Primmer*, 1698, by a German immigrant to America, Francis Daniel Pastorius. Although Pastorius kept a school in Pennsylvania at one time it seems more probable that he took his practice from an earlier spelling-book, English or German, than that he made the innovation himself: 'The Consonant of the following Syllable ought to be pronounced with the fore-going Vowel. SPELL, *Co-lour*, *Modest*... but PRONOUNCE, *Col-lour*, *Mod-dest*' (p. 16). Richard Browne, 1700, goes a step further than Pastorius and anticipates Dyche in advocating a diacritic to indicate what he regards as the apparent doubling of a single consonant after a short vowel: '*Note*, That when this mark ˘ is set over any Vowel ending a Syllable, such Vowel must be sounded short with the next Consonant following; as if the Consonant had been doubled: Thus, *bă-nish* must be pronounced *ban-nish*' (p. 33). Browne had not made this suggestion in his earlier spelling-book of 1692.

Thomas Dyche's *A Guide to the English Tongue*, 1707, advocated a form of the same solution, boldly. His method, adopted by Dilworth and both praised and scorned in later years, was to say that the stressed vowel attracted to itself the following consonant. This statement by itself would have been a contradiction of the rule, tantamount to saying that the word should be divided *hon-est*. Dyche avoided unorthodoxy by saying that in the process of being attracted the consonant doubled its power. The consonant was both attracted to the first vowel and retained by the second vowel, as if the word were *hon-nest*. But to have written the *n* twice would have falsified the spelling; so Dyche placed the mark " after the first vowel to show that the single consonant following was in sound equivalent to two consonants: *ho"-nest* (p. 24). Several hundred words are treated in this way, thereby saving both the rule and the pronunciation. Dyche's own words are:

A great Number of Words do in Pronunciation draw a Single Consonant after the former Vowel or Diphthong, actually doubling the Power of it. And this I consider'd was occasion'd by the Accent resting upon that Syllable . . . For instance in the Word *po"-pu-lous*, the Double Accent upon *O* directs the Reader to pronounce it, as if it were written *pop-pu-lous*.   (preface)

The double accent as used by Dyche appears in at least twenty-six spelling-books after him, from 1726 (Bailey) to 1855 (Paley). The apparent doubling of a single consonant is accepted, without using the accent, by four other writers up to 1861 (Mongan). Four others, including Noah Webster, reject what they variously call 'the puzzling double accent' (*First Book*, a. 1754) and 'that impotent rule' (A. Fisher, 1763, edn of 1778). Others, like John Warden, 1753, Dixon, 1728, and Johnston, 1764, accept Dyche's theory but do not use his double accent or double the consonant in print: Warden lists 600 words 'wherein a single consonant is doubled in reading' including *honest* and less obvious instances such as *sarcology* (pp. 51–68).

Other writers were reluctant to flout the rules by saying that they were subordinate to pronunciation. Harland, before 1714, represents the hesitant and compromising position of many writers. He gives the rules, 'tho' I must own, that dividing of Words into Syllables, is no where so useful, as when subservient to true Pronunciation'. In his spelling-lists, therefore, he gives the words twice, once in a column headed 'Rule' (where he gives, for example, *au-tho-ri-ty*) and again in a column headed 'Pronounce' (where the word is divided *au-thor-i-ty*) (preface, p. 31), Daniel Fisher, about thirty years later, also does not wish to forfeit the support, and custom, of those on either side of the controversy. He adapts Dyche's mark, to show where 'the Rule and Ear disagree. Any word that may be divided one Way by Sound, and another Way by the Rules of Spelling, the Scholar is directed how to understand that doubtful Division by this Mark " ; so that they who do not like the Division of Words by Rule, may with Ease teach these Tables, according to the Ear' (p. 25).

As the eighteenth century progressed more confidence was expressed in the authority of pronunciation:

1740 'As for the division of words into syllables (about which authors have made such a bustle and contest) there being no occasion for it, but when in writing or printing . . . you need only observe, that no more letters should be taken into the first line, but what are necessary to end or compleat the sound of that part of the word . . . in which your ear will be your best guide.' (Philip Sproson, p. 160)

1740 The author of *The Irish Spelling-Book* expresses his doubts in a gentlemanly dialogue. His questioner observes, 'Tho' you have laid down several Rules . . . for the due Division of Words into their Syllables, it may, perhaps, not be easy, in many Words (especially compounded, and derived ones) for a Learner rightly to perform it.' To which the author replies: 'Whenever such Word occurs, all that, you, under your uncertainty, can do, is, to make Guess work with it: You are to divide it into such a Number of Parts, and such a combination of Vowels, and Consonants, as may be conveniently pronounced together; and content your self with such a venture, whether the combinations be exactly true or not.' (pp. 52–3)

Solomon Lowe repudiates the practice with some heat:

1755 'The *Division of Syllables* is a point, which grammarians have labord with much ostentation of learning . . . and I know not what apparatus, to ascertain the thing: but, as every body, that has learnt to read, must know that they neither did (nor indeed could) attend to these niceties in learning; nor ever reapt any benefit from them afterwards; I have ventured to drop them; and have divided the syllables for the use of learners (for whose use alone it is that they are divided at all) in such manner as might best direct to the proper sounds.' (preface, p. 15)

Lowth's cool words were simple and influential:

1762 'The best and only sure rule for dividing the syllables in spelling is to divide them as they are naturally divided in a right pronunciation.' (p. 7)

John Ash, whose *Grammatical Institutes* (1760) 1763 had contained no reference to the division of syllables, remarks in his *Sentiments on Education,* 1777; 'The old method of dividing syllables begins to be deservedly exploded . . . It seems most natural to divide the syllables of a word, however compounded, just as we pronounce them' (I, 4). And Ann Fisher about the same time finds it 'amazing that Schoolmasters should have been so long hummed with the impracticable Spelling Rules of Dyche and his followers' (A. Fisher, 1763, edn of 1801, p. vi, quoting her own edn of *c.* 1777).

William Kenrick questions even Lowth's recommendation:

1773 'With due deference . . . to so good a scholar . . . a person who is already master of a right pronunciation need not be taught how to spell . . . I see no use the speaker has to divide syllables at all. Children, indeed, are taught to read by syllables, but they learn to talk by words.' (p. 26)

1785 Robert Ross (USA), like Noah Webster two years earlier, took the same view: the division of syllables is '*merely* to enable Children to pronounce them . . . When Words are pronounced with *proper Accent*, the Ear readily perceives the best

Method of dividing all Words, which are in common Use, without any Rules about the Matter.'   (p. vi)

1792   For P. W. Fogg the rules were '*fantastical dogmas* . . . long exploded, and now passing to the *limbo* of chivalry and monkery'. They should be replaced by 'new rules . . . adapted to true pronunciation'.   (I, 49)

An emphasis on pronunciation, even when supported by an acknowledgment to Lowth, could lead a teacher into strange practices. John Robinson, in *The Art of Teaching the Orthography*, 1800, and in *The New English Spelling Book* of the same year, maintained that 'The present method of dividing words into Syllables . . . is, perhaps, the parent of more corruption than any other *custom* in teaching the English language' (*New Engl. Sp. Book*, 1819, p. xiv). He quotes errors, all caused by the improper application of VCV to accented syllables, from Dilworth (*be-ve-rage* instead of *bev-er-age*), from Entick (*so-li-cit* instead of *so-lic-it*) and from Dyche, Vyse and Daniel Fisher. His own method is to arrange the spelling words in two columns:

True Orthography and most natural Division	True Pronunciation with Accent supplied
Pic-ture	Pik' - tshur
Phys-ic	Fiz' - ik
Clay-ey	Tla' - e

The last pair needs explanation. Robinson considered that from 'examining the Position of the Organs of Speech' *tl* was the correct representation of the sound made by *cl*, as *dl* was for *gl*. He prided himself on being the first writer to point this out (*Art of Teaching*, p. 47). He may have been the first to approve of the pronunciation, although an earlier phonetician, Robert Robinson, in *The Art of Pronuntiation*, 1617, had accepted it (Dobson, 1968, p. 211) and in 1587 Clement had noted it, disapprovingly (p. 13). John Robinson was himself adversely criticised on the very grounds that he had used: that many of his words were divided so badly that it was clear he had no understanding of English accentuation; that his many errors included the division of *abolish* as *a-bo'-lish* instead of *ab-ol'-ish*. It was thought he might be a Scotsman (*The Child's First Book Improved*, 1801, p. ix).

    The authority of the rules continued to weaken. Ashton and Clegg, at least as early as the seventh edition of their *The New Expositor*, 1806, first published in 1788, complained that by being required to divide *ci-vi-lize* 'the child is compelled to give two different sounds to the same syllable, in spelling the same word . . . When the learner has spelled the word, as it is divided above, he will naturally put it together thus, *cy-vy-lize*, that is, he will give to every syllable, a long sound' (preface). John Hornsey, 1806, applied the same argument to *dolorous*, and Hazlitt, 1810, to *document*. American teachers shared in the controversy. In the nineteenth century they seem always to have favoured the authority of pronunciation, but in 1793 Foster Waterman had defended the rules. Like many writers on this subject he is stronger on denunciation than on reform: 'All the Spelling Books, I have ever yet seen, are deficient in one capital point, the division of syllables; and some writers have licentiously discarded all rules.' His own rules are traditional, except that he maintains, against the older view, that 'a syllable is naturally ended in a consonant' even if the vowel is long. Thus he concedes the point most frequently made against VCV (vol. II, preface and p. 14).

Albert Picket, 1804, of Manhattan, is one of many who acknowledge a debt to Lowth. He too describes the problem of VCV, which is not resolved by following Lowth's advice: 'There is a difficulty in dividing certain words, so as to lead children to a right pronunciation of them. When *tacit* is divided *ta-cit*, a child is apt to pronounce it as if written *tace-it*. But it must not be divided *tac-it*; for *tac* makes *tak*, and this is still worse' (p. xi). Picket's tiny classroom problem illustrates very well the consequences of the (as it would seem to us) excessive analysis and excessive regulation from which teachers were trying to free themselves. Liberation was slow. Even as late as 1831 Ingram Cobbin, in England, had thought that he was the first to advocate division of syllables according to pronunciation, until he read Lindley Murray. Murray in fact attributes the recommendation to Lowth 'and others'; he himself states the traditional practice in no fewer than eleven rules (Murray [1795] 1802, Part I, Chap. 2). At the same time Henry Young is trying to modify CC, saying that because the first vowel of *custard* is short the division should be *cus-tard*, not, as CC would normally require, *cu-stard* (p. 214). G.F. Graham, 1862, and W.L. Robinson, 1868, are unusual in retaining the term 'division of syllables'. Graham's rules are traditional, except that he also says that a long vowel must end a syllable (*ca-ble*) and a short accented one 'attracts a following single consonant' (*bev-y*) (p. 5). The idea of proper beginnings has long since vanished; the ear is the sole arbiter and the rules are all but dead.

Even when the rules were dead there remained the question of VCV. Thomas Dyche would have been happy to see how his often ridiculed suggestion received a kind of Solomon's support from a writer who was unlikely to have heard of it. R.G. Latham, 1841, discusses VCV without reference to rules or to teaching: 'In certain words, of more than one syllable, it is difficult to say to which syllable an intervening consonant belongs.' In *river* does the *v* belong to the first or second syllable? A long-standing question. Latham's answer is that when a consonant is used initially, as in *pa-* (*a* sounding as in *fate*) the sound of the consonant 'may be called the sound of breath *escaping*', and when the consonant is used finally, as in *-ap*, the breath of *p* is cut off: 'it is the sound of *p*, minus the breath'. This, Latham says, holds for all consonants: 'In the formation of syllables I consider the sound of Breath Arrested belongs to the First, and the sound of Breath Escaping to the Second Syllable . . . The *whole* Consonant belongs neither to one Syllable nor to the other. Half of it belongs to each' (pp. 125–7).

The last stage of the rules is reflected more clearly in an earlier work, B.H. Smart's *A Grammar of English Sounds*, 1812. In a note on the sound of *a* as in *fate* Smart says:

'It is by habit that we learn the syllabical division of words in pronunciation. Thus we come to know that *vapour* divides into *va-pour*, where the *a*, being final in the syllable, has the present sound; while *vapid*, we learn, divides into *vap-id*, where the *a* is not final in the syllable, and therefore has not the present sound.' (p. 91)

Two hundred years earlier VCV would have prescribed that *vapour* and *vapid* were divided *va-pour* and *va-pid*. As many previous examples have shown, eventually the fact that the two words were pronounced differently led to the rule being modified. The new interpretation of the rule said that when the first vowel was short and stressed the consonant went with the first syllable (*vap-id*); but as a descriptive statement this was cumbersome, open to question and of little use to the teacher, who could be his own judge of 'habit'. By 1845 syllables could be divided without any reference to rules: 'The pupil should first pronounce the syllables separately, and in the next breath combine them with the proper accent . . . [he] will soon be able to read the longest words in the lists; and to divide and read similar words wherever he may meet them' (Scottish School Book Association, *The Child's First Book, no. 3*).

It is surprising that few writers apply the rules to the division of a word at the end of a line. *The Writing Scholar's Companion*, 1695, refers to it in discussing the hyphen and there are about six references during the eighteenth century. Matthew Beasley, 1812, and Sutcliffe, 1815, are unusual in giving the rules without mentioning spelling or pronunciation: they apply them solely to the division of a word at the end of a line – yet another indication of their weakening influence.

It took a long time for the dispute about rules to die away. During the 120 years between 1580 and 1700 they were put forward without reservation in a little over half of the relevant texts, and this proportion was only slightly reduced during the next fifty years. During the seventy years between 1751 and 1820 the proportion fell to rather more than a quarter, and over the thirty years from 1821 to 1850 to one-tenth. There were always writers in addition who stated the rules incompletely or with reservations; as the volume of firm support weakened so the number of reservations increased, but during the last period, 1821–50, even this modified support had practically vanished. Their life-cycle illustrates one development of the idea of a rule: from a prescriptive regulation to a description of regularities. The rules were derived from a way in which it was thought classical Latin had been pronounced. Their application to the spelling of Latin caused little difficulty because, the pronunciation of Latin being unknown, conflict between spelling and assumed pronunciation could easily be resolved. When the rules, by then divorced from their origin in pronunciation, were applied to the teaching of English spelling the position was different. The orthography of English was inconsistent; the spelling was not fixed; pronunciation was live and variable. Nor could the rules be restricted to the formal mechanisms of spelling. Spelling was the preliminary to, or dominant companion of, the teaching of reading. The consequent strains showed in the number of exceptions to the rules and in disagreements among teachers about how they should be applied. The strains were increased through the attention paid by teachers to 'accent', represented by Dyche's textbook of 1707. A cognate development later in the eighteenth century was the popularity of elocution, which also focused the attention of teachers onto spoken English. The rules for the division of syllables had survived so long only because all rules were respected. The application of a rule was considered to be a main teaching-procedure. Under long exposure to the strong light of actual usage the prescriptive authority of the rules had steadily weakened; in a descriptive role they were inadequate and unhelpful; they withered and died.

CHAPTER THREE

Reading, spelling, pronunciation: the skills

Kinds of spelling

Until the end of the eighteenth century spelling was often, and from then until the 1830s occasionally, defined just as 'dividing words into their syllables':

1580a 'To divide syllables in a word [is] called spelling.'
(William Bullokar, *Booke at Large*, p. 44)

c. 1625 'The dissolution of wordes into syllables commonly termed spelling.'
(Thomas Hayward, fol. 89b)

1710 'Q. What is spelling? A. Dividing words into Syllables.'
(John Urmston, 1700, p.5)

1825 'The division of words into syllables and of letters into syllables is called spelling.'
(Samuel Oliver, p. 7)

Unless this meaning of *spelling* is borne in mind it is impossible to understand, for example, Elisha Coles' boast in the preface to his spelling-book:

1674 'The Rule that I lay down is brief and plain and easie: viz. All words must so be spell'd, as they are afterwards to be pronounc'd. But this they [the Masters] dare not venture on, for fear (forsooth) of straying from the common road, or slighting of a rule that was made and intended only for the Latin tongue. See. I have broke the ice.'

Yet Coles' lists of over 6000 words contain no innovatory spellings in our sense of the term; it is in the division of syllables that he is departing from the rules and from Latin precedents.

It is not obvious that merely dividing a word into its syllables has much to do with what we call spelling: it would seem necessary to form the syllables with the correct letters, and this is often explicitly stated:

1596 'Thou hast but two principall things to learne, to spell truly any word of one syllable, and to divide truly any word of many.' (Edmund Coote, preface)

1640 'By spelling I understand the due ordring of syllables in a just proportion, as they are to be together comprehended under their severall accents: or a certain way of attributing to every syllable its true quantity or measure in the number of letters therto belonging: whether as an integrall part of a word, or constituting the whole. To this is requisite first to know the number of syllables in every word, then their division.'   (Simon Daines, p. 62)

(1677) 1716 'True and exact Spelling . . . is, the rightly dividing of Words into Syllables, giving to each Syllable its own due Letters.'   (N.S., p. 3)

1833 'Spelling is the art of rightly dividing a word into syllables, or expressing it by its proper letters.'   (A. Bobbit, p. 5)

Until early in the nineteenth century the great majority of definitions and descriptions assume that spelling is an analytical process. As late as 1817 James Andrew defines it as 'the art of reducing words to syllables, and syllables to letters. Reading is the converse of spelling' (p. 4). But the first stages of teaching spelling, whether from the hornbook or from an elementary textbook, were synthetic. The pupil would learn first the vowels, to each of which he would put the consonants in turn: *ab ac ad . . . ba ca da.* He would go on to form three-letter syllables, *bab, bac, bad,* and so 'through the monosyllables' to words of two, three and four syllables, up to whatever number of syllables the writer's common sense or ingenuity led him. This synthesising aspect of spelling is first explicitly stated by Isaac Watts, 1721: spelling is 'the Art of composing Words out of Letters and Syllables, either in Reading or Writing' (p. 26). Watts is quoted by Nathan Bailey, 1726, who calls spelling as defined in this way 'component spelling', to be distinguished from 'distributive spelling [which] is to take Words asunder according to their proper Parts, in Order to shew their true Pronunciation and original Formation' (Part 2, p. 22). Similarly *The Irish Spelling Book* begins an interesting discussion with the following exchange:

1740 'Q. What is Spelling?
   A. *Spelling* is an *Art,* which shews, 1st, How to divide Words already made, into Syllables and Letters. 2dly, How to join Letters and Syllables together, so as to compose Words by them.
   Q. Which of these two Sorts of Spelling is preparatory to *Reading*?
   A. Both, viz. the dividing of Words already made, into Syllables and Letters; and, out of these, to make up the same Words again. As, in Spelling the Word *Merciful,* we say, *m-e-r, mer; c-i, ci, merci; f-u-l, ful: merciful.* So that the Word is first divided into its Parts, and then set together again.'   (pp. 10–11)

But these 'two Sorts of Spelling' are, in the author's view, parts of spelling considered only as the division of syllables. He continues immediately

'The Word *Spelling* is frequently used to signifie the Writing of a Word, either from the Sound in its Pronunciation, or from the conception of its Characters formed in the Mind: – And, when a Man writes the Word without adding any wrong Letters, and without lessening or changing the proper ones in it, he is said to Spell well, or truly. *Spelling* in this Sense, is obtained chiefly by much Reading of Books, and a careful Observation of Words therein.'   (p. 11)

The discussion continues in question and answer, establishing that 'Spelling, or dividing Words into Syllables' is not so easy as it might seem: a knowledge of the derivation of words is needed to prevent, for example, *Ab-ra-ham* from being 'falsly spelled' *A-bra-ham*. Ability to divide syllables correctly is important for two reasons: (i) 'Somewhat of the Sense of the Original . . . is preserved; and so helps one to a clearer Notion of it's Meaning', and (ii) a wrong division leads to a wrong pronunciation. If a boy were to divide *position* incorrectly, as *pos-it-i-on*, 'he wou'd certainly pronounce [the word] as wrongly in Speaking . . . So that, without true Spelling, our very speaking itself wou'd be improper, and hardly intelligible' (pp. 13–14).

Such emphasis on the division of syllables makes it seem almost as if spelling in the 'modern' sense is scarcely being taught. This is not so. To us it may seem that the only natural way in which to spell, say, *petition*, is to begin at the beginning and name each letter in turn. Up till the middle of the eighteenth century a quite different way of thinking obtained, almost unquestioned. This way of thinking can be represented, in our terms, by the following steps. When our eighteenth-century teacher is consciously spelling *petition* he (i) mentally sees, or hears, the word and probably says it to himself. He then (ii) divides it mentally into syllables according to the way in which he says it, but governed by rules. As he hears it, in his mind's ear, it may be divided *pe-ti-ti-on* or *pet-it-i-on*, but the VCV rule will direct him to the former. He then (iii) expresses these separate syllables in speech or writing. He has been drilled in the formation of syllables (*pa, pe, pi . . . ta, te, ti*) so he can write or say *pe-ti-ti-on* without further difficulty. It is only at this stage of expressing each syllable that spelling, in its literal sense, is required. The final stage is (iv) to put the syllables together, to write or say the whole word: *petition*. He has now correctly spelled it. Spelling therefore is primarily the division of syllables; its minor role is, in Coote's words, just 'to spell truly any word of one syllable'. As is not uncommon at this period both *word* and *syllable* can refer to any small unit, whether meaningful or not. Coote, introducing a list that includes *bor, dop, gug, mur*, tells his reader, 'You may teach your Scholer, to cal these words syllabls.' Though they are not all words themselves they 'are used in English words' (p. 3). As John Matlock had said in *Fax nova artis scribendi*, 1685, a manual of penmanship, 'When you can spell a Word of one Syllable, it will be no difficult Matter to spell Words of many, if you know how to divide them' (p.

18). George Fisher, 1700, describes the spelling of *petition*, dividing each syllable in turn: 'You must say *P-e* spel *pe*; then say *t-i* spel *ti* which you must put to *pe* thus *pe-ti*. Then *t-i* before a vowel spel *si*, *pe-ti-ti*. And *o-n* spel *on*. All which make *pe-ti-ti-on*' (p. 31).

Fisher's use of *spell* here introduces a further complication in our attempt to ascertain what the pupils actually did. His instruction that *ti* before a vowel is to be spelt *si* shows that *spell* is here equivalent to 'pronounce' or 'read aloud'. This is a long-standing sense of the term. The *Oxford English Dictionary* records the transitive sense 'to read (a book, etc.) letter by letter', but the word seems to have been used intransitively in this sense also. In *The Writing Scholar's Companion*, 1695, two kinds of spelling are defined: 'Spelling may be understood two ways (i) either the true sounding of each word of one Syllable, according to the Vowels or Diphthongs. (ii) Or the dividing of words aright into distinct Syllables' (p. 18). In the first definition the 'true sounding' of a word must refer to the saying of a word, that is to reading it aloud. In the Bodleian fragment of a spelling-book, *c.* 1673, the teacher is having described to him the sequence of tasks he must give his pupil so that 'he can spel upon the book'. The expression 'spell upon the book' seems at first to be a contradiction, because 'upon book' means 'with the book open, using the book'. The expression is most unlikely to mean 'name the letters of the word that you see in front of you', because such naming-exercises were carried out when the alphabet was being learned, and the mere enumeration of the letters of a word you are looking at is a futile task if the names of the letters are known. The expression cannot here mean 'divide the word into its syllables', because the surviving pages of the fragment show that its main, if not its whole, concern is with monosyllables. To spell upon the book must here mean 'to read letter by letter', but not, as one of the illustrations in the fragment shows, letter by letter in the order in which the letters occur. To spell upon book turns out to be a familiar method of reading: 'When they meet with a long syllabl that is hard, to bring them to understand it, teach them to take it piece meal: as if, *strap*: begin thus, *a,p*, *ap*; *rap*; *trap*; *strap*' (p. 32). Spelling upon book is both a kind of spelling and a kind of reading, and it is in this sense that Fisher says *ti* is to be spelt *si*. As the emphasis on the division of syllables began to weaken, so more attention was given in the definitions to the literal aspect of spelling. Kirkby, 1746, like Watts, offers a definition that makes no reference to syllables: 'The Repetition of all the Letters of which any Word consists, and with which it ought to be wrote, is called the Spelling of that Word' (p. 20). Some years later James Dun of Edinburgh, also without reference to syllables, says that spelling is just asking 'What are the Letters which make the sound [such and such]?' (a. 1766, p. xii). Lowth, following Johnson's dictionary, sees the division of syllables as a technique appropriate only to reading, not to writing:

1762 'Spelling is the art of reading by naming the letters singly, and rightly dividing words into their syllables. Or, in writing, it is the expressing of a word by its proper letters.'   (p. 6)

In *A Short and Easy Introduction to English Grammar*, 1786, designed for Miss Davies' boarding school in Hackney, spelling is defined much as by Lowth but without reference to the division of syllables:

Q. What is Spelling?
A. Spelling is the art of reading, by first naming singly the letters that form a
   Syllable, then pronouncing that Syllable; and if there are more than one in a
   word, joining them together as you go on, to form that word. Thus, for example,
   Parsimony, P-a-r, Par; s-i, si, Parsi; m-o, mo, Parsimo; n-y, ny: Parsimony.
                                                                          (pp. 3–4)

Lowth had distinguished oral from written spelling. In the former letters were named; the latter was to 'express a word by its proper letters'. Although references to the division of syllables were still common, the synthesising aspects of spelling were receiving more attention:

1789 '. . . the Uniting of Letters into Syllables, and Syllables into words.'
                                                                     (Sewell, p. 2)

1792 '. . . to combine the proper letters in forming words.'   (Fogg, p. 3)

1794 '. . . the art of forming words of letters.'   (Wright, p. 65)

1806 '. . . the art of spelling, or joining syllables together in words.'
                                                               (Torkington, preface)

1812 '. . . naming the letters of which a word is composed, beginning with the first,
and going on regularly to the last.'   (Angus, p. 16)

Until about 1830 the division of syllables remained a common enough practice to be worth attacking. William Bearcroft, 1828, an advocate of dictation, says of his spelling-book:

'It is intended that pupils shall not do more than *name the letters* of the words, as they are correctly pronounced to them by the teacher. This kind of spelling is . . . nearly assimilated to that of manuscript, (which is the ultimate object of spelling) and the gradation . . . natural and easy, compared with the mode of sounding each syllable separately and afterwards uniting them to form words.'   (preface)

For most teachers the practical method of dividing syllables was to follow pronunciation rather than a set of rules surrounded by exceptions but there were many, even into the nineteenth century, whose thoughts ran in the opposite direction, valuing the rules as a means of teaching pronunciation:

1707   'Spelling takes Words asunder in such convenient Parts as may best direct to the true Pronunciation of the whole Word together.'   (Dyche, p. 116)

1711   'Spelling being the parting Words into convenient Parts, in order to shew their true Pronounciation; or for decency of Writing.'   (Greenwood, p. 255)

1802   'Spelling is the art of dividing words into their proper syllables, in order to find their true pronunciation. The best way of dividing words for children, is to divide them so as naturally to lead the learner into a right pronunciation.'
(Abner Kneeland (USA), p. 17)

(a. 1816) c. 1820   'Words are taken asunder into convenient parts, in order to shew their true pronunciation and original formation. This is called spelling.'
(John Smith of Norwich, p. 17)

These definitions are circular, if the person who is to be informed of the correct pronunciation is the person who divided the word. As dividing the word correctly depended almost entirely on pronouncing it correctly in the first place the division was not going to produce new information for the person who had made the division. In so far as the division displayed the correct pronunciation, it was useful to someone else. What aided pronunciation was not making the division but seeing a word already divided. Hence the almost universal practice in the spelling lists of dividing the words, by hyphens or by spaces, into their 'correct' syllables.

Sir Thomas Bernard, in the third edition, 1815, of his *The Barrington School*, 1809, describes how the spelling-books used in the school are read three times, each time exercising a different kind of spelling. He makes no mention of the division of syllables. The 'common method' of spelling, which he considers a waste of time, is to repeat all the previous syllables of a word after each new syllable has been spelt. 'Unreiterated' spelling is to spell each syllable as it comes, without accumulation. 'Previous' spelling is spelling a word previous to, and as a prerequisite for, reading it. Spelling 'off book' is supplying, without the book, the letters of a word that the teacher has given; spelling 'on book' means here 'reading the letters in the book, and pronouncing the word which those letters compose' (pp. 82–4). By the 1830s the definitions of spelling have largely disappeared from the textbooks. Their obsolescence is caused partly by changes in the teaching of reading, discussed below, but mainly by an overdue recognition on the part of the teachers that definitions are of little, if any, help to young children. Spelling was treated as a self-defining activity: naming the letters of a word. Nevertheless W.L. Robinson in 1862 still distinguishes two senses of the term, to distinguish 'two different operations . . . first the uttering either the names or powers of the letters in due order with a view to suggest the pronunciation, and secondly the writing down words in the manner usual with educated people of the time' (Intro.). He maintains that children learning to read ought not to be troubled with spelling in the latter sense.

Spelling-lists

In the hornbooks and early spelling-books the alphabet was nearly always followed by lists of syllables. Until the end of the eighteenth century between 70 and 80 per cent of the relevant texts give these lists; between 1801 and 1850 the proportion drops to 50 per cent. The change reflects a slowly changing point of view. The syllable was no longer seen as the unquestioned stepping-stone to the word; rather it represented an artificial and unnecessary stage in learning to read or to spell, and children increasingly began their learning with one-syllable words, which they might often meet straightaway in sentences. The seventeenth- and early-eighteenth-century books that did not include syllable lists were usually concerned particularly with orthography and pronunciation; they were more directly intended for the teacher, and their elementary material was presented in a setting of phonological discussion rather than as tasks for pupils.

The simplest lists comprised the vowels followed by the consonants in alphabetical order: *ab eb ib ob ub*, and so on, together with the reverse pattern *ba be bi bo bu*. The syllables were printed in lines so that all the combinations containing a given vowel formed a column. The children learnt by heart (or learnt to form quickly) both lines and columns. Usually the lists continued with three-letter combinations: *bla ble bli blo blu*, and *abl ebl ibl obl ubl*, often with four-letter ones: *stra stre stri . . . atch etch itch*, etc. These four-letter combinations were usually restricted to those which could begin, or to those which could end, a word, a consideration important in teaching the division of syllables (above, p. 75). Syllables were most frequently classified and listed according to the number of letters in them. The standard statement that there could be up to eight letters in a syllable was illustrated by sentences such as *I do say, that brave knight brought strength* (Lye, 1671, p. 74). By the middle of the eighteenth century one-syllable words were increasingly distinguished from syllables, and separately treated. The teacher who enjoyed classification could give himself great pleasure, and his pupils great trouble. John Brooksbank, 1654b, provides, without rubric, lists of which the nineteenth, presumably a classification by diphthongs, includes the sequence *peemb poomd peamn poamp rayms reynd royng rawnc rewnk*, and the twenty-first list combines with the diphthongs elaborate beginning and ending combinations of consonants: *squewngls throwrlds thwoortls schairkld . . . sklaulcht* (pp. 26, 28). Quite what the children were supposed to do with these monstrosities we do not know.

Thomas Crumpe, 1712, having listed the usual two-letter syllables, classifies three-letter syllables in six ways. The basis of his classification is to break down a syllable such as *mer*, in *merry*, to *me-* plus *-er*, both of which had been learnt in the two-letter lists, to which is joined *-ry*. From this first type of three-letter syllable he builds up lists which include *su-per-an-nu-a-ted* and *non-con-for-mi-ty*. His second kind of three-letter syllable has the form VCV, from which he builds up to *li-cen-ti-ate*, a not very happy illustration of the syllable *ice*. Four-letter syllables he classifies according to eight combinations of vowels, diphthongs, silent *e* and consonants. Five-and six-letter syllables are each classified in ten ways; longer ones are listed without classification, the last group comprising just *strengths, brought'st* and *streights*.

Phonetic criteria are regularly used in the classification of monosyllables, but seldom of syllables alone. Those teachers who could handle distinctions of sound had already discussed them in relation to the letters of the alphabet, and surprisingly little is said about the syllables beyond a recognition that the vowel sounds of *ab eb ib* differed from those of *ba be bi*. There are exceptions. The author of *'The Child's First Book' improved*, 1801, lists syllables according to three rules (p. xii):

1. The vowels are to be sounded long when they are alone, or when no consonant follows in the same syllable;
2. Vowels are short in all syllables ending with a consonant (some exceptions);
3. Vowels are long when *-e* ends the syllable (*babe*).

The author of *A Key to Spelling*, 1825, says that his arrangement of syllables is unusual because of the attention he pays to 'sound'. His lists look like any others, but he treats, for example, the difference between *pra* and *arp* as one in the sounds of the two vowels, whereas customarily they would have been distinguished merely as CCV and VCC. Unfortunately we are left to assume that *arp* is to be sounded as in *harp*, and to wonder whether *pra* is to be sounded as in *pram* or as in *prate* (p. 23).

Characteristic of those books which classify syllables, but more extensive than most, is Solomon Lowe's *The Critical Spelling-Book*, 1755. Lowe's basic criterion is the number of letters in a syllable, but this is accompanied by a further classification according to the position of vowels and consonants. His two-letter syllables are distinguished as VC (*ab eb . . . oz uz*) and CV (*ba be . . . zo zu*). Then follow alphabetical lists on the VCC pattern to be learnt horizontally and vertically. The last segment of the lists is:

asp	esp	isp	osp	usp
ast	est	ist	ost	ust
ath	eth	ith	oth	uth
ats	ets	its	ots	uts
axt	ext	ixt	oxt	uxt

There are similar lists on the CCV pattern (*bla ble . . . wro wru*). Four-letter syllables are listed as VCCC (*acht . . . ucht* horizontally; *acht . . . aths* vertically) and as CCCV (*chla . . . chlu* horizontally; *chla . . . thwa* vertically). Five-letter syllables are listed as VCCCC (*angth . . . utcht*) and CCCCV (*schra . . . sphru*).

The treatment of syllables, as distinct from one-syllable words, varied little during the years. Although by now old-fashioned, Goold Brown in 1821 is still listing *ab eb* and *ba be*, and a much later work, *Reading Analysed*, 1857, is built entirely on the syllable. The first nine lessons list all the VC syllables (*ab*); then each of the consonants is put before each VC syllable (*bab*). From the twenty-sixth lesson -*e* is added to the syllable already formed (*babe*) and from the thirty-fifth lesson words of 'irregular spelling' are introduced. The number of syllables is not important; long words are used, as they had been by Crumpe, provided that all their constituent syllables have been met already. The method is systematic in much the same way as many seventeenth- and early-eighteenth-century books, but it is less mechanical, in that nonsense combinations are avoided. But the teacher's words would not have sounded unfamiliar two centuries earlier: 'Shew me *ab* . . . Spell *ab* (without looking) . . . What does *a-b* spell?' (p. 1). The main objection to the method, pointed out in the book itself, is that it delays the introduction of common words. *He, go, so* are not met until lesson 26; *and* not till lesson 27; *the* in lesson 29 and *to* in lesson 35.

Objections to meaningless syllables were presumably held by some of those teachers who omitted them from their spelling-books, but the high status of the syllable is shown by the fact that it is not until the end of the eighteenth century that the objection is made explicit, and very timidly. Joseph Brown, about 1790, lists a few syllables, but says they are not helpful in teaching, which ought to begin with real words (p. 19). Edward Dearle, 1791, avoids that 'universal and (methinks) unprofitable mode, a train of letters thus used: *ba, be, bi* . . . which, like the alphabet regularly and formally taught, children soon say by rote, and not with judgment' (preface). But he dare not defy the convention completely, and apologetically includes just one page of two-letter syllables. Lady Fenn, in 1797, says that 'to compile syllables is an *ignoble toil*' but nevertheless useful. Teachers hesitated to deny the syllable its separate treatment, partly because it had always been so treated, partly because it was still felt to be a functional component of words and of their pronunciation, and partly because many syllables were words and the syllable could not, therefore, be given up entirely. The hesitation is apparent in a list, in Henry Innes' spelling-book of 1835, which he heads '*Do*, &c., pronounced as Syllables. *Do, to, is, as, my, by*' (p. 4). Innes is unwilling to treat *do* just as a word, because it is also, and potently, a syllable. He lists no syllables as such, but their influence is still there.

The listing of syllables, as of one-syllable words (below, p. 101), could create classroom problems about which the books are normally silent. Such comment as there is, like Dilworth's, is very general:

(1740) 1751 'Great Care is taken to avoid all such *Words* . . . which might tend to excite loose and disorderly Thoughts, or put Youth or Modesty to the Blush.'

(preface)

George Fisher, however, in 1700, after listing *cac cec cic coc cuc* through to *zac zec . . . zuc*, omitting *fac fec . . .* etc., says, 'As for the Letter *f* for a modest reason these Words relating thereunto shall suffice, *ac-tor, affec-ti-on* and *fic-ti-on*' (p. 11). The point of his first example is obscure. A misprint is more probable than a sniggery joke.

Learning the monosyllables

Monosyllables received special treatment for various reasons. They were regarded as units in the formation of compound words; they were numerous; they were easy when regular, and simple reading-passages, whole books in fact, could be made from monosyllables alone. They could also be difficult, with a Saxon individuality that defied classification and contrasted with the smooth uniformities of a Latinate vocabulary. Behind the special treatment often given to monosyllables lay the assumption that there was a cumulative relationship between linguistic units.

Insofar as there was little, or only a blurred, distinction between meaningless syllables and one-syllable words it was easy to assume that one-syllable words composed polysyllable words. If a child knew his syllables he would be able to read any one-syllable word; if he knew all, or the commonest, monosyllables he would be able to read words of many syllables. Unless the assumption was applied to a carefully selected vocabulary it was confusing and unhelpful, as in a nineteenth-century textbook in which the teacher is told 'to explain to the child that these two-syllable words are only two little words joined'. Unhappily the list to which this instruction is applied includes *utmost, virgin, weather* and *zany* (*The Illuminated London Primer*, 1845).

Until about 1730 the monosyllables were usually listed in alphabetical order, often classified also according to simple phonetic criteria. After 1750 phonetic criteria were more frequent than any other. Either of these criteria would be combined with classification by the number of letters: occasionally before 1730, frequently thereafter:

> *(1740) 1751* 'If it be reasonable, in the order of *Words*, to begin with those of one *Syllable*, as all *Spelling Authors* agree: it must be also granted as reasonable, that *Monosyllables*, which consist of various Quantities of *Letters*, should be taught in the same order, proceeding gradually from Words of *two Letters*, to Words of *three, four, five*, &c. *Letters*.'   (Dilworth, preface)

Consistent and extensive phonetic criteria are used in *The Best and Plainest English Spelling-Book* of about 1700. The syllables and monosyllables are listed according to eight 'rules', by which is meant statements of regularity (pp. 2–7):

1. Syllables and monosyllables containing a short vowel: that is, a vowel followed by a consonant (*ab, apt*).
2. Those containing a long vowel, i.e. preceded by a consonant (*ba, go, truth*).
3. Monosyllables under rule 1 which contain one or more silent letters (*bread, move, fierce*).
4. Similar monosyllables under rule 2 (*sea, womb, high*).
5. Monosyllables containing proper diphthongs (*aid, Paul*).
6. Monosyllables containing anomalous vowels, consonants or diphthongs (*s* in *was*).
7. Monosyllables containing *le* or *re* preceded by a consonant, in which the *e* must be sounded 'not so full as *el* & *er* nor so shrill as *il* & *ir* but between both (*treble, acres*)'.
8. Monosyllables containing *ci, si, ti*, etc. which are sounded as *sh* (*ancient, Asia*).

The listing of monosyllables, and the criteria by which they were classified, were matters far more important to seventeenth- and eighteenth-century teachers than we can easily imagine. The value of long lists was taken for granted, on grounds expressed by Samuel Edwards, 1765: 'The best Rule has been found by Experience to be the actual Spelling of large Catalogues, in order to get the Habit of spelling truly; but the Arrangements of Words according to their Sounds seems to contribute thereto' (p. 35). In 1753 John Warden praises Loughton's grammar for listing 'all the regular words of the same kind . . . in one table', such as those words 'wherein *c* before *e* or *y* has the sound of *s*' (preface, p. vi). The energy and ingenuity that the teachers put into their various classifications require us to study them in more detail than we would otherwise wish. Any attempt to understand what the teachers were trying to do, and what the children were supposed to do, means that we must look at the way in which these lists were structured. A few illustrations of a few types of classification follow in chronological order:

1707   Thomas Dyche lists over 2200 monosyllables alphabetically, by vowel and final consonant(s). The effect is that of rhyme. His first list begins *blab crab drab*, his second *back hack jack*. This second list contains the sequence *hiss kiss miss piss bliss*, which attracted comment. The third list comprises monosyllables ending in silent *e*, and the fourth those containing diphthongs. For all their rhyming, Dyche's lists are alphabetic, not phonetic. The words were meant to look, as well as to sound, alike. Elisha Coles, thirty years earlier, had put *bet, debt* and *sweat* into the same list; Dyche gives *bet* and eleven other three-letter words in *-et*, but *debt* and *sweat* are not there. Dyche's own comment about his method is: 'I have given the Monosyllables in Rhyme because I thought, that, not only the gingling of the Words wou'd be a Temptation to the Young Learner, but withal that placing Words of the same kind together wou'd be a considerable Help to his Memory.'   (preface)

1734   Henry Boad is the first to comment on Dyche's 'gingling'. He himself classifies monosyllables by part of speech or by the presence of features such as silent *e*, double *l*, or *ti* and *si*, which cause uncertainty in pronunciation. This method he thinks 'much better than a long detail of jingling syllables, that, in schools among boys, are apt to create too great a mixture of mirth and folly, both in studying and saying to the master; which, let him do his best, he cannot prevent in some waggish boys, when they study *hiss, kiss, miss,* &c.'   (preface)

1740   Philip Sproson also comments on Dyche's method. Dyche, and Bailey, he says, did not take 'the same pains in distributing the monosyllables into classes, according to the number of their respective letters, as they did in gingling them together, according to the *sameness of sound* . . . Can a child be brought readily to pronounce *skrew* and *shrew*, because they are of the same sound with *dew* and *few* . . . Certainly no.' In his own method the monosyllables are 'brought into distinct tables, *according to the number of letters in each word*: and subdivided into classes, according to *the easiness of their pronunciation*'.   (preface)

(1740) 1751   Thomas Dilworth, whose spelling-book was more popular even than Dyche's, lists over 1900 monosyllables in an explicit classification that is important because it was so often used by later writers. Onto a basic classification by the number of letters he imposes one that is partly phonetic, partly alphabetic:

List I   VC or CV (*am, be*)
List II   CVC (*dab*), CCV (*cry*), VCC (*act*)
List III   CVV (*see, law*), C + diphthong (*pea*)

List IV   CVCC (*rich, next*)

List V   CCVC (*blab*)

List VI   CVC + silent *e* (*babe*)

List VII   C + diphthong + (*laid*); CC + diphthong (*glue*)

List VIII   Words of five letters or more containing only one vowel (*throb, strong, length, strength*)

List IX   As List VIII but ending in -*e* (*bribe, strange*)

List X   As List VIII, but containing a diphthong and sometimes final *e* (*frail, cleanse*)   (pp. 3–21)

1756 Daniel Fenning recommends his practice, which he considers novel, of listing words by meaning: *Cake, Tarts, Ball, Tops* for boys and *Cup, Pan, Pot, Dish* for girls. His was by no means the first spelling-book to follow this practice. Henry Dixon, 1728, had grouped the monosyllables as 'the most natural and easy Things to the Apprehension of Children': parts of a house; tools; eatables; 'terms used in play'; and a similar arrangement is found in *The Child's New Plaything*, 1742; in Benjamin Martin's *An Introduction to the English Language*, 1754; and in *The Royal Guide* of about the same date.

During the latter part of the eighteenth century Dyche's 'gingling' methods, what Fenning had called 'perpetual jargon', continued in America and in Britain to be a matter of controversy. John Peirce, 1782, quotes and agrees with Fenning: the rhyming lists are 'dull, dry, and tiresome both to the Child and his Teacher' (preface). Noah Webster, on the other hand, liked the jingle for the very reasons that others had advanced against it: 'All the words in the same column being sounded alike, when a child has the sound of the first, the others will naturally follow' (1783, p. 29). But John Clarke of Grantham gives the most vivid picture of the teacher's difficulty:

1772 'Most Writers of Spelling-Books have, with infinite Pains, given a great Number of Tables of Monosyllables running in a continual Jingle; as, *Rack, pack, jack, lack, sack*, &c.; by which Means the Learner, having the first Word, runs through the Whole of that Set of Rhymes mechanically, without once looking in the Book . . . being at a Stop by the Discontinuation of the Jingle, the Master perhaps awakens him by a Blow, which obliges him to confess that he does not know what the next Word is; the Master tells him, and now having got Possession of another catch word, he very readily runs through that set of Chimes, but is most likely looking about the School the whole Time, instead of on his Book . . . He takes so very little Observation of the Form of the Letters or Word, that if any Word, which he could so glibly repeat on seeing it in these rhyming Tables, was pointed out to him, he would be quite at a Loss to read or even to spell it properly, its Appearance not having been sufficiently imprinted on his Mind.'   (preface)

The listing of monosyllables became less frequent during the nineteenth century as children were encouraged to read simple words and sentences without spelling. But the systematisers, alphabetic and phonetic, were still active:

1804   Lindley Murray keeps to the jingler's view that uniformity of material helps children to learn. His lists are 'arranged according to the length or shortness of their syllables' in order to prevent the learner from being 'perplexed and retarded by a constant recurrence of discordant sounds'.   (Introduction)

1821   In America Goold Brown lists the monosyllables by the number of letters and classifies them alphabetically with greater ardour even than Dilworth: 'Three letters combine in seven ways, and form seven classes of words bearing a close analogy to each other.' His expectation is that 'the child may catch the analogy, and pronounce the rest accordingly'.   (preface)

a. 1824   Adam Keys, in *The Rhyming Primer*, approved of rhyme and developed an ingenious method of combining rhyming lists with sentences providing a context. He set out rhyming words in short columns, the last word in each column forming part of a sentence read horizontally:

	rust	*cot*	*lo*		*bell*	*too*	*go*
	crust	*dot*	*so*		*fell*	*shoe*	*no*
I	must	not	go,	I	tell	you	so

Two more tables on the same pattern comprised the lesson, which was designed for a group of six children. Each child read one column of three words, spelling the italicised words before they were read, until all the children had read all the columns. The children then took it in turn to read the three sentences, half a sentence at a time. In these sentences they might meet words additional to those in the columns.

1838   William Birkin extensively lists 'monosyllables and dissyllables ... classified and arranged according to their sounds'.

1846   David Tower of Boston lists the monosyllables according to twenty-two vowel sounds and twenty-three 'consonantal elements'. Among the latter, for example, he lists 56 words with 'the combination [i.e. the sound] TSH, CH in *much*, and TCH in *catch*'.   (p. 56)

1870   J.M.D. Meiklejohn, stressing yet again that many monosyllables could not be read phonetically, added a startling comment: 'No wonder that the lower classes, who possess so few brain-residua, find it difficult to learn to read; and that even the middle classes find it difficult to learn to spell.'   (p. 26)

After the monosyllables

Words of more than one syllable were usually classified as 'dissyllables' and 'polysyllables', but the latter term was sometimes used, as by Solomon Lowe, 1755, for all words that were not monosyllables, and sometimes, as by John Clarke, 1772, only for words of four or more syllables. Most writers included these lists, but Thomas Tuite is noticeable in giving reasons for omitting 'the usual Tables of Words of several Syllables, which make up the greatest Part of Spelling-Books'. The lists 'do not seem to depend on, or have Connexion with any Rule' (preface).

The spelling-lists of the eighteenth century were almost all formed according to the number of syllables in a word; only in the second half of the century was any attention given to grouping by phonetic criteria also, the lack of which was strongly condemned by Lowe (p. 3). In 1707 Thomas Dyche introduced a practice that set the pattern for the rest of the century. He grouped alphabetically words of a given number of syllables by what he and later writers all called 'accent', that is, by stress:

Two-syllable words accented on the first syllable   (*turtle*)
Two-syllable words accented on the second syllable   (*prepare*)
Three-syllable words accented on the first syllable   (*cucumber*)
Three-syllable words accented on the second syllable   (*anchovy*)
Three-syllable words accented on the third syllable   (*maccaroon*)

and so on up to whatever number of syllables, four, five or six, the author chose in order to indicate the level of difficulty in his book. Dyche took his pupils to seven syllables, and though he included words as specialised as *eleemosynary* and *pusillanimity* he avoided the pretentious absurdities of some authors who compiled their lists from a dictionary: *supererogatoriously* (Hodges, 1644); *theologicopoliticus* (Ellis, 1719); *anthropomorphitanianismicaliation* (Barrie, 1794, p. 263). Proper names, especially biblical ones, were commonly listed in the same way, and few writers could resist the display of virtuosity required by *Mahershalalhashbaz*, even if their pupils suffered, like young Rob the Grinder, from 'a perpetual bruising of his intellectual shins against all the proper names of all the tribes of Judah' (Dickens, *Dombey and Son*, chap. 39). Dyche, however, also makes a point of including proper names 'frequent in our ordinary News-Papers' (preface), and Dilworth, 1740, while omitting 'all superfluous *Hebrew* and *obsolete Names*', includes in his lists *Ormskirk* and *Ormus, Alfreton* and *Alicant*.

Grouping by the stressed syllable was most frequent between 1720 and 1800, and seems again to have been popular in the 1830s. The use of stress as a criterion of classification receives no critical comment until 1865, when William Davis makes explicit the objection, which must have been obvious to earlier teachers, that words accented on the first syllable (*quadruped* is his example) are not necessarily easier than those accented on the second (his example is *vehement*). Secondary stress was not discussed; at best it was briefly referred to, as in *The Irish Spelling Book*. Usually it was ignored, as by J.F. Denham, 1834, who treats *diversification* as being accented only on the fifth syllable, or it was equated with vowel length, as by D.B. Tower,

1846, who puts *abbreviation* into a sub-class of those words which are accented on the fourth syllable: namely those which have the second syllable long and the third syllable short (p. 136).

The compulsive systematisers, who combined phonetic criteria with the incidence of stress and the number of syllables, were able to confuse their most attentive readers. Albert Picket, 1804, goes further than Lindley Murray's spelling-book of the same year. Picket follows, and adds to, Walker in numbering the vowel sounds. He then lists words by the number of their syllables, the position of the stressed syllable, and the pattern of vowel sounds. For example: of three-syllable words with the first syllable stressed some have in each syllable the second sound of the vowel. *Blun der buss* and *blus ter er* contain the second sound of *u* and the second sound of *e; bur den some* contains the second sounds of *u, e* and *o*. Picket's method forces his patterns to become more and more exclusive. His pupils are to learn that there are two, and only two, instances of the vowel pattern 2,2,1,4,2,2,2 occurring in seven-syllable words stressed on the fifth syllable: *impenetrability* and *immensurability* (p. 90) . . . All these words are part of lists meant to be studied, if not learnt by heart.

John Sharp, a teacher in Berwick in 1781, is unusual in refusing to list words by the number of their syllables. He says that *understanding* is easier to read and to spell than *eye* or *laugh* or *reign*. He groups his words in seventy-five sections; the criteria by which they are graded have to be inferred. The first two or three items in eight sections are:

Section 1. *Ba, be, bi*
       10. *Stunn'd, shunn'd, blurr'd*
       20. *A-li-en, ab-sti-nent, a-da-ment* [sic]
       30. *Place, truce, spice*
       40. *Ab-bey, a-stray, as-say*
       50. *Ab-bre-vi-a-tion, a-bo-mi-na-tion*
       60. *Be-lief, brief, chief*
       70. *Wright, wrought, wrangle*

Almost everyone assumed that it was easier for children to spell and to read long words if the syllables were divided in print, normally by hyphens. A few teachers express doubt: 'The general way of teaching Children to spell, by spelling Books wherein the Syllables of words are divided by Hyphens is neither a sure nor profitable way . . . It is a great ease to the Master indeed, but little profit to the Scholar' (Joseph Aickin, 1693, A5). John Clarke, 1772, echoed by Thomas Hastie, 1780, shares the view and gives a reason for it:

'The Tables . . . in every Spelling-Book hitherto made public, have had their Syllables divided by a Number of Hyphens . . . which gives each Word such an extended and different Appearance to what it bears when closely printed for reading, that it is, I believe, the sole Cause of that stammering Hesitation and Diffidence, perceivable in most People, who have not had a liberal Education . . . the Pupil's first Acquaintance with Words in this divided Manner makes him dubious whether they are the same Words or not, when he again sees them close in reading Paragraphs.'

(preface)

An interesting practice grew up in which words were listed in two forms, divided and whole. Richard Hodges, 1644, had put towards the end of his book an exercise in which words that had been first met in a divided form were listed whole, for revision practice. George Robertson of London, 1651, had divided the words in early lists but had left later ones whole. Elisha Coles, 1674, had printed the words, in his fourth list only, in two columns, the first headed 'Read', the second 'Write'. In the first column the words were spelt phonetically, and divided; in the other they were whole and in standard spelling:

Read	*Write*	
a-mun	*almond*	
sur-jun	*chirurgeon*	
cur-ridge	*courage*	(pp. 84–6)

The final stage in the evolution of what became a widely used technique appears in Nathaniel Strong's *England's Perfect Schoolmaster*, the first edition of which, 1674, has not survived. Strong listed words of two, up to six, syllables both divided and whole, and both in standard spelling (1681 edn, p. 22). Exactly the same practice was followed by Edward Young, 1675 (1710 edn, p. 27), and by N.S. in 1677, where he says that the pupil is to 'spell' the divided words and 'read' the undivided ones (1716 edn, p. 4). Many later writers follow the same practice; it then dies away but was revived by Honoria Williams in 1817 (pp. 147f and 161f). These parallel listings of the same words, divided and whole, were related to the teaching of spelling, in the sense of that term which equated it with the division of syllables. *The Irish Spelling Book* gives an indication of the appropriate method:

1740 'The Spelling Books which have come out of late, do only set forth Words of several Syllables divided already; which management seems not so proper to the design, *viz.* of teaching Children to divide them. For, the chief Business therein, is not to make or put together Syllables into Words, but to divide Words already made, into Syllables. And therefore, it may be more useful to place each as formerly, twice, in 2 Columns; the whole Word in the first, and the same with its Divisions over against it on the right Hand in the other: When the Learner hath, by the help of those Divisions, prepared his Task appointed, and is to perform it to his Teacher, it will be of use, if he be obliged to cover the Divisions of the Words with a Label of

Paper, and to spell the undivided words only. For, if he is to spell upon Words as divided already into their Syllables, let those Words have ever so many of them, his Work will be but little more than Spelling Words of one Syllable only, and consequently less improving.' (p. 105)

The parallel lists were linked also with the teaching of pronunciation: the divided form of the word was a guide to its pronunciation, which could be tested by making the children read aloud the undivided form. But for some teachers the better way of teaching the pronunciation of 'irregular' words was to display them in a 'regular' phonetic form. Irregular and regular forms were then shown in parallel columns headed 'Write' and 'Read', or in equivalent ways:

1766	'True Orthography'	'True Pronunciation'	
	precision	*preeseez-yin*	(Buchanan)
1783	'Written'	'Pronounced'	
	sovereign	*suv e ran*	(Noah Webster)
1800	'Orthography'	'Orthoepy'	
	cell	*sell*	(Fulton and Knight)

The method is open to objections, which were often raised, but it was reinforced by the older and widely supported practice of drilling children in 'exercises of false spelling' and 'false English' (described in chapter 7).

In a few British and in many American books, syllables are divided not by hyphens but by blank spaces, a method first found in Evans, 1621. Porterfield, 1695, divided syllables by a point. Mrs Trimmer, in the preface to *The Little Spelling Book*, about 1786, says that syllables are best divided by commas, which are easier for children, but in fact her text uses hyphens. Commas are used in the anonymous *Spelling Lessons* of 1797. An elaborate way of indicating the syllables of a word without dividing it at all was introduced into spelling-books by Benjamin Martin in 1754. Instead of listing the whole word twice, divided and undivided, he gave just the last letter of each syllable except the final one: '*diagonal i a o*; *parallelopipedon a l e o i e.*' The same method was followed by John Clarke, 1772, with acknowledgement to Martin. Clarke calls it 'an Apparatus', and advocates it on the grounds that 'it will absolutely oblige the Scholar to study his Lesson before he comes to repeat it to his Master, a Thing too often neglected in most Schools, as the Learner will be at a sad Loss to divide his Words into Syllables, if he has not taken some Pains beforehand' (preface). The apparatus also met Clarke's objection, quoted above, to dividing words by any method. The most magnificently impractical scheme is that of Richard Roe, 1829, who divides syllables by a small vertical line, indicates degrees of stress by one, two or three accents, and expresses 'the rhythmical classification' of words by musical notation. One illustration is scarcely explanatory, but is enough:

$$un \mid phil'' \mid o \mid soph''' \mid i \mid cal' \mid ly \quad = \quad ♪ ♫ \mid ♫ ♫ \qquad \text{(p. xxv)}$$

It is scarcely possible to exaggerate the reliance placed on lists and on the 'particulate' theory of learning that they exemplify. Their lack of context seems obvious to us, but as late as 1863 Robert Robinson, an experienced inspector, when stating the objection could say only that the method was 'nearly extinct' (p. 100).

Rules for spelling

'Rules' for spelling are often referred to, and sometimes enumerated at length, but there is little that can be said about them, because the writers give no constant meaning to the term 'rule'. Usually the rules are just statements about how particular letters are to be pronounced, or when they are silent, in particular circumstances; about the behaviour of particular combinations of letters; about the spelling of particular words or classes of word. The statements are derived more from the point of view and preoccupation of the individual writer than from any common stock of knowledge or teaching-procedures. To this there are two exceptions: the significance of final -*e*, and the pronunciation of *si* or *ti* followed by *on*. These are regularly discussed.

> *1674*   E at the end of words no sound doth make,
> Only in these which for Example take
> [*Clo-e, Ju-bi-le, Ga-li-le*, etc.]
>
> *Ti* writ before a vowel, commonly,
> Doth make it self in sound equal to *si*.
>
> (Henry Preston, pp. 4 and 3)

Final *e*, when preceded by a consonant and a vowel, was also taken as a sign that the preceding vowel was long, and a rule that distinguished, for example, between *fat* and *fate* was frequent, as in Tuite, 1726: 'Note, that tho' *e* in the end of a word be not pronounc'd; it lengthens the syllable; and softens the sound of *c* and *g*' (p. 16). Tuite then has to deal with the many exceptions to which the rule, as he formulates it, gives rise.

In many cases the rules for spelling are taken to be the rules for the division of syllables. At other times a rule is framed as advice:

1688 'Consider how many sounds are in your Word, and so many syllables it contains; as *Hu-mi-li-a-ti-on* contains six syllables, because there are six several sounds in it.'   (Osborn, p. 86)

Sometimes a rule is blunt and highly particular:

c. 1750 '*P* must be written between *m* and *t*; as in *exempt.*'
                                                                (Hammond, p. 45)

Owen Price, 1665, gives fifty-six rules, of which the first says that if *j* and *v* are followed by a vowel they are consonants, and the last says that *ui* 'sounds *y* in *guide* . . . [etc.] and sounds *u*, in *recruit* . . . [etc.]'. Some rules, like those of Price, are primarily concerned with pronunciation; others with spelling, as is one section of Isaac Watts' rules and observations:

1721 '*Ch* at the end of a Word, after a short Vowel, always takes *t* before it, as *catch* . . .except some very few common Words, as *much* . . .'   (p. 88)

Until 1775 rules of spelling, of varied kinds, appeared in about 70 per cent of the relevant texts. The proportion had remained constant for nearly 200 years. Quite suddenly it dropped. Over the next 30 years the proportion was a little over 15 per cent, and it remained at that level until the middle of the nineteenth century, by which time a more sophisticated approach was current: that children should frame rules on the basis of regularities that they had perceived for themselves (Robert Robinson, 1863, p. 102). It is understandable that teachers, with increasing competence, should cease to rely so much on rules. There were so many exceptions to most rules of any useful generality that pupils found little help in them, and the opinion was growing that in any case young children did not easily learn through the application of rules. Such considerations would readily, if gradually, persuade teachers to drop the rules, and in so far as spelling-rules were equated with rules for the division of syllables they declined proportionately from the middle of the eighteenth century. But the disappearance of spelling-rules from the textbooks is so sudden that one looks for a clearly distinguishable cause in the 1760s. None is apparent.

Two eighteenth-century schemes of work

Two teachers in the middle of the eighteenth century describe their very different approaches to the sequence of work. The author of *The Irish Spelling Book*, 1740, is one of the few teachers who shared Brinsley's view that the first teaching of spelling and reading should be oral. Later in the sequence he uses spelling-lists, but more sparingly and with greater discrimination than most:

'A METHOD, *for teaching a young Person to read the English Tongue*. Before a Boy ever so much as looks on a Book, let him be taught the Letters of the Alphabet, only by the Ear and the Eye; that is, let him carefully listen to the Sound of each; and, at the same Time, observe the Teacher's Mouth in pronouncing them. Let him thus first learn the Vowels, and then the Consonants.'

The pupil then learns the sounds of the letters; syllables; CV and VC; diphthongs, proper and improper; one-syllable words; words of two to four syllables:

'All these, as well as the Letters, are to be learned off Book . . . In the several Steps, whether of single Letters, or Words of various Syllables, the Teacher may look on the Book; whence he is to pronounce each to the Learner deliberately, and distinctly, and make him do the same after him . . . Reading, like spelling, is first to be gotten by the Ear only; and, tho' it is afterwards to be improved by Art, yet, at the first Beginnings, the many Observations and Rules necessary for correct Reading, are but burdensome to young Children, and of no use to them; since all they can do, is meerly by the Imitation of Sounds; and this learning off Book, thus far at first, is certainly the best way for *them*; because a single Attention to Sounds, is more easy to their tender Minds, than a double one in attending both to *them*, and the Characters denoting them.' Then let the boy 'be taught on Book, what he did before, without it; That is, learn to pronounce the Sound of each Letter, according to the Character denoting the same . . .

When a Boy hath gone over the *Little Play-Book* twice or thrice, and can, not only spell thereon readily, but also, from a silent Conception in his Mind, without spelling aloud, can pretty well express Words of one or more Syllables, he is then prepared for a higher Step,' i.e. put him into *The Irish Spelling-Book*.

(*The Irish Spelling-Book*, pp. 335–6, 339)

James Dun, in the long and interesting preface to his *The Best Method of Teaching to Read and Spell English*, a. 1766, sets out the principles to which he attaches most importance and the teaching-sequence that implements them. His general principles are (1) to begin with words that are absolutely regular, in the sense that they are pronounced in the way children would expect; (2) to build into the exercises material that unobtrusively revises earlier work; (3) to give special emphasis to the pronunciation of *c* and *g*, the first big difficulty, and to introduce other difficulties progressively. Throughout the book he stresses the importance of graded, progressive work. His teaching-sequence follows the usual route through letters and syllables, stressing the cumulative nature of reading and the importance of the first 'united sounds': the sound of *a* added to the sound of *b* gives the united sound *ab*. He deliberately treats syllables and regular one-syllable words together, commending the method of testing a child's reading by covering up the first or last letter of a syllable, so that *dwarf* is tested by showing the child *arf*, then *warf*, then *dwarf*. If the child fails at any point he is sent back to learn again the syllables of the appropriate number of letters. The converse exercise is to build up syllables from the vowel: *la, pla, spla*. Dun relies so much on the accumulation of letters that even his section on the division of syllables, which he approves of, contradicts the customary method. He says that *jovial*, if it cannot be read at once, is to be taken letter by letter, *j, jo, jov, jovi, jovia, jovial* (p. 126), but the customary treatment would have been to divide first *jovi-al* (VV), and then *jo-vi-al* (VCV).

Spelling and reading

The works already quoted show that for 300 years diverse and often conflicting views were held about the relation between spelling and reading. Our attempt to understand what the pupils and their teachers were doing, especially in the sixteenth and early seventeenth centuries, is complicated not only by this diversity but by other factors. Not all the evidence we need was ever put on paper. The hornbooks and early battledores, in continuation of Roman and monastic practice, passed straight from the alphabet and a few two- or three-letter syllables to the Lord's Prayer. The ABCs might have more extended devotional matter and might list some monosyllables, but the methodological gap between knowledge of the syllables and mastery of the reading-matter is still, to our eyes, very wide. We do not know how it was bridged. We assume that children learnt the alphabet and how to read the syllables, learnt by heart the Lord's Prayer, the Creed, the Commandments and whatever else there was, through being made to repeat them. They were then dependent on parent or teacher for help in applying these widely separated skills to the reading of new material. To the extent that intelligent children can teach themselves to read, the only essential provision was reading-material, largely the primer,[1] some of the psalms, and the catechism. If the children had already learnt by heart the passage they were trying to read they would teach themselves more easily; but most would need help, and we do not know in any detail what form that help commonly took.

Even in the seventeenth-century spelling-books there are gaps, not so much in the provision of material, which the teacher was expected to supplement, as in our understanding of what was to be done with it. Lists of words occur without any rubric. We do not know whether they were to be

---

[1] The term 'primer' was not applied to a purely secular first reading-book until about 1800. It originally contained only devotional or church-related matter.

read aloud by the pupil; to be learnt just for the spelling; to be learnt by heart in their order. The reason for this lack of guidance is often economic. There was no point in increasing the size, and therefore the price, of a spelling-book by including in it instructions that most teachers would find unnecessary. Rubrics were kept to the minimum. George Robertson, in the middle of the seventeenth century, provides another possible reason for the cryptic form of some elementary textbooks. He had a method of teaching that he wanted to keep to himself. It was convenient to have, and to sell, printed copies of his material, but how the material was to be used could be known only by applying to him for 'some directions which I shall be willing to impart' (above, p. 82). As the market for textbooks expanded, both in numbers and geographically, such a possessive attitude was no long practicable. The convention governing the composition of a textbook (that it was designed for the teacher as well as for the pupil) became clearer, and it paid to write directions for the teacher as well as to provide material for the pupil. A teacher in the country would not come to London to consult an author about his methods, although his doing so is precisely the fiction that underlies Brinsley's *Ludus Literarius*, 1612. But it takes Brinsley's quite exceptionally spacious treatment of practical matters to make the fiction convincing.

   From late in the sixteenth century until late in the nineteenth the variety of views about the teaching of reading and the teaching of spelling is complex and difficult to assess. It is possible here only to document some of this variety and one or two of the lines of thought that are suggested by the textbook evidence. The strongest line of thought is that spelling should be taught before reading; hardly less strong, but less documented, is the view that reading should precede spelling. In practice both views blend with the opinion that spelling and reading should be taught together, and this opinion can hardly be separated from the view, implicit in that which has been quoted in relation to the division of syllables, that spelling and reading are not two skills taught at the same, or adjacent, times, but one virtually undifferentiated skill. Mixed with these interdependent views is a fluc-tuating emphasis on the importance, for the theory of learning and for the practice of teaching, of studying units, whether letters or words, as wholes, and not in the atomic, particulate form that most theory took for granted. Closely related to this emphasis on wholeness was a pedagogical emphasis on the value of context: that letters and words were best remembered and understood if they were met in a context (often pictorial) where they were being used and had meaning. The emphases on wholeness and on context combined to reinforce the view that reading should be taught without spelling.

These issues are discussed here under separate headings, but this necessary constraint in presentation runs the risk of making the practices of teachers seem more clear-cut than they normally were and more consistent than they could be in any age during an ordinary hand-to-mouth teaching life.

Spelling before reading

In spite of gaps in our information about teaching-methods it is probable that most teachers from the middle of the seventeenth century until late in the eighteenth, and many thereafter, thought that spelling was a skill to be mastered before pupils learnt to read:

1654a 'Your lowest Form being thus perfect in spelling, you must now enter them in the next . . . wherein they are to learn to read, what they formerly spelled.'
(Brooksbank, p. 23)

1660 Numeral letters and abbreviations 'may easily be performed *after he can readily spell,* which when he can do, he may profitably be put to reading, but not before'.
(Hoole, p. 19)

1673 'Let him spell before he read.' (Obadiah Walker, p. 108)

1692 'The Learner being perfect in Spelling, let him now learn to read.'
(Hawkins, 1694 edn, p. 51)

1707 'After we have gone through the Letters of the *Alphabet*, he must instruct them in the true Spelling of Words, and the Distinction of Syllables . . . From this they may proceed to the Reading of Words as they are joined together in a Sentence.'
(Talbot, 1817 edn, p. 92)

The view is expressed less often during the eighteenth century but, on the evidence of the texts, the practice continued. It is described in Solomon Lowe's preface to his spelling-book of 1755 and is taken for granted in Samuel Johnson's New York grammar of 1765: 'When we can readily pronounce Words off without Spelling; and go on without Hesitation . . . we are said to *read*' (p. 4). The whole sequence from letters to reading is taken for granted also in a report from America shortly before Independence: in 1774 John Harrower, Scottish tutor to Colonel Dangerfield's family in Virginia, reported that when he first met the three sons, 'the youngest boys I got in ABC and the oldest just begun to syllab'. The oldest, Edwin, aged ten, has just 'intred into two syllables in the spelling book, Bathourest his second son 6 years of age in Alphabete and William his third son 4 years of age does not know the letters'. In two weeks Harrower had 'the two youngest spelling and the oldest reading'.[2]

Not surprisingly the method had its failures:

a. 1740   'When once a Child is got into the Bible, the Spelling-Book is thrown aside as an useless Book; so that by that time he is advanced as far as *Deuteronomy*, he cannot divide his Words, or Spell as well as he could six Months before.'

(J. Jones, p. 28)

1785   'Children should be pretty expert in Spelling, before they make a Business of Reading.'   (Ross (USA), p. viii)

1808   James Pike's *The Columbian Orthographer* carries a recommendation praising the book because it contains no reading-matter: it gives 'a death wound . . . to the painful, incorrect practice of directing children to *read lessons*, before they are able to *spell* and *accent* common words of three syllables'.

1810   'It is a fine thing to know how to read; but we must know how to spell first. We cannot read until we can spell.'
(Quoted by Dowling, 1968, p. 63, from George Wall's *The Hibernian Preceptor*, I, 47)

1810

> . . . humming students gilded primers read;
> Or books with letters large and pictures gay,
> To make their reading but a kind of play—
> 'Reading made Easy', so the titles tell;
> But they who read must first begin to spell.

(Crabbe, *The Borough*, XXIV)

1821?   'It is quite useless to put a child at reading till he can spell and pronounce, without aid, the syllables and words he must meet with.'

(Goold Brown (USA), 1827 edn, p. 4)

1831   And if you can't read, pray endeavour to spell,
                   For by frequent spelling you'll learn to read well.
(George Hillard, *The Franklin Primer*, quoted by Nila B. Smith, 1965, p. 58)

1849   'After the alphabet, spelling is the first thing to be taught; master the spelling-book, and the pupil is prepared to read, but not till then.'

(Almon Ticknor (USA), p. 5)

1851   'All Spelling-books have for their object to teach children, by writing letters, to enunciate words; and thus to learn the art of reading.'

(Connon, 1851, preface)

---

[2] Quoted from Edward Riley (ed.), *The Journal of John Harrower, an Indentured Servant in the Colony of Virginia, 1773–1776*, 1963, by E. Jennifer Monaghan, 'Noah Webster's Speller, 1783–1843: causes of its success as reading text', Doctoral dissertation, Yeshida University, 1980, p. 50.

The small number of American texts studied here suggests that American teachers maintained the priority of spelling more actively than did their English contemporaries.

Reading before spelling

The opposite view, that children should learn to read before they are taught to spell, is perhaps implicit in the apparent practice, already mentioned, of going straight from the alphabet and a few syllables to continuous reading. But as we do not know quite how 'straight' the pupil went we cannot assume that the teachers followed any particular method, or that spelling was not part of it. Mulcaster might have given us some clear information, but does not. Spelling is not one of the five components of his *Elementarie* (p. 53), and his regular expression 'true writing' refers usually to orthography, in the sense of a symbolic system for the representation of speech sounds. Mulcaster says that he is listing his five components in their sequence, of which reading and writing are the first two, as they had been in his *Positions*, 1581. In both books the only mention of spelling, by that name, links it directly with reading: 'daily spelling, and continuall reading'. Mulcaster's approach, therefore, seems to have been that in which spelling is taught as an integral part of reading. The hornbooks and ABCs, however, do give us reason to suppose that the emphasis on reading was stronger, and that on spelling weaker, in the sixteenth century than in the two following centuries, when uniformity of spelling was more desired. This seems to have been the approach of Thomas Tryon, 1695, who was critical of 'the common Method' of teaching children to read (presumably one that emphasised the spelling of syllables); he considered it 'not only tedious but difficult'. His suggestion for a quicker method was to teach the letters, then 'to spell a little in the *Primmer*, which may be done in a quarter, or half a Year', and then, without any reference to syllables, 'in any Book that treats of Temperance and Vertue', to read up to three words, or as many as a child can repeat, the child pointing to each word as he says it. After two or three hours a day for eight to ten weeks children should be able to read (p. 86). Tryon, it seems, was looking back to earlier times, as was a later teacher:

1759 'Of all the methods to teach to read *English*, I know of none so fitting to be used as the good women and masters formerly taught by; that was, after their battledore, to learn the Primer, and proceed to the Psalter, Testament, and Bible.'

(Yeomans, p. 2)

Before long the view that reading should precede spelling was absorbed by the view that reading should be taught without spelling, but the older view was still occasionally expressed: Fries, 1963, quotes a statement of it from *The Common School Journal* for 1842.

Reading with spelling

Throughout the period there is evidence that some teachers systematically taught reading and spelling together, and common sense (twentieth-century common sense) would suggest that many more did so than made any statement about their methods. Those seventeenth-century spelling-books that included even short passages of connected reading usually placed them at the end of the book, after the spelling-lists. From about 1695 there is a change. It becomes more frequent, and is soon almost the rule, for passages to be placed after each section of the spelling-lists. This alternation of spelling-lists and reading-passages strongly implies that the teaching of spelling and the teaching of reading were kept in close relationship, and its increasing frequency during the eighteenth century suggests a general change in teaching-methods, encouraged by the increasing number of pages that a textbook could afford to offer. More space was available, and it was now possible for reading-matter to be graded. The change in teaching-methods was a change of emphasis rather than the product of innovation; the close integration of reading and spelling was at no time an unfamiliar idea:

1588 'After that he hath spelled his lesson, he shall reade the same . . . If he bee exercised in spelling and reading his lessons . . . when he shall have ended his first booke the Catechisme, he wil be able to pass through the Primer commendably without spelling.'   (William Kempe, p. 225)

(1673) 1677 'Let every word in every Lesson be *first distinctly spell'd*, and then, *and not till then*, read; yea, let it be both spell'd and read, *again and again*, and no new Lesson given, till they are very *perfect* in that.'   (Lye, preface)

1728 'It will be very proper, when a Child can spell his Lesson well within book, to make him read it before he be put to learn another Lesson; and after he has gone through the Book in this manner, that he can read it perfectly, he should be made to spell without book, half a dozen Words, more or less, according to his Capacity, to employ his idle time in the School, while he proceeds to learn to read larger Words within book, in some good Spelling-book.'   (*Instructions for beginners*, preface)

a. 1766 The pupil 'may learn spelling with reading, because the one helps the other'.   (James Dun, p. xii)

1815 'Reading and spelling is taught forwards, backwards, syllabically, &c.'
          (Report of the British and Foreign School Society, November 1815, p. 37.
     Quoted by Gordon and Lawton, 1978, p. 130. The singular verb suggests that
               reading and spelling are thought of as a single process.)

1828 'In beginning to learn to read, the teacher must read the lesson over and over to the pupils, and thoroughly explain it to them . . . He must do the same with spelling lessons, and cause the pupils to read them . . . prior to requiring them to learn to spell them . . . The earlier tables of spelling are to be used as reading lessons; and at first they may be used only as such. It will be well to take a reading and a spelling lesson alternately; and not let the pupils advance in the reading beyond the corresponding spelling.'

(Butter, pp. 5–6)

1839 'The process of learning to spell our language is so imperceptibly lost in that of learning to read it, that the two can best be considered together.'

(Horace Mann (USA), p. 44)

1846 David Bates Tower (USA) describes a compromise between 'the conflicting opinions of the best methods of teaching a child to read, whether *letters* or *words* shall take precedence . . .' namely 'giving the child only a *few letters* before he is called upon to read *words* composed of those *few letters*. Thus the child is taught words long before he has mastered the whole alphabet; and yet *no words* are given him, of which he has not *previously* learned the *letters*.'

(Quoted by Nila Banton Smith (1934), 1965, p. 110)

Reading without spelling: context and wholeness

The textbooks have frequently shown how widespread was the particulate view concerning the nature of learning: that knowledge was most clearly apprehended, most accurately controlled and most firmly acquired when it was presented in the form of particles that could be systematically aggregated. It was necessary therefore for the teacher to believe also that small, short or unitary things were easier to learn than large, long or complex ones. So general was this view that those who differed from it attract our attention. In its strictest form the view was, of course, a narrow one that the experience of teaching might modify in practice. But in so far as language textbooks illustrate practice, whether grammars of English or of Latin, spelling-books or reading-books, the particulate view was often stated:

1677 'The best way of teaching to read is by calling every Letter by some name. As for example: if thou wert to teach a Child to read this sentence *And the Word was made Flesh* thou wouldst not point to it with thy finger, and tell him this word is *and*, this *the* . . . but thou wouldst call every letter by some name, and teach him that *a, en, de*, spells *and*; *te, ach, e*, spells *the*.'   (*The Child's Bible*, preface)

Even Henry Edmundson, who recognises the importance of learning words in a context and wonders whether it would have been better if he had written his book (an introduction to languages, and especially to Latin) not only in the form of lists but also 'in Syntax, and some Composure of good

Sense' (i.e. in passages of continuous prose), gives as his first reason for not having done so a typical expression of the particulate prejudice: 'Perhaps single Words are more *orderly* learned before Construction, as *Letters* before *Joynt-hand' (Lingua Linguarum*, 1655, sig. A6). But the particulate view was questioned occasionally, and in contexts other than that of elementary English teaching. Vivian Salmon has drawn attention to the work of Joseph Webbe, *c.* 1560 – *c.* 1629, a scholarly advocate of teaching Latin without grammar. Webbe's method includes treating units of discourse, which he calls 'clauses' but may be phrases or sentences, as wholes, not subjected to any grammatical analysis. In one place Webbe compares clauses to the letters of the alphabet: the letters are learnt as wholes and then combined to form words; the clauses are to be learned as wholes, and then combined, in translation and in composition (Salmon, 1964, p. 20).

Edmundson, and others who were influenced by Comenius, treated together two ideas that we tend to separate. On the one hand is the context, primarily verbal, in which a word is used and on which it (in varying senses) depends; on the other is the setting, the occasion on which a word could be used, together with its associations. Comenius held that people learn better (i.e. the intellectual process is more accurate) when the matter to be learnt is given a verbal context, and they learn better (i.e. more easily, because they are interested) when the matter is given a (frequently pictorial) setting. These ideas were sometimes associated with the practice of teaching reading without spelling. This was not such an unorthodox proposal as teaching Latin without grammar, because it could, if desired, be restricted to the earliest stages. If children were to learn to read syllables and words as wholes, and not letter by letter, it was believed that an accompanying picture would somehow fix the word in the child's mind. The picture and the word were regarded as two ways of representing what was almost always a material object; each representation was a whole. Because the pictures interested the children, motivation (a quite different concern of teachers and one that did not necessarily question the particulate assumption) and interest were associated with 'wholeness' methods.

The importance of context is occasionally discussed in the books, and it is implicit in the gradual disuse of the long spelling-lists, in their replacement by sentences and reading-passages for even the two-letter words, and in the practice, common in the nineteenth century, of prefixing a reading-passage with a spelling-list of words drawn from it. The teaching of reading without spelling is one application of a psychological and pedagogical theory that always had supporters: that wholes could be apprehended directly, and were not just the aggregation of those parts into which they could be most easily analysed. The perception of a picture can readily be taken as another application of the theory, but the relation of picture to reading, in a conjunction of these two applications, was only tentatively attempted, as by Charles Hoole, before the middle of the nineteenth century. Until then the picture was usually just a means of arousing interest. The important pedagogical opinion was that some things, especially words, are best learnt as wholes and not analysed into their components. This opinion was closely associated with the view that things are learnt more easily if they are met in a verbal context, especially if the context suggests a familiar setting of interest to the learner. The importance of interest and the importance of wholeness are both expressed in the use of pictures, and both reinforced the idea that reading could be learnt without spelling.

Edmundson's reliance on analogy,[3] which is a form of context, was expressed earlier in the preface already quoted, in which he hesitantly rejected another form of context:

1655 'The best way to gain attention is to *quicken* and *awaken* it, and the best way to that is to deliver things *fit* and *worthy* to be observed. *Naked* and *bare* Words without any *Analogy* to other Words, or to the things they signifie, have nothing to *fix* their observation, but are *loads* and *tortures* to the Memory; whereas *Analogy* . . . yeilds a *clearer* and *fuller* notice of them to the Understanding.'

(*Lingua Linguarum*, sig. A4)

George Snell, 1649, had invoked context first in connection with the names of the letters: 'It is a harder tax [i.e. task] to learn the names of several letters alone, that have no agreement in sound with the names of which they are called, then to pronounce the naming of them with the syllables in which they are set' (p. 21). The children's first reading should not be in devotional texts. Their primer should be easy and 'not bee made of the Mysteries of Faith, and matters of Religion, which are things above all capacitie of Infants'. The sequence he suggests provides an unusual link between reading and reasoning and is also an attempt to provide an everyday context for what is read:

'First . . . teach them single names; as *father, mother* . . . *apple, sugar* . . . *hand, finger*: then bring them to propositional sentences; as, *the milk is hot* . . . thence to reasoning causal; as, *this broth will bite your tongue, becaus it hath pepper* . . . Lastly, let him read illative Reason: as, *My father is angrie, therefore hee will chide.*' (pp. 10–11)

[3] The term 'analogy' was much used in eighteenth-century spelling-books and grammars for the radical and literal elements that words had in common. This use was continued into the nineteenth century especially in America, as by J.U. Parsons, 1836 and 1837, whose 'analogical classification' grouped *educate, education, educated* on the one hand, and on the other, *hosanna* with *manna*, and *banana* with *bandana* (1837, p. 9).

Snell must not be pressed too far into the role of reformer. He is applying common sense in an area governed by convention, and he still accepts that words must be 'rightly divided *syllabatim* . . . that the scholar may the better learn the hard work of dividing syllables' (p. 13). James Greenwood, an admirer of Comenius, describes the kind of spelling-book he would like to see but does not wish to write:

1711 'This book ought to contain not only single *Syllables* and *Words*, but *Sentences* and *Stories*, for by the coherence or agreement of the Parts of the Sentence, the Sense of the Words is better perceiv'd, and the Sense of the Words being known, the Pronounciation of them will be more easily and plainly understood.'
(p. 232)

Similarly in *The Child's Instructor:*

1797 'It is found by experience that a child will learn to spell the monosyllables when they occur in lessons which contain some meaning, much sooner than where the words are jumbled together, without conveying any ideas; therefore, the charm of *drab, crab, grab*, &c. is, in this book, generally avoided.' (preface)

George Nicholson's otherwise conventional *The Juvenile Preceptor*, 1803–7, includes a recognition that context is important. Nicholson does not share the view, but it is one he cannot ignore: 'Some tutors put their scholars immediately to read the words in sentences, making them quite perfect in one sentence before they proceed to another . . . and use detached words [i.e. those occurring in the passage to be read but listed separately as well] as exercises in spelling' (vol. I, 2nd edn, 1805, p. 28). Nicholson's own method is to read the 'detached' words first, then the passage.

Stress on the importance of context shades into stress on the importance of meaning:

1812 'It is found, that children will perform their spelling lessons, from a common spelling book, tolerably well, without being able to write a note, or a letter, with correctness. This is in part owing to the want of practice, to the difference in the appearance of printed and written words, and, principally, to the circumstance of their not having associated any ideas with the words which they have learnt to spell, and to their having no knowledge of the application of such words.'
(Beasley, preface)

(1850c) 1853 'From the very beginning the pupils should be exercised on the meanings of the words . . . All that ought to be looked for is, an answer which shows that they attach an idea to the word or expression . . . Thus, *no* might be treated in the following manner:- he said, *no* ! *No* Shoes, *no* moon, &c. It would be absurd [for the teacher] to say that *no* was the opposite of *yes* or *some*; or that it was an *interjection*.'
(McLeod, pp. 4–5)

Hoole, in his translation of the preface to Comenius' *Orbis Sensualium Pictus*, 1659, makes the first explicit claim in English that in the context of a picture words may be read as wholes, without spelling. He maintains that by looking only at the titles to all the pictures 'Reading cannot but be learned; and indeed too, which thing is to be noted, *without using any ordinary tedious spelling, that most troublesome torture of wits*, which may wholly be avoyded by this Method.' Mathews, 1966, maintains that Comenius did not, as he is often said to have done, advocate that reading should be taught from whole words instead of from letters. The preface shows that Comenius accepted the normal starting-point of letters and syllables, but it is equally clear that he also believed that at an early stage, even after an alphabetic grounding, a whole-word approach was desirable. What Comenius says is not free from ambiguity. In his own book, *The Petty Schoole*, of the same year, Hoole names 'Mr Roe and Mr Robinson' as teachers and authors of spelling-books (p. 12; see below, Bibliography 1, under *Robinson*). The books have not survived, but John Newton, 1669, also links the two, together with 'Mrs Jone Travel at the *Dial* in *Little-Britain*', as successful teachers who have influenced his own methods (sig. b2 verso), and Thomas Lye, 1671, names 'Mr Row' among those from whose work (by implication, their books) he has benefited (prefatory epistle). Hoole refers later, suggesting that the method has disadvantages, to 'Mr R . . . whose way was to teach to read presently without any spelling at all' (p. 19).

Francis Lodwick, 1686, disapproves of 'the usual way of teaching to spell', which is 'to dismember every syllable . . . into many Syllables, by expressing every Letter apart' by its name, each name forming in itself a syllable; whereas teachers should teach their pupils 'to express every Syllable entire at first Sight; without dismembring it' (p. 243). This passage is quoted by Philip Sproson, 1740, with approval, although he is 'not exactly agreeable' to Lodwick's plan (p. viii).

Joseph Aickin, a teacher in Londonderry influenced by Comenius, does not wish children to learn single syllables or one-syllable words by spelling them, but by reading them as wholes, and he provides pictures to support this approach; nor does he wish words in spelling-lists to be divided, either by hyphens or by spaces. Children are 'to read without spelling':

1693 'Let the Children be able to sound the force of every syllable, without first saying the Letters of it over . . . It is the Master's care that must inculcat the true method of spelling: and that children may be able to read without spelling, I have added two long Tables of Polysyllables, a Table of words illustrated by their Pictures, to imprint the true notion of Reading in their memorys and understandings; for the very looking upon the thing Pictured, suggesting the name of the thing, doth tell the children how the word is to be read: for I have found it many times a hard task, to bring children to read, who nevertheless could spell to admiration.'
(sigs. A6 verso, A7)

But words that are hard to read may have to be spelled first:

'That thou mayst be able to read a sentence distinctly, I advise the[e] first to spell every hard word silently to thyself, and then to pronounce it with an audible voice; for easie words thou canst read on first sight: and by following this method thou shalt at length be able to read the hardest word, without the toyle of dividing it into syllables.'   (pp. 67–8)

Other expressions of the same view continue:

1705   The Art of Spelling contains 'a method how to teach to read without any spelling at all'.   (title-page)

1726   'When the learner spells a word, it will be very proper for him to take particular notice of it, that he may know it even by sight, when he sees it again, as he knows a man . . . at the second sight, by the notice he took of him . . . at the first.'
(Thomas Tuite, p. 79)

1777   'The most obvious method of teaching Orthography seems to be to exercise the memory and recollection of learners . . . In this method children . . . form to themselves in their minds, as it were, a *picture* or *image* of words. The letters . . . constitute, as it were, its [the word's] figure and features: they cannot recollect the one without the other.'   (Edward Owen, preface)

1790   Samuel Freeman of Boston provides lessons 'to read without spelling'.
(p. 19)

The Edgeworths' *A Rational Primer* contains their only explicit statement relating to look-and-say methods, of which they have been incorrectly called the originators:

1799   'Children, who soon become impatient of the labor of spelling every word as they go on, quickly attempt to read *logographically*, and in this ambition they should be gradually encouraged.'   (p. 39, first pagination)

Logography was described in 1783 as 'the art of arranging and composing for printing with words intire . . . instead of single letters' (*OED*) and 'logographical' was used also by P.V. Lenoir in the title of his spelling-book, 1800, but applied vaguely to syllables rather than to words.

1828   'It is not, perhaps, very important that a child should know the letters before he begin to read. It may learn first to read words by seeing them, hearing them pronounced, and having their meanings illustrated, and afterwards it may learn to analyze them or name the letters of which they are composed.'
(Samuel Worcester of Boston, Mass., quoted by Reeder, 1900, p. 76, by Huey, 1908, p. 258 of the 1928 edn, and by Nila B. Smith (1934), 1965, p. 86)

In *Syllabic Spelling*, the 1829 edition of her *A Summary Method of Teaching Children to Read*, Honoria Williams advocates a method that she takes (as Lenoir had done, but without acknowledgment) from Berthaud. It is a method, directed at the nursery rather than the classroom, in which words are built up by the accumulation not of letters but of syllables that have been learnt as wholes through association with pictures.

John Miller Keagy, a physician in Pennsylvania, had advocated whole-word methods in his *The Pestalozzian Primer*, 1826, and in an 'Address on early education' in 1832 he repeated that the pupil 'should by no means be taught his letters, or spelling at first, but *whole words* should be presented to him, to be pronounced at sight' (*American Annals of Education 2*, 1832, 462–82, quoted by Mathews, 1966, p. 66). Also in America T.H. Gallaudet's unusual *The Child's Picture Defining and Reading Book*, 1830, uses pictures in a two-stage method. He avoids syllables, basing whole words on a picture, the context of which the children are encouraged to use in reading the names of objects in it, short phrases and sentences. Later in the book each picture is repeated, this time with a continuous narrative using mostly, but not solely, the vocabulary already learnt. Horace Mann, who also is sometimes said to have introduced look-and-say, says that the method is used in Europe and in primary schools in Boston. His way of describing the approach is:

1839 'The first practical question respects the order in which letters and words are to be taught; i.e. whether letters, taken separately, as in the alphabet, shall be taught before words, or whether monosyllabic and familiar words shall be taught before letters.' (p. 47)

References to whole methods become more frequent. John Smith, *c*. 1831, notes that 'we have been advised to begin with whole words', but he treats the idea as 'a greater absurdity' even than the old methods (p. 8). *The Anti-Spelling Book, a new System of Teaching Children to Read without Spelling*, 1833, presents words always in sentences and treats them so far as possible as wholes, but admits compromise: 'If the word consists of many syllables, read it syllable by syllable' (p. 16). In other texts, such as *The Syllabic Reading Book*, 1869, the whole-word approach is limited (or only explicitly applied) to two- or three-letter words. Even William Martin who disapproved of the 'absurd notion that reading may be taught without *Learning to Spell*', gives a list of eighteen two-letter words to be learnt by sight (1851b, p.10). The same recommendation is made by Denham, 1834; *An Easy Introduction*, 1845; Favell Bevan, 1857; Edward Marks, 1866. A similar line, with more emphasis on meeting words in the context of a sentence, is taken by Marian Cole, 1844; Charles Baker, a. 1855; and T.B. Smith, 1858.[4] The generally favourable view is summed up by J.S. Laurie and rather flaunted by John Ruskin:

---

[4] For J. Russell Webb's *The New Word Method*, 1846, and the *Normal Readers* based on it, see Fries, 1963, pp. 16–19; Diack, 1965, p. 48; Mathews, 1966, pp. 73–4.

1862 'Teachers have found by experience, that it is infinitely better to dispense
with analysis entirely, and to teach reading by what is termed the "Look and Say
Method".'   (Laurie, preface)

1885 'I absolutely declined to learn to read by syllables; but would get an entire
sentence by heart with great facility, and point with accuracy to every word in the
page as I repeated it.'   (Ruskin, *Praeterita*, chap. 1)

The more sceptical view was expressed by the anonymous author of a note
at the end of Meiklejohn's *The Fundamental Error*, 1870: that look-and-say
is perhaps the best method for children 'with large "individuality" and
lively imagination' and as a supplementary method for common irregular
words; but as a general method it lacks 'mental training'.

Even these scattered recognitions that wholeness was an important idea
for learner and teacher are rare when set against the great mass of spelling-
books. The particulate assumption was still influential even amongst
advocates of whole-word methods. Josiah Bumstead's *My Little Primer*,
1840, has been described as 'the first [American] reader to be based
specifically on the word method' (Nila B. Smith, (1937) 1965, p. 87) but his
Spelling and Thinking Combined, published in Boston, Mass., in 1841 and
introduced into Boston schools the same year, does not take the method
very far. He recommends 'pronunciation, *from the book*, [as] an excellent
preparative for spelling, inasmuch as it tends to impress the *form* of the
word upon the mind, and thus enables the scholar, in the absence of the
book, to *see* the word, as it were, before him' (1846 edn, p. 3). But some of
the Lancasterian methods that Bumstead recommends for teaching
spelling are particulate and mechanical in spirit. By his first method one
pupil names the word, its letters and syllables 'from the book'. In his second
method one pupil says the word *education*; the next pupil 'pronounces and
spells *ed*'; the third pupil *edu*; the fourth *educa*; the fifth *education*. In his
third method the whole class says *education*; the first pupil then says *e*; the
second *d*; the third *ed*; the fourth *u*; the fifth *edu*; the sixth *c*; the seventh *a*;
the eighth *ca*; the ninth *educa*, and so on until the fifteenth pupil says the
word as a whole again (p. 6).

The difference between this kind of particulate approach and that of the
seventeenth- and early-eighteenth-century teachers is that the earlier
methods were based on a theory of learning, itself based on a theory about
the structure of knowledge. The mechanical and particulate practices of the
early nineteenth century were based on theories of organisation, of the
handling of children in masses. The material to be learnt was broken down
into particles so that each individual child in the mass would have for
himself a small part of it. The two views are not incompatible. Many

nineteenth-century teachers continued to combine particulate assumptions about learning with particulate practices in the organisation of children, and justified the latter in terms of the former. But there had been a change of emphasis: from assumptions about the structure of knowledge and learning, to assumptions about the organisation of classes and mass teaching.[5]

The rejection of context

A few writers during the whole period reject the notion of context. John Evans, 1621, is the only seventeenth-century instance. His book is an alphabetical list of 'all English words', without definitions. He explains that he has deliberately designed it as word lists only. Because 'all bookes doe consist of words' the pupil, once he has learnt the words, can 'proceede to the reading either of the holy Scriptures, or of any other Booke'. Evans has excluded any continuous reading-matter on the grounds that his lists, 'in that they are only words, and not continued sentences, it enforceth the learner to rely wholly upon the sound of the Letters'. But he had also just said, 'In that I have sorted [the words] Alphabetically, it serveth to divers good uses, and truely the dependance which one word hath of another, draweth on the Learner with delight, and confirmeth the memorie' (dedication). The latter statement by itself could well be made by someone supporting the view that spelling should be learnt in the context of continuous reading-matter; but Evans 'dependance' is purely formal, as in the relation between (an example from one of his lists) *con tract, con trac ted, con trac ti on.* This is a very austere source of delight, even for those adept in the division of syllables. Evans must be regarded as a positive opponent of contextual learning. To repudiate the help of context was virtually to repudiate the help of meaning, which is the extreme position of John Warden:

[5] The wider background to the whole-word approach is briefly discussed by Mathews, 1966. The method had been advocated on widely different grounds, theological and psychological, by Valentin Ickelsamer in *Die rechte Weis auffs kürzist Lesen zu lernen,* 1527; Friedrich Gedike in *Kinderbuch zu ersten Übung im Lesen ohne ABC und Buchstabieren,* 1791; Joseph Jacotot in *Enseignement universelle: langue maternelle,* Louvain, 1822. See also *An Account of M. Jacotot's Method of Universal Instruction. In a letter to E.N. from B. Cornelius, Principal of the Pestalozzian School at Epsom,* London, 1830, and Joseph Payne, *A Compendious Exposition of ... Professor Jacotot's ... System of Education,* 1830, which makes it clear that although Jacotot's pupils took words as wholes initially they were soon made to divide them into syllables and then into letters. Jacotot's approach, which he did not claim to be novel, resembles that of the teachers who thought reading should be learnt before spelling, rather than that of those who taught reading without spelling.

1753 'The different sections for the instruction in reading, are calculated purely for pronunciation, and not for the meaning, which is entirely foreign to the design of teaching; because children are first to be thoroughly grounded in pronunciation: when that is once gained, then is the time to allow them to read such books as are suitable to their understanding.'   (Introduction: To the Teachers of English)

'Till [children] can read currently, they cannot comprehend the scope of any sentence; for they are at that time employed in considering the structure of words, not the meaning of them . . . I decline putting any connected discourses, by way of lessons, into this book; it being (as all of the same title ought to be) designed as a storehouse of words, wherein all of the same species being classed together, renders this affair [i.e. reading and spelling] hitherto so intricate, entirely simple and easy.'
(preface, p. xvi)

Charles Bryant, like Warden, puts great emphasis on the word by itself. Connected reading should not be attempted until single words can be read well:

1769? 'Reading at first (Emphasis and a just modulation of the voice come afterward by practice) being nothing more than knowing at sight, *that* certain combination of Letters which composes each word. For this reason, the longer [the pupil] is kept to the spelling and reading of single words, the better he certainly must read when he attempts them in composition.'   (preface)

Much the same view is expressed by John Scott in the preface to his *The School Boy's Sure Guide* (1771) 1774, and it continues into the nineteenth century with Richard Roe's eccentric *An English Spelling Book*, 1829. Roe maintains that words are best met alone: 'When words are met, for the first time, in sentences, it occasions a degree of hesitation which often continues through life' (preface). His book therefore contains no continuous reading-matter.

A more surprising repudiation of context, because it comes from a better informed source, is J.M.D. Meiklejohn's view that using context is a form of cheating:

1870 'It is frequently said that children are helped in learning to read by the meaning of the passage. This is as fine an instance of hysteron-proteron as could be wished. You must know the meaning of the passage before you can read it; but you must be able to read it before you can know its meaning. Of course . . . a child does frequently supply a word by guessing at it from the context; but it is self-evident that this is both illegitimate as an aid and hurtful to the future progress of the learner.'
(p. 24)

J.D. Morell's *Reading Teaching Itself*, 1874, makes no use of context. Words are learnt by concentrating on one combination of letters at a time, such as *oo* or *in*. He varies the consonants that follow and precede (*c-ook*, *b-ook, br-ook; h-oof, r-oof*) and 'contrasts' forms such as *hoop* and *hop*, or *in*, *it* and *lint*. Sentences and rhymes follow each exercise but the words are read initially in isolation. In 1879, although he still builds words up in this way because it is a helpful, practical method, he nevertheless believes that 'the character of our Notation prevents the formation of habits . . . The logical conclusion that our English children must learn each word as an individual is borne out by the fact that they do learn to read in this way' (pp. 32, 34).

Dictation

Teachers who believed that spelling was more easily learnt if the words were met in a context than if they were listed alphabetically approved of dictation, sometimes with reservations. The practice of dictation is seldom referred to before the nineteenth century. As children were often not taught to write, if at all, until they could read and spell fairly well, dictation was not commonly used. The two seventeenth-century texts that describe the practice do so in a way that suggests it was unfamiliar;

1687 John Chalmer gives the following advice to 'young Persons both Men and Women, especially those who have not learned the Grammar . . . You must get *somebody* to reade *softly* and easily to you according as you can *follow* him at first, *spelling* as *well* as you can your own way; And when you have *done*, let *some* who have *skill*, reade over what you have written, and *correct* it.' (sig. B1; p. 16)

1692 John Hawkins describes a technique that he says he learnt from Mr Perkes' *Art of Spelling*, a manual that has not survived: 'It would be a good Exercise for Scholars who can write, that the Master appoint one of the highest Form to read to the rest a Leaf or Page of some English Book, and so leisurely that they may write after him; and when they have done, he who read to them may mark all the faults in each Paper before they be shewn to the Master, this would bring Boys to take heed of what they write.' (preface)

The author of *The Expert Orthographist* shows that he is aware of the common objection that dictation is wasteful of time:

1704 'Let those *Scholars* who can write the *fairest Hand*, be *placed* in the *School* at such a *distance*, that they may not *overlook* one another's *Writing*; nor by any means (*at that time*) tell each other, how to spell any word; Then let the *Master*, *Usher*, or *Highest Scholar*, leisurely Dictate, or distinctly Read a Sentence of two or three lines, (*more or less*) upon some pertinent subject, not standing so much upon the *curiosity* of the *Writing* in this *Exercise*, provided it be *plain*, and *even*; And when they have done, let the *Master* take away every ones *Writing*, and examine each by it self, correcting the *faults*, according to the *Rules* and *Tables* of this *Book*.'

If it is objected that this will take too much of the master's time and that the pupils will be 'dulled' by not having enough time for play:

'I Answer, that School-time may be so well *Husbanded* by the *prudent Master*, that this *Exercise* shall not *trespass* upon the *privilege* of *either* . . . Let an *higher place* from the *Master*, and a *pecuniary Reward* from the *Parent* or *Benefactor* be discreetly, but duly administered, to encourage Industry. And this *Exercise* to be *constantly performed once a week at least.*'   (Introduction)

It is surprising how few eighteenth-century spelling-books refer to dictation. Anthony Benezet practised it in Philadelphia.[6] In Newcastle-upon-Tyne Ann Fisher quotes the recommendation that after the pupils have spent some time 'copying from Print' they should copy from the reading of the Master or one of the pupils: 'a Paragraph from the *Spectator, News Papers*, &c'. The master is to write the spelling-corrections in the pupils 'Writing-books' for them to learn at once, and the pupils copy them into 'alphabetical Pocket Books, kept for that Purpose' (A.B., 'A Letter to the Author', in A. Fisher (1745), 1750, pp. 7–8).

Dictation is more often recommended in the nineteenth century, especially after 1820. In 1801 David Morrice had prescribed class dictation of ten or twelve sentences, twice a week, the boys to exchange books and correct each others' (p. 167), and in 1807 'spelling by dictation was introduced into Ackworth School as the only part of the Lancasterian method to be adopted' (Thompson, 1878, p. 115). Matthew Beasley, 1812, included 'dictation exercises' based at first on the sounds of the letters ('Kate, call the cat') and ending with words containing silent letters (*bdellium* again). His 'promiscuous' dictation exercises included trades-men's bills, so as to familiarise his pupils with 'words in common use among Tradesmen, Mechanics, &c'. Putsey's *Juvenile Class Book*, 1818, recommends 'frequently dictating upon the slate' but gives the method no prominence. Samuel Catlow, however, in his revision of Joshua Collins, 1802, was enthusiastic about dictation when combined with summarising:

1818 'I consider the exercise of writing on slates from *Dictation* to be so effective, that I deem unsightly books of barbarous spelling to be worse than useless' (a reference to exercises of false English, below, chapter 7). 'Indeed, correct ortho-graphy, punctuation, and composition, may be learnt at the same time by reading any passage to a class of boys, allowing them to take down the heads in brief, and then to reproduce the sentiments and ideas of the original passage in their own language.'   (p. 51)

This was to be done twice a week for two or three years.

---

[6] Belok, 1973, p. 84, quoting G.S. Brookes, *Friend Anthony Benezet*, 1937.

William Bearcroft, 1824, describes how, nearly forty years earlier, he had become convinced that his conventional use of the spelling-book was ineffective. He then developed 'what he supposed was a new practice in the art of teaching', but discovered that 'necessity . . . had already suggested similar ideas to others, and Dictating soon found its way into many respectable English schools, and its superior usefulness is now generally acknowledged' (p. 2). Bearcroft's method of dictation took a course that is familiar to us. He gives a list of the marking symbols he used: a single underlining shows a spelling-error; a double underlining shows that the error is a misuse of homophones (*farther* for *father*); a wavy underlining indicates a spelling about which there is doubt: the pupil must consult Walker's dictionary. In the method described in *Dictates*, 1826, the pupil with the fewest spelling-errors to date reads a passage from the book, not giving the punctuation but pausing helpfully. The teacher then reads the passage. The pupils correct the exercises from their own copies of the book, except that the weakest pupil has his work corrected by the one who dictated. Each pupil keeps a record of his corrections in a personal spelling-book.

Henry Hopkins, in an undated edition of his 1837 *Exercises*, thinks dictation ineffective, though it is 'a practice much acted upon in some schools', but its popularity seems to have been increasing. The exercise is strongly supported by Robert Sullivan, 1842; Jacob Lowres, 1852; and by Walter Mcleod, 1853. It is used by David Bates Tower, 1846, in America, and by Joseph Cundall, *c.* 1850, in England. G.F. Graham, 1847, like Catlow, combined dictation with other language skills: 'The old practice of making pupils repeat words arranged in columns according to their accent, number of syllables, or alphabetical order, is now nearly superseded by the far preferable plan of Dictation Exercises' (preface). Graham still used spelling-lists, but attached them to a reading-passage from which they were derived. The pupils learnt the spelling-words from the list, but referred to the passage for their 'meaning and application'. The teacher later read aloud the passage and the pupils spelt the listed words, still presented in their context, either orally or on the blackboard. Similar methods, though requiring the pupils to write every word that is dictated, not just the spelling-words, are used by Alexander D'Orsey, a. 1853, who reinforces the opinion that 'the once common practice of repeating columns of words is utterly inadequate . . . All schools taught on advanced principles have adopted the method long pursued on the Continent, of giving spelling lessons by dictation' (preface). In 1861 Elizabeth Sewell, in the preface to her *Dictation Exercises*, says 'It is now generally acknowledged that English orthography is to be taught by the eye, rather than the ear', and by 1864 the *Spelling and Dictation Class-Book* is offered as a revision text in which dictation is required with no more comment than that it must be prepared at home. Sonnenschein and Meiklejohn remind teachers that 'spelling should never be taught *orally*. It is required for writing – only for the eye' and should be taught 'only by dictation' (1869b, preface).

From the letter to the word: a summary

The sounds of the letters were sometimes taught at the same time as the alphabet, but usually the shapes and names were established before any attempt was made to teach the sounds, even of the vowels. During the whole period, and especially during the nineteenth century, a small minority of teachers maintained that the sounds of letters, and pronunciation generally, could be learnt only by imitation. But for most teachers the need to analyse and classify was so strong that they put into elementary textbooks much material derived from, and appropriate only to, the adult study of pronunciation. The urge to classify, in print, even speech sounds, was reinforced during the sixteenth and early seventeenth centuries by interest in orthographical reform, and during the second half of the eighteenth and early nineteenth centuries by a predominantly social concern for acceptable pronunciation as an essential part of both private and public advancement.

The idea of power, or force, strictly applicable to consonants only, was often, throughout the whole period, equated with the idea of sound and applied to all letters. Power, however, was of more value as part of the teacher's theory than as a practical help to the learner: it was only through artifice that a teacher could represent power either in speech or in writing. To the teacher, wanting his pupil to join orally *b* and *a*, not by their names but by their sounds, the idea of power was essential. The power of the consonant *b* was to be followed by, and united with, the sound of the vowel *a*. But 'name', 'sound' and 'power' are so often confused in all but the most sophisticated texts that pupils are unlikely to have understood more than that all letters had names and that vowels had sounds.

Apart from the minority view just referred to, the general assumption was that for both spelling and reading the next step after learning the letters was to learn two-letter syllables. The skill to be taught lay not so much in memorising lists of syllables as in forming syllables out of letters. Too often, of course, the lists that were provided as practice material for putting together the sounds of the letters became drill fodder at a merely visual level, and the syllables were treated as things to be learnt for some inherent value. This inclination to give meaningless syllables value is seen in the frequent conflation of the categories *syllable* and *one-syllable word*, a practice influenced by two contrasting tendencies. On the one hand there was a tendency to treat the syllable as if it had meaning because the letters that formed some syllables also formed words; on the other hand to treat meaningful one-syllable words as if they were syllables: to treat them mechanically as combinations of letters and to ignore their meaning.

The most important skills in respect of the syllable are that in which the pupil expresses the syllable by giving its constituent letters their names, and that in which he expresses the syllable by giving its constituent letters their sounds (2.3 and 3.3, above, p. 23). If the pupil or the teacher was confused about the difference between names and sounds, the latter skill would be carried out as if it were the former, and an 'absurdity' created like those so frequently deplored.

The two-letter syllable included the two-letter word, and from the earliest times, but not frequently until the middle of the eighteenth century, sentences of two-letter words were introduced at once, often with an apology for their artificiality:

1596 'Wo be to me, if I do so.'   (Coote, p. 2, and many others)

a. 1835 'Be ye, or be I to go in?'   (*Reading made easy*, p. 10)

As an increase in the number of letters was generally supposed to entail an increase in difficulty, syllables of three or more letters followed in turn. At first the syllables often appeared merely as lists, but increasingly books provided their own connected reading-material. Coote provides lists of syllables and sentences, and makes a point of relating them to each other: 'For the more pleasure of the child, I have used such syllabls as are used for English words', and of his connected reading he says, 'This speech is made onely of the wordes taught before, where you are not to regarde the sence, being frivolous, but onely to teach distinct reading':

'Boy, go thy way up to the top of the hill, and get me home the bay nag, fill him well, and see he be fat, and I will rid me of him . . .'   (Coote, p. 4)

Favell Bevan, in *Reading without Tears*, a work comparable to Coote's in its influence, provides sentences that work systematically through vowel and consonant combinations:

1857	I had a cat	I had a bun	
	I had a mat . . .	I can run . . .	
	The cat had a mat . . .	My cat is in the tun.	(pp. 2, 10)

Coote simplifies his material only by limiting the number of letters. Bevan grades hers by controlling not only the length of the words but, chiefly, the variety of sounds the reader meets at one time. Coote's material is more difficult and more attractive; Bevan's is easier and duller.

A distinctive role amongst three-and four-letter syllables was taken by those which could be formed with the consonantal groupings 'proper' to begin or end words. The process of accretion continued. Just as the pupil was taught to combine *b* and *a* into *ba* so he learnt to combine the beginning combination *str* with the syllable *ap*, and the syllable *blu* with the ending combination *nt*. Out of a few elements – proper beginnings, proper endings, VC and CV syllables – could be formed a large number of monosyllables. The addition of diphthongs, which the pupil learnt to enumerate and to classify as proper or improper, and of final *e* extended the range of words so as to cover all 'regular' monosyllables: *bit, bait; spit, spite; split, splint*. There were left the 'hard' monosyllables, especially those containing *gh*. When these had been mastered the pupil has been equipped not only with syllables but with words also. A nineteenth-century example of this method being wholeheartedly applied is *The Word-making Primer*, 1854, which claims as an innovation its reliance on the blackboard in the teaching of reading. The consonants are listed vertically, with the vowels in a parallel column; syllables are formed, both CV and VC; a second column of consonants is added; then diphthongs; many permutations become possible. The book is composed of sentences using a vocabulary systematically built up in this way, and quickly, if optimistically, reaches: 'Steam is elastic ... you see the wa-ter-y cloud is-sue from the tea kettle.' The idea of proper combinations of initial consonants has gone; the teacher is presumed to know what is possible and it no longer matters if some possible combinations are overlooked. A similar three-fold permutation is adopted in the 'word-maker', a device comprising three overlapping cardboard wheels, described by Meiklejohn, 1879, p. 55.

To be competent in monosyllables was an achievement for the pupils. The mechanical manipulation of letters and syllables was being replaced by, perhaps, the reading of Bible stories or fables in a simplified vocabulary. But their achievement was only a brief rest at half time. They had now to master words of two syllables and more, many more. The author of the Bodleian fragment gave the teacher, at any rate, some encouragement:

c. 1673? 'This their long stay in monosyllabls wil so animate, and enable them for polysyllabls, that (through the Lords blessing) you wil be over-joyed to see the good speed which they wil run with in such a smooth, facil way.'

Thomas Dilworth expressed the common view more flatly:

(1740) 1751 '*Monosyllables* not only make the greatest part of our Tongue, but are the substantial Parts of all Words of more than one Syllable.'   (preface)

After the monosyllables new machinery was awaiting the pupils to help them manipulate the longer words. They had now to master the rules for the division of syllables and to study the lists of words divided according to these rules. The lists were supposed to conform with the rules; but both lists and rules were subject to the influence of everyday pronunciation, which was itself, on a pedantic view, supposed to be subject to the rules. In this uncertainty the pupil was guided by the inclination of his teacher, and the inclinations of most teachers, by the end of the eighteenth century, were away from rules and towards the practical authority of the best contemporary usage. But variations in spelling and pronunciation, which had, for the previous fifty years, been increasingly matters of social, linguistic and physiological dispute, roused, as they still do, passions disproportionate to their importance and as ill-informed as they were passionate. The teacher could not, by relying on contemporary usage, hope to avoid controversy.

The principal approaches open to a teacher of reading at the beginning of the nineteenth century can be listed in an order that corresponds roughly with the order in which they seem to have been practised, if only by a minority of teachers. Many approaches were used in conjunction with each other, and for this reason the term 'method', which is usually applied to them, seems to imply a firmness and discreteness of technique that is not supported by the historical evidence. For the same reason labels like 'syllabic' and 'alphabetic' and 'phonic' tend to be misleading unless they are used in a very restricted context.

A pupil needing to read the moderately difficult two-syllable word *butcher* might be taught:

1. To put together the names of the letters in order. This would, if strictly carried out, lead to the kind of absurdity that was so often deplored: the names of the first three letters together give the sound as if in the word *beauty*. The pupil's reading of the word would collapse into misunderstanding.

2. To use the powers of the consonants and selected vowel sounds (even if both were referred to as the names of letters) starting at the beginning and going straight through to the end. The teacher's difficulties would be (i) how to prevent the obvious but inappropriate pronunciation of *b-u-t* as *but*; (i) whether to treat *-tch* as a unit, so that the word was divided *b-u, bu; butch, butch; butch-er, butcher*. If proper endings, including *-tch*, had not been learnt the pupil would almost certainly take *b-u-t* together and be in trouble with *ch*. If proper endings had been learnt the sequence would be *bu-tch-er*.

3. To start with the (principal) vowel. With this word the pupil would be expected to know, or to guess, that *u* and not *e* was the principal vowel. This knowledge of course presupposes some familiarity with the letters, but so

do most of the techniques employed. To the *u* is added first the *b* and then the *-tch*; to *butch* is added *-er*. This approach makes it less likely that there will be confusion between the short and the long sounds of *u*.

4. To start at the end of the word, with *e-r*, *er*. Here again the critical point is whether the pupil can handle *tch* as a unit; if not he will be in the same kind of difficulty with *h-er*, *her* as he was when working forward with *bu-t*, *but*. If the pupil sees *tch* as a unit the sequence will be *e-r*, *er*; *tch-er*, *tcher*; *u-tcher*, *utcher*; *b-utcher*, *butcher*.

5. To apply the rules for the division of syllables. As *butcher* has two vowels it has (probably) two syllables. The consonants between the vowels form a combination proper to end a word, so they are kept together at the end of the first syllable, and the word divided *butch-er*. The reading sequence is: *-utch*, *butch-*, *butcher*. The word may already be divided, in text or list: *butch-er* according to rule; *bu-tcher* according to pronunciation.

6. To treat the word as a structure of previously learnt whole syllables. *Butcher* is not easily approached in this way because the first syllable to be recognised will be *bu* or *but*. Here again the pupil will need to have met *-utch* in his list of syllables; to *utch* is added *b*, either by name or by its power, perhaps indicated as *b'*; the final addition of *er* is easy. Here too there is no indication, in the method, of whether the *u* is long or short.

7. To follow a numerical code. In order to prevent uncertainty about the sound of *u* the word can be printed with vowels numbered according to a code previously learned by the pupil: $b\overset{2}{u}tch\overset{3}{e}r$. The pupil has learnt that the second sound of *u* is that in *put* and the third sound of *e* is that of *err*. The numbering of the vowels can be combined with any of the other sequences.

8. To read the word, divided or whole, not in isolation but in the context of a phrase, a sentence or a story: *The dog asked the butcher for a bone.*

9. To read the word, divided or whole, in association with a picture. Even by the middle of the nineteenth century it would be unusual for a child to be expected to read a two-syllable word, met for the first time, as a whole.

CHAPTER FOUR

Interpretation:
literature presented

The teaching of literature: before 1700

Indirect literary influences

This discussion of the teaching of reading has been restricted so far to what is often called the mechanism of reading; we have not been concerned with the substance of what was read. The term 'mechanism' is dangerous. It implies that a person learning to read is not concerned with, nor influenced by, the meaning of what he reads, that the process is mechanical in the sense that the reader transfers, by rule or by imitation, a set of visual symbols into a spoken or mental equivalent, to which meaning is attached only by a separate process. But such a view is implied by the practice of most teachers until well into the nineteenth century. The term is historically appropriate. At all times, of course, teachers have wanted their pupils to understand what they read, but that intention is not the same as the relatively modern view that understanding what you are trying to read helps you to recognise and to form the words themselves. The nearest equivalent in earlier times to the latter view was the occasional use made of context and setting that is discussed in chapter 3. The present question is not, primarily, what did children read, but what were they taught to read when mechanical reading had been achieved? What was offered to them with pedagogical intent? What were the intentions with which it was offered, and by what methods were they realised? But the roots of English teaching lie in many different soils, and it is necessary to ask also, however briefly, what indirect influences, at home or at school, might have helped children to develop those skills which in later times were directly developed through the systematic teaching of English literature.

It is tempting to make a firm distinction between voluntary, recreational reading and required, scholastic reading; but the distinction was never clearly made either by private teachers or by schools, and it is not clearly made today. Just as the present-day teacher of English will hope that his pupils' literary experience, taken as a whole, will include some reading at home and some freely chosen from the school or class library, so Charles Hoole in 1660 wanted his pupils to read George Herbert and Francis

Quarles, perhaps from the school library, to which he frequently refers (p. 158). In the same spirit Vicesimus Knox, headmaster of Tonbridge, produced in the 1780s an anthology of English literature in three volumes, each of about a thousand closely printed pages. Knox's books were designed for use in school but they seem to have been used more for directed private reading than for class teaching. They were widely used: Wordsworth wrote in 1810 that Knox's *Elegant Extracts in Verse* 'is circulated every where and in fact constitutes at this day the poetical library of our Schools'.[1] It was not in the interests of authors or publishers to distinguish fully between literature that was meant for schools and literature that was meant only for home reading. They aimed at both markets; children brought to school books that they had acquired at home, and these, apart from the Bible, were often the only literature in English available in the school; much teaching, especially of girls, was done at home. It is however impossible to include in this enquiry the whole of what is generally called children's literature. Some distinctions must be made, between kinds of reading-matter and, if possible, between intentions. In our own day parents may encourage their young children to read a factual and informative book about animals or boats, but their intention is to give them the educationally desirable experience of being interested and of being imaginatively stretched, as they might be by a story. In the same way the parents may read Gibbon, not for the historical facts but with much the same intention as they read the novels of Anthony Powell. But intentions of this kind are too subjective to be easily identified even at the present day, and the evidence for them in the past is seldom available. Nineteenth-century class reading-books were regularly compiled with an intention that the pupils should be informed, and they often contained factual passages about animals, but it cannot be assumed that there was no intention that these passages should not also stretch the pupils imaginatively. Seventeenth- and eighteenth-century spelling-books often contained devotional passages, such as the psalms, of great literary power, and it cannot be assumed that moral and religious training was the compiler's only motive in selecting them. The intentions of authors and teachers, although the purest criterion by which we could decide what reading-matter is relevant to this enquiry, are, in this connection, relatively inaccessible. We can do nothing more precise than direct our attention to reading-matter that is literary, in a broad sense, and is chosen with pedagogical intent. 'Literary' in this sense applies to all reading-matter offered to children not primarily because the

---

[1] 'Essays upon Epitaphs, III', in *The prose works of William Wordsworth*, ed. W.J.B. Owen and Jane Worthington Smyser, 1974, II, 84.

teacher wants them to be informed, but because she believes that reading it will bring about other, and educationally more important, changes. What these changes are will vary from one historical period to another, and from one section of society to another, but they have always included (in the language of our own times) the development of sensibility: awareness of, and responsiveness to, human, aesthetic and verbal experience. By pedagogical intent is meant a determination that is systematically carried out: more than a merely didactic attitude. We need to know also the extent, if any, to which teachers went beyond encouragement and prescription: the extent to which they explained and illuminated what was being read; whether, and how, they taught literature. Brinsley did not think of it as teaching literature, but the catechetical treatment of the Bible that he illustrates must be counted as one of the indirect ways in which his pupils gained literary experience. His questions are framed in such a way that the pupils answer in the words of the Bible:

1612 'Q. What did God in the beginning?
    A. He created heaven and earth.
    Q. When did God create heaven and earth?
    A. In the beginning.
    Q. Were not heaven and earth alwayes?
    A. No; God created them.
    Q. What a one was the earth?
    A. The earth was without forme or fashion.
    Q. Had it any thing in it?
    A. No; it was voyde or waste.
    Q. Was there nothing upon it?
    A. Yes; darknesse was upon the deepe.
    Q. Was there nothing else moving?
    A. Yes; the spirit of God moved on the waters.'   (pp. 264–5)

Chapbooks and commonplace books. The present-day teacher of English is apt, in his unhistorical moments, to wonder how it was that Elizabethan literature flourished when there was no subject called English on the grammar-school timetable. Was the influence of classical literature so strong, and the transference from the classics to English so effective, that a vernacular literature could be nourished just by a training in Latin and Greek? Or was the efflorescence sustained by the long tradition of vernacular literature without help from the schools, in which it was not apparently studied? Or was most literature the work of comfortable people, educated by private tutors and foreign travel? It is because such questions can be neither dismissed nor answered straightforwardly that it is helpful to look for influences that might, indirectly and in small ways, have developed in schoolboys a growing-point of literary and linguistic sensibility. A chance word, a phrase read or heard, can light the imagination; prose rhythms can stir the emotions; a jingle can strike sparks. It is worth looking to see whether even in familiar places some sparks might have been struck that modern teachers of English would be glad to have seen.

The most potent indirect influence on the literary development of young people must have been the Church liturgy and the Bible. Even an inattentive but regular exposure to the rhythms and imagery of heightened discourse would help to develop the aesthetic and linguistic sensitivities of children, whether they had schooling or not. To make this assumption is neither sentimental nor uncritically conventional. There is abundant evidence of such an influence on sixteenth- and seventeenth-century writers, and no evidence from our present-day knowledge of children that the development of aesthetic and linguistic sensitivity is confined to those who later express themselves in print.

Until at least the end of the seventeenth century the first connected reading for almost all children would seem to have been what it is convenient to call doctrinal: the ABC with the catechism, the primer, the psalter, the Prayer Book, biblical passages and varied prayers and graces. But we do not really know how true such a statement is, nor how far such reading-matter was all that children had. Uncertainty is caused, for example, by Thomas Newbery's work of 1563, *A Booke in Englysh Metre, of the great marchaunt man called Dives Pragmaticus, very preaty for children to rede.* This is a book of eight leaves, in clear and beautiful black letter, of which only one copy has survived. Dives introduces himself and talks about being a merchant:

> . . . false weightes and measures be execrable,
> And to the occupyers most dampnable.

He invokes all the trades:

> Al Brewers, Bakers, Butchers and Cookes,
> Al Printers, Stacioners, and sellers of bookes,

and then lists, in seventy-four four-line stanzas, the ware that he sells:

> I have to sell Carpets, chestes, coffers and locks,
> Presses and Keys, whorles spindles and rocks:
> Pyg Goose and Capons, Hennes Chickens and Cocks,
>   What wares doe you lacke? come hether to me.

The book is not a spelling-book, but is explicitly intended for children to read. Who bought it? To what use was it put? Would a child whose parents had bought it naturally take it to school, to show to the teacher and share it with other children, or would the book be 'too good' to be used in this way, or 'not the kind of thing you read at school'? Perhaps such questions cannot be answered, but the book remains very convincing evidence that, in the life of some families at least, there were opportunities for children to gain secular literary experience; and we may suppose that for every work such as *Dives*, which was expensively printed, there were many cheaper ones that have not survived, and much similar material circulating orally. Even if doctrinal material was the staple of children's reading it was not their whole experience of vernacular literature. Ballads, folk rhymes and folk tales; festival and itinerant plays; pamphlets, almanacs, broadsheets and what were later called chapbooks, provided even for the poor opportunity for verbal and imaginative stimulation. Uncle Toby testifies at a later date that they were 'handed around the school . . . all purchased with my own pocket-money' (*Tristram Shandy*, 6, chap. 32). Margaret Spufford (1981, p. 10) quotes from John Rhodes' songbook *The Countrie Man's Comfort*, 1588, where the preface says the book is 'for the Scholler of pettie Schooles the poor Countrieman and his familie', and in her own preface she speaks of the ordinary seventeenth-century parishioner as being 'exposed to a steady hail of printed pamphlets of news, political and religious propaganda, astrological prediction and advice, songs, sensation, sex and fantasy'. Of chapbook literature generally she says. 'It has plenty to feed the imagination' (p. 249) and her own book provides evidence for the statement, as does Louis B. Wright's *Middle-class culture in Elizabethan England*, 1935, which refers also to a slightly more prosperous level of society. Even if they kept out of the ale-house, young people would meet what Puttenham deprecatingly calls 'old Romances or historicall rimes, made purposely for recreation of the common people at Christmasse diners and brideales, and in tavernes and alehouses and such other places of base resort' (1589, Book 2, chap. 10). In many parts of the country until the present day oral tradition has remained a distinctive literary influence on children. The influence can justifiably be called literary because it is expressed through strongly rhythmical and patterned language that carries a symbolism more powerful than its surface meaning. It is no debasement of the term 'literary' to use it so broadly.

Books of commonplaces and aphorisms in Latin were a familiar part of grammar-school education and of the furnishing of an educated home. Such collections appeared also in English, but we do not know so well as we do with the Latin ones how far they were used in school. During the seventeenth century English was used increasingly in textbooks of Latin

and in the teaching of Latin generally. As translation out of English into
Latin became more common, English aphoristic and proverbial compilations that had been published earlier for general use tended to supplement
and sometimes displace the similar Latin schoolbooks that had for a longer
period been a standard source for Latin themes. Such English collections
are the first two works in a series promoted by John Bodenham:
Politeuphuia: Wit's Common Wealth, 1597, and Francis Meres' *Palladis
Tamia: Wit's Treasury*, 1598. These followed the usual pattern, grouping
under broad thematic headings short sentences, similes or examples:

1598 'The Turbot, the Skate, the Raie, and the Puffen being most slow fishes, yet
have often found in their bellies the Mullet, being the swiftest of al fishes, which
they take by cunning and policie: so many by Art and skill do far excell those that be
mightier in riches and strength.'

'The young Cuckow being a bastard devoureth the legitimate birdes, and the dam
too: so many brought up with great cockering, as Cockneys bee, overthrow their
educators.'   (Meres, fols. 58, 59 verso. From Pliny)

The sixteenth-century editions of these works make no reference to their
possible use in schools. However by 1699, if not in some of its many earlier
seventeenth-century editions, *Politeuphuia* was stated to be 'for the use of
schools'. John Newton in his rhetoric of 1671 says that the schoolboy refers
to it for help with his Latin themes, 'and if he find any thing there, all his
care is to translate it Grammatically true' (preface). Hoole in 1660 (pp. 163,
165, 182, second numeration), but writing about his practice in the 1640s,
and William Walker in 1669 (p. 38) both refer to *Wit's Common Wealth* (i.e.
Politeuphuia) as a schoolbook, and Hoole couples with it the even more
adult *Golden Grove*, 1600, by William Vaughan. William Walker's work of
1669, although a Latin textbook, is also a collection of short and sometimes
vivid sentences for translation into Latin. Their artificiality gives them an
element of fantasy:

A tall Man with a long neck in a white doublet, killed two Sparrows sitting on a high
house with one stone.

She views her wrinkled face in a broken glass, and washeth her yellow Teeth with
red wine.

He holds three Eggs in one hand: and reads a long letter in a little space.
                                                                        (p. 84)

It is a little surprising that there should be (from a modern point of view, at
least) more to stimulate the imagination in short sentences designed to
accommodate a particular grammatical feature (the agreement, in Latin,

between adjective and noun) than in the longer, more realistic, dialogues with which Walker's book ends.

As with *Politeuphuia*, Francis Meres' *Palladis Tamia* has added to its title-page by 1634 that it is 'more particularly published for schools' and in 1663 that it is 'chiefly for young schollers'. Even if such works were used only as texts for translation and as quarries for material to be used in Latin themes, and even though Comenius scorned them as a 'botcherly mingle-mangle of collections out of others' (*A Reformation of Schooles*, translated by Hartlib, 1642, p. 30), they must also have served indirectly as anthologies of varied and sometimes lively writing in English; as did also those like Robert Cawdrey's *A Treasurie or Storehouse of Similies*, 1600, which were drawn mainly from the Bible and intended to be aids not only for moral but also for doctrinal teaching. Cawdrey's vast collection, under about 400 headings and covering 860 pages of text, is good for browsing in, and although it was 30 years since Cawdrey had taught in a grammar school it frequently has a pedagogical tone. No single extract can represent such a book; this gives something of its flavour:

1600 'As in fishing, when the fishes bee deceived with the baite, have the Hookes in their mouths, men draw them, and make them follow, whither so ever please them: Even so God withdraweth mightie Tyrantes, from executing their devises, and from obtaining their enterprises.' (p. 748)

In addition to the printed collections we know of 'hundreds of miscellanies' that survive in manuscript, 'generally assembled by gentlemen with a casual interest in poetry', and at least in one instance, by a teenager, Tobias Alston, between 1637 and 1639.[2] To make your own collection of poetry was not uncommon, and implies discussion, comparison and exchange of poems between families and friends. There is no reason to suppose that such a powerful influence on the formation of literary taste was confined either to adults or to the conspicuously well-to-do.

Rhetorics in Latin; logics in Latin and English; Latin verse in English. To what extent, if at all, were rhetoric and logic in sixteenth- and seventeenth-century schools studied with intentions or potential effects indirectly equivalent to those later brought together within the subject 'English'? This unfamiliar question makes it necessary for familiar material to be treated here in an unfamiliar way, and the variety of the material requires that its treatment should be blunt, if it is to be brief.

Rhetoric, logic and grammar had been grouped together as the trivium

[2] Donald W. Foster, *TLS*, 24 January 1986, p. 87.

because they provided an academic training in what are now called communication skills, and the skills were those used in what by the end of the sixteenth century had come to be called the professions. The teaching of grammar, in Latin, had become for most teachers a self-contained routine that only occasionally recognised that it could have a broader linguistic and literary role. Its part in the development of English teaching is discussed below, but one grammar should be mentioned here because it is important for its indirect bearing on the teaching of literature.

Alexander Gill, high-master of St. Paul's School, published in 1619, and revised in 1621, *Logonomia Anglica*, a grammar of English. The work is uncharacteristic because it is written in Latin, primarily for foreigners; because it advocates, and its English examples are written in, a reformed orthography of Gill's own devising; and because it treats the figures of speech as a form of syntax, thus bringing the main substance of school rhetoric within the compass of grammar. The work is important because in his seven chapters on figurative syntax Gill quotes extensively, and predominantly, from contemporary English poetry: more than eighty times from *The Faerie Queene*, and sometimes from *The Shepheardes Calender*, from Sidney, Sir John Harington, and from *The Poetical Rhapsody*. There are single quotations from George Wither, Samuel Daniel, and from Stanyhurst's translation of the *Aeneid*, and from an unidentified Scots poem which he calls *Reus Machiavellus*.[3] *Logonomia* is not likely to have been used by English schoolboys but it is convincing evidence that the headmaster of a famous school was ready to bring English literature into at least one aspect of his teaching. It does not follow that Gill introduced English literature into his teaching at St. Paul's, but it is unlikely that the idea would have shocked him.

Rhetoric and logic, though regarded as separate disciplines, had several skills in common, which were sometimes treated as part of one discipline, sometimes of the other. Their interrelatedness was frequently discussed, but need not concern us here (Howell, 1956, *passim*). We can adopt the view expressed by John Newton: logic and rhetoric 'have such a natural dependance on one another, that they are not fit to go asunder' (1671a, preface).

Because a training in expression relied largely on the imitation of literary models, some rhetorics provided indirect, but occasionally powerful, literary experience and a training in the interpretation of English. Adult books on rhetoric, addressed to the lawyer, the preacher, the public

---

[3] In chap. 23: see Danielson and Gabrielson's note in their edition of Gill, II, 230.

speaker, the letter writer, treated it as a purely expressive skill; but the teacher of rhetoric to schoolboys, for whom imitation was the principal method, was bound to consider also its interpretative aspect. The boys had to study examples of the figures that they were learning to use. The figures were first defined, then illustrated by sometimes extensive quotation. The study of these quotations necessarily raised such questions as: What does it mean? What is the author seeking to do? Does this passage in fact illustrate the figure under discussion? How might the author have expressed himself without using the figure?

Textbooks of rhetoric were frequently written with an eye on both school and adult use. On the whole those written by schoolmasters were primarily for school use, those by members of other professions were for university use and for lawyers and preachers. But the distinction is very loose. Rhetoric was taught, or was supposed to be taught, in every grammar school. The position of logic is less clear. It was usually regarded, for example by Brinsley, as a university subject, but as early as 1588 William Kempe taught it at Plymouth grammar school, in close association with rhetoric, and as late as 1671 John Newton wrote his *An Introduction to the Art of Logic* specially for schools. Newton's work was part of a sustained programme to provide textbooks in English 'for the use of English Schools, and all such who having no opportunity of being instructed in the Latine tongue, do however desire to be instructed in the liberal sciences' (1671a, t.p.). Newton's logic, though itself outside the grammar-school tradition, indicates that logic, for some schools at least, was still within that tradition. Newton himself says in his *School Pastime* 'Logic . . . is also taught in some Schools, though not in all' (1669, B2), and in the preface to his rhetoric, 1671, he says that rhetoric and logic 'are the Arts and Sciences of which Children are the least capable . . . Logick is generally looked upon as *Noli me tangere*, an Art by no means to be taught in Schools . . . but . . Rhetorick is permitted the Grammar Master without controle.' Logic, which he called 'the last and highest' of the sciences, might be taught at the top of the grammar school or at the university.

We do not know enough about the extent to which reference to English literature might have been made in the teaching of Latin and in the study of rhetorics written in Latin. Significance is sometimes given to the quotation by Charles Butler in his Latin rhetoric of 1597 of two stanzas from Spenser's *The Ruines of Time*, published in 1591. But Butler is not so much drawing attention to a contemporary English poet as illustrating accentual verse, which he could not illustrate from classical Latin sources. He is also illustrating alliteration which, though found in classical Latin, was a particular feature of the preclassical Saturnine accentual Latin verse to which Butler's mention of (Livius) Andronicus shows that he is referring. It seems unlikely that a teacher of Latin who had a personal interest in contemporary English literature would not supplement the Latin illustrations with English ones drawn from his own reading, even if only from translations. Would a master who was reading Ovid with a class not read them some of Golding's (1567) or Sandys' (1626) translations of the *Metamorphoses,* even if he did not like Churchyard's translation of *De Tristibus* (1572)? If he was reading Virgil would he make no reference to Phaer's (1562), Stanyhurst's (1582) or Ogilby's (1649) translations of the *Aeneid?* No doubt teachers in the sixteenth and seventeenth centuries kept closer to the textbook (much of which their pupils had to learn by heart) than we do, but it would be very odd if no Tudor and Jacobean schoolboys were touched in school by the literature of their own times. We know that translations were used. There is however a difference between reading a prose translation of Ovid's *Metamorphoses,* such as Brinsley produced in 1618 'for the ruder places of the land . . . chiefly, for the poore ignorant countries of Ireland and Wales', and the illustrative use of verse translations as English poems in their own right. To the latter there are few references but, remembering in 1660 his own teaching of more than twenty years earlier, Charles Hoole recommends 'Chapman's English translation of Homer [which] will delight your Scholars to read in at leisure', and of the 'several Translations of Virgil into English verse' he particularly praises Ogilby, and wants 'his larger book' in the school library (1660, pp. 196, 179, second numbering). He also encourages verse-writing in English, modelled on Sandys' Ovid and on George Herbert (p. 158).

Some indication of mid-seventeenth-century attitudes can be inferred from Ralph Johnson's *The Scholar's Guide,* 1665. Most of the book, which is written in English, is concerned with the writing of Latin, and the use and imitation of Latin authors; the examples are all in Latin. But where Johnson is referring to a literary form for which there is no satisfactory classical equivalent he recommends not only modern writers in Latin but also writers in English: for emblems and acrostics, Quarles; for allusions, Fuller; for essays, Joseph Hall, Bacon, and Owen Felltham's *Resolves;* for characters, Blunt, Overbury and Joseph Hall. For translation as a 'poetical exercise' the only authors named are Sandys and Ogilby. Johnson's *The Scholar's Guide* is imitated, and often copied verbatim, in *Lucerna Scholastica or, the Scholar's Companion,* by J.B., 1680. Johnson's recommendations are repeated, with the addition of 'Herbert's Temple' for anagrams (p. 31).

Speculation about the practices of perhaps exceptional teachers is of limited value, but it is prudent to bear in mind the possibility (if it cannot be regarded as a probability) that the schoolboy's training in Latin and Greek literature was sometimes supplemented by quotation, at least from English authors. Such a method might be idiosyncratic and would not have any regular place in a textbook, but by the middle of the seventeenth century there is a little further evidence, from rhetorics, that English could occasionally be introduced into a Latin text. Thomas Horne's Χειραγωγία, *sive manuductio in aedem Palladis* was published in 1641 and again, after his death, in 1687. Unless they were added in the later edition, Horne included in his discussion of imitation a handful of English examples, set into a Latin commentary. They are not English versions of a Latin text; the model and its imitation are both in English. First, an example of the imitation of a syntactical pattern:

1641 'There is not so much misery in want, as trouble in satiety. Sic imitamur: *There is not so great calamity on earth, as happiness in heaven.*'   (p. 102)

The imitations are then extended to longer passages. A speech by rebels excusing themselves to a general is paralleled by the address of a son excusing himself to his father:

'*Worthy General, We call God and Man to witness, that we have neither taken up Arms against our Countrey, nor to endanger others* . . . Sic imitamur, Filius fingitur se excusare: *Dear Father, Both Men and Angels bear me witness, that I never willingly entred upon any practice, either to discontent you, or offend others* . . .'

(pp. 105–6)

In 1651 Horne produced a rhetoric in both Latin and English: *Rhetoricae Compendium, Latino-Anglice*, of which twenty-two pages are in Latin and seventeen in English. The English 'epitome' consists of very brief examples of the figures: '*Metaphors* . . . the tempest of war; flowers of Oratorie; the wounds of grief' (p. 29). More substantial illustrations, which come a little closer to providing a possible quickening of the pulse, are given in a small posthumous Latin work by Thomas Farnaby, *Troposchematologia*, 1648, based on his own *Index Rhetoricus*, 1625, but with English examples added:

> I' th' place of proper words, a Metaphore
> Puts their resemblance: How the waves do *roare*!
> The fields do *laugh* and *sing*: Did you behold
> Their *lightning* steel? Vertue now waxeth *cold*.   (p. 7)

One of Farnaby's longest illustrations is of the figure *Incrementum*:

> From low beginnings Incrementum rises
> T'a lofty pitch: Could Hel forbear these vices,

> Not gape to swallow them? Could th' earth indure
> Their foot-steps? Is the ayre grown so impure
> To give them breath? Can Heaven behold their riot
> With patient eyes? Or can the gods be quiet?   (p. 21)

There were more than forty rhetorics and more than fifty logics in Latin printed in England (many of them written by continental authors) during the sixteenth and seventeenth centuries. On the evidence of the textbooks, and disregarding speculation, those that were used in school could have had some, but only a little, influence on the pupil's appreciation of his mother tongue. Far greater would have been the influence, under a good teacher, of the regular discipline of translation, both into and out of Latin.

The logics in English, like those in Latin, provided brief, usually manufactured, examples of the terms in which analysis was carried out and of the type of argument that could be employed. The examples were not limited to sentences about Socrates; they were sometimes as vivid and as potentially stimulating as the more literary examples in the rhetorics:

1551 'To barke is proper to a Dogge, and onely proper and evermore proper. *Ergo* who soever hathe power or rather an inclination to Barke, that same is a dogge. And again, whatsoever creature is a dogge, that same hath powre or rather an inclination to bark.'   (Thomas Wilson, *The Rule of Reason*, Bviii)

In his section on fallacies Wilson mocks some false arguments by comparing them to a 'folish fonde reason, and madly invented argument: Jobson and Robson looked through an hedge, & the one saw the other: Ergo they two are both nigh of kindred' (Sv). To the 1553 edition of his logic Wilson added thirty-five lines, acknowledged, from Nicholas Udall's then unpublished play *Ralph Roister Doister*, but as with Butler's use of Spenser this was an illustration of a point that could not be made from classical Latin, the ambiguity of alternative punctuations:

1553 'An example of soche doutbful writing, whiche by reason of poincting maie have double sense, and contrarie meaning . . .

> Swete maistresse, wheras I love you nothing at al,
> Regarding your richesse and substaunce chief of al,
> For your personage, beautie, demeanoure, and witte,
> I commende me unto you never a whitte . . .'   (fol. 66 verso)

Much more interesting, and surprising, as a source of small, indirect literary experience in English is Roland MacIlmain's 1574 translation (and adaptation) of Ramus' logic. In this short work MacIlmain quotes in English about ninety passages, drawing mainly from Virgil, Ovid, Cicero and the Bible, which are more substantial than the two-line illustrations he also provides. The second chapter of Ramus' first book, 'Of the cause efficient', takes as its main illustration: 'The father also, and the mother which engendrethe, and the nursses which bring up, ar causes efficients.' This leads MacIlmain to a quotation from *Aeneid*, Book 4, in which Dido denies that Aeneas can be the son of Venus or Anchises:

> O false Aenee thy self why dost thou fayne,
>   Of Venus fayre the goddes sonne to be:
> Or that Anchise which dardam hight by name.
>   Thy author was by waye of parentie,
> For dreadfull Caucasus did thee begett
>   On terrible and ragged rockes in filde:
> And raging Tygres noryshes was sette,
>   To geve the sucke of udder rude and wylde.   (p. 19)

In his discussion of the syllogism MacIlmain gives as an example of the 'negant speciall':

> 'He that deceyveth a loving mayde is not to be praysed:
> Demophon is a deceaver of a loving mayde, as Phyllidis:
> Demophon therefore is not to be praysed.
>   Phyllis thus inferethe in Ovide.
> For to deceave a mayde of tender age,
> Which trustethe in thee, it is no vassalage,
> Nor craftie gloire: For her symplicitie,
> Had rather have the constant love of thee.
> I Phillis bothe a lover and a mayde,
> Am by thy wordes (false Demophon) deceaved:
> God graunte therfore which dwells in hevens hye,
> For thy deceipte, that thou rewarded be.'   (pp. 89–90)

Apart from Abraham Fraunce's *The Lawiers Logike*, which was in no way a school text but is significant for its extensive quotation from Spenser and Sidney, other logics in English keep more strictly to formal analysis and illustration. Even Zachary Coke, who is writing for those of 'the meanest capacity' and says at first, in encouragingly splendid language, that logic '(with Grace) recovers us to our Primogenial condition, unclouds the masqued mind, plows up, and unseals the depths of Reason, Evolves the hidden *Idaeas* of things, and unties the knottiness of every emergency', even he, when his exposition is under way, puts it again in businesslike terms: 'Logick is the directory of the thoughts, making them regular, that whatsoever is conceivable of a thing may be drawn to a right summe, for an orderly process in them, and to avoid confusion' (p. 8). Such an approach does not preclude literary illustrations, but the usual kind of illustration is straightforwardly technical. Dudley Fenner and Samuel Wotton in their separate translations of Ramus illustrate the same type of syllogism as MacIlmain illustrated, above, but their interests are not in literature:

1584 'Negative special is:
> No right Papist is a true subject:
> Some right Papist is a Jesuite:
> Therefore:
> Some Jesuite is not a true subject.'   (Fenner, C3 verso)

1626 'No murtherer hath aeternall life abiding in him.
> Every one, that hateth his brother, is a murtherer.
> Therefore
> None that hateth his brother, hath aeternal life abiding in him.
>   I Joh. 3, 14–15'   (Wotton, p. 167)

Even John Newton's *An Introduction to the Art of Logick*, 1671, which is written for schools and addressed 'To the Teachers of English', is a stodgy compilation, thinly illustrated, the flavour of which can be judged from the headings of chaps. 17–23 in Book 1:

1671   'Of the manner of having. A thing may be said to be *had* eight several waies.
> Of a proposition
> Of the opposition of categorical propositions.
> Of the Æquipollency of categorical propositions.
> Of the conversion of propositions.
> Of modal propositions.
> Of hypothetical propositions.'

Apart from MacIlmain's version of Ramus it would seem that logics in English, though like the rhetorics they might provide the occasion for studying short and stimulating passages of English writing, were not designed to do so, and seldom did. One book, however, has a direct bearing on the teaching of interpretation: Joshua Oldfield's *An Essay towards the Improvement of Reason*, 1707. It is an unusual work in that it regards logic as 'in a sort Necessary to give us a right Apprehension of Rhetoric' (p. 130) and in its simultaneous treatment of both understanding and expression it almost suggests an integrated study of communication. It is discussed below in chapter 6.

Direct literary influences

Rhetorics in English. Rhetorics written in English (excluding the large number that were designed as aids to preaching and were illustrated solely from the Bible) could be expected to provide firm evidence about the teaching of English. Their significance has been recognised since Foster Watson wrote in 1908:

'It is almost impossible to estimate the high usefulness of this now obsolete school discipline in enlarging the vocabulary and in directing the expression of the more educated English people of the seventeenth century. Unless the school and university training in rhetoric are borne in mind, an important factor in accounting for the wealth of imagery and expression in the English literature of the sixteenth and seventeenth centuries is overlooked . . . English Literature was taught first in connexion with rhetoric.' (1908, pp. 452 and 453)

and again in 1909, more cautiously:

'It is in connexion with the subject of rhetoric that we recognise the nearest approach to the study of English literature as a subject of teaching and culture in the seventeenth century.' (p. 25)

Foster Watson, however, did not distinguish between rhetorics written in Latin and illustrated from Latin literature and those written in English, which might still draw largely on familiar classical passages, translated into English. Nor did he distinguish two aspects of rhetoric on which emphasis varied from book to book: rhetoric as a direct training in composition, and rhetoric as the study of literary models at a particular stage of that training. The skills directly taught through rhetoric were expressive; the interpretative skills were a recognised and sometimes valued by-product, to which we, however, tend to attach more importance than did sixteenth- and seventeenth-century teachers.

The literary models in the rhetorics were of two kinds: those illustrating kinds of figure and those illustrating kinds of discourse. The former were brief and occasionally vivid, but their influence, though potentially powerful, could only be intermittent and indirect. Nevertheless, like the anthologies they provided small doors through which the reader could enter the private garden of imaginative experience and verbal excitement. Richard Sherry, 1550, used the metaphor of the garden: as knowledge of flowers increases one's pleasure in a garden, so knowledge of the figures would help 'our youth . . . whyle they wander by them selves, readynge at all adventures sundry and varyous authors'. Knowledge of the figures is necessary for interpretation: 'Onles we wil be ignorante in the sence or meaninge of the mater that excellente authors do wryghte of, we muste nedes turne to the helpe of schemes & fygures' (dedication). Once again, however, we would wish to know how far the writer is thinking of Latin and Greek literature, and how far, if at all, of English. Sherry states explicitly that his book will help in the reading of the Bible, but many of his other examples are translations or paraphrases of classical authors, especially Cicero. Most of them are brief:

> '*Metaphor*: I have but lately tasted the Hebrue tonge.
> *Metonymy*: Oxforth (some say) hath not forsaken all popery.'
>
> (pp. 40, 42)

One illustration, however, has a particular tone and force, the emotional charge of which could make it memorable. It is an example of the figure 'enumeration', expanded from the basic sentence 'We thanke the[e] of thys warre.'

> 'The treasure spente upon the Barbariens, the youthe broken wyth laboures, the corne troden downe, the cattel driven awaye, stretes and vyllages every where set on fyre, fieldes lefte desolate, walles overthrowen, houses robbed, temples spoyled, so many olde men chylderles, so manye orphanes, so manye wyddowes, so many virgins shamefully defiled, the maners of so many young men made worse by leude liberty, so many men slayne, so great mourning, so many good artes loste, lawes oppressed, religion blotted, al thynges of god and man confounded, all good order of the citie corrupted: I say all this heape of myschiefs that riseth of war, we mai thanke the only of it, which wast the beginner of this war.'   (p. 65)

Henry Peacham, writing 'especially for studious youth', explains the figure 'aporia', and illustrates it from Ovid:

> *1577* '*Aporia*, when we shewe that wee doubt eyther where to begin for the multitude of thinges, or what to say, or doe, in some straunge and doubtfull matter. *Dianira* hearing that her husband *Hercules* loved a Lady called *Iolea*, and also that he woulde very shortly bring her home to his house, where *Dianira* was, she was so vexed with this newes, that she could not tel what to say, nor what to doe, but cast her doubtes afore hand, and demaunded of her selfe what way she were best to work, thus. If that shee come, quoth shee, shal I complayne, or shall I hold my peace, shall I retourne to *Calydon*, or shall I tarry still? Or shall I get me out a dores, and let them have their will.'   (Mi verso)

Abraham Fraunce's *Arcadian Rhetorike*, 1588, is illustrated throughout from Sidney's *Arcadia*, which it quotes on almost every page. It also quotes the opening line of *Piers Plowman* as an example of 'polyptoton' (E4 verso) and quotes also from Spenser. But here, as in his logic, Fraunce was not writing for schools. He was a lawyer, a poet and a protégé of Sidney and his family. He represents the practice, initiated by Ramus, of drawing illustrations from modern languages as well as from the classics, a practice that influenced rhetorics written for schools. John Hoskins' *Directions for Speech and Style*, written about 1600 but not published until this century, is similarly illustrated by more than 180 quotations from, and references to, *Arcadia*, a copy of which he gave to a young man, presumably a pupil. The copy was annotated by Hoskins with *M* for metaphor, *des* for notable description, and *dc* for poetic decorum. Hoskins' *Directions*, although it is a rhetoric, classifying the most important figures in a novel way, is more explicitly a manual of composition, and especially of letter-writing, than are most rhetorics. The manual, and his annotations of *Arcadia*, exemplify clearly the universal belief that facility in expression was learnt through an understanding of the figures and through imitation of their use.

John Sergeant, who is writing 'for young Scholars, and others of all sorts, enabling them to discuss and imitate the Elegancy in any Author they read', illustrates each of his 130 figures by examples in Latin, in English and from the Bible. He draws much on Blount:

1657 '*Similitude* This comfort in danger was but like the honey that *Samson* found in the Lyon's jaws, or like lightning in a foggy night.'   (p. 211)

'*Oxymoron* If they are silent they say enough.'   (p. 122)

'*Agnomination* You are like to have but a bare-gain out of this bargain . . . Bolder in a buttery then in a battery.'   (p. 106)

In choosing examples from these texts one naturally picks those which stand out a little by their sharpness. Not all the illustrations provided by the writers would make much imaginative impact on a schoolboy, and sometimes we can risk a modern judgment that they would have done little good to his taste.

In the same year as Sergeant's rhetoric there was published post-humously an elaborate work, Joshua Poole's *The English Parnassus*. The anonymous author of the preface says, with more truth than is usual in such places, that nothing of the kind had appeared in English. The work has Latin precedents: books of epithets, synonyms and phrases all designed as helps to the composition of Latin; but Poole's ardent concern was to encourage his pupils to write English verse. His book is arranged in four sections: (i) lists of rhyming words; (ii) about 30,000 epithets grouped under substantives alphabetically arranged; (iii) something like 5000 quotations and phrases grouped under headings such as 'Elephant', 'Fairies', 'To laugh', 'To sail'; (iv) expressions useful in various forms of letter-writing. It is the third section that concerns us here, and especially the list of authors that Poole gives as those 'principally made use of in compiling this work'. The list includes 'Comedies and Tragedies, many'; Virgil, Horace, Lucan, Ariosto and Ovid in translation; Ben Jonson, Shakespeare, Drayton, Herbert, Spenser, Quarles, Daniel; Sandys, espe-cially; Chaucer, Chapman, Carew, Habington, Sir John Denham, Wither, Donne, Waller, Milton, Robert Burton. The book contains the components of a substantial and loosely thematic anthology; but that cannot have been how Poole saw it. The extracts, which seldom carry any indication of their origin, run into each other without demarcation, and are mixed with phrases and snatches from varied sources. The pupils could have used the book only as a quarry. What caught their attention might be a fine phrase or a fine passage, but it was as building-material that they were expected to examine it. Poole was more interested in teaching his boys to write verse than to read it. The two activities went together, but in this context, at least, the expressive function was the more important. It is difficult to show the odd character of Poole's book from only a short quotation: its oddness is cumulative and is apparent particularly under the headings that carry the most quotation. The following verses, in Poole's paragraphing, come from the middle of 160 lines under the heading 'Evening':

1657   Nights black contagious breath
        Already smoaks about the burning crest
        Of the old feeble and day-wearied Sun.
        The waining of the Sun. The bat doth flie
        Her cloistered flight to sullen Hecats summons
        The shade born Beetle with his drowsie humme
        Hath rung nights yawning peal,
                Seeling night,
        Skarfs up the tender eye of beauteous day.
        When like Elinar with his evening beams
        The Sun hath turn'd to gold the silver streams,
                The treble shades begin to damp
        The moistened earth, and the declining lamp invites to silence.
                Light thickens
        And the Crow makes wing unto the woods,
        Good things of day begin to droop and drowse,
        Whilst nights black agents to their preys do rowse
        The west but glimmers with some streaks of day.
        Now spurs the lated traveller apace
        Unto the timely Inne,
        When as the Nightingale chanteth her Vesper,
        And the wild forresters couch on the ground,
        The long shades of the hills appear,
        The Sun is fled to Thetis bed,
        When night entombs the dying light,
        What times the gray flie winds her soultry horn
                The Even-star bright
        Towards heavens descent had slopt his burnisht wheel.   (pp. 285–6)

The English Parnassus was sufficiently popular to have further editions in 1677 and 1678. Hoole, a school-fellow of Poole's, recommends it for use in the fourth form (p. 159) and it was known to Solomon Lowe (1755, p. 8n). Poole's own English rhetoric, 1663, which applies the figures to the exercise of varying, relates solely to expression and is discussed below (p. 275) as is Thomas Hayward's attack on Poole's teaching-methods.

The last of the seventeenth-century English rhetorics to contain a substantial discussion of the figures is John Newton's *An Introduction to the Art of Rhetoric*, 1671. The figures are illustrated for the most part from the Bible, but also from the *Arcadia*, once from Quarles' *Argalus and Parthenia*; by two lines from Spenser's *Ruins of Time* (part of the passage quoted in Butler's Latin rhetoric; above, p. 143), by a couplet from a (doubtfully authentic) verse letter of Donne's, and occasionally from less literary sources, as in his illustration of 'epanados' (more memorable than is its definition). Epanados is defined: 'An *Epanados* is, when the like sound is in the beginning and ending of the divers sentences, an *Anadiplosis* coming between.' Newton's pupils would have learnt already that an '*Anadiplosis* is, when a like sound without intermission is repeated in divers sentences, that is when it ends one and begins another.' But rather than work that out they would prefer the illustration of epanados:

> Whether the worst, the child accurst,
>   Or else the cruel mother?
> The mother worst, the child accurst,
>   As bad the one as th'other.   (pp. 112, 114, 115)

Newton's pupils would have had to scratch their heads less if he had used the definitions given by Peacham a hundred years earlier:

1577   '*Epanados*, when we iterate by partes the whole spoken before.
    Anadiplosis, when the laste worde of the fyrst clause is the fyrst word of the
    second.'   (Si and Jiii)

In those rhetorics, written in English, which emphasised the imitation of particular types of writing or oratory the model passages were sometimes long enough to have formed a small prose anthology, but the exercises were conventional and formal, the models often dull. Thomas Wilson, 1553, provides a model, in about 1500 words, 'of commending King David, for killing great Goliah'. Slightly longer models in Wilson commend justice, and the study of law; a letter of about 8500 words comforts a mother on the death of her two sons (Wilson's former pupils) and a letter of nearly 11,000 words, based on Erasmus, is designed to 'perswade a young ientleman to Mariage'. Of finer quality is one of Wilson's examples of amplification, the technique to which he gives most attention. His model amplification on Lowliness has rather more power than does a merely technical exercise:

1553 'If lowelinesse and Charitee maintayne life, what a beaste is he, that
throughe hatered will purchace deathe? If God warneth us to love one another, and
learne of him to be ientle, because he was ientle and humble in harte: howe cruell are
thei, that dare withstande his commaundement? If the subiect rebell against his
kyng, we crie with one voyce, hang hym, hang hym, and shall wee not thynke hym
worthy the vilest death of all, that beeyng a creature, contempneth his creatour,
beyng a mortall manne neglecteth his heavenly maker, beyng a vile moulde of claie,
setteth lighte by so mightie a God, and ever livyng Kyng? Beastes and birdes
without reason, love one another, thei shroude, and thei flocke together, and shall
men endued with suche giftes, hate his even christian, and eschewe companie?
When Shepe dooe straie, or cattell doo strive one against another, there are Dogges
ready to call them in, yea, thei wil bite them (as it hath been full often seen) if twoo
fight together: and shall man wante reason, to barke against his lewde affeccions, or
at the least shal he have none to checke hym for his faultes, and force him to
forgeve?'   (fol. 64 verso)

Richard Rainolde's *The Foundacion of Rhetorike*, 1563, comprises nineteen
model prose passages illustrating different forms of discourse, such as
fable, historical narration, praising. The pieces are complete in themselves,
up to 2000 or 3000 words. One of the shortest is the fable of the shepherds
and the wolves, from Aesop. Following the fable come the customary
generalising and moralising comments, with expansions, explanations and
other procedures that students were expected to imitate; these occupy 36
times as much space as the fable itself. The remaining model passages, such
as *It is not like to be true, that is said of the battail of Troie* and *The Dispraise of
Domicius Nero Emperour of Roome*, are similarly weighed down by
consequential apparatus. Rainolde's rhetoric, though important as the
first of its kind in English, is, in comparison with the collections of
commonplaces, heavy in substance, style and exposition.

    Lazarus Piot's translation of *The Orator*, by Alexandre Le Sylvain (also
called van den Busche), 1596, on the other hand, makes racy reading but is
intended for adults. Its collection of passages comprises historical set
speeches, with their replies, and forensic accusations or statements: a thief
justifies his theft and the priest, whose horse the thief had stolen, replies; a
husband justifies the murder of his wife 'for having lost two of his children,
the one by fire, the other by water'. The collection is unlikely to have been
used in school.

    That part of Thomas Blount's *The Academie of Eloquence*, 1654, which
was not taken from the (then unpublished) work of Hoskins comprises a
large collection of model letters; 'Formulae Majores, or Common Places';
and 'Formulae Minores, or Little Forms'. There is little difference
between the two latter except that the commonplaces are arranged

thematically; the formulas are meant to be used as they stand or to suggest phrases which could be used in similar contexts:

1654 'The amazed Sun hid his face behind a mask of clouds.'   (p. 136)

'Whetting his tender wit upon the sandy stone of her edging importunity.'
(p. 133)

'By exquisite methods of cunning and cruelty, I must be compelled first to follow the Funerals of my honor, and then be destroyed.'   (p. 137)

The commonplaces might serve the same purpose, but tend to offer a thought rather than a phrase:

'Speech is nothing else but an expression to another man of the images one hath within himself.'   (p. 97)

'Though the surging sea hath moved the humors of my body, yet it hath not power to change the inclinations of my mind; for I love you no less at *Antwerpe* (where I am arrived) then I did at *London.*'   (p. 57)

Newton's rhetoric contained a collection of model passages as well as examples of the figures. The passages are representative of the rather forced writing that schoolboys had to study. In any assessment of the influence of the English rhetorics it must not be forgotten that the bulk of a pupil's reading was of this quality. The first passage demonstrates also Newton's application of logic to rhetoric, what he describes as the sixth way of arguing rhetorically:

1671 'Let the proposition be: *Youths are not to be bridled with rigid discipline.* The *Reason: Because they are not the better for rigour but the worse.* Omitting the *Major,* place it Logically thus: *Youths are worse for the rigour of discipline, therefore they ought not to be kept under a rigid Discipline.* Oratorically thus.

You erre greatly if you think that a youth may be improved by severity and fear of discipline; for though they may by an austere carriage seem to be reclaimed, yet really and indeed, they become thereby the more dissolute: Go to experience, and you shall find them, to be commonly the worst of all others, who have passed their youth under the most severe discipline. As a torrent may for a while be stopped by an overthwart bank, but while it stops, it is but gathering its more strong floud, by which when the bank is broken, it doth redeem the length of its cessation, with its more raging flux: so youth being bridled under cruel pressures, after it is once freed from those lawes by w[h]ich it was restrained, it doth become the more violently insolent; and drowneth the Soul in the pursuite of those Syren snares from which it was before debarred: for we alwaies desire forbidden fruit, and to enjoy what we cannot obtain.'   (pp. 56–7)

The second passage is an example of amplification 'by Enumeration of parts':

'Instead of saying, *this valley is set forth with all the imbellishments that low ground is capable of*, one may say:

The rich fields of corn and green meadows lie in several divisions intercheckered like great beds of flowers, and fresh glass pots in a large garden. The corn-fields look as if the roots which were hid in them complained, that by mistake of their own strength, through a great desire of being fruitful, they had sent forth more stalks than they could well support, and the overladen ears encreased that oppression; the sweet grass grew up so thick in the meadows, that it seemed to be straightned for want of room, and yet crouded closer to make way for those fragrant flowers of all sorts which grew up with it; and these mingling their various colours as they best fitted the several greens which they found there, made a shew like a rich carpet, where grass was the ground, rarely made up with beautiful Embroideries of flowerwork.'   (p. 89)

Spelling-books. Until the 1680s fewer than half the spelling-books gave space (on average about one-third of the book) for any continuous reading-matter. The material was exclusively doctrinal until the late 1660s, when secular but still strongly moralistic material began to appear. Sometimes the writer's concern was more with the difficult proper names of the Bible than with doctrine:

1640 'Onely here for the further practice of little ones, that their parents may need to buy them no other book for the reading English, we have here annexed ... the first Chapter of *S. Matthew*, to inure them a little to those Hebrew names.'

(Daines, p. 66)

Some attempt might be made to lessen the difficulty of the language, but not of the ideas, either by paraphrase or by versification:

(1690) 1705   Except that you be born again,
Of Water, and the Holy Spirit;
Salvation you cannot obtain,
Nor everlasting Life inherit. *John* 3, 3–7

But must assuredly be cast
(With Devils and the damned Crew)
Into those Flames that ever last,
Your Pains and Torments to renew. *Matthew* 25, 41, 46

(Scoffin, p. 67)

Sometimes sectarian rancour and enthusiasm determined the selection of reading-matter, as in the spelling-books of Benjamin Harris, 1679; Edward Clark, 1680; Elisha Coles, 1689; Benjamin Keach, 1693, and others. Hence 30 pages of 'A Prospect of Popery' (Harris, 1716 edn) and 174 pages of 'The Image of Antichrist' (Clark, 1682 edn).

From the 1660s doctrinal material was supplemented by lists of proverbs, which in Latin had always been valued for elementary reading-practice. In the English spelling-books they represent the transition from doctrinal to fully secular material. T.H., 1667, provides a representative selection, in which the following are grouped under the letter *N*:

> No longer pipe, no longer dance.
> Nothing so certain as death.
> Necessity hath no Law.
> New Lords, new Laws.
> Need makes the old wife trot.
> None so proud as the enricht begger.

Other selections are in Fox and Hookes, (1670) 1673; *The Compendious School-master*, 1688; Hawkins, 1692. Moralising couplets, used as writing-copies either in copybooks or in spelling-books, served a similar purpose, for a wide age range:

1675 Drink, Dice and Drabs, three dangerous Dees, do call
       For a fourth D, which fourth is worst of all.   (Cocker, p. 15)

1707 *Xerxes* survey'd his mighty host with tears,
       To think they'd die within an hundred years.
       But by his own ill management we see
       They're all destroy'd and dead in less than three. (Dyche, p. 143)

In the anonymous *Thesaurium*, 1689, the secular moralising took the form of 'Lessons for Children . . . fitted for the fore-and after-noon of every day in the week. Being wholesome precepts containing several vertues necessary to be instill'd into young people' (p. 57).

In John Bunyan's *A Book for Boys and Girls*, 1686, the usual situation is reversed: instead of being a spelling-book containing reading-matter it is a reading-book containing a few pages of spelling-matter separately headed *An Help to Children*. The spelling-matter, in which only twenty-four words are listed, together with boys' and girls' names, was omitted in the second edition, 1701, and subsequently when the book was retitled *Divine Emblems*. Although the verses each end with a moralising 'comparison', their starting-point is always everyday life, as their titles show: *Upon the Boy on his Hobby-Horse; Upon the Boy dull at his Book; Upon the Sight of a Pound of Candles falling to the Ground*. One of the shorter poems, omitted in 1701, is:

> *Upon the Horse in the Mill*
> Horses that work i' th' Mill must hood-wink't be;
> For they'l be sick or giddy, if they see.
> But keep them blind enough, and they will go
> That way which would a seeing Horse undo.

Comparison

Thus 'tis with those that do go *Satan's* Round,
No seeing man can live upon his ground.
Then let us count those unto sin inclin'd
Either beside their wits, bewitch'd or blind.   (No. 28)

During the last twenty-five years of the seventeenth century the spelling-books slowly change: their reading-material ceases to be exclusively doctrinal and relaxes occasionally into a merely moralising attitude. Towards the end of the century the stage is reached when the writer of a testimonial in *The Compendious School-master*, 1688, can praise the author because his 'Method will pleasantly charm Squirrel-pated Boys into a love of Learning'. This work, although it contains doctrinal and sectarian material, is perhaps the first spelling-book to contain some unmoralising secular, if politically biased, reading-matter: a poem on the Great Fire, 1666, and the 'resurrection' of London on 29 May 1683, Oak Apple Day. More significant is *A Play-book for Children*, 1694, by J.G., the first spelling-book to contain nothing but secular reading-matter. The author is thinking of children with a freshness that seldom appeared in elementary textbooks:'I am not ignorant of the Swarms of Books for Children, already Printed, as Primers, Tutors, &c. Yet I could never find one, that both for Matter and Method was wholly suited to that tender Age' (preface). Existing books, he says, contain too much, the pages are too large, often in 'black Print', and the matter cannot be understood by the children. The spelling-lists in his own book, which measures about 130 by 80 mm., have only twelve words on a page, six when the words are long. The reading-material is in the form of three series of sentences, each sentence in a series beginning with a different letter of the alphabet. The sentences are short at first: 'Apples are for Chil-dren, that know the Let-ters', but increase in substance: 'A Wolf is a wild Beast big-ger than most dogs, that will kill the poor Sheep if they be not watched.'

The use of secular material is continued in two books that must have appeared within a few years of each other. T.W.'s *A Little Book for Little Children*, a spelling-book published some time in Queen Anne's reign, contains no doctrinal matter. It includes two lively alphabet rhymes: '*A* was an Archer, and shot at a Frog . . .' and a less well-known one that severely says, under G and H:

Goats are stinking Creatures, and selfwill'd
Hogs good for nothing are till they be kill'd.

In addition there are riddles and the well-known puzzle verses beginning 'I saw a Peacock with a fiery Tail.' The second, and in most ways conventional, work is Harland's *The English Spelling-Book revis'd*, of which the third edition was published in 1719. It contains the Church Catechism, and graces, but it also contains more than forty pages of passages from English literature. The author apologises for 'this Miscellaneous Collection' being 'somewhat different from the Nature of a Spelling Book' and containing 'abstruse' matter; but because children are influenced by what they read he has chosen passages of the highest quality. If his judgment in the choice of passages has failed he hopes 'the Reader will be so kind to consider, that Persons employ'd about this Affair [presumably teaching] are not always sent from the great Seminaries of Learning'.

Harland's choice includes passages from Quarles, Tillotson, Waller, Garth, Dryden, Blackmore, Cowley, Prior, from L'Estrange's *Aesop* and from *Hudibras*. Shakespeare is represented by seven lines from *Othello* ('Good name in man and woman . . .'), Milton by eleven lines from *Paradise Lost* (Book 5, 277–87). It is difficult to assess the importance of Harland's book. He realised that his reading-material was unusual, but he did not claim to be an innovator following any policy. His book is in two parts, the spelling and simple reading-matter 'collected and digested for the weak apprehensions of children in their first steps to learning'; the grammar and the literary selections, still for children, but 'when their capacities are grown stronger'. This second part, he adds, 'may be of use to older people'.

From the evidence quoted it seems as though secular reading-material, often heavily moralising, of a more extended form than the usual short sentences, began to appear in the spelling-books during the 1680s, and that pieces of a lighter or more literary nature (according to the maturity of the intended pupil) appeared for the first time towards the end of the seventeenth century.

In this enquiry as to how far, if at all, children and especially schoolchildren, during the sixteenth and seventeenth centuries had any kind of teaching in, or exposure to, literature in English, only the evidence of the spelling-books is clear, so far. We do not know enough about the impact of oral traditions, or about the extent of purely recreational printed literature for children, to do more than speculate about their influence. For grammar-school pupils the evidence of Latin rhetorics and of English and Latin logics has some relevance, but the influence would be patchy and indirect.

The teaching of literature: eighteenth century, to 1770

After the end of the seventeenth century spelling-books cease to be the most important source of, and evidence for, school reading. Secular recreational reading was beginning to be provided, as never before, for schools; writers on education were urging schools to encourage the reading of literature; anthologies for school use were beginning to appear. By the 1770s the teaching of English literature in school had become a matter of normal educational discussion. The enquirer, however, still has some difficulty in describing the results of his enquiry. He wants to know not only what was taught but how it was taught. In this wish he must not run too fast. Increasingly during the seventeenth century young people at school and at home had from one or another of the sources just described an opportunity of meeting some literature in English. In the opinion of most teachers and parents this experience was meant to improve their competence in mechanical reading; to strengthen their religious practice, their moral outlook and their everyday behaviour; to give them some useful general knowledge; and, all else being equal, to bring pleasure. The reading of English literature, taking the term broadly, was a private activity, a recreation, even if it was encouraged at school. It was not seen as a skill, and was not therefore taught. It was available; it was met incidentally; it was presented; but it is premature to ask about methods of teaching.

The enquirer can do no more at this stage than show the setting in which these reading-opportunities were presented, and give some indication of the reading-matter itself. In attempting this he can offer little more than an annotated booklist. The methodological element, which is the fire and the salt of his narrative, has yet to be added.

Early in the eighteenth century the position changes in that anthologies for school use begin to appear. Pupils no longer have direct acquaintance with literature only in the spelling-book or fragmented in rhetoric; it is now available in its own right. But it is still, on the whole, presented rather than taught. It is only towards the end of the eighteenth century that methodology is discussed. There is however a difference in this respect between the eighteenth and the seventeenth centuries. The bare presentation of literary material is in the eighteenth century accompanied by much comment on its benefits and dangers, on what is suitable and what is safe. This part of the present chapter therefore, although it too is partly booklist, leads on to the teachers' often salty opinions about the educational effects of literature. In the nineteenth century this discussion continues, and is supplemented by explicit consideration of method.

Spelling-books. Spelling-books of which the reading-matter was wholly doctrinal continued to appear until the 1760s. *The British Instructor*, 1763, was one of these, perhaps because it was intended primarily 'for the use of the poor Negroes and others abroad, especially in *Virginia* and *South Carolina*'. A similar evangelical intention lay behind William Turner's *The Art of Spelling*, 1710, which was dedicated 'to the Honourable Society for Propagating Christian Knowledge', and Benjamin Harris' *The New English Tutor Enlarg'd*, which appeared about the same time. Harris' is a work of such intense sectarian vehemence that even after more than two and a half centuries it can threaten the reader's equanimity. Other spelling-books of the period 1700–60 that use only doctrinal reading-matter are the anonymous *The London New Method*, 1711, Daniel Fisher's *The Child's Christian Education*, a. 1750, which, because a child 'cannot be perfected by what he does not understand', seeks in its selections to remove 'that tedious Obscurity which must needs render the Reading of the *Bible* at large so irksome and discouraging' (preface) and Thomas Smith's *An Easy Spelling Book*, which had a sixth edition in 1764. Others during the early part of the eighteenth century contained both doctrinal and secular (usually moralistic) material in about equal proportions. The two most popular, Henry Dixon's *The English Instructor*, 1728, and Thomas Dilworth's *A New Guide to the English Tongue*, 1740, provided mostly doctrinal material, supported by fables and moral sentences:

1728 '*An Old Crab and a Young.* Child (says the Mother) you must use yourself to walk streight, without skewing and shailing so every Step you set: Pray Mother (says the young Crab) do but set the Example your self, and I'll follow you.'

(Dixon, p. 93)

1740 '*Life is short and miserable*
        Ah! Few and full of Sorrow are the Days
        Of Miserable Man: His Life decays . . . [etc.]'   (Dilworth, p. 132)

A similar combination of biblical passages and fables is found in William Markham's *An Introduction to Spelling and Reading English* and in the more thoughtful *Instructions for Beginners*, both published in 1728. It is sad that Markham's book was popular enough to be revised and reissued as late as 1867, whereas the anonymous *Instructions* was not, so far as we know, reprinted.

The spelling-books in which the reading matter is wholly, or almost wholly, secular vary in tone more than in substance. William Ronksley's *The Child's Weeks-work*, 1712, addressed 'To the judicious teachers of English Schools', is distinctive in both tone and substance. It contains only one page of spelling, on the grounds that 'Orthography . . . is rather to be learnt by one's own Observations, than by any Rules whatsoever' (preface). It comprises simple verses, presumably written by Ronksley, riddles, proverbs, fables, jests, precepts for health and behaviour. The verses are arranged for each day of the week, two or three stanzas morning and afternoon:

> In School, I say,
> You need but stay
>   From *Eight* to *Ten*, then Play.
> From *Two* to *Four*
> You Learn; no more
>   But just *Four Hours* a Day.   (p. 4)

The book is relaxed, original and free from sanctimoniousness.

This small group of spelling-books illustrates almost the whole range of poetry thought suitable for children. There is characterless versification:

(1736) 1754   Behold the soft, the pleasing Smiles,
              That crown the Parent's tender Care,
              And well reward the early Toils
                Their wise and prudent Conduct share.   (*First Book*, p. 119)

There are divine songs, from Watts, Pope's equally popular *Universal Prayer*, extracts from Thomson's *Seasons*, Young's *Night Thoughts*, and a grim passage from Book 12 of *Paradise Lost* (Scott, 1771). In spite of concessions to interest and amusement most of the reading-matter is what the teachers think children ought to have, or at least what they ought to like. It is *The Child's New Play-Thing* that is unusual in offering 'Stories proper to raise the Attention and excite the Curiosity of Children', such as *St George; Guy of Warwick; Fortunatus; Reynard the Fox*. This book seems also to have been popular: it had its first American edition within two years, 1744, and frequent British and American editions until at least 1819.

The proportion of reading-matter in these spelling-books declines as the publication increases of school anthologies, simple works of history, natural history and tales for home reading. In twenty-five spelling-books that appeared between 1710 and 1771 about 45 per cent, on average, is allotted to continuous reading-matter. The average for the first ten of these books, to 1740, is just under 50 per cent, whereas the average allocation for the last ten, from 1755, is just over 25 per cent. Increasingly spelling-books keep to spelling, readers keep to reading-matter, and only the grammars retain their compendious function as linguistic hold-alls.

Rhetorics. During the early years of the eighteenth century the attitude of teachers of rhetoric began to change. Joseph Trapp, lecturing in Oxford, criticised the traditional approach:

1742 'As I am now on the Subject of Figures, I can't help making a Remark or two upon those Books of Rhetorick that are usually read in Schools ... Surely there's no

Necessity that an Art designed for the Refinement of the Minds of Youth, should be treated of in so rough a Method, so full of dry, logical Definitions, as must be hard for Boys to understand, and much harder to remember. Nor is there any Need of all those Subdivisions of Figures, one under another, which, when Boys have once made themselves Masters of, before they have Judgment enough to use them, they think their Business is to adorn their little Performances with these sort of Flowers, as they call them.' (Joseph Trapp, *Lectures on Poetry*, p. 53, translating his own *Praelectiones Poeticae*, vol. I, 1711, p. 66)

The emphasis of teachers was no longer directed almost solely to composition; they began to look on literature as more than a source of models for the teaching of expression; their texts were not always confined to a summary analysis of the figures; illustrative quotations were fuller and not tied to the figures. The development was gradual. It is apparent in the outlook of Anthony Blackwall, whose intention in *An Introduction to the Classics*, 1718, was 'to reform *Rhetorick* from the Rubbish and Barbarism which it lies under in the common Books' (preface). The old summary tradition however was continued in schoolbooks for a long time: Bland, 1706 and 1708; Stirling, 1733; Martin 1737; Daniel Turner, 1771. Other rhetorics, of the same summary style, are included within English grammars: Gildon, 1711, second edition 1712; Lowe, 1737; Daniel Turner, 1739; Burn, 1766; Fenning, 1771. Such rhetorics were by then of little importance as sources of even fragmentary literary experience. The newer style of rhetoric had taken over and strengthened the textbook's potential value as a small anthology. This new approach to rhetoric, in which more attention was paid to the study of literature, and especially modern literature, was strongly influenced by French rhetoricians (Howell, 1971) of whom Charles Rollin, although not himself an innovator, was the most quoted by British school-teachers. Rollin's lectures were first published in 1726–8 and the English translation, *The Method of Teaching and Studying the Belles Lettres*, 1734, helped to popularise the latter expression. It is significant that in 1748 Adam Smith lectured both on rhetoric and on *belles lettres* and that Hugh Blair, who in 1760 had been appointed to a chair of rhetoric, was in 1762 appointed to a chair of rhetoric and *belles lettres*.

A consequence of the new approach that is especially relevant to the schools is the growing readiness of teachers such as Blackwall, who would hitherto have been drawing almost all their illustrations from Latin and Greek, to include many from English literature. In 1704 Richard Spencer had produced *Suada Anglicana*, a rhetoric written in English especially for schools, in which the illustrations are nevertheless all in Latin. In 1739, however, John Holmes' school-text *The Art of Rhetoric made Easy*, whilst dealing exclusively with the Bible and Latin and Greek authors in Part 1, quotes extensively in Part 2 (a summary of Longinus) from Thomson's *Seasons*, 'which, according to Longinus' *Criterion of Sublimity*, have upon a repeated Perusal irresistibly forced my Attention and lasting Admiration' (II, p. 40). An equally surprising, although later, exception to the summary style of rhetoric is found where it would not be expected, in William Gordon's compendium *The Young Man's Companion*, to which rhetoric had been added by the fourth edition, 1765. The practical value of compendia such as Gordon's lay in the chapters on letter-writing, measuring, gardening, and in those, intended for the solitary student, on arithmetic, geometry and trigonometry; if rhetoric was included it was normally the barest summary of the figures. Although Gordon's rhetoric shows signs of being derived from other works, especially Dodsley, it is unusual, for a book 'adapted to the lowest capacity' (p. 26), in its substantial and wide-ranging verse illustrations, commonly of about six lines each. Milton is quoted most frequently, then Prior; Dryden's translations; Denham, Pope, Thomson, Gay, Cowley. Shakespeare is represented by three passages, only the first of which occurs in Dodsley and in Blackwall: *Twelfth Night* (II. iv: 'She never told her love'); *Romeo and Juliet* (V. i: 'I do remember an Apothecary . . . make up a Shew'); *Othello* (IV. ii: 'You, Mistress . . . keep our Counsel')

The juxtaposition of old and new approaches to the teaching of rhetoric and to the teaching of literature is seen in two volumes of *The Circle of the Sciences*, published, and perhaps written, by John Newbery, 1746. One, *The Art of Rhetorick*, is no derivative summary; it bears the mark of individual judgment and choice. Its emphasis is on the classics in translation: Demosthenes, Cicero, Sallust, Homer, but it also includes passages from Addison's *Cato*, from *Paradise Lost* and from *Julius Caesar*. The latter is particularly interesting, not for the passages – the speeches of Brutus (III. ii: 'Romans, countrymen, and lovers . . .') and Antony ('Friends, Romans, countrymen . . .') are obvious choices in a book dealing primarily with oratory – but as a rare instance of a textbook passage being analysed. Antony's speech is broken into on six occasions by editorial paragraphs describing the reaction of the crowd, showing what in Antony's words had caused the crowd to react, what in their reaction had caused Antony to continue as he did, how Antony's words reveal his intentions (pp. 80–92). The other Newbery volume, *The Art of Poetry*, in later editions titled *Poetry made Familiar and Easy*, cautiously makes pleasure at least as important as instruction:

1746 'The whole Aim and Intention of POESY is to *please* and to *instruct*. In order to please, it borrows from Nature every Thing that is gay and delightful. It adorns its

Diction with Number and Harmony; and it never fails to employ the *Marvellous* and *Pathetick* in their proper Place. And in order that it may instruct . . . it describes and exposes to View . . . Virtue in all its Beauty and Perfection, and Vice in all its most abhorrent Shapes.'   (preface)

The book is conventional in that it deals, in question and answer, with rhyme, metrics and types of poem: 'The *Song* admits of almost any Subject, but the greatest Part of them turn either upon *Love* or *Drinking*', as the lively examples show. The elegy is represented by Pope's *Elegy to the Memory of an Unfortunate Lady*; satire by Dryden's *Mac Flecknoe*. The book is most unusual in that it nearly always gives complete the works that it uses as illustrations, and it gives no illustrations of dramatic verse, because satisfactory extracts would be too long. The exceptions are illustrations of epic verse: Virgil, Homer, Milton. Such respect for the integrity of poems is rare in elementary books and is characteristic of the good judgment of the unknown compiler.

In the teaching of older students rhetoric was still more closely linked to Latin and Greek authors than to English ones. But new attitudes were current here also. In the preface to Dodsley's *The Preceptor*, 1748, compiled expressly for school use, 'though for the higher classes', can be seen an easing of the old rote learning of the figures and their illustrations. Once Dodsley's students understand a figure the teacher should not only explain its textbook illustrations but require the students 'to exemplify it by their own Observations, pointing to them the Poem . . . in which an Example may be found, and leaving them to discover the particular Passage by the Light of the Rules which they have lately learned' (preface, p. xxii). In addition to the rhetoric, *The Preceptor* contains sections on reading and speaking that serve as a small anthology. Reading for Dodsley is reading aloud and the passages are chosen for that purpose, largely from the periodicals and miscellanies. The section on speaking is unusual in the range of its extracts from Shakespeare: *As You Like It, Julius Caesar, 2 Henry IV, Henry V, Henry VIII*, and 'several Scenes from *Timon of Athens*, somewhat altered, and thrown into one'. The prose passages are all from Nathaniel Hooke's *Roman History*.

The relation between English and the classics and, in the context of these rhetorics, the respective status of Shakespeare, Milton and Pope is shown in a comparison of three rhetorics of this period. Part 2 of *An Introduction to the Classics* (1718, but here cited from the second edition, 1719) by Antony Blackwall, a grammar-school headmaster, is a reforming rhetoric (above p. 163). John Lawson's *Lectures concerning Oratory*, 1758, are the published form of lectures to a university class, to whom he apologises for speaking in

English. He takes 450 pages for 23 lectures, of which those on the history of rhetoric and on modern Latin poetry are excluded from this analysis. Thomas Gibbons' *Rhetoric*, 1767, is also a set of lectures, at about the same academic level, given in a dissenting academy to an audience of young men most of whom were hoping to enter 'the learned professions'. In their published form Gibbons' lectures occupy nearly 480 pages.

Of all the quotations and references in these three works the proportions taken from writers in English, excluding the Bible, are: Blackwall 37 per cent; Lawson 44 per cent; Gibbons 30 per cent. Within these English quotations the percentages are:

	Shakespeare	Milton	Pope
Blackwall	11	40	–
Lawson	12	29	18
Gibbons	2	21	11

Latin and Greek authors in translation (sometimes accompanied by the original) are still a more frequent source of illustrative quotation than are writers in English (Pope and Dryder
counted among writers in English). This was natural for Blackwall and Lawson, but Gibbons was relatively free from the classical presuppositions of a university teacher.

The difficulty of assessing the status of English literature relative to Latin and Greek, in school, is further illustrated in an English grammar of the same period. John Houghton, 'master of a private grammar school', wrote an *Introduction to English Grammar* in 1766. He followed the not uncommon practice of providing literary passages as examples of parsing, including extracts from Proverbs, Revelation and two substantial passages from *Hamlet*. Houghton is concerned that his pupils should read English literature, however questionable his use of it might sometimes be. He discusses, as a model for his pupils, how to interpret a passage from Edward Young's *A Vindication of Providence*, which he calls a 'supposed difficult Passage', and recommends that pupils should be 'taught to analyze, and give the Sense of' papers from the *Spectator* and *Guardian*, and to read Dodsley's *Fables*. Yet in an appendix where he gives some views 'upon Education in general', and especially on the importance of Latin and Greek, he makes no reference to English at all. By 'good Learning' he says that he means '*principally* CLASSICAL LEARNING in it's greatest latitude' because it is 'intimately connected with every thing that is truly valuable in *human Life*'. He then adds a note saying that in stressing the classics he 'would not be understood to exclude' certain subjects from the grammar school. These subjects are 'Arithmetic, Algebra, or the Elements of Mathematics . . . Geography . . . by way of Amusement' and writing. He does not mention English grammar, although he is writing a textbook for it, nor literature, despite the attention he gives it. It does not necessarily follow that Houghton wanted English to have an unimportant place in the curriculum, but the omission is striking and hard to explain except on the grounds that he considered English a classical subject in the broadest sense. This may seem unlikely, but there is some support for the suggestion in Blackwall's *An Introduction to the Classics.* When Dodsley, in adopting Part 2 of Blackwall's work for his own *Preceptor,* says that he has added more illustrations to it, it might be assumed that he added illustrations from English works, which would not be relevant to Blackwall's subject. But, as we saw, 40 per cent of Blackwall's illustrations are from English writers: the same proportion as in *The Preceptor.* Dodsley's additions were more than offset by his omissions, and there are slightly fewer quotations, for English, Latin and Greek authors taken together, in *The Preceptor* than in Blackwall's book. Blackwall's illustrations from English writers, which it must be assumed he considered in some sense classical, come, in order of frequency, from Milton (15), Tillotson (6), Spenser, Shakespeare (4), Prior, Addison, Cleveland, Roscommon and Congreve. These are quite separate from over 20 quotations from Dryden's translations of Virgil and Juvenal. The term 'classical' needs to be watched with care and not interpreted too narrowly. Although Johnson defined 'a classic' as 'an author of the first rank; usually taken for an ancient author', he also defined 'classical' not only as 'relating to antique authors' but also as 'relating to literature'. (Cf. George Chapman, 1773; below p. 206.)

Three writers of verse for children

The clearest evidence for the teaching of English literature in school must come from anthologies compiled primarily for school use: but as it is impossible to make a firm distinction between children at home and children at school it will be useful to consider first the work of three writers of verse for children: Isaac Watts, Thomas Foxton and Nathaniel Cotton. They can be considered as representing gradations in the pedagogical importance, for this study, of poetry written for children in the first half of the eighteenth century. Watts' verses appeared in countless anthologies and were widely read in school; Foxton's appeared in some school anthologies but were less popular and had, it seems, largely dropped out by the end of the century; Cotton's, though very popular, seem to have been read at home more than at school. The works are:

> Isaac Watts, *Horae Lyricae*, 1706. Eight British editions in the first thirty-seven years; many editions until at least 1854.
> Isaac Watts, *Divine Songs*, 1715. Twenty-one editions in the first thirty-seven years; a hundred editions by 1850 (*DNB*); many editions, British and American, thereafter.
> Thomas Foxton, *Moral Songs*, 1728. Fourth edition 1743; issued also with Watts' *Divine Songs* as late •1781.
> Náthaniel Cotton, *Visions in Verse*, 1751. Eleven editions in the first thirty-six years; many editions, British and American, until at least 1821.

In 1706 Watts is writing for young people who 'have been allowed to Sin beyond the Vicious Propensities of Nature, plung'd early into Diseases and Death, sunk down to Damnation in Multitudes' (preface). Nevertheless he is trying to overcome the prejudice that poetry, especially for children, is light and trivial, that 'all that arises a Degree above Mr *Sternhold* is too airy for Worship, and hardly escapes the Sentence of *unclean and abominable*' (preface, third edition 1715). His attitude is pleasantly indicated by what must have been quite a racy comment, that 'the Book of the *Revelations* seems to be a Prophecy in the Form of an *Opera* or a Dramatic Poem' (*ibid.*). The *Divine Songs* were carefully written 'so that you will find here nothing that favours of a Party: the Children of high and low Degree, of the Church of *England* or Dissenters, baptized in Infancy or not, may all join together in these Songs'. Nearly all his verses have a slightly detached tone that is very different from the evangelical rhetoric of his own preface to *Horae Lyricae*, and from most contemporary religious exhortation. It was this unusual detachment, sincere and simple, sharpened by the occasional vivid phrase ('Let Dogs delight to bark and bite') that gave Watts' poems their immense popularity. He said of his own 'slight specimen' of *Moral Songs* included in the *Divine Songs*: 'My Talent doth not lie that way' (preface) and he elsewhere praised Foxton's *Moral Songs composed for the Use of Children* as being near to what he had in mind.

Foxton's verses, although they all 'display the Beauty of some Moral Virtue, and shew the happy Consequences of a due Regulation of the Passions' (preface) have, like Bunyan's, their starting-points in the everyday life of children: *On the Flying of a Paper Kite; Upon a Boy's being whipp'd at School; On some Boys seeing a Lion, a Leopard, and other wild*

Beasts at a Show.[4] Nathaniel Cotton's *Visions* are remote from the flying of kites. The first three of the eight visions are 'Slander'; 'Pleasure'; 'Health'; later a ninth was added, 'Death'. Each vision includes an allegorical description of its abstract subject in an avuncular and sometimes caressing tone. The poems are nearly always addressed to girls:

> My lovely Girl, I write to you;
> And pray believe my Visions true:
> They'll form your Mind to every Grace;
> They'll add new Beauties to your Face.   (Vision 1)

We do not know to what extent volumes of verse by individual authors were used in school at this period; at a guess, Watts' and Foxton's volumes would sometimes, and Cotton's seldom, be used as a whole in school. The usual school-text was an anthology.[5]

Anthologies

Until late in the nineteenth century there are special difficulties in identifying and evaluating the evidence of anthologies. If each piece in a school anthology had been chosen (being a complete work) or extracted (being part of a work) by a compiler who was following a known policy, commercial, educational or evangelical, and had a reasonably broad acquaintance with available literature, it would be possible to make useful inferences about the compiler's opinions, the popularity of particular works and authors, and changes in the kinds of literature considered suitable for study in school. But these conditions seldom obtain.

Very often a piece in an anthology was not taken directly from its parent work but from another anthology. The primary judgment and selection of the piece was made not by the compiler of the anthology under consideration but by a different person, at an earlier time and perhaps following different criteria. All that can be inferred is that the later compiler thought the piece suitable; it is not possible to infer that he thought it more suitable than alternative pieces by the same author, or of the same kind.

Often the text of an anthology piece has been altered: by omission, simplification, bowdlerisation. If these alterations had been made by the compiler they would be evidence concerning both his literary and his pedagogical judgment; if they were inherited, perhaps without the

---

[4] Two of Foxton's least moralising poems are included in *The Oxford book of children's verse*, ed. Iona and Peter Opie, OUP, 1973.

[5] Four of Cotton's poems are in *The Oxford book of children's verse*, two of them, including one of the fables on which his popularity mainly rested, from editions later than 1751.

compiler being aware of them, their evidential value is restricted. Furthermore the pieces in some anthologies carry no author's name or any indication of their source. Sometimes the compiler's own work is silently included. To trace the genesis of such pieces, and thus to establish their full evidential value, is a considerable task. For lack of such information it is usually necessary to take the contents of an anthology at their face value: the compiler thought them suitable. We seldom know how far he was exercising a considered choice.

In the eighteenth and nineteenth centuries, as in our own, certain poems, sometimes the only poem by which an author is widely known, become anthology pieces. They are not for that reason inferior. They are anthology pieces because they make a quick and strong appeal, and these qualities make them useful in school. But these qualities are possessed by verse that is superficial and thin, as well as by verse of substance. The very qualities that give the verse its substance may, in the compiler's judgment, counteract its immediate appeal and thus reduce its chance of inclusion. Anthologies therefore tend to perpetuate on the one hand the more trivial of those poems which make a quick and strong appeal, and on the other hand those few which have been accorded the conventional status of unquestioned masterpiece, whether or not they appeal much to schoolchildren.

In comparing one anthology with another it is natural to consider how many extracts from particular authors occur in each. An anthology that contains twenty pieces by Milton and three by Pope is presumably compiled according to criteria different from those behind one in which there are twenty pieces by Pope and three by Milton. But the security of such a judgment is affected by the length and autonomy of the pieces. If one compiler is working in the tradition of the old aphoristic collections he thinks of a 'piece' as the expression of a single thought or a single rhetorical beauty, which is unlikely to exceed six or eight lines. If a second compiler has as his model a collection of whole poems he is likely to choose from *Paradise Lost* or the *Essay on Man* longer and sustained passages that have something of the coherence of a complete poem. Twenty passages of Milton chosen by the first compiler might offer the reader no more than the second compiler's three passages. To assess the weight of a particular author in a number of different anthologies merely by counting lines would, however, be as crude as by counting extracts. Both types of information are needed because they are relevant to the pedagogically important question how far poetry in general, and certain kinds of poetry in particular, can adequately be taught from extracts. In an enquiry such as this it is impracticable to study in such detail even the more fully documented nineteenth-century anthologies, and the complex uncertainties surrounding most of the earlier ones would make it difficult for even a sophisticated analysis to produce useful conclusions.

The difficulty was recognised at the time. Thomas Hayward, reviewing previous anthologies in the cantankerous preface to his own collection *The British Muse*, 1738, complains that attributions are not given; there is too much translation; texts are altered or taken from secondhand sources; pieces are short and scrappy. Of *Belvedere*, 1600, a collection of nearly four and a half thousand fragments, he makes the scholastically relevant comment: 'There is . . . so abrupt and sudden a hurry from one idea to another in every chapter . . . that the sentences slip through the reader's apprehension as quicksilver through the fingers' (p. vii).

School anthologies. James Greenwood (later Sur-Master at St. Paul's School) compiled *The Virgin Muse*, 1717, while he was 'teacher of a boarding school at Woodford, in Essex'. The book is dedicated to nine 'young ladies', and its tone is in many ways that of the home, not the school. Such an anthology is needed because 'you will hardly find any Collection of Poems, that you can prudently put into the Hands of the Youth of either Sex' without meeting something '*Shocking* to *Good Manners, Difficult* to be *Understood,* or very *Trifling* and *Silly*'. There is nothing in the book that is not 'strictly *Modest,* and truly *Poetical*' (preface). What gives the work its particular interest for us is a statement later in the preface: 'I have endeavoured to make it a compleat Book for the *Teaching to Read Poetry*.' The context makes it quite certain that *read* here does not mean merely 'read aloud' or 'perform'. This is the first expression in a textbook of the idea that poetry could be taught, and not just presented to pupils; but there is a danger of exaggerating its significance. Only in the study of foreign languages, principally Latin, Greek and Hebrew, is there evidence before now of texts being scrutinised and 'taught' in order to bring out their meaning. We may assume that the practice of teachers of the classics would carry over, in this as in so many ways, to the study of an English text, but there is no evidence before Greenwood's anthology that it did so. His book is, if not a landmark, at least a benchmark in the development of the teaching of English.

The Virgin Muse opens with two appropriate pieces: *The Virgin*, by 'Mrs Philips' (Katherine Philips, the matchless Orinda, herself a product of a girls' boarding school) and *Virtue*, by the Earl of Roscommon, whom Johnson, quoting Pope, called 'the only moral writer of King Charles's reign'. The authors most frequently represented among the 126 pieces are

Cowley (20), Milton (19), Dryden (17), Waller (9) and Garth (7). Neither Shakespeare nor Pope appears. There is no change in the second edition, 1722. The teaching-aids that Greenwood offers are simple enough. There is an 'Alphabetical Index, explaining all the hard Words; for the Use of the younger Sort of Readers', in which the explanations are one-line definitions like those often attached to the lists of hard words in the spelling-books. Greenwood's other and more distinctive aid is 'Notes explaining some difficult places'. All the notes are brief. Most of them explain classical allusions or expressions such as : 'Indian Leaf: *Tea*; Flying Towers: *Ships*; Accursed Disease: *The Small-Pox*'. Fuller than most is his note on the line at *Paradise Lost*, Book 7, 426, in which birds 'rang'd in figure wedge their way'. Greenwood comments, 'Birds are often observed to make Figures in their Flight; the Crows in the shape of a Wedge' (p. 179).

The school anthologies next published are noticeable for their high proportion of prose, to which more than three-quarters of the space is given, and for the fact that the compilers of six of them come from the north:

John Warden (Edinburgh)	*A Collection*	1737
Anon.	*The Edinburgh Entertainer*	1750
James Buchanan (a Scot)	*The Complete English Scholar*	1753
Ann Fisher (Newcastle)	*The Pleasing Instructor*	1756
Anon.	*The Moral Miscellany*	1758
D. Burgess (Berwick)	*The Entertainer*	1759
Joseph Priestley (Yorks.)	*Rudiments of English Grammar*	1761

The prose extracts are almost entirely from the periodicals, especially *The Spectator, Tatler, Guardian, Rambler* and *The Gentleman's Magazine*, and from works of history and geography. The verse selections are too few to carry much significance, but it is noticeable that none of them includes any Milton and that they all include some Pope, if only *The Universal Prayer*, which appears in five of them. Shakespeare is allowed seven pieces by Burgess; elsewhere Shakespeare is represented only in Warden, by one passage (*King Lear*, IV. vi, Edgar to Gloucester: 'Come on, sir, here's the place'), and by Priestley (Wolsey's farewell). There is little prefatory or pedagogical comment except from Ann Fisher, and what there is shows that moral considerations carry far greater weight than others. Buchanan's selection includes fables and passages from Job and the Psalms, and the ever-popular story of Joseph, because young people have 'no Collection proper to improve their Minds in virtuous Knowledge, or make them acquainted with the English language in general'. Buchanan reminds teachers that the prose passages give them 'an opportunity of inspiring

Youth with the warmest Sentiments of Virtue', and when he refers to 'several beautiful Poems by our best Poets', which he has included 'to give Youth a Taste of reading Verse', he recommends them because they refer to monotheism, patriotism and the duties of husbands and wives (preface, pp. viii-xi).

Ann Fisher, in *The Pleasing Instructor,* emphasises morality in the beginning of her preface: 'The sole View of the Editor . . . is to exhibit a *connected Plan of Morality* . . . free from that incoherent Jumble so remarkable in all Collections of this kind.' She then hopes that 'the young Reader . . . will acquire a *true* Taste to [sic] an Ease and Elegance in his *Native* Tongue'. She goes on to consider the education of girls, many of whom lack all books in school and do sewing because there is nothing to read. She writes with increasing force about the need for girls to develop 'a Taste for the Beauty and Propriety of the Mother Tongue', and above all for their need to understand what they read; to understand:

1756 '. . . the *Nature* and *Kinds* of Words with their Connections and Dependencies upon one another. That many women read *much* and yet *not* to Edification is, chiefly, because they are ignorant of *these* Connections and Dependencies . . . and thereby *misled* in the Sense of what they are about to trace, especially in *circumstantial* Authors, or such as the Generality call *dark* and *obscure* Writers . . . They feel an Entanglement, though they *know not* what or where.'
(preface)

The Moral Miscellany has many sources in common with Ann Fisher's book but lacks any comparable discussion of teaching. It is meant to be 'very useful in schools, and . . . peculiarly suited to such persons as cannot afford to purchase those works from which the collection is made'. This comment, in the same words, appears in Burgess' preface and is one of many references to the self-educators who shared with the schools an important part of the market. The compiler has 'taken care to insert several Stories, Visions, and Allegories, which impress the imaginations, and fix the giddy roving minds of youth more than any other species of composition'. He sounds as if he were a schoolmaster. The *Miscellany* had a second, unchanged, edition in 1765 and is recommended by John Houghton in his English grammar, 1766. Priestley's small collection of pieces illustrates the section on style attached to the first edition of his English grammar but subsequently omitted. Most space is given to Pope; Young and Shakespeare are the only other poets represented.

Four further collections contain only verse:

James Burgh	*The Art of Speaking* (1761)	1763
John Drummond	*A Collection of Poems*	1762

| Anon. | *The Poetical Miscellany* | 1762 |
| James Elphinston | *A Collection of Poems* | 1764 |

Burgh and Elphinston do not state that their books are meant for school use, but they were both schoolmasters and the texts show that they have their pupils as well as 'youth' in mind. Here again the northern influence is apparent: all the named compilers were Scots. The emphasis of Burgh's book is on public speaking and reading:

> 'A youth should not only be accustomed to read to the master, while the general business of the school is going on, so that none but the master, and those of his own class can hear him, but like wise to read, or speak, by *himself*, while all the *rest* hear.'
>
> (p. 14)

Burgh's passages are arranged under seventy-six 'passions', from 'tranquillity' to 'death'. Their emphasis is on classical writers in trans-lation, Shakespeare, Milton, Addison, Pope, Swift.

Drummond arranges the passages in Part 1, which are short (he calls them 'sentences') anonymously and thematically; in Part 2 authors are given, Milton with twice as many as either Shakespeare or Pope. Elphinston's 169 passages are arranged in 11 genres (fables, allegories, elegies) in which Shakespeare, Milton and Thomson are not represented. The most favoured genres are 'Didactic Essays' (35); 'Odes' (34) and 'Hymns' (29). *The Poetical Miscellany* is the most interesting in this group. It makes a conventional attack on the drudgery of studying Latin and Greek for seven or eight years 'in order to acquire a smattering' and hopes 'that every sensible and unprejudiced Parent will be better pleased to hear his Son repeat fifty lines of Milton, Pope, Young or Thomson, than five hundred of Ovid or Virgil'. The emphasis on morality is weakened; among the 'several important Purposes in Education' that the book can serve, the first is to present the 'distinguishing Beauties of some of the most eminent of our Poets'; the second is to show the 'Force and Beauty of our Language', and only the third is to impress upon the pupils' minds 'many noble Sentiments' (preface). More than 40 per cent of the book is given to Milton (50 pages) and Young (91 pages) but by the third edition, 1778, Milton's share has been slightly, and Young's very greatly, reduced. Pope's share is slightly increased, but the main change is a wider coverage of authors.

Some school anthologies were designed especially for elocution and dramatic production. The two-volume *Miscellanies in Prose and Verse*, 1739–40, by Daniel Bellamy, father and son, is made up of fables, and plays that had been performed by the 'young ladies of Mrs Bellamy's school'. *A Help to Elocution and Eloquence*, 1770, is composed of three essays illustrated by extracts from Shakespeare (*Julius Caesar, Othello, Hamlet, Lear*), Otway, Rowe and Milton; by verse and prose passages, each prefixed by the name of the emotion most appropriate to it, and by a wide range of prose and verse for 'Reading and Declaiming'; periodical essays; letters; history; Tickell; Collins; Gray, Gay, and Pope's *Universal Prayer*. The work is explicitly a textbook 'designed to form the minds of youth to a true taste in reading . . . for the use of schools'. So also is John Drummond's second anthology of 1780 (first edition 1771) where the extracts are glossed every three or four lines by promptings such as 'fawning', 'contempt'. The index to these marginalia contains 178 items (passions) from 'abhorrence' to 'wonder'.

The difficulty of using the evidence of school anthologies was described above. That there should be this difficulty is itself important: the anthologies are our main source of information about what literature was read in school, and it is frustrating to be so severely limited in assessing the purposes they were meant to serve and the values they represent. The limitations can be illustrated by three works that it would be interesting to compare in detail. They are anthologies of verse and prose appearing about the same time, one in Scotland, one in England and one in Ireland:

> Arthur Masson: *A Collection of Prose and Verse*, fourth edition, Edinburgh 1764; another edition at Ayr, 1796.
>
> J.N., *Select Lessons in Prose and Verse*, Bristol, 1765; ten editions to 1807.
>
> Samuel Edwards, *An Abstract of English Grammar*, Dublin, 1765, of which pp. 110–67 are 'Examples for the Learner's Exercise in true and living Speech'. No further editions.

Masson and Edwards were certainly teachers, and J.N. seems to have been one. The anthologies are alike in the type of literature they draw on: the Irish and Scottish ones give no sign of their national origins except, perhaps for Masson's three extracts from Home's *Douglas*. They all include work by Shakespeare, Milton, Thomson, Addison (*Cato*), Pope and papers from the *Spectator*. Masson is distinctive for his reliance on the periodicals and on short stories; J.N. for his inclusion of many extracts from Tillotson's sermons and for the higher literary quality of his selections; Edwards for the large proportion of scriptural and devotional writing, for the grading of his material over a wide age range and for his recommendations for further reading. All but three of J.N.'s pieces carry an attribution of some sort, but over 40 per cent of Edwards' and over 50 per cent of Masson's are unattributed. Masson includes some of Addison's hymns without attribution. If he took them direct from the *Spectator* he might not know who wrote them; but why then did he not put them with the twelve other extracts that he attributes to the *Spectator*? If he took the hymns from one of the numerous selections either of Addison's work or of the *Spectator*, he would probably know who wrote them. If he took them from another anthology, in which they were unattributed, he may not have known that they came from the *Spectator* or that they were by Addison. Addison was so widely commended to schoolboys as a stylist and as a moralist that it is not without interest to know whether the inclusion of his work in a school anthology was a contemporary judgment reflecting and endorsing his reputation (and with significant pedagogical implications) or whether it unknowingly repeated such a judgment made many years previously. These freewheeling judgments were common. Masson included the *Spectator*, no. 159, a popular anthology piece usually given the title *The Visions of Mirzah*, which Burns, who used Masson's book in school, called 'the earliest composition that I recollect taking pleasure in'. The piece is included also in an anthology by Alexander Barrie, which had its second edition in 1781. It does not follow that Barrie took it from Masson, but the title of Barrie's book, *A Collection of Prose and Verse*, is identical with Masson's. Barrie includes, as did Masson, not only such customary pieces as Dryden's *Alexander's Feast* and Pope's *Universal Prayer* but three unusual pieces: *An Abridgment of the History of the Bible*; *A Jewish Story concerning Abraham*; *Abraham's Soliloquy upon receiving the Command to sacrifice his Son Isaac*. It seems likely that Barrie had Masson's book in his hand as well as in his mind, but he has in no way just taken over Masson's selection: his extracts from Milton and Shakespeare are all different from Masson's and he gives several hundred lines from Edward Young, a poet not represented in Masson.

Until more is known about the status and genealogy of their components the educational significance of most of these anthologies can be gauged only by the face value of what they offer, although we can be sure that they vary in significance as much as they do in literary quality.

Of the three anthologies just considered, the humblest is the most interesting, because Edwards tells us something about how it is to be used. His was a small private school, with one usher. It was an English school in that it taught no Latin and prepared boys 'intended for business'. It was not entirely successful. He refers to the failure of Dublin parents to understand what he is doing, and he regrets that the number of older, full-time pupils (his 'regulars') is smaller than when he started. His approach is individual. He has formal sessions on Tuesdays and Saturdays when the boys make complaints, in writing, about each other, 'both the Plaintiff and Defendant being allowed to make the most they can of the Cause, with all their Witnesses' (p. xxi). Boys in debt to each other are allowed a period of respite before being required to pay up. Bystanders at fights are liable to be punished along with the 'boxers'. 'In Cases of Defamation some Brand of Infamy is put on the Offender; usually a Spit on the Face or a Pandy.'

The collection of passages in Edwards' *Grammar* represents the transition from the older figure-of-speech rhetoric to the newer elocutionary approach to literature, and also the transition from mainly biblical to secular passages. Although the *Grammar* was published in 1765 it represents the views Edwards first expressed about thirty years previously. Edwards, though virtually unknown and in no sense a scholar or widely read, is thoughtful and articulate. Among the passages he selects some appear without any attribution; others are partially identified. He seems to be using as sources a few works that he knows (from which he is making his own selection) and other people's collections (from which he takes pieces about which he knows little or nothing). The rhetorical part of the book, pp. 75–85 and 106–9, describes in doggerel couplets twelve tropes and forty-five figures ('A Synathraesmus sums up Things in brief: / At once she's *Widow, Strumpet, Bawd,* and *Thief'*). The reading-passages, pp. 110–67, are preceded by a twenty-five-page section on 'true Pronunciation' and expressive reading and speaking, a large part of which is a classification of 'the Passions and Emotions of the Mind' that determine how and with what gestures a passage is to be spoken. The passages are grouped according to the emotions they express, but they do not differ much from any contemporary selection made for classroom, and therefore mainly oral, use. The elocutionary framework is dropped for the oldest class, and it is only at first that it is obtrusive in the notes attached to each piece: 'Shew Desire with your Hands; and decline the Head a little at *faint*; stretch out the open Hands towards the *Earth*, with a gentle Movement of springing at *flee* . . .' (p. 128). The passages are arranged for three classes. No indication is given of their ages, but the youngest are assumed to be able to 'read tolerably' (p. vi). Edwards' policy is to provide 'easy, pleasant and instructive Lessons . . . such as the *historical Parts of the Bible,* the *Descriptions of Animals* and its *Supplement, Croxal's Aesop* and Dr *King's Pantheon* . . . *Cambray's Telemachus, Select Papers in the Spectator, News Papers, Translations of the Classics* and *Some Pieces of English Poetry,* &c.' (*ibid.*). The reference to newspapers, as distinct from the periodicals, is unusual. The boys are to be 'led through' these passages several times, with 'proper Instruction . . . for reading in an easy and distinct Manner'. In the lowest class the boys are made 'to beat at the Stops' when they read (p. x). This practice always involved the reader in making a gesture to mark the punctuation, but Edwards quotes approvingly Sheridan's rejection of the common requirement that the reader should count, or beat, one for a comma, two for a semi-colon, three (or even four) for a colon and four (or even eight) for a full stop (pp. 73–4). Edwards' emphasis is on the realisation of the text in performance. He is concerned with the meaning of the text only so far as it indicates the emotion that the performer is to express. Just what emotion the text does suggest, and the evidence for differing interpretations, is not discussed, but is indicated by a controlled use of emphasising italics. Edwards draws the reader's attention to this 'novel Attempt' whereby he will 'boldly mark what seems emphatic; and shall also superadd, in some Places, what Fancy suggests to be suitable Action' (p. 111). His use of italics is not just the observance of a typographical convention; it is part of his interpretation of the piece. On this evidence Edwards' response to literature is not very sensitive. It avoids elocutionary excesses but it often kills the delicate relationship between emphasis derived from the metre and emphasis derived from the sense. One of his shorter pieces shows the method:

> When, after Battle, I the Field have seen
> O'erspread with *ghastly* Shapes, which *once* were Men;
> A *Nation crush'd*, a *Nation* of the *Brave*
> A *Realm* of Death, and on *this* Side the Grave;
> Are there, said I, who from this *sad* Survey,
> This *human Chaos* carry Smiles away?
>   (p. 160; Young, *Love of Fame*, Satire 7, lines 59–64)

If Edwards' limitations are due in part to his naivety it is to the same quality that we owe his readiness to discuss the details of his work. Would that more, and more sophisticated, teachers had been so open.

Edwards' use of newspapers is not unique:
a. 1752 Pupils 'should read a good weekly *newspaper*, and their teacher shou'd explain everything they don't understand therein'.   (John Williams, p. 15)

1754 'When Boys are advanced to the Study of History, it may be proper to make them read some Newspaper constantly, as it is published.'   (Gough, p. xv)

William Chown in 1788, stressing the importance of understanding what you read, urges young people to study 'even a common Newspaper' (p. 21). In 1790 the Massachusetts *Sentinel* reported that in the reading-school at Boston newspapers were 'to be introduced occasionally, at the discretion of the Masters' (Butler, 1969, p. 494) and at Newark, in Canada, Richard

Cockerell wanted to teach reading from the newspapers instead of from the Bible.[6]

Other anthologies. The next group of texts shows how inappropriate it is to attempt a firm classification according to their use in home teaching or in school teaching; their use by learners under instruction and by those instructing themselves; by children and by adults. Some collections, of course, are intended solely for adults, some for very young children, but in between there is a range of texts for which the intended readership is loosely defined. Commercial considerations that had always applied were being reinforced by rapid social and economic changes. Publishers were careful not to specify the market too narrowly.

At one extreme of this middle group is Charles Gildon's collection *The Complete Art of Poetry*, 1718. It makes no reference to schools or to youth, and its two volumes would be expensive. Yet its tone is instructional: it gives unusual space to Shakespeare (about 150 pieces); its second volume is 'a collection of the most beautiful descriptions, similes, allusions'. It could very well have served older pupils both as an anthology and as a guide to the writing of verse. At the other extreme is *Little Master's Miscellany* (1742) 1748, which, though 'designed for the improvement of the youth of both sexes' is domestic in tone. More than half the book is given to dialogues 'between Master Joseph and Miss Patty' on (amongst other topics) lying, fishing, deformity and tulips. There follow fables in verse and 'moral songs' of the kind that appear in the spelling-books. Between these extremes there is a group of anthologies 'for youth', of which one, Goldsmith's two-volume compilation, *The Beauties of English Poesy*, 1767, is, in spite of the expense, offered to schools also. It aims to show 'our youth, particularly . . . what is beautiful, and inform them why it is so'. Goldsmith is writing for a wide market but his emphasis is on young people:

'As to the short introductory criticisms to each poem, they are rather designed for boys than men; for it will be seen that I declined all refinements, satisfied with being obvious and sincere. In short, if this work be useful in schools, or amusing in the closet, the merit all belongs to others.'   (preface)

Goldsmith's assessment of his own contribution is a fair one, as his criticisms show:

Il Penseroso and L'Allegro: 'The imagination shewn in them is correct and strong . . .'

[6] Marie Tremaine, *A bibliography of Canadian imprints, 1751–1800*, U. Toronto Press, 1952, p. 445.

Gray's *Elegy*: 'A very fine poem, but overloaded with epithet . . . The latter part of the poem is pathetic and interesting.'

The Rape of the Lock: 'Perhaps the most perfect [production] in our language. It exhibits stronger powers of imagination, more harmony of numbers, and a greater knowledge of the world, than any other of the poet's works.'

Poems as long even as Prior's *Alma*, Denham's *Cooper's Hill* and Johnson's *London* are given in full. Chaucer, Spenser and Shakespeare are not represented, nor is there any further work by Milton. Goldsmith's comments naturally fail to explain to his readers why the beauties are beautiful, but they are a rudimentary form of teaching literature. He was too busy a journalist to produce considered and consistent comments about the teaching of literature, but his well-known views about the novel represent those of many teachers (below, p. 204).

A number of varied anthologies were compiled for 'youth' but contain no reference to schools or teaching. *The Young Student's Assistant*, 1752, is oddly named as it seems to be addressed largely to the governess. It is based on Rollin and 'other approv'd Oeconomists' and it is to the former that a number of advices are attributed, of which the fourteenth is, 'ENDEAVOUR to fortify her [the girl's] *Reason* early; and to be sure to avoid the inflaming of her *Imagination*'. The commonplace but important view expressed in this advice carries little significance in a work that is wholly derivative. *The Beauties of Poetry Display'd*, 1757, is a two-volume thematic collection ('Abandoned'; 'Absence'; 'Accent'; 'Advice'; 'Advocate'; 'Aeolus'; 'Aetna' . . .) of very short extracts, preceded by a derivative account of the origin of poetry and poetic forms. *Poems Moral and Divine,* c. 1760, contains complete poems, including Pope's *Messiah, Universal Prayer* and *Ode on Solitude*; Addison's metrical psalms; and Bishop Ken's morning and evening hymns. *Poems for Young Ladies* (1767) 1770, another of Goldsmith's compilations, also includes devotional verse, in which, he says, English poetry is deficient, together with moral verse, of which we have more, and entertaining verse, to which he allots half his space; but he takes care that 'innocence may read without a blush'. Nineteen writers are represented, Addison with most pieces, then Edward Moore's *Fables* and Collins' *Eclogues*. There is no Shakespeare. Most of the entertainment is provided by Young, Ogilvie, Parnell, Glover, Cotton, Gay and Philips.

These last few anthologies are of importance only as evidence that English literature, conventionally defined, was available in a form thought suitable for children and young people: mainly but not solely those who could afford to go to school. Only three of the anthologies so far considered, Greenwood's *The Virgin Muse*, Goldsmith's *Beauties*, and Gildon's

Complete Art of Poetry, give any indication of how literature might be taught, and Greenwood, the only schoolmaster of the three, alone puts into the text any attempt at detailed explanation. This is not to say that teachers using other books did not explain what their pupils were reading; there is no evidence. The attitude of most writers is that implied by the terms 'beauties' and *'belles lettres'*. The identification of figures of speech was being replaced by the identification of fine passages and fine images. Goldsmith might think it appropriate (and possible) to ask what made them fine (and this was an unusual question in an educational context) but neither he nor the teachers took the question any further.

The newer approach to literature, in the name of *belles lettres*, is explicitly followed in the anonymous *The Art of Poetry on a New Plan*, 1762, a greatly expanded version of *The Art of Poetry*, 1746 (above, p. 164). The 1762 version, which is between two and three times as full as the 1746 one, is more pedagogic in tone. Much of the additional matter takes the form of 'such reflections and critical remarks as may tend to form in our Youth an elegant taste, and render the study of this part of the Belles Lettres more rational and pleasing' (t.p.). But the added material lacks the crisp authenticity of the 1746 writer. Its judgments are bland and pedestrian and add little to the extracts they accompany. Even the tributes to morality are tired: 'As the Church is the School for Religion and Piety, so would the Theatre, under due encouragement and proper inspection, become a School for Morality and Virtue' (II, 149). It is only in the chapter on epic and heroic poetry, expanded tenfold from 1746, that the commentary comes at all to grips with the verse, two-thirds of which is by Homer (in Pope's translation) and Virgil (Dryden or Pitt). *Paradise Lost*, 'in which Milton seems to have rivalled and excelled all other Epic poets' (II, 318), is given much less, but still respectful, treatment.

Copybook anthologies. The many copybooks compiled by writing-masters continued to fulfil something of the function of an anthology. Eighteenth-century ones often included longer extracts than had the earlier books, but the tone remained moralistic. The aim of George Shelley, 1712, is 'more to make Youth *Virtuous* than *Witty*'; Thomas Ollyffe's *Miscellaneous Sentences*, 1719, will moderate the 'levity' of youth and will promote 'virtue and sobriety'; Prideaux Errington says boys would rather copy verse than prose, because verse 'will further their virtuous Inclinations, and promote the Interest of Religion'. Joseph Longman's *Sentences*, 1786, is unusual (and he claimed that there had been no book like it 'for near a century past') in being a thorough anthology: 'the beauties of Addison, Johnson, Rollin,

Wesley'. It was designed 'particularly for the improvement of youth, in good sense, and correct English', but the extracts seldom exceed six or seven lines and are often much shorter. The copybooks begin with sentences of one or two lines, arranged alphabetically. The selections in eighteenth-century works are narrower and of less literary value than those of the previous century. In John Tapner's *The School-Master's Repository*, 1761, the first of eighty sentences for *A* is: 'A Youth that would transcend, must ever mind to mend', and the last sentence under *Z* is: 'Zeal beyond Reason, is always out of Season.' In many of the books longer passages follow, up to ten lines each, and occasionally one stands out with a force that might catch the copyist's attention:

'It is affirmed of an English King, That he can do no Wrong, because he can do nothing but what the Law impowers him to do; for he hath all Things subjected to his Authority while he acts according to Law; yet there is nothing left to his Arbitrary Will.'   (Ollyffe, 1719, p. 19)

A future English king, George IV, ended his own copybook in 1767, at the age of five, with what might be regarded as a complementary maxim: 'Solid sense is always to be preferred to wit' (Gumuchian, 2727).

CHAPTER FIVE

Interpretation: literature taught

The teaching of literature: eighteenth century, from 1770

In the 1770s there was a quite marked change in teachers' attitudes to literature. Not only did they now reckon to teach it, as well as present it, but they began to see that it had value for ordinary children as well as for those in educated homes. J. Butler's *Proposals*, 1772, look ahead to both developments. He analyses society into seven classes: (i) 'those bred to independent fortunes'; (ii) those 'intended for the professions'; (iii) the army; (iv) mercantile employment; (v) mechanic trades; (vi) labour; (vii) service. The children of labourers, who may start work at the age of seven or eight, can learn to read if they are well taught, and they would be better taught if the mistresses were better paid. All children should learn to read, because only then would employment opportunities be opened up and the dissociation between labour and learning ended. Their reading should not be solely vocational:

1722 'Many of the passages of Poetry, the most admired by the best judges, have been such as have touched the bosoms of the very Vulgar. It is not with coarse humour only that these are pleased, but often with true pleasantry and peculiarities of character. Their Souls are, too, susceptible of the tenderest sensations from stories, movingly told.' (p. 84)

More emphasis on the teaching of literature meant more emphasis on teaching children to understand what they read. T.M., in *The Grammarian's Vade-Mecum*, describes 'a striking defect':

1774 'Youth of both sexes are suffered to read on uninterrupted, provided they pronounce properly, and place the accent or emphasis right, without examining minutely, if they really comprehend the meaning of common words. It is too often taken for granted, they do; but by very mortifying experiments (even on some young gentlemen of sixteen years of age) the editor has found this to be an error of the first magnitude.' (p. 65)

It is convenient to treat as a group the works published between 1771 and 1801. In the years just before 1802 there appeared a number of texts that both sum up many trends of the previous thirty years and also indicate future developments: Lindley Murray's school anthologies, 1799, 1800 and 1801; Mavor and Pratt's anthology, 1801, and the Edgeworths' discussions of the teaching of literature, 1798, 1801 and 1802, with which must be considered their later *Readings of Poetry*, 1816. The texts in this group were nearly all written specifically for school use; the few that make no reference to schools have such a strongly implied pedagogic purpose, as well as a generally didactic one, that it is reasonable to assume that schools would use them.

In addition to the school-texts the number of books for children's recreational reading was increasing throughout the period. Most of them had a didactic and moralising purpose, as stated in title or preface, but it is at present impossible to say how far they were used in school. Lady Fenn's simple spelling-books and grammars, although set in the home, were certainly used in school; of her reading-books a few seem directed solely to the home. Most children's books of the time assume a domestic setting for their readers and an audience of varied ages. If they were read in school it would perhaps be mainly in the many small schools chosen by parents who could not afford a governess but wanted something better than the dame school. In those homes where the parents could afford to buy books there was more reading, and more reading aloud, than there is now, and some of the literary and linguistic education of young children that we expect schools to provide was accepted by parents and schools as the responsibility of a literate home. The range of children's books that was available at the beginning of the nineteenth century has yet to be studied systematically, although much has been written about a few familiar authors. Many works by authors unknown except to collectors would be important for any close consideration of the development of children's literary experience, sensibility and competence.

Rhetorics. During the last thirty years of the eighteenth century seven grammars were published that contained elementary rhetorics, but these merely enumerated the figures of speech, an approach that was becoming old-fashioned. A brief rhetoric of the same type, though more fully illustrated, forms part of John Ash's *Sentiments on Education*, 1777. More akin to the newer style of rhetoric was Seally's two-volume *Belles Lettres for the Ladies, c.* 1773, an imitation of Rollin. Three substantial and important works, although they were intended for adult, especially academic, readers are relevant for their influence on school-teaching both in Britain and in America. These are George Campbell's *The Philosophy of Rhetoric*, 1776; Hugh Blair's *Lectures on Rhetoric and Belles Lettres*, 1783; and John Walker's *Elements of Elocution*, 1781. Campbell's book was written at intervals from 1750, most of it while he was Principal of Marischal College, Aberdeen, and Professor of Divinity. Blair's lectures were given in their earliest form in 1759 in the University of Edinburgh, and Walker's in 1778–9 while he was what we would now call a visiting lecturer at Oxford. Campbell's work is the more profound, but it was to Blair and Walker that the writers of school-texts turned. An abridgment of Campbell was made for schools, without prefatory comment, by Alexander Jamieson in 1823, nearly fifty years after the publication of the original, but Blair's lectures, now called essays, appeared in an abridged form the year after they were published and in at least twenty-four later issues in England and America. The abridgment was not made specially for schools, but they were part of its intended market.

Spelling-books and compendia. Some six spelling-books or compendia published between 1771 and 1779 contain selections of verse and prose, usually comprising about a quarter of the book. The passages are frequently taken from magazines and are of slight literary value, except in two books. The first, John Hewlett's *An Introduction to Reading*, the earliest surviving copy of which, in a fourth edition, 1798, contains extracts from Cowper, Crabbe and Goldsmith, was frequently reprinted till 1816. The second, *The British Spelling Book*, Part 1 (third edition 1799) takes nearly all its verse from Watts, and its prose includes passages from *Sandford and Merton*, Chesterfield, Hugh Blair and the *Spectator*.

Anthologies

The most numerous texts in this period are collections of passages for use in teaching. One or two for younger children were intended for home reading as much as for school; some of the elocutionary collections were intended also for the private pupils whom their authors visited. But more than fifty texts were explicitly or by clear implication designed predominantly for school. That so many school anthologies were published within thirty years is evidence that English literature was widely read, if not taught, in schools during the later decades of the eighteenth century.

Elocutionary anthologies. The elocutionary collections, with two exceptions, derive either from John Walker or from William Enfield's *The Speaker*. Walker, retiring from the stage at the age of thirty-six, ran a school for two years and then taught part-time, it seems, at a number of schools; he also compiled an English dictionary that became a standard work in the nineteenth century and wrote textbooks on various aspects of English teaching. Enfield was appointed at the age of twenty-nine to teach *belles lettres* at Warrington Academy, where he stayed until it closed thirteen years later.

The Speaker was probably the most widely used of all school anthologies. Forty-two years after its publication the Edgeworths could say, rather loftily, 'we are informed that this is an established school-book, and we see in private families that it is in every body's hands' (1816, p. vi), and it continued to be issued regularly until at least 1858. In the first edition Shakespeare was represented by thirty-eight pieces, a quarter of the total and far more than the next most frequently chosen authors: Sterne (11), Pope (10), *Spectator* (7), Akenside (6) and Thomson (5), with whom must be ranked Gray in respect of the *Elegy*, the *Hymn to Adversity* and the *Eton College* ode. Enfield's preliminary essay on elocution contains standard advice, but a second essay, *On Reading Works of Taste*, added between 1782 and 1799, gives some picture of Enfield's approach to the teaching of literature. He treats the varied purposes for which people read as either 'the improvement of the understanding' or 'the exercise of the imagination', and books consequently are either works of knowledge or works of taste. His descriptions of the qualities which make up a perceptive reader and of those which make for good writing are expressed in the belle-lettrist abstractions of the time but in a platitudinous and tautological form. He wanted his students to understand what they read, and to enjoy it and be able to criticise it, but he seems able to help them only by gestures towards 'conformity to nature', 'variety of conception', 'sublimity, beauty and novelty'. The pieces in his anthology spoke for themselves much more effectively.

The arrangement of most of the elocutionary anthologies was 'promiscuous'. In some of them prose and verse pieces were separated; in some the pieces were grouped according to the type of performance they required: 'Narrative, didactic, argumentative, oration, dialogue, description, pathetic' (Enfield, 1774 and 1780; Cresswick, 1789). Others followed Walker's psychological classification of pieces by the type of attitude or emotion they expressed or, as William Scott put it, 'the modes of utterance peculiar to different movements of the mind' (1779, preface). Walker's *Elements* lists more than seventy 'passions' (e.g. sneer, raillery, shame, gratitude, sickness), and the same type of classification is used also in his *The Academic Speaker*, 1789, and by William Scott and by Cresswick. Out of the twelve collections that can reasonably be compared Shakespeare is given most space in eight. One of these twelve, on the other hand,

Sheridan's and Henderson's Practical Method, gives fifteen extracts from Gay's *Fables,* compared with four from Shakespeare and eight from Milton. The *Spectator* and other periodicals provide much of the prose, and the collections show individual tastes such as Enfield's eleven pieces from Sterne (both *Tristram Shandy* and *A Sentimental Journey*) and John Adams' numerous extracts from Thomas Percival's *A Father's Instructions.*

Apart from advice about performance little is said on how the collections are to be used. John Walker makes a comment that shows that the idea of a literary textbook was still novel:

1777 'As the compiler had frequent occasion to teach pupils in classes, he found it necessary that each of them should read in the same author, and attend to the same passage at the same time . . . This method of teaching required a book of a small size and price, with as much variety as such a book would admit of.'   (preface)

Mary Weightman approves of 'the present universality of committing pieces to memory, and learning to recite them with propriety and grace' (1787a, preface), but the contrary view is expressed by Cresswick:

1789 'It has been a custom too prevalent to make children learn by rote longer passages from authors, to whose very expressions they could not annex an idea . . . Parents are often led astray by the selfish desire of having a wonderful child to exhibit: but these monsters very seldom make sensible men or women.'
          (preface)

Cresswick's method is for the children to learn by heart a short passage; write it later from memory; correct their version by the original and then make a fair copy. This they should do on two mornings a week for four or five years.

Although it was a commonplace of elocution that the reader or reciter could perform properly only if he understood his text, the manuals give him little guidance on how to do so. The advice they give concerns performance. Although the performance must be governed ultimately by an interpretation of the text the manuals' advice is nearly always at one remove from it. They give advice on how to express a particular emotion but they do not discuss what it is in the text that indicates the appropriateness of that emotion. The most that they achieve is a slight reference, as when the author of *Sheridan's and Henderson's Practical Method,* anticipating Joseph Warton, touches on the meaning of the first line of Gray's *Elegy.* He describes how 'the late Mr Henderson used to read *The curfew tolls the knell of parting day*':

1796 'The words *the knell of parting day* he delivered as if they were placed between a parenthesis, and if the scholar will repeat the line in the manner it is generally printed, and afterwards in the method adopted by that gentleman, we are convinced his own judgment will at once see the great superiority of the latter.'

(p. 2)

Joseph Robertson's three works, primarily guides to reading aloud, pay more attention to the meaning of what is to be read than do most elocutionary collections. Robertson is not teaching the pupils how to study a text but he is doing more than just point out its beauties.

General anthologies: works by Vicesimus Knox. A group of works by Vicesimus Knox, of which six are anthologies, should be considered together:

Essays, moral and literary		1778; 1779
Liberal Education		1781
Elegant Extracts (prose)	(cited as *Prose*)	1783
Elegant Extracts (poetry)	(cited as *Poetry*)	c. 1784
Elegant Epistles	(cited as *Epistles*)	1790
The Poetical Epitome		1791
The Prose Epitome	abridgements of above	1791
Models of Letters		1794

One of Knox's essays, added to the third edition of his 1778 volume, is 'On the Best Method of Exciting Literary Genius in Boys who Possess it'. There he states some of the views that influenced the schoolbooks he was compiling at the time, especially the importance of imaginative literature and the relative unimportance of commentary and explanation:

'Instead of exercising the understanding only at a very early age, I think, a considerable share of attention should be paid to the cultivation of the fancy. For this purpose, the most entertaining story-books should be read as an amusement. The more romantic, the better adapted to the purpose. The popular histories of giants and fairies, enchanted castles, and ideal beings of uncouth form, and whatever strongly strikes the imagination, or deeply affects the heart, is calculated to vivify the latent seeds of embryo genius. Many of those little books, which are sold by itinerant pedlars to children and servants, and which are thought too despicable to deserve the attention of the learned, have constituted the mental food of our sublimest writers in the age of infancy.'

He stresses again that the books must be read 'merely as a matter of entertainment . . . it would be ridiculous to read them as a task . . . they enable the soul to feel its lively energies expanding to strength and maturity'. It comes as something of a surprise, so soon after his consideration of 'the infant fancy', to find that he is speaking especially of Milton and Shakespeare:

'An objector may urge, that a young boy will often be at a loss to understand them. But let not this be regarded. Let him read on, and pass over what he does not understand ... his genius will be called forth much more powerfully, by dwelling on what he understands, and receiving a proper impression from it, than by stopping to develope difficulties with the coldness of a critic.'

(1778; 4th edition 1784, no. 72)

For prose reading Knox recommends *Robinson Crusoe, Don Quixote*, oriental tales from the periodicals, and those parts of the Bible 'which are so beautifully distinguished for simple sublimity and unaffected pathos'. In an earlier essay, 'On Novel Reading' (no. 18 in the second volume, 1779) discussing the reading of boys, he distinguished between romances, e.g. works by Fielding, Richardson, Smollett, Cervantes, of which he approves, and novels. He thinks novels are insipid, but he is unusual in saying that they do no harm: 'The futility of the modern Novel precludes its power of causing any other mischief, than the consumption of time that might be more usefully employed.' In *Liberal Education* he touches on organisation: 'As English cannot always conveniently be read in schools, and during school hours, it must be read in private by boys who wish to acquire a perfect knowledge of it' (p. 134). But, as will be seen, Knox is assuming three distinctions: between a classical school and an English school; between reading English and being taught English; between prose and poetry. In the classical school, where the boys are reading English in private, they are also being taught to take a page of the *Spectator* and parse it as is done with Latin and Greek (1781, p. 132). He is particularly scathing about the teaching of poetry, which he wishes to be taught, as well as read, in the classical school:

'The mode of pursuing the study of poetry, received in some schools, is certainly absurd and inefficacious. It is usual to place in the boy's hands some superficial treatise, intitled the Art of Poetry. This puzzles him with rules which he hardly understands, and presents him with a train of dry and unentertaining ideas ... What can be expected when a youthful genius is put under the guidance of such critics as Byshe [sic] and Gildon?'   (1781, p. 193)

What then should the teacher do? He should read aloud to the boys and then give them Milton, Shakespeare and Pope to read, keeping to the great poets until the boys' taste is formed (p. 194).

In the prefaces to the anthologies Knox's attitude is more cautious: 'Since Poetry affords young persons an innocent pleasure, a taste for it, under certain limitations, should be indulged ... There is no good reason ... why the mercantile classes, at least of the higher order, should not amuse their leisure with any pleasures of polite literature' (*Poetry*, preface). The books are 'calculated for classical schools, and for those in which English only is taught' (*Prose*, preface to second edition), and would 'be useful to young persons . . . while they were cultivating an acquaintance with the ancients' (*Epistles*, preface). In the preface to *Poetry* Knox shows that his earlier and more general remarks about the teaching of literature must not be given too 'liberal' an interpretation. The extracts 'may be usefully read at ENGLISH SCHOOLS *in classes*, just as the Latin and Greek authors are read at the *grammar-schools*, by explaining every thing grammatically, historically, metrically, and critically'.

The books are fat octavos: both *Prose* and *Epistles* contain over 1000 pages in their early editions; *Poetry* contains 900 pieces, *Prose* more than 800. It was not only a price of 5 guineas that made abridgments necessary. In each anthology the material is divided into four books, but the classification is necessarily imprecise. In *Poetry* and in *Prose* the first book is for 'sacred and moral' pieces, and the fourth book contains 'humorous, facetious pieces' (*Prose*) or 'an appendix of ludicrous poems' (*Poetry*). Although 'ludicrous' carries its earlier sense of 'recreational' it is surprising to find Watts' *Divine songs* here among the epigrams, songs and ballads. The age range for which the anthologies are intended is so wide that almost any kind of writing could be appropriate, and many ephemeral authors are represented by a single extract. In *Poetry* authors given particular attention, judged quantitatively, are: Pope, pre-eminently, a quarter of the 127 extracts being from his *Homer*; Spenser, 100 extracts, most of them short descriptive pieces; Milton, Shakespeare, Thomson, between 30 and 40 pieces each (*Lycidas, Il Penseroso* and *L'Allegro* being given in full). In *Prose* a third of the 128 extracts are from the sermons of Hugh Blair; there are 68 extracts from the periodicals, of which 22 are from the *Spectator*, and substantial quotation from James Harris, Robert Bolton's *Letters*, Hume and Smollett.

In spite of their size and price Knox's anthologies were popular: *Poetry*, by itself, had at least fifteen British editions to 1824 and at least three American ones to 1826. *Prose* also had about twelve British editions to 1824, and four American ones to 1826. *Epistles* had about twelve editions in Britain, but none, apparently, in America. In addition there were British and American issues of the three anthologies together. The abridgments seem to have been less popular, the only one to have a second edition being *The Poetical Epitome*. It would be useful to know more about the publishing and sales history of these influential books, many editions of which are undated. Is it a sensible guess, for instance, that the full volumes sold well because there was nothing like them, but the abridgments were in competition with many of the anthologies described below?

General anthologies: for home and for school. The remaining works illustrate
the variety of anthologies which were directly or indirectly intended for
school use. Of those indirectly intended for school, a first group were
probably directed principally to the home:

Beauties of English Prose	1772
The Amusing Instructor	1777
Beauties of Fables	1780
Fenn: *The Rational Dame*	[1790?]
Modern Beauties	1793
Mavor: *Youth's Miscellany*	1798
Mavor: *The Juvenile Olio*	1796
Mental Amusement	1797
Mavor: *The Nursery Garland*	1801
Mavor: *A Father's Gift*	1805

Only two of these require notice. *The Rational Dame* is 'a companion for
young mothers' to enable them to answer children's questions, especially
on natural history, but it was also introduced in Ackworth School as a class
reading-book in 1800. *Mental Amusement* is of interest for its eighteenth
chapter, 'On Education and Books', a conversation between two mothers.
Mrs Danby fears that 'religious truths are almost frittered away' in what
young people read. Mrs Aikin thinks that such truths can be found also in
secular literature, but they both agree in condemning 'romances and
novels' on the grounds that they are read 'too early in life, when the heart
embraces fictions as reality, and in time loses its sympathy for real objects of
distress, when they are not tricked out in the trappings of sentiment' (an
argument put forward at the same time by the Edgeworths, below, p. 209).
Mrs Danby wants no more than 'our whole family library, which had been
formed in the reign of Queen Anne' and consisted of 'two large Bibles and
three small ones – *The Whole Duty of Man* – *The Complete House-wife* – and
our only romance was Bunyan's *Pilgrim's Progress*'. Mrs Aikin thinks this
'rather a confined collection' (pp. 75–81).

A second group of anthologies was probably intended more for school
than for home:

The Polite Preceptor	1774
The Polite Preceptor	
(a different work)	1776
The Poetical Preceptor	1777
Devis	1782
G. Wright	a. 1782

Tomkins	a. 1785
Andrews	[a. 1800]
Wisdom in Miniature	1785
Elegant Poems	1791
J.B. Webster	*c.* 1800
Aikin	1801
Beauties of Modern Literature	1802

Several of these explicitly state that they are for use in school, but in style and sometimes in content they are derived from the tradition of home reading. Because authors and publishers were deliberately aiming at both markets it is natural that there are books that belong equally to either of the categories into which they might be put. Wright's *The Young Moralist* is a compilation 'from various miscellanies' designed to be 'a pleasing antidote to the poison' imbibed by young people from 'the noxious ingredients which modern novels, romances, and suchlike publications, are principally made up of' (preface). *Wisdom in Miniature* is difficult to classify. It is a collection of short, aphoristic pieces, without sources; they are grouped under various headings: e.g. 'Envy and Detraction', 'Of the Government of the Passions', 'Wealth, Luxury and the Pursuit of Pleasure'. The book is explicitly for schools, and was immensely popular, with British editions until at least 1845 and American ones until at least 1833. Characteristic of these collections are Webster's *The Domestic Instructor* and Lucy Aikin's *Poetry for Children*. Webster's anthology 'for private families and public schools' is distinctive for its emphasis on the exotic, as recommended by Knox and of established popularity in the periodicals. Lucy Aikin's 'short pieces to be committed to the memory' are pedagogic in tone but undirected as between home and school, as is the collection *Elegant Poems*, which comprises only Pope's *Essay on Man* and *Universal Prayer*; Gray's *Elegy* and *The Fatal Sisters*; Blair's *The Grave*. There is no preface, nor any indication of its intended readership. The selected poems are all frequently represented in school anthologies.

General anthologies: for school. Of thirty-five collections made for school use during this period only about half contained a substantial proportion of verse; these are analysed below. Of the remainder some were wholly prose, such as J.H. Moore's *The Young Gentleman and Lady's Monitor, c.* 1760, containing passages from the periodicals and the Bible, very popular also in America (Belok, 1973, p. 57) and W.F. Mavor's *The British Nepos*, 1798, biographies of famous Britons, reprinted until 1838, in America as well as in Britain. Many collections were mixed, usually containing more prose than verse; such were: *Essays in Prose and Verse*, 1774; Cresswick's *The*

Lady's Preceptor, 1792, and in America Webster's *A Grammatical Institute*, Part 3 (*An American Selection*) and the collections by Bingham, 1794; Caleb Alexander, 1797; and Mathew Carey, 1800.

Two themes recur in these anthologies (or one theme with its inversion): a fear of passion, and a preoccupation with morality. The elocutionists had immobilised the passions by pinning them down in lists and talking about them, but the anthologists were handling free material. Even though by 'passion' they usually mean no more than 'feeling' the word retains always its suggestion of a power that it is difficult to control. But what is poetry, what is fiction, without feeling?

1792   'The design of Poetry is to excite the passions, and to give us a perfect and substantial pleasure; but it ought not to stir up any passion but those which it is of consequence to keep in motion[,] never such as are contrary to wisdom and virtue.'
(Cresswick, p. 274)

(1794) 1797   The compiler 'has not given place to romantic fiction . . . Pleasing and interesting stories, exemplifying moral virtues, were judged best calculated to engage the attention and improve the heart. Tales of love have not gained admission.'   (Caleb Bingham of Boston, preface)

1801   The poems 'wake . . . no passion, except what the purest hearts may feel; they fan no flame, that youthful innocence need blush to own.'
(Mavor and Pratt, preface)

At this period, and until well into the nineteenth century, three responses were commonly made by school anthologists to the question of how to handle the potential power of imaginative literature. The most frequent response was to restrain literature, both poetry and prose fiction, by imposing on it a straitjacket of moral comment and interpretation. A similar result was achieved, for fiction especially, by the converse practice of putting factual instructional material (geology, geography, natural history) into an overtly fictional framework. The third response, applied mainly to poetry and less evident in eighteenth-century texts than in later ones, was to treat literature as a vehicle for memory training. J.H. Moore, 1784, favoured the first response, recommending 'books abounding with moral instructions', and Lindley Murray expressed it in words that even in late-eighteenth-century conditions must surely have been piously unrealistic:

1800   'Perhaps the best reason that can be offered, in favour of poetical selections for the use of young and innocent minds, is, the tendency which they have, when properly made, to preserve the chastity of their sentiments, and the purity of their morals.'   (preface)

Views of this kind, applied to poetry and to fiction, were common. Their tone could be cool, as when Mme de Genlis says, in her translator's words, that her dialogues are all written 'in a language perfectly simple, always sacrificing imagination to morality' (1800, p. 24) or it could be shrill, as when David Morrice cries, 'The less the little works you select have the spirit of *romance* in them . . . the better . . . [You should avoid] that intoxicating, reason-perverting, and effeminating poison of the mind, termed Novels' (1801, p. 137). Hannah More is sometimes associated with such views, and she certainly deplored the awfulness of novels being read aloud by a girl to a workshop of milliners, and even in hospital wards ((1799) 1800, p. 31), but her objections were thoughtful. She was worried that girls, especially, were damaged intellectually as well as morally by superficial reading:

'The imagination being liable to be worked upon, and the feelings to be set a-going, much faster than the understanding can be opened and the judgment enlightened . . . girls who have been accustomed to devour a multitude of frivolous books, will converse and write with a far greater appearance of skill as to style and sentiment at twelve or fourteen years old, than those of a more advanced age who are under the discipline of severer studies.'   (pp. 120–1)

She deplores 'the swarms of *Abridgments, Beauties* and *Compendiums*' that promote superficial knowledge: 'This extract-reading, while it accommodates itself to the convenience, illustrates the character of the age in which we live.' Vanity and an appetite for pleasure encourage 'little snatches of ornamental reading', whereas what is needed is 'dry, tough reading' (pp. 122–3; 126).

Lucy Aikin is opposed to the rationalising materialism of Lindley Murray but she shares the current fear of novel-reading, on grounds not unlike those advanced by Hannah More:

1801 'Since dragons and fairies, giants and witches, have vanished from our nurseries before the wand of reason, it has been a prevailing maxim, that the young mind should be fed on mere prose and simple matter of fact. A fear, rational and laudable in its origin, of adding, by superstitious and idle terrors, to the natural weakness of childhood, or contaminating, by any thing false or impure, its simplicity and innocence – has, by some writers, and some parents, been carried to so great an excess, that probably no work would be considered by them as unexceptionable for the use of children, in which any scope was allowed to the fanciful or marvellous.'   (preface)

She goes on to ask whether novels are not educationally more harmful than fairy tales: 'whether a romantic sensibility be not an evil, more formidable in magnitude, and protracted in duration, than a wild and exalted fancy'. This debate about the educational effects of imaginative literature was continued throughout much of the nineteenth century and is reflected in the texts yet to be considered.

Some of the anthologists, especially those in America, seek out modern work, and contemporary poets are represented more quickly than the repetitious nature of the anthologies might lead one to expect. Wordsworth's *The Pet Lamb*, first published in 1800, appeared the following year in Lindley Murray's *Introduction to the English Reader*. Burns, from the editions of 1786 and 1787, appears in John Adams' *The English Parnassus*, 1789; in Hodgson's *The Hive* (1799) 1806, and in Mavor and Pratt's *Classical English Poetry*, 1801.[1]

The American anthologists increasingly but irregularly draw on American sources, in prose more than in verse. Noah Webster, 1785, excluding anonymous passages, uses only addresses to Congress and two pieces from Tom Paine, but in the third edition, 1787, he changes the title to *An American Selection* and the contents shed much European literature in order to emphasise 'the Geography, History, and Politics of the United States'. Joseph Dana, although his anthology of 1792, *A New American Selection*, echoes Webster, scarcely uses American writers, relying mostly on Vicesimus Knox's *Elegant Extracts*. In Caleb Bingham's *The American Preceptor*, 1794, and in its sequel *The Columbian Orator*, at least half the sources are American. Matthew Carey's *The School of Wisdom*, 1800, although highly political and republican in its attitude, draws mostly on European writers.

Analysis of the anthologies, 1771–1801

Although, for reasons already given, any analysis of the anthologies must be confined to their superficial aspects, it may be of interest to see the result of an attempt at some comparative figures. In Table 6 the anthologies are listed in chronological order and are marked '(Pr)' if they contain prose pieces also. The analysis is limited to verse; prose pieces are too diverse in their sources and too often unattributed. 'Pieces' may seem rather a simpering term, but it was regularly used by the compilers: the pieces are not all extracts; many are whole poems. The number of verse pieces in each anthology is shown in the last column and includes the number (in round brackets) of unattributed pieces. The poet, or poets, most frequently represented appear in column 1; the next most frequent in column 2, and so on for the first four ranking places. The figures in these columns show the

---

[1] The four pieces in Adams are 'On the happiness of an active life', i.e. stanza 2 of *Despondency*; 'An address to the Deity in the view of Dissolution', i.e. *A Prayer in the Prospect of Death*; 'On the influence of gloomy and stormy weather on the author's mind', i.e. stanzas 2 and 3 of *Winter, a Dirge; Inscriptions upon the Monuments of Thomson, Milton and Gray*. In Hodgson, the *Epistle to a young Friend*; in Mavor and Pratt part of *The Cotter's Saturday Night* and *A Winter Night*.

Table 6. *British school anthologies, 1771–1801*

		Order of frequency			no. of pieces incl. (unatt.)
	1	2	3	4	
1776 Perry (Pr)[a]	{ Milton, Pope, Shakespeare } 8	Gay 5	Thomson 3	–	58
1777 *Poetical Preceptor*	Shakespeare 76	Milton 29	{ Pope, Thomson } 20	{ Addison, Rowe } 11	200
1781 Barrie[b] (Pr)	Milton 7	Shakespeare 5	Addison 3	–	42 (22)
1783 *Beauties* (Pr)	{ Cunningham, Shenstone } 4	{ Eliz. Carter, Drummond, Goldsmith } 2	–		33 (8)
a. 1785 Tomkins	Pope 6	Thomson 5	{ Eliz. Carter, Cunningham } 4	{ Addison, Gray, Milton } 3	65 (12)
1789 Adams	Pope 20	{ H. and M. Falconar } 15	Cowper 12	Thomson 9	185
1793 *Bee*	Cowper 5	{ Pope, Thomson } 5	{ Akenside, Eliz. Carter, Mason, Young } 3	–	58
1793 Scott (Pr)	Shakespeare 8	Thomson 7	Milton 6	Goldsmith 4	66
1796 Hill	Doddridge 9	Anne Steele 7	Cotton 6	{ Simon Browne, Jos. Fawcett, Watts } 5	128
a. 1798 Holland (Pr)	Watts 26	Thomson 13	Shakespeare 7	Byrom 6	158

Anthology	Poet 1	n	Poet(s) 2	n	Poet(s) 3	n	Poet(s) 4	n	Total
1799 Hodgson (Pr)	Cunningham	4	T. Bedingfield, Cowper, S. Johnson, Pope, Shakespeare, Capt. E. Thomson, Thomson	2	—	—		—	42
1799 L. Murray[c] (Pr)	Cowper	9	Thomson	8	Pope	6	Addison, Young	5	56
1800 L. Murray (Pr)	Young	5	Goldsmith, Ogilvie	4	Barbauld, Parnell	3	Gray	2	37
1801 L. Murray (Pr)	Watts	12	Cotton	7	Pope	3	—	—	57
1801 Mavor (*Garland*)	Watts	11	Cowper, Thomson	6	Cunningham, Pope	5	Barbauld, Eliz. Carter, Mavor, Parnell	4	114
1801 Mavor *New Speaker*[d] (Pr)	Mavor	3	Ogilvie, Pratt, Charlotte Smith, Thomson	2	—	—		—	28
1801 Mavor and Pratt[e]	Langhorne	19	Pratt	9	Cowper, Cunningham, Pope	8	Parnell	7	286
1801 L. Aikin	Pope	22	Dryden	17	Addison, L. Aikin	10	Darwin, Gray	7	180 (13)
1801 *Elegant Selections* (Pr)	Wolcot	7	Gray, Pope	4	Cowper, T. Warton	3	—	—	67 (23)

Note:
a (Pr) = prose pieces also
b Pieces by Addison are all from *Cato*.
c There is no Shakespeare in any of Murray's anthologies.
d Poets represented by only one work include Johnson (*Vanity of Human Wishes*), Pope (*Messiah*), Parnell (*Hermit*).
e Epic and dramatic poetry are excluded by the compilers.

Table 7. *Authors in Table 6*
by frequency of representation

by number of rankings		order
Pope	12	1
Thomson	11	2
Cowper	7	3
Shakespeare	6	4
Addison	5	5=
J. Cunningham	5	5=
Milton	5	5=
Elizabeth Carter	4	8=
Watts	4	8=
Goldsmith	3	10=
Young	3	10=

number of pieces by which each author is represented. Often in the case of a small anthology the fourth place, and sometimes the third, cannot be significantly allocated. The warning must be repeated that the number of pieces is only a partial indication of the potential influence of an author. Gray's *Elegy* for instance is often the only work of his to be included, and the representation of Young probably does not do justice to his influence.

A number of obvious factors make it dangerous to press these figures very far. There are too few anthologies for statistical treatment, some with many unattributed pieces; the anthologies are intended for readers of varying, if overlapping ages; three of the anthologies reflect the opinions (and the self-esteem) of one editor, W.F. Mavor, and another three those of Lindley Murray. Editorial criteria vary: Elizabeth Hill models her selection on Watts' *Divine Songs*; Lindley Murray excludes Shakespeare, and others exclude dramatic verse. Nevertheless, allowing for all these factors, it is of some interest to see the extent to which individual poets are represented (Table 7). That Pope and Thomson should at this time be considered more suitable for school reading than Shakespeare is not surprising. Cowper, from the impression on reading the anthologies, would seem to have been equally approved by teachers, but the figures do not bear this out; the impression is both confirmed and modified by the figures for the nineteenth century in Table 9.

John Walker and John Wesley. The pre-eminence given to Pope in verse and to Addison in prose is expressed also in John Walker's *English Classics Abridged*, 1786. Walker says that he is following the advice of Knox to confine young people to three or four authors. His selections are therefore limited to Pope (*Essay on Criticism*; *Essay on Man*), Addison and Milton (*Paradise Lost*). Addison's essays are 'particularly adapted to young people' because they entertain while they instruct, and 'tend to form a just taste'. Pope's *Essay on Criticism* is chosen because in spite of its faults 'its beauties are so predominant as to make it justly the favourite of all readers ... and ... under the direction of a Christian tutor, it may be read with great advantage'. In all the selections the reader 'will be candid enough to excuse any slight alterations of the authors ... when he considers to whom the selections are addressed'. In each of Pope's poems about a tenth has in fact been omitted, but *Paradise Lost* has not just been tinkered with: it has been systematically abridged. Thirty-six per cent is retained overall, but continuity is kept through intermittent prose summaries, on average two in each book. Walker, unlike twentieth-century examiners, does not emphasise Books 1 and 2. The book of which he retains most is Book 8 (57 per cent); least is retained of Books 3 and 10 (21 per cent and 19 per cent).

John Wesley had conducted in 1763 what may be called the same operation on Milton. Wesley's intentions had been not so much to shorten as to simplify, because 'this inimitable Work, amidst all its beauties, is unintelligible to abundance of Readers'. He therefore omitted 'those lines, which I despaired of explaining to the unlearned'. Wesley and Walker had different immediate purposes but they had in common the desire to make *Paradise Lost* more accessible. Naturally Wesley retained more than Walker did, 81 per cent overall, whereas Walker kept only 36 per cent; but they differ also in their judgments about the proportion to be retained in individual books. The book of which Wesley retains most is Book 6, and he retains least of Book 1. Walker puts Book 6 tenth in the order ranked by the proportion of text that is retained, and Book 1 fifth. A curious feature of the comparison is that Walker, who might have been expected (because he was only abbreviating the text) to retain roughly the same proportion of each book, varied the proportion far more than Wesley, who was simplifying and might therefore have been expected to vary the amount of his retentions with the difficulty of the text. But the range of Walker's retentions is 38 points, from 19 per cent (Book 10) to 57 per cent (Book 8); whereas Wesley's range is only seventeen points, from 72 per cent (Book 1) to 89 per cent (Book 6). There are too many variables even in these similar operations for any conclusion to be drawn other than that Wesley's and Walker's judgments about the poem differed considerably, and even that conclusion is uninformative until we know (should anyone think it worthwhile to investigate it) how far the passages excluded by Wesley are amongst those excluded by Walker.

Teachers' comments on English reading, 1698–1801

During the eighteenth century the evidence from textbooks is supplemented by much comment from writers on education. To list merely the titles of the relevant books would be unhelpful. A collection of quotations can be misleading because the context is missing; nevertheless these expressions of opinion are important. They show that writers who are thinking of varying kinds of pupil (those taught at home, in the upper forms of grammar schools or as students, in the lower forms of grammar schools and private schools, in specifically English schools, and in charity schools) are increasingly giving thought to what pupils should read and, less often, to the question whether they can be helped, or taught, to read more fully. The following extracts therefore are arranged chronologically with an indication, as concise as possible, of their context. The full title of the work from which the extract comes, which is often informative, is given in Bibliography.

1698 Robert Ainsworth is proposing a small boarding school to be used by 'Gentlemen, Tradesmen, and all Persons, who do not design their Children for Scholars'. In part the education is to be vocational, including book-keeping; in part social: 'learning the Art of a decent *Carriage* and *Comportment* with a Dancing-Master'. Latin would not be taught. Instead the pupil would concentrate on 'reading the best ENGLISH *Writers*, polishing and perfecting his ENGLISH *Style*'.

(p. 30)

1701 Francis Brokesby, who is discussing grammar-school and university education, says in passing that grammar schools do little to fit boys for trade except that they 'help them to spell English better, by that knowledge they get in Latin' (p. 4). His approval of the teaching of English poetry is cautious. He is comfortable with the teaching of prosody, and with heroic poetry or hymns, both of which recommend virtuous actions (p. 25). He is less comfortable with dramatic poetry, but will allow its 'sparing use' provided it is not such as will 'provoke laughter, or evaporate the mind into froth and vanity, or excite some amorous passion' (p. 112). Less conventional is the importance he attaches to pupils being taught to understand what they read. His fear that children will be deceived by dishonest or inaccurate writing is the prosaic counterpart to his fear that their morals will be corrupted by 'prophane or lascivious' verse: 'We should endeavour that Childrens Notions of things from the first may be as clear and true, as their age is capable of forming . . . Now tho' it be impossible, but that such as converse with the Vulgar should imbibe vulgar Errors: Yet when we take occasion to discover to them, how much they are deceived by relying on such Authors; they will afterwards become more inquisitive into the truth of things, and not suffer themselves to be imposed on for the future, nor easily give credit to what is told them that is rare and strange, till they have Reason or better Authority to confirm the truth thereof.' (p. 56)

1712 The second edition of Gildon's *A Grammar of the English Tongue*, 1711, contained 'An Essay on an English Education', itself part of a longer 'Reasons for an

English Education'. The author, in spite of his wish to strengthen the teaching of English, sees poetry in education as serving merely a moral purpose. His view is so narrow that it seems to caricature the worst aspects of this kind of educational and literary criticism: Locke 'knew very well that Numbers had a natural Power on the Soul; and, therefore, that it will be impossible wholly to banish *Poetry* from Mankind . . . The Question therefore is, Whether this Art, which we have found to be in our very Nature, shou'd be Rude and Barbarous, or Polite and Regular. The first can give nothing but a rude and barbarous Pleasure, the later has been, may be, and always indeed ought to be, directed to the Advancement of Virtue, and the Improvement of our Manners, by correcting the predominant Passions of the Mind, an Indulgence of which produces so much Evil to Humane Life, or to the Praise of God, which wonderfully raises and inflames the Soul with Divine Love and Ardour. The first is done by *Tragedy*, and some part by *Comedy*; the later by *Hymns* and *Psalms*.' (pp. 20–1, first enumeration)

1713 Henry Felton, writing in 1709 for 'a young Nobleman of sprightly Parts', is very general in his recommendation of English authors, and of the miscellanies, all of which are 'admirable'. He does not expect too much from his pupil; he expresses the accepted view that 'a good Taste is to be formed by reading the best Authors', and he looks to the time 'when Your Lordship shall be able to point out their Beauties'. (p. 150)

1713 At the opposite end of the social scale is the reading-list suggested in *Lessons for Children . . . for the use of a charity-school in the country*. The writer supports the view that 'Children would sooner come to read *English* well, if they were not constantly kept to read the Bible, but were sometimes put to read other Books.' A reading-list follows: twenty-six items, a few of which are sufficient to suggest the tone of them all and the extent to which reading in such a school might attain variety:

No. 2 *Dr Clark's three Practical Essays on Baptism, Repentance, and Confirmation.*
No. 5 *A Persuasive to a serious Preparation for Death and Judgment.*
No. 8 *A Dissuasive from the Sin of Drunkenness.*

1714 John Edwards expresses a similar awareness of human sinfulness, in respect of which the enjoyment of literature is a trivial distraction. The opening words of his survey of human knowledge and learning are: 'We live in a dark World, and are misled into wrong Conceptions of things, because the ignorant and insane have here the majority of votes.' It is only natural, therefore, that his chapter on poetry should begin: 'Verse is Words put into a *Wanton-Posture*; it is *Playing* and *Fidling* upon them. If we will speak truly and impartially, 'tis Violence put both on Words and Things . . . All Versifying is unnatural, strain'd, and out of order' especially rhymed verse. '. . . This Poetic Age hath prov'd the most Atheistical and Immoral' (pp. 17–18). It is necessary to bear in mind that such views were sincerely held and were as influential in the education of children as the more congenial praise of literature that we like to quote.

1730 A similar fear of poetry is expressed by John Clarke, Master of the Grammar School at Hull, in the second edition (1730) of his *Essay upon the Education of Youth*, 1720. He approves of children being taught to write English, which is 'of infinitely more Use and Importance than the Writing and Speaking of Latin' (p. 116), but he disapproves of poetry because it tends to lead boys into ruin and debauchery (pp. 69–70). In his *An Essay upon Study*, 1731, although conceding that a knowledge of Latin and Greek poetry 'furnishes the Mind with a most delicious and charming Entertainment' (p. 46) and that 'it is, indeed, the highest and noblest of all Diversions' (p. 194), he nevertheless expresses what appears to be his stronger opinion that 'it can not, I think, be made subservient to any *important* Purpose of Life, where Prose will not do as well, or much better' (*ibid.*).

1731 Thomas Stackhouse, writing with the grammar school in mind, suggests that teachers should 'have some of our best Authors, both in Verse and Prose, read in a *Classical* manner to their Pupils, and Exercises of all Kinds perform'd in their *Mother Tongue*' (p. 195). The implication of 'classical' is that the English text should be studied closely in the way that Greek and Roman schoolboys were supposed to have 'had their own Authors read to them, their Beauties pointed out, and the Stile and Order of the whole Composition laid open and desected' (*ibid.*).

1733 Isaac Barker, a teacher in Whitby, says in the preface to his English grammar that the pupils, once they have a general knowledge of grammar, 'should spend much of their Time in reading the easiest and most instructive Histories, whether true or fabulous, and be directed in the *Course of their Reading* to make such Observations upon the *Language* as are most material'. The suggestion that the reading should provide substance for teaching is even more unusual than the recommendation that the pupils should read fiction. The context makes it clear that Barker is writing about English, not Latin.

1743 James Barclay is one of the few teachers who question whether the journals are suitable for the younger pupils in a grammar school: 'In reading, I would always put such *English* books in their hands as they were fond of, and understood. Our *Spectators, Guardians*, and the like . . . are above the apprehension of children.'

(p. 64)

a. 1747 William Foot, writing also about the grammar school, takes the opposite view: 'A Master should esteem it an important Part of his Business, to bring his Pupils to speak, and write *English*, properly and neatly. To which End they should often read to him some Author, (the *Spectator* for Example) that is a Standard of good Style.'

1748 Caleb Fleming's *A Modern Plan* is only indirectly concerned with the curriculum, but it is meant to be read by young people. One section of the work, 'Of the Imagination', seems to suggest that some of the moralist's anxiety about the effects of imaginative literature derives from the power of dream imagery: poetry and romances and dreams belong to a world where feelings are 'too strong':
'*Tutor* [Imagination is] that power of the soul, by which it formeth images of things; which it does thro' means of impressions made on the brain, by sensation . . . In your sleep, when you have dreams, they are of this sort; which, when you awake and consider them as only the workings of the imagination, you regard them but as dreams . . .
Youth Is it then of great use?
Tutor It is; but then it may give wrong characters or marks of things, and so be very harmful.

Youth When may I know it to be harmful?
Tutor When it paints objects in false colours, or in too strong ones.'

(pp. 21–3)

1748   James Todd observes that writers on education have hitherto concerned themselves with 'People of Quality . . . while the more obscure Gentry, as well as those in low life have been intirely neglected' (Intro.). He gives some indication of the reading he would recommend for those more interested in 'Arithmetick and Practical Geometry than what is stiled the polite literature': a 'syllabicating Catechism for a spelling Book', then *Proverbs*, Aesop, the New Testament, selections from the *Spectator*, Pope's *Essay on Criticism*. Ballads should be read only at home (p. 64).

1750   S. Butler, 'a gentleman of Bristol', is uncertain about the novelty of his remarks, 'for Treatises upon *Education* are so numerous, that it is a Matter of some Difficulty to write upon the Subject' (p. 114). One of Butler's recommendations is that grammar-school boys should read some English literature in school: 'It frequently happens that a Boy hath not had so much as one *English Author* recommended to him all the Time he hath been at School; and if he hath read any English Book besides the *Bible*, and the *Translations* of the Classicks, it must have been done chiefly at a *leisure Hour*, and very seldom by the Direction of his Master. There are many Boys in the highest Class of some Schools, who hardly know that any thing hath been wrote in our own Language worth reading, unless a *Play* or a *Spectator* hath accidentally fallen in their Way . . . How easily might an Hour or two be allotted each Day at a *Grammar School*, for the Study of *English;* without hindring such a Progress in *Latin* and *Greek*, as is necessary . . . What if an *English Exercise* were appointed each Week, or rather more often, in our *Schools* and *Universities*; and were to be spoken in publick?'   (pp. 54–5, 69)

a. 1752   John Williams' recommendation of newspapers was quoted above, p. 178. For the reading of 'beginners' he recommends Bolingbroke, Swift, Addison, Dryden's prefaces; the Earl of Orrery's Letters; Sir William Temple's essays, and 'speeches in Parliament' (p. 24). For more advanced pupils his suggestions are so numerous as to be unselective.

1754   Benjamin Martin, discussing the curriculum of an English school, attacks the practice of using the Bible as a reading-book: 'When a Youth can mutter over a Chapter . . . full of hard Names, (as the Tenth of *Nehemiah* is the usual *Test*) he is then reputed a notable Proficient, and represented to his Parents, as the *Captain of the School.*' The disrepute into which the Bible falls as a schoolbook 'bedrivelled, daubed, and pulled to Pieces' may foster deism and infidelity.   (preface)

1756   Thomas Sheridan the younger, writing from the point of view of a teacher of elocution, deplores the neglect of English once boys 'are got into Latin' (p. 97). He recognises that the status of English as a subject is affected by the quality of its teachers: 'Nor can it be doubted, that if the means of acquiring skill in the English were as easy and common, if it could be taught by as certain rules, and the preceptors were as knowing in that as in the learned languages, infinitely a greater number would apply themselves to a critical study of that, both from views of interest and inclination, than to the others' (p. 223). He uses the same argument in the *Heads of a Plan for the Improvement of Elocution* in his *A Course of Lectures*, 1762.

1759 Goldsmith objects to the romances in which a dissolute youth is followed by a wealthy marriage: 'The old story of Whittington, were his cat left out, might be more serviceable to the tender mind, than either *Tom Jones, Joseph Andrews*, or an hundred others . . . Were our school-masters, if any of them have sense enough to draw up such a work, thus employed it would be much more serviceable to their pupils than all the grammars and dictionaries they may publish these ten years.'

(*The Bee*, No. 6)

1767 William Ward, writing of his own grammar school in Yorkshire, joins in the general commendation of the *Spectator*: 'We, at this School, have daily Occasion to observe this [the conformity to rule of Addison's style] in our Teaching; for we make much Use of the *Spectator* as an English Classic.'   (preface, p. x)

1770 James Buchanan, discussing the curriculum of 'an English grammar-school', urges that English literature should be taught, but the method he describes is rudimentary: 'youth should be constantly exercised in reading some of the best English classics . . . The master should point out to them the beauties in style and sentiment, and give them a taste of poetry' (p. 116). In an important paragraph he expresses not only the usual view that literature helps 'to inculcate the principles of religion and morality', but the more profound view (later to become almost a platitude) that literature develops both the emotions and the intellect; its most beautiful passages 'tend to mend the heart, at the same time that they enlighten the understanding' (*ibid.*).

1770 In the same year Ann Fisher was making robust recommendations to her pupils in the spirit, if not in the style, of Buchanan: 'For Ease, Elegance, Invention, and Humour, read *Addison*; for Ease and natural Humour, *Swift*; for Conciseness, Elegance, and nervous Sense, *Hume*; for the most flowing, florid, metaphorical Stile, *Seed*; for the truest, boldest, poetic Stile, *Shakespeare*; for an expressive, rich, glowing Stile, *Hawkesworth*, particularly his Eastern Stories in the *Adventurer*.'

(p. 41)

1772 Especially interesting is J. Butler's *Proposals for an Amendment of School Instruction*, which includes the most detailed account yet offered of a method of teaching English literature. The author's main themes are that Latin should be taught only to those who can profit from it, and that all children, even the poorest, should be taught to read, so that the able ones would not be debarred from self-improvement. The proposals for English teaching are too full to be discussed in detail here, but they are so potentially important for the development of the subject that they must be described. 'English' is for the author unquestionably the name of a subject. He refers to the part of the day 'allotted to English tuition' (p. 48), and to the 'Master for English', who would seldom be capable (he says) of teaching much else (p. 62). His general proposals are arranged for younger boys, for the middle school and for higher classes; his proposals for English teaching (and he is concerned almost solely with literature) are based on the 'Collection'. This is a graded anthology of pieces, beginning with two-line verses or aphorisms and extending through extracts of increasing length to whole works. He speaks as if the Collection would be largely, if not wholly, verse. It would last a pupil at least the three years he spent in the first class, and perhaps the next three years, in the second class. In schools of more than two classes (about forty boys in all) more provision would have to be made. He believes that the needs of schools are so individual that a generally used textbook (collection) would not be practicable (p. 29) but that neighbouring schools might co-operate by making manuscript copies of pieces that they found useful and thus building up a shared collection, which might even find a commercial publisher (p. 35).

For younger boys, who have a 'strong imitative faculty', the extracts should exemplify 'an habitual clearness, as well of thought and discourse as style and writing'. Such extracts would make it easier for the teacher to counteract 'the bad habits . . . of fancying you understand what you don't, or understanding by halves, or of being inattentive to, or absent from, what is set before you as an object of understanding' (p. 11). The author is careful not to condemn strong feelings: 'Neither will warmth of style be inconsistent with the simplicity so much insisted on: it is the union of these that touches the heart' (p. 13). But 'even the forcible and sublime style, and that of the passions if highly figurative, is to be withheld from the lowest class, and not to be produced to youths afterwards, but as their faculties advance and ripen, to meet and fully comprehend it . . .' The youngest boys 'are not to be accosted *from a book*, in strains much above or very different from what they have heard in speech' (p. 12).

In the middle school 'before almost any entire poems were read, might not extracts be made from them, complete in themselves, and quite intelligible?' The only example the author gives is Pope's *Man of Ross* (*Moral Essays*, 3, 250–90), a frequent anthology piece. Then could come 'Poems and Works of Imagination. Longer and entire poems . . . addressed chiefly (in all instances but that of the highest class in the greatest schools) to the imagination, will be respectively adapted, as they are proper, to the use of every forme above the lowest' (p. 28). The implication that the most senior pupils have transcended imaginative literature is puzzling. 'Adapted' means 'applied'; it does not imply alterations to the text. For the older pupils the writer also expects 'abundant other English reading out of school-hours and at home' (p. 56).

The author differs from most eighteenth-century writers on education in priding himself on giving attention to practical matters. He sees himself as promoting the ideas of Locke, and transferring them from the private home to the (private) school. He realises that it will be difficult to find good teachers of English: 'No Master almost has regarded English; but all have stuck to Latin' because 'extraordinary negligence in a Master, must, in the case of English, soon manifest itself' to the parents, who are more able to detect shortcomings in a teacher of English than in one of Latin (pp. 101–3).

The author makes what must be a very early reference to the difficulty of assessing competence in English. In subjects like geometry and arithmetic, which he calls 'determinate acquisitions, where every step of the progress is distinctly marked', it can be 'more certainly known that neither the master nor the scholar has been idle' than is possible when judging 'proficiency in English learning'. Even so, in geometry and arithmetic 'it would be very difficult to come at a knowledge of the progress made, and . . . generally for want of able Examiners, less would be known of this progress, be the tests ever so determinate, than in that of literature', where the parents can judge (pp. 61–2). The author's practical advice refers also to the teaching of reading: to train the pupils 'to *carry the eye forward*, and become perfect master of the following clauses of a sentence ere you pronounce that directly before you' (p. 38). He advises the teacher to interrupt as little as possible while a child is reading, and he gives a timetable for the organisation of two reading-periods of three-quarters of an hour each, in a four-hour morning, for each of two classes of twenty pupils, when they are 'called up'. The fourth hour is 'to be set apart, besides looking over exercises, for the master's interval of ease and recovery from his fatigue' (pp. 47–9).

The modernity of this unusual book strikes most readers, but we must be careful in drawing a conclusion from it. It is not so likely that the author was wonderfully in advance of his times as that he was exceptional in formulating and putting together in print ideas that would be congenial to an imaginative teacher, either of the eighteenth or of the twentieth century.

1773   George Chapman's detailed description of work in the grammar school at Dumfries (*A Treatise on Education*) is a reminder that the teaching of English and the teaching of Latin and Greek were not necessarily incompatible. He uses the term 'classical education' very broadly. In saying frequently that 'a classical education is the most effectual means of giving a young man a critical knowledge of his mother-tongue' (p. 78) he seems conventional, but in a classical education he includes English language and literature, the figures of rhetoric, English history, and the history and geography of Greece and Rome (p. 80). He stresses the gradation of work. Latin is not started until the age of ten; till then the work is largely English grammar and composition, with carefully selected English reading. For some years rhetoric and poetry can 'scarce be comprehended by children' (p. 169). 'Novels . . . and that species of poetry which is most apt to inflame the fancy, and to seduce the mind, or to divert it from serious studies, are to be kept from children as long as possible.' Horace and Virgil are approached through criticism and through English literature: 'Select passages from Trapp's Lectures, Newbery on Poetry, The Preceptor, Rollin's Belles Lettres, and the Elements of Criticism, are carefully read and illustrated; then the best English poets . . . such as Thomson, Pope, Milton, are put into their hands from the school library' ('A Sketch of the Author's Method', in 1792 edn, p. 16).

1775   Chapman cautions us not to expect a narrowly classical pattern of work in all grammar schools, but George Croft is probably more representative of grammar-school heads. In his *General Observations concerning Education* he makes a rather irritable defence of classical learning. He offers the customary reasons, except for one that is unusual in its desperation: boys who are incapable of making much progress in any subject might as well study Latin: 'If it be said that too much time is engrossed in the laborious Task of Learning dead Languages, we should first take into the account the Youth, the inexperience, and the imbecility of the learners, and we should consider how little Progress they would be able to make in any other branch of Knowledge' (p. 7). Croft wishes his boys to spend two hours a week in 'the reading of periodical papers, and other useful Compositions of English Writers in Verse and Prose', but the main purpose of this reading would be to counter 'the barbarous dialect' of the locality (p. 5).

1777   Joseph Priestley's *A Course of Lectures on Oratory and Criticism*, although it is a blend of the old and the new rhetorical methods, shows considerable insensitivity towards literature. Its insights are psychological and in Howell's words leave 'the poetic principle unrecognized'. The literary education of the students at Warrington would not be much advanced by a lecturer who believed that: 'Poetry and works of fiction make a high *entertainment*, when they are made nothing more of; but they make a very poor and insipid *employment*. Infinitely preferable were it to be confined to the study of geometry, algebra, or law, without even having a glimpse of any thing more amusing, than be condemned to pass one's life sleeping over history, romances, poetry, and plays.'   (Lecture 18)

c. 1781 W. Richards, in *Youth's General Instructor*, which is in effect a pamphlet advertising his academy at Shadwell ('boarding with a bed-fellow, £20 p.a.; single £25'), includes in his curriculum 'theatrical entertainments . . . provided the Plays are judiciously selected' and 'with a sparing Hand, some particular *Virtuous Novels*, and ingenious *Fictions*, such as the *Adventures of Telemachus*' by Fénelon, and his fables; *The Travels of Cyrus*, by A.M. Ramsay (Chevalier Ramsay), and Croxall's *Mythical Amusements*.   (p. 16)

1784 Lady Fenn's *The Female Guardian* contains a list of eighty-one English and four French titles that form 'Mrs Teachwell's Library for her young Ladies'. These include many periodicals; the grammars of Lowth and Ash; *Elegant Extracts* (no details); *The Speaker*; *The Beauties of Poetry Display'd*; Aikin's *Miscellanies*; poems of Cotton, Parnell, Elizabeth Carter; Young's *Satires (Love of Fame)*; *The Seasons*; Akenside's *Pleasures of Imagination*. But there is no mention of Shakespeare, Milton or Pope, and none even of Cowper, who might have suited Lady Fenn's rather low-keyed recommendations.

1785 Thomas Reid, in his *Essays on the Intellectual Powers of Man*, while praising the powers of the imagination, expresses a view that would, and did, restrict the teaching of literature: 'The human imagination is an ample theatre, upon which every thing in human life . . . is acted. In children, and in some frivolous minds, it is a mere toy-shop.'   (Essay 4, end of chap. 4)

1794 William Milns, in *The Well-bred Scholar*, is concerned chiefly with composition and with literary texts as models for writing in various genres. He urges that the texts should be studied. The teacher should not only 'point out and explain . . . the particular beauties of the chosen passage, but . . . show how naturally they rise out of what went before, and how admirably they prepare the way for what is to follow them. The attention . . . should also be directed to the less showy, but more important succession of just ideas, solid arguments, and sensible observations' (pp. 30–1). In praising particularly Thomson's *Seasons* Milns makes the interesting comment, which would not be endorsed today, that descriptive poetry is the most popular with boys. There would perhaps be more support for his view concerning elegies (*Lycidas*; Gray; Pope) that 'this sort of poetry is not very essential towards forming the taste of youth' (p. 132). Critical and pedagogical judgments of this kind, however simple, are nevertheless rare at this period and are a sign of the maturing of English as a subject and the growing professionalism of its teachers.

a. 1798 Further signs of development are apparent in the collection by Thomas and John Holland, *Exercises for the Memory and Understanding*. Nearly 100 pages are given to 'examinations'. These are questions not only on the passages in the anthology but on other books as well. 'Questions on Mrs Barbauld's *Lessons for*

Children' begin: 'Of what are books, papers, pens, ink, leather and pins made?' The questions on Mrs Barbauld's *Hymns* begin: 'Why should we praise and bless God? What gives light by day? By night? What warble in the shade?' The questions on *Sandford and Merton* would test a pupil's knowledge of the story: 'How might an hippopotamos be mortally wounded?' (p. 480).

1798–1817   The teaching of literature is taken further than any previous writer had achieved in the works of Richard Lovell Edgeworth and Maria Edgeworth:

> 1798   *Practical Education* (R.L.E. and M.E.)
> 1801   *Moral Tales* (M.E.; preface by R.L.E.)
> 1802   *Poetry Explained for the Use of Young People* (R.L.E.)
> 1816   *Readings on Poetry* (R.L.E. and M.E.)
> 1817   *School Lessons* (R.L.E.)

They see the teaching of literature as much more than a question of what should be offered children to read. Literature, and poetry in particular, needs to be explained, and explanation is at least a large part of teaching. The Edgeworths were of course writing for parents, but for parents who were acting explicitly as teachers; they were considering children in a literate, comfortable home, but the children's responses were genuine and childlike. The parent-teacher's attitude, and most of the method suggested by the Edgeworths, could be transferred into a small classroom. Their starting-point was the belief that children do not understand, even imperfectly, even a half of what they are required to learn by heart (1816, preface). This bold and important statement must, however, be set in the context of what children were required to learn by heart. The Edgeworths' illustration is the opening lines of Pope's (so-called) *The Man of Ross*, chosen because 'there are no lines perhaps which are more frequently given to children to learn by rote' (1816, preface):

> But all our praises why should Lords engross?
> Rise, honest Muse! and sing the Man of Ross.

Two girls of eight and ten could not understand the first line because they did not know the meaning of 'engross'. Although the Edgeworths do not refer to the inversion in the first line, which one would expect also to cause uncertainty, they do not conceive of difficulty as being caused only by vocabulary: 'The pleasure that we receive from the remote allusions or metaphoric language of poetry depends, in a great degree, upon the rapidity with which we pass over a number of intermediate ideas, and seize the meaning of the author; but children find much difficulty in supplying the elisions of poetic thought and diction' (1802, preface). The teacher's aim in removing misunderstanding is to promote enjoyment, but that is not his sole aim: 'We have disclaimed and reprehended all attempts to teach in play. Steady, untired attention is what alone produces excellence' (1801, preface). The Edgeworths disagreed with the common view, expressed by Enfield, that instruction and enjoyment were separate responses to separate kinds of reading. They saw instruction and enjoyment working together in the teaching of literature, so that (and here there is an optimistic leap in their argument): 'those, who have tasted with the keenest relish the beauties of Berquin, Day, or Barbauld, pursue a demonstration of Euclid, or a logical deduction, with as much eagerness, and with more rational curiosity, than is usually shown by students who are nourished with the hardest fare, and chained to unceasing labour' (1801, preface). An unusual recommendation is that 'perhaps the first introduction to poetry should be obtained from prose', on the lines of Mrs Barbauld's prose hymns, one of which is quoted, along with a short passage from Gilbert White and references to the Old Testament and to Fénelon's *Telemachus* (1802, preface).

The practice of explaining poetry to children is defended against a number of possible objections, the chief of which is that 'matters of taste and sentiment are not cognizable by the laws or amenable to the tribunal, of reason'. Some teachers have been led to fear 'that they may destroy what they call genius and originality in their pupils . . . by endeavours to examine, analyse, and reason on any works of taste or poetry'. Such teachers just present their pupils with poems that they ought to admire. Consequently 'the pupil is either compelled to feign admiration which he does not feel, or he is left in despair of his own taste and abilities because he cannot comprehend what has never been explained to him, and what he is forbidden even to examine'. By contrast, what is needed is 'an education which shall give independence and energy by teaching young people neither to admire nor to despair, without reason' (1816, preface).

The authors pick up also the much-discussed theme of fiction, from an unusual point of view. 'Sentimental stories and books of mere entertainment . . . should be sparingly used, especially in the education of girls.' This is not only because of the danger of 'creating a romantic taste'; more important is the fact that such reading 'has an effect directly opposite to what it is intended to produce. It diminishes, instead of increasing, the sensibility of the heart . . . The imagination, which has been accustomed to . . . delicacy in fictitious narrations, revolts from the disgusting circumstances which attend real poverty, disease, and misery; the emotions of pity, and the exertions of benevolence, are consequently repressed precisely at the time when they are necessary to humanity' (1798, p. 334; cf. *Mental Amusement*, a. 1798, above, p. 191). It is in their recommendations for reading that the unrepresentative nature of the Edgeworth family circle is most apparent, and they were not unaware of it themselves. They believed that the conduct of children educated at home is more directly influenced by what they read than is the conduct of children at school: 'For pupils who are intended for a public school . . . no great nicety in the selection of their books is necessary' because at school they will mix with such a variety of children that they cannot avoid encounters with vice (1798, p. 324). Suitable reading at or soon after the age of seven would include voyages, travel, *Robinson Crusoe, Gulliver's Travels*; up to the age of nine or ten the diet is strengthened: the reviews; *The Annual Register*; Enfield's *Speaker*; *Elegant Extracts*; papers of the Manchester Society and the French Academy of Sciences; Priestley's *History of Vision*; Franklin; Lavoisier; Erasmus Darwin (1798, pp. 335–41). The view is again expressed that descriptive poetry is especially suitable for children because 'no labour of attention is demanded, no active effort of the mind' (1798, p. 366). Yet this kind of poetry is suspect just because it is easy: 'From time to time it may be an agreeable amusement [but] our object is . . . to strengthen the habits of attention, and to exercise all the powers of the mind. The inventive and reasoning faculties must be injured by the repetition of vague expressions, and of exaggerated description, with which most poetry abounds' (1798, p. 367). Richard Edgeworth, in particular, believed that children 'cannot improve their reasoning faculty by poetic studies' (*ibid*. p. 666), and his share in the work of 'explaining' poetry is powered by a desire to bring out as much rationality as the poem possesses.

Poetry Explained discusses *The Youth and the Philosopher*, by William White-head; Gray's *Elegy*; *L'Allegro* and *Il Penseroso*; Collins' *Ode to Fear*, and *Henry V*, V.iii. *Readings on Poetry* follows the same method and has the same purpose 'of enlarging their [children's] understanding, and forming their taste for literature' (1816, preface). The poems discussed, all taken from *The Speaker*, are: Pope's *The Man of Ross*; Gray's *Ode on a distant Prospect of Eton College*, the *Hymn to Adversity* ('not easily to be understood') and *The Bard* ('still more difficult'); Joseph Warton's *Ode to Fancy;* Parnell's *Hesiod* (omitting the framework of Pandora); *Paradise Lost*, Book 5, 153–204 (regularly known as 'Adam's Morning Hymn'). Some of the very short extracts and sentences that form the first part of *The Speaker* are treated in the same way.

The type of explanation is simple. It is concerned mainly with vocabulary and literary allusions, sometimes with syntax. Comparisons are made with other poems and social and moral comments are frequent. The comments are those of a widely but loosely read father, not those of a scholar. To give a full view of Edgeworth's approach requires more illustration than is possible here, but its strengths and weaknesses can be illustrated by a summary of his 'explanation' of the *Hymn to Adversity*, the first three stanzas of which are reproduced here in the continuous form, and in the text, adopted by Edgeworth from *The Speaker*:

> Daughter of Jove! relentless power!
> Thou tamer of the human breast,
> Whose iron scourge and tort'ring hour
> Affright the bad, afflict the best.
> Bound in thine adamantine chain 5
> The proud are taught to taste of pain,
> And purple tyrants vainly groan
> With pangs unfelt before, unpitied and alone.
> When first thy sire to send on earth
> Virtue, his darling child designed, 10
> To thee he gave the heavenly birth,
> And bade thee form her infant mind.
> Stern rugged nurse, thy rigid lore
> With patience many a year she bore.
> What sorrow was, thou badd'st her know, 15
> And from her own, she learn't to melt at others' woe.
> Scared at thy frown terrific fly
> Self pleasing Folly's idle brood,
> Wild Laughter, Noise, and thoughtless Joy,
> And leave us leisure to be good. 20
> Light they disperse, and with them go
> The summer friend, the flattering foe,
> By vain prosperity deceived,
> To her they vow their truth, and are again believed.

Edgeworth says that this is a classical poem: 'The object of the poem is moral, and as it relates more to the higher ranks of men, than to those of inferior station, the lesson it *inculcates* or enforces has something awful and sublime that commands attention.' He then summarises the moral of the poem. He explains 'Daughter of Jove', and comments, perhaps confusingly, that the words 'relentless power' 'are placed equivocally in this sentence: the sense requires that they should relate to Adversity; but the construction connects them with Jove'. Explanations follow of 'iron scourge' (line 3), 'tort'ring hour' (line 3), 'adamantine' (line 5), 'purple tyrants' (line 7), 'unpitied and alone' (line 8). On lines 9–10 he comments: '*Virtue* is put out of its proper place, merely to excite attention, and to give an air of poetry to what would else be plain prose.' 'Lore' (line 13), 'scared' (line 17) and 'summer friend' (line 22) are explained. 'She' (line 14) is referred to 'Virtue'; 'they' (line 21) is referred to 'Laughter, Folly, &c.' The error in Enfield's text, 'deceived' for 'received' (line 23), is pointed out: '*deceived* makes absolute nonsense of the whole stanza'. This is a patchy kind of explanation, but it is the first demonstration, among the texts considered in this survey, of a sustained attempt to 'teach' a poem.

Richard Edgeworth is more at home in the reading-book that he wrote for the school established for the poor by his son Lovell. The object of *School Lessons* is 'to comprise common and general instruction in a few words, to avoid detail, and to excite curiosity'. This it does with a freshness and a realism that are striking. The early lessons are packed with information: 'Three of the most deadly poisons that are known, Sugar of Lead, Corrosive Sublimate, and Arsenic, are like white sugar' (p. 59). A second part of the book, for more advanced pupils, is composed of fables, well illustrated, and (a regular feature of many kinds of textbook) a 'heathen mythology'.

1801 In *The Order and Method of Instructing Children*, published when he was twenty-three, George Crabb shares the uncertainty felt by many of his contemporaries about the power of imaginative literature, but he is more open than most in expressing his puzzlement: 'It seems almost a paradox for human nature to delight more in fiction than in reality' (p. 130); what is so independent of our understanding 'ought only to amuse, instead of which it fascinates children. It prevents the proper use of their mental faculties' (p. 132). Fiction is innocent and 'ought not to be refused', provided children fix their main attention on what is real. Novels and romances, which 'ought to be the most proper books to be put into the hands of youth', are now amongst the most improper. Current novels have to be classed merely as fiction: 'they cannot with propriety be placed any higher'. Human nature is 'painted in exaggerated colours . . . the representations in novels . . . are calculated to fan the flame already too violent in the mind of youth towards personal attractions' (pp. 134–6). He recommends, therefore, that the human body should be studied in school so as to remove this 'incessant thirst for obscenity' (p. 148).

1802 Joshua Collins, the retired headmaster of a grammar school and author of *A Practical Guide to Parents and Guardians, in the right choice and use of books*, is in no doubt about novels: 'of whatever complexion' they should be banned from school because with 'that sort of reading . . . it is impossible to foresee to what an extent it will be carried' (p. 25). His recommendations are predictable: Trimmer; Barbauld; Mavor; Watts; Lucy Aikin; Knox's prose and verse epitomes; Lindley Murray's *English Readers; Spectator*; Gay; Thomson; for girls *Mentoria*; Mrs Chapone's *Letters for Young Ladies*; Cresswick's *The Female Reader* (which he attributes to 'Mrs' Cresswick); de Genlis. He gives a list of 'English classics' for the library (by implication at home rather than at school) with little significant comment except a query whether Dryden, whom he mentions not under 'poetry' but under 'miscellaneous' with Montesquieu, Soame Jenyns and Blackstone, is too 'political' (pp. 119–48).

Three lines of thought are particularly apparent in this sequence of quotations. The first is the largely conventional hope, vague but not entirely vapid, that reading of the right kind will have two beneficial, but unconnected, results: heightened moral sensibility and a good prose style. The second line of thought, growing stronger during the century, is a more reflective consideration of the influence of literature on young people. On the one hand there is a recognition of the enlarging power of the imagination; on the other an apprehension that this power may dangerously unsettle both belief and conduct. The force of the emotions is recognised, admired and feared. The attractions of fiction and fantasy are admitted, but they are not comfortably distinguished from the seductions of falsehood. The third line of thought, also growing in strength, is that the teacher ought (to be able) to teach: that it is not enough just to present literature for reading at home or at school, without explanation or comment. It is by now being admitted that children often fail to understand what they read; that explanation is necessary, and that the teacher is responsible for providing it. These lines of thought do not, of course, disappear with the century. Henceforward they are a permanent part of the English teacher's consciousness.

The teaching of literature: nineteenth century

During the early years of the nineteenth century, school literary texts began to change. Many of them became more explanatory, more didactic. By the middle of the century some of them were directed towards public examinations. The texts were for institutional reading only: the distinction between home and school reading, for older pupils at least, was being sharpened. The texts are also more numerous. For both these reasons they must be discussed now in broader terms than has so far been necessary and with only occasional reference to their American equivalents.

Home reading. Compared with the earlier period, the nineteenth century provides many more books designed almost solely for home reading. If they were used in a school it would be in one so small and selective that it would be virtually an extension of the governess's schoolroom. This at any rate is how it seems; but we are forced again to acknowledge that we do not know much about the books used in any type of school. Even if these books were used only at home they could not be ignored here. They are relevant to the teaching of English in that they influenced the development of some children's literary taste and linguistic skills, and they exist in their hundreds. The field of children's literature raises many questions of aesthetic interest, such as that implied by Coventry Patmore's test for inclusion in his anthology *The Child's Garland*, 1862. The poems, he wrote, should have 'actually pleased intelligent children', but the application of the test 'excluded nearly all verse written expressly for children' (preface).

Questions such as this cannot be pursued here. It is possible only to indicate, by three works, the strength of three themes of educational importance: children's understanding of poetry; the pressure of religious convictions; the use of poetry as a vehicle for, or a solvent of, factual information.

Jane Harvey's *Poems, Original and Moral*, a. 1820, and her *Sacred Hymns*, 1818, have the same preface. It assumes that in writing for children imagery is usually a source of difficulty and can hardly be combined with simplicity:

1818 'In poetical pieces, written expressly for the use of children, the three points which appear to me of chief importance are, 1st, To suit the sentiments and language to the bounds of their capacities; 2ndly, To render them so attractive as to induce their committal to memory; and 3dly, To give them sufficient elevation to prolong that remembrance to a later period of life: the *first* point, by nearly precluding all imagery and embellishment, enhances the difficulty of the other two.'

(preface)

Favell Bevan's *The Peep of Day* is a fervent instructional reading-book, which *Reading Without Tears* was later designed to precede. Written for children between three and five, it is:

1833 'A little work . . . not in *size*, but in the humility of its contents. It aims at the superlative degree of littleness . . . It desires to be among books, as the humming bird among birds.' The child under its influence will: 'give evidence of his immortality by willingly hearkening to discourse concerning the INVISIBLE, – the ETERNAL, – the INFINITE. The simplicity of the language may seem unworthy of the sublimity of the subject . . . and some may smile at the contrast; – but the little one will not smile – except with joy to hear of his Heavenly Father, and of his incarnate Redeemer.' (preface)

Charlotte Smith's *Conversations Introducing Poetry*, 1804, the first volume for children of five and upwards, the second for older children, is an introduction not to poetry but to natural history. Appropriate poems, by Charlotte Smith and her friends and occasionally by better known writers, are inserted into the text. The first conversation is about the greenchafer, the ladybird, the snail, fish in a river, and bees; each topic preceded by a verse. In the second volume the reader is introduced, rather surprisingly, to Burns: 'The poetry of Burns, though all of it is not exactly desirable for our present poetical studies, is much of it so excellent' that *On Scaring some Water Fowl in Loch Turit* is included; but even that poem is 'not equal to *The Cotter's Saturday Night*' (which is not included).

The dominant tone throughout books for home reading is one of moralising: sometimes so heavy-handed that it is difficult for us to picture a relationship between adults and children that gave it a natural place. But children seem to have accepted it, and to have submitted it to that wonderful metabolism that protects them from too rich a diet of benevolence.

School-based reading. There is some evidence during this period of what books were read or recommended in school, but much more evidence of this kind would be produced by a systematic search.

1815 John Shoveller, in an outline of the course at his academy, doubts the value of learning 'classical [English] literature' by heart: it is not popular and has no influence on the memory. The brief timetable he gives allows plenty of English grammar (6 a.m. to 8 a.m. Mondays and Fridays for the youngest class) and composition (2 p.m. to 5 p.m. Mondays and Thursdays for the first (oldest) and second classes). His 'repetition of English lessons' and 'declamations' refer to these activities. His recommendation for holiday reading is an easy gesture towards '*The Spectator* and other moral essays of the same kind, some of the best poetry, . . . Johnson's *Lives of the Poets*, and Plutarch's *Lives*, should be in the library of every youth.' That is to say, his pupils should buy the books for themselves. (p. 85)

1816 The anonymous author of *A Practical Treatise on Day-Schools* allows one hour a day for 'English Reading, Grammar, Exercises and Composition'. The reading he specifies is, for ages eight to nine *Sandford and Merton*; for nine to ten Lindley Murray's *Reader*; for ten to eleven *The Class-Book* (probably Phillips, 1806); and for the next three years, in turn, one book each of natural history, geography and English history (p. 101).

1830 In *The Juvenile Reader's Assistant*, an unsophisticated book drawing largely on John Walker's *Rhetorical Grammar* but also recording the practice of 'the Misses Wilmshurst's Seminary, Cromwell House, Maldon', a sequence of reading is outlined for children aged three onwards: the pictures in Clark's *Primer* (i.e. Galt, a. 1821); Trimmer's *A Spelling Book for Young Children* (probably Part 1 of *The Charity School Spelling Book*); her *Easy Lessons; The Progressive Spelling Book* (improbably the anonymous one of a. 1810; not otherwise identified); Lindley Murray's *Introduction to English Reading*; Blair's *Models of Juvenile Letters* (i.e. Phillips, 1811); Lindley Murray's *The English Reader*. Outside the sequence but also used in the seminary are John Platt's *Literary and Scientific Class Book* and Enfield's *Speaker*. (pp. 37–48)

1844   James Pycroft's *A Course of English Reading* seems to be intended both for the home student and for the undergraduate. Its 5 pages, out of 312, on English literature are unhelpful. To read *Paradise Lost* 'is the duty of all – the pleasure of a few . . . *Eloisa to Abelard* is the most immoral and impious poem ever sanctioned' (p. 305). Even in his second edition, 1850, all Pycroft has to say about Wordsworth is: 'Admired by all his brother poets. See Coleridge's *Biographia Literaria*. Read *The Excursion.*'

1872b   E.A. Abbott recommends for the youngest classes, 'not to be studied but to be read at home' and lightly examined at school, *Sandford and Merton, Robinson Crusoe, Swiss Family Robinson, Evenings at Home*, some of Aesop and Hans Andersen. If the task is not pressed too hard 'we need not anticipate a boyish reaction against the enforced study of fiction'.   (p. 9)

Rhetoric and belles lettres. The texts are of three types: advanced rhetorics, mainly for university use; school rhetorics; domestic discussions about poetry, some of them substantial enough to be used in school. These last are the most interesting. They are similar to the Edgeworths' *Poetry Explained* and *Readings on Poetry* and are similar in tone, though not in content, to Lucy Aikin's *Poetry for Children* and Charlotte Smith's *Conversations introducing Poetry*. George Gregory's *Letters on Literature, Taste, and Composition, addressed to his Son*, 1808, are artificial in the sense that the son, whether real or not, is an artifice. The book is in the tradition of *belles lettres*: refined discussion of style, the sublime, the pathetic, figures of speech, genres, illustrated from the classics and from modern European literature. Its two volumes would scarcely fit it for a school-text, but it covers topics that were treated in school. In Esther Hewlett's *The Young Reviewers; or, the Poems Dissected*, 1821, the children are reviewing not their books but their conduct. The poems discussed are considered as expressions of, or exhortations to, moral behaviour. The first poem, *Evening Reflections. A Maxim of Pythagoras*, begins:

> Let not soft slumber close your eyes
> Before you've recollected thrice
> The train of actions through the day.

The children ask to have the meaning of the poems explained, and Philip, who is attending a neighbouring academy as a day-boy, describes how he learnt Gray's *Elegy* in one afternoon, but because he had not paid attention to the meaning he made a fool of himself on breaking-up day by declaiming, 'The *cuckoo* tolls the knell of parting day'. Expectations raised by the terms 'reviewers' and 'dissected' are not satisfied. The poems are explained and the children write about them, but the discussions and reviews are concerned not with the meaning of the verse but with its moral significance. *The Gentleman's Magazine* justly said of this book, 'Deprecating as we do, every tendency to infantine pedantry [we prefer] more simple modes of instruction' (vol. 92.1, Feb. 1822, p. 155).

John Aikin's *Letters to a Young Lady on a Course of English Poetry* are simpler, in that the form of the book does not require a forced reciprocity from the young lady. Aikin writes amiably about Pope, Milton, Dryden, Swift, Young and others but makes no mention of Shakespeare. His attitude to literature is much that of Gregory, but more relaxed and, in one respect, almost flippant. He is omitting, he says, 'any grave lectures upon the moral use of poetry' although he will point out passages helpful to the young lady's moral development. He has some difficulty with the topic of love, much in evidence in poetry, but she is not to worry too much:

1804 'Love in poetry is a more harmless thing than love in prose. The more of fancy is mixed with it – the more it is removed from common life – the less is its influence over the heart and the conduct; and it is probable that the refinement and elevation of sentiment fostered by a taste for poetry may prove a protection from that light and vulgar passion which enters merely at the eyes, and is too sensual to be disgusted with coarseness and stupidity.'   (p. 4)

Poetry without Fiction: for Children, 1823, it is explained, means poetry without fairies. The book is an application to children between the ages of three and seven of the Edgeworths' *Poetry Explained* and endorses not only contemporary prejudice against fairies but also the Edgeworths' wish to teach children to 'appreciate *sense* rather than *sound*'. This intention is carried out by questioning that is persistent but not penetrating. Fiction, unfortunately, is not entirely excluded. A poem on the setting sun pretends that the sun goes round the earth because this idea is 'more level to their [the children's] comprehension'; it can be corrected later. The author's relaxed attitude towards facts has a sounder counterpart in her understanding that 'the capacities of children vary considerably as to the *age* at which they unfold themselves . . . It is of little consequence that children should read or spell, or do anything else at any particular age' (pp. vii, x). Children's moral and religious development, however, should be cultivated through poetry, even by mere versification, which is all the author calls her own work. Her 'lines on *Mamma's Headache* . . . committed to memory, will recur on some similar occasion, and produce an exercise of self-control, by no means unimportant' (p. xv). She quotes also 'an amiable and sensible young friend' who declared that Parnell's *The Hermit* 'learnt in infancy had done more towards establishing a confidence in the wisdom of Providence than any of her more dry reading' (p. v).

Conversations on Poetry, again taking place in a family of children, whose ages are not stated, is more thorough than usual in its explanations, but the conventional setting forces both father and children into artificiality. The explanations concern figurative language particularly. Clara asks, about a passage in Mrs Barbauld's prose hymns, 'Papa, what do people mean when they talk about metaphor?' Father's explanation includes the opinion that metaphor, being 'the natural style of the imagination and the passions . . . is always used, and generally with correctness, by the untutored inhabitants of uncivilized countries', partly because they have insufficient words (p. 8). After discussing many examples of metaphor father says:

1824 'It is better for young people to acquire a taste for plain, simple and unadorned truth – for simple description of natural objects – before they enter much upon that which requires so great an exercise of the imagination as good metaphorical poetry necessarily does.'   (p. 24)

He does not discuss any possible inconsistency with what he had earlier said about the untutored and uncivilized. One of the daughters then leads into a discussion about truth and beauty, but they soon return to *On a Sprig of Heather*, from Joanna Baillie's *A Collection of Poems*, 1823, and an explanation of *erica vulgaris* and the shyness of moorfowl.

Among the school and advanced rhetorics, Alexander Jamieson's *A Grammar of Rhetoric*, although written for schools, is endowed with, or suffers from, the comprehensiveness characteristic of late manuals of rhetoric. Its virtue is that it professes to encourage individual judgments about literature:

1818a 'The young student . . . so far from learning to suspend the exercise of his own judgment, is taught to investigate the grounds upon which those principles [i.e. those regulating the standard of taste] are supported, and in comparing them with the simple dictates of his own mind, to form, from the various sources which reading and reflection may afford him, the elements of rearing for himself a standard of taste, to which, in more matured life, he may refer . . . productions of the fine arts, or of polite literature.' (Intro.)

In the same year Jamieson published *The Rhetorical Examiner*, a volume of 1560 questions based on the grammar, many of which are direct and stimulating:

No. 355 How may an author be perspicuous without being precise?
No. 370 Distinguish the terms *austerity, severity, rigour*.
No. 522 Give an example and its analysis of a *complex* sentence conveying the dullest species of the unintelligible.
No. 709 Give an example of a trite simile from Shakespeare's *Coriolanus*.
No. 923 Does the number of incompetent critics furnish a plausible objection against criticism?

William Enfield of Newcastle, 1809, Cecil Hartley, 1822, and William Pinnock's *Catechism of Poetry* enumerate and illustrate genres: the first two at length, the last briefly. William Barron's *Lectures on Belles Lettres and Logic*, 1806, were delivered regularly at St Andrews between 1778 and his death in 1803. The seventy-one lectures cover much the same field as Jamieson's *Grammar of Rhetoric*, with the interesting addition of a chapter on the psychology of word order. Barron is speaking to university students, with no reference to the work of the schools, in spite of the substantial overlap in this area between the work of Scottish universities and some schools. His references are to classical and modern European literature, including *Tom Jones*, of which he approves. Richard Whately's *Elements of Rhetoric*, 1828, written for 'unpractised teachers' while he was still an academic, has school as well as college students in mind, but as it is concerned almost entirely with the expressive aspects of rhetoric it is considered in chapter 6, below. Alexander Bain's *English Composition and Rhetoric* is likewise primarily about composition, but Bain attaches importance to 'rhetorical analysis' and gives sample analyses of both prose and verse. He comments on four lines of Campbell's *The Pleasures of Hope:*

1866   At summer's eve, when Heaven's aerial bow
            Spans, with bright arch, the glittering hills below,
            Why to yon mountain turns the musing eye,
            Whose sun-bright summit mingles with the sky?

These lines contain a description individualized by the point of time given ('at summer's eve'), and enlivened by circumstances of action – '*spans* with bright arch', '*turns* the *musing* eye', '*mingles* with the sky'. The touches conveyed in '*bright* arch', '*glittering* hills', '*sun-bright* summit', are graphically selected, and can be easily realized; if there be anything to object to, it is the three-fold iteration of the one idea of light.   (p. 288)

Although Bain chose these lines because they 'exemplify the Poetic Figures and Qualities', it is noticeable that he does not name any of the figures, whereas eighteenth-century teachers would have made their pupils name the figures before they did anything else. In Bain's hands it is linguistic functions generally, not just those designated by traditional names, that are being analysed. In 1887–8 Bain rewrote the whole work, and this analysis disappeared.

Literary history

Until the development of public examinations in the 1850s there was no large market for histories of English literature. The establishment of the first chairs of English in English universities (University College, London, 1828; King's College, London, 1835) did not at first give much encouragement to literature (D.J. Palmer, 1965, chap. 2), and the Scottish universities and schools had their own rhetorical tradition in which the formal history of literature had little place. School anthologies sometimes included short biographies of selected authors, and these were also published separately, as in Frances Rowden's *Biographical Sketches of the most Distinguished Writers . . . for the use of schools*, 1820. Chambers' Educational Course included Robert Chambers' *History of the English Language and Literature*, 1836, and in 1848 Thomas Budge Shaw, an Englishman teaching in Russia, published in London the *Outlines of English Literature*, which he claimed to be 'the first attempt to treat, in a popular manner, questions hitherto neglected in elementary books'. Shaw's claim was supported by the popularity of his book, which, edited by others after his death as *The Student's Manual of English Literature*, 1862, had many editions in England and in the United States. Nearly as popular was *The History of English Literature*, 1853, by William Spalding, Professor of Rhetoric at Edinburgh and then at Aberdeen, which was also used in American schools (Applebee, p. 18). By the middle of the century the number of histories was increasing rapidly. G.L. Craik's adult six-volume *Sketches of the History of Literature and Learning in England*, 1844–5, had been reduced first to two volumes (*A Compendious History . . .*) in 1861 and then to a single volume, *A Manual of English Literature*, 1862. W.F. Collier's *History of English Literature*, 1861, though said to have been used in Massachusetts schools (Applebee, *ibid.*) makes heavy reading, and its 538 pages (even the $10\frac{1}{2}$ given to American Literature, in an appendix) must have been unbearable.

Two other biographical manuals were designed for schools: the Irish Commissioners' *Biographical Sketches of Eminent British Poets*, 1851, and *Biographical Outlines of English Literature*, 1862, by David Pryde, an Edinburgh headmaster. These works agreed with Collier that 'the history of English literature is essentially biographical, for true criticism cannot separate the author from his book' (1861, preface). At a more elementary level was the anonymous *Guide to English Literature . . . in the form of Question and Answer*, 1862; more advanced were Robert Demaus' *Introduction to the History of English Literature*, 1860, and Joseph Angus' *The Handbook of English Literature*, 1865.

Anthologies

Elocutionary anthologies. Anthologies with an emphasis on elocution, though few in number, continued to appear during the nineteenth century. Many of them form part of manuals, and it is in the context of performance (discussed in chapter 6 below) that they are of particular interest. Their contents differ from those of the general school anthology in obvious respects. There are more dramatic pieces, with a stronger representation of Shakespeare than hitherto. A third of James Wright's passages (1814) are given to Shakespeare and he is prominent in Harcourt Bland, 1863; Carpenter, 1869; and Ross, 1869. There are more speeches, classical and modern, and more quasi-dramatic verse narrative, often very poor. There seems to be a shift away from figures of speech (retained nevertheless by Linnington, 1833) and from the analysis of kinds of emotion made popular by John Walker. Most texts were designed for adults as well as for schoolchildren, with an increasing emphasis on public performance by children. But the performance was static; recitation, not drama: 'Every modification of an oath, all drawing of swords and daggers, wounding and dying, are totally unfit for boys in a schoolroom' (Brewer, 1842, preface). The influence of Walker is very strong: explicit in James Wright, J.S. Knowles, Hindmarsh, Linnington and Sullivan. About two-thirds of these elocutionary texts, a much higher proportion than in other anthologies, come from Ireland, Scotland and the north of England: an indication perhaps of a wish not only to speak well but to be considered well spoken. As in other types of British anthology American authors are increasingly drawn-on during this period. Washington Irving appears in the 1820s; Brewer, 1842, includes American prose and verse; Sullivan, 1850, draws on Ebenezer Porter's *Rhetorical Reader* and on several 'excellent American works on Popular Education'. Bland uses Washington Irving, Longfellow and Poe; Armstrong, 1866, uses Longfellow, Poe and William Cullen Bryant; Carpenter uses Whittier and Longfellow; while Ross has a short section of 'Poetry of the American Internecine War'.

General anthologies. Many compilers continue to express anxiety lest poetry should corrupt the young. Poetry, unless it is specifically religious, is felt to be potentially subversive of morality, but the opinion is seldom expressed in terms clear enough to allow argument or refutation:

1814 'Nothing will here be found, which can contaminate the purest mind, or reasonably offend the most rigid . . . Preference has been given to such pieces, as breathe the purest strains of Religion and Morality.' (Elizabeth Mant, preface)

Elizabeth Hill's *A Sequel to the Poetical Monitor* continues to subordinate literary qualities to moral exhortation:

a. 1815 The compiler's choice 'has been directed not so much to those pieces which are distinguished by superior genius and beautiful poetry, as to those which exhibit lively and pointed descriptions of the deformity of folly and vice, and the beauty of wisdom and virtue.'   (preface)

The compiler of *The Moral and Poetical Miscellany, c.* 1819, while accepting that 'poetry is an amusement', and recognising 'the powerful and pleasing sensations which it excites in the imagination', nevertheless states the particular purpose of his collection as 'to convey morality in the most enticing dress'. *Sacred Poetry*, 1835, prepared for the Irish national schools, takes the moralising process to an extreme. The anthology was compiled 'for the peasantry of Ireland'. It followed 'the practice of throwing important truths and precepts into a poetical form, for the purpose of being committed to memory . . . Poetry of this description . . . becomes a record of facts and of precepts, which a man carries constantly about with him.' Throwing exhortation into a poetical form is exemplified by the first stanza, out of two, of a representative poem in the Irish anthology:

> *For a very little child in sickness*
> Almighty God, I'm very ill,
> But cure me, if it be thy will:
> For thou canst take away my pain,
> And make me strong and well again.   (p. 53)

It was not only naive verse that was thought suitable for carrying a message, and the message was not always a moral one. F.C. Cook's *Poetry for Schools*, 1849, was an introduction to 'the great classical poets of England'. It was intended especially for children seeking apprenticeships, and for pupil teachers, but the broadest hope of the compiler ('one of Her Majesty's Inspectors of Church Schools') was that the 'children of the peasantry and artisans' would come to understand and 'sympathise with sentiments and principles by which well educated persons are influenced' and 'to understand and sympathise with the views of their superiors'. Because such children 'are frequently at a loss to understand the forms, which persons of cultivated minds are accustomed to use in expressing their thoughts' they are open to persuasion by the 'socialist infidel'. Cook is unusual in politicising the teaching of literature so overtly, but he is less unusual in his exclusion of Pope and Dryden because they lack 'passages for the moral and religious principles of which I would willingly make myself responsible' (preface).[2] The compilers do not discuss, or seem to recognise, any difference between religious poetry and versified doctrine. Anthologies such as *Selections of Poetry*, 1862, combine a strong representation of Milton and Cowper with an equally strong representation of William Josiah Irons, Robert Murray McCheyne and Augustus Toplady. The hope

---

[2] A memorandum, 'Suggestions on reading books', written by Cook for the SPCK in 1850, is printed in Goldstrom, 1972a, Appendix 5. It refers to collections of prose passages only, and maintains a confident balance between religious education and vocational preparation.

that religious and moral training can be reinforced through poetry is expressed during the whole period, often in language disproportionate to a juvenile anthology:

1846   The anthology contains 'only such pieces as would elevate the mind, purify the affections, and inspire the reader with religious emotions, a devotion to Nature – to Home – to Country, and embue him with the spirit of universality and charity, and a pure and holy love of every living thing'.   (*The Gem Book*, preface)

Such emphatic statements of the compiler's position are not common. More often the moralising assumptions are lightly touched on, or implicit in the selection. It is not until Palgrave that literary values are explicitly given priority over (but not in opposition to) moral values. Palgrave's attitude is best seen in *The Children's Treasury*, to which nothing is admitted 'which does not reach a high rank in poetical merit'. His aim is 'to give pleasure, high, pure, manly (and therefore lasting)'. But the moralising force of these three characteristic epithets is less important than the pleasure given by the poems. Writing of himself Palgrave says:

1875   'Poetry, for poetry's sake, is what he offers. To illustrate the history of our literature, to furnish specimens of leading or of less-known poets, to give useful lessons for this or the other life, to encourage a patriotic temper – each an aim fit to form the guiding principle of a selection – have here only an indirect and subsidiary recognition.'   (preface)

What is subsidiary for Palgrave is important for many other school anthologists, but few of them enumerate their aims as explicitly as E.C. Lowe, headmaster of Hurstpierpoint, whose attitude to poetry is not uncommon after the middle of the nineteenth century:

1868   'If through the Lyrics of our glorious English tongue some of our youngsters are encouraged in their love of animals, quickened to observe the beauties of nature and to read her parables, confirmed in domestic affection, trained to good humour and sympathy, and rooted in attachment to old England, *The Young Englishman's First Poetry Book* will have realised all that its compiler could desire to accomplish by so humble an instrument.'   (preface)

Walter Stirling's *The Poetical Moralist*, a. 1814, distinguishes slightly between boys and girls. Although 'purity of thought should be most particularly regarded' for young people generally, and although he has expunged every passage that might prove injurious, there are poems more suitable for boys 'as uniting information to guide, morality to instruct, and piety to support them', whereas for girls, by implication, there is no need for information: 'Religion is the best guardian of the feminine virtues.' Some anthologies are compiled solely for girls. Mrs Barbauld's *The Female*

Speaker, 1811, which is one of 'those useful and unpretending publications ... for which the routine of education, particularly in schools, will always create a demand' (preface), is noticeable for continuing in its section of 'select sentences' the earlier aphoristic tradition noticed above (chapter 4) and alive still in copybooks such as John Holland's *Definitions*, 1804, which contains fifteen pages of 'Sentences from Shakespeare, Milton, Pope, Thomson, Cowper'. Similarly Mrs Burroughs' *The Monitor of Youth*, 1807, comprises 652 quotations in alphabetical order, beginning with Sir Joshua Reynolds: 'Every *Art* is worthy of notice, that tends to soften and improve the mind.' Martin Smart's *The Female Class-Book*, 1813, takes care 'to avoid, except with the most rigid moderation, all those subjects on which too lively a curiosity might be indulged ... on the principle that it is not by filling the minds of girls at school with perpetual ideas of love and courtship, that the best wives and mothers are likely to be produced'. The 'prurient writing' found in other anthologies is excluded (preface). John Platts' *The Female Monitor*, 1823, is a collection of exactly the same kind, but he carefully claims that it is distinct from both Smart and Barbauld.

Analysis of the anthologies, 1802–1870

For reasons already discussed (above, pp. 169–71), it is difficult to analyse the contents and to assess the significance of the 114 anthologies listed in Table 8. An attempt is made, in the limited form used for the earlier period, to identify the poets whose work was most frequently chosen. The frequency of a poet's appearance is to some extent a measure of his or her popularity; but by whom is this popularity assessed? In some cases the anthologies are compiled by teachers who give educational grounds for their selection; in some the compiler is a benevolent onlooker, outside the classroom; in others the compilation is an anonymous commercial production. A commercial origin is necessary for any textbook, and benevolence is not necessarily a handicap, but often the selection of pieces, and hence the evidence for their popularity, represents the opinion of teachers only indirectly.

The presentation in Table 8 is the same as in Table 6. Very minor poets are not identified or discussed. Three of the anthologies appeared after 1870, two of them by Palgrave, who had compiled an earlier collection, and one by Hales, who had been an important influence on English teaching before 1870. The names of some, usually later, poets are italicised on their first appearance in the table, which is not necessarily their first appearance in any of the anthologies. In Table 9 the number of ranking positions held

Table 8. *British school anthologies, 1802–1870*

	Order of frequency				no. of pieces including unattrib.
	1	2	3	4	
1805 Button	Button 35	Cowper 10	Wolcot, *Southey* 5	Watts 4	96
1805 J. Smith[a] (Pr)[b]	Shakespeare 8	{Goldsmith, Home, Pope} 5	{Addison, Thomson} 3	–	96 (16)
1805 Cottle	Cowper 28	Young 17	Cottle 16	Pope 11	236 (34)
1807 Evans	{Bowles, Linn, Rogers, Southey} 8	C. Smith 7	*Coleridge* 6	{W. Fox, Langhorne} 5	222 (16)
1808 Wemyss	Cowper 25	Beattie 14	{Pope, Young} 10	{Goldsmith, Thomson} 9	200 (16)
1808 *Classical Selections*	*Campbell* 8	{*Burns*, Cowper, Ossian, P. Pindar, Scott, Southey, K. White, *Wordsworth*} 3	–	–	109 (31)
1809 Angus[c]	Thomson 7	Home 4	Grahame 3	–	67 (10)
1809 Mylius	Lamb 27	C. Smith 22	{Fawcett, Gay} 12	{H. More, Watts} 9	202
1810 Mylius	Shakespeare 40	Pope 25	Cowper 18	{Milton, *Scott*} 16	304

Date / Compiler	Author	No.	Author	No.	Author	No.	Author	No.	Total (authors)
1811 Barbauld (Pr)	Cowper / Pope	8	Shakespeare	6	Milton	5	—	—	74 (5)
1813 Angus	Thomson	33	Grahame	26	Richardson / Shakespeare	6	Young	5	163 (21)
1813 Pinnock[a]	Cowper	6	—	—	Goldsmith	11	Shakespeare	9	32 (11)
a. 1814 Stirling	Pope	13	Thomson	11	Milton	20	—	8	224 (16)
1814 Wright	Shakespeare	34	Gay	20	Collins / T. Warton	10	Addison	4	103
1814 Mant[a]	Cowper	14	Bowles	10	*J. Montgomery*	5	Gray	7	177 (11)
a. 1815 Hill	H. Moore	9	Cowper / H. More	5	Barbauld / Cowper / T. Gisborne / M. Robinson	5	—	4	101 (25)
1815 Earnshaw	Bidlake	6	Williams / Pindar	5	—	—	—	—	175 (49)
1815 *Twenty-six …*	Cowper / Watts	3	J. Newton / J. Stennett	2	—	—	—	—	26
a. 1816 Ewing	Shakespeare	34	Pope	12	Campbell	11	Young	7	137 (2)
1817 Carey (Pr)	Pope	17	Goldsmith	9	Bloomfield / Shakespeare	3	—	—	58 (20)
a. 1819 Guy (Pr)	Gay	9	Pope	5	Cowper / Cotton / Watts	4	—	—	81 (21)
1819 Ewing (Pr)	Watts	7	Campbell / Hogg	5	Grahame	4	—	—	53 (3)
1820 McLaren (Pr)	Shakespeare	8	Colman	3	Cowper / Milton	2	—	—	32
1822 Hort	Thomson	22	Charlotte Smith	14	Cowper	13	Bloomfield	8	166 (53)

Table 8 (*cont.*)

	Order of frequency				no. of pieces including unattrib.
	1	2	3	4	
1822 Pennie	Pennie (8)	Pope (6)	Campbell, Cowper, Milton, Scott (4)	–	177 (36)
a. 1823 Knowles (Pr)	Campbell (16)	Shakespeare (12)	Milton (9)	*Byron* (6)	119
1823 *Poetical Gems*	Bucke (9)	J.M. Neale (5)	Cowper, Rogers, Scott, I. Walton (4)	Collins, Gray, Milton (3)	93 (10)
1823 Thomson (Pr)	Cowper (8)	Beattie (5)	Grahame, Thomson, Watts (4)	Campbell, J. Montgomery (3)	75 (4)
a. 1824 Hindmarsh[a] (Pr)	Shakespeare (16)	Byron (10)	J. Montgomery (9)	Cowper (8)	203 (13)
a. 1825 Carpenter (Pr)	Shakespeare (7)	Cotton, R. Graves (4)	Addison, Cowper, Jenyns, Young (3)	–	102 (27)
a. 1826 Hewlett (Pr)	J. and A. Taylor (22)	Cowper (19)	J. Montgomery (15)	Thomson (14)	270 (33)
1826 White[a] (Pr)	Byron, Campbell (9)	Cowper (8)	Shakespeare (6)	Milton (5)	64 (4)

1826 Angus	7 Shakespeare	6 Pope, Richardson	5 Cowper	4 Akenside, Campbell, Carnegie	133 (34)
1829 Hinchcliffe (Pr)	9 Cowper	7 J. Taylor	6 J. Montgomery	4 Gay	102 (25)
1830 Winks[a] (Pr)	7 Cowper	3 Shakespeare	—	—	37 (6)
1831 McCulloch (Pr)	4 *Hemans*, Southey	3 Campbell, Milman	—	—	58 (5)
1831 Bransby[a,d] (Pr)	6 Cowper	5 Thomson	4 J. Baillie, Rogers	—	72 (2)
a. 1832 Campbell (Pr)	6 Hemans	2 Barbauld, Darwin, Pollok	—	—	45 (9)
1833 *Readings*	10 Scott	7 Croly, Milton, J. Montgomery	6 Rogers, Wordsworth	5 Addison, Campbell, Hemans, Southey, Thomson, K. White	191
1833 Linnington	9 R. Montgomery	8 Southey	6 Byron, Campbell	5 Hemans	164 (9)
1834 Innes	10 Byron	6 Shakespeare	5 Campbell	3 Innes	78 (17)
a. 1836 *Poetical Selections*[a]	7 Byron	6 Scott	4 Campbell, Cowper, Roscoe	—	67 (9)
1836 Batt	18 Wordsworth	11 Hemans, J. Montgomery	8 Cowper, Scott, J. Taylor	6 M. Howitt	296 (40)

Table 8 (*cont.*)

	Order of frequency				no. of pieces including unattrib.
	1	2	3	4	
a. 1837 W. Graham	Byron 5	Cowper / Rogers / Scott / Wordsworth 3	–	–	55 (2)
1837 Easy Poetry[a]	Bowles 9	Wordsworth 6	Watts 3	Burns / Cowper / Hemans 2	120 (68)
1837 McCulloch (Pr)	J. Taylor 3	Ken / Watts / Wordsworth 2	–	–	19
1838 Allen	Byron / Scott 13	Coleridge 11	Cowper / Milton 10	Lamb / Shakespeare / Wordsworth 8	150 (2)
1838 Martin (pages)	Byron / Moore / Wordsworth (12)	Scott / Shelley (10)	Bloomfield (9)	Coleridge / Southey (6)	(121 pp.)
(1838) 1850 Reading Book (Irish) (Pr)	Cowper 7	J. Montgomery 6	Sigourney 4	Bowring / Barton / Hemans 3	112 (38)
1839 Leitch (Pr)	Campbell 4	Bowring / Scott / Watts 2	–	–	39 (6)
1839 Payne	Cowper 22	M. Howitt 13	Wordsworth 9	J. Montgomery / Southey 7	202 (37)

Collection	Poet	n	Poet	n	Poet	n	Poet	n	Total
c. 1840 Dunn and Crossley (Pr)	Shakespeare	6	Byron, Cowper	3	—	—	—	—	69
1840 Scottish First Collection (Pr)	Campbell	3	Beattie, Pollok, Shakespeare, Scott	2	—	—	—	—	29
1841 Scottish Second Collection (Pr)	Byron	7	Burns, Campbell, Cowper, Scott, Thomson, Wordsworth	2	—	—	—	—	32
1841 Johns[a]	Shakespeare	9	Milton	6	Wordsworth	5	—	—	70 (2)
1842 Brewer[a] (Pr)	Shakespeare	19	Brewer	11	Byron, Cowper	10	Hemans, Milton	6	220
1844 Conybeare	J. and A. Taylor	6	(Ballads)	4	Southey	3	Coleridge	2	20
1845 Payne (1)[a,c]	Cowper	15	Wordsworth	10	Byron	8	Coleridge, Milton	7	168 (7)
1845 Payne (2) (pages)	Milton	(60)	Chaucer, Shakespeare	(17)	Goldsmith, Pope	(15)	Spenser	(14)	(205 pp.)
a. 1846 Specimens[a]	Shakespeare	11	Cowper	8	Milton	7	Gray	5	143
1846 Hartley (Pr)	Shakespeare	10	Byron	7	Hemans, H. Smith	5	Campbell, Scott	4	97 (9)
1847 Thackeray[a]	Cowper, Milton, Shakespeare	8	Gay	5	Collins, Darwin, Gray, Pope	4	Akenside, Shenstone	3	134 (11)

Table 8 (*cont.*)

	Order of frequency				no. of pieces including unattrib.
	1	**2**	**3**	**4**	
1847 Routledge/ Mylius[f]	Scott (10)	Hemans (8)	J. Montgomery, Gay (6)	*Bryant*, Logan, Watts (4)	167 (22)
1849 Cook (1)	Wordsworth (6)	J.M. Neale, Southey (5)	Cowper, Herbert, Keble, Milman, R. Montgomery (4)	–	67 (4)
1849 Cook (2)	Shakespeare (22)	Milton (20)	Cowper (18)	Thomson (14)	84
1849 Guy	Bryant (8)	Moore, K. White (5)	Cowper, *Clare* (4)	Heber, Hemans, M. Howitt, C. Smith (3)	112 (13)
1849 McLeod	Campbell, Cowper, Hemans (3)	Heber, Scott, Southey (2)	–	–	34 (1)
a. 1850 Sessional (Pr)	Thomson (11)	Watts (10)	J. Grahame (8)	Cowper, H. More, Pope (5)	86 (2)
a. 1850 Bell (Pr)	Shakespeare (19)	Byron (15)	Campbell (10)	Hemans (8)	203 (2)
1850 McLeod	Scott, Shakespeare (4)	Cowper, *Macaulay* (3)	Hemans, Milton, J. Montgomery, Morehead, Thomson (2)	–	50 (3)

1851 Chambers	{M. Howitt, Watts} 6	Cowper 4	Milton 3	—	79 (15)
1851 Hughes	Wordsworth 19	Hemans 16	*Longfellow* 15	Campbell 12	248 (9)
(1849) 1851 *Selections* I (Irish)	Shakespeare 13	Cowper 12	{Moore, Pope} 11	Byron 10	258 (15)
1851 Gilfillan[a]	{Shakespeare, Milton} 9	Chaucer 7	Herrick 6	{Blair, Cowper, Drummond, Harington, Herbert, Jonson, Pope, Sackville, Thomson, Watts} 4	201
1852 *Choice*	J. Montgomery 5	{Heber, Hemans, J. & A. Taylor} 3	—	—	74 (24)
(1849) 1852 *Selections*, II (Irish)[a]	Wordsworth 23	Thomson 21	Cowper 18	{Hemans, Scott} 13	502 (29)
1852 *Class Book*	Shakespeare 16	Milton 12	{Cowper, Thomson, Wordsworth} 8	Spenser 6	94 (1)
1852 Guy (Pr)	Shakespeare 35	{Byron, Collins, Littleton, Pope} 3	—	—	70
†1853 *Book of English Poetry*[a]	Shakespeare 8	Milton 7	Pope 6	{Campbell, Cowper, Longfellow, Rogers, Wordsworth} 5	283 (10)

Table 8 (*cont.*)

	Order of frequency				no. of pieces including unattrib.
	1	2	3	4	
a. 1854 Hartley (Pr)	16 Byron	16 Shakespeare	14 Campbell	4 Southey	88
1854 Buchan (Pr)	6 { Cowper, Shakespeare }	5 Milton	3 { Burns, Longfellow, Wordsworth }	–	79 (2)
1856 Bowman	10 { Byron, Scott }	9 Wordsworth	8 { Pope, Shakespeare }	6 { Campbell, Shelley, Southey }	210
1856 *Poetry Book*	8 E. Follen	4 { Barton, M. Howitt, Wordsworth }	–	–	66 (35)
1857 Constable, *Advanced English*[a] (Pr)	12 Shakespeare	7 Wordsworth	6 { Byron, Cowper }	5 Milton	74
1858 McCulloch (Pr)	5 Longfellow	3 A.P. Paton	2 *Tennyson*	–	36 (9)
1860 S.R.	10 Longfellow	8 Hemans	6 { Bowring, Byron }	5 { E. Cook, J. Montgomery }	177 (44)
1861 Palgrave[a]	41 Wordsworth	32 Shakespeare	22 Shelley	13 Scott	288 (12)
1861 *Selection I*	10 { Moore, Shelley }	5 J. Taylor	4 { Cowper, Hemans }	3 Longfellow	98 (17)

Year / Source	Poet 1	No.	Poet 2	No.	Poet 3	No.	Poet 4	No.	Total
1861 T.B. Smith[a] (Pr)	Longfellow Shakespeare		Byron	12	Bryant Campbell Southey	8	Milton Tennyson	7	144
1861 Shorter (1)	Wordsworth	14	Shakespeare Shelley	38	Byron	23	Cowper	16	413 (8)
1861 Shorter (2)	Wordsworth	5	Coleridge Longfellow Shakespeare	9	E. Cooke J. Montgomery T. Shorter	7	*Blake* M. Howitt Swain	6	194 (12)
1862 M'Gavin	Stallybrass		M. Howitt	9	Clare Cowper H. F. Gould W. Sugden	5	–	3	157 (11)
1862 Selections	Irons	9	Cowper	15	Milton	14	McCheyne Thomson Toplady	11	138
1862 Junior Reader	Campbell		Hemans	5	Scott	4	–	3	39 (6)
1862 Inglis	Milton	8	Byron Cowper Shakespeare	22	Wordsworth	12	Burns	9	435 (12)
1862 Patmore	Wordsworth	7	Cowper	16	Shakespeare	10	Campbell Southey	8	177 (22)
1863 Curtis[a]	Shakespeare		Campbell	12	Scott Wordsworth	6	–	5	89
1863 Laurie	Cowper Wordsworth	3	Campbell	9	Southey Tennyson	6	Scott	4	102 (8)
1864 E.D.	Wordsworth	10	Cowper	14	Longfellow	12	Campbell Hemans	11	267 (35)
1863 Bland[a] (Pr)	Shakespeare	3	Byron	11	Hemans	5	Knowles Longfellow Milton Tennyson	4	76 (3)

Table 8 (*cont.*)

	Order of frequency				no. of pieces including unattrib.
	1	2	3	4	
1865 Pollard (Pr)	Longfellow 3	Shakespeare 2	—	—	29
1865 *Readings*	Shakespeare 9	Milton 6	Cowper, Dryden, Pope 5	Byron, Campbell, Goldsmith, Southey 4	179
1866 Armstrong	Shakespeare 6	Wordsworth 4	Bryant, Buchanan, Hemans, Scott 3	—	51
1866 *Words*	Wordsworth 21	Longfellow 18	Cowper 11	Hemans, Tennyson 9	150
1866 Bilton (Pr)	Shakespeare 14	Byron, Cowper 5	Milton, Scott 4	Longfellow, Macaulay 3	55
1867 Stevens and Hole (Pr)	Dryden 3	Addison, Bloomfield, Campbell, Goldsmith, Shakespeare 2	—	—	61
1868 Trench	Wordsworth 9	Milton 8	Shelley 6	Blake, Beaumont and Fletcher, W. Drummond, Scott 5	310 (23)

Year / Editor	Poet 1	No.	Poet 2	No.	Poet 3	No.	Poet 4	No.	Total
1868 Lowe	Wordsworth	14	Cowper	10	Burns Campbell	6	Hood	5	91 (7)
1869 Davis	Byron Longfellow Wordsworth	7	Moore Shakespeare	6	Campbell Pope Scott Southey	5	Burns Coleridge Cowper Goldsmith	4	89
1869 Carpenter[a] (Pr)	Shakespeare	6	Wordsworth	4	Bryant Buchanan Hemans Scott	3	–		51
1870 Cornwell	Shakespeare	9	Southey	6	Campbell Cowper Hemans A. and J. Taylor	5	–		151 (15)
1872 Hales[a]	Milton	4	Dryden Gray	3	–		–		28
1875 Palgrave (1)	Wordsworth	9	Scott	8	Blake Cowper Campbell	5	–		84 (11)
1875 Palgrave (2)	Scott	7	Blake Wordsworth	5	Campbell Cowper	3	–		84 (9)

Notes:
(a) Gray's *Elegy* is included, usually complete, in these collections.
(b) (Pr) = prose pieces also
(c) Angus 1809: the entry for Thomson is an estimated equivalent for the twenty-one pages from *The Seasons* that are selected, and that for Grahame an estimated equivalent for nine pages from his *British Georgics*.
(d) Bransby 1831: an enlarged edition of a collection first published in 1814.
(e) Payne 1845: from the fourth edition, 1859. This entry refers to Part 1 of the collection, the next entry to the more advanced Part 2.
(f) This revision by Routledge of Mylius, 1809, is virtually a fresh selection.

Table 9. *Authors in Table 8 by frequency of representation*

	A rankings	B order	C rankings (weighted)	D order (weighted)	E average rank (weighted)	F order
Cowper	67	1	181	2	2.7	4
Shakespeare	53	2	182	1	3.4	1
Campbell	36	3 =	82	5	2.3	8 =
Wordsworth	36	3 =	114	3	3.2	2
Milton	32	5	74	6	2.3	8 =
Scott	29	6	72	7	2.5	6 =
Byron	28	7	83	4	3.0	3
Hemans	26	8	54	8	2.1	11 =
Pope	21	9	52	9	2.5	6 =
Southey	19	10	40	11	2.1	11 =
Thomson	18	11	42	10	2.3	8 =
Longfellow	14	12 =	36	12	2.6	5
J. Montgomery	14	12 =	30	13	2.1	11 =

by each author is shown in column A, and column B gives their order: a first rough measure of popularity. But to give equal credit to a fourth-ranking position and to a first is unsatisfactory. Column C therefore attempts to measure the quality of the rankings by showing the weighted number of ranking positions: a first position counting as four, a second as three, a third as two and a fourth as one. Column D shows the order produced by this weighting. It is desirable to have a single measure that will combine the influence of both raw and weighted scores, that is, the number and the quality of the rankings. By dividing column C by column A a figure is derived that represents the average weighted rank, column E. This figure creates a fresh, 'final' order in column F.

These decimal manipulations suggest, of course, a degree of precision that is unreal. Nevertheless, if they are not pressed too far they provide some information about the views of compilers of verse anthologies for the young. Column A shows that Cowper has 25 per cent more rankings than Shakespeare; column C modifies that statement by showing that Shakespeare, when he is chosen, is represented by practically the same number of pieces as is Cowper; column E combines the two statements into a third that puts Shakespeare's popularity above Cowper's, although by the first statement it had been below it. The figures show also that Shakespeare, Wordsworth and Byron, on these criteria, form the most popular group; a second group is composed of Cowper, Longfellow, Pope and Scott; a third of Milton, Thomson and Campbell; a fourth of Montgomery, Southey and Hemans. The change in Cowper's position, from first in column B to fourth in column F, is caused not only by the popularity of Wordsworth and Byron during the second half of the century but also, in part, by the fact that Cowper is represented by passages from his longer works, and these passages tend to be lengthier, and fewer in number, than those selected from poets who wrote more lyrics than did Cowper.

Campbell is the extreme case of a poet frequently selected but not given a high status numerically (column C). Longfellow is at the other extreme: a 'late' poet (he does not make a ranking until 1851) whose high status numerically more than compensates for the comparatively low number of times he is ranked.

The data in Table 9 can scarcely be compared with those in Table 7, which refers to a much shorter period; but it is noticeable that although the early pre-eminence of Pope and Thomson is not maintained they do not lose their popularity during the nineteenth century to the extent that is sometimes asserted. During both periods Milton keeps a middle position numerically but Addison and James Cunningham fail to keep theirs. Watts, rather surprisingly, does not appear in Table 8 after 1851 and does not make Table 9.

Poets who are ranked in this analysis but are not among the thirteen most frequently quoted include Burns (seven rankings), Gay and Shelley (six), Gray and Young (five), Blake (four), Dryden (three), Chaucer, Clare, Macaulay, Spenser, Tennyson (two). Other poets are steadily represented in the anthologies but not sufficiently to be ranked. Crabbe appears in ten collections between 1805 and 1845; Keats appears first in Esther Hewlett's *The New Speaker*, a. 1826 (*Fancy*, lacking its first eight lines, as *Ode to Fancy* and its author as 'Keate') and in ten later collections, including Payne, 1856, where also he appears as 'Keate', represented this time by the sonnet on Chapman's Homer.

Many anthologies during this period included some work by American writers. Franklin and Washington Irving are the most frequently quoted prose writers; Lydia Huntley Sigourney, who appears in at least fourteen British collections between 1837 and 1864, is probably the most quoted poet before Longfellow. Timothy Dwight and John Blair Linn are included in Evans, 1807; William Cullen Bryant and Longfellow first appear in 1833; Poe in 1836; Whittier in 1851; W.B.O. Peabody occasionally in the 1850s and 1860s. One or two anthologies proclaim their use of American authors. J.F. Winks' anthology began as *Choice Pieces, from British and American Authors*, and then became *The British School Book . . . selections . . . from the most approved standard writers of Great Britain, Ireland and America*, but the American element is nominal. *Readings in*

Poetry, 1833, contains 'specimens of several American poets of deserved reputation'. Amongst the twenty represented are James Kirke Paulding, Carlos Wilcox, Richard Henry Dana, Nathaniel P. Willis, and Richard H. Dana, as well as others better known in Britain. In *Youth's Poetical Instructor*, 1847, most of the passages, unattributed, are taken from monthly publications and it is not easy to say from which side of the Atlantic they come. The modest standard of this collection can be judged by a stanza from the anonymous poem addressed to *The Electric Telegraph*:

> The Post Office destroy'd will be;
> For where's the use of writing,
> When back the answer comes by thee
> Whilst queries we're inditing?

T.B. Smith's *Choice Specimens of English and American Poetry*, 1861, draws on nine American poets, of whom J.R. Lowell is the only one not represented in earlier collections.

Readers

Single texts. The reading-books considered in this enquiry are only a small proportion of a large number. Some of them continue where the spelling-books left off: they reverse the balance of the spelling-book and give most of their space to reading-passages, with only a few spelling-exercises. Most texts provide spelling-practice, if at all, only in the vocabularies that precede the reading-passages. These vocabularies list the difficult words, divided into syllables, often accented, defined and identified as a part of speech. The pupils were usually expected to learn these lists, but not by heart, before reading the passage. These single reading-books are not part of a series. They are designed for an age range of several years, elementary or advanced. Some readers are general in that they aim to cover many different topics, in prose and verse, fact and fiction. Others have a dominant theme: religious or moral development; reading aloud as a performance skill; travel and geography; natural history; agriculture; manufactures. The passages are often accompanied by questions requiring simple recall or, more rarely, reasoning, and nearly all the books stress comprehension.

By the beginning of the nineteenth century the production of such textbooks was becoming a worthwhile commercial operation. One of their most colourful promoters was Sir Richard Phillips. As a young man he had spent a year as an usher in a Chester school and two years running a commercial academy in Leicester. He then sold hosiery, pianos and books, and settled as a writer, under many names, and publisher of popular manuals. In spite of his radical views and a prison sentence for selling Paine's *The Rights of Man*, he became Sheriff of London. His *Reading Exercises for the Use of Schools*, a. 1813, nominally by the Rev. David Blair, one of Phillips' ghostly designations, contains prose and verse extracts from 'the numerous books . . . written for children within the last twenty years', most of which, he adds, he has been obliged to alter. Joseph Guy, father and son, in London and William Angus in Glasgow represent the increasing number of private schoolmasters whose talents and profits lay, at least equally with teaching, in the production of textbooks. Angus' *Juvenile Pieces, in Prose and Verse*, 1815, contains spelling-lists of the usual kind; prose and verse passages marked with vertical strokes to indicate 'rhetorical pauses' not shown by punctuation; 'select sentences'; homophones; a list of all words used in the reading-passages whose pronunciation might cause difficulty; and an appendix 'containing the history of Joseph, and an abridgment of Watts' Preservative from the Sins and Follies of Childhood and Youth'. The variety of its contents, and those of similar texts, is not necessarily a sign of indiscriminate or hack compilation. A set of the books could serve pupils who were at different stages of instruction, and each pupil could make his one textbook serve for several stages. The parents of Angus' pupils were not likely to spare much money for textbooks; a prudent policy like this brought him more pupils than the policy, followed by practitioners at a more prosperous level, of specialising the textbooks and requiring the pupil to buy more of them.

Adam Keys, whose *Rhyming Primer* had had some novelty of method, produced also an elementary reading-book, *The Excitement*, 1831, 'adapted to the self-corrective method of teaching to read'. This method is a variation of the common practice of making children stand in a line and read a sentence each in turn. In the usual practice, when a pupil made a mistake the next in line was asked to correct it; if he failed the opportunity passed down the line until a pupil made the correction. The successful pupil then 'moved up' to a position above that of the pupil who originated the mistake. In Keys' system the pupil making the original mistake moves at once to the bottom of the line and the correction is made not by the pupil next in line but by the class as a whole. Keys recommends the method because it prevents quarrels between the erring reader and his supplanter. In most texts of this kind methods of class organisation are not discussed except as they relate to the teachers' main concern: that the children should understand what they read. *Spelling, Questions and Stories*, 1825, is closely related to object lessons. Questions (animal, mineral, vegetable, manufactured?) are asked about words in spelling-lists and in stories. It is a sensible book, leaving much to the judgment of the infant teacher: 'The answers which the children will give ... will suggest fresh words to spell, to talk, to enquire and to think about' (Part 2, Intro.). James Campbell, a teacher in Dundee, contrasts his 'system of mental exercise', that is, thinking about the meaning of what you read, with 'bare reading' (*The Child's Economic Instructor*, Part 33, [1829] 1852 edn, preface). Ingram Cobbin, 1831, writes that 'the *interrogatory method* of teaching, now so much in use, is highly valuable', although his own use of it seems very restricted:

Text: 'Cam-els are bred in the East, but they are not known all o-ver the East, but on-ly in Per-sia, Tur-key . . .'

Question: 'In what part of the world are camels bred? In what parts of the East are they known?'   (p. 23)

Restricted the questions may be, but opening up a simple text in this way was felt to be an innovation and an educational advance. Cobbin, who had been educated at Hoxton Academy, was secretary to the British and Foreign School Society and was informed about teaching-methods. More detailed questioning, associated with Lancasterian methods, had been familiar since early in the century but was seen as an aspect of mechanical reading and was itself mechanical. A work contemporary with Cobbin's shows the process. The sentence to be read is 'It is bad for men to do any ill.' A child reads and spells the first three words. Teacher: 'It is what?' The child reads, 'It is bad for men.' Teacher: 'Bad for whom? What is it for men?' The child reads, 'It is bad for men to do any ill.' Teacher: 'To do any what? What is bad ... What is it for men? For whom is it bad? What is it bad for men to do? Any what? Who are not to do any ill? What is it for men to do any ill?' (Gall, a. 1832, p. 37).

Feverish questioning of this kind was not used in the more advanced stages of teaching comprehension, and there seems to have been a gap of some years between the initial popularity of mechanical questioning and the general use of questioning with older pupils. It is almost as if the crudities of mechanical questioning had created a prejudice against a questioning approach to the teaching of literature.

William Fletcher, master of Woodbridge Grammar School, in *The Child's Handbook* treated questioning as a skill in need of advocacy:

1837 'For ages ... instead of treating the young as sentient beings, capable of judgment and reflection, they have been governed and directed as mere machines ... Rendering them distinguished for retentive memories rather than cultivated understandings, has been almost the exclusive business of the teacher.'

(pp. 7 and 9)

The children, he says, should be asked 'first, such questions as they might propose themselves . . . and next, such as might be put on the part of the teacher' (p. 16).

That children should enjoy what they read seems by now to be taken more for granted: the point is seldom discussed in the prefaces. A strangely contrary view, however, is expressed by George Fulton:

1826 'From upwards of forty years' experience in Teaching, I have formed the opinion, that to begin a child's instructions with lessons conveying meaning and amusement, may deceive parents and instructors, leading them to believe that the pupil is making rapid improvement; while . . . his mind has been taken up with the amusement afforded him; and the words he has appeared to read have made so little impression, that perhaps he will hardly be able to recognise one of them in any other book.' (p. 12)

Fulton, although he was writing as an elderly man, was an innovative and perceptive teacher, and as the book in which he states his principle contains more than a hundred pages of well-chosen prose and verse one is left to suppose that it applies only to the very first stages of learning to read.

If a single text has to represent this group of elementary readers it would be one without pictures or questions, containing prose and verse passages, mostly without attribution, suited to the interests of children in comfortable homes. Such is *The Child's Reader*, published together with *Pleasure and Profit* in 1843, from which representative titles are : 'Good Manners' (hortatory); 'The Rattlesnake' (informative); 'The Basket-Woman' (prose story); 'The Old Man's Comforts' (Southey's poem beginning, 'You are old, Father William', later transformed by Lewis Carroll).

During the early decades of the nineteenth century there was an increasing emphasis on the factual and informative, sometimes accompanied by an explicit rejection of fiction and verse, as in *The Class Book*, 1806, by David Blair (i.e. Sir Richard Phillips), which condemns 'Speakers' and 'Readers' and 'Beauties' as 'compositions which do not teach any thing, which are often unintelligible to young persons, and which . . . leave the mind in a state of listless curiosity and total ignorance'. According to Phillips (nearly fifty years before Dickens' *Hard Times*, 1854), 'the greatest possible number of facts ought to be submitted to the observation of children' (preface). This emphasis on factual knowledge came to be strengthened by what was seen as a need to provide vocationally directed reading-matter for the poor, especially the rural poor. C.W. Johnson's *The English Rural Spelling Book . . . intended as an introduction to the English language; and to the first principles of the practical and scientific cultivation of the soil*, 1846, ranges from a picture alphabet through spelling-lists to simple agricultural chemistry and miscellaneous verse and prayers; and the Irish Commissioners produced about the same time their *Agricultural Class Book; or, how best to cultivate a small farm and garden.* The factual and the technological are stressed also in P. Jamieson's *The Juvenile Library or School Class Book, c.* 1820, which includes extracts from books classified as *Mineralogy, Botany, Natural History, Trades and Inventions* as well as from history, geography and poetry. The scientific and technological extracts ('Biscuit baking at Deptford'; 'Fire damp and safety lamp') occupy half the book.

Other readers in the same spirit are:

1821   John Platts: *The Literary and Scientific Class Book.*

1827   J.M. M'Culloch: *A Course of Elementary Reading in Science and Literature,* which expresses the compiler's view that 'a class-book for an initiatory school should consist of lessons on useful subjects rather than of rhetorical passages'.

(preface)

1837   R.T. Linnington: *The Scientific Reader and Practical Elocutionist.* The extracts are not all scientific. There are sections of 'classical modern poetry' (no Wordsworth or Coleridge), dramatic, oratorical and comic pieces. There are more than 500 questions ('in accordance with the Catechetical System which has been so long and so successfully practised') on the scientific pieces: 'What is meant by Attraction?' 'Is fire a real substance?' 'At what angles do the crystals of frozen water form?'

1841   *Elementary Instruction,* which is aimed to gratify children's 'thirst for information', avoids the catechetical method, 'it being considered that interrogation should be regulated by the judgment of the teacher, and the progress of the pupil'. The contents range from the multiplication tables through 'different kinds of meat' to poems and hymns (Watts, Hemans, the Taylors).

1845   The Irish Commissioners' *Reading Book for the Use of Female Schools* includes historical and poetical pieces, but its emphasis falls equally on the factual ('The manufacture of pins and needles') and on the vocational ('Duties of a housemaid').

1851c   William Martin, in his *Intellectual Reading Book,* invokes 'the intellectual method of teaching' (by which is meant that children should be helped by questioning to understand what they learn) and 'Divine Poesy, as one of the most efficient engines in the culture of the feelings'. The book illustrates the junction, but not the fusion, of the moral and the instructional. Each section of the book is in two parts: the first, 'religious and moral lessons'; the second, 'intellectual lessons', dealing with such things as canals, whales, national industries. Poetry is represented by twenty-four poems; twenty-three by Martin himself and one by Prince Albert.

1857   *Constable's Advanced English Reading Book* has sections of prose and poetry preceded by seven sections on, e.g., zoology; vegetable products; social economy; law, property and constitution.

The utilitarian and factual character of so many reading-books is derived from diverse points of view: a desire to bring contemporary and technological themes into children's school reading; a concern for vocational relevance; an assumption that factual reading was all the working classes could safely be given, or all that they were capable of benefiting from; the belief, less widely held, that writing that was in both spirit and form prosaic was morally superior to, or at least safer than, imaginative literature. The older emphasis on enjoyment was not lost, but in school-texts it was subdued. One work in particular is noticeable for preserving it. *The National Reader*, by the Rev T. Clarke (i.e. John Galt), 1821, professes to combine not the instructional and the moral but 'instruction and entertainment', which Galt says are the two objects of every juvenile book; for 'it is necessary to engage the imagination, if we would cultivate the understanding, of youth'. If more teachers had shared this wise opinion there would have been less emphasis on the educationally harmful opposition, strong at the time, between intellectual and affective responses to literature. Galt was not, of course, excluding or repudiating moral influence: it could arise from instruction or from entertainment, and his selection of pieces on natural history favoured 'such animals and insects . . . as, from their habitudes, furnished a moral from whence youth might learn the virtue of benevolence' (preface). In a rather more old-fashioned tone and in deliberate opposition to current trends A.M. Hartley compiled an anthology 'from Belles Lettres, and the works of imaginative authors' in preference to 'dry selections from scientific and ratiocinative authors' (1846, preface).

Readers in series. The readers that appeared in series express most of the tendencies already discussed. Many are concerned primarily to strengthen the pupil's Christian, and often a particular doctrinal, stance at the same time as they provide vocationally useful information. Some aim to provide a broad, simple education in geography and history, with a little natural history and physical science; others emphasise not only science but also technology and manufacturing industry. Some are concerned also with the pupils' future status as citizens, and set out to introduce them to economics and government. Seldom is anything provided just in order to give pleasure. All the readers directly or indirectly express an intention to influence the pupils' moral development, and in most of them the moral development includes, unsurprisingly, an acceptance of the society, and of that position in it, in which the pupils find themselves.

The readers published before 1870 were a response to a need for popular rather than mass education. Their compilers had to assume that the pupils might have the Bible, and occasionally little else, to read at home or, at worst, in school. Variety, therefore, was important. So was quantity. Because the books would be read again and again by the same child they should contain as much as possible. But they had also to be cheap. For commercial reasons it suited the publishers, and for organisational reasons it suited the schools, that the books should be produced in a graded and coherent series: one book for each year, up to four, five or six years. A series sometimes had to be increased by supplementary volumes or by bridging volumes intercalated into a series because there was a gap in the level of difficulty between the texts for consecutive years. The passages, which might be grouped thematically, were usually accompanied by questions and, in the early volumes of a series, by spelling- and vocabulary lists.

The series came from three overlapping sources. Some, throughout the period, were issued by commercial publishers but were known by the names of their authors, from whom the initiative may or may not have come. In many cases (e.g. William Pinnock, John Cassell, J.S. Laurie) it is difficult to distinguish author from publisher. A second group of readers, especially during the 1840s, was compiled, sometimes by named authors but more often anonymously, on behalf of governmental or denominational bodies such as the Commissioners of National Education in Ireland and the National Society for Promoting the Education of the Poor in the Principles of the Established Church. These bodies sometimes published the books themselves but more often worked through commercial publishers. From 1860 the initiative passed to the publishers. Their series were sometimes anonymous, sometimes by named authors. The more advanced the book the more likely that the compiler would be named. About sixty titles are marked RS in Bibliography 1; these should give a representative impression of the earlier series. Their number increased after 1870; by 1876 there were at least fifteen series of readers fitted to the Revised Code (Goldstrom, 1972a, p. 167).

The readers are documents of great social and educational interest, but not in a way that is central to this enquiry. Apart from political economy, they added little that was new to the kind of material that might be read in an English lesson, but they greatly extended its range, especially in elementary technology. The nature of the books largely determined how they could be read in class. The important variable was the teacher's skill in questioning, but, on the evidence of the texts, this was not expected to go further (nor were most teachers perhaps capable of going further) than questions on recall and simple vocabulary. The manuals and the questions in the readers show little awareness of what was to become a commonplace: that questions, from pupil and from teacher, were the growing-points of the children's classroom education.

The readers must here receive less attention than their number and social importance might seem to require. Detailed study of them must wait also until more bibliographical information is available. Meantime the content of many of the readers has been most usefully set in its social and political context by J.M. Goldstrom in *The social content of education, 1808–1870*, and little can be added here to what he says. Goldstrom classifies the principal themes of the readers as: (i) Christian theological instruction; (ii) class structure; (iii) domestic and vocational training; (iv) the outside world; (v) good and bad conduct.

American readers. American readers and anthologies resemble the British ones in their emphasis on morality and in the increasing prominence given to factual, technological and vocational information. They differ in giving greater emphasis to geography, especially the geography of America, and in their greater emphasis on American writing. This natural desire to give prominence to American authors was expressed without denigration of British writing and with only occasional overestimation of American, as when Noah Webster, in strengthening the American content of the early editions of his *An American Selection*, claimed that 'the writings which marked the revolution . . . are perhaps not inferior to Cicero and Demosthenes'.[3]

The freshness of American readers could be appreciated in Britain. In 1827 John Pierpont of Boston compiled *The National Reader*, stressing that it was for American youth, for whom no British reading-book was or should be suitable. An Englishman living in Thetford, Norfolk, read in a Sheffield newspaper a review of Pierpont's book, sent for a copy and reissued it for English schools. He considered it to be:

1829 'A vast improvement on similar books, which are at present used in Great Britain; I found the matter better adapted to the sprightliness of youthful fancy, and more attractive to the eagerness of youthful curiosity . . . The pious reflections seemed to me of a character more inviting to juvenile readers; and devotional pieces, free from the stiffness of age, and the rust of antiquity.'
(E.H. Barker, preface to the London edn, 1829, of Pierpont's *The National Reader*)

Other early collections with a patriotic bias are *The American Poetical Miscellany*, 1809, which 'introduces' the work of little-known American writers, and *The American Prose Miscellany*, 1809, which is notable also for

---

[3] 1809 edition, quoted by Nila B. Smith, (1934) 1965, p. 49.

its inclusion of Mirabeau, Voltaire, Diderot, La Rochefoucauld and Marmontel in translation. Joseph Richardson's *The American Reader*, 1810, is 'wholly from American authors'; Samuel Worcester, (*c.* 1830) 1847, chooses American authors rather than, for example, Mrs Barbauld, whose style he considers 'unnatural and in bad taste', but he does include Goldsmith, Hemans, Addison and Wordsworth. Lyman Cobb's *North American Reader*, 1835, is restricted to American writers, and B.B. Edwards in the same year, although he includes 'the wisdom married to immortal verse' of Coleridge, considers Johnson and Blair 'not suitable' and Shakespeare, Milton, Thomson and Cowper 'not necessary' compared with the 'manly sense' of Jeremiah Evarts and the 'Ciceronian elegance and dignity of Robert Hall'. It was natural that on the whole the more vocational and factual readers relied on American sources and the more literary ones on British and translated European classical sources. Yet it is surprising that Abner Alden's *The Reader*, (1802) 1822, not an advanced collection, contains 21 pieces by Pope, out of 67; less surprising that Warren Colburn's *First Lessons in Reading and Grammar*, 1832, should be drawn entirely from Maria Edgeworth and Berquin, or that of the 120 pieces in Charles Merriam's *The American Reader*, (1828) 1829, 61 should be by British authors, including Gray's *Elegy*, 1 speech from *Julius Caesar*, and 6 poems by Felicia Hemans.

American readers have been studied more thoroughly than have the corresponding British texts. They reflect more directly, and more quickly, cultural changes that were nearer the surface of society than in Britain. The American readers, more even than the British ones, are social rather than pedagogical documents. When President Eliot of Harvard described them in 1891 as 'ineffable trash' because they offered not real literature but scraps, he failed to understand what the books were doing and how important they were (Reeder, 1900, p. 57). But in spite of the analyses, such as those by John A. Nietz and his students (1953, 1961), by Charles Carpenter, 1963, and by Michael V. Belok, 1973, it is difficult to assess the potential influence of the readers on the teaching of literature as it is envisaged in this enquiry. Like many of the British texts, most American readers were little concerned with imaginative literature: they were compressed, and sometimes digested, collections of informative reading.

We do not know yet how to assess the educational significance of readers. It is useful to have broad impressions quantified, as that the proportion of religious (as distinct from merely moral) matter in American readers before 1775 was 83 per cent; that it dropped to 22 per cent between 1775 and 1825, to 7.5 per cent over the following fifty years and to 1.5 per cent between

1875 and 1915 (Nietz, 1953). More penetrating is the kind of study carried out by Stanley W. Lindberg in *The Annotated McGuffey*, 1976, where the effects are studied of both commercial and educational influences on a single series, the six volumes of *The Eclectic Readers*, first published in 1836 and described by Applebee as 'virtually universal for the next fifty years'. This kind of analysis, however, needs to be supported by information about how the readers were used. Their educational significance depends as much on what the teachers did with them as on the nature of their contents.

Imagination, understanding, memory

Imagination. The three lines of thought discussed above (p. 193) in relation to eighteenth-century texts continue into the nineteenth century. The influence of literature on behaviour and its role in promoting religious, moral, patriotic and even political attitudes were also touched on above. Although still a matter of steady concern, it is discussed less often in early-nineteenth-century texts than is the closely related topic of the imagination, especially as manifested in the novel.

Edward Mangin's *An Essay on Light Reading*, 1808, is an attack on the novel, which he takes to include 'romances, histories, memoirs, letters, tales, lives, and adventures', all of which, except romances 'profess to be resemblances of truth . . . representations of manners and persons actually living, or who have lived'. The grounds of his attack are two-fold: that such works misrepresent the truth, and that 'the first ambition of the inexperienced youth who reads these deleterious memoirs is, to emulate the principal personage' (p. 42). Mangin is writing about young people of seventeen or eighteen, and a particular target for his attack is *Tom Jones*: 'in our seminaries of education, many young persons . . . know more of the site of Mr Allworthy's house, and its environs, than they do of Athens or Rome . . . and are intimate with every corner in Molly Seagrim's bedchamber' (pp. 33–4). He praises Goldsmith, at length and in capital letters, as 'a moral instructor'. Robertson, Hume, Richardson, Cowper, Gray, Beattie, Collins and, especially, Langhorne, are also approved reading; Pope and Swift are as bad as Fielding and Smollett. Mangin's concluding statement is more balanced than his opening attacks and might be approved by some modern critics of television: '*Light reading*, of a certain kind, is . . . "the thief of time"; and, as the expression is usually understood, essentially injurious to the growth of private and public virtue' (p. 212). It has always been easy for cultivated people to say things like that.

Observations on Works of Fiction in general and particularly those for childhood and adolescence, 1813, is addressed to all who write for a living, and its comments on 'the inundation of juvenile literature, which seems ever ready to pour in upon our nurseries and school-rooms' (p. 39) are not directed towards schools. The writer praises Maria Edgeworth's stories and *Sandford and Merton*, but finds the anonymous *Julietta, or the Triumph of mental Accomplishments over personal Defects* rather 'overstrained'. She considers writing for adolescents difficult because 'so much instruction has already been imbibed', and she expresses what was to become a familiar complaint: 'It might be wished that the English *stock-books* for adolescence kept pace with those for childhood' (p. 65).

Three writers in 1818 expressed views about the educational importance of imagination. William Enfield, 1818, writing in 1793, regretted that modern education 'is calculated, almost solely, for the exercise and improvement of the understanding and memory, and makes little provision for the cultivation of other faculties of the mind ... as if our whole business and our whole enjoyment consisted in *thinking*, and nature had designed us neither to *feel* nor to *act*' (p. 3). Enfield argues that imagination is the controlling force in aesthetic activities, amongst which he includes gardening, poetry and architecture, and that the beneficial effects of aesthetic experience transfer to the moral field (p. 11). His closing words are: 'I only wish to recommend the cultivation of the powers of Imagination and Taste, in conjunction with those of the understanding.' William Godwin agreed: 'The imagination is to be cultivated in education, more than the dry accumulation of science and natural facts' (1818, p. 4).

Henry Gray Macnab, on the other hand, in *Analysis and Analogy recommended as the means of rendering Experience and Observation useful in Education*, 1818, is, amongst other concerns, attacking 'the destructive power of imagination', but it is unlikely that his interpretation of the term is the same as Enfield's. For Macnab the imagination is the centre of irrationality. He refers to it much as earlier generations had referred to enthusiasm: 'Victims to the delusive and destructive power of imagination ... slaves to caprice and fancy, excited to passion and prejudice ... have endeavoured to undermine *the strongholds of Religion, Virtue and genuine Science* ... The imagination ... extinguishes the mild and pleasing light of reason' (p. 2). He sharply distinguishes 'instinctive' and 'intuitive' powers from imagination, and much of his essay is a discussion of these powers in relation to science.

Similar fears, in quite a different context, are expressed in *Hints on Reading*, 1839, by M.A. Stodart. The hints are addressed to young girls in the form of letters, one of which, about poetry, is more deeply considered than is usual in such exhortations. It discusses the relation between truth and poetry. The imagination is both powerful and a potential enemy to truth and therefore to religion: 'The pleasures of imagination have been described in prose and verse. A volume might be written upon its evils . . . Where there is much imagination, there ought to be a superior quality of judgment to hold it in rein . . . Let such as possess imagination . . . daily seek for strength from above, to cast down imaginations.' Truth is the essential quality to be pursued in education, and although not all poetry is falsehood 'very much of worldly poetry is calculated to blind the eyes of those who believe not, as well as of those who believe' (pp. 54–60). The poet most strongly recommended is, a little surprisingly, Spenser.

The educative importance of the imagination was maintained with especial vigour by E.H. Barker, who wrote in the preface to his English edition of Pierpont's *The National Reader*:

1829   A teacher would have greater success 'if he conveyed his instruction more through the imagination than through the judgment of the pupil, – if he aimed more at captivating the heart, than at improving the mind . . . if he relied more on the living spring of natural feelings . . . than on the inculcation of didactic principles, however wise . . . The imaginative POET, rather than the ratiocinative PHILOSOPHER, is required for the instruction of youth.'

Barker expresses himself strongly, but he is putting forward a minority view, in opposition to a state of affairs later described by Catherine Sinclair in the preface to what has been described as 'an almost revolutionary novel for children', *Holiday House*:

'The minds of young people are now manufactured like webs of linen, all alike, and nothing left to nature . . . All play of imagination is now carefully discouraged, and books written for young persons are generally a mere record of dry facts, unenlivened by any appeal to the heart, or any excitement to the fancy.'

(Quoted by Carpenter and Prichard, *The Oxford Companion to Children's Literature*, 1984, s.v. *Holiday House*)

A writer on 'Books for Children' in the *Quarterly Review* saw the forces opposed to the proper use of the imagination as those of too narrow a morality. The increase of population and changes in education at the end of the eighteenth century had the effect that 'the age soon began to demand something more and something better':

1843   'Much of the monotonous repetition of spelling-book, dictionary, and grammar, in which children's minds had been kept . . . was repealed . . . Besides original works of great merit, our young people were furnished with extracts and compilations from the best classic and old English writers, and with abridgments from the first standard authors . . . [but] because their predecessors had appealed almost exclusively, and sometimes most perniciously, to the imagination . . . the marvellous and the romantic, even when free from all impurity, was condemned by some as useless, by others as false; and one of the most striking features of this change of system may be characterised as the predominance of a more direct moral teaching . . . It may be justly questioned whether . . . in banishing the world of fiction, and advancing one of reality in its place, we have not sometimes dismissed a protector, and introduced an enemy.' (*Quarterly Review*, 71, p. 56)

Comments of this kind express a permanent tension between two groups of educational attitudes: on the one hand those which tend to mistrust human nature and seek to control it directly, and on the other those which tend to trust human nature and seek to control only the environment in which it develops. During the middle decades of the nineteenth century it was perhaps true to say, with H.G. Robinson, a trainer of teachers, 'The culture of the imagination . . . appears in these days to be rather underrated . . . Some people seem afraid of this faculty . . . The tendency of earnest middle-class Englishmen is to compress truth, to square and shape it into formulas and to confine it within party limits' (1860, pp. 429–30). The Revised Code of 1862 marked some easement of this narrowly utilitarian attitude but, as Goldstrom points out, there were still inspectors who thought that 'extracts from the English classics and specimens of high-class poetry are neither fitted for the age of the scholars, nor useful to their present or their future career' (Goldstrom, 1972a, p. 168, quoting Report of the Committee of Council, 1866–7, p. 129).

Understanding. Amongst the anthologies and reading-books of this period there is an irregular but perceptible development in the way the pieces are presented and in what the compilers expect the teachers to do. In broad terms the change is from appreciative comment (sometimes rather vacuous) to explanation; from explanation to questioning; from questioning to judgment and evaluation.

The Understanding Reader, by Daniel Adams, a teacher in Leominster, Massachusetts, is one of the early texts that make explicit what teachers are thought to have neglected:

(1803b) 1805 'Would it not . . . be proper, to add to what is usually understood by *learning children to read*, the *learning of them to understand*? Is no regard to be had to the definition of words? to the sense of the writer? to the exercises of reflection? to the fixing of the attention? and to the cultivation of the memory?' (preface)

Adams' book is aimed at 'that most necessary habit of READING WITH ATTENTION' but the questions that are attached to a few passages require nothing more demanding than recall. Adams makes the same point in his *The Thorough Scholar*, where he expresses a view unusual for his times:

1803a 'Universal Axiom in Education: That METHOD in teaching, which most naturally leads Youth into reflections of their own, and which most readily calls forth the operations of their own minds, is BEST.' (preface)

John Evans, in *The Parnassian Garland*, 1807, prefaces each extract with 'a very few remarks [which] have a considerable effect in preparing the understanding' because 'a mere general *Title* has not sufficient interest to attract the attention, especially of Youth, whose ideas, on most topics, are loose and indefinite' (preface). Thomas Wemyss, 1808, is writing for parents, in the expectation that his pupils may first read his anthology at home. He recommends the Edgeworths' *Poetry Explained* and says what he thinks explanation involves: 'Pointing out the meaning of the words, and the substance of the sentiment, with the adaptation of the one to the other, and the difference between poetical and prosaic language. Let inversions be marked and ellipses filled up' (preface). Pinnock's *Universal Explanatory English Reader*, 1813, is more detailed, if more mechanical. Each sentence in an extract is numbered. The extract is preceded by definitions of the difficult words that appear in the text, where they are italicised; each defining word is numbered according to the sentence in which it occurs. A similar method, apart from the numbering, is followed in *The Moral Poetical Miscellany*, 1819, and in many other collections.

J.M. M'Culloch, in *A Series of Lessons in Prose and Verse*, 1831, attacks elocution on various grounds, including its tendency to encourage children to read without understanding:

'Till within the last few years . . . the qualification most highly valued in a Teacher was a practical acquaintance with some popular theory of Elocution; and the chief . . . end aimed at in Teaching, seems to have been – to burden the memory of the pupil with 'Rules' and 'Extracts' utterly unsuited to his capacity. No one who has escaped the misfortune of toiling through the works of the fashionable Teachers of the last generation, their 'Speakers', 'Rhetorical Readers', 'Pronouncing Vocabularies', &c. – can form any conception of the ingenuity that has been extended in rearing up barriers in the Scholar's way.' (preface)

He hopes that 'the time is nearly gone by, when children of seven and eight years of age are to be compelled to waste their time and their faculties on such preposterous and unsuitable exercises as enacting dramatic scenes, reciting parliamentary speeches, and reading the latest sentimental poetry' (*ibid.*). A change will improve the morals of young people also, especially if they no longer meet so much of three authors, whom he names, one supposes, as different types of undesirable influence:

'It is truly deplorable to think of the amount of bad morality and false religion that must have been disseminated among the youth of this country, through the medium of school-books which were mainly compiled from such writers as Shakspeare, Chesterfield, and Hume.'   (*ibid.*)

M'Culloch links explicitly two opinions that many compilers of anthologies and readers expressed separately: that children should be taught to understand what they read, and that what they read should be useful. He says of his book:

'Being intended for schools, where the Teacher makes it his business to instruct his Pupils in the *meaning* of what is read, as well as in the "art of reading", it has been compiled [from] only such lessons as appeared well adapted to stimulate juvenile curiosity, and store the mind with useful knowledge.'   (preface)

He gives directions to the teacher on a number of points of method:

'Endeavour to get the Pupil to understand the meaning of every lesson he reads . . . aim at getting him to understand the *scope* of the lesson and the *amount* of information contained in it, rather than the mere meaning of the leading words that occur.'   (p. vii)

The teacher is to emphasise the derivation of words, and M'Culloch lists Latin and Greek roots and prefixes that are to be learnt. The pupil is to record all words of more than four syllables and all 'peculiar' words. M'Culloch also provides 'elliptical lessons', a technique that is discussed below in chapter 7. In his fourth reading-book he just recognises that the attempt to explain everything fully may interfere with the pupil's reading: 'The Explanatory System of Instruction, though eminently helpful to the intellectual culture of the pupil, is yet apt, when uninterruptedly pursued, to interfere with speedy progress in the mere art of reading' (1837d; 1858 edn, preface).

Richard Batt also claims to be a follower of the 'explanatory system'. His *Gleanings in Poetry*, 1836, is arranged in a loose thematic form that derives its strength from his view that compilers of school anthologies have 'strangely overlooked' pleasure, and its weakness from his view that 'Poetry is capable of rendering almost *any* subject more inviting, and often more instructive than prose' (preface, p. xxv). He offers, for example, under the theme 'Clouds', a pedestrian poem by S.C. Hall, followed by a prose passage on the formation of clouds from W. Mullinger Higgins' *The Earth*; Coleridge's *Fancy In Nubibus*, untitled, with another passage from Higgins; Antony's 'Sometime we see a cloud that's dragonish . . .' with omissions (*Antony and Cleopatra*, IV. xiv. 1–11) and a long note by the compiler quoting Sir Humphry Davy; and finally Shelley's *The Cloud*, accompanied by an extract from the compiler's journal of a tour in Northern Ireland in which he quotes two snatches of verse. The 220 lines of verse in this section of the anthology are accompanied by more than 1200 words of prose. These prose appendages seldom explain the text; usually they provide a factual, informative diversion, expressing Batt's view, argued in a long and interesting preface, that:

'Reading books for juvenile minds should consist chiefly of judicious selections from approved works on the general history of nations, biography, physical geography, natural history, astronomy, and the elements of general science. These subjects have been almost entirely neglected in many schools of respectability; I am aware that they are *now* brought more prominently into view, but in many seminaries for children of the middle classes of society they are still kept almost or altogether in the shade of obscurity.'   (p. xvii)

It is interesting to find Batt, a Quaker teaching in a Quaker school, saying that young people will get more from science 'recorded in an inviting and impressive manner' than from what are '(to them) dry and repulsive disquisitions on the principles of religion and virtue' (p. xxiv). In applying his views to the teaching of poetry Batt inevitably chooses much inferior work, but he is eloquent on what poetry has meant in his own life, and his pursuit of it for the anthology was strong enough to make him write to Wordsworth, Southey and James Montgomery for permission to print their verse (p. xxxvi). It is also interesting to find a teacher in a middle-class school referring with respect to the superior range of modern topics offered by the elementary school reader.

More detailed teaching is described by Walter McLeod. In his *The First Poetical Reading Book*, 1849, each poem is preceded by a list of words, the spelling and meaning of which are to be learnt; the anthology is to be used, he says, like a class reader. The poems are learnt by heart at home; then they are explained and read in class and written out on slates. Explanation involves paraphrase: 'Besides the usual examination on the meanings of the words and phrases, and the sense of each separate sentence or verse, the children should be accustomed to state, in their own words, the substance of the portion which they have read . . . or, in other words, to turn the poetical description into prose' (Intro.). Tension between literary and informative modes is apparent also in Edward Hughes' *Select English Poetry*, 1851, where every poem has a prose introduction and the anthology ends with an appendix of Greek, Latin and Saxon roots. Hughes expresses the tension: 'The Intellectual System of Education is now too firmly established to require anything to be said in its favour. But it may be doubted if those who have adopted it have not . . . neglected the Imaginative

Powers' (preface). He gives two pieces of advice to the teacher: the pupils should be brought to understand the poems 'as far as grammatical and logical structure is concerned' and for their historical and geographical content; but the poem should also 'be felt and appreciated through that mysterious contact of mind with mind in which all true teaching consists' (preface). Similarly William Pollard, in *The Ackworth Reading Book*, 1865:

'You may either teach elocution, dwelling upon the beauties of style, the structure and force of sentences, the power and meaning of figures of speech, the effects of emphasis, of modulation of the voice, and of tone generally; or you may teach historical, geographical and scientific facts. But the attempt to teach both in the same lesson, and by means of the same book, must prove a failure.'   (preface)

The Irish Commissioners' *Selections from the British Poets* would, it was hoped, 'invigorate the intellectual faculties of the pupils, sharpen their critical perceptions, exercise their memories, improve their taste for reading, and call their moral powers into vigorous action' (Vol. 1, 1821, preface). Referring to a group of poems, *Paradise Lost, The Task, The Seasons, The Excursion*, Robert Bloomfield's *The Farmer's Boy* and Clare's *The Village Minstrel*, the compiler says, 'It is the Christian spirit by which they are pervaded that constitutes their principal value ... In the workshop of the artizan, the cottage of the peasant [the works of] our Descriptive and Moral poets ... should be the study of the poor and humble after the toils of the day are over' (Vol. II, 1852, Intro. to section on the seasons). These results were to be pursued by procedures that are described in outline. The class is to read poetry on at least one day in the week. The teacher reads the poem, part of its biographical introduction and part of the introduction to the group ('Sacred', 'Didactic and Moral', 'Descriptive') in which it comes. He explains the allusions and points out expressions that need to be emphasised in reading aloud; he explains the meaning of the poem and what the writer was trying to achieve. He then questions the class about the author's life and discusses what critics have said about him. Only then 'each of the pupils should ... be required to read, either the whole, or a portion of the piece'. Recitation and further practice in reading aloud should follow, with more questioning on the vocabulary and grammar of the poem. Eighteenth-century textbooks may have been intended to present literature rather than to teach it, but by the middle of the nineteenth century attempts were certainly being made to 'do' literature thoroughly.

Criticism, in the weak sense of forming a judgment, is implicit in many of the learning-procedures so far described, but the term itself is rare. An unusual example occurs in a volume of *Examinations composed for the Pupils at Ormskirk Classical and Commercial School*, 1804. These are sets of questions on prescribed parts, mostly grammatical, of particular textbooks, but the final question is just 'Required a criticism of the following stanza' – nine lines of verse. One of the textbooks to which the *Examinations* refer is stated to be David Irving's *The Elements of English Composition*, which describes in separate chapters stylistic qualities such as clarity, strength, harmony. Four of its later chapters are given to what is in each case called 'Critical examination of a passage in the writings of . . .' (Addison, Swift, and others), in which the passage is scrutinised in terms of the qualities described earlier. It seems virtually certain that this is the procedure envisaged at Ormskirk. It is noticeable, too, how quickly Irving's book was used. It was published in 1801 and the Ormskirk pupils had used it for long enough to have been examined on it, and for the questions to have been published in 1804.

The Ormskirk questions have a bite, both linguistic and critical, unlike any school textbook of the period. Instead of accepting, and asking the pupil to repeat, the customary definition of a sentence as making complete sense the book asks: 'Strictly speaking, does the phrase *if I love* convey a complete sense?' (p. 31). The questions press the pupils to think about the meaning of what they read: 'What is the precise meaning of the following phrases? . . . Supposing the emphasis to be placed on different words in the following sentence, of how many different meanings do they admit: "Will you send for the book to-morrow yourself?"' 'Correct the following examples and point out the canons of criticism to which they relate . . . Do figures of speech imply any thing uncommon or unnatural?' The quality of the Ormskirk questions shows when they are compared with Richard Phillips' *Five Hundred Questions*, 1824, which also covers Irving's *Elements*, but with questions much more narrowly related to the text.

Textbooks had hitherto given few examples of questioning as an aid to the teaching of understanding: it was left to the teacher to devise his own. But during the early years of the nineteenth century it was increasingly recognised as a practice that could be generally applied and illustrated in textbooks. Usually the questions expect the pupil to find, or recall, facts or expressions in the passage, and sometimes to explain them; a few questions expect the pupil to make inferences; fewer still are designed to elicit judgments. All types are represented in the following example of questioning, good and bad:

1813d 'By what name should we distinguish the error which those gentlemen committed in refusing to wait till the Tiger was properly secured before they attacked him?'

(Pinnock, *Universal Explanatory English Reader*, p. 84. The story,

retold from the *Asiatic Review* of 1802, does not contain any word equivalent to
'rash' or 'foolhardy'.)

1814 'Q. Was our Lord much followed? A. Yes. Q. Had he any enemies? A. Yes,
the wicked Jews. Q. Why did they hate him? A. Because he preached up humility.'

(National Society, *Questions* . . . 1836 edn, p. 43)

The importance of questioning seems to have been appreciated, or at least
publicised, by mothers and governesses earlier than it was by the writers of
textbooks. Of particular interest is the anonymous *Aids to Developement*,
1829, in which a series of dialogues exercises the linguistic skills of young
children. The opening conversation is a demonstration that textbooks are
not necessary: it is a form of object lesson, and an exercise in what was in
later days to be called lateral thinking. Mother shows a visitor how a small
boy can respond to the question 'What can you do with this stool?' The boy
sits on the stool, stands on it, turns it upside down and sideways and puts it
in other positions, expressing in words each action as he performs it. A more
advanced exercise is an attempt to teach empirically the nature of figurative
language. Mother takes five lines from *The Seasons*, of which the first two
are:

> 'Tis done! dread Winter spreads his latest glooms,
> And reigns tremendous o'er the conquered year.

Mother:	What is, to reign?
Fanny:	To rule, to govern.
M.	And who is said to do this?
F.	Winter.
M.	Can winter govern?
F.	No.
M.	Who are said to reign?
F.	Kings.
M.	Yes; and what does that imply?
F.	That the people do what they please, and that they make them obey.
M.	But can this apply to winter?
F.	Yes, Mamma.
M.	Over what does he reign?
F.	Over 'the conquered year'.
M.	What do you mean by 'conquered'?
F.	Overcome [etc. Winter 'overcomes' all vegetation]. (pp. 204f)

John Smith of Liverpool, in his *A Key to Reading*, 1830, gives several
sequences of questioning, modelled on what he had seen in the Edinburgh
Sessional School under John Wood. In the sequences, which Smith says he
used with a small group of children, it is the questions that are important;
the answers are idealised in that they are the product of unrecorded

explanation and discussion within the group. The following is part of a sequence on the first stanza of Gray's *Elegy*:

Q.   What is the meaning of *parting day*?
A.   That the daylight is departing.
Q.   Then you do not conceive that the word *parting* is an adjective to the word *day*, as *meeting-day*, *wedding-day*, &c.?
A.   No: I think it is the participle of a verb implying the parting away, or departure, of the daylight.
Q.   Why do you say *daylight*? The word is *day*.
A.   Yes: but a complete day includes all the twenty-four hours, and that portion of the day, only, seems to be meant which is distinguished from the night by the sun's light, which is departing.   (pp. 35–6)

Further examples:

(1832) 1836 ' "One evening, when his father and mother were drinking tea". What is meant by *tea* in this sentence? Ans. It is water, with an herb, called *tea*, steeped in it. What is meant by *drinking* tea? Ans. Swallowing it.'

(Warren Colburn, Boston, preface)

1851   (On Cowper's *Boadicea*)

When the British warrior queen,
    Bleeding from the Roman rods,
Sought, with an indignant mien,
    Counsel of her country's gods . . .

Q. What other preposition might be used for *of* (line 4)?

Such the bard's prophetic words,
    Pregnant with celestial fire,
Bending, as he swept the chords
    Of the sweet but awful lyre.

Q. Why *bending*?   (Edward Hughes, p. 4)

1852   (On *Macbeth*, Act One)
Q. 1. What is the subject of this play?
Q. 7. What may be observed of the witches?
Q.13. Describe Lady Macbeth's character.
Q.15. What creation of character has Shakespeare displayed in this drama?

(G.F. Graham, p. 143)

1854   (On *The Cotter's Saturday Night*)
Q. 1. What are the signs of *this* chill November day's close?
Q. 2. What day of the week is it?
Q. 3. Why is the Cotter glad when Saturday night comes?
Q.33. Who will quote Joshua XXIV.15 to me?   (A. W. Buchan, p. 251)

E.A. Abbott gives an example from the teaching of older pupils:

1872b 'The practical way of answering the question, "What is to be taught in English?" is to open an English book, and, imagining ourselves in a class-room, to ask what would our boys require to be taught in order that they might understand the passage before us.'

He takes ten lines from the opening scene of *Richard II*:

<blockquote>

K. Rich. High-stomach'd are they both, and full of ire,
     In rage deaf as the sea, hasty as fire.
Boling.   Many years of happy days befall
     My gracious sovereign, and most loving liege!
Mow.   Each day still better other's happiness,
     Until the heavens, envying earth's good hap,
     Add an immortal title to your crown.
K. Rich. We thank you both; yet one but flatters us,
     As well appeareth by the cause you come,
     Namely, to appeal each other of high treason.
</blockquote>

Abbott deals first with grammatical points, which he admits are here irrelevant (the parsing of 'befall' and 'better'; the use of 'but') and then with 'other questions, natural and important':

'What does *appeal* mean here? How did it come to have that meaning? Can we illustrate it from the words *repeal, appellation*, or any others? Here, then, comes in derivative etymology. Again, what is the exact meaning of *high-stomach'd*? How does it differ from *angry*, or *haughty*? This opens up the question how we can ascertain the exact meaning of a word, and it naturally introduces the subject of synonyms. We shall find that boys require to be asked, What is meant by the 'heavens envying earth's good hap'? and such a question at once introduces metaphor. Then, under the same head, there are other questions connected with diction – why is the *sea* selected as the representative of deafness? Why say full of 'ire', and not 'anger'? Under what circumstances would *ire* be more appropriate than *anger*? Then, is a boy to read, 'In rage, deaf *ás* the sea, hasty[4] . . . as fire'? and if not, on what principle are we to lay the accent on *deaf*, and on the first, instead of the second, syllable of *hasty*? Lastly, when these and similar questions have been asked, it is surely reasonable for a teacher to ask whether King Richard is right in arguing that, because two of his subjects accuse one another of high treason, therefore one of them is necessarily a flatterer. And thus, in the most natural way possible, we open the door to Logic.'   (pp. 23–4)

It may be commented that even here studying the meaning of the text is not yet an autonomous pursuit. It gains strength, if not respectability, from its association with etymology, logic and figures-of-speech rhetoric. But a style of teaching that seeks support from established disciplines is distinguishable only in trivial ways from a style that tries to stretch the

---

[4] The sense seems to require 'hasty' to be printed 'hastý'.

pupils intellectually and train them to make connections between aspects of experience that they have met in separate contexts. That is what Abbott was demonstrating.

Memory. Until recent times educators have always valued memory training, and teachers of literature have been amongst those who practised it. Learning by heart, in all subjects, was a useful form of pedagogic and, it was hoped, mental discipline, which could easily be administered and could be justified by reference to ideals more noble than that of controlling the unruly. The teacher of literature had his own justifications, or rationalisations, of which the least important was the social accomplishment of apt quotation. A common justification was the belief that, by learning in childhood fine verse that you did not like, you would accumulate for your preoccupied years as an adult a store on which you could draw with gratitude. The most powerful justification was that in order to appreciate fine verse you had to know it so well that you virtually knew it by heart. All these views are implied, at various times, in nineteenth-century anthologies; the view that does not appear until later is that the pupil, not the teacher, should choose what he will learn.

An argument against requiring young children, at least, to learn poetry by heart is cogently stated in *Aids to Developement*:

1829 '*Mrs Sandhurst* I have been accustomed to set my children to learn by heart little poems which are written expressly for the purpose, do you object to this?
  Mrs Eustace I confess I do . . . What is generally called poetry for children, in order to be made comprehensible to them, is brought down to so low a standard, that all which ought to be distinguished in poetry, is necessarily lost.'   (p. 15)

Two anthologies refer to the fluctuations in teachers' attitudes. Alexander Allen's *Select English Poetry* emphasises memory:

1838 'The earliest advantage which is to be found to arise from the practice of learning and reciting passages of poetry, is an improvement of this faculty. Some respectable teachers have underrated the importance of a strong memory, and have thought more of quick apprehension and general smartness in their pupils. These appearances, however, are often fallacious, and sometimes scarcely conceal the weakness of a memory barely retentive enough for ordinary purposes.'
                                                                    (preface)

Edward Hughes, 1851, writes of what he considers an excessive reaction against memory training, which was given too much importance in olden days, but 'it has been too hastily assumed that verbal memory is not worth cultivation' (preface). A position frequently taken by teachers was that children would virtually memorise anything that they had studied thoroughly. Charles Bilton's expression of this view illustrates also what 'thorough study' could mean when applied to literature: 'It is recommended that before any piece be committed to memory, it should be made the subject of many lessons in grammar, be thoroughly *manipulated*, so to speak, parsed, paraphrased, and analysed, and then the committing to memory will be found to involve little or no exertion' (1866, preface).

The absurdities of most manuals of memory training are outside our consideration, but one, which takes some of its illustrations from the teaching of poetry, may represent a class of book that must have influenced teachers of English. John Millard's *The New Art of Memory, founded upon the Principles taught by M. Gregor von Feinagle*, 1812, claims in its third edition, 1813, to have been used at Ampleforth. The book is memorable for at least two of its illustrations.

At a public demonstration a girl of eleven:

'... repeated fifty stanzas of four lines each, from the second part of Mrs More's *Sir Eldred of the Bower*. These she repeated consecutively, and in any order desired. On any remarkable word being mentioned, she determined the stanza, the line, and the place of the line, in which it was to be found; and also how many times the same word occurred in the Poem.'   (p. 22)

An account is also given of how to memorise the first stanza of Goldsmith's *The Hermit* (also called *Edwin and Angelina*), then a frequent anthology piece:

> Turn, gentle hermit of the dale,
>   And guide my lonely way
> To where yon taper cheers the vale
>   With hospitable ray.

'We must here reflect, and imagine that we see a *Hermit* standing on the *Tower of Babel*, and turning round with inconceivable rapidity; a very large *taper* is placed upon his head. Angelina is walking by the tower and calling out loudly to the hermit "to guide her lonely way"; the *taper* cannot fail to suggest the remainder of the stanza.'   (p. 173)

Such commercialised remnants of classical rhetoric have a horrible fascination for us, quite different from, but nearly as powerful as, their popularity with nineteenth-century Corn Exchange audiences. The American equivalent of Millard is Lorenzo D. Johnson's *Memoria Technica*, 1846, although his subject matter is mainly historical and his procedures obscure. It takes a long time, for example, to work out why in his system CHEESE is a mnemonic for the fact that blister-plasters were invented in 60 BC (3rd edn, 1847, p. 45).

Memory training is only one of those instrumental uses of poetry that have always been favoured by teachers whose own response to literature is uneasy or negative: poetry for grammatical analysis or paraphrase or as an emulsifying agent for moral direction or for factual instruction. Typical of many texts is *The Sunday School Reader*, 1858, planned so as 'to illustrate each prose Lesson by a piece of poetry, suitable for committing to memory, or for . . . dictation'. Less common is the approach of Mavor's *English Spelling Book*, 1801, which includes in its 1807 edition a poetical version of the 'Rules of the Humane Society for recovering drowned persons', with an appropriately worded recommendation that the verses should be 'given, a small portion at a time, as tasks to be committed to memory'. The 102 lines begin:

> When in the stream, by accident, is found
> A pallid body of the recent drown'd . . .   (p. 134)

Authors, set books and examinations

The single-author text as an examination set book – *The Prologue to the Canterbury Tales* – is still a familiar publication. There had been single-author texts since the 1770s: cheap editions of British classics; versions of *Paradise Lost* and Young's *Night Thoughts*; *Beauties* of Johnson, of Sterne, and many others. Such works became more frequent and more specifically intended for schools, as the nineteenth century progressed. In 1818 W. Johnstone, of an academy at Stanmore, London, could comment on 'the numerous cheap editions of the standard authors', which he preferred to books of extracts, and he was preparing a list of authors and works suitable for school use (p. 56). School editions of Shakespeare, edited for performance and not for examinations, go back to the eighteenth century (they are considered in Chapter 6). As nineteenth-century examination texts they were usually studied without reference to performance and even without recognition that they had been written for the stage.

Five individual works, already published separately, were brought together by John Evans to form a limited anthology, *The Poetic Garland*, 1808. Its 'biographical sketches and explanatory headlines' suggest a pedagogic intention that must, judging by the works selected, have been peculiarly gloomy. In the words of the title page the collection comprises 'Porteus on Death, Blair's Grave, Gray's Church-Yard, Cunningham's Pile of Ruins, and Noyes's Distress'. John Corry's *The Beauties of Cowper*, *c*. 1820, is a selection for school use but carries no notes or questions. Joseph Hine, who compiled a *Selection from the Poems of William Wordsworth, Esq.* in 1831, was a teacher, and his work was meant as a classbook. He particularly says he wishes each pupil to have a copy. Hine explains his choice of poet on the grounds that Wordsworth 'has an uncommon sympathy with all that conduces to the formation and preservation of purity in youth'. William Angus, also a teacher, compiled *The Beauties of Paradise Lost*, 1841, for 'young readers', without referring directly to school use and with no teaching-aids except his favourite marks to indicate 'rhetorical pauses and emphases'. The book would be used by private students of elocution as much as by pupils in school.

During the 1850s public examinations were instituted: the College of Preceptors in 1853; the Home and Indian Civil Service in 1855; the Royal Society of Arts in 1856, and in 1858 the London matriculation examination and the Oxford and Cambridge local examination. The examination syllabuses immediately gave rise to textbooks that implemented their prescriptions and sometimes caricatured their intentions. McLeod's edition of *Spring*, 1863, is a representatively conscientious text. It is 'specially intended for pupils qualifying for the Oxford Local Examinations, in June', and its emphasis on grammar follows the regulations for that examination, which prescribes 'the *Analysis* and *Parsing* of a passage taken from "Spring" in Thomson's *Seasons*', together with questions on it. McLeod calls his book a manual: he tells Thomson's life, quotes Samuel Johnson (7 pages) and then gives 31 pages to the analysis of sentences. The poem follows, with notes that can be classified, in McLeod's terms, as critical, explanatory and grammatical. For the first 300 lines of the poem there are 111 notes; thirteen are 'critical', in that they make comparisons with other poems or make evaluative judgments about Thomson's text. Sixty-seven notes are explanatory (of allusions, figures of speech and the meaning of words) or informative (about the plover, the zodiac, the rainbow, the Golden Age). Thirty-one notes are grammatical, sometimes technical and sometimes a mere shake of the head (on line 21: 'Thomson plays sad havoc with his adjectives and adverbs'). McLeod provides what the examiners say his pupils need. The most significant aspect of his book is not that it illustrates the difficulty of examining literature at an unsophisticated level but that it implies the existence of candidates studying without much help and of teachers of limited general education. The heaviness of the annotation in these texts varies more with the editor than with the work which is annotated: McLeod and Bromby on average provide four notes for every ten lines, Robinson and Connon fewer than two. There is much concern with etymology, frequently gratuitous and sometimes over-confident, as in one of McLeod's notes on *The Deserted Village*:

> The man of wealth and pride,
> Takes up a space that many poor supplied;

Space for his lake, his park's extended bounds,
Space for his horses, equipage and hounds.

'*Note* The *horse* is supposed to have been so named from his obedience and tractableness, the obsolete Saxon word *hyrsian*, signifying to obey . . .'

McLeod's note continues with references to Horsa, brother of Hengist. This kind of irrelevance was encouraged by the examiners. They emphasised etymology because they shared the contemporary academic interest in philology. They used (one could say exploited) this interest in language, together with the respect traditionally given to the study of grammar, as a means of stiffening the study of English literature. They believed that stiffening was necessary because, a few individuals apart, they still thought that the intellectually disciplined study of any literature required the kind of close linguistic analysis through which their own success in Latin and Greek had been achieved. John Hunter's preface to a school edition of *Paradise Lost*, Book 1 expresses in a mild form the common academic view: 'An attentive reading of even one book only of this noble poem, with, now and then, something like the critical examination employed in classical study, ought to be supposed a useful means of disciplining the intellect, and cultivating the taste.' C.W. Connon's preface to his edition of *Paradise Lost*, Books 1–4, puts it more cogently:

1855 'In many respects the complete Mastering of the Paradise Lost will be found to involve the same sort of collateral information as is necessary to the intelligent reading of the ancient poets. The mere words, being those of our mother tongue, may not demand any particular care; but the appreciation of their relations and nice dependencies requires as much thought, and as delicate a perception of the beautiful, as any thing in Homer or Virgil . . . In the higher class of English poets, if we have any other aim in reading them than mere amusement, we must voluntarily subject ourselves to the same deliberate study as we have to submit to in the Classical writers from necessity. It is only after dwelling on the poet's words, and, as it were, brooding on their etymology, their history, their grammatical structure and arrangement, and above all, *their allusive import, and moral significance*, as distinguished from their mere dictionary significance, that they become pregnant and full of meaning, and that we can truly be said to understand.'

Some publishers put out plain texts, like the SPCK's 1859 edition of Book 1 of *The Excursion* and their 1870 edition of Gray's *Odes*, but most texts were annotated, and adopted a tone they were to hold for a hundred years, audible in their titles, recorded in full in Bibliography 1, below: for Milton, C.W. Connon, 1858; for Goldsmith, McLeod, 1858, and C.P. Mason, 1865; for Wordsworth, H.G. Robinson, 1863, and C.H. Bromby, 1864.

More general textbooks also appeared, to meet the anxieties of parents and teachers about the progress of the pupils 'in this age of Competitive Examination', as William Chambers put it in 1866. Chambers' *Miscella-*

neous Questions, with answers. Embracing science, literature, and arts, has sections on 'Language, literature &c.' ('What is Philology? What is meant by "liberty of the press"?') and on English literature ('What change took place in English literature in the reign of Elizabeth?' 'Mention the most noted prose writers of this [variously specified] era'). The work is designed for cramming, and though representative of many is itself uninteresting, except for a startlingly ignorant comment about American literature, which had for many decades been distinctively represented in English anthologies: 'Q. Has literature been successfully cultivated in the United States? A. Yes; but only in recent times, when there have been numerous writers, whose works exhibit the same characteristics as those of their English contemporaries' (p. 143).

The examiners of the 1850s and 1860s paid particular attention to four areas. Summarising, occasionally analysing, and quoting an argument is the skill most frequently required:

1858 'Give the substance of Burke's examination of Locke's opinion concerning darkness.'   (RSA)

'Give concisely the plot of *King Lear*. You may adopt the style of an ancient Chronicle down to the close of Act 3. From that point employ the language of modern narrative.'   (Oxford)

1860 On *The Excursion*: 'Give a view of the argument of the fourth book entitled "Despondency Corrected", and illustrate it by quotations.'   (RSA)

Almost as frequently required is the explanation of vocabulary, expressions and allusions:

1858 On Chaucer: 'Explain the words:- *chevalrie, arwes . . .*' and nineteen others.
                                                                      (RSA)

On Pope: 'Explain the following passages, giving the context in each case:

> When the dull ox, why now he breaks the clod,
> Is now a victim, and now Egypt's god.'

and 5 others.   (RSA)

On *King Lear*: 'Explain the allusions in the following passages:
  Thou shalt have as many dolours for thy daughters as thou canst tell in a year.'
                                                                    (Oxford)

Their third emphasis was on character:

1858 'Describe the character of Laertes.'   (RSA)

1859 'Compare the character of Macbeth with that of Lady Macbeth, and illustrate your comparison by references and quotations.'   (RSA)

Paraphrase, the fourth technique that the examiners concentrated on, was used to test both expression and interpretation. Bromby, in his edition of *The Excursion*, Book 1, echoes their views on the importance of paraphrase: 'an almost indispensable instrument of education when a pupil knows no other language except his own', but his judgment is suspect when he goes on to say that paraphrase is made more difficult by 'the paucity of English synonymes'. The Oxford examiners keep paraphrase as a means of testing comprehension:

'Give the sense of the following passages in ordinary prose, explaining more particularly the portions which are printed in italics:-

France in choler parted!
And the king gone to-night! *prescribed his power!*
Confined to exhibition! All this done
Upon the gad!'

The RSA examiners sometimes give eighteen lines of Chaucer or Spenser to be turned into modern English and prose order; at other times they require the candidates to 'briefly express the sense' of a passage ' in plain prose', which leaves uncertain the proportions in which paraphrase and summary are to be combined.

Public examinations in English were now established, and their influence on the work not only of intending candidates but of all, even young, children was assured. Its development belongs to the study of the comparatively recent history of English teaching.

J.W. Hales and E.A. Abbott

J.W. Hales' *Suggestions on the Teaching of English* can be regarded both as the most complete and sensitive expression of the various approaches developed during the previous forty years, and also as the first modern statement about the teaching of English. But such a comment tends to jerk his work into the wrong kind of prominence. It was important work, but other teachers had led up to it. Hales had stated the case for English as a subject in the chapter on the teaching of English that he contributed to F.W. Farrar's *Essays on a Liberal Education*, 1867. In 1869 he wrote the 'Suggestions', reprinted as an introduction to his anthology of 1872, *Longer English Poems*. Hales illustrates his suggestions from Scott's ballad 'O listen, listen, ladies gay' (*Rosabelle*) in Canto 6 of *The Lay of the Last Minstrel*.

He states first two general principles: 'Nothing should be told a pupil which he can think out or find out for himself', and that methods should vary according to the ability of the pupils: 'With a very low form it might be well to dwell simply on the story . . . to see that that is thoroughly understood' (1872; 1874 edn p. xv). He then turns to *Rosabelle*. It should be learnt by heart, out of school, with 'some attention to elocution . . . To be fully appreciated, it should be heard by the outer ear, and so by the inner.' The pupils should see 'that reading [aloud] is in a manner interpretation'. The teacher should then concentrate on the general meaning of the ballad, which Hales analyses into four parts: stanza 1; stanzas 2–6; stanzas 7–11; the last 2 stanzas; then the poem as a whole. He stresses how frequently people fail to understand what they read, especially verse. Pupils should learn to question themselves, 'Do I really understand?' They should write down their difficulties and submit them to the teacher, and make written abstracts of poems. Hales then discusses what he calls 'minor, subsidiary matters': allusions; historical background; prosody; grammar; etymology; biography; submitting a passage (an argumentative piece by Wordsworth, Shelley, Pope or Milton) 'to the formal processes of logic'. He envisages the teacher asking, 'Might *Rosabelle* have been written in blank verse? Could *Paradise Lost* have been effectively written in the metre of *Rosabelle*?' In teaching meanings 'definitions must be perpetually asked for. The furnishing of them will often tax the pupil's powers of intelligent expression to the utmost.' Metaphor, simile and personification are 'very important terms', but Hales does not spend much time on them. Finally the older pupils should make 'an attempt at criticism', and he offers, in respect of *Rosabelle*, such critical ideas as 'simple vigour . . . no personal intrusion . . . no vain cries and groans . . . the awful plainness' of the old ballads.

Hales makes it clear that he is illustrating, from 'a not extra-ordinary piece of English writing', only the kind of work that can be done. He is not suggesting that *Rosabelle*, or any other poem, should necessarily be worked over so fully. But the comprehensiveness of his treatment derives from the energy and earnestness of his times, as does his concluding exhortation:

'After some such lesson as that just attempted . . . will not the intelligence of the pupil have been thoroughly exercised? Will not his previously acquired knowledge have been called into use and arranged better? Will he not have added something to that better ordered store? Will he not, while awaking to a pleasant consciousness of what the power of his mind is . . . learn also how much there is that is beyond his reach, and how, of what lies within his reach, the better part may not be won "without dust and heat": learn the great lesson . . . that there is nothing to be achieved without sincere, undaunted, never-wearying industry?'   (p. xxxvii)

E.A. Abbott, headmaster of the City of London School, in his lectures *On Teaching the English Language*, goes into greater detail than Hales. He sees the interpretation of metaphor as being a principal source of difficulty to schoolboys, and the 'expansion of metaphors' as an essential teaching-exercise. He takes as an example Pope's lines from the *Essay on Man* (4, 9–12) 'in which the poet is asking where the plant of happiness is to be found, whether... "twin'd with the wreaths Parnassian laurels yield, / Or reap'd in iron harvests of the field"'.

Abbott comments:

1872b   'I thought an average boy of average ability might be expected to see that *iron* was a very unusual epithet for *harvests*, and that "iron harvest" must be a metaphorical expression.'

He then shows in a series of steps how the metaphor can be expanded until it means: 'As the reaper cuts down the corn, so war reaps his harvest of iron-clad warriors who are struck down in death.' To Abbott's surprise none out of a class of fairly able fifteen-year-olds 'could either expand the metaphor, or even give the meaning correctly' (pp. 38–9). This, he thinks, is one of the areas where pupils most need to be taught how to read with understanding, to interpret. The exercise, and the teacher's surprise, are yet another indication that we have reached comparatively recent times.

The evidence quoted in this chapter is sufficient to show that increasingly during the nineteenth century pupils in some schools read literature in English and were helped in class to understand and judge what they read. But the teachers who thought work of this kind worthwhile were not numerous, and they were not, with rare exceptions, found in classical schools, where the general attitude was that described by Skeat as obtaining in the 1850s:

'No portion of our literature was ever explained to me at any of my five schools. It [English literature] was then considered as a thing altogether apart from our ordinary curriculum, and only to be seriously regarded when in the privacy of our own homes.'   (W.W. Skeat, *A Student's Pastime*, 1896, introduction; quoted by J. McMurtry, 1985, p. 137)

CHAPTER SIX

Expression and performance

The skills

Before 1700 it is difficult even to guess how much attention was paid in school to the skill of expressing yourself orally, in English and in your own words. We may assume that in a sixteenth-century school for young children the pupils, if they were happy with the teacher, would want to talk and might be encouraged to do so. But we may not assume that such encouragement would be part of any intention to develop their expressive skill. What we know of attitudes to children, to learning and to language make such an intention most improbable. In sixteenth-century grammar schools the boys were often forbidden by statute to speak English even out of school, though the prohibition was probably not meant to be absolute and was always impracticable. It signifies the importance attached to Latin, not necessarily a low status accorded to English.

The main task of the schoolboy student of rhetoric was learning how to express himself orally and in writing in Latin and, to a lesser but steadily increasing extent, in English. The component skills of expressive rhetoric can be summarised; they were not, of course, exercised consecutively:

   (i) Having a supply of ideas and arguments to put forward. One way of making sure that you had overlooked nothing was to use a checklist, derived from Aristotle, which purported to present all the fundamental questions that could be asked about any matter.

  (ii) Having a supply of words in which to put forward your ideas and arguments. This meant not only the possession of a wide vocabulary but also skill in recognising and handling slight differences of meaning.

 (iii) Being able to arrange what you said or wrote in a way that best showed its coherence and logical cogency.

 (iv) Being able to arrange what you said or wrote in a way that also made the most persuasive impact on your hearers.

  (v) Being able to make what you said or wrote not only persuasive but also delightful in itself, by choosing an appropriate form of discourse (parable, speech, letter); by the use of figurative language and turns of speech.

(vi) Being able through the use of voice and gesture to increase the persuasiveness of what you said.

A prerequisite for the oral exercise of these skills was an adequate memory, and techniques for memorisation were from classical times part of rhetoric until Ramus, and many after him, gave them a separate and usually inferior status. A noticeable feature of the teaching, from a modern point of view, was a disregard of the pupil's originality. The term 'invention', which designated the first of the skills just described, carried more of its literal meaning than it does now. The pupil was expected to 'come upon' to discover, what already existed in the work of earlier, authoritative writers; only to a small extent, if at all, was he expected to be creative or original.

The dominant method of teaching was through imitation, and it was the provision of literary models for imitation that made the rhetorics a fragmentary but important source of reading-matter (above, chapter 4). By the eighteenth century the component skills of rhetoric were beginning to be differentiated. The preacher, whose distinctive skills had received attention early in the seventeenth century, continued to require 'pulpit' rhetorics. Oratory was for the public figure, local and national, and not only for the politician and the lawyer. A new development was the consideration given to the skill of conversation as a social accomplishment, but not yet as a skill related to employment. During the second half of the eighteenth century the rhetorician's traditional concern for delivery and performance was extended and particularised under the name of elocution. Manuals of elocution appeared frequently between the 1760s and the 1830s. They were stimulated at first by the general interest in language characteristic of the second half of the eighteenth century, but they were maintained by the more powerful influence of a social and geographical mobility that enhanced the importance of London English and correct pronunciation.

The schools reflected this extension of oral skills by increasing attention to reading aloud; to recitation; to the declamation of set speeches on public occasions; and to dramatic presentations, if not performances. There was differentiation also in the written skills. Letter-writing, always the most widespread application of rhetoric, was treated in a greatly increased number of popular manuals, and was taught in schools as a practical skill. The theme and the essay gradually detached themselves, though never completely, from the imitation of literary models. Verse-writing was practised but little discussed, and had little connection with prosody. Prosody retained for a long time its double reference: to speech sounds and to metrics. The elocutionists took over its first function and the grammarians kept their inappropriate grip on the second. Free, or original, composition was rare: only a very confident teacher would let his pupils write freely, in verse or in prose.

The evidence for these developments is less abundant and less direct than it is for other aspects of English teaching. Much, insofar as it relates to imitation, is implied in the discussion of models in chapters 4 and 5. The teachers seldom go farther than saying what parts a theme ought to have and what kinds of topic are suitable. The detailed, and interesting, aspects of the teaching of expression are too individual (to both pupil and teacher) to be put into a textbook. The pupil's product, sometimes published and sometimes surviving in a fair-copy book, is evidence only for what the teachers would have liked their pupils to be able to do unaided. What the textbooks do provide is a sequence of statements by teachers who wish to emphasise a particular aspect of expression. They write within the framework of traditional rhetoric, but the specialisation that they favour is steadily loosening that framework.

Individual writers: sixteenth and seventeenth centuries

The earliest text considered in this enquiry was written by a schoolmaster in order to help his pupils to express themselves in English, orally and in writing, both as an end in itself and as a preliminary to composition in Latin. Leonard Cox's *The Arte or Crafte of Rhetoryke*, which was first published about 1524, and certainly before 1532, is a classical rhetoric in that it derives from Cicero and many of its illustrations are translated or paraphrased from him. But, although some rhetorics written in English may have been intended solely as aids to the composition of Latin, there is no doubt that Cox was explicitly concerned with English. He is writing for pupils who may:

'. . . eyther be advocates and proctoures in the lawe or els apte to be sente in theyr prynces Ambassades or to be techars of goddes worde in suche maner as maye be moste sensible and accepte to their audience.'

But he is not thinking only of the privileged and the successful. His pupils include also 'all them that have any thynge to prepose or to speke afore any companye what somever they be' (Aii verso). It is necessary, he says, for speakers, especially preachers, to give some thought to technique. If they speak without

'. . . invencyon and order with due elocucyon great tediosnes is engendred . . . by occasyon where of the speker is many tymes or he have endyd his tale eyther lefte almost alone to his no lytle confusyon or els whiche is a lyke rebuke to hym the audyence falleth for werynes of hys ineloquent langage faste on slepe.'   (Aiii)

Cox's method is conventional. It proceeds by analysis (of the principal ideas) and by illustration. There are no exercises in the book and no discussion of what the pupils should do. He analyses first the idea of an 'oration'. The 'theme' of any oration must be one of four kinds: logical, demonstrative, deliberative or judicial. Each kind is further analysed. For example, a logical theme must be either simple or compound. If simple, it should have four 'places or instrumentes': the definition of the 'thyng' (topic); the causes; the 'partes' (its structure); the effects. The illustration he gives is 'What thyng Justyce is'. Of a compound theme the distinctive feature is that it must be true or false. This leads Cox into a description of the difference between rhetoric and logic:

'The Logycyan in disputynge observythe certayne rules for the settynge of his wordes beynge solycytous that ther be spokyn no more nor no les then the thynge requireth and that it be even as playnly spoken as it is thought. But the Rhetoricyan seketh abought and boroweth wher he can asmuche as he may for to make the symple and playne Logycall argumentes gay and delectable.'   (Aviii)

Cox then analyses the structure of an oration into four parts: 'the preamble; the tale or narracion; the provinge of the matter or contencion; the conclusion' (Bi verso). It is not necessary to pursue these analyses, or those of other rhetoricians. They vary according to the tradition being followed, and can be pedantic in detail. When they are combined with the technique of imitating model passages it is not difficult to guess at the teaching-sequence: (i) learn one or more of the categories formed by the analysis; (ii) study and learn by heart some illustrations of that category; (iii) imitate, at first orally and then in writing, one of the models, using a simple and familiar topic or situation; (iv) write a theme on a topic or situation that has been treated by an earlier author; (v) compare your theme with what was written by the earlier author; (vi) learn by heart the earlier theme. Models, as was seen in chapter 4, might sometimes be from English literature, but the exercise was normally directed towards the learning of Latin. It is clear that English played a substantial part, but it is difficult to tell when that part was subordinated to Latin and when it was encouraged in its own right. That it was so encouraged is beyond doubt.

   Cox restricted his manual to the skills of finding and arranging words; he did not discuss ornament or the figures. Richard Sherry, 1550, some of whose illustrations were quoted in chapter 4, gives particular attention to the figures, knowledge of which, from our own 'great fludde' of literature, is necessary for expression:

'Not only must we chose apte, and mete wordes, but also take hede of placinge, and settinge them in order . . . To chose them oute finely, and handsomlye to bestow them in their places . . . is no easy thynge.'   (pp. 18–20)

Thomas Wilson's illustrations of the figure amplification were quoted above (pp. 153–4). He strongly advocates a plain style, and makes fun of an 'ynkehorne letter' from a Lincolnshire man soliciting a benefice, which begins: 'Ponderyng, expendyng, and revolutyng with my self your ingent affabilitee, and ingenious capacitee, for mundane affaires: I cannot but celebrate and extolle your magnificall dexteritee, above all other' (Yii verso). Wilson uses the term 'composition', not to designate either a piece of writing or a teaching-subject but in the Latin sense out of which these uses arose:

1553 'Composicion . . . is an apte joynyng together of wordes in suche order, that neither the eare shal espie any ierre [i.e. jar], nor yet any man shalbe dulled with overlong drawing out of a sentence, nor yet muche confounded with myngelyng of clauses, such as are nedelesse, beyng heaped together without reason, and used without nomber.' (Yiv verso)

The term 'composition' is liable to cause misunderstanding: its other sense in sixteenth- and seventeenth-century writing about language is the process by which compound words are formed; it is in this sense that Mulcaster calls the nineteenth chapter of his *Elementarie*, 'Of Composition'. He did not reach that part of his programme that might have discussed composition in the sense of written expression.

Thomas Blundeville's *The Arte of Logike*, 1599, illustrates the share that logic could have in the teaching of expression, and also how different from ours were the presuppositions and methods of that teaching. Blundeville, following an earlier sixteenth-century logician, is showing the different 'proofs' that can be adduced in respect of the 'theame or proposition' *Man ought to embrace vertue*. Nine proofs are formulated in relation to the subject, 'man'; eleven in relation to the predicate, 'virtue'; and three in relation to both subject and predicate. Each of these twenty-three proofs is expressed in two forms: 'after the Logicall manner with short speech' and 'after the Rhetoricall manner with copious speech'. Whether or not he learnt any logic, a schoolboy carrying out an exercise of this kind would be extending his skill in the precise control of language. One example is necessary, but one is sufficient. The second proof for the subject is 'from the Etimologie', first in its rhetorical, then in its logical, formulation:

'It becometh everie creature that is made of the slime of the earth to be voide of all arrogancie and pride, to bee lowlie, humble, and obedient to his creator, and to embrace vertue in observing the law of God devoutly and religiously, wherefore man called in latine *homo*, of this word *humo* (that is to say) earth, or rather slyme of the earth, taking his originall from so base and vile a thing ought to bee humble and voide of all pride and arrogancie, and to love vertue above all thinges, being alwayes obedient to God his creator, and readie to do his most holy precepts and commandements.

Logically thus

Every sensible creature that is created of the slyme of earth ought to be obedient to his Creator and to embrace vertue, therefore man ought to bee obedient to his creator, and to embrace vertue.' (sig. P2)

The year after Blundeville's logic was published William Vaughan, in *The Golden-Grove*, attributed to logic qualities that might equally have been claimed for rhetoric. They certainly relate to confidence in expressing yourself. Vaughan answers his own question: 'What maketh youths to speake so boldly & roundly? Logike' (chap. 40). We can assume that logic, so far as it was taught in school, had a much more direct influence on boys' ability to express themselves than it had on their appreciation of literature.

Brinsley, 1612, has more to say about the teaching of expression than about any other aspect of English. The impression he gives overall is that English was important, but was not regularly taught in its own right. It was a necessary and valuable, but in day-to-day practice subordinate, accompaniment to the teaching of Latin, which was the grammar schools' defining task. Nevertheless Brinsley's statements are strong. Amongst the 'chiefe points aimed at' is 'to grow in our owne English tongue . . . to utter their minds in the same both in proprietie and puritie' (General Contents, no. 32). He looks for 'continuall . . . growth amongst all my Schollars, in their English tongue as in the Latine. And not only for the reading of it, but also for understanding it, and abilitie to utter their mindes of any matter, wherewith they are acquainted, or which they learne in Latine' (p. 21). He thinks that the grammar schools neglect expression in the mother tongue, which is regrettable not only through national pride but because 'very few' grammar-school pupils 'proceede in learning, in comparison of them that follow other callings' (p. 22). All the methods, except one, that Brinsley suggests for teaching English expression derive from Latin. The exception is the standard practice of summarising the sermon: in a few key sentences by those who can only just write; in a full analysis by the pupils in the highest form. But this practice is referred to by Brinsley only briefly as part of language-teaching; he sees it principally as a technique in the teaching of religion (pp. 255-8). His other recommendations are letter-writing in English (seldom attempted, he says, in grammar schools); 'the reporting of a Fable in English, or the like matter'; drafting Latin themes in English (p. 186); and principally in every aspect of translation out of Latin: 'reading forth of Latine into English, first in propriety [i.e. grammatical accuracy], then in puritie [of English]' (p. 23). Brinsley stresses translation, through which his pupils will 'attaine variety and copie [abundance] of English words, to expresse their minds easily' (p. 107) and 'reading . . . forth of Latine into a good English stile' (p. 175).

Brinsley also discusses, in a most interesting passage, the relation between imitation and originality. He is thinking entirely of the teaching of Latin, but he expresses a view that strongly influenced the later teaching of English: if a pupil knows by heart models of good writing he will eventually have more to say for himself than if he is left from the first to rely on his own inadequate resources. The pupils should 'have first the most excellent patterns, & never to rest until they have the very patterns in their heads, and as it were ever before their eies; for then they will be able to go forwards of themselves with delight' (p. 209). They are 'to learne each Author so perfectly, as to say every worde without booke, as much as is possible, that the verie phrase and matter of their Author may bee their owne to use perpetually' (p. 210). If they rely too much at first on their own 'Invention in making Epistles, Theames, Verses, disputing' the resulting work will be 'nothing but froth, childishnesse and uncertaintie' (p. 210).

Hoskins, as reproduced by Blount, 1654, has more to say about the techniques of written expression than have most rhetoricians. He discusses everything in relation to the figures, but his advice (directed by Blount, at least, 'to the youth of both sexes') is practical. Sometimes it is general: Sir Philip Sidney's method '(besides reading *Aristotle* and *Theophrastus*) was to imagine the thing present, that his pen might the better describe it' (Blount, p. 37); sometimes in detail, as in the use of 'distinction' to show exactly what you mean:

1654 'If there be any doubt or ambiguity in the words, it is better left out than distinguished. But if you are to answer former speeches, that imply any doubtfulness, you may disperse all clouds . . . with *Distinction*. As being charged you have brought very light reasons, you may answer, *If by light you mean clear, I am glad you see them; if by light you mean of no weight, I am sorry you do not feel them* . . . But as ambiguity is not onely in words but in matter; so both wayes it is taken away by *Distinction*. Sometimes it is in single words . . Somtimes in coherence of Sentences, by reason of the relation of each word to other.'		(Blount, pp. 37–8)

Joshua Poole's strange work *The English Parnassus*, 1657, was described in chapter 4. It is an enormous quarry out of which his pupils could carve and assemble their own English verses. What makes the book strange is the vast amount of material set against the weakness of Poole's conception of poetry. He was, as he says himself, no poet, yet he was enthusiastic about writing poetry in English. He seems to have expected the boys to write verse as a recreation, not in class (Proeme, third and final paragraphs). In its arrangement of epithets the book resembles the gradus that helped schoolboys to manufacture Latin verse. In schoolboy Latin verse, however, cliché was a virtue, and Poole shows no awareness of its dangers in English:

'*Ice* Slippery, chrystal, glassie, transparent, shining, crusted, congealed, thick-ribd, chilling, stiffnd, benumming, united, glistering, rigid, hanging.' (p. 115)

'*Swine* Beastly, nasty, fulsome, noysome, loathsome, miry, dirty, uncleanly, sordid, wallowing, greedy, hungry, grunting, dull, bristled, wastful, rooting, tumbling, rolling, sluggish, lither, drowsie, gluttonous.' (p. 198)

The school practice of writing English verse was not an eccentricity of Poole's. Unless there had been support for it there would not have been two issues of the first edition of his book, and two subsequent editions. His book was still well enough known to be attacked by Thomas Hayward in *The British Muse*, 1738. Hayward's objection is that Poole is encouraging what Hayward, eighty years later, considers a bad style: 'the pompous insignificance and empty swell of pedantry and bombast'. Hayward had no difficulty in finding examples of it: '[Poole's] scholars might learn . . . when they took a nest, to call the birds, *The Summer's waits, the air's feathered parishioners, the woods' wild burgesses, the living ships with feathered sails* . . . Fine language to improve the style of youth' (pp. xii, xiv; Poole, pp. 260–1, before the misnumbered sequence).

In 1663, at least six years after his death, Poole's *Practical Rhetorick* was published. It is modelled on Erasmus' *De Copia* and is designed to develop fluency and variety in both English and Latin. It is practical because it deals with the expressive, and not with the interpretative, aspects of rhetoric. The technique, standard in the teaching of the classics, is that of 'varying' both vocabulary and syntax. It involves, if carefully taught, judging equivalences of meaning and of tone. The book comprises variations on only six sentences, each set of variations filling between thirty and forty pages. The first sentence to be varied is *Love overcometh all things*. The simplest form of variation is to make *Love* 'Cupid' or 'Venus' son', or 'the blind God', or 'the Paphian Prince', or 'the Cyprian Queen's blind Boy'. *Overcometh* is varied as 'conquereth', 'tames', 'vanquisheth', etc. *All things* is varied as 'everything', or 'no few things', or 'many things', or 'great things' (pp. 1–3). The syntactical form is also varied: 'There is nothing, that is not overcome by love'; 'What overcomes all things, if not Love?' But systematic elaboration through the figures soon strains the idea of equivalence: 'Me thinks, I hear Love speaking, and thus vaunting himself of his strength and power: "Hercules was strong even to a Miracle; yet so did I effeminate him; that in Woman's apparel he spun in the company of the other Sex"' (p. 23; italics and reversed italics omitted).

Obadiah Walker's *Some Instructions concerning the Art of Oratory*, 1659, makes unusual allowance for the student's own ideas. Although he is careful to warn the student against leaving what Walker calls his 'fancy' to chance – 'gazing about, and waiting as it were, what may by sudden Enthusiasm drop into it' – he does recognise the importance of 'fancy', even if it means that the student must revise what he first wrote:

'In inventing take heed of torturing your fancy too much at first; either in the quest of more curious matter, or in setting it down in the exact form . . . What orderly matter therefore, it [sc. the Wit] shall (unforced) offer you, set down; that by this, as a lower step, the Fancy may ascend, and scrue it self up to something more choice; which it cannot so easily mount unto at the first, without taking, by the way, this meaner rise. But then we must take the pains of twice writing, that the second Copy may cast away (according to its better Provision) what is ordinary and common in the former . . . It is convenient therefore, often to break off the thread you are spinning; and set your imagination on work afresh, upon some other new circumstance, as if nothing at all had been meditated before. All which variety of in-cohering matter is to be joynted and set together in the second review.' (pp. 10 and 13)

Walker's advice is to use other men's thoughts only after you have exercised your own, and the first step in composing is 'the *setting down* your Inventions confusedly; and the transcribing out of other Authors of what fits your purpose' (p. 17). There is a freshness in Walker's approach that inclines one to treat his books as something of a landmark, the sign of a new direction. He warns his students about the correct placing of 'only' (p. 100); he advises them to read aloud what they have written: 'to try whether the words be well placed, and the numbers well fitted, and the phrase enough perspicuous, an *audible recitation* of them is not to be omitted' (p. 113). Advice of this kind is new to the textbooks written in English. It is hard to know whether it is new only because such advice had not previously been thought appropriate for a textbook or whether it was new advice. In his later book *Of Education*, 1673, Walker treats invention in broader terms, but the emphasis is the same. The teacher should not thrust his pupil 'upon fishing in Books at first'; the pupil should:

'. . . set down what is suggested by his memory or fancy concerning his subject, be it considerable or no. The Soul will by litle and litle heat, and wind it self, unto higher conceptions; and in transcribing, he may reject what is too obvious.'

(pp. 130–1)

Walker is here speaking of Latin, but this scarcely matters because one of his earliest recommendations was 'invent in English before in Latin, confusedly before in order, then chuse the best, put it in order, turn it into Latin, and then file and polish it' (p. 108). Even if this practice would be abandoned in the later stages of learning Latin it seems likely that Walker envisaged initial composition in English throughout most of the grammar school. He certainly recommends that each pupil should 'compose and pronounce [orations] hansomely, at least in his own language', and 'understand and practise (though not much, except he have a considerable dexterity in it) *Poetry* . . . but his fancy as well as expressions will be low and mean' (p. 109). This sounds like the promotion of composition in English, but the phrase 'in his own Language' is ambiguous: it seems to mean 'in English', but it might mean 'in Latin of his own making, not in Latin copied from a model'.

Charles Hoole, though a less imaginative teacher than Walker, was active in promoting the use of English, tightly tied, however, to Latin. His pupils imitate Aesop in English before translating their imitation into Latin (1660, p. 64, second numbering); they expand on Terence, in English (p. 141); they imitate Cicero's letters, in English (p. 146); they follow the usual practice of writing their Latin themes first in English (p. 185); they 'learn to compose English verses', imitating English verse translations of Virgil, Ovid and Mantuan (p. 158); and, as a rather rarified climax, to imitate in English, Latin, Greek and Hebrew, '*Anagrams, Epigrams, Epitaphes, Epithalamia, Eclogues, Acrosticks, and golden verses*' (p. 201).

Another sign that new directions were being opened up in the 1660s is a collection of 'school-boys' exercises and divertisements' published in 1672 under the title *Ludus Ludi Literarii*, edited by R.S. It contains forty-seven speeches, most of them in English, spoken at, or prepared for, 'breakings-up' in a school near London in 1671. The editor says that this collection is, so far as he knows, 'the first *Essay* of this nature that ever came in print, or has been made by any one'. He justifies the work on the grounds that boys 'are seldom, or never, put upon the making of Orations in their Mother-Tongue, but always, or generally, in *Latine* . . . If a Master shall indeed *inlarge* and *inrich* the *Inventions* of his young Schollars, and put a sharpe edge upon their Fances' – this is good work, although he himself would prefer to do other things than run a private school. The best method is 'by setting them certain *Copies* and *Patterns* of dilating upon any kind of Subject, *pertinently*, and *pleasantly*, (or of *Theames* and Subjects so dilated on)'. This is better than trying to teach by rule. He apologises that many of the subjects are 'petite', but he approves of light things if they are not profane. Titles include: 'Upon a Mince-Pye'; 'Upon Boyes going to School, that are not intended for Schollars'; 'Upon a Quakers Wedding'. The speeches are competent, but have been, one must suppose, edited before or after delivery. Three of them were reproduced, without acknowledgment, in Curson's *The Theory of Sciences Illustrated*, 1702.

Robert Blau's *Praxis Oratoria*, a. 1696, is a collection of Latin speeches, with English translations, performed but not, it seems, written by schoolboys. Every boy who had made even a start in Latin was required every year to deliver in public at least one of these speeches, such as: 'In praise of learning'; 'Upon the Cocks and their Game'; 'Against the Indulgence of Mothers'. The collection is worth noting because Blau recognises that 'it is not only usefull (tho not usual) but most necessary to practise such Declaimings in our Mother Tongue, for any who would make a desireable progress in their Studies' (preface). Each speech is followed by a song or chorus, in Latin and in English, set to a familiar tune such as *Chevy Chase* or *Phyllis full of harmless thoughts beneath the willow tree.*

Joshua Oldfield's important *An Essay towards the Improvement of Reason* discusses within the framework of logic both expressive and interpretative skills, and their interaction. The book derives from Oldfield's teaching to young men in training for the ministry. Though parts of it apply only to Latin, the bulk of it relates explicitly to English, which he thinks has been neglected. He wants to enable his students '*rightly* to take what others deliver, and *justly* to express what we ourselves intend' (p. 125). Thinking perhaps especially of sermons, he maintains that it is difficult to make oneself understood. He sees, unusually, how dependent meaning is on context:

1707 'Propriety of expression . . . is not so easie a Matter, as is commonly tho't, nor so justly perform'd as is generally presum'd . . . Men seem to be commonly much in the Dark about each others Meaning . . . oft contending about *Words*, where they are really agreed about *Things* . . . We should therefore endeavour to find out *such* Words, and put them *so* together, as that Persons of a Moderate Capacity, who have the requisite Furniture . . . may, or indeed must, apprehend the design'd Import.'
(p. 137)

If people do not understand, it must be because they twist or disregard the words, or through 'not regarding the *Contexture,* or such other determining Circumstances as have been mention'd' (p. 137). Most of what Oldfield says can be found within the classical tradition or in Locke, to whom he expresses an obligation. What is new is its application to English.

Some eighteenth- and nineteenth-century teaching-methods

From early in the eighteenth century written expression received incidental treatment in many types of textbook, principally in grammars, spelling-books and manuals of self-improvement. Separate works of what may loosely be called traditional rhetoric continued to appear, but in small numbers and at long intervals after the middle of the century: Holmes,

1739; Ward, 1759; Gibbons, 1767. As early as 1731 John Clarke, who had earlier recommended 'the Writing of *English Epistles* as well as *Latin*, for their Improvement in their own Language; a thing to be regarded and taken care of' (1720; edn of 1730, p. 116) had doubted the value of rhetoric in the teaching of expression:

1731 The rhetorician's rules 'signify not very much ... they extend little further, than only to caution a Man against such gross Faults, as Persons of any extensive Knowledge, very conversant in good Authors, can hardly be guilty of, and consequently are of no very great Use'.

From the schoolmaster's point of view:

'A readiness of Invention, wherein the Talent of Eloquence chiefly lies, is a natural Gift, capable of Improvement indeed from Use and Exercise, but of very little, if any at all, from any Rules I have ever yet met with.'   (pp. 184–5)

In 1762 Adam Smith was recorded as saying in a lecture, the substance of which he had first given more than ten years earlier, 'Systems of rhetoric, both ancient and modern ... are generally a very silly set of books and not at all instructive' (1763; 1963, p. 23). In the grammars, especially, the old rhetoric survived, sometimes dealing briefly with invention, arrangement, ornament and delivery, more often in a form reduced to the figures of speech, which kept their position because they were easy to teach and hard to learn. Michael Maittaire's grammar, 1712, is an exception: his pages on 'Composition' give more attention to clarity and simplicity than to figures.

A number of practices common in the classroom are confusingly interrelated. They are all derived from the teaching of rhetoric but they lost their coherence as the skills of rhetoric were fragmented and separately taught. These practices were taken over by the grammarians and used for general linguistic training; but they were also recommended by teachers of composition and *belles lettres*. They include imitation; varying the structure of sentences without (much) changing the meaning; paraphrasing; transposing both prose and verse out of an 'artificial' into a 'natural' order; using and interpreting elliptical writing; rewriting verse as prose.

Imitation. Imitation had been from the earliest classical times considered the best way of training the speaker and the writer. It was advocated by most of the seventeenth-century writers already discussed and throughout the eighteenth century. John Urmston was characteristic in teaching his pupils 'the genuine *Idioms*, and natural *Dress* of their *Mother-Tongue*, by accustoming the Scholar to read, or copy out Books, which have been written by the Masters of our Language' (preface). Imitation was advocated both by a traditionalist like John Holmes ('an attentive and sedulous imitation', 1739, preface) and by the more adaptable Rollin. There were few who questioned its value or the view of Thomas Reid that 'the imagination of a child, like the hand of a painter, is long employed in copying the works of others, before it attempts any invention of its own' (1785, Essay 4, chap. 4). Even a sensitive writer like Goldsmith could envisage the pupil 'having amassed a fund of beautiful metaphors and exquisite descriptions' being 'at length set to compose something' (preface to Wiseman's grammar). Too often school composition was virtually the rearranging, in a limited number of conventionally treated genres, of a limited range of conventionally standardised expressions.

Henry Felton, writing in 1709 when his pupil John was thirteen, described the benefit of leisurely and discriminating imitation, and made the much less frequent point that study of a model did not preclude a student's writing from being authentic:

1713 'Reading these celebrated authors will give Your Lordship a true Taste of good Writing, and form You to a just and Correct Style . . . I would not recommend any of them to a strict Imitation: That is servile and mean, and You cannot propose an exact Copy of a Pattern without falling short of the Original: but if Your Lordship once readeth them with a true Relish and Discernment of their Beauties, You may lay them aside, and be secure of Writing with all the Graces of them all, without owing Your Perfection to any. Your style and Manner will be Your own.'
(p. 206)

Flattery apart, this is good advice. At a humbler level the author of *An English Grammar, wrote in a plain and familiar manner*, published in Antigua about 1750, wanted young people to be 'taught *English* by grammatical rules, and *composition* by the bright patterns of stile above quoted'. The model he most strongly recommended was Swift, who 'stands foremost of all our *English* writers; because his language is concise, and yet clear; nervous, but yet harmonious; simple, but so *perfectly elegant*, that it is hardly possible to add, take away, or alter a *word* . . . without obscuring his sense, or weakening his expression . . . Mr *Addison* stands next in rank' (pp. 72, 70).

David Williams, 1774, seems inconsistent in his approval of imitation. He first praises the study of Shakespeare:

'It is owing to our being able to read and understand the plays of Shakespear, that our manner of writing has in some instances rather improved than degenerated; and that . . . we have some authors who compose with the truest elegance and who might dispute the palm of fine writing with the best of their predecessors.'   (p. 151)

Soon afterwards (p. 162) he is saying that for pupils to begin with the imitation of a favourite author is the usual, but an incorrect, practice. They ought to go straight to Bacon, Blackstone and Kames. His point presumably is that imitation of the best (even if you find it dull) is effective whereas imitation of anything less than the best (even if you admire it) is not.

William McCartney, 1792, and William Milns, 1794, represent two opposing attitudes in their commonest forms. McCartney wants model passages to be read 'as often as may enable the learner to write from memory'; the learner is then to imitate the model, not slavishly, on a similar subject. His first draft is to concentrate on the thought; a second draft is to concentrate on the language, and third, even fourth, drafts may be necessary (p. 13). William Milns objects both to learning by heart and to imitation because they combine to weaken a pupil's confidence in his own writing. Learning 'the most brilliant passages in works of genius' will fill his mind 'with a confused jumble of glaring images, and . . . give him such wrong impressions of . . . excellence' that his own work suffers (1794, p. 30).

During the nineteenth century teachers relied little on imitation: the practice seems to have been dropped almost suddenly at the beginning of the century. George Scraggs, however, writing for unsophisticated readers in 1802, provides model passages from named authors and advises his pupils: 'Often clothe the thoughts of a good writer in your own words' (p. 174). The most notable later exception is G.F. Graham, whose *English, or the art of composition*, 1842, is 'founded on the application of the principle of IMITATION to the simplest expression of thought'. Graham wanted his pupils in the early stages to imitate syntactic patterns and the construction of paragraphs, but later he provides model fables and themes and an analysis of *Spectator* no. 411. He follows the same method in his more advanced textbook *English Style*, 1857. In both books he is not just echoing eighteenth-century practice: he is adapting it to his own times, and the difference is apparent in the style of his linguistic and psychological assumptions.

Varying. The customary method of varying was illustrated above (p. 275) from Poole's *Practical Rhetorick*. More common, slightly more practical, and only slightly less harmful, was the restrained and perhaps sarcastic form offered by John Twells in *Cicero Redivivus:*

1688 'Whereas in *English* the ignorant Many are used to write thus, *I have not received a Letter from you this Twelve-month*: a lover of quaintness and elegancy will raise himself above the common level, and express himself on this, or some such-like manner . . . *The sun hath once completed his yearly circuit, since you grac'd me with a letter.*'   (Quoted in Baldwin, 1944, II, 400)

Varying was a technique in the teaching of Latin style. It was not wholeheartedly incorporated into the teaching of English. William Meston in

1823 recommends that students should 'change daily two or three sentences of an English book into all the forms they admit' (p. 74), and Alexander Reid provides exercises in which the pupil has to 'vary the expression in the following sentences by changing the parts of speech', as '*Wisdom* is better than *riches*' becomes '*To be wise* is better than *to be rich*' (1839; 1869 edn., p. 35). Such exercises may appear in grammars or in composition texts.

Paraphrase and prosing. Paraphrase, both oral and written, was a recognised method of simultaneously exercising pupils in interpretation and expression. As it required no special books it is often recommended but not much discussed; its value is taken for granted, as by Benjamin Franklin, in *Proposals relating to the Education of Youth in Pennyslvania*, 1749, and by Henry Bright, 1783. Bright makes it very clear, as it later ceased to be, that paraphrase was not summary. One of his model paraphrases is only 8 words shorter than the original's 132 words, and his second model is longer than the original by 50 per cent. A representative account of the practice is given by Joseph Guy:

1813 'Outlines of Fables, intended to assist the young Learners in their early attempts at Composition, both written and oral. The Tutor should first read over one of Dodsley's Fables deliberately to his Pupils; and with the following outlines to refresh their memories, they may be expected to reproduce the same on a slate or paper. In their attempts at oral composition, each pupil should stand up and recite the substance of what the tutor has read, in his own words. The Classes should be exercised weekly, in one or more of the following Fables.'   (pp. 110–11)

The outlines are brief staccato summaries, riddled with blanks, and thus providing an additional preliminary exercise, that of 'supplying the ellipses' (below, p. 340). Paraphrasing was closely associated with metaphrasis, the traditional task of rewriting verse as prose, or prose as verse. Lawson, 1758, commends, for English, 'putting into Prose such Passages as please me most [he instances *Paradise Lost*, Book 2], imagining that by this Practice I shall gradually transfuse some Part of their Spirit into my own Speech and Writing' (p. 312). Milton is especially subject to this treatment, as in Metcalfe, a. 1771, where the opening lines of *Paradise Lost* appear as:

a. 1771 'Sing, heavenly Muse, of Man's first disobedience, and (of) the Fruit of that forbidden Tree, whose mortal Taste (*or* the mortal taste of which Tree) brought . . .' etc.   (Appendix 1, 'Of Poetry turned into Prose')

Similarly James Wood, 1777, has a chapter, 'Verse turned into Prose', in which his first, and even more futile, illustration is also from *Paradise Lost*. The technique was commended by Lady Fenn, 1784, and by James

Waddell, 1799, on the grounds that the exercise prevents a pupil from 'being imposed upon with bombast and fustian which too often passes for sublime' (p. iv), but it was not generally popular until the middle of the following century, when Richard Hiley prescribes 'Mutation of poetry into prose', in which 'as much as possible, the exact *meaning* and *spirit* of the original must be retained. *Poetical terms* and *idioms* must be carefully excluded' (1848, p. 154). Equally insensitive are Robert Armstrong, 1853 and Roscoe Mongan, 1864 ('much of the luxuriance of poetry may be pruned away in prose . . . Endeavour to give the author's exact meaning': p. 211). Yet for all the obvious objections against it the practice was respectable enough to be endorsed by Alexander Bain, both in the first edition of his *English Composition and Rhetoric*, 1866 (preface) and in *On Teaching English*, 1887, (chap. 3).

Paraphrase and prosing cannot be separated clearly from transposition.

Transposition and prosing. Transposition was not, by that name, one of the figures of syntax. It was a pedagogical modification of expolition, which was defined by Peacham as: 'When we abide still in one place, and yet seeme to speak divers things, many tymes repeating one sentence, but yet with other wordes, sentences, exornations, and fygures' (1577, Piv verso). Transposition derived its pedagogic power from the assumption that there was a natural order of words in a sentence, an order that was therefore in some sense fundamentally correct. Transposition was 'the placing of Words out of their natural Order, to render the Sound of them more agreeable to the Ear' (Dilworth, chap. 13) and was practised as an aid to the acquisition of a flexible style. It was discussed by Obadiah Walker in 1659, and by William Baker in 1724, but it was during the second half of the eighteenth century that it became a commonplace in the teaching of written expression and of grammar (A. Fisher, (1745) 1750; Merriman, 1750; Priestley, 1761; Owen, 1777; Webster, 1784; Sewell, 1789 and at least twenty others before the end of the century). James Buchanan, however, was responsible for presenting transposition from quite another point of view, one that trivialises it. Buchanan believed 'the clearest and purest Writers use the fewest Transpositions, and that they are more allowable in Poetry than in Prose' (1762, p. 217). He believed not only that there was a 'natural' word order but that the natural order was that of English. In his *A Plan of an English Grammar-School Education* he gives examples of how the 'artificial' order of Latin is transposed into the natural order of English:[1]

---

[1] Vernaculars regularly seem to their speakers to be expressed in a natural order. See Padley, 1985, pp. 142, 311. Kenrick is unusual among British grammarians in preferring 'habitual' to 'natural' (1773, p. 17).

1770 'The artificial, rhetorical, or inverted order of a Latin sentence, is rendered into its natural order, agreeing with that of the English by construing it grammatically . . . 'When she heard that I stood at the door, she made haste'. *Postquam ante ostium me audivit stare, approperabat.* Natural order thus: *Postquam audivit me stare ante ostium, approperabat.*' (pp. 129–30)

Buchanan's concern for transposition related more to interpretation than to expression. He seems to have thought that artificial word order and ellipses caused especial difficulty in reading an English author, and above all in reading Milton. His *The First Six Books of Milton's Paradise Lost, rendered into Grammatical Construction* is an extraordinary but influential work. After explaining 'for young readers, chiefly' the difference between artificial and natural order he expresses the hope that when they have read the first three or four books of *Paradise Lost* in his version 'even youth, who but know the parts of speech, by carefully comparing the context with the natural order . . . will . . . become tolerable masters of ellipsis and transposition'. When they have read six books they will be competent to read 'every English classic, whether in prose or verse' (pp. 14–15). Buchanan's 'natural order' for the opening of Book 2 is:

1773 'Satan sat exalted high on a throne of royal state; which far outshone the wealth of Ormus and of Ind, or all places where the gorgeous east with richest hand showers on her kings barbaric pearl and gold; he was by merit raised to that bad eminence; and uplifted thus high from despair beyond his hope, he still aspires beyond thus high; being insatiate to pursue vain war with heaven; and though untaught by success, he thus displayed his proud imagination.' (p. 91)

Buchanan respects Milton only in giving his text the largest type and the most prominent place on the page. The transposed version is printed below Milton's text, and Buchanan's notes below that. But Buchanan has made that sad shift of emphasis which the routine of teaching tends to bring about. What began as a help to understanding and to flexible expression became an end in itself – the tolerable mastery of ellipsis and transposition. The pursuit of this mastery entailed prosing because amongst the works that school pupils were likely to read the verse was more 'artificial' than the prose.

Transposition and prosing continued to appear in nineteenth-century textbooks but not with the same frequency as during the later decades of the eighteenth century. Blanch Mercy, 1799, describes transposition as 'throwing words out of their natural order, as in poetry' (I, 82) and in the same year the American *Practical Exercises* commends 'ornament' so long as it does not detract from 'perspicuity':

1799 'The natural order of words and members in a sentence is that order, in which the thoughts arise in the mind, and is generally the most perspicuous; but they may not unfrequently be transposed without occasioning obscurity, and the strength and elegance of the period be greatly promoted.' (p. 13)

Examples follow of Milton and Pope transposed. In America Samuel Dearborn's *The Columbian Grammar*, 1795, and in Britain *The Complete Young Man's Companion*, 1798, give exercises of this kind, and George Scraggs, in a manual of composition designed for 'common capacities' in 1802, gives models of 'transposed or varied sentences'. He alone avoids suggesting that the 'unnatural' order is slightly incorrect.

The purpose of these exercises is described by the anonymous author of *Exercises of Transposition*, 1818. In teaching composition, he says, it is not so much ideas that are wanted as 'an ability of clothing them in suitable words'. It is easier to rearrange the words of an existing passage than 'to form one entirely new'. Transposition is thus a preliminary exercise for composition. His exercises are paragraphs in which the order of phrases and clauses (and often of words within clauses) is jumbled. To our eyes the exercise is reduced to a mere puzzle; to him, 'words, sentences, paragraphs and chapters, necessarily pass under a *critical* review by the student a number of times, before they are organised; and of consequence he becomes practically acquainted with the structure of language' (preface).

An odd variation of the practice, advocated by no other teacher, is William Angus' 'Rhyming couplets transposed', which also turns the exercise into a puzzle. His pupils are given:

> *1812* Her even lines show her steady temper,
> Polish'd as her brow, and neat as her dress. (p. 302)

They are supposed to transpose this back into its original form, presumably:

> Her even lines her steady temper show,
> Neat as her dress, and polish'd as her brow.

The exercise itself is unimportant. More significant is the fact that we know of it only because Angus was also a writer of textbooks. Other teachers, equally ingenious, wrote no books. We are reminded that the textbooks are not a full record of what teachers did, nor even of their best practices.

A late example, in 1834, of the earlier treatment of transposition is McCulloch's exercises in 'Conventional Order and Rhetorical Order . . . Transpose the prepositions in the following sentences, in as many ways as the sense will admit . . . Convert by transposition the following rhetorical sentences into conventional sentences' (pp. 158–68). These exercises occur in a grammar; transposition has lost the connection it first had with the teaching of written expression. In the same year the American teacher

Expression and performance

Richard Greene Parker used transposition without any reference to its original meaning but only to a combination of paraphrase and prosing. A section of his *Progressive Exercises in English Composition*, under the heading 'Transposition', begins: 'The ideas contained in the following poetical extracts may be written, in the pupil's own language, in prose' (p. 25). In about 1850 'Scott's Transposition' was listed as in use by the Society of the Holy Child Jesus.[2] The book has not been identified.

Elocution

Howell, 1971, discusses the complicated shift during the early eighteenth century in the meaning of 'elocution'. In Latin, and in Ciceronian rhetorics written in English, 'elocution' had meant style, especially in relation to the use of the figures and tropes; the term for rhetorical delivery, including gesture, had been *pronuntiatio* or *actio*. In the shift, which Howell convincingly relates to the emerging science of phonetics, 'pronunciation' was restricted to what is now its modern sense and 'elocution' referred to voice production, delivery and gesture. There was naturally some overlap between the terms and the change of meaning was not uniformly applied.

Although interest in elocution had been growing during the first half of the eighteenth century, Sheridan is often thought of as its initiator, and he did not discourage the belief. The chief topics on which he lectured were: rules for correct pronunciation; articulation; the management of the voice in the expression of feeling; and gesture. He addressed himself to adults, but specially to teachers only in his *Elements of English*, 1786. He was a good lecturer, but his success was in large part created by the social conditions of his time. The educated, and those who aspired to education and its rewards, were increasingly aware of the importance of speech, and increasingly able to compare, unfavourably, a national or regional way of speaking with the supposedly pure speech of the educated Londoner. During the later decades of the century many people were affected by what John Martin in 1798 called 'the present rage for speaking in public, on all sorts of subjects, by almost all sorts of persons' (p. 24). Leigh Hunt records his membership, about 1804, of 'a club of young men, who associated for the purpose of cultivating public speaking' (*Autobiography*, chap. 7), but the rage affected paterfamilias as well as his sons, and continued to do so, at varying levels of society, during most of the nineteenth century. J.T. Sinnett, in a grammar first published in 1848, defends the space allotted to oratory in a book

[2] Information from John P. Marmion.

'intended for the MILLIONS' on the grounds that 'the PEOPLE are just as capable of feeling . . . as the Aristocracy', and must be helped to express themselves in public affairs (1853 edn, p. 79).

Three aspects of elocution, much older than the elocutionary fashion itself, concerned the schools: reading aloud; correct pronunciation; public performance. Pronunciation, it was recognised by most teachers, could not be learned from a book. The best that could be done was to list and illustrate the sounds of the vowels (usually in a spelling-book), to arrange spelling-lists phonetically, and to provide a numbered key to the vowel sounds, the numbers being printed above the text to be read (Sheridan, 1762, Lecture 2; Kenrick, 1773; John Walker, 1791). The grammars sometimes included lists of words whose pronunciation caused difficulty or social embarrassment. During the nineteenth century there was a regular flow of manuals, adult but often made to look as though they could also be used in school, in the old orthoepic tradition. Such were Benjamin Smart, 1810 and 1812; Thomas Ewing, a. 1816; James Knowles, 1829; David Charles Bell, 1845.

Latin recitations, declamations and public orations had always been part of grammar-school and university education, but we do not know to what extent they were delivered in English during the sixteenth and seventeenth centuries. It is likely that they followed the same kind of development as the performance of plays in English (below, pp. 297f.) and, if the comment in *Ludus Ludi Literarii* quoted above (p. 277) is accurate, they were not frequent. By the early decades of the eighteenth century such performances in English were a regular part of school life, especially in the academies:

a. 1811 'The task of the younger boys . . . consisted in learning to read and write their mother tongue grammatically; and one day in the week . . . was set apart for the recitation of select passages in poetry and prose . . . Each scholar . . . ascended the stage, and said his speech, as the phrase was. The speech was carefully taught him by his master, both with respect to its pronunciation, and the action deemed suitable to its several parts.' (Quoted from Alex Graydon, *Memoirs of a Life passed in Pennsylvania*, 1811, by Sol Cohen, 1974, p. 510)

That account of mid-eighteenth-century practice in America is characteristic also of British schools.

Just as the teacher of rhetoric had found himself under a compulsion to analyse and classify the figures of speech, and the teacher of grammar to classify adverbs and interjections, so the teacher of recitation and oratory was compelled to enumerate the emotions ('passions') that the speaker's material might express. Ward, 1759, listed 54 passions; Burgh, whose list acquired nearly definitive status, 76; Drummond 75; Walker 60. The practice continued into the nineteenth century with James Chapman,

1821; Innes, 1834, who built up a list of 127; and Hartley, 1846. These lists were the points of reference for two kinds of advice: on what gestures to use, and how to modulate the voice. Advice on the use of the voice usually took the form of marginal comment, such as those below (p. 296) quoted from Lawrie, 1779. An early eighteenth-century example, which still keeps close to traditional rhetoric, comes from Curson's compendium, which is directed also to older school pupils and includes school orations taken from *Ludus Ludi Literarii*. He quotes an unnamed author on gesture:

1702 'The hand is to be *held out* when we speak of Begging: *Up* when we speak of Praying... *Clapping* the *Hands* together when speaking of Wonders: *Opening* one or both hands, when making a thing plain or explaining... *The first Finger turned down* for urging and pressing as it were: *Put up* for Threatning: the *middle Finger* put out for reproaching: the *left Thumb* touched by the Index of the right hand for reasoning and disputing.'   (pp. 111–12)

Charles Bland, writing also for schoolboys, gives advice on the use of the eyebrows: 'You must not raise them *both* at every turn... nor *lift up* the *one*, and *cast down* the *other*; but for the most part they ought to remain in the same *Posture* and *Equality* that *Nature* hath given them' (1708, p. 34). When linked with an itemisation of the emotions the advice, to schoolboys, takes this form:

1765 'JOY, if sudden, is expressed by clapping the Hands, leaping, open eyes, irregular Smiles, and a loud Voice. It improves into TRANSPORT or ECSTACY...' etc.
                                                    (Edwards, p. 95)

Edwards was a provincial teacher on a small scale. John Walker was a highly influential metropolitan teacher who set out to provide 'a regular system of Gesture, suited to the wants and capacities of school-boys'. He recognises the difficulty of relating movement and gesture to the expression of feeling. He does not try to describe gestures appropriate to each emotion, but seeks 'such a general style of action... as shall be easily conceived and easily executed; which, though not expressive of any particular passion, shall not be inconsistent with the expression of any passion' ((1789) 1801, pp. v-vi). He provides drawings of schoolboys in the act of performing a number of basic gestures, and he builds his advice on these. Walker's approach is artificial, but it is a carefully thought out artifice that, given the conventions, left the speaker a measure of interpretative freedom. Most textbook commentators, however, prescribed powerful but vague treatment for single words or phrases. Two nineteenth-century examples must stand for many. In the first R.T. Linnington provides a commentary on how to recite a (very bad) poem called *The Captive*, which he has chosen as an illustration of the style of 'plaintive expression with intense feeling'.

This is the third stanza, with Linnington's advice:

1833   '(c) He smiles in scorn and turns the key!
                     He quits the grate, I knelt in vain!
              (d) His glimm'ring lamp still, still, I see, –
                     'Tis gone – and all is gloom again.
              (e) Cold, bitter cold! no warmth! no light!
              (f)   Life, all thy comforts once I had;
                     Yet, here I'm chain'd, this freezing night,
                     Altho' not mad! no, no! not mad!

(c) *Disappointment.*

(d) The speaker should look anxiously in the supposed direction of the object, and keep his eyes fixed on it for one or two seconds, after he has uttered the word *see*, suspending his voice at the same time.

(e) The feeling of cold is represented by shuddering, and contracting the shoulders, and clasping the hands.

(f) *Repining*, requiring a plaintive tone with much feeling. A speaker should, however, at all times, be careful to avoid a *whining* cant, which is too frequently mistaken for pathetic expression.'   (p. 59)

Gilbert Austin, 1806, applying to school use Joshua Steele's *Prosodia Rationalis*, carries the encoding method to its limits. He is trying to give precise instructions for both voice and gesture. The text, Gay's *The Miser and Plutus*, is accompanied by three aids: small drawings of the reciter's posture; a code printed above the line, indicating the possible movement of the hands; another code, printed below the line, for the feet. Symbols for pitch, speed and volume are listed separately. It would have been better to set the piece to music.

Teachers who tried to encode directions for the use of voice and gesture, especially those who used pictures or diagrams, were seeking a form of indirect imitation. The reader, who had no teacher to watch, obeyed the code and worked out for himself what he would have seen and heard a teacher do. But even such a regulated form of imitation was repudiated by some: it was not regulated enough. James Wright considered in 1814 that

'. . . the imperfect plan of teaching Elocution by mere imitation is now at length happily and fully exploded. [To proceed with rules and examples] . . . is now considered to be the readiest and only correct method by which an eloquent delivery can be taught . . . [He has therefore] been forced to reject all compilations hitherto dignified with the title *Exercises in Elocution*, as useless.'

Wright was not only trying to rival Walker and Burgh; he tried to find in sentence structure a basis for the rules by which he wished to teach. His twenty rules relate to the speaking of compact (periodic) sentences; parentheses; loose sentences; 'sentences which have parts corresponding to

parts' (antitheses); the enumeration of a series. The pieces in his collection
are printed with the numbers of the appropriate rule printed above the line
and are marked with accents to show Walker's rising and falling inflections.

Talking, debating, making speeches and reading aloud

Talking and debating. During the eighteenth century there began to appear
occasional references to the value of children's talk, even in school. They
are scattered and disconnected, but worth recording. James Barclay
recommended that the master should ask the children:

1743 '. . . how they would have behaved, and what they think of any action or
expression. This . . . leads them to ask a thousand little questions of which one would
scarce think them capable . . . It encourages them to speak freely what they think . . .
Such conversation with children is surely better than keeping them at a distance.'

(p. 19)

John Williams, a. 1752, suggested rather hopefully that children at
boarding school might be encouraged to talk to each other at night and
summarise the day's work (p. 13). He does not say whether this
conversation should take place in the dormitory or amongst the few pupils
strong enough to have seats near the fire. John Rice, 1773, a teacher of
elocution, writes: 'The reading books is, indeed, a great *help* to knowledge;
but of very little effect in improving the mind, if not assisted by
conversation' (p. 43; he expands the point in the following pages). Lady
Fenn, as often, expresses the mother's point of view as much as the
teacher's. She says that when children are interested they will speak with
vivacity, 'even compose little narratives, which they relate with the utmost
energy of expression'. She does not discuss any formal encouragement of
these narratives; her interest is in the reading-passages in her book. But
these passages are composed 'of such prattle as we hear from the dear little
people when amusing themselves . . . They are supplied with Lessons in
their own infantine *language*' (1797, Part 2, preface). 'Prattle' is much in
vogue at this time. William Godwin, 1805, refers only to the teacher, who
should 'prattle' to children, 'expatiate' upon some points, 'introduce quick,
unexpected turns, which, if they are not wit, have the effect of wit upon
children' (preface). Godwin does not refer to the children's talk but the tone
of his comment implies that the teacher's wit is reciprocated.

More formal conversation was also practised. In 1816 Ackworth School
had a discussion group for teachers and pupils that considered topics such
as, 'What is it that regulates and fixes the wages of labour and the price of

everything bought or sold?' In 1821 the group was formally constituted as the Association for the Improvement of the Mind (Thompson, 1879, p. 165). In 1822 Mr Dunnett, 'lecturer in oratory' and teacher of elocution at Mr Ambler's academy at Canterbury, published a debate conducted by his pupils on the topic 'Was Caesar a good man?' The chairman was Master Henry Stickals and there were twelve speakers. The style is flowery and orotund, but underneath the editorial and publicising pencil there is an undercurrent of boyish attitudes. No vote was taken. The chairman concluded by expressing his own opinion that Caesar was not a great man (*Debate*, 1822).

Debating is not talking, but it is not, or should not be, a succession of set declamations in the old rhetorical tradition. A study of early school debating societies would show how far they encouraged authentic personal expression and how far, if at all, they were related to classroom activities.

Making speeches. A formal speech required the same care with delivery as did recitation and reading aloud, and preparing pupils to make set speeches followed the pattern already described. Many newspapers, in America and Britain, carried accounts of school functions like this report of an 'exhibition with dramatization' at Marblehead Academy, Salem.

1794   'The entertainment was opened with an Oration, by Master Watson, on the subject of heroism; in which a pleasing and useful contrast was drawn between the characters of Caesar and Washington.'
(*Salem Gazette*, 16 September 1794, quoted by Butler, 1969, 162–3)

Pupils would hardly ever make a speech extempore, but there continued well into the nineteenth century the convention that they should be able to write one. Buchanan quotes an anonymous contributor to George Turnbull's *Observations upon Liberal Education*, 1742, as maintaining that students ought 'to speak every Day their unwritten Thoughts on any Subject in English'. Buchanan disagrees: Let them 'first deliver their written Thoughts . . . whether extemporary or studied'. His method for training extempore fluency is to make his pupils study passages from good writers that have been put by the teachers into incorrect English. The pupils make an improved version, study it, 'and then deliver it extempore. This is in a great Measure delivering their own Compositions' (1762, pp. xx–xxi).

No doubt a confident master would let an able boy draft his own speech for a public occasion, but it would be closely edited. An unusual instance of this is *Musae Berkhamstedienses: or poetical prolusions by some young Gentlemen at Berkhamsted School*, 1794, of which a corrected edition was issued in 1799. This second edition, responding to a reviewer's scepticism, records the extent to which the author of each piece received assistance. In the second edition there are thirty pieces, of which six are original compositions in Latin and twelve are translations into Latin. Of the English pieces nine are original (two by adults) and three are translations out of Latin. The preface to the first edition makes it clear that though these 'exercises' were all written for 'what is called Speech Day on 2 October, 1793' they were not all delivered; nor did the author necessarily speak his own piece. Four of the seven original English pieces written by boys were unaltered, and one received only 'a few touches' in one part. This particular piece, *Liberty, an allegorical poem,* by Edward Walford, gives a schoolboy's response to recent events in France: the execution of the king and the terror of 1793. The temple of Liberty is seen in a dream:

> A Goddess, outward lovely to the eye,
> Grac'd the bright fane; her name EQUALITY.
> But horrors round her fly, and black despair,
> Stern ministers of death, and bloody war . . .
> Through the thick murky gloom my eyes survey,
> By the pale lamps which spread a mournful day,
> *The Rights of Man,* and *We are equal all,*
> In golden letter grav'd upon the wall.

One asks how far the triteness of the epithets is caused by a teaching-method that relies too much on imitation, and how far it reflects a view of poetry in which originality is little valued in comparison with the harmonious manipulation of what is familiar. Other contributions raise the question more strongly: *An Adieu to Berkhamsted School* ('much corrected') opens: 'Scholastic Dome farewell! I must depart!'; *Robinson Crusoe's Soliloquy* ('unaltered') begins:

> Ten times already this slow-moving sun
> Around the globe its annual course has run.

But the question is loaded with hindsight and detracts from the value of the unusual Berkhamsted initiative. To see that initiative in proportion look only at a much more ordinary example of what a late-eighteenth-century teacher thought his pupils should perform. These are the opening and closing sentences of a short schoolboy speech:

> *The Response*
> *To be delivered by one of the senior scholars on behalf of all.*
> Permit me, Sir, in the Name of my young Companions, my Fellow Students here met together, unanimously to express our hearty Concurrence in following the Directions you have so amply laid before us . . . Fired with a Love of Glory, and an ardent thirst for Praise, which we are assured is the grand Criterion to mark a noble

Mind, we will constantly exert our utmost Abilities to attain to Excellence in every laudable Pursuit; thereby to ensure your Approbation, and recommend ourselves to *public esteem,* (Sewell, 1789, p. 133)

Reading aloud. In sixteenth- and seventeenth-century rhetorics reading aloud, in English, received little attention. As a performance skill it was treated under oratory or declamation; as evidence for, and as a form of, interpretation it was not yet considered significant by teachers. Howell (1971, p. 154) considered Steele's *Spectator* no. 147, of 1711, both a sign of, and a stimulus to, increasing concern to make the reading in church of the Book of Common Prayer more lively. Steele wonders why the clergy are unable to read better words that they read so often:

1711 'This Inability . . . proceeds from the little Care that is taken of their Reading, while Boys and at School, where when they are got into *Latin*, they are look'd upon as above *English*, the Reading of which is wholly neglected, or at least read to very little purpose, without any due Observations made to them of the proper Accent and Manner of Reading.'

In 1721 Isaac Watts included in his *The Art of Reading and Writing English* a chapter on 'Directions for Reading' (14) and one on 'Reading Verse' (20), which brought together, at a level suitable for schools, the best customary advice. Watts claimed no originality, but these chapters, combined with his chapter on 'Emphasis' (15), were timely: they were reprinted and recast and included in numerous anthologies, spelling-books and grammars until well into the nineteenth century. His advice is simple, concise, light in tone and sensible: observe the meaning ('Let your Voice humour the Sense a little'); read in a natural, not in a special, voice; clarity is more important than volume; don't hurry; avoid both monotony and sing-song. Watts' most influential advice, however, is a powerful half-truth, repeated countless times in the following eighty years: 'The great and general *Rule* therefore of reading *English* Verse, is to pronounce every Word, and every Sentence, just as if it were Prose' (p. 76). He qualifies this advice in two ways, omitted or, in the case of the second, rejected, by many later writers:

1721 'At the end of every Line, where is no Stop, make a Stop about half so long as a Comma, just to give notice that the line is ended. II. If any Word in the Line happen to have two Sounds, chuse to give that Sound to it which most favours the Metre and the Rhyme.' (p. 77)

By this he means, in his examples, that 'glittering' may be pronounced 'glitt'ring', and that in the couplet 'Were I but once from Bondage free / I'd never sell my Liberty' the last word must be pronounced 'Libertee', whereas if it were to rhyme with 'sky' it 'must be sounded as ending in -*i*'. Watts' advice for avoiding a poetry voice was popularly taken to mean just that verse should be read as if it were prose. His qualifications were ignored and the advice became a harmful oversimplification.

Unnatural reading was a constant matter of complaint and caused the teachers much difficulty. Bishop Burnet, writing in 1668, had urged that children 'should be taught to pronounce fully and plainly, without peeping-tone, or chirping' (1761, p. 12) and many echoed him, including John Mason: 'The greatest and most common fault of all, is reading with a Tone.' He quoted Watts and recommended that pupils should practise reading aloud from *Pilgrim's Progress* because it is 'writ in a familiar Stile, that comes nearest to that of common Conversation . . . The great Rule is . . . to *follow Nature, and avoid Affectation*' ((1748) 1761, pp. 14, 35). But as Peter Walkden Fogg wrote twenty years later:

1796 'Those who have treated these subjects [emphasis, pause, tone, etc.] best have as yet produced little beyond the simple direction – "Follow nature". This is perfectly just indeed, but scarce merits the name of a rule; because all men of sense keep this constantly in view, whatever they undertake; and because perverse habits are generally mistaken, by those they enslave, for nature itself.'

(II, Dissertation 13)

Sheridan is frequently critical of the schools, sharing the teachers' own dissatisfaction with the indistinctness of young people's reading. Indistinctness, he says, is caused by:

1762 '. . . too great precipitancy of speech. And this takes its rise in England, chiefly from a bad method of teaching boys to read . . . The prize to boys, who have made any proficiency in reading, seems to be destined to the swift; they set out at a gallop, and continue their speed to the end, without regarding how many letters or syllables they drop by the way; or how many words they justle into one another . . . To this hasty delivery . . . is owing that thick, mumbling, cluttering utterance, of which we have too many examples.' (Lecture 2)

Although it was sometimes attributed to him, Sheridan avoided the crude statement that verse should be spoken as if it were prose. Certain elements should be treated in the same way in both prose and verse: the pronunciation of words, emphasis, 'pauses relative to the sense only', which he called 'sentential pauses'. The elements distinctive to the speaking of verse were 'the movement of the voice from accent to accent; laying no stress on the intermediate syllables'; and 'musical pauses', those at the caesura and at the end of a run-on line. A reader or speaker who observed these rules would avoid 'the usual fault of introducing sing-song notes, or a species of chanting into poetical numbers' (*Rhetorical Grammar*, 1781, p. 135).

John Walker, whose influence was eventually decisive, gave the popular form of Watts' advice an endorsement so prohibitively lukewarm that the misconception eventually disappeared:

1781 'For those . . . whose ears are totally deficient in a true taste for the music of poetry, the best method . . . is to read verse exactly as if it were prose: for though this may be said to be an error, it is certainly an error on the safer side [than "sliding into a whining cant"].' (II, 174)

It was still necessary at the end of the century for Joseph Robertson to restate what Watts had actually said:

1799 'Verse should be read as verse, and prose as prose . . . If the last word of any line is passed over with the rapidity of an unaccented syllable, the measure will be totally annihilated, and the poetry absurdly reduced to mere prose.' (p. 9)

The argument continued during the nineteenth century and into our own day because the question is a real one. But nothing was added to it at the school level, and it need not here be pursued further.

A second question was related both to reading aloud and to recitation: how far should the performer enter into the thinking and feeling of the author whose words he was speaking? Sheridan gives his answer in general terms:

1762 'As soon as we perceive . . . the full meaning . . . of any sentence, we shall be able to express that meaning to others, in the same manner, and with the same propriety and force, as if it proceeded from the immediate sentiments of our own minds.' (Lecture 1, p. 11)

Samuel Edwards, writing solely about schools, puts it more sharply:

1765 'No person can *read* well till he come to *speak* what he sees in the Book before him, in the same *natural* Manner as he speaks the Thoughts which arise in his *own* Mind; therefor he must understand what he reads.' (p. 87)

No one of course doubted that the reader must understand what he reads, but it does not follow from this axiom that he should identify himself with his author. William Cockin disagreed with Sheridan: he drew attention to the difference between an '*original* speaker' and 'a *repeater*'. The former speaks with more feeling, because he is expressing ideas which he himself has chosen; the latter with less feeling because he is merely passing on what someone else has chosen to say:

1775 'The manner of our delivery in reading ought to be inferior in warmth and energy to what we should use, were the language before us the spontaneous effusion of our own hearts in the circumstances of those out of whose mouths it is supposed to proceed.' (pp. 7–8)

The view that Cockin is contradicting is not, in fact, the view that Sheridan had advocated. Cockin is contrasting the situations of the original speaker and the repeater: only if the repeater could enter into the situation of the original speaker (which he cannot) would his delivery rightly be as passionate. Sheridan does not say that the reader should try to enter into the situation of the original speaker: only that he should read the words as if they were his own. Sheridan's reader *creates* his own imaginative situation, from which he draws the force of his delivery, but it is his own equivalent, not a reproduction, of the original speaker's situation.

Lawrie, in *The Merchant Maiden Hospital Magazine*, 1779, makes a heroic attempt to show at the school level how a passage should be read. Emphasis is shown by italics; modulations are noted in the margin. In a passage of nearly 600 words one word in every 5 or 6 is italicised and there are about 40 marginal directions. A single sentence must suffice to show what a teacher would be expected to pass on to her girls. The topic is *Woman*:

1779   Text: '*Remember* thou art made man's *reasonable* companion, *not* the slave of his passion: the end of thy being *is* not merely to gratify his desire, but to *assist* him in the toils of his life, to *sooth* him with thy tenderness, and *recompense* his care with *soft* endearments.'
    Margin: Begin this with a middle note, but strong voice: continue almost equal 'till the word *sooth*, at which fall softer and lower to the end of this sentence.'
                                                                    (p. 18)

Complaints about monotony persisted throughout the nineteenth century, on both sides of the Atlantic. In *Mansfield Park*, when 'the subject of reading aloud was further discussed' Edmund and Crawford agree about 'the total inattention to it, in the ordinary school-system for boys' (chap. 34), and Allison Wrifford, a representative voice from Concord, deplored:

1834   '... monotony, or monotonous school-tone, precipitancy and indistinctness, and the reverse, a lifeless, drawling of speech ... The practical teaching [of reading] is the least understood and most neglected, of all the branches of our school education ... The main drift ... of all common schools is evidently confined ... to the mere practice of reading as fast as possible and calling all the words by their right names, and in their right order, and this, without much regard to sense or comprehension.'   (pp. 11, 9)[3]

Robert Robinson in Britain quotes other inspectors, including Matthew Arnold, who agreed that the main cause of bad reading was the poor quality

---

[3] The reference to the 'name' of a word recalls seventeenth-century discussion about the names of vowel sounds.

of what the pupils had to read. In a lengthy discussion Robinson suggests that teachers should pay more attention to phrasing ('grouping the words'); that children reading in an 'irregular tone' should be asked to say, in a conversational voice and without looking at the book, the words they had just read; that the teacher when hearing reading should only listen and not follow in the book, thus keeping herself alert for indistinctness (1863, chap. 1). The discussion still continues.

Dramatic work

Dramatic work is relevant to the teaching of both expressive and interpretative skills, but it has not in the past been linked especially to the teaching of English; nor is it solely so linked today. It has by its nature left few early records of how it was conducted. We know that plays were performed, and we can infer from the circumstances of a production some of the motives behind it, but we lack the kind of evidence from the teachers themselves that is provided by the prefaces to textbooks. It would be desirable, but difficult, in the sixteenth and early seventeenth centuries, to distinguish between performances by near-professional boy actors and choristers and those by pupils in the associated grammar schools. It would be desirable also to distinguish between public performance (the school play) and the use of dramatic methods in teaching a classroom subject, usually Latin, such as those described in Samuel Shaw's *Words made Visible*, 1678-9. A further distinction needs to be made between the performance of a play, perhaps privately within the school, and the reading in class of a dramatic text, or of a text in dialogue meant merely for reading or for a static performance analogous to the concert performance of an opera. In assessing educational significance we need to be able to compare, perhaps, the situation of a Merchant Taylors' schoolboy of 1582 acting before the queen in full feminine gear hired from the Revels Office with that of a boy from the same school in 1861 playing a female part in male evening dress (Motter, 1929, p. 120).

School performances of Latin plays, especially at Christmas, were common and sometimes prescribed by statute. St Paul's performed a Latin play at Greenwich in 1527 (Watson, 1908, p. 323); Terence and Seneca were performed at Westminster in the 1540s and Latin and Greek plays at Shrewsbury in the 1560s (Baldwin, 1944, I, 177-8, 389). The 1566 statutes of the grammar school at Norwich prescribe at least two comedies at Christmas, and at Sandwich there was to be a Latin play, the parts to be learnt 'at vacant times' (*ibid*, 416, 344).

It is difficult at present to know to what extent plays in English were acted by ordinary schoolchildren. Ought we to be surprised, for example, that some time between 1699 and 1715 the boys of Clerkenwell charity school put on a performance of *Timon of Athens* and that as a consequence the Bishop of London was asked to withdraw the master's licence (M.G. Jones, 1938, p. 9)? It is difficult also to know how far the plays were spectacles put on to impress the public and recruit new pupils, and how far they had any direct educational purpose. The spectacular school play does not lack educational value. Present-day arguments between the proponents of a public performance, on the one hand, and of drama classes in the school hall on the other, concern the effectiveness of the time-taking school play in relation to these values. But we have no reason to suppose that such considerations affected the school play even in the seventeenth and eighteenth centuries: it seems to have been an activity independent of, and not in competition with, the classroom.

Popular dramatic tradition is so strong in England that it is sensible to suppose that plays in English have always been performed in schools. Ian Lancashire records the performance at Winchester, before 1450, of an interlude, *Occupation and Idleness*, which, he says, was 'undoubtedly a school play' (1984, p. 283). T.H.V. Motter, 1929, could not trace plays performed in English earlier than those given at Ralph Radclif's school at Hitchin in the years after 1546, and the only evidence he quotes, from John Bale in 1557, leaves uncertain the status of comedies with Latin titles, such as *De Patientia Griseldis* and *De Melibaeo Chauceriano* (Motter, p. 226). Nicholas Udall's *Ralph Roister Doister* was written for performance by Winchester choir-school boys in 1561; at Eton in 1561 Malim recorded the headmaster's freedom to put on plays in English in addition to the Latin ones, provided they had 'acumen et leporem' – sharpness and humour. Such fragments of information seem to be the most that is available. These plays would all have been public performances: it is the rehearsals that would have been interesting educationally.

During much of the seventeenth century there is no evidence of public performance, although we are told that Eton did put on plays during the Commonwealth (Motter, p. 51). John Mason's idiosyncratic play *Princeps rhetoricus . . . the Combat of Caps*, performed by his pupils in Camberwell, was described in 1648 (Northup, 1912) and *Lingua, or the Combat of the Tongue and the Five Senses for Superiority* had been performed at the Free School, Huntingdon (with Cromwell in the cast) before it was published in 1657. In 1671 the author of *A Model for a School for the Better Education of Youth* gives explicit approval for school acting, but as a recommendation, not a statement of actual practice. He divides the 'pleasant part' of the curriculum into 'solid learning' (which includes arithmetic, gardening, and English as an aid to learning Latin) and 'complemental qualities' taught during 'intermissions'. These include dancing, singing and instrumental music. The 'frequent acting of Interludes would much improve Children in Audacity and Carriage', but it is not clear whether the plays would be in English. The only example the writer gives is a dramatisation in eight comedies of the whole of Comenius' *Janua Linguarum*. The model is professedly an ideal but it is related to the then well-known progressive school at Tottenham High Cross, with which the author was in some way connected.

Obadiah Walker, 1673, and Francis Brokesby, 1701, both commend acting, but they are referring to the social education of young gentlemen rather than to a school curriculum. And they are cautious. Walker insists that the plays should be 'of good subjects, well garbled [i.e. sifted, cleansed] and discreetly handled' (p. 110), and Brokesby, under the heading 'recreations', allows the acting of comedies or tragedies 'if rightly chosen or compos'd' (p. 112). After the Restoration there are records of Beaumont and Fletcher's *Love's Pilgrimage* being performed at Merchant Taylors' in 1665 and of Dryden's *Cleomenes* at Westminster in 1695. We know of *Julius Caesar* at St Paul's in 1712, of an English play, *The Jesuits*, at Charterhouse in 1724, of *Cato* at Reading School in 1731. In Scotland *Henry VIII* was performed at a school in North Berwick in 1727, and *Julius Caesar* at Dalkeith in 1734. *Cato* was performed at Perth in 1724 (Scotland, 1969, 1, 85), at Whitehaven in the 1770s, and at the English School in Worcester, Mass. in 1787 (Butler, 1969, p. 276). The academy at Hackney was renowned during the eighteenth century for its school plays, and especially for its triennial public performances of Shakespeare; *Macbeth* in 1739; *Henry IV, Part 1* in 1748, 1764 and 1777; *Julius Caesar* in 1774; *King Lear* in 1783. Other plays performed included Thomas Tomkis' *Albumazar* in 1747, and John Hughes' *The Siege of Damascus* in 1765 (E.A. Jones, 1934).

Some evidence of practice outside the grammar schools is provided by two works, one by Daniel Bellamy and the other by Bellamy and his son of the same name. *The Young Ladies' Miscellany*, 1723, is a made-up volume of dramatic material, produced for, and on sale at, Mrs Bellamy's school at Temple Bar and at the 'College-Boarding-School, in Bury' kept by the elder Bellamy's sister Mrs Hannah Wood. The preface, defending 'Dramatic Representations' against parental apprehensions, argues that the education of girls is concerned too much with their appearance ('Tis pity that the favourite Works of Nature should be nothing but moving

Pictures') and not enough with developing their minds and their judgment. If dancing is acceptable, why not acting; learning should be enjoyable; drama will train the memory. Then follows a short 'Essay on Pronunciation', mostly concerned with the expression of various emotions, illustrated by short passages from Rowe's *Tamerlane*, from Addison's *Cato*, from Dryden's *The Spanish Friar*, and from *Macbeth* and *Julius Caesar*. Next are two plays by Bellamy, with separate title-pages; one, *Vanquish'd Love: or, the Jealous Queen*, had been performed by the schoolgirls and the other was to be performed 'as one of their Annual Publick Exercises'. The later two-volume *Miscellanies in Prose and Verse*, 1739–40, includes plays suitable for young ladies, four of which are stated to have been performed at Mrs Bellamy's school, now moved to Kingston on Thames. As their entries in the *Dictionary of National Biography* show, there was nothing unorthodox or raffish about the Bellamys (even if Mrs Bellamy, not to be confused with Mrs George Anne Bellamy, had been, as seems likely, an actress). Nor do they write as if acting plays in a girls' school was a novelty: their defensiveness is no more than a conventional reassurance for parents.

The range of eighteenth-century opinion about drama was wide. Isaac Watts was only thirteen years older than the elder Bellamy but his outlook was very different. In *A Discourse on the Education of Children and Youth*, 1753, he concedes that morally satisfactory and even profitable plays could be written, but

'It is too well known, that the comedies which appear on our stage, and most of the tragedies too, have no design to set religion or virtue in its best light, nor to render vice odious . . . Besides, there is nothing that will pass on our theatres that has not the mixture of some amorous intrigue . . . modesty is in certain danger there.'

((1753) 1798, section 9)

This kind of objection, to the professional stage, could be countered in respect of schools, as in Samuel Werenfels' lecture at the University of Basel, published in England in 1744 as *The Usefulness of Dramatic Interludes in the Education of Youth*. The English translator comments: 'This Oration may be consider'd as a Just *Encomium* on those schools among us, whose *Dramatic* Interludes (whether in *Latin*, *French* or *English*) have already been introduced with proper Choice; and prompt others to the like Practice' (preface). The plays should be 'Chast, Rational, Decent', and love is not necessary for the plot (p. 19).

It is surprising that Thomas Sheridan, an actor, the father of an actor and the son of a schoolmaster, had nothing to say about dramatic work in school. The answer may be supplied by John Walker, himself an actor turned teacher:

1789 'Though the acting of Plays at schools has been universally supposed a very useful practice, it has of late years been much laid aside. The advantages arising from it have not been judged equal to the inconveniences; and the speaking of single speeches, or the acting of single scenes, has been generally substituted in its stead. Indeed, when we consider the leading principle and prevailing sentiments of most plays, we shall not wonder that they are not always thought to be the most suitable employment for youth at school; nor, when we reflect on the long interruption to the common school-exercises, which the preparation for a play must necessarily occasion, shall we think it consistent with general improvement . . . The acting of a play is not so conducive to improvement in Elocution as the speaking of single speeches.'

Walker states his objection to school plays: the actor's skills, especially the 'nice discrimination of the passions', are too complex and too difficult for schoolboys, and are of little importance in school life:

'In short, it is speaking rather than acting which school-boys should be taught; while the performance of plays is calculated to teach them acting rather than speaking.' (pp. xii-xiii)

Walker was writing about a development that he hoped was taking place: it suited his own views on the teaching of elocution. If he was correct it was not for long, judging by a facetiously ferocious attack in the *Monthly Mirror* for December, 1798, on the danger of encouraging young people to think they are successful actors. The article is headed 'School-Plays':

1798 'At this season of the year, we have sucking *Hamlets* and *Romeos* by wholesale. And now, therefore, it will not be amiss to caution fathers . . . against the encouragement of PLAYS IN SCHOOLS . . . Westminster School led the way; Reading, Hackney, Burlington, and Soho followed; the smaller academies next caught the infection . . . a *mania* that rages with alarming violence throughout the kingdom. Even our *ladies*' boarding-schools have not entirely escaped the influenza . . . Virgil is neglected for Shakspere, and Ovid for Otway . . . This *boys' play* is a public and abominable nuisance.'

One well-known advocate of the school play at this time was Richard Valpy, headmaster of Reading School for fifty years, whose comment was: 'The propriety of acting Plays at School, however sanctioned by the practice of many ages . . . has lately been questioned by some writers' (1804, preface). Valpy thought the plays were valuable and without 'detrimental consequences'. Between 1795 and 1825 he produced his own versions of *The Critic, Hamlet, King Lear, Henry IV, Parts 1* and *2; Henry VI; King John*, and *The Merchant of Venice*, which can be taken as typical of his treatment. He claimed that his principal object was 'to retain, as far as he thought it consistent with grammatical correctness and moral delicacy, the language of SHAKESPEARE'. Nevertheless he cut out the 'more than

Mahometan violence' that obliges Shylock to renounce his religion: 'The liberality of the present times revolts at the idea of arming the followers of the Prince of Peace with the weapons of destruction.' Most of Act 5 is omitted, as had been Act 1 of *King John*. The episode of the rings is 'inconsistent with that purity of style and sentiment, which does so much credit to the present taste of the British Nation'. Liberties such as those taken by Valpy have been 'not only exercised, but justified and applauded in Dryden, Tate, Cibber, Garrick, and Colman'. He will be justified, he says, if he 'can shew the possibility of making a new progress in the purification of the Stage'.

The evidence for school performances in English (some of them house plays) as recorded by Motter, continues during the nineteenth century: *The School for Scandal* and *The Rivals* at Eton between 1811 and 1822, *A Midsummer Night's Dream, Julius Caesar, Cato, Box and Cox* between 1830 and 1850. A scene from Sheridan Knowles' *The Hunchback* was given at Merchant Taylors' in 1857; a scene from *Hamlet*, in Greek, in 1858; *The Taming of the Shrew* in 1865 and *The Merchant of Venice* in 1867. At Winchester *Hamlet* was performed in 1866, *Macbeth* in 1867, and *King Lear* in 1868. Motter's material is drawn from a limited number of prestigious schools, but there is no reason to suppose that they were highly unusual.

The static performance or reading of a dramatic text was much more frequent than a full production. The texts range from those meant for quite young children, such as Mary Ann Killner's *Familiar Dialogues for the Instruction and Amusement of Children of Four or Five Years Old, c.* 1782, to P.I. Marshall's *Dramatic Pieces, calculated to render Young Ladies amiable and happy; when their School Education is completed*, which was praised by Sarah Trimmer. Similar works are Barbara Hofland's blank-verse *Little Dramas*, 1810, written for a girls' boarding school, and the anonymous *Dramatic Dialogues for the Use of Young Persons*, 1792, attributed to Mary Pilkington. The author describes these dialogues as stories without the 'said she', not intended for performance and not in rivalry with Mme de Genlis, whose *Theatre à l'Usage des jeunes Filles*, 1779, had been translated as *Theatre of Education*, 1781. Mme de Genlis' plays are described by their English editor as 'only moral treatises brought into action', but she herself intended them to be performed. More prosaic are the three plays in *The Theatre of Youth*, published in Huddersfield about the end of the eighteenth century. They are moralistic and the dialogue is stilted, but the action proceeds at a fairly crisp pace and there are a few rudimentary stage directions. Arnaud Berquin, whose collection *L'Ami des Enfans* appeared in an English translation in twelve volumes in 1783, merely put stories into dialogue form, but plays were made from them, as *The Honest Farmer, a drama in five acts*, 1791. Maria Edgeworth's *Little Plays for Children*, 1827, were meant mainly for acting at home, as were collections of plays by Julia Corner between 1854 and 1865.

Biblical subjects were often given quasi-dramatic treatment, but with caution and little expectation of performance. Hannah More explained in the preface to her blank-verse *Sacred Dramas*, 1782, that some of the long speeches retarded the action because she 'rather aspired after moral instruction than the purity of dramatic composition'. Nevertheless the plays were meant for school use and remained popular for eighty years.

Many small plays appeared in children's magazines. They did not aspire to theatrical energy but they could easily be given a classroom performance. Characteristic of many is *The Little Foreigner, or The Folly of Prejudice: a drama in one act*, which came out in the *Juvenile Magazine* for January 1788. A French boy of eleven comes to an English family to improve his English and encounters, from the English children, unconvincingly violent prejudice, which is with equally unconvincing suddenness overcome by the intervention of their father. He concludes the play with the observation that 'a national prejudice is a sure indication of a narrow mind'.

On the limited evidence of this enquiry it would seem that during most of the nineteenth century there were many dramatic and quasi-dramatic texts for young children but few for older ones, unless they were at a school with a dramatic tradition. It is probable that most teachers followed Walker's advice and did not venture beyond the dramatic extracts in the anthologies.

Written expression

William Nelson, 1952, in an important article on 'The teaching of English in Tudor grammar schools', provides evidence that some sixteenth-century schoolmasters were actively concerned with the quality of the English into which their pupils translated Latin, and saw themselves, explicitly, as teaching English expression. Nelson maintains that the teachers forbade the speaking of English at school not because they were indifferent to English but because they wished particularly to give the boys practice in speaking the colloquial Latin that was not to be found in the classical texts studied in the classroom. He quotes from Nicholas Grimald's translation of Cicero's *De Officiis*, 1553, a passage in which Grimald, recognising that someone speaking his mother tongue does not necessarily 'bestowe his wordes wiseleye, orderly, pleasauntly, & pythiely', hopes that the pupils will read this translation 'advisedly, and with good leasure, thre, or foure, or five times . . . as well in the english, as the latin, to weygh well properties of words, fashions of phrases, and the ornaments of bothe [languages]' (p. 124). So close does Nelson make the relation between translation out of Latin and the teaching of written English that he goes so far as to say: 'The beginning of the teaching of English in the grammar schools as a separate study was therefore not an independent growth but an amputation' (p. 143).

Such an exaggeration does not weaken the importance of translation in the hands of a teacher who cared about English. Translation and imitation (discussed above, in chapter 4) were throughout the sixteenth and seventeenth centuries the main formal practices through which schoolboys learned to write English.

Imitation as a technique was traditionally supported by a classification of the kinds of writing and by an enumeration of the qualities that made for good writing. Both procedures were common in the early nineteenth century, usually as a framework for practical advice on composition, but they were less common in the eighteenth century, when composition was given comparatively little attention. Enumeration of genres is not infrequent, but in itself it is unhelpful and susceptible to endless and sterile variation. A slightly more practical kind of enumeration is seen in one of the earliest examples, P.K's *The Scholar's Instructor*. The classification ('Colloquies, Essays, Fables, Characters, Themes, Epistles, Orations, Declamations, &c') is accompanied by advice, particularly on those types of writing which would be frequent in school:

[*1707?*] '*Essays* . . . Express the Nature of the Subject you insist upon, in Two or Three short Descriptions or Definitions; shew the several kinds of it, also the Causes, Adjuncts and Effects of each kind; Use no Tautology but choose Language, Metaphors and Allegories, which adorn this Exercise very much.

    Fable . . . Let your Stile be short, witty and facetious, and the Phrase be good.

    Character . . . A facetious and Witty Description of the Nature and Qualities of a Person, or some sort of People . . . Let all be witty and pleasant, with tart nipping Jerks about their Miscarriages or Vices.' (p. 66)

At the end of the century William Milns, 1794, who keeps his pupils mainly to 'Letters, Fables, Themes, Orations', makes an unusual attack on the customary advice to make letters 'easy and natural', to write as if the recipient was present in person. His objection is just that children will take 'natural' to mean 'colloquial'. 'The idea of being *easy and natural*, has occasioned greater errors in the epistolary style than a total disregard, or ignorance of every rule' (p. 34). Advice of this kind during the nineteenth century is mostly provided under the broader heading of themes, which are considered below.

The categories of rhetoric, even when ostensibly referring to language or style, are based on an analysis of human behaviour and emotions. Thus the language used to describe qualities of writing, and often kinds of writing, is subjective and imprecise. Ogilvie, 1774, classifies compositions as 'simple, perspicuous, sublime, nervous, correct', whereas Irving, 1801, and most writers use terms such as these for styles: the concise opposed to the diffuse; the simple to the affected; the nervous to the feeble; the vehement, the plain, the neat, the graceful, the florid. William Banks, in *The English Master*, 1823, analyses human powers (e.g. attention, perception, abstraction, conception) and relates imagination specifically to literature: 'It is the peculiar province of this faculty to form new combinations . . . *Meg Merrilies* . . . is as much a creature of imagination as any of the characters in *Paradise Lost*' (pp. 230–1); but his discussion of style is not related to these faculties. It is centred conventionally on clarity, purity, precision and propriety. Alliteration perhaps preserved the names of the four central qualities on which teachers concentrated as: purity, propriety, precision and perspicuity, but they were not distinct. David Williams, 1850, in discussing purity gives as examples of 'vulgar provincial' expressions, 'bamboozle', 'bang up' and 'hum-drum' and provides lists of 'inelegant' and the corresponding 'elegant' terms: 'give up', 'shut out' and 'shun' are corrected to 'yield', 'exclude', 'avoid' (pp. 8–10). Similarly 'perspicuity or clearness' can hardly be distinguished from 'precision', under which he discusses the use of 'between' for 'among', and 'back' for 'ago', pleonasm ('personal interview') and other types of looseness. Such analysis was, in two senses of the term, academic. It was made by rhetoricians writing for university students rather than for teachers in school (even Bain, in 1866, has chapters headed 'Intellectual Qualities of Style' and 'Emotional Qualities of Style'), and it remained a self-contained descriptive system largely unrelated to the practice of expressive skills. The needs of schools were better met by the bluntness of Abbott's *How to Write Clearly*, 1872, a work that nevertheless acknowledges a debt to Bain.

Throughout the eighteenth and nineteenth centuries teachers of composition attached most importance to clarity, whatever they called it, and the author of *Of Education* seems to attribute this attention particularly to his own times:

1734 'It is amazing, to see how little the *English* Language has been cultivated in the common Course of Education. If of late Years there has been a greater Demand than formerly for Exactness we must attribute it to the exceeding Purity of Mr *Addison's* Writings.' (p. 15)

Addison's style was held up as a model for more than a century. William Chambers, born in 1800, 'carefully scrutinised the papers of Addison and other writers sentence by sentence, in order to familiarise myself with their method of construction';[4] but it is of course debatable how far Addison himself modified popular opinion about style and how far he exemplified, with especial skill, a change of taste that was developing generally. In the schools there is no doubt that Addison provided the standard of clarity, and the teachers' pursuit of it is apparent in most of the methods discussed in the rest of this chapter.

The general assumption was, in Zachary Coke's words, that 'When a man hath soundly and well thought on a thing, it enableth him exactly and in order to teach and write it' (1654, p. 8). Or, as Abraham Tucker put it, 'a clear conception produces clear expression'. Tucker however himself questioned the assumption: 'Perhaps', he continued, 'it may be truer that clearness of expression become habitual will produce similar clearness in our conceptions' (1773, pp. 100–1). Perhaps it is even truer that influences are exerted in both directions and that it is unhelpful to try to measure their respective strengths.

A quality that received only occasional notice but is of interest to us because of later developments in the teaching of expression is what we often call 'originality'. A better term however is 'authenticity'. Few people, schoolchildren or adults, are original except in relation to their own narrow circumstances. To judge writing authentic is not to claim for it any originality; it is authentic through being personal; its language is powered by the writer's own feelings and interests, not by obedient imitation of a model. If the writing is authentic, it is argued, it will be structurally and stylistically better (even when ungrammatical) than if the topic had been prescribed and governed by rules. These are twentieth-century ideas, but they go back to radical eighteenth-century thinking about childhood and to the rare teacher in earlier centuries who realised the educative power that could be tapped by drawing on children's real interests.

John Rice comes very near to expressing what we would consider a modern view. He is recommending that children 'should first learn to write and read their own Words and Sentiments'. To the objection that these would be ungrammatical he replies:

1765 'No Matter: let the ill Construction of their Language, and the Impropriety of their Sentiments, be gradually corrected together: By which Means they may also

---

[4] *Memoir of William and Robert Chambers*, 1872, quoted by Q.D. Leavis, *Fiction and the reading public*, 1932, p. 111.

acquire a Stile, or Method of expressing themselves on any Subject with Ease, and in *their own Way.*'

Few people, he says, can do this, and business and personal letters are composed:

'. . . of the Phrases and Turns of Expression, taken from popular Writers, or those generally in Use.' Classical scholars have 'as little Stile of their own, as the Illiterate: Their Verses being little better than *Centos*, and their prose Writings a strange Jargon or Mixture of different Idioms and Scholastic Phraseology.'   (p. 11)

Much less explicit is Henry Bright, whose sequence of work is largely conventional: but he commends as a stimulus for writing Comenius' *Visible World* and 'a Collection of select Aenigmas', because of 'the singular Alertness and Quickness of Thinking evident in such Children as are versed in aenigmatical Exercises' (pp. 4–6). For older pupils he commends Addison, but also gives advice about composition that he himself seems to find surprising:

1783 'I really think it more adviseable to follow no Rules at all . . . First be Master of the Subject . . . then having rang'd his Ideas in an orderly Method, use the Words which first offer, and provided they be suitable to the Matter, evermore rising and falling with it, being intelligible, and easy, natural and unaffected' he will achieve a good style.   (p. 82)

This is the way to 'an agreeable Style', a more relaxed way than that offered by most of Bright's contemporaries. Amongst these was William Milns. He bases his teaching on rhetoric but believes that if his pupils have a topic that interests them 'a little skilful management will make all the rules of rhetoric appear to be the result of the learner's own observations: he will almost fancy himself the inventor of the art' (p. 17). Such an empirical approach to rhetoric is suggested by no other writer and it is a pity that Milns did not describe it.

The Edgeworths might have been expected to discuss the question of originality but their only comment is Maria's, in chap. 22 of *Practical Education*, that a child should be encouraged 'to give an exact account of his own feelings in his own words'. It is such a passing comment that one does not know whether Maria takes the principle for granted or does not consider it important.

Meston, 1823, cautiously discusses a student's personal approach to writing. An important element in composition, which has been 'long neglected both in our schools and colleges', is the imagination: 'A premature attention to the rules of criticism would nip it in the bud.' Provided his imagination is moderated by reason, the student 'may exercise his fancy on any subject that he pleases ... Let him put his performance into the shape of a harangue, a dialogue, a letter, or an essay; only let him agree with the teacher beforehand on the subject and the form' (pp. 68, 72). More typical of the ordinary teacher were John Davis' efforts, by reading the class a story of which they had gradually to build up an outline, to help his pupils 'to undertake that terrible task of writing their own thoughts' (1830, p. 196). Whereas at the untypical junior school of Bruce Castle, with the purpose of: 'cultivating and directing the imagination . . . the pupils are encouraged to the task of oral composition, the teacher acting simply as an amanuensis, and no nonsense is ever found to be dictated' (Fry, 1838, p. 246).

Richard Whately also relates the quality of a composition to the interest of the writer in his subject, but, like Meston, he does not think the teacher should relinquish his control of the subject matter:

(1828) 1841   'An exercise composed with diligent care by a young student, though it will have cost him far more pains than a *real* letter written by him to his friends, on subjects that interest him, will be very greatly inferior to it. On the *real occasions* of after life ... he will find that he writes both better, and with more facility, than on the *artificial* occasion, as it may be called, of composing a declamation.'

Provided 'a most scrupulous care' is taken 'in the selection of such *subjects* for exercises as are likely to be *interesting* to the student', and on which he has some information, he should be encouraged 'to express himself (in correct language indeed, but) in a free, natural and simple style; which of course implies ... such a style as, in itself, would be open to severe criticism ... The composition of boys *must* be *puerile*' (pp. 24–7).

The most frequently taught form of written composition was probably letter-writing, as the great number of manuals testify, from the seventeenth century to the twentieth. The writing of 'epistles', the art form of letter-writing, was a component of classical rhetoric. Locke recommended that schoolboys should be taught to write letters, and his advice was followed, usually in the form described by William Foot, where the master dictates model letters, which are then imitated (a. 1747, p. 13). Nevertheless letter-writing is little discussed in the present enquiry: the manuals were written according to a uniform pattern and raise no questions of teaching-method. Little is said, either, about the writing of verse, although there are indications that this was a more important activity than we realise. It is often advocated, but as a recreation. No one discusses how it should be taught in school, except as an exercise in metrics. Yet one H.B. published in 1589 *Certen Observacons for Latyne and Englishe Versyfyinge*, of which only a single leaf has survived. Caleb Vernon, who died in 1665 at the age of twelve and a half, had been writing at school 'an *English* Poetical Exercise on a solemn subject' (John Vernon, 1666, p. 18), perhaps in the way that Joshua Poole encouraged his pupils to take (above, p. 151). Samuel Parr's school at Stanmore 'gave more than usual attention to English Composition' and allowed the boys to compose English verse (*DNB*), as did Boyer at Christ's Hospital.[5]

The theme and the essay were once distinct forms of composition. 'Theme' was the older, classical term that originally covered all forms of pupils' prose and verse composition. It was taken for granted that such compositions would be reasoned, impersonal and serious. The 'essay', a term not used for an art form before Montaigne and Bacon, carried for a long time its literal sense of an attempt: a piece of writing that did not profess to be finished or systematic. It resembled a meditation in being personal, even conversational; it did not seek to prove anything. It was not considered a suitable exercise for schoolboys.

This clear distinction became blurred. It never disappeared, but 'essay' became the dominant, and eventually the only, term used in schools. Various factors weakened the distinction: chiefly that a topic could be treated either as an essay or as a theme. Montaigne wrote on cruelty and Bacon on superstition, but either subject could be treated as a theme. A second factor was the reputation of Addison. He called some of his papers 'essays' (*Spectator* no. 476) and they could all easily be so regarded. This, as it were, let the essay into school. A further factor was the gradual rejection during the nineteenth century of the seven-fold structure to which the theme had traditionally been restricted. A prescribed structure that was more than Beginning, Middle and End was felt to be too rigid; but as an essay also required a beginning, middle and end the difference between theme and essay was further weakened. By the time the essay had lost some of its personal quality and the theme had lost most of its formal structure the terms no longer signified a clear distinction.

This development can be illustrated concisely :

[1707?] '*Essay*: a short Discourse about any Vice or Virtue.
       Theme: a Discourse amplifying a Subject, by shewing the Meaning, and proving the Truth of it.'   (P.K., pp. 65–6)

1739 The seven parts of a theme are 'Proposition; Reason; Confirmation; Simile; Example; Testimony; Conclusion.'   (Holmes, Part 2.2)

This same seven-fold structure was taught by John Walker, 1801; P.H. Pullen, 1820; John Davis, 1830; E. Johnson, 1830; R.G. Parker, 1832; Alexander Reid, 1839. Themes were 'regular' in so far as they required, or

---

[5] For incidental references to verse-writing see Hoole, 1660, p. 157; Aickin, 1693, p. 28; Bell, 1769, Book 3; Butler, 1772, p. 57; Bright, 1783, p. 83; Armstrong, 1853, Part 2, p. 150.

could be fitted into, such a structure; whereas the essay 'cannot be reduced to the same rules' (Walker, p. 132). Yet the compositions of pupils in a Sheffield academy on 'Are the passions an advantage or disadvantage to Man?' are described as essays (Abraham, 1805).

1823 '*Theme*: all exercises in composition.
        Thesis: a theme whose subject is a proposition, such as, "Virtue is its own reward".'
(B.H. Smart, pp. 71, 92)

1830 Advice on 'making a Theme, or, as it would more properly be called, an Essay upon a given Theme or Subject'.
(E. Johnson, p. 2)

1834 'Two evenings [a week] for themes [such as] *The Lawfulness of Rebelling against an Unjust Law; Tithes; On the Conduct of England to Uncivilized Nations.*'
(W.E. Forster, aged sixteen, in T. Wemyss Reid,
Life of W.E. Forster, 3rd edn, 1888, reprinted 1970, p. 65)

1850 'Themes, or prose essays, I wrote so badly, that the master was in the habit of contemptuously crumpling them up ... The essays must have been very absurd, no doubt [but] there was an absurdity in giving us such essays to write. They were upon a given subject, generally a moral one, such as *Ambition* ... I suspect that the themes appeared to [the master] more absurd than careless.'
(Leigh Hunt, *Autobiography*, chap. 3)

Soon after the middle of the nineteenth century the broadening of the meaning of 'theme', anticipated by Smart in 1823, had begun. 'Theme' and 'essay' were becoming interchangeable, as by Leigh Hunt. In 1853 the Armstrongs, although they distinguished theme and essay, suggested as essay subjects some which would earlier have been treated as themes: e.g. 'The Arctic Expeditions, in connection with their influence upon science' (Part 2, Book 3); and G.F. Graham was treating as themes the topics 'Anger' and 'Revenge' (1857, Part 4), which Bacon had treated as essays. In 1864 Roscoe Mongan is still distinguishing essay and theme, but at the same time Alexander Bain is saying that the essay is 'essentially an exercise in thought or knowledge' (1866, chap. 3), which is what used to be said about the theme, and William Johnson (Cory), a master at Eton, is asking how a 'constraining and chastening discipline' can be applied to the schoolboy 'essay', of which he gives as examples 'The character of Germanicus', and 'The growth of imperial absolutism' (1867, pp. 355–6). The essay is now reasoned, impersonal and serious, but writing in English can still be seen as necessarily undisciplined.

William Johnson wanted to prevent 'the amorphous generalities of the young essayist' and 'the cyclic monotonies and platitudes of that "original composition" which school reformers dislike'. But he doubted whether these defects could be prevented if schoolboys were to write in English:

1867 'The use of the English language by itself has been, if I am not misinformed, tried and found wanting in Scotland and in New England; the fruit of essay writing has been shallow and tasteless fluency . . . We need an exercise which cannot be written quickly, which is sure to give the censor [i.e. the teacher] plenty to do, which will bring two minds, the older and the younger, into stimulative contact, which forces us to distinguish between the thought to be expressed and the manner of expression.' (p. 356)

It is that final criterion that shows Johnson's belief that schoolboys can achieve disciplined writing only through the exercise of translation, and leads to the principal reform he suggests: that French should take the place of Latin. The French 'are in Literature the legitimate heirs of the Romans. . . . The wisdom of the English cannot be by a classical or a critical method of instruction made to filter slowly into the understanding of a young student' (p. 362).

Public examinations focused teachers' attention on a form of writing that, whatever its subject, was forced by circumstances to be an essay:

1856 'Describe the feelings of the English in regard to the Church, at the accession of Henry VIII.' (Royal Society of Arts, *English History*)

'State your views of Othello's character and illustrate them from the play.'
(RSA, *English Literature*)

1858 'Contrast the life of a soldier with that of a sailor both in peace and war.'
(Cambridge Locals, junior, *English Composition*)

By 1876 the term 'essay' had appeared in the rubrics, and the Oxford and Cambridge Board instructed their candidates to 'Write an essay on . . . *The effects, good and bad, of railways on civilisation*' (*English Grammar and Composition*).

Composition was unpopular in school, and the reasons given, by the teachers, tell us something about the teaching and perhaps explain why the skill was not taught in every school. Even as late as the 1840s 'composition was virtually unknown' in the voluntary schools of Nottingham (Wardle, 1971, p. 71). Thomas Percival says that the composition of themes 'is always irksome to boys, and seldom well executed by them; because a grave, didactic, and methodical discourse is not suited to [them]'. He thinks boys would prefer to write 'tales and fables, with moral reflections' (1775, edn of 1781, preface). Priestley in 1761 had regarded as 'very frivolous' what he calls the common objection to composition in English: that boys are not supposed 'to be capable of so much reflection as is necessary to treat any subject with propriety' (preface). John Walker, on the other hand, accepts without demur that some pupils have 'almost an invincible repugnance to this sort of exercise' (1801, Introduction), which E. Johnson and many other attribute to 'the common dilemma of having *nothing* to say' (1830, p. 4).

The same dislike seems to have been common in American schools. Richard Graham Parker told the American Institute of Instruction in 1838 that composition is 'loathed and execrated' because the pupils think that they are expected (and fail) to produce work of a polished quality; and Charles Morley says composition is unpopular because it is dull (1838, preface). His remedy is to involve the pupils more, to make them think for themselves, 'to investigate thoroughly and accurately', but his textbook is more ordinary than this prescription suggests. G.F. Graham in England, in 1842, would have agreed with Percival. Composition is disliked because pupils are made to 'plunge at once into a sea of abstraction' and write on topics such as 'perseverance, government, ambition' on which they 'cannot possibly have formed *any* ideas'. Graham's remedy also is to start them with 'a plain narrative or description', especially fables and historical writing. It was, in fact, quite common practice to start pupils on retelling or paraphrasing a story. Conversely they were often given the outlines of a tale that they had to flesh out, and sometimes they were given both:

1817 'To compose a narrative of any kind [the pupil] must have some facts to narrate: the Tale ... supplies him with those facts, which he is afterward to relate *in his own language and manner* . . . with such assistance as he may derive from the subsequent Skeleton of the same Tale. . . . After having once or twice attentively perused the Tale, he is then (without having any further recourse to the original) to write down the same story, partly from memory, partly from his own invention, aided by those *Hints* and *Questions* which he will find in the Skeleton.'

(John Carey, preface)

Carey's tales were modern equivalents, with humans (often children) instead of animals, of fifteen of Aesop's fables from Dodsley. The first of his skeletons, which shows the eighteenth-century origin of the tales, begins:

Dick Dulby – son of herdman – brought up (where and how?) – twelve years old – never at school – ignorant (to what degree? Give an instance) – Billy – gentleman's son – eight years old – read well – three years at school – (with what disposition to learning?).

Carey's props for the young writer (the fable, the tale, the skeleton, the hints and questions) illustrate the general, if not universal, belief that children's inventiveness, which Carey recognises, could neither order itself, nor express itself, without continual adult help. Teachers believed that giving help meant analysing whatever material or process the pupils were studying. Hence many of the extravagances of grammar and rhetoric. In logic, where analysis had a more real function, there was less extravagance, and it is a pity that so much teaching of English was based on rhetorical pseudanalysis and not on the tauter analysis of logic. Part of the common, and disputed, area between rhetoric and logic had been Disposition (Arrangement, Method), and it was this aspect of composition that the seven-fold structure of Walker and his followers was meant to teach. Earlier writers on elementary logic, especially Isaac Watts and the author of John Newbery's admirable *Logic Made Familiar*, treated method in relation to communication, and hence to expression. Newbery's definition would have been a good starting-point for the teaching of themes, but except for a few like John Rippingham, 1811, teachers did not follow that course. The definition runs:

1748 'Disposition, or the Art of Method, is the Ranging a Variety of Thoughts on any subject in such an Order as is fittest to gain the clearest knowledge of it, to retain it longest, and to explain it to others in the best Manner.'

(p. 152, italics omitted)

The six- and seven-fold schemata were only part of the teaching-sequence that Walker was the first to describe systematically. Various teaching-sequences were discussed by his contemporaries. George Crabb, a more thoughtful man than Walker, maintained that children's learning was too dependent on memory and not enough on 'giving strength and vigour to the operations of thought'. His sequence in the teaching of written expression was: simple sentences; the use of connectives; descriptions (of a knife, a top, animals 'beginning with the horse'); skeleton outlines ('heads'); narrative; reproduction; summaries of history and biography; argumentative writing. Also:

1801 'They should even be called upon to form a character, from what they know of men and manners, and make such a concatenation of events as will form a short story; to which they should affix a moral, drawn entirely from their knowledge of the world.'

(pp. 165–75)

Walker's *English Themes and Essays*, on the other hand, which appeared at the same time as Crabb's book, is for teachers only. It assumes that 'we must not expect [young people] to invent matter; what they write must be infused into them' (preface) and is composed of pieces illustrating the following sequence of work:

1. The pupils reproduce a short narrative that has been read to them. They are given also an outline of the narrative, on paper. The outline is a series of key words with spaces between them that the pupil is required to fill.

2. Sketches in narrative, with detached sentences: for a backward

class who have difficulty in using connectives. The pupil reproduces a short piece (read to him) first in detached sentences, then in
connected narrative.

3. Reproduction of a story that has been told twice, once in outline,
   once in full.
4. 'Regular subjects' according to a schema, the full form of which is
   to be learnt by heart: Definition; cause; antiquity or novelty;
   universality or locality; effects.
5. Themes, according to the seven-fold schema.
6. Easy essays. The pupils reproduce an essay that has been twice
   read to them. In the second reading each paragraph is accompanied
   by a sentence summarising it.

The difference between Walker's approach and that of Crabb is striking, as
is Walker's almost total reliance on reproduction. His pupils have little, if
any, chance of expressing their own ideas in their own words.

John Rippingham, 1811, develops three stages of theme writing:
'Definition', which comprises neutral, descriptive statements on, for
example, flattery; 'Definition with Judgment' permits the addition of
admonition, e.g. 'Beware of flattery'; 'Definition, Judgment and Argument' comprises a treatment of the topic in full.

George Jardine, 1818, writing mainly for university students, arranges
themes in four graded positions (pp. 291–324):

1. Those requiring factual recall (of his lectures) and the ordering of
   material: 'On what grounds may philosophy be distinguished from
   other forms of knowledge?'
2. Those requiring the ability to 'arrange and classify' knowledge,
   e.g. 'How may the books in a library be arranged, according to a
   natural or an artificial classification?'
3. Those requiring judgment and reason, e.g. 'Do holidays promote
   study?'
4. Those requiring the 'higher processes of investigation', e.g. 'To
   discover the state of Egypt in respect to government, science, and
   art, in the time of Moses, and the only *datum* given him [the
   student] is this single fact – that fine linen existed in Europe at that
   period.'

Graham, 1857, starts his sequence from far back: words; propositions;
sentences; definition; writing 'on a subject'. His book is built on this
structure and contains excellent illustrations and exercises. About this
time, however, the schematic type of teaching-sequence seems to lose

favour. Teachers base their work either on the qualities of good writing or on a grammatical approach to idiom and usage. E.A. Abbott's *How to Write Clearly*, 1872, does both. His fifty-six rules, much subdivided, are arranged under the two headings 'Clearness and Force' and 'Brevity'.

The teacher's response to his pupils' written work was seldom discussed. It was thought of as 'correction' rather than as 'appraisal'. William McCartney's first attempt in 1791 to describe his method of teaching English was so vague that he had to publish another in the following year, particularly in order to clarify his advice about correction. His practice seems to have been to return written work with the errors marked but not corrected. The pupil makes his own corrections 'before they are corrected publicly', which must mean that the teacher uses his pupils' work as teaching-material. McCartney argues that giving back work in which the corrections have been made by the master is of little value, even if the pupils are required to study the corrections. 'The improvement observable in the versions which boys write arises from additional skill insensibly acquired by reading the language, and the mere habit itself of writing; but very seldom from any precise effect occasioned by a master's corrections' (1792, p. 18).

The last section of John Walker's *English Themes and Essays* is called 'Hints for correcting and improving juvenile composition'. Here and in his introduction a picture emerges of the method by which the sequence described above is carried out. The pupil writes a first draft on loose paper. Next day he copies it, with amendments, onto the lefthand page of an exercise book. He reads the theme, without interruption, to the teacher, who then takes it sentence by sentence and shows the pupil 'where he has erred, either in the thought, the structure of the sentence, the grammar of it, or the choice of words. Every alteration . . . should differ as little as possible from what the pupil has written' (p. 222). The pupil then makes a fair copy on the righthand page of his exercise book. Walker does not say what happens then, but one assumes that the teacher at some time checks on the fair copy. Walker understandably advises that classes for composition should be as small as possible.

There is less textbook evidence for the teaching of composition than for any other aspect of English. This is understandable and proper. The skill of interpretation is limited by a finite (even if unknown) number of 'possible' interpretations: the words are there. The skill of expression has no such limits: the words are not there. The initiative must always be with the pupil. Even the most prescriptive teachers, wanting imitation rather than authenticity, had few general ideas with which to direct their pupils, and even these ideas, such as purity and precision, were necessarily imprecise. In the first part of the nineteenth century some textbooks did profess to teach composition, but they had few successors. If the writer tried to be analytical and detailed his book was too rigid; if he was relaxed and accommodating it said no more than was obvious to common sense. The teacher of composition, having moved out of the strictly regulated apartments of rhetoric, was better off on his own. If he wanted a home, as sometimes happened during the second half of the nineteenth century, he shared accommodation with grammar.

Very few teachers, from amongst those who wrote about the subject, believed that children had, in their own fashion, the power of authentic expression. It was generally assumed that children could do only what they had been taught to do, and that children's learning, in so far as it was more than memorisation, was an intellectual activity that required from the teacher correspondingly analytic methods. Composition therefore tended to be an exercise only for senior pupils, for those who 'have for some years been carefully educated in a progressive course of scientific studies' (James Butler, 1828, p. 95). Prescriptive and analytical methods of teaching composition did not reach those intuitive and aesthetic forces that can give even simple personal writing a measure of authentic literary quality.

CHAPTER SEVEN

Linguistic control

Until the end of the eighteenth century

English grammar and Latin grammar

It is a familiar but unavoidable difficulty when discussing the teaching of English that all the skills are so interdependent that there are objections to taking any one by itself. Learning to control language is of course an aspect of all the skills so far considered, but it has historically considerable autonomy. Almost without exception our seventeenth- and eighteenth-century predecessors believed that linguistic control, in English, was achieved through the study of grammar, and it is grammars that provide most of the evidence on which this chapter is based. In a previous work[1] I have described the principal contents of the early grammars, their relationship with Latin, their treatment of the parts of speech, and, less fully, of syntax, together with the grammarians' attempts to reform the categories. The present chapter deals with the aims and methods of the teachers in developing linguistic skill and with the various exercises they used in partial isolation from the teaching of expression and interpretation; but the content of the grammars must be briefly considered, as must the evidence that some teachers were dissatisfied with the traditional system and made efforts to reform it.

The grammars, as textbooks, included much more than parts of speech and syntax. In the same way as many spelling-books acted at an unsophisticated level as manuals of literacy and general knowledge, so the early grammars regularly included some orthography, the figures of speech, correct usage, Latin and Greek roots, homophones, punctuation, versification and letter-writing. During the nineteenth century the more peripheral topics were dropped, but their place was often taken by philological matter or by rhetorical matter related to composition. The grammars continued to imply, through their contents, either that grammar narrowly defined was dry and difficult (and this was often explicitly admitted) or that grammar should not be narrowly defined.

[1] *English grammatical categories, and the tradition to 1800*, Cambridge University Press, 1970, henceforth *EGC*.

Until the end of the eighteenth century teachers, even though they acknowledged that their pupils were studying a language that they already understood, were rarely able to conceptualise the differences in method between studying your own language and learning a foreign one. Consequently most teachers continued to ground their teaching of English grammar on the same categorical framework and methods as were used for Latin. The influence of Latin pervades every aspect of the English grammars. Although familiar in outline this influence has subtle effects that need further examination. In the present context, however, it is enough to recall one of its grosser manifestations: the declension of English nouns and adjectives. Latin nouns formed cases by inflection. The most obviously equivalent function in English was that performed by prepositions. It was therefore understandable that the meaning of 'case' should be extended to cover the combination of preposition and noun, and John Henson, in the middle of the eighteenth century is not unusual in giving the declension of *man* as:

	Singular	Plural	
Nominative	a man	men	
Vocative	o man	o men	
Accusative	a man	men	
Genitive	of a man	of men	
Dative	to a man	to men	
Ablative	from a man	from men	(p.6)

So powerful was the idea of case that the articles themselves were sometimes given cases. Thomas Tomkis, a Fellow of Trinity College, Cambridge, in an unpublished English grammar written in Latin in 1612, declined them in the singular:

Nominative	A, the
Vocative	O the
Accusative	A, the
Genitive	Of a, of the
Dative	To a, to the
Ablative	From, etc. a, the

The plural of *the*, he says, is the same in all cases as the singular, whereas *a* (and this is a really extraordinary comment) lacks a plural entirely: 'caret omnino plurali'. Tomkis is not alone. The articles are declined also by Entick, 1728; Wiseman, 1764; and Egelsham, 1780. The inappropriateness of a Latin model is even more dramatically evident when an English adjective is declined in the tabular form customary in teaching Latin. This example comes from John Stirling's *A Short View of English Grammar*, 1735:

	Nom.	Voc.	Acc.	Gen.	Dat.	Abl.
Singular						
Masculine	wise	wise	wise	wise	wise	wise
Feminine	wise	wise	wise	wise	wise	wise
Neuter	wise	wise	wise	wise	wise	wise
Plural						
Masculine	wise	wise	wise	wise	wise	wise
Feminine	wise	wise	wise	wise	wise	wise
Neuter	wise	wise	wise	wise	wise	wise

(A4 verso)

The influence of Latin affected methods as well as materials. John Burn, 1766, describes how when the master is reading a piece of English in class (five or six lines a day) he should tell his pupils 'to take their Dictionaries and prepare it, so as to be able readily to give the several meanings of every word in it, and likewise the several parts of speech' (preface).

A further difficulty for the teacher was the generally accepted view that the grammars of modern European languages, and of Latin, ancient Greek and Hebrew, were variations of a general grammar common to most languages, and even of a universal grammar common to all. Such a view obscured the distinctiveness of first-language teaching, inhibited attempts to develop a grammar and a mode of teaching appropriate to English-speaking pupils, and tended to keep English subordinate to the elaborate and prestigious grammars of the classical languages. Teachers did not know how to distinguish what seemed to be universal functions, such as naming and predicating, from contingent features such as inflection. Because English grammar was thus kept in close relationship to Latin grammar it was assumed, by circularity, that English grammar was a good preparation for Latin. During the seventeenth century, and occasionally in the eighteenth, grammars appeared that tried to link English and Latin so closely that they were, with varying degrees of deliberation, grammars for both languages.[2]

There were other constraints on the teacher of English. If English grammar were to be reformed, the teacher of Latin would have to spend more time teaching elementary grammar. It was in the interests of the Latin teachers to discourage the English teachers from tinkering with grammar. The awkward relation between the two shows in the reforming English grammars such as the 1776 edition of John Newbery's *Grammar and Rhetorick* and Smetham's grammar of 1774, which contain both an English grammar and 'an English grammar for Latin'.

---

[2] For example John Hewes, 1624; Joshua Poole, 1646; Mark Lewis, *Essay* (1670?) and *Institutio*, 1670; William Clare, 1690; John Entick, 1728; Alexander Adam, 1772. See *EGC*, pp. 152–62.

Although nowadays we think of Latinate English grammar as being precise and narrow in scope, it contained a kind of ambiguity that teachers of English still face. From classical times teachers of grammar had held mixed opinions about the relationship between the study of language and the study of literature: a mixture expressed by the word 'grammar' itself (letter; letters). Grammatical rules are derived from, and need to be illustrated by, language in use. Even if a grammarian thought that grammatical rules were axioms he needed authors (authorities) from whom he could illustrate how the rules were exemplified and (with relish) how they were broken. One sense of 'grammar', therefore, as in 'grammar school', included literature; while in a narrower sense the subject was confined to the forms and structures of Latin and Greek. Grammars of English until the end of the nineteenth century illustrate both senses, and English teachers today have a corresponding difficulty in deciding whether to teach forms and structures only as they arise in their pupils' daily use or whether to isolate them in artificial contexts and teach them in a concentrated, systematic way ('back to formal grammar').

What the pupils were expected to learn

In the seventeenth and eighteenth centuries most pupils, and until 1870 at least some pupils, were expected to learn the grammar by heart. Often the book was printed in two sizes of type: essential matter, to be learnt verbatim, in large type; amplifications, with which the pupil was expected to be thoroughly familiar but not word perfect, in smaller type. Sometimes, in still smaller type, notes were included for the teacher. Hoole's prescription for the Latin teacher is typical:

1660 'Let them begin the *Accidents*, and go thorow it, and *the whole Latine Grammar* at twelve parts, onely construing and giving an account of the by-Rules, but saying all the rest by heart . . . Now in repeating these parts, I do not enjoyn that onely one boy should say all, though I would have every one well prepared to do so; but that one should say one piece, and another another, as you please to appoint either orderly throughout the Form, or picking out here and there a boy at your own discretion.'   (pp. 77–8)

Such dependence on memory was criticised:

1700 'Let none mistake me, as if I thought the *Latin Grammar* altogether useless; for I think it very useful, as a Repository, to be often consulted in our reading as we do our *Dictionaries* . . . but to oppress the Memory by getting so much by heart, is so far from promoting Learning, that it is a very great hindrance to it: for one Word shuffles out another, but one Sense does not drive out another: and therefore Sense is a more faithful Preserver of all words, than an overcharg'd Memory.'

(Lane, pp. xv-xvi)

In Ussher's English grammar of 1785 'the slavish method of committing a whole book to memory, which is generally done with very little assistance or improvement of the understanding, is totally rejected; and grammar is rendered . . . an object and exercise of the intellectual faculties' (preface). William Milns' objection is more subtle. Boys who have '*to say by heart* a great number of Latin rules' before they have read any Latin 'are naturally led, in their future studies, to continue their attention to words alone' (1794, preface). It was no doubt this concentration on words, to the neglect of ideas, that led to the fact, regularly deplored by teachers and parents, that after years and years of learning Latin boys could still understand scarcely anything of it.

In the English grammars it was often laid down that only the rules were to be learnt by heart; but this could still be a considerable task. John Collyer, 1735, says, 'Only the large Print is to be got without Book'; but this would mean memorising more than 10,000 words. James Gough, 1754, making the same arrangement, requires about 5600 words to be learnt; an American, Alexander Miller, 1795, requires over 11,000 and at least 10 other eighteenth-century grammarians make similar requirements. Blanch Mercy, 1799, justly claims that her book is unusual in 'giving the pupil *little to learn by heart*, but *much to put in practice*' (preface).

The grammars were usually organised in four parts called: Orthography (or Letters); Etymology (or Words); Syntax (or Sentences); Prosody (or Pronunciation and Versification). Pronunciation was sometimes separate from versification as a fifth part, Orthoepy. Outline grammars in dictionaries, spelling-books and compendia often omitted syntax. The main substance of the grammars comprised: (i) Definitions and examples of the parts of speech, with in most cases their subdivisions, and rules relating to case inflection, plural, feminine and comparative forms. (ii) Paradigms of regular verbs (their moods and tenses) and lists of 'irregular' (usually strong) verbs, with their past tense and past participle. (iii) Rules of syntax, with exercises of 'false English'.

Definitions. It was conventionally supposed that children understood grammatical categories through learning their definitions, and the sections of a grammar that had to be learnt by heart always included general statements such as:

1700   'A Conjunction is an Undeclin'd part of Speech, used in joyning Words and Sentences, together; so as to shew what Relation one notion hath to another.'
(Richard Browne, p. 109).

1711   'A *Preposition* is a Part of Speech, which being added to any other Parts of Speech, serves to mark or signify their State or Reference to each other.'
(Greenwood, p. 71)

1677   'A *Verb* is a part of Speech, that joyneth the Signification of the Words together.'   (Newton, p. 12; an unusual definition)

1735   'The Verb or Affirmation is a word that affirms something of the subject or agent, either of being, action or suffering.'   (Collyer, p. 49)

(1760) 1763   'A *Pronoun* is a Word used *instead* of a Noun, to avoid the *too frequent* Repetition of the *same* Word.'   (Ash, p. 36)

As the parts of speech did not form mutually exclusive categories, their definitions, as the first three examples above show, could be of little assistance to any learner who was dependent on them. Even when the general statements took the form of descriptions rather than definitions the teachers themselves realised that children did not learn from them. Two complaints out of many:

1670   'Doubtless the Doctrine of Grammar is too subtile for Children; because it is communicated by Logical Definitions in the Etymologie, and by the signification of words in the Syntax, neither of which Children can reach, who cannot use Abstraction . . . How unintelligible these Logical Definitions are to Children, those know that have been toyled with them . . . Consider whether it is not unintelligible to say, "A *Verb* signifies *doing, suffering*, or *being*": The Notion of Action and Passion are out of a Child's reach . . . Do you think a Boy would judge, that *have sate* is a Verb, because it signifies *doing*?'[3]   (Mark Lewis, *Essay*, pp. 1 and 3)

1794   ' It is next to impossible to make the definitions of verbs even tolerably clear to children.'   (*A Short English Grammar*, p. 15)

Even in Latin and Greek brief definitions had always been inadequate. Partly for this reason, and partly through the teachers' unquestioning reliance on analytical methods, most parts of speech were submitted to elaborate and sometimes grotesque subdivision. Dionysius Thrax had discussed twenty-eight kinds of Greek adverb, and Priscian twenty-six in Latin;[4] the *English Accidence*, 1733, gives forty-one in English. Horne Tooke lists thirty-eight 'kinds' of conjunction in order to illustrate 'that farrago of useless distinctions . . . which explain nothing' (1829 edn, I, 3).

[3] The equivalent passage in the 1674 edition, p. 18, runs: 'I would fain see that Master which dares to stand by these Descriptions, as useful to Children; or that will undertake to justifie them against such visible marks, as may be laid down by Particles in the English Tongue, to know the parts of speech by'.   [4] *EGC*, pp. 102–3.

As with the elocutionists' analysis of the passions, this procedure had no limits. Even when, as with the pronoun, the subdivisions recognised syntactic and formal criteria, they could only reflect the complex, difficult and internally inconsistent nature of the traditional category.

Parsing. Just as the parts of speech were the most important features in a school grammar of English so parsing was the most important exercise for the pupil. It could be conducted at three levels. The simplest was just to say to what part of speech a word belonged. The second level, often called grammatical or etymological parsing, was to add information about the subdivision into which the word could be placed (proper noun; adverb of quantity), its number and gender. The third level, syntactical parsing, was to add information about the function of the word in its sentence ('subject of the verb . . . governed by the preposition. . . . '). Case could be a constituent of either grammatical or syntactical parsing.

Parsing was, of course, an exercise familiar in the teaching of Latin, but it does not for some time appear in seventeenth- and eighteenth-century English grammars as regularly as might have been expected. William Bullokar, 1586, gives Latinate rules for parsing, but no examples. The first examples come in the fourth edition, 1674, of Wallis' grammar of 1653, where he provides a praxis on the Lord's Prayer and the Apostles' Creed, examples which are closely followed by Greenwood in 1711 and by Owen, copying Greenwood, in 1732. A praxis was a worked example: an exercise for the pupil to read through, remember and apply to the parsing exercises that the master would give orally. John Collyer refers to parsing as 'an exercise well known in Latin schools', which suggests it is less familiar in the English schools for which he is writing. He describes his own practice:

1735 'In Parsing let the young Scholar read deliberately the verse, sentence or sentences that he is to parse, then if the words are not in the natural order let him put them so, supplying words that are omitted, and throwing out such as are redundant.' (p. 122)

The exercise of parsing does not allow much variation. Collyer's plan of combining it with transposition, resolution and supplying the ellipses is followed by others at that time (Turner, 1739; Buchanan, 1753) but was not standard practice. It seems to have taken a long time for parsing to be treated as a matter of course and to have a generally accepted name. Noah Webster, 1784, describes it and adds in a note, 'This is called *parsing*' (p. 87), and in 1798 John Sedger also explains the procedure at length but gives it no name (pp. 114–15). Until 1800 the exercise is often called 'grammatical resolution', although in 1793 John Hornsey adds that it is by now 'more generally called parsing'. Other terms are 'construing' (*Grammarian's Vade-Mecum*, 1774; Chown, 1788), 'exemplification' (*Rudiments of Constructive Etymology*, 1795; Lindley Murray, 1797), 'grammatical analysis' (Harrold, a. 1787; *Only True Guide*, 1799), 'governing' (Giles, 1803) and 'the parts of speech delineated', a model praxis after which the pupil's task is to 'account for the Words in the following Sentences' (Bettesworth, 1778). Henry Bright brings several terms together in his instruction that the pupil 'should often analyse English in a parsing Praxis' (1783, p. 7).

Syntax. Syntax, in the teaching of elementary Latin, comprised rules relating to concord (e.g. the agreement between adjective and noun in gender, number and case) and government, or construction, which determined the case of nouns and pronouns 'governed' by particular verbs or prepositions. The notions of both concord and government implied inflected forms, and in so far as syntax was thought of as just concord and government it was understandable that English grammarians should think that English had little or no syntax:

1586 'As English hath few and short rules for declining of words, so it hath few rules for joining of words in sentence or in construction.'   (Bullokar, p. 53)

1654 'Here should follow the Rules of Concord, and Construction: but becaus there is little, or no variation in the parts of the English tongue: they are altogether needless.'   (Wharton, p. 60)

1706 'If it be expected from me that I should now proceed to the Regular Construction of these Parts of Speech which is Grammar; I must tell thee beforehand, I shall make but blind Work of it (as others have done before me) it being as impossible to do such a thing well, as it is impertinent to undertake it at all, from the Nature of our English Tongue . . . To make a Grammar in a Language whose declinable Parts of Speech are without suitable Variations, is, in my Opinion, like exercising a Company of Faggot-Sticks, that have no Motion.'
                                    (*The English Scholar Compleat*, p. 26)

Similar views were expressed by Daniel Farro, 1754, and Samuel Johnson, 1755. Up till the end of the seventeenth century about half the English grammars contain syntax; between 1701 and 1750 all but two or three of them do; between 1751 and 1800 the proportion is over 75 per cent. These variations do not mean that teachers were changing their views about syntax: they reflect the increase during the second half of the eighteenth century in the number of compendia, companions and manuals, especially of letter-writing, in which a sketchy and derivative grammar, limited to the parts of speech, was thought sufficient.

English syntax was taught through rules, the most important of which were learnt by heart. The rules were usually grouped according to the part of speech they mainly concerned. The number of rules varied greatly, according to whether the writer was heavy-handed in his use of a Latin model; whether he treated as distinct rules each of the many exceptions to the main rules; whether he tried to bring under a syntactic rule specific items of usage and idiom; whether he had much understanding of, or interest in, this branch of grammar.

George Wilson's *Youth's Pocket Companion*, 1756, contains an unoriginal but representatively simple grammar in which the syntax 'is confined to a few short and easy rules' dealing with: the sentence (simple and compound); nominative before verb (with exceptions); genitive before noun (*John's horse*); adjective before noun (with exceptions); adjective before another adjective attached to a noun (*a very good old man*); article before noun; nominative of pronoun before verb, accusative after (with exceptions); double singular nominatives requiring a plural verb; singular nominative with plural verb (*the committee have . . .*).

Most commonly there were between fifteen and twenty-five rules discussed, sometimes at length. The 109 rules of Jane Gardiner, 1799, and the eighty-eight of John Kirkby, 1746, are exceptional. The teachers tended to be at a loss over syntax. Their pupils did not need the easy rules, because they already observed them in practice, and the difficult rules were complex, questionable and specialised. It was only in the nineteenth century, when more attention was given to the sentence, and grammar was often linked with composition, that syntax provided the pupil with skills which he could study and practise.

Correction of false English. After parsing, the most generally used exercise was the correction of 'false English': sometimes the correction of spelling, sometimes of syntax, often of both. Such exercises were first applied to the teaching of English syntax by Ann Fisher of Newcastle. She made the claim herself, and her contemporaries supported it, but the idea, she said, came from an anonymous male correspondent writing from Carlisle in November 1749, and signing himself A.B. He addressed her as 'Sir', which was natural if he did not know her, because the grammar was published at first anonymously and later as by 'A. Fisher'. A.B. enclosed a short essay 'On the Method of Teaching', in which he suggested that as 'in learning *Latin*, making Exercises from FALSE CONCORD, is reckon'd the most expedient Method, to a thorough Knowledge of SYNTAX' so 'Exercises of *bad English* under the few Rules we have, after the Manner of *Clark's* or *Bailey's Examples for the Latin Tongue*, must needs be altogether as requisite to a critical Knowledge of our *own*.' Ann Fisher accepted the suggestion and the exercises that he enclosed. The first set of exercises are grouped according to the nine rules of syntax provided by Fisher (which A.B. presumably saw in the first edition of the grammar, not yet traced), and a second set are 'promiscuous', the pupil not being told what rule is being broken. The first three promiscuous exercises require the pupils to correct:

(*1745*) *1750*   The Ministers preaches, but Sinners hears not.
              The stout Soldier Sword have been the proud Enemies Ruin.
              Thou and me is both accused of the same Fault.   (p. 129)

Ann Fisher was the first to apply the technique to the teaching of English syntax, but it had already been used in the teaching of spelling. William Baker, in *Rules for True Spelling and Writing English*, had included '*rude Examples* to most of the Rules'. Baker's sentences were grouped at first by rule, then randomly in verse passages:

a. 1724   My *deer* and only *Sun*
                  Now that thy Infant *Yeers ar dun* . . .   (p. 105)

The teachers advocating exercises of this kind were, at their best, applying a method that might have been thought up at any time. It was the same as that invoked in 1747 by Lord Orrery, who wrote in a letter, concerning Johnson's *Plan* for his dictionary: 'I would have a collection of bad phrases, as well as of good, as I would see a bad building to avoid the faults in it.'[5] No spelling-books before 1750, and few later, printed exercises for correction in this way but the teachers regularly taught from errors made by their pupils in class (see *The Irish Spelling Book*, 1740, pp. 342–3). At the end of the eighteenth century and in the early nineteenth there were published a striking number of textbooks devoted solely to the correction of error, mainly in spelling and syntax, sometimes in punctuation; more rarely in the use of figurative language. So much importance was attached to this seemingly trivial technique that it is worth recording the principal works:

> *Exercises, instructive and entertaining, in false English*, 1787
> Elisha Ticknor (USA), *English Exercises, in which sentences, falsely constructed, are to be corrected*
> James Alderson, 1793 and 1795
> John Fawcett, 1796
> Lindley Murray, 1797b
> *Practical Exercises* (USA), 1799
> Charles Allen, 1800

[5] Quoted by J.L. Clifford, *Young Samuel Johnson*, 1962 edn, p. 288.

John Hornsey, 1818
John Smith, [c. 1825]

Three of them are alike in forming small anthologies, clouded by orthographical distractions. The 1787 *Exercises* are facetious and anecdotal; Alderson relies partly on contrived letters ('My dear Charles, You ar arrivd at an aje kapabl of distinggwishing the luvlenes of vertshu and deformety of vise'), partly on distorted extracts from Blair, Chesterfield, Sterne and others. Allen has a section 'Didaktik, preseptiv, and morral', which includes Addison on 'the importanse of a good edjukashun' and a section of 'Poetre', which includes obfuscated passages from Cowper, Shakespeare, Scott and Gay. Some of these books were extremely popular. The 1787 *Exercises* went to at least twenty-one editions by 1841; Alderson's 1793 volume had had twenty-five editions by the same date and was reprinted as late as 1864; Lindley Murray's was in print in Britain until the 1860s and in America until the 1880s.

Like many elementary texts the 1787 *Exercises* had been used in the author's own school. They were planned with thought:

1787 'Some Passages are made exceeding faulty, with a View to put Boys upon studying the current Sense of what they are about to write, and thereby insensibly to accustom them to an Exertion of the Powers of the Mind on Subjects, where Reading, Speaking, or Composition are concerned.'

The boys had to do more than correct the spelling: the exercises were also:

'To accustom Boys to mark over every Word, its Part of Speech, to divide such Words as are capable of a Division into Syllables; to place the proper Accents over every Vowel and Syllable; and to dash all the emphatical Syllables or words.'   (preface)

The teaching-sequence is also described. 'The first Scholar, or Captain of the Class' collects the exercises of the first class and gives them to the master, who looks at them, saying aloud his reasons for each correction he makes. The class, who have been listening carefully, then correct their own versions of the exercise, which have been returned to them, while the master is going through the same procedure with the second class. When the first class have made their corrections they parse each word in the passage. The work is handed in again and the master 'would do well to note down the Number of Faults in each Exercise, in a Book provided for the Purpose'.

Most exercises in false English concerned errors of syntax. Between 1750 and 1800 they appeared in about eighty texts, of which more than half dealt only with syntax and about twenty with syntax and spelling. Both types of exercise attracted comment, usually favourable, and the authority of Lowth was invoked. In discussing the teaching of expression he had said that pupils must:

1762 '. . . be able to judge of every phrase and form of construction, whether it be right or not. The plain way of doing this, is to lay down rules, and to illustrate them by examples. But besides shewing what is right, the matter may be further explained by pointing out what is wrong.' (preface)

Lowth's own practice was better than that of most teachers who followed him. In the notes to his grammar he quotes named authors who violate the rules he is describing; he does not invent improbable errors. The same practice is followed, at a more discursive level, by Philip Withers in *Aristarchus*, about 1790.

P.W. Fogg, 1796, describes frankly the failure of his method. The exercise to be corrected is: 'Thi gospil maiks every man my naibour.' A boy brings up as his first answer 'The gospil makes every man my naibour', whereupon the master underlines 'gospil' and 'naibour' and sends him back. The boy corrects these to 'gospill' and 'nabour'; the master then lends him a dictionary, but he continues at fault with 'naibur'. The boy complains that he cannot find the word in the dictionary, so the master writes beneath it the numbers of the relevant rules, 31 and 56. Rule 31 says: 'Before *gh* and *gn* we do not write *ai* but *ei*, except in *arraign* and *campaign*.' Rule 56 says: '*Ei* has generally the *seventh* sound; but before a *silent g* it has the fifth.' The boy then produces *neighbur*, so 'the master has to put it down *neighbour* and set him an additional exercise' (pp. v-vi).

James Rothwell maintained that his pupils preferred the correction of false English to any other exercise (1797 edn, p. 139). It was certainly popular with teachers in England and in America:

1790 'The master may . . . read short sentences in false grammar, and the scholars write, from the master's dictating, in as correct a manner as they can . . . I have practised this with the greatest success, and find it very apt to produce an emulation among scholars, and therefore not unworthy the attention of the English masters.' (Daniel Pape, p. 37)

William Woodbridge of Connecticut explains the purpose of the exercises:

1800a 'The only method of becoming correct in language is *carefully to observe* our mistakes . . . Every one who wishes to speak or write his language correctly, *must parse* that language – and carefully correct a variety of exercises of incorrect grammar, under all the rules of syntax. He must not only know it wrong; but know the reason why.' (p. 28)

Lindley Murray, here as in many contexts speaking for teachers who were too preoccupied or too unreflective to examine their own methods, says as much as can be said in support of these exercises:

1797b 'The principles of knowledge become the most intelligible to young persons, when they are explained and inculcated by practical illustration and direction . . . The rules [of syntax] require frequent explanation; and, besides direct elucidation, they admit of examples erroneously constructed, for exercising the student's sagacity and judgment. To rectify these, attention and reflection are requisite; and the knowledge of the rule necessarily results from the study and correction of the sentence . . . By discovering their own abilities to detect and amend errors, and their consequent improvement, the scholars become pleased with their studies, and are animated to proceed.' (Introduction)

Murray's argument assumes that people acquire a skill by first learning by heart the rules that govern its application. To this extent he was like all his contemporaries. But he was more aware than they that to apply rules is not necessarily easy or straightforward. His support for exercises in faulty English, because it stated the importance of explanation and illustration, and because Murray's books were so influential, helped to weaken teachers' dependence on the merely authoritative application of rule. But this influence was also damaging to the teaching of literature and composition. In a section headed 'To promote perspicuous and accurate writing' Murray first provides exercises in which a single word is to be corrected, then long expressions for general overhaul. One of these is meant to help the pupil 'to avoid the injudicious use of technical terms':

1797b 'Most of our hands were asleep in their births (sic), when the vessel shipped a sea, that carried away our pinnace and binnacle. Our dead-lights were in, or we should have filled. The mainmast was so sprung that we were obliged to fish it, and bear away for Lisbon.' (p. 144)

Murray's 'correct' version in the separately published *Key* is a sad affair:

'Most of our *sailors* were asleep in their *apartments*, when a *heavy wave broke over the ship*, and *swept* away *one of our boats*, and *the box which contained our compasses*, &c. Our *cabin windows were secured*, or *the vessel would have been* filled. The mainmast was so *damaged*, that we were obliged to *strengthen* it, and *to proceed* for Lisbon.' (p. 119)

Some teachers objected to these exercises, usually because of their artificiality, designed more to keep the children busy than to make them think:

1771 'As to examples of *bad English*, I not only think that they make a very awkward appearance, but I am even of opinion, that they may have a very bad effect.

They are more likely to perplex a young Scholar, and to confirm an old one in error, than to direct the judgment of the one, or correct the bad habit of the other.'   (Fenning, p. vi)

Similar criticism is made by Joshua Story, 1778, and by J.G., 1796. These exercises in false English, however fatuous, were based on a theory about learning. They are distinct from attempts, increasingly frequent in Britain and America from about 1780, to correct 'vulgarisms'. Daniel Staniford, for example, in the fourth edition of his grammar published in Boston, Mass., in 1797, gives grammatical errors from the Bible and famous authors separately from vulgarisms of pronunciation such as 'Brumejum' for 'Birmingham', 'meenyal' for 'menial', and the equally familiar 'Izzen-tit true?', with its reply 'It is forzino [as far as I know].'

Punctuation. Punctuation was taught in spelling-books, elementary readers, rhetorics, grammars, compendia, dictionaries and sometimes in separate pamphlets such as *A Treatise of Stops, Points and Pauses*, 1680, written for schools, and Monteith's *The True and Genuine Art of Exact Pointing*, 1704, written for lawyers. It was taught for two different purposes. For composition it was important to know how particular stops were related to rhetorical and syntactical structure: how the stops should be used. For reading aloud it was enough to know how long to pause (for breath, it was often supposed) at each kind of stop. These two approaches were usually combined, but in different proportions. Spelling- and reading-books made perfunctory reference to the function of the stops, while grammars analysed them in detail.

The extent to which syntactical and rhetorical structure was discussed varied with the assumed maturity of the reader. Most of the school-texts deal only with the most obvious structures. Representative examples come from one seventeenth- and one eighteenth-century schoolmaster, who are perhaps above the average level of sophistication.

Charles Butler in his grammar of 1633 makes no mention of counting, only a general reference to relative duration. The period 'is a point of perfect sense, and perfect sentence: which, in the last word, falleth the Tone of the voice below its ordinary tenour, with a long pause'. The colon 'is a point of perfect sense, but not of perfect sentence: which falleth the Tone of the voice, with a shorter pause'. Semi-colon 'is a point of imperfect sense, in the middle of a Colon or Period: commonly, when it is a compound axiom; whose parts are joined together, by a double, and sometime by a single, conjunction.' Butler here illustrates also types such as: '*They ate, they drank; they bought, they sold; they planted, they builded*' (p. 59). The comma 'is a point of more imperfect sense, in a simple axiom, or in either part of a compound: which continueth the tenour of the voice to the last, with the shortest pause'.

The Goughs, 1754, also represent thoughtful teaching of punctuation. They give the counting-rule in the spelling part of their grammar and the structural rules in the syntax. After describing five uses of the comma they turn to the semi-colon. It is used, they say, when part of a sentence is dependent (in meaning but not in syntax) on a previous part, e.g. '*He was proud, haughty and contemptuous; a Fault very common to the Nobility.*' If the dependent part of the sentence is 'contrary or exceptive' to the previous part a semi-colon separates them: '*He was a good Poet; but an ill Man.*' In particular the semi-colon is used 'when several Sentences . . . have an equal Dependence on the same Word, or Sentence . . . as, *He was of high Birth; of a warm, enterprizing, factious Disposition; greedy of Power, Honour, Riches.*'

The Goughs' discussion of the semi-colon and colon continues in this style. They based their teaching on the application of rules, with the minimum of illustration. Joseph Hutchins, 1788, in Philadelphia, also relies on rules but is unusual in the quantity of illustration he provides, making this section of his grammar equivalent to a simplified version of Robertson's *Essay on Punctuation*, 1785.

What may be called the performance aspect of punctuation was taught in two forms. By the usual method the pupil was told to pause at a comma for as long as it took to count one, at a semi-colon for two, at a colon for three, and at a full stop for four. David Fordyce, 1792, is unique in adding an additional two if the stop is an exclamation-mark. A variation, found independently in *A Treatise*, 1680, and in Noah Webster, 1784, is to make the ratio 1 : 2 : 4 : 6, thus making the pause for the full stop six times as long as the comma. The other form of teaching prescribes a ratio derived from musical notation:

1640 'I remember my singing-Master taught me to keep time, by telling from 1, to 4, according to the nature of the time which I was to keep . . . The same course I have used to my pupils in their reading, to inure them to the distinction of their pauses, and found it no lesse successful.' (Daines, p. 71)

The proportions that Daines in fact describes are 1 : 2 : 3 : 6, and if the period comes at the end of a paragraph it is to carry a pause equivalent to twelve commas. Mark Lewis, in *Plain and Short Rules for Pointing Periods*, about 1675, compares the period to a minim, the colon to a crotchet, a sub-colon (semi-colon) to a quaver, and a comma to a semiquaver (p. 2), which gives the ratio 1 : 2 : 4 : 8. Robert Lowth is also quite explicit in the comparison, though he chooses different notes: 'The Semibrief, the

Minim, the Crotchet, and the Quaver' (1762, p. 158), and the same illustration is used in *The Only True Guide*, 1779 (p. 37). Between 1770 and 1800 at least ten other grammars adopt the ratio 1 : 2 : 4 : 8, but without any reference to music. They express the ratio by saying that the semi-colon represents a pause twice as long as that of a comma, a colon a pause twice as long as a semi-colon, and a full stop a pause twice as long as a colon. Arithmetical insecurity may have led some teachers to think that this ratio was equivalent to the rule 'count to four', but this seems unlikely and one, at least, Matthew Raine, says clearly that for a period you count eight. The ratios are not important except as a small piece of teaching-method and as yet another example of the teachers' dependence on rules, even in quite inappropriate contexts. The obvious and sensible comment is seldom made:

1765 'The Time of the foregoing Stops is stated by some in the Proportion of 1, 2, 3, 4, 8; and by other, of 1, 2, 4, 8, &c. which seems much too large. It is best therefore to regulate them, according to the Nature of the Subject; which must be left to the Judgment of the Reader or Speaker.'   (Edwards, p. 73)

The parts of a sentence. By the middle of the present century the analysis of simple and complex sentences, at the school level, had become so stereotyped an exercise that it was difficult for teachers to envisage alternative methods or a time when no method had been thought necessary. But the system of analysis was a late-nineteenth-century synthesis of several earlier lines of thought.

Until the end of the eighteenth century, sentence analysis was not a teaching-exercise, although all the components of the analysis had been identified, and discussed in a variety of contexts and under various names. Some of these names derive from a logical, and some from a grammatical, tradition of analysis.

Sentence had at first rhetorical rather than grammatical associations and is discussed surprisingly seldom by seventeenth-century grammarians. Its essential components were a nominative case and a verb, and its essential characteristic was regularly expressed by the difficult concept of completeness of meaning. By the middle of the seventeenth century the logical division of the sentence into subject and predicate was being used in some grammars.

Nominative (case) was the usual, grammatical, term for what was later called the 'subject' – originally a term of logic and metaphysics. For example: in *to be an able Grammarian requires some study*: '*to be an able Grammarian* . . . is the Nominative Case to the Verb *requires*' (Houghton, 1766, p. 28).

Agent was sometimes used in the eighteenth century for the material category (the person or thing indicated by the subject) but more often for the grammatical category. The two were often confused, especially in a passive construction, as by Mayne, 1799, who says that in *Her gown is torn by a nail* 'nail is the agent, and the *gown* the object of that agent' (p. 41). Similarly Mercy, (1799) 1801: In *I am loved by her* 'her' is the agent (p. 58).

Accusative (case) or objective case were the normal terms before 'object' came into common use in the second half of the eighteenth century. Even then the term was not wholly familiar: Vyse, 1776, can only refer to 'the Noun or Pronoun which receives the Force of the Active Verb' (p. 107), Farro, 1754, to the 'affected name' (p. 321) and Henson, 1756, to 'the substantive governed of the verb' (p. 28).

Consequent was the correlative of *antecedent*; *patient* the occasional correlative of *agent* (*British Letter Writer*, 1765, p. 9; Bayly, 1772, p. 36).

Verb was used without misunderstanding both for the part of speech and for the part of a sentence. The verb 'be' was sometimes given its logical name 'copula'. That part of a sentence which followed the copula was given no special name: in an analysis of *I am the Duke of Norfolk* the words after *am* are called just 'the nominative after the verb' (Duncan, 1731, p. 59), and this was the normal expression. A frequent practice was to apply to the parts of a sentence the terminology of the parts of speech. Thus Raine, 1771, describes one possible structure of a simple sentence as: adjective and noun; verb and adverb; adjective and noun (p. 116).

Clause, until late in the nineteenth century, carried a wide meaning, corresponding more to 'expression'. A clause need not contain a finite verb; the term was applied to any group of words that possessed some semantic and syntactic unity:

1627 'We call a clause, a perfect member of speech, consisting of one or more words rightly knit unto other members, either before; or after; or both before and after.'   (Joseph Webbe, *Lessons and Exercises out of Cicero Ad Atticum*, A3)

When Puttenham says, 'The members of language at large are whole sentences, and sentences are compact of clauses' (p. 76) he is not referring to subordinate clauses. What the twentieth-century teacher calls 'clauses' were, of course, recognised, but as part of the syntax of different parts of speech. The use of conjunctions and relatives was described without reference to the idea of subordination or dependence.[6] In the same way sentences containing more than one finite verb were described as compound: 'A compound *sentence* is two or more simple *sentences* joined

---

[6] Interesting exceptions are Mark Lewis, 1674, and William Ward, 1765; *EGC*, pp. 474–8.

together; either by *conjunctions, adverbs,* or *relative pronouns*' (Waddell, 1799, p. 57). The complex sentence, requiring the idea of subordination, was not yet felt to be a necessary part of the teacher's equipment. Lowth, for instance, gives two examples of a compound sentence, distinguished not by any hierarchical difference but by the type of connective: 'Blessed is the man, *who* feareth the Lord' and 'Life is short, *and* art is long' (p. 133).

The following representative illustrations show the treatment of what were later to be called substantival, adjectival and adverbial clauses, and the application of 'clause' to units lacking a finite verb:

(1670b) 1674 'We have Infinitive Moods, Gerunds, Supines, Participles, Apposition, Vocative Cases, and Interjections. These are all contracted Sentences ... They are depending clauses: Their dependency is ellipted.'

(Mark Lewis, *Essay*, p. 1; *EGC*, pp. 474–5)

1700 'A whole Sentence is often taken as one aggregate Substantive of the Neuter Gender, and third Person singular; and then it may be the Nominative Case before a Verb, or the Accusative after it, a Substantive to an Adjective, or an Antecedent to a Relative: as for Example, *He who is vertuous is content with his Condition, which is the true property of Riches.*' (Lane, p. 78)

1731 'Very often in a Sentence, after the Subject of it, is another Sentence interwoven by way of Parenthesis, joined with that Subject by the Pronoun relative ... [and] bears the Part of an Adjective to the Subject, as *Persons, who say there is no God, are Fools.*' (Duncan, p. 46)

1764 'Whole Sentences are often considered as one word; as, *What I tell thee, is certain; I know, that thou art a good boy.*' (*A Real English Grammar*, p. 66)

1765 'Of whole Sentences used as substantives ... "I know *that my Redeemer liveth*". *That my Redeemer liveth*, denotes *that which is known*, and therefore is a kind of accusative case.' (W. Ward, p. 489)

1793 'A compound sentence is made either by a conjunction, adverb, or pronoun relative: as *Learning, which refines human nature, is the best treasure*' etc.

(Huntley, p. 31)

1795 In the sentence '*Israel loved Joseph more than all his children, because he was the son of his old age; and he gave him a coat of many colours*: This is a compound sentence, consisting of four simple sentences: 1. *Israel loved Joseph more*; 2. *than* (he loved) *all his children*; 3. *because he was the son of his old age*; 4. *and he gave him a coat of many colours*. The first and second are connected by the conjunction *than*; the second and third by the conjunction *because*; the third and fourth by the conjunction *and.*' (Alexander Miller, N.Y., p. 112)

1799 In 'a house *large* enough for my purpose' *enough for my purpose* is referred to as 'a clause depending on' the adjective *large*. (Gardiner, p. 73)

James Elphinston, for all his idiosyncrasies, discusses the analysis of the sentence in more forthright terms than are used by most of his contempo-

raries. His own summary illustration, itself summarised, shows the parts of
a simple sentence as:

1765	Introductory particle	*In this manner*
	The subject	*the donor*
	The operative medium (verb)	*makes*
	The object direct	*the donation*
	The circumstance (adverb)	*duly*
	The object indirect	*to the donee*

In a 'complex' form of this simple sentence the subjects and objects might
each have 'a qualifier joined', or be expanded 'by an incidental sentence
introduced by an apposited or agreeing noun, relative pronoun . . . or when
any part or incidental sentence is multiplied by a conjunction'. The
resulting illustration, a sentence of sixty-two words, adds, for instance, to
donee a 'qualifier' containing two finite verbs: *a person of undoubted
character, and who not only deserved very well of the donor, but will make the
best use possible of the donation* (II, 185–6). Despite these finite verbs
Elphinston is not requiring that a sentence of 'complex form' should
contain what we might call subordinate clauses. By 'complex' he means
something more like 'fully expanded'; and he is not using 'complex' instead
of 'compound', for he goes on to say a compound sentence is one composed
of several simple or complex ones.

Like Elphinston, the author of *A Real English Grammar*, 1764, was aware
how difficult it could be to keep interpretative control of a complicated
sentence, and that students needed help. He quoted a sentence of the kind
that caused them difficulty:

'*So that if, when we consider the different duties of Life, we also consider their
importance, we will not hesitate to prefer such as concern a future state, to those which
regard only the present.*'

He considers the main causes of difficulty to be that 'the order of many
words [is] very elegantly and emphatically changed' and that the relatives
and conjunctions are often 'huddled together'. The reader's task is to
identify the subjects and verbs and to see how the parts of the period are
connected with each other: to 'consider them Grammatically [and] restore
them to their natural order'. The reader 'ought to read it to himself thus':

'(Some circumstance going before is) *so* (convincing), *that we will not then hesitate
to prefer such duties as concern a future state, to those duties, which duties regard only a
present state, when we consider the different duties of Life.*'   (pp. 75–6)

The author's reference to relatives and conjunctions shows that he is
thinking of their connective function, but he is governed by the idea of

'natural order', which he applies to the clauses. Natural order is the only relationship between clauses that he considers, and he thus forgoes the assistance that was eventually provided by analysis of the clauses' functional relationship. Elphinston and this anonymous author both represent a transitional stage of teaching. The old reliance on varying and transposition could do little more than develop a feel for structure; a more rigorous technique was needed, and the necessary instruments were familiar; but they had yet to be brought together into an analytical system. William Ward had come nearer than anyone to forming such a system. He had discussed relative clauses by name in his speculative account of the pronoun (1765, p. 138); his examples of noun clauses were quoted above; what were later called adverbial clauses are illustrated in his discussion of conjunctions that require a following subjunctive, as in: '*I will not let thee go*, EXCEPT THOU BLESS ME'; and in: '*There mingle broils,* / ERE *this avenging sword* BEGIN *thy doom*' (p. 497).

The forms of analysis described or suggested by Ward and Elphinston were made explicit at the end of the century by the Abbé Gaultier, a French refugee who ran a school in London and published textbooks in both English and French. Gaultier describes how teaching his pupils to make summaries grew out of his method of analysing a sentence[7] and developed into a visual demonstration of an author's style. He describes sentences in the same way as Elphinston, both their overall structure (simple, complex, compound) and their internal structure (subject, verb, direct and indirect objects, each with its adjuncts or modifications; and a fifth element, the determinative, answering questions such as when, why, where). Gaultier goes beyond Elphinston in his description of the compound sentence and in his explicit reference to subordination: 'an assemblage of sentences, of which one is principal and every other is subordinate'.[8]

Gaultier's subordinate sentences are of three kinds: those that *modify* nouns; those that *determine* the attribute (verb); those that modify nouns and also determine the attribute. The first stage in making an abridgment, called 'analysing the paragraph', is virtually describing clause analysis:

1800 'If the paragraph consist of a simple or of a complex sentence, find out the subject, attribute and adjuncts. If the paragraph consist of a compound sentence, or several split sentences, find out the principal, and then the subordinate sentences, which either modify a noun, or determine the signification of the attribute.'

(pp. 17–18)

[7] *EGC*, pp. 486–9.
[8] Padley, 1985, p. 313, discusses the influence of the Port Royal grammars on the idea of subordinate clauses.

But Gaultier's examples show that subordination for him is both semantic and syntactical. He analyses the following paragraph:

'Nothing can please many, and please long, but just representation of general nature. Particular manners can be known to few, and therefore few only can judge how nearly they are copied. The irregular combinations of fanciful invention may delight awhile, by that novelty of which the common satiety of life sends us all in quest; but the pleasures of sudden wonder are soon exhausted, and the mind can only repose on the stability of truth.'

He calls 'Nothing . . . long' the 'principal' sentence because the other two relate and are subordinate to it; for the sentence

'*Particular manners . . . few*, &c is subordinate of [i.e. depends on the notion of] *motive*; it expresses the *reason why* nothing but just representations . . . can *please* MANY . . . The sentence *Irregular combinations, &c* is also subordinate of *motive* . . . All these sentences may be joined in one by prefixing the conjunctive word *because* to each subordinate sentence.'   (p. 25)

By the end of the eighteenth century the ground had been fully prepared for the analysis of sentences in the form that it eventually took towards the end of the nineteenth century.

Exercises. The commonest types of exercise have already been described: parsing, transposition and the correction of faulty spelling and syntax. The textbooks give a first impression that apart from these there was little for the pupils to do except learn by heart. Such an impression is certainly false, but it is difficult to say how false. Economic and educational factors are closely related. To the extent that books are expensive, and therefore scarce both for poorly paid teachers and for their pupils, teaching-methods will tend to be oral whether or not it is educationally desirable that they should be. If even rough paper is scarce the tendency will be reinforced, and it is only partly modified by the use of slates. English textbooks until well into the nineteenth century, and even then not for the poor, contain few of the exercises, to be written by the pupil, that a later abundance of paper made damagingly available. The early textbooks give an imcomplete picture of what the pupils did, if only because they show almost nothing of the oral questioning that, it must be assumed, did take place. However subservient the children, however limited the teacher, however much he relied on the question-and-answer form in which many textbooks were designed, it is most improbable that he or she took no initiative to find out how far the class had understood, as well as how much they had remembered. It is equally improbable, or nearly so, that a reasonably conscientious teacher, having discovered things that a pupil did not understand, should not give him a task that would help to clarify them. The attitudes towards children of sixteenth- and seventeenth-century adults have been much discussed because they seem so different from our own. But the differences relate to the behaviour of children and to methods of upbringing. Just as parents with authoritarian attitudes could still express love for their children, so teachers could have used oral and spontaneous exercises as supplements to the spelling-book and grammar, even though the extent of such work cannot now be measured.

During the second half of the eighteenth century textbooks begin to provide instructions that indicate the probable nature of much oral teaching. James Murray's grammar includes, with separate page-numbers suggesting that they were also issued separately, thirty pages of 'grammatical exercises'. They are printed without any rubric:

a. 1771 'The Future. I will write a Letter, Letters have been written by me, thou wilt play, he shall write, ye have written, they had written Letters, they shall be written by them, I wrote a Letter . . .' (p. 13, second numbering)

One supposes that the pupil had to put into a future tense those sentences which were not future, to handle 'will' and 'shall' correctly; to name the tense of each verb. At the end of the exercises Murray adds a note:

'The Teacher must instruct his Scholars to apply the Exercise to the Grammar Rules, as there are no particular Directions given sufficient to direct a young Scholar how to apply them. It was thought proper to leave this to the Master.' (p. 30)

It looks as though pupils are beginning to expect guidance from the textbook, as well as from the teacher, about how to carry out an exercise. A similar set of exercises, on the rules of grammar, is provided in Raine, 1771. John Shaw also shows how closely the idea of an exercise was linked to the application of rules. Shaw sees himself as returning to the model of Latin teaching after a period when English teachers have strayed:

1778 'A custom has . . . unaccountably prevailed for a long series of years, to pay no attention to the study of Grammar . . . To have been taught only to read their own language with ease and fluency has been reckoned sufficient for the purpose of an English education.' (preface)

In Shaw's method:

'The young persons under my care, as soon as they have learned perfectly by heart the declensions of the nouns and pronouns, and the conjugations of the verbs . . . are taught to form the exercises to be rectified by the rules of etymology . . . They are put to turn a certain portion of those that are to be rectified by the rules of syntax into correct English, by way of an evening exercise at home . . . The succeeding day they account for the grammatical construction of each word in it.' (preface)

It is not easy to keep in mind that Shaw is talking about the teaching of English. Joshua Story's grammar, 1778, contains 'English Exercises' which, like Shaw's, prescribe, not demonstrate, what the pupil has to do: 'Write down the plural of . . ., the possessive case of . . ., the superlative of . . .' It is only at this time that such hitherto oral exercises are beginning to be included in the textbooks. The implications are that more boys are expected to have copies of their own, that more written work is done in class, and that homework is being more regularly required.

William Sewell gives one example each of twenty-three exercises, with the comment that it is left 'to the judicious Instructor to enlarge them at Pleasure'. He goes on to describe what he does in class:

1789 'Once a Week, I give the first Scholar an Exercise on his Slate; which he reads audibly and distinctly to the Rest. After a Pause to give them Time to consider the Nature of the Exercise, the first Scholar spells each Word of the Exercise . . . pointing out the Stops and Marks . . . while each One copies the Exercise on his Slate, as the first Scholar dictates to them.'

The teacher then explains to what aspect of grammar the next exercise is related. The pupils write the exercise, 'each One keeping his Performance close to himself'. Those who complete the exercise correctly 'receive the Applause' of the others, and when the teacher has looked at each slate the successful pupils help the others with their corrections. When the teacher has checked the corrected exercises the pupils 'copy them fairly into their Books'. The rough work is done on the slate; the paper book is for fair copies (pp. 91–112).

In the 1790s such exercises became more frequent. John Sedger's praxis on his grammar, although in question and answer, is also a model for the teacher's own questions: 'The learner should be able to answer such questions as follow' (1798, p. 91). *The Pupil's Friend*, a. 1799, contains thirteen pages of questions on grammar, 'the Answers to be supplied by the Learners' (p. 103), a clear extension of the conventional praxis. Blanch Mercy recommends a variety of exercises, including: constant questioning; identification of parts of speech by structural criteria ('How are you to know what *part of speech* a word really is? By attending to the *office* of it in the Sentence': II, 116) and paraphrase. James Waddell provides an even wider range of exercises and 'finds that variety of example is the only thing which accomplishes the pupil'. Waddell found it 'impossible . . . to carry on his classes with advantage, without some such exercises' (preface). It can be seen from William Angus' *Epitome* of 1800 that exercises in something like their modern form are an accepted part of a textbook. He provides five types, with answers given separately:

Improper expressions	He lives in the second *flat* of Mr T.'s land.
Redundancy	He was received with *marked* applause.
Improper ellipsis	To play cards.
Bad arrangement	Theism can *only* be opposed to Polytheism or Atheism.
Ambiguity	He sent him to kill his own father. (pp. xxxii–xl)

Ellipsis, though originally a figure of syntax and, in the purest practice, taught as an aid to the development of style, had fallen into the hands of the grammarians, whose examples of 'elliptical syntax' were often as trivial as this from Raine: 'The Bell rings at six (of the clock).' The eighteenth-century grammarians' treatment of ellipsis represents a deterioration in teaching-method. They take a rhetorical exercise and use it in such a way that it encourages (if it encourages anything) bad writing rather than good. The exercise was based on the generally held view that in the 'full and perfect' form of an expression every word was present that the grammatical form permitted. In one of Greenwood's examples '*Drink ye White or Red Wine?*' is an elliptical form of '*Drink ye White Wine, or drink ye Red Wine?*' (1711, p. 221). It was not maintained that the full form of an expression was stylistically better, or necessarily desirable. *Suppression*, the alternative name for ellipsis, was proper but artificial; the full form was 'natural'. It followed therefore that children should be able to tell when an expression was elliptical and to 'supply' the words that had been 'omitted' or were 'understood'. They learnt rules telling when words might be left out, and they learnt, unavoidably, that in some way it would be more natural, perhaps better, to say 'What Man is that Man?' than to say 'Who is he?' (Greenwood, *ibid.*).[9]

During the second half of the eighteenth century more than thirty of the texts studied here contain exercises on the ellipsis, usually arranged according to the part of speech that is being suppressed. The standard definition said that ellipsis was 'the elegant suppression . . . of one or more words, to avoid disagreeable repetitions' (Dearborn, USA, 1795) – the notional repetition, one must remember, of words that would not in fact have been spoken. Usually the exercise, supplying the ellipsis, is straight-forward. Sometimes a writer like Alexander Miller, also in America, offers examples of a speculative kind: 'rode (*through,* or *through the space of*) ten miles (*in*) an hour' (1795, p. 76), but it was unusual for any teacher to recognise the possibility of alternative completions.

Tautology, under the name of *pleonasm*, had also been a figure of speech, but was by late-eighteenth-century grammarians regarded as 'rather a fault

[9] For the background in medieval and humanist Latin grammars to the English treatment of ellipsis see Padley, 1976.

than a figure' (Fogg, 1792, p. 247) and some books contain exercises in 'tautology or repetition'.

James Buchanan is one of the few authors to give tautology much attention (twenty pages). One sentence is enough to illustrate the exercise, which by definition takes up more space than it is worth. The passage, to be purged of tautology, comes from an essay on parental duty:

1762 'The second Order of Duties regard the intellectual, and *regard the* moral Life of their Children, or *regard their Childrens* Education in such Arts, and *in such* Accomplishments, as is necessary to qualify *their Children* for performing the Duties *their Children* owe to themselves, and *owe* to others.'

(p. 233, here freed from additional errors introduced for correction)

Here again one needs to keep in mind that the words to be removed as tautologous were not in fact used. They have been introduced merely so that they can be taken out.

Vocabulary. The teaching of rhetoric had always included the acquisition of a copious vocabulary: through reading, through the practice of expression, and through exercises such as varying. In elementary textbooks of English the acquisition of vocabulary is not discussed but it is implicit in the spelling-lists, especially those arranged thematically, and in those accompanied by brief definitions; in the frequent lists of homophones and of noun and verb forms distinguished by stress (*'conduct, con'duct*); in the illustrations, more common towards the end of the eighteenth century, of derivation from Latin and Greek (e.g. Wynne, 1775; Webster, 1784). Many of the spelling-lists contained absurdly irrelevant words, such as J.G.'s choice, for 'junior classes', of 'fascine', 'scholium', 'ichorous' and 'ochimy', but however wasteful the method the teachers' dictionary-hunting took both them and their pupils outside their everyday vocabularies. The spelling-dictionary had been a standard help in school at least since the publication in 1765 of John Entick's immensely popular volume. The main purpose of the dictionaries was to show how words were spelt: the definitions were kept to one line at most and were sometimes omitted. The dictionaries were often treated as spelling-lists, and the pupils were required to learn not only the spelling but also the definitions. Nineteenth-century objections to this practice are quoted below.

A private tutor, T.M., 1774, provides an unusual example of vocabulary work in (very genteel) action. He complains that even sixteen-year-olds have a poor vocabulary.

1774 '[Even] if they do barely understand any *simple term* expressing an *idea*, how few can give you *two*, or more changes of words to express the same *idea* . . . The following practice is therefore affectionately recommended to Parents, Guardians and Tutors . . . It is thrown into dialogue, to render it the more familiar.

Practical Dialogue

Pupil I *have* a very fine *house*.

Master Pray, Miss, do me the favour to give me some other word, instead of *have*, to express the same idea.

P. Lord, Sir! why you make a perfect child of me.

M. Pardon me, Madam; this subject, however trifling it may appear . . . [is important, e.g.] For I *have*, you may substitute, I *possess*, I *enjoy*, I *occupy*, I *hold*. *Vid. Johnson's Dict.*'   (pp. 66–8)

Word formation was touched on in most grammars, usually in explanation of compound and derivative words. Less often there is a separate discussion of prefixes and suffixes, leading on to derivation from Latin and Greek, as in the second part of Greenwood's grammar of 1711, which illustrates both approaches (giving also a chapter to the origin of British place names) and in chapter 11 of Part 3 of Buchanan's *British Grammar* of 1762. The history of the English language, touched on by Gill and Wallis, comes into the school grammars with Gildon and Greenwood, who are using Wallis, but interest in both history and dialect shows earlier, at a less sophisticated level, in John White's *The Country-Man's Conductor*, 1701, which includes 'some examples of the English of our ancestors, and also of our western dialect'. Interest was strengthened by Benjamin Martin's *Institutions of Language*, 1748, is seen in Newbery's *Pocket Dictionary*, 1753, and was reinforced by Samuel Johnson's dictionary and its imitation by Nathan Bailey. At the school level Charles Wiseman introduced sections on the history of English proper names and on 'A comparative view of the English language, both ancient and modern', which discusses Latin, romance languages, Welsh and Dutch (1764, pp. 388f). M'Ilquham, 1781, and Bullen, 1797, included short historical sketches of English; Corbet, 1784, offered 'Observations on the ancient and modern languages of England'; Bicknell, 1790, drew on Martin; Fogg, 1796, included a dissertation on the 'History and Character of the English Language'; Patrick Lynch, 1796, hoped 'to enliven the dry and uninteresting subject of Grammar, by introducing historical notices of its gradual improvements' (preface, p. xi). The stimulatingly speculative work of Horne Tooke was not read by schoolboys but its influence, acknowledged or not, is apparent in very many of the school grammars.

Attempts at reform

In school English grammars belonging to the first half of the twentieth century the parts of speech are stated with some firmness to be: noun, pronoun, adjective, verb, adverb, conjunction, preposition and interjection. Because these parts are found in Latin grammars also it is generally thought that there has been an unbroken and unquestioned system of parts of speech since classical times: a system that, in spite of its appalling inconsistencies, it is even now difficult, for school purposes, to alter. In so far as English 'grammar' in school comprised the parts of speech it was, until the 1950s at least, accepted for its convenience in teaching other languages, or it was reluctantly tolerated, or it was irresolutely rejected. Many of our earlier predecessors, however, between 1730 and 1780 tried to ease their pupils' inherited burden of Latin categories by simplifying the technical terms and by modifying the Latin system of parts of speech.

Technical terms. Sixteenth-century teachers had sometimes replaced Latinate terms with English ones, partly to simplify them, partly to show that the English language could encompass a technical vocabulary. Hart's proposals in 1551 had included 'joiner' for the hyphen; 'rest' for the comma; 'asker' for the note of interrogation; and in 1561 he added 'time' for tense and 'manner' for mood. Ralph Lever's *The Arte of Reason*, 1573, proposed a range of vernacular replacements for the standard terms of logic ('witcraft') including 'saywhat' for definition. At the end of the seventeenth century Joseph Aickin was still urging English teachers to invent 'English tearmes, proper for all Sciences' (preface), a challenge that Gildon thought he (and presumably Brightland) were meeting in respect of grammar:

(1711) 1712 'Our End being the teaching only the present *English Tongue*, we had no Regard to any Term whatsoever, which had not an immediate Regard to that: by this means we believe we may say, That we have deliver'd the Learner from some Scores of Hard Words, impos'd in other *Grammars*.' (preface to second edition)

By the 1780s the reforming impetus was dying away, and all that Alexander Murray can say, giving both traditional and reforming terms ('adjective'/'quality'; 'verb'/'affirmation'), is that the latter 'convey a clearer idea of their nature and use to an English Scholar than the first, which are not English words and cannot be understood independently of a definition' (1785, p. 4, printed 14). John Shaw expresses, with some exaggeration, an opinion widespread in the 1770s:

1778 'Most of the writers' of English grammars 'since Dr Lowth's publication . . . seem to have departed as much as possible not only from the rudiments, but the terms made use of in Grammars of that tongue, and have chosen to put their materials into any form, rather than suffer them to fall in with the Latin plan . . . Many of the technical terms are changed for others equally if not more abstracted and perplexing: and thus a new kind of grammatical language has been invented.'

(p. v)

Simplified terms in common use were:

Letters, Words, Sentences instead of orthography, etymology, syntax. From 1700.

Name instead of noun (substantive). From 1695.

Adnoun instead of adjective. From 1695 and frequently until at least 1858.

Adname was occasionally used in the same way. From 1711.

Quality instead of adjective. From 1711.

Affirmation instead of verb. From 1712.

Personal instead of pronoun. From 1646.

Foregoing or *leading state* instead of nominative.

Following state instead of accusative. Both from 1711. These two changes were more than verbal: they represented an intention, initiated by Wallis, 1653, to avoid saying that English nouns had cases.

Time instead of tense. Occasionally in Latin grammars from the 1560s, and in English ones from about 1617 (Hume).

Parts of speech. In English grammars published before 1801 there are 297 direct or implied enumerations of the parts of speech, sometimes more than one enumeration being given by the same author, even in the same book. These enumerations, so far from being uniform, fall into no fewer than 58 different systems. This is because in the English grammars the Latin system of eight parts of speech was modified for various reasons, in various ways, variously combined. Noun substantive and noun adjective were treated as two distinct parts. The articles could be treated as distinct parts; as attachments or signs of the noun; as adjectives; as particles; or they could be excluded altogether. The participle could be treated as a distinct part of speech; as an adjective; as part of the verb. Adverb, conjunction, preposition and interjection were often grouped together in the single category of particle. The interjection was often denied the status of a part of speech; sometimes it was included within the adverb. Further subordinate categories were created by the inclusion of, for example, the interjection within the adverb when the adverb was itself included within the primary category of particle; or when the participle was included within the adjective, which was itself included within the noun. Many of these systems are put forward by only a single author, sometimes as an explicit reform, sometimes as an apparently casual variation the uniqueness of which would have surprised him. For instance the author of *The Young Mathematician's Logic*, 1760, proposes the following system of six parts: Substantive (including pronoun substantive); Adjective (including pronoun adjective, article and participle); Verb; Adverb (including interjection); Conjunction; Preposition. No single characteristic of this system is unique. The pronoun substantive (*he*, etc.) and pronoun adjective (*his*, etc.) had been divided in at least one earlier grammar; the interjection had been included within the adverb in three earlier grammars; the article had been treated as an adjective in six, and the participle in two. But this particular system, which is quite explicit, happened to be unique, and to remain so. Variations such as this show that the parts of speech did not form the coherent system of mutually exclusive word classes that was implied by their use in teaching. These variations demonstrate also how difficult it was for the teachers to make sense of the Latinate categories and how their restless attempts to introduce small improvements led to a proliferation of systems.

Because many of the Latin categories were so unsatisfactory when applied to the teaching of English, attempts were also made to improve the system radically, usually by reducing the number of parts.[10] There were two lines of thought: one stemming from an interest in language and universal grammar, the other from the teacher's practical need for a grammatical system designed for first-language teaching. The former line of thought led to systems such as Dalgarno's (the noun as the only part of speech, because all words were in origin nouns); Lodwick's three-fold classification into Words of Action, Words of Quality and Words of Help; James Harris' system of four primary parts: Substantive, Attributive, Definitive, Conjunctive. The second line of thought led to the many grammars – more than forty – in which the parts were reduced to four: Substantive, Adjective, Verb and Particle. But the teachers' attempts at reform failed, largely because no one was able to make a real category out of the particle. It was a purely notional combination of adverb, conjunction, preposition and interjection (and often the article), all of which retained their primary functions and definitions even in their professedly subsidiary roles.

Nevertheless the attempts are important evidence of teachers' dissatisfaction with the traditional Latinate system, and of their efforts to reform it. Only the most radical thinkers, however, could break out from the categories that had conditioned everyone's thinking about language. The Latin system seemed sufficiently close to the nature of English to make it hard to overturn, while at the same time it was manifestly inappropriate for

---

[10] Padley, 1985, p. 129, notes in the vernacular grammars of Europe 'a general tendency everywhere as the eighteenth century approaches to simplify the parts of speech, whether on pedagogical or philosophical grounds'.

teaching. The radical thinkers went too far for the teachers. The teachers, by not being radical enough, were forced back onto the categories they would have liked to change.[11]

The nineteenth century

Many nineteenth-century grammars were ordinary, routine productions. Their contents and their methods scarcely distinguish one from another and they are interesting only because they show the extent to which eighteenth-century practices could still be maintained even during a period when ideas about both language and teaching were being actively debated.

Ordinary grammars and established methods

Mrs Thackwray's *A Grammatical Catechism*, which had its second edition in 1813, is typical of the more thoughtful of the ordinary grammars. The preface to the first edition regrets that young ladies find grammar so dull (it lacks 'external allurements'). Mrs Thackwray relies on Lindley Murray and on frequent questioning: Part 1 of the book is in question-and-answer form. Forty-two pages are given to the parts of speech, the verb having ten pages; word formation is just mentioned, before nine pages of syntax and four pages on punctuation and the use of capital letters. In Part 2, added in the second edition, the parts of speech are considered again, with discussion of case, mood, tense and some reference to other languages (twenty-seven pages); a table of abbreviations, a summary of the parts of speech, and a parsing praxis make up the remaining ten pages.[12]

Part of the ordinariness of the ordinary grammars lies in the uniformity of their systems of parts of speech. The grammars published before 1801 employed fifty-eight different systems.[13]

The most frequent was a system, No. 9, of ten categories: Substantive; Adjective; Article; Pronoun; Verb; Participle; Adverb; Conjunction; Preposition; Interjection. Next most frequent was system No. 10, which

---

[11] The grammarians' treatment of the parts of speech and their attempts at reform are more fully discussed in *EGC*. Among the most interesting of the reforming school grammars are: A. Lane, 1695 and 1700; William Loughton, 1734; Solomon Lowe, 1737; Ann Fisher, 1745; James Gough, 1754; Samuel Edwards, 1765; Thomas Smetham, 1774; H. Ward, 1777.

[12] Among other representatively ordinary grammars are: Hannah Kilham, 1818; W. Putsey, 1821; William Angus, a. 1825; William Harrison, a. 1834; W. Shatford, 1834; Richard Dunnock, 1836; *Grammar of the English Language*, 1837; L.A. Donatti, 1839; Alexander Wilson, a. 1842; Richard Wilson, 1845; Hugo Reid, 1850; John Cassell, 1855; W.K. Farnell, 1858; J.C. Curtis, 1867.

[13] *EGC*, chap. 8, with appendices 1 and 2 slightly revised. The numbering of the systems in *EGC* is continued here.

differs from system 9 only by including the participle within the verb. Systems 9 and 10 were used in 35 per cent of the grammars published between 1586 and 1800; but during the first quarter of the nineteenth century they were used in nearly 90 per cent. Between 1825 and 1850 there was more innovation in the textbooks and system 10 lost much of its popularity. The proportion using systems 9 and 10 dropped to about 70 per cent and fell a further 10 per cent between 1850 and 1870.

Learning the grammar, or part of it, by heart seems to have remained the ordinary practice until the middle of the nineteenth century, and to have been not infrequent thereafter. By 1863, however, a school inspector in Ireland can say that it 'is now abandoned by all except the very worst teachers' (R. Robinson, p. 267). Many teachers continued, during the first part of the century, to distinguish by typography or by prescription a main text that had to be memorised. If the author of *The Plainest . . . Principles*, 1812, is to be obeyed strictly it would seem that the boys of Bridport Grammar School were expected to memorise about 12,000 words, and about the same amount is required by J.W.R., 1839, who defends himself: 'Grammar is not a light study . . . it must be so accurately learned, that your mind may, at any moment, be ready to apply its rules, otherwise how can you write and speak with propriety?' (Address to his pupils). One of the severest prescriptions is that by Henry Young:

1832 'The rules of the grammar should be committed to memory, not in a superficial manner, but so as to be repeated without hesitation. In order to accomplish this, the pupil should go over them until he is perfect . . . The mind, in its unexpanded state, cannot fully comprehend the nature of things; but if rules be indelibly imprinted on the memory, the learner will have in store a valuable quantity of raw materials for time and a matured judgment to digest.'　　　　(p. xxii)

Many seventeenth-century teachers would have agreed with that.

J.W. Gill's *First Steps in English Grammar*, 1854, of thirty-two pages, is designed to be learnt entirely by heart. Boys in the first class take the book home 'to write out and parse one or two of the sentences', and carry out other exercises. In the second class the boys take the book home 'very nearly every night and commit a small portion to memory'. In the third class the grammar is used as an occasional reading-book, and the boys ask each other questions on it. Gill grounds his practice on the belief that children in the first class of an elementary school cannot 'by themselves' follow explanations that require 'the application of logical reasoning'.

Contrary views about learning grammar rules by heart are also expressed. One of the most interesting attacks, because it is also constructive, is by 'a schoolmaster' in *A Practical Treatise on Day-Schools*:

1816 'The inefficient manner in which this important and ornamental branch of education [English grammar] is usually taught in day-schools, is really astonishing; very few of those who pretend to learn it, being ever able to distinguish one part of speech from another. The general method of studying it, if it deserves such a title, is to commit it to memory only; or if a few exercises are written, they are almost always corrected by the master, who himself is frequently unable to give any other reason for the alterations he makes, than, that the words do not read well . . . To teach grammar with proper effect, in a numerous school, requires a regular plan, which should be undeviatingly pursued . . . If grammar has never been taught, or only [inefficiently] it will be proper to allot half an hour, or an hour a day to it, for some time, even at the expence of other studies. Then arranging all the boys of the school in one class, with the exception of such as are really too young, let the teacher begin by explaining to them what a noun or substantive is, not merely by saying, it is the name of whatever we can see, understand, or discourse of, but by producing numerous examples of each kind; then by requiring each boy to give an example, continuing this round and round as long as time will allow. The second lesson will be for explaining and exemplifying the article.'

As soon as about ten boys are able to distinguish the parts of speech they are taken separately and taught the second stage of the sequence: subdivisions of the parts of speech, gender, number, case, mood, tense. Then they move on to syntactical parsing, from which they go first to easy written exercises, in answering which they have always to quote the relevant rule; then to more difficult ones. From these they 'proceed' to the examples under 'Purity, Clearness, Strength, and Precision; and afterwards to original Composition'. After two years the master will have seven 'grammar forms', each of seven or eight boys, corresponding to the seven stages in the sequence. If the master is singlehanded he must

'. . . make use of the boys of each class, alternately to help prepare the next lower . . . Each boy will not have the trouble oftener than once a week . . . Indeed it will be no injury to the boys so employed, but rather an advantage, as, while they are assisting the lower class, they are refreshing their own minds.'   (pp. 54–61)

William Hill, 1833, repudiating 'the Host of Grammar Books, with which society has been pestered, during the last seventy or eighty years', says that his own is written in the language of the classroom and can be understood without being learnt by heart (preface), and R.H., 1851, wishes no part of grammar to be 'forced on the memory of the pupil', who should be trained to understand (p. xxii). Henry Butter's *Inductive Grammar* states more emphatically than any the argument against excessive memory work:

a. 1843 The pupil's memory 'is taxed, but his reasoning faculties remain unoccupied . . . When the scholar is required to apply what he has obtained from his grammar, he possesses only a chaos of nouns, declensions, conjugations, moods, tenses, &c. from which he must select the necessary directions for his present purpose.' (preface)

The pupil should be trained 'to make his own deductions', that is to frame his own rules, 'from the nature of the language', thereby strengthening not only his reasoning powers but also his interest.

Throughout many texts, not only grammars, and especially in America, there is from the early years of the nineteenth century an increasing emphasis on the importance of the pupil's own reasoning and judgment. This approach is apparent in England in 1806, when John Bullar, in his *Thoughts on the subject of education at school: addressed to his friends*, wrote: 'If the teacher can but succeed in leading his pupil to THINK, and to INQUIRE, he will indeed have exerted himself to a happy purpose.' Explanation is important because children 'have learned grammar, as a parrot has learned the few syllables with which he imitates human speech' (p. 13).

In America the importance of independent thought was associated specifically with freeing children from the obligation to obey rules blindly:

1867 'It is not the province of the grammarian to legislate in matters of language, but to clarify and arrange its forms and principles by a careful study of its analogies as seen in the usage of the best writers.' (Samuel S. Greene, preface)

Children, Greene says, do not improve just by knowing a rule. Rules 'become valuable when the child has reached such a degree of development as shall enable him to comprehend their application'.

That there are other forces governing the use and teaching of language, less palpable but more potent than grammatical rules, is illustrated in an odd episode described by Enos Cobb, an American teacher, in a discussion about purity of style:

(1820) 1821 'A grammarian, who had discovered a new system of teaching, invited a number of ladies and gentlemen to his room, to hear him give an explanation' of the power of the preposition; 'and, in elucidating his system, he gave the following low and vulgar sentences, among many others equally unpleasant:

> *The cow runs round the barn*
> *The sheep broke through the fence*
> *The swine wallowed in the mire*

These were so disgusting to his company, that they left him as soon as they could conveniently excuse themselves.' (p. 85)

Even though 'disgusting' probably meant no more than 'distasteful' the reaction of an audience interested in grammar to these regular and grammatically faultless sentences surprises us now, and seems to have been memorable at the time. To use farmyard animals in the illustration of a grammatical rule was so offensive that the audience were unable to consider the rule at all. We cannot be sure, of course, that the audience were not so bored that they made a slight lapse of taste a pretext for making their escape.

Exercises

False English. The popularity of these exercises, immense during the 1790s, continued until about 1820. They were less frequent during the following twenty years and had practically ceased to appear by 1855. By the nineteenth century the exercises had become more realistic and related more to syntax than to spelling, although pupils were still occasionally required to correct sentences such as '*A farmer as in is granerry 10 qwarter of wheats*' (Gilleade, 1816, p. 174). The correction of false syntax was still defended on the paradoxical grounds that 'a correction of the exercises renders the student conversant with the best modes of speech' (Dyer H. Sandborn, USA, 1836, preface to 1840 edn). Lennie praises it, rather unconvincingly:

a. 1816 'When the individuals in a class are all expert in detecting errors, they are apt (each through eagerness to be *first*) to bawl out the word all at once, and thus make too much noise. This inconvenience, however, being unavoidable, should be endured, at least occasionally; for, after a while's rigid attention, an exercise of this description has a fine effect upon them.'   (p. 88)

John Walker, 1805, thought that if such exercises were to be given they should be kept apart, as by Lindley Murray, from the correct form of the sentences, which should be available, to the teacher only, in a separately published key. By this means the pupil would be forced to search in his textbook for the rule that determined the correct form. In the anonymous *English Grammar* of 1810, however, it is just this reliance on rule that is rejected (and therefore all parsing and false syntax exercises) in favour of learning 'by examples'. The author builds his whole book on this principle, but he seems inconsistent: he particularly praises Lindley Murray; yet Murray stresses the application of rules to the correction of false syntax. Dependence on rules was criticised more clearly by William S. Balch, in America:

1839 'Reasons instead of rules should be taught to scholars, that they may rely more upon themselves, and the convictions of their own minds, and the facts of the case, for the correctness of their positions, than upon mere rule . . . Human authority has been too obsequiously obeyed.'   (preface)

At the same time Allen and Cornwell, in England, were calling exercises in false syntax a 'pernicious practice' (1841, preface). The practice was dying away, but it never vanished. In 1871 it was still sufficiently familiar for a writer to include among the recommendations of his book that 'no bad grammar *to be corrected* has been introduced' (*The Young Student's English Grammar*, preface).

Vulgarisms were treated separately from the correction of false syntax. They were a regular feature of all sorts of manuals, British and American. Christopher Earnshaw, for example, in Yorkshire, disapproves of:

1817 'He lives *aback* (at the back) of the shambles.
It was very difficult to *agree* (reconcile) the two accounts.
A *bettering* (more respectable) sort of person.' (p. 71)

Daniel Powers, 1845, in Massachusetts, provides first a 'vocabulary' of vulgar or obsolete expressions such as 'above-board' ('applied to a person whose income is more than his expenses') and 'chipper' ('lively, as "he is a *chipper* fellow" '). Later in his grammar he lists 'words and sentences so low, that we thought it expedient not to admit them into the vocabulary'. These include 'blazes' ('the horse ran like blazes'); 'hopping mad'; and 'nation' ('a nation fine horse').

Similar exercises 'to avoid low expressions' are given by Meilan, 1803; Thomas Roome, 1812; and C.W. Connon, 1845. It was generally agreed, in Britain and in America, both by those who were seeking to improve themselves and by the teachers who were helping them, that vulgarisms had to be eradicated, if only on prudential grounds. For an unquiet moment the Hon. Samuel Best, Rector of Abbots-Ann, glimpsed the alternative possibility that the upper classes might adopt the language of the vulgar. In the preface to his grammar 'for the use of village schools' he wrote:

a. 1852 'The classically-educated man cannot, if it were desirable, so ignore his education as to address a congregation in the jargon and patois of the village ... We may and ought to raise them to our standard; we cannot, without profaneness in sacred things, descend to theirs.' (4th edn, 1857)

Parsing. As parsing is tied to the system of parts of speech, the exercises in the nineteenth century are even more monotonous than they were earlier. Few voices question their usefulness. In the United States Joseph Wright, 1838, is quoted as saying that parsing is generally unimportant (Goold Brown, 1850, 1875 edn, p. 103) and Daniel Powers in Massachusetts, 1845, considers it 'more than useless to Pupils under the age of fifteen'. Similarly cautious comment is made in England by Hyde Clarke, 1853, who describes parsing as 'an educational process of very limited utility'.

In the ordinary grammars syntax continued to be taught as a series of rules, most writers keeping to the division between concord and government, and offering between 20 and 30 rules. Those who tried to go beyond the traditional division emptied the term 'rule' of any meaning by trying to apply it to repetitive or idiomatic features, to which there was no end. Hence the 58 rules of William Clark, 1835; the 77 of James Douglas, about 1860; and the 423 of J. Taylor, 1804.

Exercises such as those described earlier in this chapter were used in an increasing number of textbooks during the nineteenth century, and by about 1860 it was commonplace, under the influence of examinations and inspectors' visits, for any text, even a literary one, to include questions and tasks. Sometimes separate books of exercises were issued, on the lines of Lindley Murray's: the anonymous *Exercises of transposition to Walker's Themes and Essays*, 1818; James Wilkins' *Grammatical Questions, with notes*, of the same year; Sir Richard Phillips' *Five Hundred Questions*, 1824; and John McQueen's *Easy Exercises in English*, 1869. One familiar type of exercise, transposition, acquired an independent status that enabled it to appear in grammars or manuals of composition or as an adjunct to interpretation. It was at its best valued as a means of teaching linguistic flexibility, but it seldom rose above the insensitive mechanism of the eighteenth-century examples. Such exercises are given by Angus, 1828; T.J. Wiseman, 1846, and Maurice Kavanagh, 1859. A characteristic instance;

1852 'Transpose or vary: *The brother deserved blame more than the sister.*
The Roman State evidently declined in proportion to the increase of luxury.'   (W. Martin, p. 102)

A characteristic rubric shows the exercise free from its earlier preoccupation with theories about the natural order of the parts of a sentence: 'Vary the arrangement . . . trying which form is most clear and harmonious' (*English Grammar and Composition*, 1853, p. 164).

One exercise, not common but heavy with harm for the future, is used in William Angus' *Supplement*, 1828: 'A New Method of Exercising the Pupil on the Signification of Words, by finding out their Opposites'. The pupil is given a list of words, by part of speech, for each of which he has to give the opposite. Angus' examples are; '*Ability*: incapacity; weakness, bodily or mental. *Abrogation*: enactment; enforcement' (p. 178). In spite of Angus' description it is unlikely that he was first to devise such an extension of the common exercise of supplying synonyms, but his is the first textbook, amongst those consulted, to contain the exercise. It appears also in J. Harris' *Easy Exercises*, 1862, and in John McQueen's *Easy Exercises in English*, 1869. No exercise has done more to blunt the capacity for making the very linguistic and logical discriminations that it was meant to develop. It gives point to J.S. Laurie's warning that teachers use too many exercises that take the place of any real understanding of the subject: 'a serious danger by which school literature is threatened' (1862, preface).

Elliptical exercises. During the nineteenth century there is a significant change in the use made of elliptical exercises. Earlier they had been designed on the assumption that the fullest possible form of an expression was the most correct. The elliptical exercise was thought of as developing style. By the mid-nineteenth century it was a verbal exercise in the form of a puzzle, meant to develop linguistic control. The pupil's skill lay in choosing for the blank space a word that fitted the syntactical structure of the sentence and was consistent with its meaning. The Irish commissioners' *English grammar* includes the following exercise as part of the section on syntax:

(1836) 1838 'When the morning of life —— over your head, every thing around you —— on a smiling appearance. All nature —— a face of beauty, and —— animated with a spirit of joy; you —— up and down in a new world...' etc.   (p. 102)

Such exercises were thought to train verbal flexibility in a way that would develop both interpretative and expressive skills. An Irish inspector, Robert Robinson, wrote in an English grammar, 'The meaning of any passage [in a verse anthology] will be easily detected by children if they are in the habit of filling up ellipses, analyzing and transposing sentences' (1863, p. 297), and Richard G. Parker told American teachers: 'As an intellectual exercise ... I know of nothing more useful than the practising of pupils in supplying the ellipses, so as to reduce a form of expression to grammatical rule ' (1839, p. 128). Other teachers using the exercise in this way include William Martin, 1852 and George Currey, 1856; in America John L. Parkhurst, 1820. The exercise took various forms.

G.F. Graham used it in the teaching of metrics. The pupil is to fill the blanks in the following anapaests with words of the prescribed pattern of stressed (–) and unstressed ($\smile$) syllables:

1862   We may (–) through this (–) like a child at a feast,
            Who but (–) of a sweet, and then (–) to the rest;
            And when (–$\smile$) begins to ($\smile$) dull in the east,
            We may (–$\smile$) our wings, and be off to the west.   (p. 259)

And Charles Morley, 1838, in America, amongst a variety of elliptical exercises, makes his pupils complete verses from which whole lines have been omitted. George Simpson, a Bristol teacher, produced an entire textbook of *Elliptical English*. He considered that 'the study of the English language will, henceforth, take a prominent position in our first-class schools' through 'the importance which is attached to it in the Oxford and Cambridge Middle Class Examination'. His book begins with 'elliptical sentences' ('Their —— are —— in bed'); then with a change in the meaning of ellipsis it provides what are in effect outline narratives, each blank representing not a single word but a break in the story:

1858 'Travelling—— Scotland—— ravine—— woman—— "Alas, my child"—— —— intense —— object —— tears —— sight —— "My good woman, what ?" ' etc.

(p. 43)

More characteristic of the exercise in the form it maintained for many years are those in E. Hughes' *A Series of Composition Exercises*, 1869. The simplest are of little value, even as vocabulary exercises, because they provide no context: 'I see a ——.' The most advanced would permit some disagreement and discussion: 'Fields are surrounded by ——, and we go in through the ——, for it is wrong to go over the ——.'

The value of works such as this depended on the teacher's linguistic sensitivity. If, as most of the eighteenth-century teachers taught, there was only one word that could correctly fill a blank, the exercise merely reinforced stereotyped expressions and did more harm than good. If the pupil felt free to suggest one or more words that might fit the blank, a number of useful questions arose. Did the suggested word fit the structure of the sentence? Did the resultant meaning fit the context? If more than one word could be inserted were there grounds for preferring one to another? These possibilities were seldom realised, even in the twentieth century. A potentially valuable method of training inferential skill and of enlarging vocabulary was restricted to the endorsement of banality.[14]

Vocabulary, etymology and history of the language

The types of exercise described earlier in this chapter continued during the early decades of the nineteenth century. Lists of synonyms were frequent ('ale-house, public-house, inn, tavern': Andrew, 1817) and later textbooks

---

[14] In modern 'cloze' procedure the reader has to supply words that have been omitted not because they are key words but according to a previously determined order. The same kind of inferential skill is required as in elliptical exercises, but the technique is intended to provide a measure of the 'readability' of a text rather than to teach either interpretation or expression.

sometimes show how such lists would be used in oral work: 'Distinguish between . . . *evident, obvious, plain, conspicuous, visible*' (*English Grammar and Composition*, 1853). Portions of the dictionary were still learnt by heart, as Eliza Chamberlain, 1846, expected her children's dictionary to be used, but the practice was criticised:

1810 'The common use made of Dictionaries in most Schools, is a great hindrance to improvement; for, by making Boys get off a certain portion of spelling and explanation each day in the order of a Dictionary, a great deal of time, genius and application is sacrificed.'   (George Wall, preface)

Wall reckons that even if a boy learnt thirty words and definitions a day it would take him five years to work through the dictionary, by the end of which time he would have forgotten half. W. Johnstone, 1818, in advocating the teaching of 'verbal definition', warns against learning the dictionary by heart, and in the same years John Hornsey carries to its extreme conclusion the paradox of 'false spelling'. In his *English Exercises*, a book composed entirely of muddled spelling, he refers to the dictionary as 'a book that I never allow any boy to have in my school' (preface).

Many teachers, however, tried through exercises of various kinds to enlarge vocabulary. Thomas Carpenter produced what was in effect a selective spelling-dictionary: forty-eight daily lessons each containing about twenty words.

1813 '*Thursday*
    S. *Dràper*, a dealer in cloth
    A. *Doùble*, twice as much or many.
    S. *Extràction*, lineage; a drawing out' etc.

The items were learnt overnight and repeated the following day by individual pupils; the week's work was recapitulated by the class as a whole, in chorus, every Monday morning. Anna Jameson produced a children's dictionary of about 3800 words, on the lines of a glossary by Maria Edgeworth 'in one of her admirable early lessons'. The dictionary attempts no indication of pronunciation or grammatical classification, and its definitions are short. Its very first entry, however, shows that brevity can lead to logical and moral non-sequiturs of an inappropriate kind: 'TO ABANDON, is to leave or go away from: an *abandoned* man or woman means a *very wicked* man or woman.'

The Pestalozzian object lesson also developed vocabulary and expression generally. The following leisurely sequence is part of a lesson on a piece of glass:

1830	'*Teacher*	Is there any other glass in the room?
	Pupil	Yes. The windows.
	T. (closes shutters)	Can you see the garden now?
	P.	No.
	T.	Why cannot you?
	P.	We cannot see through the shutters.
	T.	What can you say then of glass?
	P.	We can see through it.
	T.	Can you tell me any word which will express this quality?
	P.	No.
	T.	['Transparent'] What do you understand about a substance from the word?
	P.	That you can see through it.' etc. (Mayo, p. 6)

From about 1830 the most frequent means of expanding a pupil's vocabulary was through the study of Greek, Latin and Germanic roots, often combined with exercises in the formation of sets of words from the same root, as in John Smith's *A Key to Reading*:

1830   'Q. What is a scribe?
          A. A writer.
          Q. How would you express to write *in* or *on*, as in a book or on a monument?
          A. To inscribe.
          Q. What noun have you from that verb?
          A. Inscription.
          Q. What would express to write *to*, in the sense of to attribute to, but using the same root?
          A. To ascribe.
          Q. Express to write *of*, or *concerning*.
          A. To describe.
          Q. The noun?
          A. Description.
          Q. Its adjective?
          A. Descriptive.
          Q. What is an animal called which is not described or classed in natural history?
          A. A nondescript.' And so on, through *indescribable, scripture*, etc.

                                                              (pp. 38–9)

Lists of roots had been common in grammars and spelling-books since the middle of the eighteenth century, and a growing interest in comparative and historical linguistics broadened their range and strength. Exercises in word formation, at an elementary level, became less mechanical. Thomas Arnold's is more sophisticated in its brevity than most:

1844 'Exercise 62. Without-aid (*aidless*). Sick-in-the-brain (*brain-sick*). What does *brain-sick* mean? (*disordered in mind*). Without brains (*brainless*). One-who-claims (a *claim-er* or *claim-ant*). Adverb and abstract substantive from *dainty* (*daintily, daintiness*).' (p. 70)

More representative of ordinary practice are Henry Young's exercises in 'verbal analysis . . . the reducing of words to their elementary significations (*need-less-ness*)'.

The attention given to Greek and Latin roots was extended to 'Saxon' or 'Anglo-Saxon' forms, with frequent reference to Horne Tooke. In 1815 Sutcliffe included in his grammar an appendix on derivations from Anglo-Saxon, and in his 1821 edition he added 'Specimens of changes induced on language': passages from Ulfilas, Wyclif and Caxton. William Graham's *Exercises on the Derivation of the English Language*, 1829, is meant to fill a gap between English and Latin: 'The greater proportion of those who attend an English School in a Provincial Academy, never attend the Classical Master . . . In many Latin Schools there is seldom a reference made to our own language.' Although Graham praises 'the light which has been struck out by Tooke and his followers, in the dim path of Gothic literature' he is sceptical about many of the derivations he provides, although they are 'given on learned authorities' (preface).

Etymology had by the 1820s ceased to carry its seventeenth- and eighteenth-century reference (in school grammars) to the classification and inflections of words; it now referred to their derivation and formal history. Henry Butter's *Etymological Spelling Book*, 1830, was constantly reissued and revised and school textbooks of etymology were published by William Graham, 1829 and 1836; Angus, 1840; Wilson, 1842; G. Manson, 1846. Allen and Cornwell claimed in 1841 that their grammar was perhaps the first schoolbook to teach the formation of Saxon derivatives, and William Barnes' school grammar of 1842 practically coincided with theirs. During the 1840s there appeared also the anonymous *Etymological Guide to the English Language*, and *The Little Linguist*, 1846, an elementary grammar, boldly called itself 'a complete guide to English philology'. 'Philology' was a term handled with respect. Mrs Thackwray added to the second edition of her grammar material 'from writers on philological subjects' and in 1858 William Farnell fears that 'hypercritical philologists' will find his grammar too perfunctory, C.P. Mason's grammar of 1858 included a section on etymology, as did many during the second half of the century: William Manneville, 1851; Eves, a. 1852; Hyde Clarke, 1853; Alexander Bain, 1863; William Nicholson, 1864.

There was nothing new in an interest in languages but it had seldom been expressed in schoolbooks before the 1820s. The popular manuals, derived from encyclopedias, kept the subject at what was by then an old-fashioned level:

1811c 'The language of savage nations is . . . very limited; they are able to call a few hundred things by their names: to express some qualities; and name a few modes of action; but they express more by gesture than by sound . . . The most ancient languages consisted of two or three hundred monosyllables . . . The first sounds used by savages, were mere cries of pleasure and pain . . . called INTERJECTIONS.' (Phillips, 1828 edn, s.v. *Grammar*)

Shepherd, Joyce and Carpenter include in their manual of 1815 a long chapter on language, and James Andrew's grammar of 1817 contains in tabular form information about the main features of twenty-eight languages (Hindostanee has sixty letters). Sutcliffe has already been cited; William Banks, 1823, adds to his speculations about the origin of language and writing twelve pages on the history of English; John Reid, in a note to his school grammar of 1829, recommends Horne Tooke, and Alexander Murray's *History of the European Languages*. The most abundant writer at the advanced school level is R.G. Latham, the first part of whose *The English Language*, 1841, is 'a historical and analytical view'. In 1849 he published the *History and Etymology of the English Language for the Use of Classical Schools*, and his *Handbook*, 1851, had a similar section on 'the history and analogy of the English language'. At a more popular school level G.R. Gleig wrote, about 1850, a whole textbook on the *History of the English Language*, and during the 1850s at least a dozen school grammars contained chapters on the history of the language. By the 1860s the historical study of English had been established in school for more than twenty years and there was nothing unusual in the appendix on 'pure English as understood from the history of the language' in Edward Higginson's grammar of 1864 or in the six pages of Anglo-Saxon paradigms included in Dalgleish's grammar of 1866. It was however a little unusual for the interest of schoolboys to be solicited by statements such as: 'The evidence that the *Abrenuntiatio Diaboli* is Westphalian is less conclusive than that conveyed by the names Frekkenhorst and Essen' (Latham, a. 1861, p. 16).

The previous chapter illustrated the emphasis given by examiners to the grammatical aspects of literature. Language, with which grammar was equated, was examined at an earlier period, and more fiercely, than was literature. The first London Matriculation paper in English was sat on 10 October 1839. There were five questions to be answered in three hours.

The first was a multiple question on the sounds of the vowels, the organic formation of consonants and the inconsistencies of English orthography. The second question asked merely: 'What is the probable origin of the indefinite and what of the definite article?' It is in the final question that the examiners become pressing, if not hectic:

'Define a Verb. Explain the origin of the form of the preterite tense in English, and point out accurately its signification, distinguishing it from the aorist.

Give the preterites and perfect participles of the following verbs . . .

Of what verbs are *sodden* and *fraught* the participles?

Mention Wallis's well-known rule for the use of *shall* and *will* in the different persons; and give a full explanation of the meanings of these verbs.

Is it correct to say "He says he shall go", "Do you suppose you shall go?"

Do the phrases, "He thought he should go" and "He thought he would go" mean the same thing?

Does the line of Byron, "I ought to do and did my best" appear to you to contain a solecism?

Would "I ought to have done" necessarily imply that I have *not* done?

Are such phrases as "The performing a promise" inaccurate and why?

What is the difference of meaning between "I intended to write" and "I intended to have written"? (Quoted by Stephen Potter, 1937, appendix)

It is obvious that questions such as this would influence the kind of teaching given in school and the kind of textbook written to support it. But it is not enough just to say that the examination influenced the schools. The schools influenced the examiners also. Both parties were responding to the powerful claims of philology for a leading place in the curriculum. Philology, at the school level, tended to reinforce the dry, overanalytical pedagogy from which, by the 1830s, the teaching of young children, at least, was just beginning to free itself.

Innovation and development

There are four main areas in which the teaching of linguistic control developed during the first three quarters of the nineteenth century: the use of functional criteria in describing the parts of speech; innovation in naming and grouping the parts of speech; giving pupils more initiative, through so-called 'inductive' methods; the analysis of sentences.

Syntactic criteria. Syntactic criteria for determining the parts of speech had been commonplace in Latin teaching since at least the early sixteenth century. The noun substantive, for example, had been distinguished from the noun adjective on the ground that it could stand alone, whereas the adjective needed some word like 'man' or 'thing' to accompany it. Syntactic criteria passed into the English grammars and were used regularly, but infrequently, throughout the seventeenth and eighteenth centuries.[15] It is to this criterion that Cobbett refers when he quotes 'grammarians' as teaching that if you can meaningfully put 'the good' before a word that word must be a noun. Cobbett rejects the criterion for the feeble reason that expressions like 'the good sobriety' make no sense. His own vague prescription is: 'You must employ your mind' (1818, Letter 3). W.G. Lewis, 1821, quotes Cobbett but prefers to use as a syntactic test the words 'I think of a . . .' put before the word under consideration (p. 8). Similarly Charles Lyon, 1832, defines a verb as 'a word before which the nominative cases of the pronouns may be used' (p. 35). B.H. Smart, 1831, uses the syntactic criterion in more general terms, applicable to any part of speech: 'It is not *what* a word signifies that determines it to be this or that part of speech, but *how it assists other words in making up the sentence*' (p. 39). But even that admirable sentiment could have odd applications. In his *Manual* of 1847 Smart uses practically the same words but immediately follows them with the statement that in '*He was taught geography*' the last word must be an adverb. Prudently he adds a note 'to prepare the teacher for modes of view otherwise likely to startle him hereafter' (p. 101).

Smart commends Lindley Murray for his occasional use of syntactic criteria: that a substantive can be known by being able to have an article in front of it. But he blames Murray for his more usual philosophical definitions, incomprehensible to children (p. 266n.). What was at issue was not so much whether definitions should be dependent on some conception of meaning, but whether the customary definitions of technical terms were of any help to children. Syntactic definitions, as well as the customary ones, used the concept of meaning: a substantive was 'able' to have an article in front of it only to the extent that the result was meaningful.

Many teachers in the middle of the nineteenth century, whatever kind of definitions they offered, relied on an exercise, developed during the previous century, known as 'supplying the ellipses' (above, p. 353). They applied it to the learning of the parts of speech. T.J. Wiseman, for example, requires the pupil to supply a verb for the blank in '*The Nile ——its banks at certain marked periods*' (1846, p. 58); W.D. Kenny requires adverbs in '*The —— he reads, the —— he studies*' (1858), p. 113); B.H. Smart requires prepositions in:

---

[15] *EGC*, pp. 289–92 *et passim*.

1847 'The older our habits, the greater the difficulty —— changing them. We find little difficulty —— changing new habits . . . But every day fastens a habit more strongly —— us, and renders us less capable —— not complying —— our inclinations, whether good or bad.'   (p. 51)

When badly framed, the exercise merely encouraged glibness and cliché, but when linked with a demonstration of the function of a given part of speech it was an improvement on the so-called philosophical definitions. Elliptical exercises of this kind are used by William Manneville, 1851; Seacome Ellison, 1854; J.C. Curtis, 1867 and J.S. Laurie, 1868; and in America by James Brown, 1836, and R.G. Parker, 1839. An interesting instance occurs in Mrs Marcet's *Mary's Grammar*, 1835. In the earlier part of the book Mrs Marcet, in the person of Mary's mother, had met the usual difficulties when she began her discussion of the preposition with the standard definition: 'Prepositions serve to connect nouns together, and to show the relation between them.' Then, however, she puts a book on the table, a stool under it, and elicits from Mary the appropriate words to express the spatial relationships between book, table and stool (Lesson 13). When it comes to parsing mother sets a sentence containing a blank: '*Put the doll —— her bed*', and asks Mary not to provide a word that might fill the blank but to say what part of speech any word would be that could fill it (Lesson 16). This is a subtler method than the usual one.

The reforms of James Brown of Philadelphia started from a similar view of the parts of speech: that they should be classified not by meaning but by their position in the structure of the sentence. Meaning is an unreliable guide:

'Even the *constitution* of the *United States* cannot be understood by two impartial statesmen in the *same* way . . . The *British grammarians* have attempted what can never be accomplished; namely a consistent classification of words upon their *significations* . . . The proper course in forming a system of grammar , . . is to divide the words of a sentence, not according to their dictionary signification, but according to their constructive principles.'   (1836, pp. xvi, xxv)

Brown effectively retains, under new names, the substantive and the verb; his five other parts of speech express various forms of syntactical relationship, obscurely described. He tried to found his grammar on 'constructive principles' but his authentic perceptions, and his hope that reform could begin in the primary school (1836, p. xviii), were drowned in whirlpools of overelaboration: new terms, inadequately explained, some-times for familiar categories, sometimes for new ones inadequately thought through. He tries to defend his self-indulgence in the invention of technical terms, but his ideas are merely obscured by calling language 'phrenod' and a sentence 'gnomod'. Few readers would have had confidence, when they reached it, that the 'steronepoecormeclade' would give more help in understanding the structure of 'I went *from* him *to* them', which illustrates it, than they could get from an ordinary textbook. But underneath the nonsense there lies what could have been the foundation of a useful approach to teaching elementary grammar. In his *An English Syntascope* Brown develops a scarcely coherent system of symbolising the structure of a sentence. The system is taught by means of an apparatus, the syntascope, of his invention. In describing the system he discusses also the parts of speech. He sees that what they are, and how many they are, depend on the basis of classification. Although many bases are possible 'there is but one which is *sound*; there is but one which is *calculated* to give you the true *constructive principles* of your language: that one is . . . the *construction* of the language' (1839, p. 66). This self-evident statement is not as impressive as Brown would have liked us to find it, but the point he is trying to make was, and remains, important.

Naming and grouping the parts of speech. During the nineteenth century, as during the two preceding centuries, teachers and linguists tried to improve the classification of the parts of speech: usually by moving the traditional categories into a fresh grouping, occasionally by trying to establish an entirely new set of categories. In about twenty grammars the authors merely tinker with the status of the article, the participle and the interjection. The participle is usually included within the verb, sometimes within the adjective; the article is included within the adjective, the noun or the pronoun or, like the interjection, is denied any status.

Some teachers were dissatisfied not so much with the categories as with their names. John Sherman, 1826, in America, who wished his grammar to be 'wholly divested of scholastic rubbish', called the verb 'assertor', the interjection 'ejaculation', and the adverb 'appendant'. In England J.B. Davidson and others used 'forname' for the pronoun, 'describing word' for the adjective, and 'connecting word' for the conjunction. William Manneville used the well-established 'adnoun' for adjective and the innovatory 'prenoun' for article, while William Barnes, 1842, returned to an older tradition by using 'Saxon' terms: 'name-word', 'deed-word', 'mode-word' and 'bindword'. James Brown's attempt at a radical terminology is described above. Less enterprising was the British author of *Universal Grammar Illustrated*, 1835, who was writing only for teachers and 'their properly prepared' pupils. He introduces, specially for English, a new category called the 'plusortal' ('many sorts'), which seems closely to resemble the adverb but to be different from his 'particle', which seems closely to resemble the preposition.

Nearly all teachers who advocated reform of the parts of speech thought that their number should be reduced. If one part could, apparently, 'be' another part, the distinction between them must be unreal and could be abolished. Only one nineteenth-century teacher seems to have followed the opposite course: to reduce the number of overlapping categories by making the overlaps into separate categories. Christopher Earnshaw, 1817, takes a small step in this direction by adding to the ten parts of system 9 (above, p. 346) the auxiliary verb and the relative pronoun as parts in their own right. Amongst those who wish to reduce the number of parts the influence of Horne Tooke is naturally strong. Henry Rogers, 1838, lecturing to students at University College, London, maintained that a knowledge of one's own language and skill in composition both depended on 'an inductive process' strengthened by direct instruction. He fully accepted Tooke's view that only noun and verb are necessary parts of speech (Lecture 2). Those who followed Tooke were nevertheless usually obliged to subdivide their primary categories. John Kigan, 1823, divided his primary category of noun into four, and his verb into six: 'The classes of our primary words are founded upon the nature of the things which they respectively represent ... The classes of our secondary words, are founded on the uses which we make of them' (pp. 81–2).

A more frequent grouping into three parts of speech is put forward by seven nineteenth-century writers. The most common classification is into noun, verb and particle, which in various forms goes back to Gill, 1619, and several eighteenth-century grammarians.[16] It is used by Dominique St Quentin, 1812; David Booth, 1837; Hyde Clark, 1853; by the author of *Manual of the Analysis of Language*, 1856, and by the author of *Observations on Grammar*, 1824, written for Leeds Grammar school, who uses 'adverb' instead of 'particle'. A similar system of 'noun', 'relative word' and 'sign' is put forward by D.W. Elmore, 1830, in the USA but it is described too briefly to be convincing. Relative words 'relate to other words' and include adjective, verb and adverb; signs include the verb 'be', prepositions and conjunctions. Hugh Doherty in England, 1841, also provides a thinly described classification into 'nouns' (including some pronouns and some parts of verbs), 'adnouns' (including inflected forms of verbs and everything that modifies a noun) and 'subadnouns' (adverbs, prepositions,

---

[16] *EGC*, Systems 22, 42, 46, 48.

conjunctions). J.B. Thompson, writing for beginners, gives a basic classification into 'entities' (nouns) and 'existences' (verbs), but he feels so strongly about the particular absurdity of 'disjunctive conjunctions' that he makes two further categories: 'disjunctions' and 'conjunctions'.

Most of these writers were teachers, trying to make better sense of what their pupils were required to learn. Some, like A. Scott, 1820, made no attempt at innovation but nevertheless modified their teaching in response to current ideas about language. Scott keeps to a conventional nine-fold system, because it is useful; but he quotes with approval the relativistic view that the parts of speech are derived not from differences in things but from our ways of regarding things (p. 53). That the innovators failed because they were asking the wrong questions is not important to us, who are still not sure what are the right questions. That they tried is important, because they preserved, in however small a way, the principle that things should not be left unquestioned merely because they are very old or very difficult.

Pupil's initiative and 'inductive' methods. Closely related to the use of syntactic criteria was an innovation, particularly among American teachers, that relied on what was called, with various differences of meaning, 'induction'.

John Sherman, 1826, of Trenton Falls, N.Y., aimed to work 'upon principles of inductive investigation . . . and be guided . . . solely by *established facts*'. He attacked the conservatism of Lindley Murray: 'I thank God that I live in a country whose forefathers were driven to a wilderness, because they were *innovators*' (preface). In its simplest form the inductive method was another restatement of the view, which teachers have always found it difficult to act on, that we understand an explanation of a thing more easily if we have first met, and examined in our own way, instances of the thing itself. Alexander Reid, for example, in his grammar of 1837, deliberately provides no exercises on the rules of syntax: he wants his pupils to find for themselves, in their daily reading, examples to illustrate the application of a given rule. When John Wood, in Edinburgh, commended an 'inductive' approach to grammar he meant that definitions of the parts of speech should not be given until the pupils had collected from their reading words that seemed to have something in common (1828, chap. 17). Similarly B.H. Smart:

1831 'In an elementary grammar, no definition, and no *part* of a definition, should be brought forward, till absolutely required by the examples that are immediately to follow it. In teaching a child, it is the greatest absurdity in the world to set out with *general* principles, when the business is, to reach those principles by the examination of particulars.'   (p. 42n.)

Smart would have been more consistent with the principle expressed in his second sentence if he had said in his first sentence that the examples should precede, not follow, the formulation of the definition. But his 'absolutely required' implies an empirical process of some kind. Other British teachers were making the same point at this time. Henry Rogers, in a lecture in 1837, taught that both grammar and composition depend on 'an inductive process' (1838, p. 19) and Allen and Cornwell claimed for their widely used grammars: 'The Rules or Definitions are in all cases inductions from given examples . . . The whole course is, strictly, one of Induction and systematic Progression' (a. 1846, preface). Their method, however, was not one of strict induction. It was circular, in a way that they no doubt felt to be necessary at an elementary level. The material out of which the pupil was to build up inductively and 'discover' the category had been processed in such a way that the logical work had been done before he met the exercise. All the pupil had to do was to acknowledge, not discover, similarities. In their own illustration the examples are preceded by the name of the category to be discovered, and the relevant words are already drawn to the pupil's attention. Their method is that described by Smart, with its limitations:

a. 1846 'Verbs. EXAMPLES. The boy *strikes* the dog. The dog *barks*. The child *sings* a song. The cat *runs*. The bird *flies*. EXPLANATION. These words, *strikes, barks, sings* . . . are called Verbs. They are all words which mean *doing* something . . . A Verb is a word which denotes BEING or DOING.' (1855 edn, p. 13)

Henry Butter's attack on excessive memorisation, in his *Inductive Grammar*, 1843, has already been quoted (above, pp. 348–9). His remedy, which he calls induction, seems to be vitiated by a double misunderstanding. The method will 'induce [the pupil] to make his own deductions . . . from the nature of the language' (preface). If Butter was unclear about the difference between induction and deduction, and believed that an inductive method was one that persuaded the pupil to learn, it is not surprising that what his pupils do is much what they had always done. He goes on to explain to the teachers that the pupils should read the textbook explanation of the noun, and then find the nouns in the accompanying sentences. William Martin, 1852, is no more successful. Although he refers in his preface to 'the application of those *Rules of Grammar* which the pupil has been taught to discover for himself' there is little sign in his text of such a process. Much more practical is R. Robinson, 1863, whose manual abounds in common sense. He insists, like others before him, that the names of the parts of speech must not be introduced until their functions have been met and understood (p. 269).

In American texts there is greater emphasis on an inductive method, but no greater agreement than in Britain about how best it should be used. The feeling common to all its advocates was that children should so far as possible make their own inferences from facts that they had encountered in as natural a way as possible; the teacher should build on the child's reasoning power rather than on his memory. Richard W. Green sums up his views in the statement, 'The pupil is compelled *to make his own grammar*', but his first illustration of the questioning that he regards as the essence of induction shows how far he is from any real discovery method:

1829 '*Teacher* (holding up a book)   What do you see?
    Pupil   A book.
    T.   Is that the name of it?'   (p. 13)

Dyer H. Sanborn, 1836, whose grammar is described as 'embracing the inductive and productive methods of teaching', seems, like Henry Butter, to take the term to mean inducing children to work, or perhaps introducing work to them. His first forty lessons dealing with the parts of speech are 'preceded by explanations written in the lecture, talking style . . . by way of Induction' (preface). Bradford Frazee claims that inductive methods are in harmony with the teaching of Pestalozzi. The common method of teaching, says Frazee, is 'more like that of teaching birds to talk or sing, than that of teaching reasoning beings'. In the teaching of composition the teacher should not follow 'the beaten track of *thinking for the pupil* by furnishing him with lists of words and broken sentences'; the pupil should be '*taught how to think* for himself, to write his own lists of words and broken sentences' (1844, preface). Frazee is giving his pupils more initiative, but there is nothing specially inductive about his method. His recognition of children's reasoning power is not carried through in any way more specific than that followed at that time by any other good teacher.

It would seem, though further evidence is needed, that in both America and Britain the term 'inductive' was irrelevant and misleading, because it was often misunderstood. Even its critics failed to see what was important. Smith B. Goodenow, principal of a New England high school, wrote in 1839 that 'induction' was only a 'plastering up' of the errors of Lindley Murray. But it was more than that. It was a signal that teachers wanted children to draw more of their learning from their own experience, and to express it (to a limited extent, no doubt) in their own words. As the Glasgow teacher Alexander D'Orsey put it, the teaching of grammar fails because 'theoretical explanations are deemed sufficient, without the practical employment of the pupil's tongue and pen' (1842, Part 2, preface). Goodenow is himself criticised, along with others, by John Goldsbury, also in America: 'The present age is distinguished, above all others, for its different theories of English grammar . . . No theory of English grammar, essentially or fundamentally different from that of [Lindley] Murray, can be safely adopted.' But Goldsbury does not regard himself as particularly conservative. He thinks that he holds a middle position: 'Taking the *language* as it is, and the *Murray system* as it is, he would endeavour to interpret the former by the latter' (1846, preface).

Others in America and in Britain, while still 'taking the language as it is', tried to shift the teachers' attention away from the details of grammar towards the linguistic and psychological processes behind expression. Samuel S. Greene, superintendent of public schools in Providence, puts the theory more successfully in his preface than it is illustrated in his grammar:

1854 'In the presentation of a subject like that of English Grammar, the first question which naturally arises, is that of the point of view from which it shall be examined. Shall the forms of language be regarded as direct results from thought . . . Or shall they be looked upon as possessing in themselves, regardless of their origin, all that is necessary to guide a successful investigation?'

Greene rejects any form of grammar that is merely seeking 'to know what a word or expression is from its external aspect – its termination, position'. The writer's task, 'an idea being given . . . is, to find as well an appropriate expression as to decide upon the nature and classification of the latter' (preface). It was this point of view that linked the teaching of grammar to the elementary teaching of composition. At first the link had been mostly through exercises in the correction of error. John Davis' book of exercises on Murray, 1830, includes 8000 words of text in which punctuation is to be corrected. These are followed by narrative outlines and the procedure described in the previous chapter. M. Rice's *An Initiatory Step to English Composition*, 1835, is virtually a grammar: it assumes that expression is the converse of analysis and is trained by it, and G.F. Graham's *Helps to English Grammar*, 1843, provides sentence patterns (subject: verb: adverb of time: verb: adverb of manner) for which the pupil has to provide appropriate sentences ('The water now boils furiously') (pp. 78f.). More stiffly, Samuel S. Greene wants the teacher to build up on the blackboard, from the pupils' suggestions, sentences such as: 'Lamb —— the lamb —— the lamb ran —— the young lamb ran —— the young lamb ran quickly' (1854, p. 111). Jacob Lowres, whose *Companion to English Grammar*, 1862, is also a 'guide to composition', puts the familiar exercise of varying sentences onto a grammatical basis and designs them specifically in the control of the relative pronoun, in the use of a participle instead of a conjunction, or in the use of the passive (pp. 47f).

Talk about induction was only one sign of a wider tendency. Both British and American textbooks in the middle of the century show that some teachers were beginning to trust a little more in the linguistic ability of children – to believe that children naturally have such ability. The belief is expressed in those grammars where the pupils are led to see (if not to 'discover') the functions of the parts of speech for themselves, rather than by learning to apply a definition; and in those composition exercises that allow the pupils some initiative – not much perhaps, but more than they had previously been expected to possess.

The analysis of sentences. Parsing, primarily a form of classification, also took account of relationships between words (qualifying, governing) and thus resembled the analysis of a sentence into its parts. Because no distinction was regularly made between expressions which contained a finite verb and those which did not (both being called clauses) sentence analysis, although mainly concerned with the relations between phrases forming the subject and predicate of simple sentences, also took account of the relations between the sentences that formed part of a complex expression. It was only after 1870 that this last procedure came to be separately designated 'clause analysis'.

Throughout the nineteenth century the simplest form of sentence analysis continued to be the division into subject and predicate. The subject of a sentence was still occasionally called the 'agent' (Pullen, 1820) or the 'actor' (Oliver, 1825) and for a long time the terms varied with the writer. 'Predicate' could mean 'an Adjective or Participle agreeing with . . . the Nominative' (Andrew, 1817); it often designated only the finite verb, even when it was followed by further expressions, as in 'Birds *build* nests' (Lowres, 1862). The verb was still sometimes called the 'attribute' (Hiley, 1832; Bobbit, 1833) but the eighteenth-century term 'affirmation' had disappeared. There was much variation in the treatment of what followed the verb. In the sentence just quoted 'nests' could be called the 'object'; or 'the case after the verb' (Goold Brown, 1850); or the 'modification of the predicate' (Hallock, USA, 1842). Pullen calls it the 'action' and defines it as 'an OBJECT or SUBJECT on which the agent operates'. After the mid-century, a frequent practice was to confine the term 'object' to what follows a transitive verb. What follows an intransitive verb was called the 'completion' (Graham, 1862; Armstrong, 1868b) or the 'complement' (Dalgleish, 1866). Subject, object and completion could each be accompanied by 'dependent or qualifying words' (Crabb, 1808); by 'attributes' (Currey, 1856); or by 'adjuncts' (Allen, 1813; Nicholson, 1864). The verb too could have adjuncts, but more usually, and increasingly in the latter half of the century, these were called 'extensions' (Mongan, 1864), less frequently 'enlargements' (Higginson, 1864; Armstrong, 1868).

The close connection between parsing and analysis is more clearly seen in the grammar by Edward J. Hallock, of Vermont, than in the British grammars, although several of them come near to his word-by-word analysis. Hallock, it should be noted, names no part of speech. He analyses the sentence: '*The poor mariner contemplated the horrors of his situation with a look of absolute despair.*'

1842	'*Mariner*	subject
	the, poor	modifications of the subject
	contemplated	predicate
	horrors, with, look	modifications of the predicate
	the, of situation	modifications of *horrors*
	a, of despair	modifications of *look*
	his	modification of *situation*
	absolute	modification of *despair*' (p. 142)

During the first part of the nineteenth century the practice is continued whereby sentences are analysed without using the idea of subordination. George Crabb, 1808, describes eight ways in which sentences 'may ... be so amplified or extended by each other, as to become periods, as several agents and actions ... may be connected together, so as to form one whole' (p. 168). The eight types of sentence are named according to the function of their connectives: conditional; disjunctive; causal; consecutive, etc. He supports this analytical approach with a synthetic one:

1808 '*Preceptor* Give me a plain simple sentence, Henry about boys learning lessons.

Hen. "Boys learn lessons".

Pre. Now amplify this sentence by attaching some good quality to the boys.

Hen. "Good boys learn lessons".

Pre. Now attach some word to the verb to express their manner of learning.

Hen. "Good boys always learn lessons".

Pre. Now annex some word to the object to indicate whose lessons they learn.

Hen. "Good boys always learn their lessons".

Pre. Now make this a complex sentence, by speaking of the lessons which are set to good boys.

Hen. (Silent)

Pre. "Good boys always learn the lessons, which are set them". Can you give me a conditional sentence, George, about contentment and happiness?

Geo. (Silent)

Pre. "If a person be contented, he will be happy". Give me the same sentence in a negative form, with the conjunction.

Geo. "Unless a person be contented, he will not be happy".' (pp. 186–7)

A. Hope, 1806, defines a compound sentence as consisting of 'two or more simple sentences, connected by conjunctions, or relatives, or both'. The term 'complex' is seldom used in this connection; when it is, it still carries no implication of subordination: 'When the members of a compound sentence are complex they are subdivided into clauses' (William Allen, 1813, edn of 1824). Similarly Mary Ann Tuckey, 1829: '*The ox knoweth his owner —— and the ass his master's crib; but Israel doth not know —— my people doth not consider.* This complex sentence has two members, each of which contains two clauses' (p. 66).

M. Rice provides 'exercises in analysis' in which his pupils have to divide sentences into appropriate units, and designate them. One of his examples, divided but not designated, shows that an embedded sentence is not given a distinctive status:

1835 'A taste —— for useful knowledge —— will provide —— for us —— a great and noble entertainment —— when other entertainments leave us.'   (p. 103)

Analysis into subordinate clauses (adjectival, substantival, adverbial) became such a grotesquely elaborated and dominant exercise that it is reassuring to remember that these teachers, and others such as Alexander D'Orsey and Ernest Adams, managed without it. What came to be the standard form of clause analysis was said at the time (Tilleard, 1855, p. 3; Dalgleish, 1865, preface) to have been introduced into England in 1852 by J.D. Morell from Carl Ferdinand Becker's *Deutsche Grammatik*, 1829, translated into English in 1830. Morell's grammar of 1852 was very influential but it was not the first to draw explicitly on Becker. In 1847 J.H. James had published *Elements of Grammar, according to Dr Becker's System*, and there are signs of Becker's terminology in Allen and Cornwell, 1841. Becker's system seemed then more of a novelty than it now appears to have been. Bain refers to it in 1863 as the 'recently introduced system of the Analysis of Sentences', but all the elements of the system can be seen in earlier English grammars. The distinction of the system lay in its tight conception of subordination, in the special status it gave to the presence of a finite verb in a clause, and in its strict limitation to three types of clause. By 1858 Morell's system had been subjected to the analytical fervour of C.P. Mason and his followers, fully developed only after 1870, and most teachers and examiners seem to have welcomed what they thought was an intellectual discipline (for older pupils at least) that gave added importance to the study of grammar. The tightness and dryness of the system were apparent. Matthew Arnold commented, 'It can hardly have been by the deliberate judgment of men of sagacity that that meritorious work, *Morell's*

Analysis of Sentences, was made the intellectual food of girls of sixteen.'[17] Hugh Doherty went so far as to say that many of the difficulties of grammar were cherished by teachers out of self-interest, and that this self-interest was an expression of a disturbed society:

1841 'The principles of language are, at best, a very dry study; but the confused methods of metaphysical grammarians have rendered it eminently repulsive to the young mind, and unfortunately, the private interests of school-masters induce them to perpetuate those difficulties which render their assistance absolutely necessary. This is a natural consequence of *incoherence* in social organization, which aggravates all the miseries of poverty and ignorance.' (preface)

There was nothing new in the grammarians' restrictive use of the term 'grammar', but such a conception of the subject has always been an obstacle to the teaching of linguistic control. The better part of the grammatical tradition shows when John Hunter, for instance, in his 1848 preface calls grammar 'a gymnasium of the mind', and when Thring wrote in 1852, 'Grammar will be found the readiest way to lead even the most uneducated to intelligent thought.' Such teachers were thinking not of nail-biting analytical niceties but of English grammar in the broadest sense, which the best of its teachers had always tried to hold on to: the study of how one's own language works.

[17] 'The Twice-Revised code', in *Fraser's Magazine*, 1862, p. 237; reprinted in R.H. Super, *Matthew Arnold: democratic education*, Ann Arbor, 1962.

CHAPTER EIGHT

English: the development of a subject

The term 'English'

One of the purposes of this enquiry was to examine the often made statement that there was little or no teaching of English before the final decades of the nineteenth century. When was English first taught? The preceding chapters provide the materials for an answer, but they show also that the question should be expressed differently, and that it is necessary to consider the term 'English' itself: a more ambiguous one than might be expected.

Francis Clement was quoted above (p. 5) as addressing 'the English teacher' in 1587. Although he was writing for teachers of reading and spelling, the expression he uses sounds as if he thought that there was a subject called 'English', however narrow in scope. It is reasonable, and probably accurate, to interpret him in this way; but there is a slight doubt. It is possible that what Clement thought of his readers as teaching was not a subject, but a language: English, not Latin. He may have been using 'English teacher' in the sense of Coote's 'Schoolmaisters of the English Tongue' (1596, A2). But such doubts are overrefined. Neither Clement nor Coote was concerned with English as contrasted with, or analogous to, any other language. They were, and were writing for, in Mulcaster's words, 'such people as teach children to read and write English' (1582, p. 53). At this date basic facility in the *language* was the *subject*.

The expression 'English schoolmaster' was, or formed part of, the title of several seventeenth-century elementary books: Robert Edwardes, 1591; Edmund Coote, 1596; Elisha Coles, 1674; John Hawkins, 1692; James Porterfield, 1695; T. Lydal, 1701. It is also used, referring to people, by Samuel Hartlib, 1646 (Webster, 1970, p. 114); John Newton, 1671b, preface; in *Hortus anglicanus*, 1683 (t.p.). Such people are also called 'teachers of English' by Richard Hodges, 1644 (sig. o4b); Charles Hoole, 1660 (*The Usher's Duty*, p. 1); John Newton, c. 1669 (preface) and 1671a; Richard Browne, 1700 ('our English teachers . . . are too illiterate to adapt things proper, out of a running and continued method': preface). Equivalent descriptions are '[those] who undertake the teaching of English'

(Brooksbank, 1654a, p. 10); 'instructors of Youth, in the English tongue' (Osborn, 1688, preface); 'those who pretend to teach English' (Browne, 1692, preface); 'the School-masters of the English Tongue' (Aickin, 1693, preface); and Christopher Cooper's *The English Teacher*, 1687. In this last case 'teacher' (like 'tutor' in many other book titles) means both the person who teaches and the manual that can take his place.

There are many references to teachers being licensed 'to teach English': David Palmer at Watford in 1607 (O'Day, 1973, p. 121); John Shuttle 'to be the English Schoolmaster at Albany' in 1665 (Sol Cohen, 1974, 1, 353); twenty-two masters subscribed for English in the diocese of Lichfield and Coventry between 1690 and 1699 (Alan Smith, 1975, p. 10); William Wheelwright, 'English master licensed to teach children in the English language' in 1693 (*ibid.*) and Edward Clark 'to teach an English School' in 1696, and three others in 1698 (Alan Smith, 1976, pp. 124–6).

The English teacher implied the 'English Scholar', and this term is regularly used in seventeenth-century titles or prefaces: Evans, 1621; Edward Young, 1675; *The Compendius Schoolmaster*, 1688; *Thesaurium*, 1689.

The term 'English school' was applied first to schools for reading and spelling: English in the narrowest sense. In Ireland it implied that teaching was to be predominantly in English, not Irish, and O'Raifearteaigh (1950, p. 130) quotes from an Act of 1537 that enjoined the priest to swear, 'I will teach or cause to be taught an English school.' In England the term carried, in addition to its earliest use for a reading (and therefore elementary) school, a slightly later use for a school in which Latin was not taught but other subjects might be learnt well beyond an elementary level. In 1627 Exeter Grammar School was refounded with a Latin school and an English school, in separate buildings (F. Watson, 1909, p. 535) and Rosemary O'Day (1982, p. 63) cites Chigwell, Lewisham, Repton and others as 'co-existing English and Latin schools'. Alan Smith (1975), describing the endowment of schools in a single diocese during a period of forty years, notes English schools at Newport, Salop, in 1660; Birmingham, 1676; Lichfield, 1677. But, as so often, it is difficult to know just at what level such schools taught.

Although Benjamin Martin says 'An English Grammar School, is a Thing unheard of in our Nation' (1754, preface) the term was used in the same year by Daniel Farro, speculatively, in the apparently backhanded remark that his grammar 'contains a Method so easy, that every *Female Teacher* in the *British* Dominions may open an *English* Grammar School, and render themselves much more useful to the Public' (1754, p. vii). There does seem to have been an 'English Grammar School' in Grafton Street,

Dublin, run by Samuel Whyte and advertised in the 1763 edition of James Burgh's *The Art of Speaking*.

James Buchanan, however, agrees with Martin, complaining in 1767: 'We have Latin Grammar Schools in most incorporate Towns; but we have not a professed English Grammar School in all Britain . . . There ought to be a Master for the English Language, in each of those eminent Seminaries of Westminster, Eaton, &c.' With his own school in mind, no doubt, he continued: 'I would not do Justice, if I did not say that the English Language, to my Knowledge, is taught with care and Propriety in several of our eminent Boarding Schools' (preface, p. xxiv). Such a school, perhaps, was that of John V. Button of Lewes, Sussex, who advertised in 1791 that he was opening 'an English grammar school', but in 1805 he described himself as of 'the classical and commercial academy', a description that his public would understand more clearly. The expression 'English grammar school' occurs also in the anonymous *A Paraphrase on the Rev. Dr Watts's celebrated Distich on the Study of Languages*. The British Library copy lacks a title-page: we are told only that the eighty lines of verse are 'addressed to the young gentlemen of the English Grammar School. By one of their school-fellows'. The English grammar school, so far as it existed under that name, seems to have been just an English School offering advanced teaching, or advanced pretensions. In 1821 an English Classical School was planned for Boston, Mass., where there was also an English High School in 1830, and an English High School was planned for Salem in 1826 (Butler, 1969, pp. 288, 291, 295).

George Snell, in *The Right Teaching of Useful Knowledge*, 1649, drew up a plan for a school in which it would be possible for a student, through English alone, to equip himself for a career in the same way as Romans did who knew Latin but not Greek. Snell's first chapter is headed 'The Teacher of the English School. Preparing Learners how to live well in their future vocation'. The school is to cater for pupils at four levels of achievement: those who are to remain illiterate; those who can use only English; those who learn other languages; those who are going to teach. It is not certain from Snell's references to English whether he would wish any literature to be read in school, but it seems unlikely. His attitude to rhetoric, and to education generally, is utilitarian: the 'reading of Histories onely for delight . . . is a prodigal consumption of precious time' (p. 257).

During the first half of the eighteenth century the terms 'English School' and 'English teacher', with its equivalents, were in regular use in Britain and in America. Edward Mills, master of the writing-school in Queen Street, Boston, petitioned the justices in 1727 that because he had previously been assessed as a 'grammar Schoolmaster', and thus exempt from public taxes, he should continue to be exempt now that he was assessed as 'an English master'. He hoped 'that Yr Honrs (who are good Judges) will allow that the knowledge of Grammar is very requisite if not absolutely necessary to Compleat an English mastr as well for Instruction to spell . . . as to write good English'. His petition was granted (Nash, 1959, p. 9). 'Teaching English' is by now something that many teachers do, and they have views about how it should be done. John White, 1701, writes of the 'method of teaching English' (preface); John Warden, 1753, of an 'irregular way of teaching English' (preface) and Masson, 1761, of 'the art of teaching English' (a. 1757; 1761 edn, dedication). In 1718 Archibald Keith received from the Edinburgh Town Council an annual payment in respect of his 'singularity in teaching of English' (Law, 1965, p. 34). John Urmston, in the preface to his Latin grammar, *A New Help to the Accidence*, 1710, regrets that 'the Teachers of our Free-Schools affect being thought Grand Schollards, above teaching *English*, which alone would be Business enough, and do more Service than many of them do by teaching Latin', and he goes on to tell how the bookseller to whom he took his plan for a work called *The Petty-School* was 'willing to print only that Part which had Relation to Teaching English'.

It is difficult to tell from such references how far 'English' refers just to the teaching of reading and how far to a subject more broadly conceived. John Collyer, of Nottingham, seems to be referring to a subject, not just to reading. He is discussing 'the discouragement the English Tongue labours under' and 'the low methods of Education, practised in our common English Schools'. He complains that English is seldom taught beyond the level of achieving literacy;

1735 'The Business of laying the Foundation . . . usually falls into unskilful hands, the effect of which is, the far greatest Part among us are, as it were, tied down to make no greater proficiency than just learning to read, for no farther advances being to be made in private Schools, and English being seldom or never taught in our free Schools, tho' some of them have two or three Masters, where should they have it?' (preface)

The fluidity of the terms shows in the *Charges and orders for the several Officers of Christ's Hospital*, where 'the Charge of the Master of the Reading School in London' includes the teaching of English grammar:

1797 'You shall enter into your School immediately after Seven o'Clock every Morning from the First of *March* to the first of *November* . . . You shall instruct such of the Children of this House as shall be committed to your Care, in spelling and reading *English*, and in the Knowledge of *English* Grammar; and bring such of them

forward in Writing and the four first rules of Arithmetic, as you may . . . think
capable of improvement.'   (p. 75)

John Warden in 1737, and his son of the same name in 1753, called
themselves 'Teachers of English' on the title-pages of their books, as did
John Drummond in 1767. In 1768 W.R. is recommending that English
should be studied at universities, where there should be well-endowed
professorships (*Oxford Magazine*, No. 1, p. 34), and in July 1781 'Mr
Stalker, the English master' dined with Boswell and his wife.[1] A few years
later James Hall, 'Teacher of the English Language, Cupar, Fife',
complained, like many before and after him, that English is neglected in
school:

> *1789* 'Do we not every day meet with scholars, who, after having finished an
> English course of instruction, can neither spell, pronounce, read, speak, nor write
> their own language, without violating either its orthography, orthoepy, principles
> of expression, or grammatical construction? In most country towns the teacher of
> Latin is caressed beyond measure, and English is only taught as being subservient to
> the *important* end of acquiring a smattering in the Latin tongue. Hence the teaching
> of English becomes the province of old women, or illiterate mechanics, in desperate
> circumstances, who fly to that, as to the last resource.'   (preface)

This exaggerated description must be balanced by the fact that in the year
in which it was written there were published William Sewell's thoughtful,
if conservative, English grammar; Noah Webster's *Dissertations*; and
school anthologies by Cresswick, John Adams and John Walker. Nevertheless the standard of teaching was generally considered low, as by Peter
Walkden Fogg in his 1796 preface, and by others.

The term 'English education' would apply, one would suppose, to what
was provided in an English School, but this is not entirely the case. 'English
education' referred usually to a vocational, and sometimes to an academic,
curriculum more advanced than that offered in most English Schools. The
term was given currency by Gildon, in the second edition, 1712, of his
grammar published the previous year, and the essay in which it occurred,
'Reasons for an English Education', may have been prompted or written by
the shadowy John Brightland. The idea of such an education dates from
before 1712: it is part of many seventeenth-century reforming tendencies,
economic and political, which sought to free from the burden of Latin those
who aimed at careers for which a university education was unnecessary or
unattainable. Robert Ainsworth in 1698 described, for 'Gentlemen,
Tradesmen, and all Persons, who do not design their Children for

---

[1] J.W. Reed and F.A. Pottle, *Boswell, Laird of Auchinleck*, 1977.

Scholars', an ideal curriculum comprising penmanship; reading 'the best English writers'; composition; accounts; mathematics; some rudiments of arts and science; 'Carriage and Comportment with a Dancing-Master'; and polished conversation (p. 30). Ainsworth's attitude is similar to Locke's, and his plans are designed for pupils of the same social level. Gildon is more academic. His 'English education' comprises grammar, rhetoric, poetry and logic, and would allow a limited place for Latin. He recognises also the 'meanness' of women's education, which contains nothing for the mind, and it is probably to him that Elizabeth Elstob refers in 1715 when she says that '*Grammarians . . . who have taken upon them to teach our Ladies and young Gentlemen, The whole system of an English Education*' should have been better informed about the history of their own language (p. iv). By 1760 John Ash is saying 'The Importance of an *English Education* is now pretty well understood . . . not only for Ladies, but for young Gentlemen designed merely for Trade' (preface). These two themes, trade and the education of women, remain central to all proposals for an English education, especially in the works of James Buchanan (e.g. the preface to his *A Regular English Syntax*, 1767). From the middle of the eighteenth century there are frequent references to the importance of geography, and the notion is being born that English, geography and history are naturally related to each other in some way that justified their being grouped together, in the twentieth century, as 'the English subjects'. John Jones, before 1740, accompanied the grammar in his *A Step towards an English Education* with 'two Essays on the Excellency of Geography', and Thomas Ewing, [1815?], and William Stewart, in 1849, both advertise themselves as teachers 'of English, Geography and History'. Samuel Edwards, 1765, regards English grammar as 'the Foundation . . . of an *English* Education', to which he would add: penmanship, accounts, literature (including the newspapers) and as much geography, chronology, history and 'natural philosophy' as there is time for (Introduction).

The expression 'an English education' was applied widely until the end of our period. The idea and its practice need investigation, and a starting-point might be the interesting comment, as yet unpublished, by Jonathan Barry, that in Bristol, at least, 'the most significant social divide was not between classical and English education, but between different kinds of English education' (private communication).

By 1813 at least a section of a school could be known as 'the English Department'. At that date James Sheridan Knowles was appointed 'headmaster' of such a department in the Belfast Academical Institution. He declined the post in favour of his father, James Knowles, who was dismissed from it in 1817 (James Knowles, 1829, preface; *DNB*). The school in East Hartford, Conn., run by Theodore L. Wright in 1834 had an 'English department' (Butler, 1969, p. 195), as did Glasgow High School in 1842, when Alexander D'Orsey was master of the department.

Evidence concerning the nature and distribution of English teaching that is drawn from the use of the word 'English' is always hard to assess. We have to decide on external grounds whether an English School is so called because it teaches reading, or because it teaches technical subjects to a modest vocational level, or because it gives an academic education that emphasises English subjects rather than, or to the exclusion of, Latin. Such evidence must be balanced also by occasions when 'English' was not used where it might have been expected:

1762 A not very well-off Virginian gentleman, needing to work for his living, could not afford to study Latin and Greek as well as 'English grammar, reading, writing . . . rhetoric, eloquence'. These are not referred to as English.

(Sol Cohen, 1974, 1, 456)

1780 John Sheild, master of an academy at Ewell, advertised among the subjects he offered 'English and English grammar'. English grammar would be considered a component of English. (Hans, 1951, p. 79)

Early nineteenth century Mr Woodgate's Academy, Honiton, which offered a 'commercial, nautical, mathematical and classical education', named history and geography among the subjects taught, but not English: only 'Reading, Writing . . . English Grammar . . . and English Composition'.

(Gordon and Lawton, 1978, p. 167)

1843 At Montpelier Academy, Vermont, the required subjects included 'Orthography, Reading, Writing, Composition, Grammar, Rhetoric', but English is not mentioned. (Sizer, 1964, p. 28)

1861 A British and Foreign School Society inspector who was invited to report on Ackworth, a school that then had what we would call a strong tradition of English teaching, reported on 'Spelling and Definition of Words; Reading; Writing; History; Geography; English Grammar and General Information', but not on English.

(H. Thompson, 1879, p. 279)

1872 Two inspectors nominated by Cambridge University to report also on Ackworth referred to reading, writing, spelling, English grammar, geography and history, but not to English. (*Ibid*. p. 293)

An alliance of components

It is evident that English was thought of sometimes as a unity, sometimes as a blend of components, one or more of which might be dominant in a particular context. At first, besides reading and spelling, there were two main components, grammar and rhetoric, overlapping but separately designated. Minor components were logic, overlapping slightly with grammar, and pronunciation, treated usually as a part of both spelling and grammar but overlapping slightly with rhetoric.

In a second stage the expressive and interpretative aspects of rhetoric tended to separate, so that there were three major components, closer together in that they often appeared in the same vernacular curriculum and sometimes, but not often, shared the name 'English'.

In a third stage the alliance was still closer in that the name 'English' was more widely applied, but each component (literature, composition, grammar) could invoke its autonomy when desired. Pronunciation was linked with some of the performance aspects of expressive rhetoric and, as elocution, was at times a major component.

In a fourth stage there were added two additional components: the historical study of both literature and language.

To talk of stages is to oversimplify what is a complex pattern of changes occurring at different times, at different speeds and with differing degrees of stability. To put dates to the stages or to the entry of particular components is to oversimplify still further; but it may be helpful to make the attempt. The result is crude, and suggests a precision that it cannot offer. The components, however, must first be examined in more detail.

With regard to literature: some children had been reading, under instruction, doctrinal and scriptural matter, in English, long before the middle of the sixteenth century. From 1550, the date of the first inter-prative rhetoric in English, they could meet a very little secular English literature in school. The amount of English literature in the rhetorics increased in time and could be supplemented during the early decades of the seventeenth century from the aphoristic anthologies and, to an unknown extent, by what it is convenient to call chapbook literature. By the middle of the seventeenth century pupils could be encouraged, by a teacher like Hoole, to read English poetry from the school library, and the everyday spelling-books were beginning to include secular reading-matter such as proverbs and general knowledge. By 1717 the pupils could have an anthology of English verse designed for school use and aimed explicitly at helping them to appreciate poetry. By 1740 the spelling-books regularly contained secular verse and short anecdotes or fables.

With regard to expression: the first expressive rhetoric in English appeared about 1525; the first manual of letter-writing in 1568, for adults. Although expression was the main concern of the rhetorics, we know very little directly about the tasks given to the pupils during the sixteenth and seventeenth centuries: they have to be inferred from the nature of the passages provided as illustrations of the figures, on which practically all the teaching was centred, and from customary teaching in Latin. The tasks can safely be taken to include: speeches, usually in a historical setting; fables; characters; essays; verse. It is also difficult to know how far these tasks were carried out in English for its own sake and how far as a preliminary to their being translated into Latin. Nor can we be sure that these two intentions are exclusive: a teacher might very well train his pupils to write with care the English they were later going to put into Latin. It took longer for the teaching of written expression to detach itself fully from translation and from rhetoric than it had taken the teaching of literature. It was beginning to happen before 1750, but it was not general until nearly the end of the century.

Pronunciation, if only an attempt to indicate the sounds of the letters, was a regular part of spelling-books and grammars from early in the sixteenth century, and could hardly fail to be part of any instruction in reading. Oral expression was a component of rhetoric in Latin, but we do not know how general it was in English before about 1730, by which time it was established in a performance role. Dramatic expression in English we know to have been part of the experience of some schoolboys from the middle of the sixteenth century, but here again we really do not know how far, if at all, it was a widely recognised part of school life before the second half of the eighteenth century.

Formal teaching of the English language intended, in part at least, for schools, is apparent from 1586, the date of the first printed grammar of English. Grammar remained during the whole of the period by far the most autonomous of the components. Table 4 shows the rapid increase in the production of new grammars from the second half of the eighteenth century. This increase was commented on at the time, but Thomas Smetham, master of an academy in London, sets it in a wider context that would include the growing importance of elocution (Table 1, group 3). Smetham says that till lately language has been neglected in England:

1774 'It is true, the political disputes, which have of late years so much engaged the attention of the public, have been the cause of rendering the improvements in the English Tongue more general than they would otherwise have been; the reason is, many men of opulence, whose youth had been too much engaged in commercial pursuits to admit of philological disquisitions, being called (on account of their pecuniary eminence) to the service of the public, when they had occasion to speak publickly, or write upon some temporary topics, found their insufficiencies with respect to language: this awakened their attention; and, though late, they have frequently entered into those pursuits, which in their youth had been neglected; and, when once the necessity of being well acquainted with our Native Tongue appeared, the rising generation was not forgot.' (preface)

A range of linguistic exercises had been developed, especially in rhetòrics, during the seventeenth and eighteenth centuries, overlapping sometimes with grammar; and by the beginning of the nineteenth century textbooks composed entirely of such exercises had begun to appear.

Tables 1 to 5 provide limited additional evidence concerning the development of English. They give a picture of the number of new textbooks, chronologically distributed; but they do not show the number of editions (far less the number of copies sold) and are therefore an insufficient guide to the volume of teaching. Table 1, however, does show, in the period 1721–70, the beginning of an increase in literary texts and in grammars and other linguistic texts. From 1771 there is a marked increase in spelling and elementary reading-texts, in literary texts, and in elocutionary, performance and grammatical texts. Tables 2 and 4 show that it is just before the 1770s that these not altogether steady increases begin, reaching a first peak in the early 1820s or, in the case of grammars, a first peak about 1800 and a second in the 1840s and 1850s.

A tentative outline development of the subject, which fuller study would refine, shows the entry into the teaching of English of its principal components:

From early times	Reading, spelling and pronunciation; some oral expression; perhaps some drama, for which there is no textbook evidence
By 1525	Some written expression
By 1550	Snatches of literature
By 1586	Grammar
By 1650	More substantial literature; more sustained written expression
By 1720	Some explicit teaching of literature; linguistic exercises in, or derived from, grammar and rhetoric
By 1730	Elocution
By 1750	More substantial dramatic work
By 1770	More sustained teaching of literature; more attention to language and written expression
By 1820	History of the language
By 1850	History of literature

It seems reasonable to say that the three main component skills of the subject: interpretation, expression and linguistic study, were being taught, separately, in small (sometimes very small) parts of the curriculum from the end of the sixteenth century. At the same time 'English' was used to designate the preliminary skills of reading, spelling and pronunciation but was not used for the main component skills themselves. One must therefore question Foster Watson's description of Mulcaster's *Elementarie*, 1582, as 'the earliest textbook on the teaching of English' (1909, p. 10). Unless the teaching of reading is treated as a main component it cannot be said that English existed as a subject as early as the sixteenth century. However a subject is defined, the relationship between its parts must be more firmly expressed in its organisation, if not in its nomenclature, than was then the case. An alliance must be formed between the components, even if each is allowed much autonomy. But it is an alliance, not a fusion. The components of English have never fused. To this day even its literary and linguistic aspects are often taught and examined separately. So the question to be answered should be something like, 'When were interpretation, expression and linguistic study taught in some systematic relation to each other?' It would be halfway to an answer to say, 'In those English Schools or Academies which taught to a level above the elementary'. To provide a date, and the other half of the answer, requires more detailed knowledge about the English Schools than we yet have. On our present knowledge it would be reasonable to put early in the eighteenth century the time at which, in some schools, the alliance between the components was systematic enough to justify calling them a subject, and to put between eighty and a hundred years later, about 1790, the strengthening of the subject and its extension to schools generally.

Most subjects derive their existence more from the ways in which we organise knowledge, or have in the past organised it, than from any reality which that knowledge represents. The image of the map of knowledge has made us think of subjects as if they were countries with boundaries, and it has prompted unreal questions as to when a subject first achieved independence. Old subject names, like arbitrary territorial boundaries, persist only because it would cause an administrative upheaval to change them. The looseness and flexibility of English as a subject are advantages, not defects. English is a model subject insofar as it allows teachers (other pressures permitting) to teach together things that, in any particular conditions, should be learnt together, to take on new components and to shed old ones.

Change and progress

There were many changes in the teaching of English during the period covered by this enquiry. As changes they are interesting and sometimes important; as evidence of what we nowadays may judge to have been progress they are unimportant. If we did not think that the ways in which we now teach fit our circumstances better than would most of the methods of our predecessors, we would not teach as we do. To judge whether teachers in 1860 made better use, in their circumstances, of current knowledge than equivalent teachers did in the circumstances of 1660 would require such an exact estimation of psychological, cultural and economic factors that it could hardly be done.

Changes within the teaching of English occur unevenly, within the subject and in time. Some are cyclical, as when we find Samuel Shaw complaining in 1778 that English grammar has been neglected. Some occur only in the work of a few individuals, and are not generally accepted: the whole-word approach to the teaching of reading, for example. Some changes are adopted by everybody and become fashions, such as learning through the correction of error ('exercises in false English').

The most noticeable and the most important changes are not confined to the teaching of English. Typical of them is the slow increase in teachers' understanding of how children learn, and in their recognition that children can have intellectual and aesthetic abilities distinctive of, and appropriate to, stages in their development. Perceptive teachers, with or without a theory, have always had a sympathetic understanding of children's difficulties in learning: amongst seventeenth-century English teachers John Brinsley, Richard Lloyd, Charles Hoole, Joseph Aickin; in the eighteenth century William Ronksley, John Newbery (an honorary teacher), Samuel Edwards, Ann Fisher, John Williams of Catherington, J. Butler (author of *Proposals for an Amendment of School Instruction*), the author of *Instruction and Amusement United*, Maria Edgeworth; in the nineteenth century William Lennie, George Fulton, Adam Keys, Alexander Jamieson, William Bearcroft, Richard Batt, William Fletcher, Alexander D'Orsey, Robert Sullivan, R. Robinson, John Wood, J.W. Hales, E.A. Abbott.

Most teachers of English, judged by their textbooks, lacked the smooth expository techniques that had been developed over the centuries by teachers of Latin. The best of them saw that most of the techniques of Latin teaching were inappropriate, but they did not know enough about the ways in which language is used to understand why. They devised alternative techniques, but in a hit-or-miss fashion that is still being systematised in our own day. Our predecessors, as a whole, were probably less well educated than the classical teachers; until the middle of the eighteenth century, perhaps. But impressions such as these are what this enquiry tries to avoid. They are premature, even as impressions, because we do not have enough information. May it not be, for instance, that during the late seventeenth and early eighteenth centuries, when English was becoming integrated into a subject, the teachers who saw its importance and helped its development were, in conventional terms, better educated than most English teachers a hundred years later when the subject was taught more widely? The efforts needed to give English the status of Latin would attract the able and far-sighted, not the hacks. On the whole it is the hacks who have received attention hitherto: their awfulness is memorable. But the so-called dame school and the pushy proprietorial 'academy' are a small part of the picture. The textbooks show more of the picture, but it is still incomplete. No teacher wishes to be judged by the books he uses; nor even by the books he writes.

Children's learning became slowly less dependent on the application of rule. For a long time pupils who were considered incapable of seeing for themselves, and remembering, some simple aspects of spelling or usage were required to perform the much more difficult task of learning by heart, and knowing when to apply, an often elaborate rule.

One of the fluctuating changes came from the age-long tension between training the memory so that children will remember what is right and training the reason so that they can work it out for themselves. The tension became less acute at the end of the eighteenth century, when it was generally accepted that children should be taught to understand what they read, but it remained intermittently active in most forms of language work and especially in the teaching of reading. We are nowadays well aware of how complex, from a psychological point of view, is the process of learning to read, but we are less aware of the extent to which seventeenth-century teachers wrestled with these complexities: the relation between reading and spelling; between spelling and pronunciation; the use to be made of the names of the letters; the relation between their names, their sounds and their powers; the status of the syllable; the relation between whole units and their parts.

Equally far-reaching changes occurred in teachers' views about what children should or might read under instruction. For long their reading was restricted to doctrinal or biblical matter; when it was extended to secular moralistic reading it was heavy and gloomy, lightened only by the humanity of animal fables. Enjoyment was gradually tolerated, but remained suspect if it was found on the children's own initiative. Slow changes came also in the teachers' attitude to imaginative literature, but in the general opinion, whatever might be acceptable at home, school reading should be serious: solid with the seriousness of morality or with the seriousness of facts.

There were corresponding changes in attitudes to what children wrote. Nearly always their compositions were dependent on prescribed imitation of specific authors or genres, and every essay had to develop according to a prescribed sequence. Only occasionally, towards the end of the period, did an individual teacher recognise children's capacity for authentic writing, drawn from their own experience. It took even longer in the teaching of composition for teachers to modify their fear of feeling than it had done in the teaching of literature. Children had always been able to meet in the Bible flights of imagination and passion, but in their own writing no childish equivalent would have been approved.

If changes such as those outlined here were contained solely within English it would be appropriate for the eventual historian of the subject to put them in a British historical setting and relate them to the experience of other English-speaking, and other European, countries. But it would be premature to attempt this now. The changes do not always reflect innovations pioneered by teachers of English. The teachers responded to movements in the culture of their times, movements that affected teachers of history, Latin, scripture, French, geography and elementary science. The changes can be viewed in depth only when we know more about the history of other subjects in the curriculum, and when the curriculum itself, which has a history, can be related to the wider cultural movement of which it is a part. It is not only for English that we need to know more about teachers' intentions and about what they did in the classroom. The significance of what they intended and what they did in English will be better assessed when English is seen in relation to the curriculum as a whole and when the curriculum is seen in relation to the culture of its time.

The present enquiry has shown, I hope, that there is plenty of evidence on which to base a history of the teaching of English, and has shown in places what some of the less familiar evidence looks like. It has also, I hope, given more detailed attention than is usual to the work of individual classroom teachers. It is the teachers who give education its history.

ABBREVIATIONS

a.	Published in or before the stated year
AAS	American Antiquarian Society, Worcester, Mass.
BFSS	British and Foreign School Society
BL	British Library
C	College
CBEL	*Cambridge Bibliography of English Literature*, 1940–57
CHE	College of Higher Education
DES	Department of Education and Science, London
DLC	Library of Congress, Washington DC
DNB	*Dictionary of National Biography*
EETS	Early English Text Society
EGC	*English Grammatical Categories* (see Bibliography 4, MICHAEL)
GB	Goold Brown, 1850 (see Bibliography 3, BROWN, Goold)
HIC	Catalogues of a highly important collection of children's books. Sotheby, London, various dates
HM	Headmaster
LTM	*Lime Tree Miscellany*: catalogues of Arnold Muirhead, antiquarian bookseller
NBL	National Book League: exhibition catalogues
NCBEL	*New Cambridge Bibliography of English Literature*, 1969–77
NLI	National Library of Ireland, Dublin
NLS	National Library of Scotland, Edinburgh
NLW	National Library of Wales, Aberystwyth
N&Q	*Notes and Queries*
NUC	*National Union Catalogue*
NYc	New York: Columbia University
NYct	New York: Columbia University Teachers' College
NYPL	New York Public Library
O	Bodleian Library, Oxford
OCCL	*Oxford Companion to Children's Literature*
PL	Public Library
SPCK	Society for Promoting Christian Knowledge
SR(A)	*A Transcript of the registers of the Company of Stationers, 1554–1640*, ed. Edward Arber
SR(E)	Do. *1640–1708*, ed. G.E.B. Eyre
TC	*The Term Catalogues, 1668–1709*, ed. Edward Arber
t.p.	Title page
UL	University Library
ULIE	University of London Institute of Education
V&A	Victoria and Albert Museum, London (National Art Library)

British texts recorded
and consulted

We know so little about the quantitative development of textbooks that it will, I hope, be useful to have even this incomplete list not only of works which have been consulted but also those which are known, even if in some cases no copies exist.

Entries have been designed in a way that should make quick reference possible. They give prominence to the author's name (or to the title of an anonymous work) and to the date (often estimated) of the earliest edition known; this date therefore *precedes* the title. The code, explained on p. 9, designating the type of text comes between the date and the title. Titles are given in full only to the extent that they describe relevant contents or intentions. All omissions within a title are indicated, but if the title as given here stops before the end of the full title this is noted, by 'etc.', only if the full title is unusually long.

The term 'edition' is used here for all printings and is not distinguished from 'impression'. Editions that have been consulted are marked *. In most cases only those editions are recorded which have been consulted, but an exception is made for potentially significant works that have received little or no bibliographical attention. Where possible some indication is given of the approximate number of editions over a given period, and at least one location is given for each edition recorded. No attempt has been made to seek out locations. The number of pages is recorded only when it is significantly high or low. The printer or publisher is recorded only if the information helps to distinguish works of closely similar titles or if it could be of local interest. Shelf-marks are occasionally given if books are difficult to identify. If no location is known to me I have given the source of the information that such an edition exists – usually the name of an author listed in Bibliography 4. Editions located in American libraries have all been consulted in microform or xerox copies. The place of publication is London, unless stated. The catalogues of a few antiquarian booksellers with specialist knowledge of textbooks are recorded, especially when an edition has not been located. The page references at the end of an entry in Bibliographies 1 and 3 are to the present work. Numbers in roman type indicate direct quotation; numbers in italic indicate reference or indirect quotation. Tables 6–9 are not indexed.

A., S.W.
[1610]* S *Most easie instructions for reading, specially penned for the good of those who are to come to yeares.* By S.W.A. Pp. 4. (BL, date 1625?; Folger, date 1610?). Alston, IV, 50 and Plate 7 for reproduction of first page.
[Anon.]
[c. 1561?] S *An A.B.C. for chyldren. Here is an A.B.C. devysed with syllabes, with the Pater Noster, the Ave Maria, and the Crede, both in Latin and in Englishe. And by this boke a man that hath good capacitie and can no letter on the boke, may*

lern to reade in the space of vi wekes, bothe Latin & Englysh, yf he geve therto good diligence . . . Also ye mai lern therbi to write English truly, and to knowe the tru ortography of the Englishe tongue. (Queen's C, Oxford); anr edn [*c.* 1565?] (Trinity C, Dublin). Reprinted E. Flugel, *Anglia*, 13 (1891)*, 461–7. Alston IV, 1–4 and Plate 1.

ABBOT, A.

[*c.* 1825] RE *The mother's primer, or first book for children.* Edinburgh: Oliver and Boyd. Chalmers, p. 117; Sotheby HIC, I, 1974, lot 5.

ABBOT, Gorham Dummer 1807–74

1848* RE *A first English reader.* Taylor and Walton. (BL; O). Also, in the same year, *A second English reader* (BL; O).

[a. 1848] S *The new English spelling book, designed to teach orthography and orthoepy; with a critical analysis of the language, and a classification of its elements.* Taylor and Walton. 2nd edn advertised in 1848.

ABBOTT, Edwin 1808–82 Headmaster of the Philological School, Marylebone

[a. 1879] G *A handbook of English grammar.* 3rd edn, rev. W. Moore (BL).

ABBOTT, Edwin Abbott 1838–1926 Headmaster, City of London School

1872a* Ex *How to write clearly. Rules and exercises on English composition.* Pp. 78. (BL).   Pp. *305, 315.*

1872b* Ed 'On teaching the English language', in *Lectures on education: delivered before the members of the College of Preceptors in the year 1871, Vol. 1.* College of Preceptors. (BL).   Pp. 215, 257–8, 267; *383*

ABBOTT, Edwin Abbott, and SEELEY, Sir John Robert 1834–95

1871* Ex *English lessons for English people.* Pp. xxiv, 292. (BL; Hull UL); anr edn 1906*.   P. 2.

ABRAHAM, J.H. (ed.)

1805* Ex *Juvenile essays: comprising, in the order of merit, the first and second half-yearly prize compositions of the pupils belonging to the Milk Street Academy, Sheffield, to which is prefixed a brief history of education and a table of the system pursued in the above academy.* Sheffield. (BL; Sheffield UL).   P. 310.

[Anon.]

1779* Ex *The accomplished letter-writer; or, universal correspondent. Containing familiar letters on the most common occasions in life . . . To which is prefixed a compendious grammar of the English Tongue . . . with a selection of some beautiful poetical epistles, and various forms of polite messages.* (BL). Alston, III, 345. Unlikely to have been used in school.

ADAM, Alexander 1741–1809 Rector, Edinburgh High School

1772* G *The principles of Latin and English grammar.* Edinburgh. (BL); 4th edn as: *The rudiments . . .*, 1793* (BL; Glasgow UL); six further British edns to 1846.   P. *319 n.*

ADAM, Alexander 'Teacher, Edinburgh'

1826* S *The infant's guide to the alphabet, and first principles of pronunciation.* Edinburgh. (BL). Advertised in 1856 as *The infant's guide to pronunciation.*

[1830?] P *The rudiments of correct reading; consisting of rules and examples adapted to the capacity of children.* Edinburgh: Oliver and Boyd, 1856* (Hull UL). Preface dated 1 January 1830.

[a. 1826]* S *The twopenny book, or infant's first lessons.* Edinburgh. Pp. 24. (BL).

ADAMS, Ernest Assistant master, University College School

1858* G *The elements of the English language.* Bell and Daldy. Pp. 183. (BL). 2nd edn enl. 1862 (BL); 25th edn, rev. J.F. Davis, 1892; anr edn 1905.

1868 G *The rudiments of English grammar and analysis.* (BL; O). 2nd edn 1871 (BL; O). Further edns to 1877 (NUC).

ADAMS, John 1750?–1814 Master of the Academy, Putney

1791* RA *The elements of reading: being select and easy English lessons, for young readers of both sexes: designed as a sequel to the spelling-book, and a proper introduction to The Speaker, or any other selection of a like nature.* (BL); 2nd edn enl. 1795 (Holtom, Cat. 49, 1985). 6th edn advertised in J. Hill's *Enchiridion lyricum,* 1819.

1789* RA *The English Parnassus: being a new selection of didactic, descriptive, pathetic, plaintive, and pastoral poetry, extracted from the works of the latest and most celebrated poets; such as* [twenty-nine names follow]. (Nottingham UL). Pp. *187, 195, 376.*

ADIE, William 'Schoolmaster in Paisley'

1769* S *A new spelling-book, in which the rules of spelling and pronouncing the English language are exemplified and explained.* Paisley: A. Weir and A. McLean. Pp. 18. (BL).

ADIS, Henry

[*c.* 1660?]* S *A fannaticks primmer, for the instruction of their little-ones, in order to the attaining to perfect reading.* (BL). Alston, IV, 60 and Plate 9 for t.p.

[Anon.]

1815 G *The adventures of Dame Winnifred, and her numerous family; or the infant's grammar.* G. Martin. Gumuchian, 249.

[Anon.]

1848 RS *Agricultural class book; or, how best to cultivate a small farm and garden.* Commissioners of National Education in Ireland: Dublin. Akenson, p. 413; anr edn 1850 (BL). Goldstrom, 1972a, p. 208. P. *242.*

AICKIN, Joseph 'Lately one of the masters of the Free-School, London-Derry'

1693 G *The English grammar, or the English tongue reduced to grammatical rules . . . In learning whereof the English scholar may now obtain the perfection of his mother tongue, without the assistance of Latin: composed for the use of all English schools.* (O); Scolar Press facsimile 1967*. Alston, I, 34–5; Vorlat, 1975; Padley, 1985. Pp. 67, 72, 75, 105, 121, 343, 373; *48, 52, 63, 309n., 383.*

Aids to development, 1829, see MAURICE, Mary Atkinson

AIKEN, John 1747–1822 Tutor, Warrington Academy

1804* B *Letters to a young lady on a course of English poetry.* (BL); 2nd edn 1807* (BL). P. 216.

1796* RA (Alexander Pope) *The universal prayer. To which is prefixed a critical essay by J. Aikin.* T. Cadell. (BL)

AIKIN, Lucy 1781–1864

1828* RA *An English lesson book, for the junior classes.* (BL); anr edn 1833 (BL).

1811* Ex *Juvenile correspondence.* (BL); 2nd edn 1816 (BL); 3rd edn 1826 (BL).

1801 RA *Poetry for children, consisting of short pieces, to be committed to memory.* (Nottingham UL); 2nd edn 1803* (BL); at least fourteen further edns to 1836. Pp. 194; *192.*

AINSWORTH, Robert 1660–1743 Teacher

1698* Ed *The most natural and easie way of institution: containing, proposals for* *making a domestic education less chargeable to parents, and more easie and beneficial to children. By which method, youth may not only make a very considerable progress in languages, but also in arts and sciences, in two years.* Pp. 31. (BL); 2nd edn 1699 (BL); 2nd edn 1736*, pp. 48 (BL). Bryant, p. 107. Alston, X, 144–6.   Pp. 200, 376–7.

[Anon.]

[*c.* 1815] RE   *The Albion primer, or first book for children.* Fairburn. Chalmers, p. 117; Gumuchian, 25.

ALDERSON, James   Master of the English Academy, Ashford, Kent

1795*G   *English grammatical exercises; comprised in a variety of examples, under the different rules of syntax.* (BL). Alston, III, 412.   P. *326.*

1793* S   *Orthographical exercises: in a series of moral letters. To which is added, a selection of essays, &c. from the best English writers.* (BL). 5th edn [*c.* 1800?] (Hull UL); 25th edn 1841 (BL); many edns to 1864.   Pp. *326, 327.*

ALEXANDER, Cecil Frances   1818–95

1858 RA   *Hymns, descriptive and devotional, for the use of schools.* (BL); edns to at least 1903.

1848 RA   *Hymns for little children.* (BL). 'Three hundred and ninety-fourth thousand' in 1871 (BL); 62nd edn 1884; edns into twentieth century.

ALEXANDER, Levy

1833 G   *The young lady and gentleman's guide to the grammar of the English language. In verse.* (BL); anr edn 1835, Hunter 1848.

ALEXANDER, Samuel

[*a.* 1830] G   *A practical, logical essay on the syntax of the English language.* 2nd edn Liverpool, 1830 (BL); 3rd edn Manchester, 1832 (BL); 4th edn enl. London, 1832* (BL; Wisconsin UL). The 4th edn was designed particularly for schools.

[ALLAN, Louisa]

1813 G   *The decoy; or, an agreeable method of teaching children the elementary parts of English grammar by conversations and familiar examples.* First published in *A present for a little boy* (Welch, 1972); 2nd edn 1814* (BL; DES); 4th edn 1819* (BL); 5th edn 1823 (Bedford CHE, incomplete); 6th edn 1827 (Reading UL).

ALLEN, Alexander   1814–42   Headmaster, Madras House Grammar School, Hackney

[1838] RA   *Select English poetry, designed for the use of schools and young persons in general.* Preface dated 1838. 5th edn 1850* (BL); 7th edn 1853; 14th edn 1866 (Harvard UL).   P. 259.

ALLEN, Alexander, and   CORNWELL, James   1812–1902

[*a.* 1846] G   *Grammar for beginners: being an introduction to Allen & Cornwell's English School Grammar.* Goldstrom, 1972a, p. 146. 11th edn 1848 (NYct); 25th edn 1855*, 72 pp. (BL); many further edns to 1888 (NUC),   P. 365.

1841* G   *A new English grammar, with very copious exercises, and a systematic view of the formation and derivation of words.* Pp. xv, 168 (BL); at least sixty British and American edns to 1880. By the 12th edn, 1847, its title had changed to *An English school grammar.*   Pp. 351; *357, 370*

ALLEN, Charles

1800* S   *New orthographical exercises, for the use of English seminaries, in five parts: in which the useful, the moral, and entertaining, of our best writers, are combined with a certain and easy mode of acquiring a just pronunciation of the mother tongue,* *as it is spoken in the best circles. Preceded by an introduction, and interspersed with several pieces on the art of reading and speaking English with propriety.* Pp. 144; preface from Southwark, 20 March 1800. (BL). Alston, VI, 551a. All the pieces are in false spelling.　　P. *326*

ALLEN, William　Of Newbury, Berks.

1813 G　*The elements of English grammar; with numerous exercises, questions for examinations, and notes, for the use of the advanced student.* GB; 2nd edn 1824★ (BL), pp. iv, 457; 3rd edn 1824 (BL; Wisconsin UL).　　Pp. 370; *368.*

ALLISON, M.A.

[a. 1847] G　*First lessons in English grammar, for the use of the nursery and junior classes in schools; with questions for examination at the end of each lesson.* 7th edn 1847, recorded by Hunter, 1848; 9th edn 1851★ (BL).

ALLOTT, Robert

1600 RA　*England's Parnassus: or the choycest flowers of our moderne poets*; in Thomas Park, *Heliconia*, Part 4, 1814; J. Payne Collier, *Seven English miscellanies*, 1867; ed. Charles Crawford, Oxford, 1913★.

[Anon.]

1808 RE　*The alphabet of Goody Twoshoes; with spelling and reading lessons.* (title from [*c.* 1825]). Chalmers, p. 118; anr edn 1822 (Bedford CHE); anr edn [*c.* 1825]★ (V&A, imperfect); anr edn [*c.* 1845] Chalmers, p. 118. Rosenbach, 598, records a Philadelphia edn of 1821.

[Anon.]

[1576] S　*An alphabet and playne pathwaye to the facultie of readinge SR*(A), II, 308, and Alston, IV, 5; sub-title added: *the spelling ABC*, 1590, *SR*(A), II, 566, and Alston, IV, 6; as *A New booke of spelling with syllables. Or an alphabet and plaine path-way* [etc.] 1601 (Trin. C, Dublin); anr edn 1610★ (BL); anr edn 1621 (Bodley); anr edn [1677], no copy. Alston, IV, 7–10 and Plate 2 for 1601 t.p.　　P. 72.

[Anon.]

1777★ RA　*The amusing instructor: or, tales and fables in prose and verse, for the improvement of youth. With useful and pleasing remarks on different branches of science.* F. Newbery. (BL).　　P. *191.*

[Anon.]

[a. 1846] RA　*The ancient poets and poetry of England.* By the compiler of *The gem book of poesie*, possibly William Martin. (Advt).

ANDREW, James　1773–1833　Principal, East India Company's Military Seminary

1817★ G　*Institutes of grammar, as applicable to the English language, or as introductory to the study of other languages, systematically arranged, and briefly explained.* Preface 24 April 1817. (BL).　　Pp. 91, 354, 368; *358.*

ANDREWS, T.

[a. 1800?] RA　*The Christian Speaker; or, elegant extracts in prose and verse; variously selected from sacred and moral writings, calculated to entertain the mind, improve the understanding, and amend the heart.* 10th edn, addns, T. Bailey, [1800?]★ (BL).　　P. *192.*

ANGUS, J.

1805 G　*The English grammar unveiled and adapted to the lowest capacity.* Workington. (O).

ANGUS, Joseph 1816–1902 Principal, Stepney College

[1865]* B *The handbook of English literature.* Religious Tract Society. (BL). P. *219.*

1862 G *A handbook of the English tongue. For the use of students and others.* Religious Tract Society. (BL copy destroyed in war).

ANGUS, William 'Teacher of English'

[a. 1813] G *An abridgement of Angus's grammar, for the use of beginners.* 2nd edn enl. Glasgow, 1813* (BL; Cambridge UL); 4th edn 1825 (Wisconsin UL); 5th edn 1829 (Glasgow UL); 6th edn 1839 (BL). The preface to the 1st edn, reprinted in the 2nd, says it is 'an abridgement of a larger work published . . . about two years ago'.

1841*RA *The beauties of Paradise Lost. With rhetorical pauses and emphases; and a brief life of Milton.* Glasgow. (Glasgow UL). P. *262.*

1840* G *A brief analysis of the English language, showing the mode of its formation, and the principle sources whence it is derived.* Glasgow. (Glasgow UL). P. *357.*

[a. 1825] G *English grammar; mnemonically arranged. Interspersed with critical notes and explanatory observations, chiefly of a practical nature: with exercises; a key; anglicisms, scotticisms, iricisms, &c.* Pp. viii, 288. 4th edn Glasgow, 1825* (Glasgow UL). P. *346 n.*

1800a* G *An epitome of English grammar. Containing* [parts of speech; syntax] *Violations of the rules of syntax; improprieties in the choice of words; errours, arising from redundancy* [etc.]. *In these errours are included, a variety of scotticisms and vulgar anglicisms . . . Calculated for the use of schools.* Glasgow. (Aberdeen UL); 2nd edn 1807 (BL). Pp. 339–40.

[1809] S *An introduction to Angus's Vocabulary and Juvenile Pieces: containing lessons for reading, spelling, &c.* (title from 6th edn). Watt; 5th edn Glasgow, 1823 (BL); 6th edn 1827* (Glasgow UL). P. *62.*

1815* RA *Juvenile pieces, in prose and verse; with lessons for spelling, and all the difficult words in the reading lessons alphabetically arranged, with their orthoepy in the opposite column. Also, an appendix, containing the history of Joseph . . . The whole intended for the use of schools* [etc.] Glasgow. (BL); 6th edn 1831* (Glasgow UL). P. *239.*

1812* G *A new system of English grammar, with exercises, and questions for examination; interspersed with critical notes and explanatory observations, chiefly of a practical nature. Also, an appendix, containing an extensive collection of vulgar anglicisms, scotticisms . . . and elements of English composition . . .The whole intended for the use of schools, and private teaching.* Glasgow. Pp. xii, 432. Preface dated 1 August 1812. (Glasgow PL; BL); 5th edn 1839 (BL; O). P. *285.*

[a. 1829] Ex *Principles of English composition.* 2nd edn Glasgow, 1829. Separate publication of a section of his *New system of English grammar?*

[a. 1815] RE *Progressive lessons for children, containing the principles of reading, on an improved plan, in three parts.* Advertised in his *Juvenile pieces,* 1815.

1800b* P *A pronouncing vocabulary of the English language: exhibiting the most approved mode of pronunciation . . . every word being reprinted – divided into syllables – and accented . . . With an appendix; containing* [classical and scripture names]. *Adapted to the use of schools.* Glasgow. 4th edn 1808, Watt; 5th edn 1814 (BL); 19th edn 1830* (Glasgow UL); Scolar Press facsimile of 1800 edn, 1969*. Alston, IV, 954 and Plate 113 for reproduction of two pages. From at least the 5th edn the title was *An English spelling and pronouncing vocabulary.*

[a. 1824] RA   *Sacred extracts in prose and verse.* 3rd edn Glasgow, 1824* (Glasgow UL). A separate publication of part of his *A selection of hymns.*

[a. 1827] RA   *A selection of hymns and sacred maxims: with an abridgment of The Economy of Human Life; the elements of reading; and exercises in spelling.* 3rd edn advertised in 1827; 4th edn Glasgow, 1831* (Glasgow UL). The preface to the 4th edn is from 'English Academy, 130 Ingram Street, Glasgow, Feb. 1831'.

1809* RA   *A selection of short poetical pieces, on various subjects. Intended for exercises in reading and recitation.* Glasgow. (Glasgow UL). 2nd edn 1813, as *A selection of poetical and dramatic pieces* (BL); 3rd edn 1821 (Glasgow UL; Wandsworth PL); 4th edn 1826* (Glasgow UL).

[1828] G   *Supplement to Angus's English Grammar; containing the principles of English composition; additional scotticisms and exercises; remarks on letter writing; and on the analogy and anomalies of English pronunciation.* 2nd edn Glasgow, 1829* (Glasgow UL). Preface dated 4 November 1828.   P. 352.

[Anon.[

1833* S   *The anti-spelling book; a new system of teaching children to read without spelling.* (BL); 3rd edn 1834* (BL); 6th edn 1834(?) (BL).   Pp. 43, 82n., 123; 69.

ARMSTRONG, Robert   'English master, Madras College, St Andrews'

1868a* G   *The narrative English grammar, with exercises and questions.*   Pp. vi, 54. Edinburgh (BL). Chambers' Educational Course.

1868b* G   *The practical English grammar. With exercises and questions.*   Pp. vi, 120. Edinburgh (BL). Chambers' Educational Course.   P. *368.*

1853* Ex   *A practical introduction to English composition, Part I.* Edinburgh: Sutherland and Knox. (BL). An 11th edn was advertised in 1862. For Part II see ARMSTRONG and ARMSTRONG.   Pp. 310; *283, 309n.*

ARMSTRONG, Robert, and ARMSTRONG, Thomas   'Master of Buccleugh Sessional School, Edinburgh'

1865* RA   *Class-book of English literature; with biographical sketches, critical notices, and illustrative extracts. For the use of schools and students.* Pp. 404. Nelson. (BL).

[1870]* B   *Compendium of English literature for the use of schools and students.* Edinburgh. Pp. viii, 154.

[a. 1862] La   *Etymology for junior classes.* (Advt.).

1858* La   *Introduction to English etymology.* Edinburgh: Sutherland and Knox. Pp. 116. (BL).

1859 La   *Manual of etymology.* Edinburgh. (BL). An abridgment of their *Introduction.*

1866* RA   *Poetical readings and recitations, with introductory exercises in modulation.* Edinburgh: T. Laurie. Pp. 96. (BL); anr edn [1878] (BL).   P. *220.*

1853* Ex   *A practical introduction to English composition, Part II.*   Edinburgh: Sutherland and Knox. (BL). *Key,* 1854* (BL).

[ARNOLD, Thomas Kerchever] 1800–53

1838* G *An English grammar for classical schools. Etymology. Parts I and II.* (BL); 2nd edn, with the addn of a syntax, 1841 (BL); 4th edn 1848 (Wisconsin UL); 5th edn 1852 (Glasgow UL).

1844a RE *A first reading book, Part I.* (O).

[a. 1844] RA *A first verse book.* Advertised in his *Spelling turned etymology,* together with *A second verse book.*

1853 G *Henry's English grammar: a manual for beginners.* (BL).

1852 La *Latin via English: being the second part of Spelling turned Etymology.* (BL).

1844b* La *Spelling turned etymology, Part I.* (BL)   Pp 81, 356–7.

[Anon.]

1762 RA *The art of poetry on a new plan: illustrated with a great variety of examples from the best English poets; and of translations from the ancients: together with such reflections and critical remarks as may tend to form in our youth an elegant taste.* 2 vols. J. Newbery. (BL). Facsimile edn, Gregg International Publ., 1969*. A much enlarged form of *The art of poetry,* 1746, attributed to John Newbery, q.v. Roscoe, J16A, questions the connection between this volume and those in *Newbery's Circle of the Sciences.*

[Anon.]

[1705] S *The art of spelling and reading made most easy. By which book alone, a child may be brought to read the whole English tongue with greater speed, ease, and delight, than by any other. In three parts. The first is designed for the less knowing tutors: and consists in a discourse of the essence, nature, and power, of letters; and by what instruments of speech they are formed . . . with a method how to teach to read without any spelling at all. II is for young beginners and contains the whole body of the English tongue . . . Part Third is designed for the bigger and more knowing children; and contains a great variety of most useful particulars, both in prose and verse . . . Useful for masters, dames, and tutors of children; but especially for such parents as teach their own children to read English. TC,* III, 484. No copy. Alston, IV, 221.   P. 122.

ARTHINGTON, Maria

1828* G *The little scholar's first grammar; or grammar made easy to the capacities of young children.* York. (BL; O).

ASH, John 1724?–1779

1760* G *Grammatical institutes; or grammar, adapted to the genius of the English tongue.* Worcester. (Worcester PL); 4th edn London, 1763(?) (O); anr edn 1768* (BL); anr edn 1779* (BL); at least sixty British and American edns in all, to 1810. Scolar Press facsimile of 1763 edn, 1967*. Alston, I, 153–92. Scheurweghs and Vorlat, 1959.   Pp. 322, 377; *54.*

1777* RA *Sentiments on education, collected from the best writers; properly methodized, and interspersed with occasional observations.* 2 vols. (BL). Alston, X, 272. Although it does not sound like it, this work is 'intended for the amusement of the English scholar, and especially of young people'.   Pp. 85; *184.*

ASHTON, James, and CLEGG, John

[1788] S *The new expositor: containing tables of words from two to seven syllables, inclusive; accented, explained, and divided, according to the most approved method of pronunciation . . . For the use of schools.* (title from 1806). No copy; 2nd edn Liverpool, 1792 (DLC); 4th edn 1800, no copy; 7th edn 1806* (Nottingham UL); 15th edn* (DES); a 44th edn, Derby: Mozley, was advertised in Birkin, 1838. Alston, IV, 868–868b and Plate 88 for t.p. of 1792 edn.   Pp. 86–7.

ATKIN, John   Master of the Grammar School, Goole

1845 G   *The practical and self-instructing English grammar.* (BL; Columbia UL).

AUSTIN, Gilbert

1806* P   *Chironomia; or a treatise on rhetorical delivery: comprehending many precepts, both ancient and modern, for the proper regulation of the voice, the countenance, and gesture. Together with an investigation of the elements of gesture, and a new method for the notation thereof; illustrated by many figures.* Pp. xix, 583, xvi. (BL).   P. *289.*

AUSTIN, Richard C.

[1864]* S   *The youth's progressive spelling and reading book. In three parts.* I [two-letter words]; II [up to three syllables]; III [more than three syllables; homophones; reading-passages]. T.M. Tripcony (BL).

B., A., see *A model for a school,* 1671

B., E.S.H.

1870*   *The Civil Service orthography. A handy book of English spelling . . . adapted for the use of schools & of candidates for the Civil and other Services.* (BL); 2nd edn 1876 (BL).

B., H.

[1589] Ex   *Certen observacons for Latyne and Englishe versyfyinge.* (O, one leaf only). *SR*(A), II 534.

B., H.

1852 G   *A introduction to aid in parsing the English language: forming also an elementary grammar . . . By an educator.* (NLS). The preface is signed H.B.

B., I.

1657* Ed   *Heroick education; or, choice maximes and instructions, for the most sure and facile training up of youth, in the way of eminent learning and vertues.* (BL). The BL copy is corrected in an early hand to 1656.

B., J.

1674* S   *Ludus literarum, the sporting of the letters: or, the scholar's recreation. Being a new invention, tending to a speedy attaining knowledge in the tongues . . . To be used instead of card-playing . . . The book of directions, with the packs of letters to be made use of in this learned recreation, are to be sold by Mr Davis, Bookseller in Oxford.* [One shilling for the book; fourpence for the pack of letters: sixpence if the counters are included.] (St John's C, Cambridge; Folger). Alston, IV, 98 and Plate 16 for t.p. in full.   P. 70.

B., J.

1680* Ex   *Lucerna scholastica or; the scholar's companion. In two parts. The first giving rules for making epistles, themes, orations, and all other kinds of oratorical exercise. The second giving directions for making all sorts of poetical exercise. And both fitted to the capacity of children.* Pp. viii, 38. (BL). Alston, VI, 104.   P. *144.*

B., J.

[1824]* RA   *The pet lamb, in rhythm, intended as an innocent exercise for the memory* *of children*. Darton. Pp. 36. (BL); anr edn [*c.* 1840], Sotheby HIC, I, 1974, lot 124; anr edn [*c.* 1860], *ibid.* lot 125.

B., L.

1847 G   *The young lady's new grammar . . . By a lady*. (O; BL).

B., R.

[1864]* S   *Spelling and orthographical exercises*. Simpkin Marshall. Pp. 48. (BL).

[B., T.]

1788 B   *Ars rhetorica; or, a compendium of rhetoric*. Chester. (Illinois UL). Alston, VI, 261.

BAILEY, Nathan   d. 1742   Master of a boarding school at Stepney

1726* S   *An introduction to the English tongue: being a spelling book. In two parts. The first* [spelling-lists, accented]. *The second* [sounds of the letters; divisions of syllables; punctuation]. *For the use of schools*. (BL); 2nd edn 1733 (Harvard UL). Alston, IV, 321–2 and Plate 46 for t.p. in full   Pp. 91; *84.*

BAIN, Alexander   1818–1903   Professor of Logic and English, University of Aberdeen

1866* Ex   *English composition and rhetoric. A manual*. (BL; Bristol UL); 2nd edn 1869 (Reading UL); 4th edn 1877 (BL); enl. edn, two parts, 1887–8* (BL). The edn of 1887–8 is entirely recast and is virtually a new work.   Pp. 218, 310; *283, 305.*

1863 G   *An English grammar* (BL); rev. edn as: *A higher English grammar*, 1872; anr edn 1879* (BL); anr edn 1904, *NCBEL*, III, 1514.   Pp. 370; *357.*

1874 G   *A companion to the Higher English Grammar*. (BL); 2nd edn 1877* (BL).

1872 G   *A first English grammar*. (BL); anr edn 1882, *NCBEL*, III, 1514. *Key*, with additional exercises, 1872 (BL).

1869 Ed   'On teaching English'. *Fortnightly Rev.* 6, 211–13.

1887* Ed   *On teaching English: with detailed examples, and an enquiry into the definition of poetry*. (BL).   P. *283.*

BAKER, Charles   1803–74   Teacher

[a. 1861] RA   *Graduated reading: comprising a circle of knowledge, in 200 lessons. Graduation 2*. 10th edn 1861 (U/Microfilms).

1848 RA   [as above] *Graduation 3*. (U/Microfilms); 12th edn, n.d. (*ibid.*)

1835 RE   *Primary lessons for children and infants' schools*. (O)

[a. 1855] RE   *Reading without spelling: one hundred short and easy lessons*. 2nd edn [1855] (NUC); 5th edn, n.d. (U/Microfilms).   P. *123.*

BAKER, William   d. 1736

[a. 1724] S   *Rules for true spelling and writing English; with useful observations on the sounds of letters and diphthongs; and the use of capitals, stops and marks*. 2nd edn Bristol, 1724* (O; NLW). Alston, IV, 317 and Plate 44 for t.p.   Pp. 53, 326; *283.*

BALDWIN, Edward, see GODWIN, William

BALDWIN, Percy

[*c.* 1824] D?   *The reading and spelling expositor; or the first steps to reading and spelling, and the elements of useful knowledge*. Advertised by Sherwood, Gilbert and Piper in a copy of John Grant's grammar. From the evidence of the books advertised, the advertisement would seem to be after 1823 and before 1825.

BALES, Peter   *c.* 1547–1610?   Writing-master

1590 S   *The writing schoolemaster: conteining three bookes in one; the first, teaching swift writing; the second, true writing; the third, faire writing . . . The second book: named, The Order of Orthographie: shewing the perfect method to write true orthographie in our English tongue . . . to be attained by the right use of this booke without a schoolemaster, in short time, and with small paines, by your owne private studies.* (O; Cambridge UL); edns in 1597 and 1600. Facsimile of 1590 edn, Theatrum Orbis Terrarum, Amsterdam, 1969*. Alston, VIII, 2–4.

BALFOUR, Clara Lucas (born LIDDELL)   1808–78   Lecturer on *belles lettres* at a leading ladies' school (*DNB*)

1852* B   *Sketches of English literature from the fourteenth to the present century.* Pp. vii, 404. (BL).

BANKS, William   'Private teacher of composition, intellectual philosophy, &c.'

1823 Ex   *The English master; or, student's guide to reasoning and composition: exhibiting an analytical view of the English language, of the human mind, and of the principles of fine writing.* (BL; Hull UL); 2nd edn 1829* (BL; Glasgow UL and PL).   Pp. 305; *358*.

1808* B   *Syllabus of lectures on belles lettres.* Glasgow, 14pp. (BL).

BARBAULD, Anna Letitia (formerly AIKIN)   1743–1825   Sometime teacher

1811* RA   *The female speaker; or, miscellaneous pieces, in prose and verse, selected from the best writers, and adapted to the use of young women.* (BL).   P. *203*.

1781* RA   *Hymns in prose for children.* (BL); at least fifty British and forty American edns to 1880. Facsimile of 1781 edn in Garland Publ. Co's Classics of Children's Literature, no. 10.   P. *207*.

1826* RA   *A legacy for young ladies, consisting of miscellaneous pieces, in prose and verse.* (Nottingham UL; BL); 2nd edn 1826, *LTM*, 21, 1958, no. 250.

1778–9? RA   *Lessons for children.* There seem to have been four sets, but their composition changed in later edns: A. *Lessons for children from two to three years old*, 1778; B. *Lessons for children of three years old, Part One*, 1778; C. *Lessons for children of three years old, Part Two*, 1778?; D. *Lessons for children from three to four years old*, 1779? A., and perhaps other series, was published also as *Instructive lessons*, and other parts of the series as *More instructive lessons* (Nottingham UL). American edns were published as *Easy lessons for children* and *Easy reading lessons for children*, Welch, 57, 58.1, 58.2. Many edns were published until well into the second half of the nineteenth century. The following have been consulted: A. 1778* (Glasgow UL); 1787* (BL); B. 1788* (BL); B. and C. 1778* (BL); D. 1788* (BL). Cf. below *A new sequel to Mrs Barbauld's Lessons*, 1796.

BARCLAY, James   Rector of the Grammar School, Dalkeith

1743* Ed   *A treatise on education: or, an easy method of acquiring language, and introducing children to the knowledge of history, geography, mythology, antiquities, &c. With reflections on taste, poetry, natural history, &c.* Edinburgh. (Glasgow UL; Reading UL; BL); anr edn 1749 (BL)   Pp. 202, 290.

BARCLAY, James   Master of an academy in Goodman's Fields; later at Tottenham

1774* D   *A complete and universal English dictionary . . . to which are prefixed a free enquiry into the origin of letters: an essay on the . . . English language . . . besides a . . . grammar of the same.* (title from 1792). (BL); anr edn 1792* (BL). At least seventeen other edns from 1782 to 1851. Alston, V, 284–7.

BARCLAY, Rachel (formerly LLOYD) 1743–92

1795* RA   *Select pieces of poetry, intended to promote piety and virtue in the minds of young people.* (BL); 2nd edn as: *Poems intended to promote*. . . 1797* (BL; Leeds UL).

BARKER, E.H., see PIERPONT, J. (USA), 1827

BARKER, Isaac   Of Whitby

[1733?]* G   *An English grammar shewing the nature and grounds of the English language, in its present state. With some general observations and directions relating to the spelling, pronouncing, and writing of it.* York. (BL). Alston, I, 63; Vorlat, 1975.   P. 202.

BARNES, William   1801–86   Sometime teacher

1842* G   *The elements of English grammar, with a set of questions and exercises.* (BL).   P. 362; *357*.

BARRE, William   Master of Shoreditch Infants School

1829* RA   *Original hymns for the use of infant schools.* Wellington, Salop. (BL).

BARRIE, Alexander   'Teacher of English in Edinburgh'

[a. 1794] S   *The child's assistant.* Noted on the t.p. of his dictionary in 1794. New edn Glasgow: Francis Orr, 1847* (NLS); anr edn Glasgow, 1856* (BL).

[a. 1781] RA   *A collection of English prose and verse, for the use of schools.* 2nd edn Edinburgh, 1781* (BL); anr edn 1800 (NLS); 23rd edn 1816 (NLS); 27th edn 1827 (NLS).   P. *176*.

[a. 1800] G   *An epitome of English grammar.* 9th edn Edinburgh, 1800 (Columbia UL, N.Y.). Alston, I, 530.

1796* S   *A spelling and pronouncing catechism.* [Edinburgh] Pp. 36. (BL; NLS). Alston, IV, 917 and Plate 96 for t.p.

1794* D   *A spelling and pronouncing dictionary of the English language, for the use of schools* . . . *To which are added, the principles of English grammar.* (BL). Alston, IV, 910 and Plate 93 for t.p.   P. 104.

1800 RA   *The tyro's guide to wisdom and wealth; designed for the moral instruction of youth: with exercises in spelling, containing about five thousand words, having the parts of speech pointed out. To which are now subjoined, the principles of English grammar. Intended as an introduction to the author's Collection.* (title from 1808 edn) Edinburgh (Jordanhill CHE); 2nd edn 1801* (BL); 4th edn 1807 (NLS); 5th edn 1808*, the first to include the grammar (Glasgow UL); 9th edn 1815 (NLS).

BARRON, William   d. 1803   Professor of Belles Lettres and Logic, St Andrews

1806* B   *Lectures on belles lettres and logic*, 2 vols. Pp. 620 + 597. (BL). Howell, 1971, *passim*. The lectures were given between 1778 and 1803.   P. *218*.

BARTLE, G.W.

1858 G   *An epitome of English grammar.* (O).

BARTON, John   'Master of the Free School of Kinfare in Staffordshire'

1634* B   *The art of rhetorick concisely and compleatly handled, exemplified out of Holy Writ, and with a compendious and perspicuous comment, fitted to the capacities of such as have had a snatch of learning, or are otherwise ingenious. By J.B.* (BL). Alston, VI, 60; Howell, 1956, p. 274.

BARWELL, Louisa Mary (formerly BACON) 1800–85.

1833 RE   *Little lessons for little learners, in words of one syllable.* No copy. Moon, 37;

2nd edn 1834; 6th edn, Grant and Griffith, n.d.* (Nottingham UL). Information about edns is erratic: Moon, 37, gives a 4th edn by Harris in 1838, while Grant and Griffith advertise a 5th edn in 1831, and *DNB* says it appeared first in 1883. A second series, according to *DNB*, was published in 1835.

BATCHELOR, Thomas 1775–1838

1809 La *An orthoepical analysis of the English language; or, an essay on the nature of its simple and combined sounds; the manner of their formation by the vocal organs; the minute varieties which constitute a depraved or provincial pronunciation . . . The whole illustrated and exemplified by the use of a new orthoepical alphabet, or universal character . . . Designed for the use of provincial schools.* Pp. viii, 164. (O; BL). A critical facsimile by Arne Zettersten, in *Lund Studies in English*, 45, Lund, 1974*.

BATE, Henry Teacher

[a. 1757]* G *A short system of English grammar. For the use of the boarding school in Worcester.* Worcester: R. Lewis. Pp. v, 44 (Liverpool UL). Inscription date 29 April 1757. Alston, I, 151a.

BATHURST, Charles 'Under-master, Sir J. Williamson's Free School, Rochester'

1846* G *Outlines of English grammar, for the use of schools.* Rochester and London. (BL; O).

BATT, Richard Teacher, Friends School, Lancaster

1836* RA *Gleanings in poetry, with notes and illustrations. First series.* Harvey and Darton. (personal). Pp. 252–3; *383.*

BAYLEY, R.S.

1843 G *The textbook of the People's College on English grammar, for the use of students.* Sheffield: People's College. Pp. 34. (Sheffield PL).

BAYLY, Anselm d. 1794

1771 G *The English accidence teaching by an easy method the pronunciation of English and the parts of speech.* (NYPL). See next entry. Alston, I, 294. Pp. *48, 50.*

1772* G *A plain and complete grammar of the English language; to which is prefixed The English Accedence: with remarks and observations on A Short Introduction to English Grammar.* (Cambridge UL); Scolar Press facsimile 1969*. Alston, I, 313. The grammar remarked on is Lowth's, 1762. P. *333.*

BEARCROFT, William 'Late Master of the Academy, Kirkby Moorside'

1824* S *Practical orthography; or, the art of teaching spelling by writing: containing an improved method of dictating, with exercises for practice; and collections of words of difficult, irregular, and variable spelling. Intended for the use of teachers.* York: Wilson and Sons, and London. (BL). P. 129.

1828* S *A short English spelling book: in which the exercises are divided into two classes; the former consisting of words in which the spelling and pronunciation agree; and the latter, of words in which they differ. Designed for the use of children in general* [and especially as an introduction to his *Practical orthography*] York and London. (BL). Pp. 94; *383.*

BEARD, George

1826 G *An introduction to grammar, with notes.* Taunton. Green, *Bibliotheca Somersetensis*, II, 151.

BEARD, John Relly 1800–76 Teacher

1854 G *Lessons in English; containing a practical grammar, adapted for the use of the self-educating student.* Cassell. (BL).

1860 RE *The rational primer; or first reader: a practical answer to the question, 'How can I learn to read?'.* Manchester, 1860 (O).

BEASLEY, Mat Of Stourbridge

1812* S *Orthographical instructions, with suitable dictation exercises, for the use of schools.* Stourbridge. Pp. 108. (BL); 4th edn as: *Dictation exercises, with suitable orthographical instructions, for the use of schools: being a new system of perfecting children in spelling.* London: Pinnock and Maunder, 1819 (Hove PL); 5th edn, London: Whittaker, 1825* (Nottingham UL).   Pp. 120, 128; *88.*

BEATTIE, (formerly BLAND), Harcourt   'Professor of Elocution, Glasgow, and teacher at the Established Normal College'

1863* P *A new manual of elocution: containing twelve original and simple rules for reading and speaking.* Stereotype edn, Glasgow: Gilchrist. Preface dated August 1863. (personal).   P. *220.*

[Anon.]

1783* RA *Beauties in prose and verse, selected from the most celebrated authors, antient and modern . . . with some original pieces. The whole calculated to exhibit the most striking pictures of virtue and vice to the minds of youth.* Stockton. (BL).

[Anon.]

1772* RA *The beauties of English prose: being a select collection of moral, critical, and entertaining passages, disposed in the manner of essays . . . The whole tending to cultivate the mind, and promote the practice of virtue.* 4 vols. (BL). The preface says the work is 'designed chiefly for the instruction . . . of the British youth . . . as a standard, or model, for . . . correct and fine writing'.   P. *191.*

[Anon.]

[1780?]* RA *Beauties of fables: in verse: selected to form the judgment, direct the taste, and improve the conduct of youth.* (BL).   P. *191.*

[Anon.]

1802* RA *The beauties of modern literature, in prose and verse: selected from the most eminent authors.* Richmond [Yorks.]: T. Bowman. (BL).   P. *192.*

[Anon.]

1757* RA *The beauties of poetry display'd. Containing observations on the different species of poetry, and the rules of English versification. Exemplified by a large collection of beautiful passages, similies, and descriptions.* 2 vols. (BL); facsimile reprint, Garland Press, N.Y., 1969. Listed in Mrs Teachwell's library: see Fenn, *The female guardian* 1784.   P. *180.*

BECK, William

[a. 1829] G *An outline of English grammar.* 3rd edn 1829. Pp. 34. GB.

BEDFORD, Frederick William 'Head-Master of the Leeds Mechanics' and Literary Institution Schools'

1852* G *Basis of English grammar for the use of schools.* Webb, Millington. Pp. iv, 41. (BL)

1858 Ex *Canons of punctuation, based on the analysis of sentences.* Nelson. (BL).

[Anon.]

1824* RA *The bee: a collection of poems chiefly designed for the young.* Dublin: J. Jones (BL); anr edn, for the Society for Promoting the United and Scriptural Education of the Poor of Ireland, [1825?] (BL).

[Anon.]

1793 RA   *The bee, a selection of poetry from the best authors. NCBEL*, II, 417; anr edn Darton and Harvey, pp. x, 192, 1795* (BL); anr edn 1797 (BL); 5th edn 1807* (personal); 6th edn 1811 (BL; Nottingham UL).

BELCHER, Joseph

1825 RA   *Poetical sketches of biblical subjects: partly original, partly selected from our most esteemed poets, illustrative of the sacred volume.* Pp. xii, 298. (BL). The work is intended as, *inter alia,* 'a task book in the higher classes of religious seminaries'.

BELL, David Charles

[1845]* P   *The art of speech and theory of elocution: including . . . an improved system of delivery; the principles of gesture, and a plan of notation, illustrated by diagrams: the whole elucidated and exemplified by eloquent extracts.* Dublin: M'Glashan and Gill. (personal). Preface dated 1 July 1845. Anr edn (?) as: *The theory of elocution* [etc.] Dublin, [1857] (BL).   P. *287.*

[a. 1850] RA   *The modern reader and speaker: a selection of poetry and prose . . . preceded by the principles of elocution* [etc.] 2nd edn Dublin, 1850* (BL). Many edns to 54th, 1881.

BELL, John   'Late teacher of grammar and the mathematics'

1769* G   *A concise and comprehensive system of English grammar. In two books. Designed for the use of schools and private families.* Glasgow. (BL). There are three books, each with its own t.p. dated 1769: *I.* is the grammar; *II. The construction of prose; III. The construction of verse.* Alston, I, 287.   P. *309n.*

[BELLAMY, Daniel] the elder

1739–40* RA   *Miscellanies in prose and verse, consisting of dramatick pieces, poems, humorous tales, fables, &c.* 2 vols. J. Hodges (BL). At the end there is an advertisement for Mrs Martha Bellamy's school, now at Kingston on Thames, and for the school in 'St Edmund's-Bury' kept by Isaac and Hannah Wood.   Pp. *174, 300.*

1723* RA   *The young ladies miscellany: or, youth's innocent and rational amusement. To which is prefixed, a short essay on the art of pronunciation . . . for . . . the young ladies of Mrs Bellamy's school, in Old Boswel-Court, near Temple Bar.* The book was sold by Mrs Bellamy at her school, and also by her sister, Mrs Hannah Wood, 'mistress of the College-Boarding-School, in Bury', Suffolk. (BL); 2nd edn 1726 (Folger L). Alston, VI, 320–1.   Pp. *299–300.*

BELLAMY, Elizabeth

1802 G   [An English grammar]. GB. Title or description?

Bel-vedere see MUNDAY, Anthony

BENHAM, William   1831–1910   Sometime teacher

[1863]* RA   *The English ballads for school reading.* (BL; Cambridge UL).

BENNETT, Richard   'Carlisle-House-School, Lambeth'

1820* RA   *Original pathetic, legendary, and moral poems, intended for young persons, being inculcative of the principles of religion and virtue, clothed in the alluring garb of amusement.* (BL).

BENTLEY, Hugh

[after 1816?] RA   *British class book, prose and verse.* Cradock. Chalmers, p. 121.

BERNARD, Sir Thomas   1750–1818

1809 Ed   *The new school; being an attempt to illustrate its principles, detail, and* *advantages.* (BL); anr edn 1810 (BL); 2nd edn as: *The Barrington School* [etc.] 1812 (BL); 3rd edn 1815* (BFSS archives).   P. 95.

BEST, Hon. Samuel

[a. 1852] G   *Elementary grammar for the use of village schools.* 3rd edn 1852 (BL); 4th edn 1857* (BL); 5th edn 1862 (BL; O).   P. 351.

[Anon.]

[1700?]* S   [*The best and plainest English spelling-book*] *The first part. Containing all the different words, syllables, & letters, in the Old English characters, of the three first usual school-books, (the horn-book, the ABC with the catechism, & the primer) & more too.* Pp. 16. (Harvard UL, lacks t.p.; here designated by caption title). Alston, IV, 192.   Pp. 100; *81.*

BETTESWORTH, John   'Master of the Academy in Quaker's Buildings, West Smithfield'

1778* G   *The English grammar epitomis'd; wherein the parts of speech are made clear and easy. Some sentences inserted, and each word therein grammatically explained, with a reason assigned for the same; to which are added the several rules of syntax, in promiscuous examples of good and bad English* [etc.]. (BL); 3rd edn [1805?] (Alston). Alston, I, 348.   P. 324.

[BEVAN (later MORTIMER), Favell Lee]   1802–78

1833 RA   *The peep of day; or, a series of the earliest religious instruction the infant mind is capable of receiving. With verses illustrative of the subjects.* (title from 1863). *NCBEL,* III, 1090; rev. edn 1863* (V&A); anr edn 1868 (V&A); anr edn 1873 (Bishop Lonsdale C). Sales were 250,000 to 1867, according to Altick, p. 388. One of a series, designed to follow on from *Reading without tears.*   P. 213.

[1836?]* RE   *Reading disentangled; or classified lessons in spelling and reading* [running title] Two series, each of seventeen sheets. Roake and Varty. (BL); 14th edn [1855] (BL); '2nd thousand' 1864 (O); anr edn 1873 (BL; O).   P. *30.*

1857* RE   *Reading without tears; or, a pleasant mode of learning to read. By the author of Peep of Day, &c., &c.* Pp. xvi, 136. (BL); anr edn 1861 (BL; O); anr edn 1864 (O); '19th thousand' 1866 (O); anr edn Part 1, 1869 (V&A); anr edn 1878 (Wandsworth PL); anr edn 1888 (Melbourne UL); '81st thousand' 1890 (O); anr edn 1924 (Bedford CHE). Facsimile pages in Chalmers, pp. 85f.   Pp. 40, 131; *123.*

[a. 1861] RE   *Teaching myself; or, an abridgment of Reading without Tears. For the cottager in his own home.* Noted in the preface to 1861 edn of *Reading without tears.*

[Anon.]

[a. 1845] G   *The Bible word-book; or, the rudiments of English grammar taught by the words of the Old and New Testament, classed according to the parts of speech, and arranged according to the number of syllables.* The 2nd edn, advertised by J.W. Parker in Johns, 1845.

BICKNELL, Alexander   d. 1796

1790* G   *The grammatical wreath; or, a complete system of English grammar: being a selection of the most instructive rules from all the principal English grammars: in two parts: I* [elementary rules] *II* [advanced rules] etc. (O). Alston, I, 450.

Bicknell's other works include *Isabella, or the rewards of good nature, a novel,* and *The Putrid Soul, a poetical epistle to the Rev. Joseph Priestley.* P. *342.*

BIDLAKE, John Purdue Teacher

1861* S *Exercises in orthography and derivation.* Allman. (BL).

1863 G *A new English grammar, combining the substance of Lennie's Principles of English Grammar, with extensive alterations and improvements, and additional chapters on derivation, analysis and composition.* (BL; O).

BIGLAND, John

[a. 1824?] S *The new pronouncing and spelling book, accompanied by a series of . . . lessons.* 5th edn Derby: Mozley, [*c.* 1824]; 8th edn [*c.* 1835]. Chalmers, p. 121.

BILBY, T. and RIDGWAY, R.B 'Masters of the Chelsea and Hart Street Infants' Schools'

1831* RA *The infant teacher's assistant, for the use of schools and private families: or scriptural and moral lessons for infants: with observations on the manner of using them.* Printed for the authors. (BL).

BILTON, Charles

1867–70 RS *The class and standard series of reading book, adapted to the requirements of the revised code.* Books 1–4, boys' and girls' edns. (O).

[a. 1868] RS *The first . . . fourth reading book; book the fifth: a poetical reader.* Advertised by Longman in 1868.

1867 RE *The infant primer for school and home use in teaching reading.* (O); anr edn, eight parts, 'adapted to the requirements of the new code, 1871', 1870–6 (BL).

[*c.* 1870] RE *The reading book for infants.* Advertised by Longman in 1870 as 'adapted to the requirements of the new code, 1871'.

1866* RA *Repetition and reading book for pupil teachers and the upper classes of schools: consisting of selections of prose and poetry from the best English authors.* (BL). P. 260.

BINNALL, Henry

1851 RE *The graduated spelling and reading book.* (O).

BINNS, John 'Schoolmaster at Bretton, near Wakefield'

[a. 1788]* S *The youth's guide, to the English language, in four parts. I. Being a new spelling book; shewing how to pronounce common words. II.* [biblical proper names]. *III.* [homophones]. *IV. A compendious English grammar: shewing in the newest manner how to divide words into syllables* [etc.]. New edn Halifax, 1788 (BL). Alston I, 442. See below, *An essay towards an English grammar,* 1800. Pp. 20–1.

BINNS, William

[1867] RE *Elementary instruction. First stage primer.* (O).

[Anon.]

1849 B *Biographical sketches of eminent British poets, chronologically arranged from Chaucer to Burns, with criticisms on their works.* Akenson, p. 231; anr edn Dublin, 1851* (BL). The collection was compiled by Maurice Cross for the Commissioners of National Education in Ireland. P. *219.*

BIRCHALL, J.

[a. 1821] RA *The monitory task book; consisting of prose and poetry, original and selected: interspersed with striking maxims and moral precepts. Designed for the use of schools.* 2nd edn Manchester: J. Gleave, 1821. NBL, 1949, no. 328.

BIRKIN, William   'Master of an academy in Derby'

1838* D   *The rational English expositor, and guide to pronunciation; containing an extensive selection of words . . . with copious and accurate definitions: being peculiarly adapted, by an analogical classification, a simple notation of sounds, and a clear illustration of leading principles, to facilitate the acquirement of an accurate pronunciation, as well as to elucidate the proper signification of words, by reference to their origin and construction.* Derby: Mozley. (Fulham PL).   P. 103.

BITHELL, Richard   'Master of the London & N.W. Railway Company's School, Wolverton'

1845* S   *Spelling taught by transcribing and dictation, in a series of exercises especially adapted for home work.* Pp. 54. (BL).

BLACKWALL, Anthony   1674–1730   Master of the Grammar School, Market Bosworth

1718 B   *An introduction to the classics . . . with an essay, on the nature and use of those emphatical and beautiful figures which give strength and ornament to writing.* (title from 1719). (BL); 2nd edn 1719* (BL); further edns in 1725; 1728; 1737; 1746; new edn ed. W. Mavor, 1809 (BL). Facsimile of 1719 edn by Garland Press, N.Y., 1969. Alston, VI, 130–5.   Pp. 163; *165–7.*

BLAIR, David, see PHILLIPS, Sir Richard

BLAIR, Hugh   1718–1800   Professor of rhetoric and *belles lettres*, Edinburgh

1783 B   *Lectures on rhetoric and belles lettres,* 2 vols. (BL); 4th edn, 3 vols., 1790* (BL); at least thirty further British edns to 1863 and at least thirty-three American edns to 1873. Ed. H.F. Harding, 2 vols, S. Illinois Press, Carbondale, 1965; facsimile of 1785 edn by Garland Press, N.Y., 1969. Alston, VI, 237–51. Abridged in 1784 and in eight further British edns to 1822, and in seventeen American edns to 1857. Alston, VI, 252–60.   Pp. *163, 184.*

BLAKE, J.   Of Hallwood Academy

1811 RA   *The universal piece writer, the reader and reciter; being a collection of detached sentences, extracts of poetry* [etc.]. Chester: T. Cutter. (BL).

BLAND, Charles

1706* B   *The art of rhetorick, as to elocution; explain'd: and familiarly adapted to the capacityes of school-boys, by way of question and answer; in English.* (BL); anr edn 1708 (BL). Alston, VI, 115.   P. *163.*

1708* B   *The art of rhetorick, as to pronunciation; explain'd: and familiarly adapted to the capacities of school-boys, by way of question and answer; in English.* (BL; Edinburgh UL). Alston, VI, 118a.   Pp. 288; *163.*

BLAND, Harcourt, see BEATTIE, Harcourt

[BLAU, Robert]

[a. 1696] B   *Praxis oratoria vel suadela victrix. Containing some select orations (both in Latine and English). Introducing one another: to each of which are subjoyned suitable citations out of good authors, for confirming of the several points, and a chorus relative to each subject.* 2nd edn enl. Edinburgh, 1696* (Aberdeen UL); 3rd edn 1703 (NLS).   Pp. 277–8.

BLAYMIRES, John   'Schoolmaster at Eccleshill'

1789 S   *The Christian's spelling book, intended for the use of schools and private families.* No copy; anr edn 1815, no copy. Alston, IV, 869.

[a. 1815] S   *The juvenile preceptor; or an easy introduction to reading, being a progressive book of monosyllables adapted to the capacities of children.* 3rd edn, Lane and Whittaker, 1815, from Tuer, (1897) 1979, p. 241, and Gumuchian, 772.

BLOUNT, Thomas   1618–79

1654 B   *The academie of eloquence. Containing a compleat English rhetorique, exemplified, with common-places, and formes, digested into an easie and methodical way to speak and write fluently, according to the mode of the present times.* (BL); five further edns to 1683. Scolar Press facsimile of 1654 edn, 1971*.   Pp. 154–5, 274; *151*.

BLUNDEVILLE, Thomas

1599 Lo   *The art of logike. Plainely taught in the English tongue . . . A very necessarie booke for all young students in any profession to find out thereby the truth in any doubtfull speech* [etc.]. (BL); anr edn 1617 (BL); anr edn 1619 (BL). Scolar Press facsimile of 1599 edn, 1967*. English Experience facsimile of 1599 edn, Amsterdam, 1969; Howell, 1956, says the logic was probably written about 1575.   Pp. 272–3.

BOAD, Henry   'School-Master at Colchester'

[a. 1734] S   *The English spelling-book, and expositor: being a new method of teaching children and adult persons to read, write, and understand the English tongue* [etc.] 2nd edn 1734* (Cambridge UL); 23rd edn enl. by T. Smith, 1805* (BL). Alston IV, 411–18 and Plate 50 for 1734 t.p.   Pp. 58, 101.

BOBBIT, A.

1833* G   *Elements of English grammar; familiarly illustrated, for the use of young people.* J. Souter. (BL). Written by a woman.

Bodleian fragment

[c. 1673?]* S   (Title lost.) A fragment of a spelling-book, 32 pp., incomplete. (O). Alston, IV, 94 and Plate 114.   Pp. 91, 132; *368*.

BOLSTER, John

1814 S   (Bolster's) *Improved spelling-book: or, easy guide to the English language.* Cork (Bodley).

BOLTON, C   'Schoolmaster'

1793 S   *The imperial spelling book; or reading made easy for the use of schools.* J. Marshall. NBL, 1949, no. 146. Alston, IV, 902, could not trace the NBL copy.

BONHOTE, Elizabeth   1744–1818   Of Bungay, Suffolk

1788* RA   *The parental monitor,* 2 vols. W. Lane (BL); 2nd edn 1790, Robin Greer, Cat. 1974, item 77; 3rd edn 1796 (BL).

[Anon.]

1801 G   *The book case of knowledge. Vol 8, Grammar and letters.* John Wallis. Gumuchian, 801.

[Anon.]

1869 RE   *A book of easy lessons for very little children. Edited by a clergyman of the Church of England.* Oxford: J. Parker. Pp. 20. (BL).

[Anon.]

1853* RA   *The book of English poetry: with critical and biographical sketches of the poets.* Nelson. (BL).

Book of juvenile poetry see D., E.

[Anon.]

1800 G   *The book of nouns, or things which may be seen.* Darton and Harvey. A miniature book with sixty-three engravings, Sotheby, Cat. 11 (1976–7), lot 572; Welch, 112.1 and 112.2, gives Philadelphia edns of 1802 and 1804; Rosenbach, 290, describes the book.

[Anon.]

[1858] RA   *A book of poetry for the young.* Burns and Lambert. (BL).

BOOTH, David   1766–1846   Sometime teacher

1831* Ex   *The principles of English composition: illustrated by examples, with critical remarks.* Pp. vi, 351. (BL); 2nd edn 1833, Parker, 1838 (USA), p. 131. Chaps. 2–4 are reprinted from his *An analytical dictionary*, 1835, the introduction to which had been written in 1830.

1837* G   *The principles of English grammar.* Charles Knight. (O; BL).   P. 363.

BOWEN, Edward Ernest   1836–1901   Master at Harrow

1867* Ed   'On teaching by means of grammar', in F.W. Farrar's *Essays on a liberal education.*

[BOWEN, T.]

1799* G   *The rudiments of English grammar, intended for the use of the Rev. T. Bowen's academy, at Walsall.* Walsall: F. Milward. Pp. 60. (O); anr edn 1806 (O).

BOWMAN, Anne

1856a* RE   (Routledge's) *New reading made easy. A first book of lessons in one and two syllables.* (BL; O).

1856b* RA   *Poetry: selected for the use of schools and families. From the most approved authors, ancient and modern.* (BL).

BRADLEY, Charles

[1809]* G   *Grammatical questions, adapted to the grammar of Lindley Murray: with notes.* Banbury (BL; O); 2nd edn York, 1818 (BL); 3rd edn 1813, GB; 4th edn York, 1818 (BL); 6th edn 1825 (BL); 8th edn 1835 (Wisconsin UL).

BRADY, John Henry

1835* RA   *Little fables for little folks; selected for their moral tendency, and rewritten in familiar words, not one of which exceeds two syllables. Designed as reading lessons, to amuse and instruct.* (BL).

1827 D   *The writer's and student's assistant, or a compendious dictionary.* (BL); 2nd edn 1830 (BL); 3rd edn [1835] (BL).

1838 G   *The writer's and student's grammar of the English language; after the model of that by W. Cobbett, but divested of all political illustrations and offensive personal allusions.* Whittaker. (BL; O). Published anonymously.

BRANSBY, James Hews   1783–1847   Teacher

1814 RA   *Selections for reading and recitation: designed for the use of schools.* (BL); 2nd edn as: *The school anthology; or selections . . . [etc.]* 1831* (personal). The 2nd edn is much enlarged.

BRENAN, Justin

1829 Ex   *Composition and punctuation familiarly explained for those who have neglected the study of grammar. For the use of the artisan and mechanic.* (title from 16th edn). (BL); 12th edn, much enl. 1863 (BL); 16th edn 1874* (Glasgow PL).

BRETT, Arthur see *A model for a school*, 1671

BREWER, Ebenezer Cobham 1810–97 'Master of the Mile End School, Norwich' [1864] RE *My first book of reading and spelling.* (BL).

[a. 1853] Ex *A guide to English composition; or, one hundred and twenty subjects analysed, and illustrated from analogy, history, and the writings of celebrated . . . authors, to teach the art of argumentation and the development of thought.* 2nd edn 1853*, pp. xvi, 426 (BL); 4th edn 1872.

1842 RA *School recitations, selected from various authors, and disposed under proper heads.* (BL); 4th edn [1845?]*, Pp. viii, 352, dedication dated 1 October 1845 (private colln).   P. 220.

[Anon.]

[a. 1823] RE *Brickley's new primer, or, mother's first gift. Being an introduction to all the spelling books.* 6th edn Dublin: J.J. Nolan (NLI).

BRIDEL, Edmund Philip 'Master of an academy at Stoke Newington'

[a. 1790] G *An introduction to English grammar, intended also to assist young persons in the study of other languages.* 2nd edn 1790, GB; anr edn 1797* (BL); anr edn [1798?]. Alston, I, 499–500.

BRIGHT, Henry 'Master of New-College School, Oxford'

1783* Ex *The praxis; or, a course of English and Latin exercises, in a series of exemplifications, from an initial one for a beginner at school, to such as are applicable to the capacities and circumstances of young academics, in order to form a proper habit of thinking, and writing, at an early time of life. For the use of youth in the lesser schools.* Oxford. (BL); new edn 1815 (Leicester UL).   Pp. 307, 324; *282, 309.*

BRIGHTLAND, John, see *Reasons for an English education,* 1711.

BRINSLEY, John 1566 until after 1630   Master of the Grammar School, Ashby de la Zouch, Leicestershire

1622 Ed *A consolation for our grammar schooles: or, a faithful and most comfortable incouragement, for laying a sure foundation of all good learning in our schooles . . . More specially for all those of the inferiour sort, and all ruder countries and places, namely, for Ireland, Wales, Virginia, with the Sommer Ilands, and for their more speedie attaining of our English tongue by the same labour, that all may speake one and the same language. And withall, for the helping of all such as are desirous speedilie to recover that which they had formerlie got in the grammar schooles* [etc.] (BL). Ed. T.C. Pollock, Scholars' Facsimiles, N.Y., 1943*; English Experience facsimile, Amsterdam, 1969. Alston, X, 36.

1612 Ed *Ludus literarius: or, the grammar schoole; shewing how to proceede from the first entrance into learning, to the highest perfection required in the grammar schooles . . . Intended for the helping of the younger sort of teachers* [etc.] (BL; O); five further edns in 1627. Ed. E.T. Campagnac, from 1627 edn, Liverpool, 1917; Scolar Press facsimile of 1612 edn, 1968*. Alston, X, 29–34.   Pp. 33–4, 137, 273–4; *112, 383.*

BRITISH AND FOREIGN SCHOOL SOCIETY

1816* Ed *Manual of the system of teaching reading, writing, arithmetic, and needlework, in the elementary schools of the British and Foreign School Society.* (BL); 2nd edn 1821; 3rd edn 1825; as: *Manual of the system of primary instruction pursued in the model schools of the* [BFSS] 1831* (BFSS archives); anr edn 1834, Goldstrom 1972a, pp. 39, 215.   P. 71.

1864 RS *Revised lesson books, for the revised code.* Books 1-6 (O). Goldstrom, 1972a, pp. 169–70.

See also DUNN, Henry and CROSSLEY, J.T.

[Anon.]

1763* S *The British instructor; or the first book for children. Being a plain and easy guide to the English language. Divided into different syllables, with proper lessons under each syllable . . . Designed for the use of schools.* (Yale UL). Alston, IV, 697 and Plate 66 for t.p.   Pp. 76, 160–1.

[Anon.]

[1765?]* Ex *The British letter writer.* (BL). Alston III, 277.   P. *333*.

[Anon.]

[c. 1820?] RE (Innes') *British Minerva primer, or London first book for children.* (Melbourne UL); anr edn [c. 1830], Chalmers, p. 138; anr edn [c. 1830?]* (Nottingham UL).

[Anon.]

[c. 1840] RE *British primer, or the young child's first book.* Derby: Richardson, Sotheby HIC, IV, October 1976, lot 1859; anr edn [c. 1845] Sotheby HIC, VI, October 1977, lot 2767; anr edn 1846* (BL). Other undated edns at Nottingham UL and Bedford CHE. Chalmers, p. 153, suggests a date *c.* 1825.

[Anon.]

[c. 1860] RA *British reading book.* Routledge. Catalogue.

[Anon.]

[c. 1855?]* S *British spelling book.* G. Routledge. Pp. 158. (private colln).

[Anon.]

[a. 1799] S *The British spelling-book, or a rational introduction to the English language . . . wherein the words are accented and divided conformably to the most approved mode of pronunciation. Third edn. Part first. For the use of schools.* Liverpool, 1799* (DES); Part 2, also of 3rd edn, is dated 1801* (DES); 5th edn 1811. Alston, IV, 942.   P. *185*.

[BROKESBY, Francis] 1637–1714

1701* Ed *Of education with respect to grammar schools, and the universities,* (BL), Alston, X, 150.   Pp. 200, 299.

BROMBY, Charles Henry 1814–1907 Principal of Cheltenham Training College

1864* RA *The first book of Wordsworth's Excursion.* With notes. Longman. (BL).   Pp. 265; *263*.

1848 G *The pupil teacher's English grammar, and etymology of the English language.* (BL); 4th edn 1852, Schmitz, I, 201. *Abridgment,* 1868 (O).

BROOKSBANK, John 'Presbyter and schoolmaster in Vine Court in High Holborn'

1651* S *An English monosyllabary. That is, the best art, that can be us'd to teach the learners, of our English tongue. How exactly, and judiciously, to read all words of one syllable . . . Made and composed for the good of the Commonwealth.* Pp. 40 (unnumbered) (BL; O).   P. 18.

1654a* S *Plain, brief, and pertinent rules, for a judicious and artificial syllabication of all English words, according to art, and the institution of the same tongue.* (BL; O). Alston, IV, 57 and Plate 9 for t.p.   Pp. 17–18, 42, 59, 113, 373; *41, 48, 50, 51, 52.*

1654b* S   *Two books more exact and judicious for the entring of children to spell, and read English, than were ever yet extant. An English Syllabary, and An English Monosyllabary. Wherein is the best art that may be, to teach the learners of the same tongue exactly and judiciously, to spell and read all words of one syllabl.* (BL). Brooksbank is here described as 'Minister and Schoolmaster in Jerusalem Court in Fleetstreet'. Anr edn as: *The compleat school-master in two books,* 1660* (BL). Here he is called 'Brocksbank'. Alston, IV, 58–9.   Pp. 96–7.

BROWN, James Robert   'Master of the Spitalfields Infants' School'

1826* Ed   *A compendium of the analytical method of instruction, adopted at Spitalfields Infants' School; with general observations on the system of infant tuition, &c.* (BL); as: *A short essay on infant cultivation,* 1826 (BL); 2nd edn, as: *An essay on infant cultivation, with a compendium,* etc. 1827*; 3rd edn as: *An essay on the cultivation of the infant mind viewed in its connection with the infant system of education,* 1828* (BL); 4th edn 1832 (BL); 5th edn as: *An essay on the cultivation of the infant mind; forming an epitome of the system of infant education,* 1834* (BL); 6th end 1838 (BL).   P. 65.

1837* Ed   *The infant school echo; or, a practical compendium of the system of infant education.* Pp. 90. (BL); 2nd edn 1843 (BL).   P. 71.

BROWN, John   'Master of an academy, Kingston, Surrey'

1809* C   *The elements of English education, containing I. An introduction to English grammar. II. A concise English grammar. III. A short system of oratory . . . VI. Miscellaneous prose selections . . . VII. A miscellaneous poetical selection.* B. Crosby. (BL).

BROWN, Joseph

[1790?]* RE   *The new English primer, or reading made easy, according to a new plan, for the use of schools, and as a first book for children.* (BL). Alston, IV, 874.   P. 98.

BROWN, T.R.

1838* La   *A treatise on the English terminations of words; with a list of the most common prefixes, and their usual significations.* Oundle: Richard Todd. Pp. vii, 25. (BL).

[Anon.]

[1841] RE   *(Brown's) Royal Victoria primer; or child's first book.* Whittaker, NBL, 1946, no. 77.

BROWNE, Richard   'Late English, and Writing-Master of Rugby in the county of Warwick; but now of the city of Coventry'

1692* S   *The English examiner: or, a spelling-book, containing, I. Rules for spelling, reading, and pronouncing of our English tongue, by way of question and answer. II.* [Spelling-lists] *III.* [Homophones] *IV.* [Miscellaneous]. *Lastly, is added the practice of reading, or the way of teaching to read by verses, that have words therein only of one syllable.* (BL). Alston, IV, 166 and Plate 30 for t.p.   P. 373.

1700* S   *The English school reformed: containing, First, rules shewing the nature of vowels, consonants, syllables, diphthongs, dividing of syllables, and of stops and points. Secondly, A praxis . . . Thirdly* [spelling-lists] *Fourthly* [homophones]. *Fifthly . . . words that are writ one way and sounded another . . . Lastly, an accidence adapted to our English tongue.* (BL); 3rd edn 1707* (BL); 11th edn 1736* (O); Scolar Press facsimile of 1700 edn, 1969*. Alston IV, 193–9 and Plate 33 for t.p. of 1700 edn.   Pp. 27, 80, 83, 322, 372; *51.*

BRYANT, Charles   'School-master in Norwich'

[1769?]* S   *A key to letters, or, a complete introduction to spelling and reading English* ... *I.* [Spelling-lists]. *II.* [Division of syllables; sounds of letters; homophones; verbs; scripture names]. Norwich. (commend. letters dated January and February 1769). (BL). Alston, IV, 714 and Plate 72 for t.p.   Pp. 20, 126.

BRYCE, A.H.

1870 RA   *Readings from the best authors.* Nelson. Catalogue.

BUCHAN, Alexander Winton   'Master of St James' Parish School, Great Hamilton Street, Glasgow'

1854* RA   *The advanced prose and poetical reader, being a collection of select specimens in English.* Glasgow. (BL); 2nd edn 1858 (BL).   P. 257.

1859* RA   *The poetical reader: a new selection of poetry for the school-room, with notes and questions.* Edinburgh. (BL); 2nd edn 1861 (BL). A reprint of the poetical part of his advanced reader.

BUCHANAN, James   'Master of the Boarding-School at Loughbury-House, opposite Stockwell, in Surry'

1762* G   *The British grammar; or, an essay, in four parts, towards speaking and writing the English language grammatically, and inditing elegantly. For the use of schools.* (BL). Published anonymously. 2nd edn 1768 (BL); 3rd edn 1779 (NLW). Scolar Press facsimile of 1762 edn, 1968*. Alston, I, 208–11.   Pp. 34–5, 43, 283–4, 291, 341; *342.*

1753* S   *The complete English scholar. In three parts. Containing a new, short, and familiar method of instructing children, and perfecting grown persons in the English tongue, and of learning grammar in general, without the help of Latin.* (BL; Hull UL). Alston, IV, 594 and Plate 56 for t.p.   Pp. 172; *323.*

1766* D   *An essay towards establishing a standard for an elegant and uniform pronunciation of the English language, throughout the British dominions, as practised by the most learned and polite speakers ... Designed for the use of schools* [etc.] (BL); Garland Press facsimile, N.Y., 1969. Alston, VI, 487.

1773* G   *The first six books of Milton's Paradise Lost, rendered into grammatical construction; the words of the text being arranged, at the bottom of each page, in the same natural order with the conceptions of the mind; and the ellipsis properly supplied, without any alteration in the diction of the poem. With notes ... to which are prefixed remarks on ellipses and transposition, exhibiting an easy method of construing, and reading with judgment, either prose or verse. Designed for the use of our most eminent schools.* Edinburgh. (BL). Published posthumously. Alston, III, 109 and Plate 36 for reproduction of Buchanan's pp. 20–1   Pp. 283–4.

1757 D   *A new pocket-book for young gentlemen and ladies: or, a spelling dictionary of the English language.* (O; Dr Williams L). Alston, IV, 674 and Plate 63 for t.p.

1770* Ed   *A plan of an English grammar-school education. With an introductory inquiry whether by the English language alone, without the embarrassment of Latin and Greek, the British youth, in general, cannot be thoroughly accomplished in every part of useful and polite literature, and qualified to make a more early, advantageous, and elegant figure in life.* Edinburgh. (BL). Alston, X, 260.   Pp. 204, 283–4.

1767* G   *A regular English syntax. Wherein is exhibited, the whole variety of English* *construction, properly exemplified. To which is added, the elegant manner of arranging words, and members of sentences. The whole reduced to practice, for the use of . . . our most eminent schools.* (BL); anr edn 1769* (O); five American edns to 1792. Alston, I, 279–85. Pp. 374; 377.

BUCKE, Charles 1781–1846

1829 G *A classical grammar of the English language.* (BL).

BUCKLEY, T.A. (Theodore Alois William) 1825–56

1854a RA *The boy's first help to reading, or selections from the best authors.* Routledge. Catalogue.

[1854] RA *The boy's second help to reading,* Routledge, (BL; O).

1854b RA *The girl's first help to reading.* Routledge. (BL).

1854c RA *The girl's second help to reading.* Routledge. (BL; O).

BULLAR, John

1806* Ed *Thoughts on the subject of education at school: addressed to his friends by John Bullar.* Southampton: Baker and Fletcher. Pp. 36. (BL). P. 349.

BULLEN, Henry St John 'First assistant master at the Grammar School, Bury St Edmunds'

1797* G *The rudiments of English grammar, for the use of schools.* Bury St Edmunds: Gedge and Robinson (BL); 3rd edn 1813, no copy; as: *Linguae anglicanae clavis; or, rudiments* [etc], rev. Charles Heycock, 1853 (BL; O); 2nd edn 1870 (BL; O). Alston, I, 501. P. *342.*

BULLOKAR, William *c.* 1531–1609 Sometime teacher

1580a* S *(Bullokar's) Booke at large, for the amendment of orthographie for English speech* [etc.]. (BL; O); ed. Max Plessow, *Palaestra,* 52 1906*; English Experience facsimile, Amsterdam, 1968; ed. J.R. Turner, *The Works of William Bullokar,* vol. III, Univ. Leeds Texts and Monographs n.s. I, 1970*. Alston, VI, 529 and Plate 37 for t.p. P. 90.

1586* G *(William Bullokar's) Pamphlet for grammar: or rather to be said his abbreviation of his Grammar for English, extracted out of his Grammar at Large.* (Reformed orthography normalised.) (O; Christ Church, Oxford); ed. Max Plessow, *Palaestra,* 52, 1906*; ed. J.R. Turner, *The Works of William Bullokar,* vol. II Univ. Leeds Texts and Monographs n.s. I, 1980*. Alston, I, 1, explains the ghostly existence (now terminated) of Bullokar's *Bref grammar.* Pp. 324; *323.*

1580b S *A short introduction or guiding to print, write, and reade Inglish speech* [etc.] (Huntington L); 2nd edn 1581 (Bath UL). Edited by B. Danielsson and R.C. Alston, *The works of William Bullokar,* vol. I, Univ. Leeds Texts and Monographs n.s. I, 1966*, which reproduces both edns. Dobson, 1968, I, 93–117. Pp. 37; *52.*

BUNYAN, John 1628–88

1686 RA *A book for boys and girls: or, country rhimes for children.* (BL); as: *A book for boys and girls: or, temporal things spiritualized,* 1701, (BL); 3rd edn 1707; as: *Divine emblems, or temporal things spiritualized,* 9th edn 1724 (BL). Many edns to 1864. Intro. John Browne, with seventy-nine facsimile pages of 1686 edn, 1889* (BL); ed. E.S. Buchanan, NY, 1928* (BL); facsimile in Garland Press Classics of Children's Literature, no. 4; in *John Bunyan, the poems,* ed. Graham Midgley, Oxford, 1980. The spelling-section of 1686, 'An Help to Children', was omitted in subsequent edns. Pp. 157–8.

BURGESS, D

1759*RA   *The entertainer; or, youth's delightful preceptor, containing a collection of the most curious and remarkable pieces of natural and civil history, poetry, voyages, fables, lives, travels, wars, battles, sieges, &c. &c. . . . An appendix containing rules for reading and study, with a catalogue of such books as are proper to form the library of the gentleman, lady, tradesman, &c. . . . The whole designed not only for the use of schools, but also for those who have neither time to read, nor money to purchase the larger works from which those ingenious and instructing pieces are extracted.* Berwick: R. Taylor. Pp. vi, 330. (BL).   Pp. 173; *172.*

[BURGH, James]   1714–75   Master of an academy at Stoke Newington

1761 P   *The art of speaking. In two parts. Containing I. An essay, in which are given rules for expressing properly the principal passions and humours, which occur in reading or publick speaking. II. Examples or (sic) speeches taken from the antients and moderns . . . with notes of direction referring to the essay.* (title from 2nd edn). (Manchester PL); 2nd edn Dublin, 1763* (BL). Alston, VI, 334–54, records twenty-two edns in all to 1804.   Pp. 173–4; *287, 374.*

BURN, John

1766* G   *A practical grammar of the English language: in which, the several parts of speech are clearly and methodically explained . . . together with rules of composition, or the proper arrangement of words in sentences, also illustrated by various examples. For the use of schools.* Glasgow. (BL); 2nd edn 1772 (NLS); 8th edn 1802* (BL). Alston, I, 271–7, records ten edns in all to 1810.   Pp. 319; *163.*

1777 D   *A pronouncing dictionary of the English language.* Glasgow. (Marietta C); 2nd edn [1786?] (Glasgow PL); Scolar Press facsimile of 1786 edn, 1969.

BURNET, Gilbert   1643–1715

1761* (1668) Ed   *Thoughts on education. By the late Bishop Burnet. Now first printed from an original manuscript.* Pp. xiv, 95. (BL); ed. John Clarke, Aberdeen, 1914 (BL).   P. 294.

BURNS, James

[c. 1867] RS   *Standard reading books, adapted to the requirements of the revised code.* (O, Books 2, 3 and 4 only).

[BURROUGHS, Mrs]

1807*RA   *The monitor of youth, and companion to manhood: or, selections to create a taste for composition.* Dublin. (BL).   P. 223.

BURROWS, Alfred J.   'Certificated master of Bosbury Grammar School, Herefordshire'

[1852]* Ed   *Notes and abstracts or heads of gallery lessons; adapted to simultaneous and class teaching. For the use of teachers in elementary schools, pupil teachers, and candidates for certificates. Part the first.* Pp. 64. (BL).

BURTON, John   'Late schoolmaster at Leicester'

1823* S   *A select yet comprehensive spelling-book, and expositor of the English language, containing nearly ten thousand of the most useful words, from one to seven syllables inclusive, accented and divided according to the purest modes of pronunciation . . . Adapted to schools in general.* John Offer. (BL).

BUSCHE, Alexandre van den (LE SILVAYN)

1596* B   *The orator: handling a hundred severall discourses, in forme of declama-*

tions: some of the arguments being drawne from Titus Livius and other ancient writers, the rest of the authors owne invention: part of which are of matters happened in our age . . . Englished by L.P. (Lazarus Piot or Pyott). (BL). Howell, 1956, pp. 336–8; Baldwin, 1944, II, 45–8.

BUTLER, Charles   *c.* 1560–1647   Master of Basingstoke School

1633 G   *The English grammar, or the institution of letters, syllables, and words, in the English tongue.* (BL; Bodley); anr edn 1634 (BL). The 1634 text was edited by A. Eichler, Halle, 1910*. Alston, I, 5–6; Dobson, 1968, I, 156–65; Vorlat, 1975.   Pp. 81, 330; *29, 41, 48, 143.*

1597* B   *Rameae rhetoricae libri duo. In usum scholarum.* Oxford. (BL); anr edn as: *Rhetoricae libri duo, quorum prior de tropis & figuris, posterior de voce & gestu praecipit: in usum scholarum accuratius editi,* 1598; anr edn 1600* (BL). At least nine further edns to 1684. Howell, 1956, p. 262.

[BUTLER, J.]

1772* Ed   *Proposals for an amendment of school-instruction.* (BL). NBL, 1949, no. 45, whence attribution (by Arnold Muirhead).   Pp. 183, 204–6; *309n., 383.*

BUTLER, James   Master of a school in Birmingham

1828* Ed   *Outlines of practical education: or, a brief statement of the course of elementary, mathematical, classical and philosophical studies, pursued by his own pupils.* (BL).   P. 316.

[BUTLER, Samuel]   Master of a boarding school in Bristol

[1750]* Ed   *An essay upon education, intended to shew that the common method is defective . . . With a plan of a new method, more extensive, and of more general use. By a gentleman of Bristol.* (BL: Bristol UL and PL). Information from Jonathan Barry. Alston, X, 213.   P. 203.

BUTTER, Henry   b. 1794?

1830* S   *The etymological spelling book; being an introduction to the spelling, pronunciation and derivation, of the English language: containing . . . above 3000 words deduced from their Greek and Latin roots: adapted for the use of classical and ladies' schools, and also of adults and foreigners.* Preface dated 26 December 1829. (BL); 21st edn 1836* (Nottingham UL); 225th edn 1859* (S.A. Library, Cape Town). Very many edns, e.g. 421st [1883?] (Leicester UL); 470th, 1880 (Fulham PL). Glasgow PL has an edn of 1948.   P. *357.*

[1828]* S   *Gradations in reading and spelling, upon an entirely new and original plan, by which dissyllables are rendered as easy as monosyllables.* Three parts. Dated from preface. (BL; O has Parts 1 and 2); 3rd edn advertised in 1830; 21st edn 1839 (BL); 35th edn 1848 (BL). Introduced into Ackworth School in 1831.   P. 117.

[1828?] S   *The gradual primer, upon an entirely new and original plan, by which young children may more easily learn words of two syllables than they have heretofore learned words of one syllable.* 10th edn 1839 (BL; O); 45th edn 1858 (BL). Part 1 of *Gradations* issued separately.

[a. 1843?] G   *Inductive grammar: being a simple and easy introduction to a grammatical knowledge of the English language. Designed for the use of beginners. By an experienced teacher.* James S. Hodson, jr, 112 Fleet Street. 1843* (BL). Published anonymously; the attribution is by BL.   Pp. 348–9, 365.

BUTTON, John V.   'Of the Classical & Commercial Academy, Cliff, Lewes'

1805* RA   *Exercises on elocution; or, poems, select and original, principally intended for public recitation: compiled and written by J.V. Button.* Lewes: J. Baxter. Pp. viii, 231. (BL). The prospectus issued for the opening of Button's 'English grammar school' in Lewes on 11 July 1791, was reprinted in 1888* (BL).   P. 656.

BYSH, John

[1822] RE   *The imperial primer, or, first book for children, intended as an easy introduction to reading and spelling.* For John Bysh: Mary Dewick. *Bookmark* Catalogue, December 1985, item 211.

C., T.

1843 G   *The keystone of grammar laid; or, the governess's assistant in simplifying that science.* (O; BL).

[CALVERLEY, Francis]

1681* S   *A pleasant spelling-piece: spelling the most variously written syllables in the Bible, or elsewhere, with such distinction, plain and delightful demonstrations, that the least reading child may quickly become perfect in spelling. With* [an introduction to Latin]. Pp. 4. (O). Alston, IV, 140a.

CAMPBELL, George   1719–96   Professor of Divinity, Aberdeen University

1776 B   *The philosophy of rhetoric,* 2 vols. Many edns in Britain and America to 1911. Abridged for schools by A. Jamieson, 1823*. Reprint of 1850 edn, ed. Lloyd F. Bitzer, Carbondale, Ill., 1963*. Alston, VI, 233.   Pp. *184–5.*

CAMPBELL, Mrs Graham

1861 G   *Louisa's metrical English grammar.* Cheltenham. (Cheltenham PL; BL; O).

CAMPBELL, James   Teacher of English, Arbroath Academy: previously in Dundee

[a. 1829] S   *The child's economic instructor. Part I.* 2nd edn Arbroath, 1829*. Pp. 24. (BL); 25th edn Edinburgh, 1852 (BL).

1829* S   *The child's economic instructor. Part II.* Arbroath.   Pp. 36. (BL).   P. 240.

[a. 1852] S   *The child's economic instructor. Part III.* 16th edn Edinburgh, [1852]*. Pp. 144. (BL).

[1832] RA   *A collection of interesting and instructive lessons, in prose and verse . . . and a copious list of Latin and Greek roots. For the use of senior classes.* Dated from the preface to the 1834 edn, 1 May 1832. But the 1834* edn carries no indication that it is not the 1st, and the preface to the 7th edn, Edinburgh, 1846* (BL), suggests that the 2nd edn was in 1842. This would make 1834 a (delayed?) 1st edn.

1832 RA   *A collection of interesting and instructive lessons, with various original exercises, intended as a sequel to The Economic Instructor. For the use of junior classes.* Edinburgh. (Dundee PL). Dundee PL have the following edns: 6th 1834; 7th 1836; 12th 1840; 16th 1842; 17th 1844; anr 1846. BL has 21st 1853*; 23rd n.d.

CAPP, Mrs

[a. 1866] G   *An easy grammar, for the use of schools.* 3rd edn, Lincoln. (O).

CARE, Henry   1646–88

1687* S   *The tutor to true English: or, brief and plain directions, whereby all that can* *read and write, may attain to orthography, (or the exact writing of English) as readily as if bred scholars . . . With an introduction to arithmetic* [etc.] (BL); 2nd edn 1699 (BL); Scolar Press facsimile of 1687 edn, 1971*. Alston, IV, 151–4 and Plate 24 for t.p. of 1687.   Pp. 72; *50, 81.*

CAREY, John   1756–1826   Master of a school at West Square, Surrey

1817* Ex   *Introduction to English composition and elocution; in four parts, viz. I. Aesop modernised and moralised, in a series of instructive tales, calculated, both as reading lessons, and as subjects for narration: II. Skeletons of those tales, with leading questions and hints, to guide and assist the juvenile writer in re-composing them: III. Poetic reading made easy, by means of metrical notes to each line: IV. An appendix of select prose.* Pp. x, 268. (BL; Glasgow UL).   P. *312.*

1809 Ex   *Practical English prosody and versification, or descriptions of the different species of English verse – gradually accommodated to the capacities of youth at different ages and calculated to produce correctness of ear and taste in reading and writing poetry.* GB; anr edn 1816* (BL). *Key,* 1816 (BL).

CARPENTER, Joseph Edwards

1868 Ex   *A handbook of poetry: being a clear and easy guide . . . to the art of making English verse . . . To which is added a new poetical anthology, and a concise dictionary of proper rhymes.* (BL).

1869* RA   *The public school speaker and reader: a selection of prose and verse, from modern and standard authors; classified and arranged for the use of public schools. With full instruction in the art of elocution.* (BL).   P. *220.*

CARPENTER, Thomas   'Master of the Academy, Barking'

1813 La   *An English vocabulary, in which the words are arranged indiscriminately; designed as a sequel to the Scholar's Spelling Assistant . . . To which are added miscellanies.* (DES); 2nd edn 1816* (BL); anr edn [*c.* 1824], Chalmers, p. 123.   P. *355.*

1803* S   *The scholar's orthographical and orthoepical assistant, or English exercise book.* Pp. 354. (BL). Includes more than 200 pp. of prose and verse in his phonetic spelling. Anr edn (?) as: *New orthographical assistant, or English exercise book,* 1807, Chalmers, p. 123.

1796* S   *The scholar's spelling assistant: wherein the words, &c. are arranged on an improved plan . . . For the use of schools and private tuition.* (BL); anr edn 1827* (BL); more than thirty edns overall to 1863 (BL) and a Toronto edn of 1867, Deverell, 1963.

[a. 1825] RA   *The school speaker; consisting of poetical and prosaic pieces, orations, dialogues &c., introductory, appropriate, and interesting . . . for the use and improvement of young persons.* 3rd edn 1825* (O).

1837* C   *The young scholar's manual of useful knowledge.* Pp. 72. (BL). Includes 8 pp. of English grammar.

[CARTER, John]

1764* D   *The complete English spelling dictionary . . . by which foreigners will acquire the true English accent; natives will be enabled to correct and shake off the false and improper dialect (peculiar to any county in this kingdom) and children may be taught to speak the language with the greatest propriety. For the use of schools.* (BL). Alston, IV, 703 and Plate 70 for t.p. in full.

CARTER, John   Of Ipswich

[a. 1797] G   *A short and easy introduction to English grammar.* 5th edn, Ipswich: G. Jermyn, 1797* (Wisconsin UL). Alston, I, 503.

CARTER, John   Of Leeds

1773* G   *A practical English grammar, with exercises of bad spelling and bad English: or, a plain and easy guide to speaking and writing the English language with accuracy and correctness. Containing* . . . [etc.]. Leeds: John Binns. (BL). Alston, I, 316.

CASSELL

1869–70 RS   (Cassell's) *Primary series. Parts 1–9.* (BL).

1865–75 RE   [Classics retold in words of one syllable]
    Pilgrim's Progress [c. 1869]
    Rare Romance of Reynard the Fox [c. 1869], Ellis, pp. 24–5.

see also FOWLER, William C. (USA)

CASSELL, John

1855* G   *The child's educator; or, familiar lessons on natural history.* In twelve parts. Pp. vi, 594. (BL). Each part contains a 'lesson on language'.   Pp. 63; *346n.*

1856–7 RS   *Educational course,* 1–6 (Advt).

[Anon.]

1852* G   *A catechism of English grammar, especially adapted for a class book. For the use of schools.* Wymondham: T. Colman. (BL). The cover title says 'By a lady'.

CATHOLIC POOR SCHOOL COMMITTEE

1860–2 RS   *Reading books, 1–5.* Goldstrom, 1972a, pp. 118, 171, 211.

1867 RS   *Burns' standard reading book, adapted to the requirements of the revised code. Books 1–5.* A simplified version of the preceding. Goldstrom, 1972b, pp. 137–9.

CATLOW, Samuel   Of a private seminary at Mansfield

1793* Ed   *Observations on a course of instruction, for young persons in the middle classes of life.* Sheffield. (Leeds UL; BL). Alston, X, 321.

1798 Ed   *Outlines of a plan of instruction . . . to which is added, a detailed view of the system of studies . . . adopted in the literary and commercial seminary established by the Rev. Samuel Catlow, at Mansfield, Nottingham. Mon. Rev.,* 27 (November 1798), 327. For Catlow's later views on school textbooks see also COLLINS, Joshua, below.

CAWDREY, Robert

1600 RA   *A treasurie or storehouse of similies: both pleasaunt, delightfull, and profitable, for all estates of men in generall.* (BL); anr edn 1609, *NCBEL*; Scolar Press facsimile of 1600 edn, 1969*.   P. 141. *See also* p. 58.

Certen observacons for Latyne and Englishe versyfyinge see B., H.

CHALMER, John   Teacher of writing and accounts

1687* S   *English orthography: or, the art of writing and spelling true English, in three parts.* Part I [Letters]. Part II [Spelling]. Part III [Writing]. (Aberdeen UL). The Glamis Castle copy is dated 1686. Alston, IV, 147 and Plate 25 for t.p. in full.   P. 127.

CHAMBERLAIN, Eliza

1846* D   (Chamberlain's) *Young scholar's new English dictionary; containing every word in common use, fully explained and accented.* (Nottingham UL).   P. *355.*

CHAMBERLAIN, T.

[a. 1856] G   *English grammar, and how to teach it: together with a lesson in spelling and reading.* 3rd edn 1856*. Pp. 24. (BL).

CHAMBERS

[a. 1845] RS   *The first book of reading, under six years old.* Advt in 1845. *The second book of reading*, advertised at the same time.

[a. 1865] RS   *Introduction to reading.* Chambers's minor educational course. Advt.

1863 RS   *Narrative series of standard reading books.* Books 1–6. (BL).

1867 RS   *National reading books*, Book 1 (Hull UL; BL); rev. series, Parts 1–9, 1873–7 (BL).

[a. 1865] RS   *Reading lessons.* Chambers's minor educational course. Advt.

CHAMBERS, Robert   1802–71   Sometime teacher

1836 B   *History of the English language and literature.* Chambers's Educational Course. Edinburgh. (BL).   P. *219*.

CHAMBERS, William   1800–83

1866* C   *Miscellaneous questions, with answers. Embracing science, literature, arts, &c.* Edinburgh: W. and R. Chambers (BL).   Pp. 263–4.

1851* RA   *Poems for young people.* Chambers's Library for Young People. Edinburgh. (NLS; BL); anr edn 1870 (Preston PL).

CHAPMAN, George   1723–1806   Master of Dumfries School

1773* Ed   *A treatise on education. With a sketch of the author's method.* Edinburgh. (BL); 5th edn 1792* (BL). Alston, X, 264–8.   P. 206.

CHAPMAN, James   'Teacher of the science and practice of elocution, Edinburgh'

1818* P   *The music, or melody and rhythmus of language; in which are explained . . . the five accidents of speech . . . illustrated with symbolical marks, and a musical notation . . . To which are added, outlines of gesture, and a selection of pieces in verse and prose.* Edinburgh. (BL). 2nd edn 1819 (formerly in the possession of Arvid Gabrielson).

[a. 1811] RA   *The orator, or elegant extracts, for the use of schools and academies; to which is prefixed, a dissertation on oratorical delivery, with an appendix, containing outlines of gesture, and examples of the principal passions and emotions.* 2 vols. 2nd edn Glasgow, 1811 (NLS); 3rd edn Edinburgh, advertised in his 1821 work: see next entry.

1821* P   *The original rhythmical grammar of the English language: or, the art of reading and speaking, on the principles of the music of speech.* Edinburgh. (BL).   Pp. *287–8*.

CHAPMAN, Thomas

[1765?] S   *The new universal and royal spelling book.* No copy. Alston, IV, 703d. [Anon.]

[1704] S   *The charity school, or reading and spelling made easy to the meanest capacity; chiefly designed for the use of all the charity schools in England; containing, I. Tables of common words from one syllable to eight, divided and not divided* [etc.] *TC*, III, 428 (November 1704) and 468 (June 1705). Alston, IV, 216–17. No copy.

CHARLES, James   Printer

[1807?] RE   (Charles's) *New and improved royal primer; or, the first book for children.* Dublin: J. Charles (BL).

[Anon.]

[a. 1805] RA   *The charms of literature: consisting of curious, scarce, and interesting pieces in prose and poetry.* 2 vols. 5th edn enl. Newcastle-upon-Tyne: J. Mitchell, 1812* (BL). Reviewed in the *British Critic* for August 1805. The collection is specifically, but not solely, for the young.

CHAUCER, Geoffrey, see MCLEOD, W., 1871; MORRIS, R., 1867.

[Anon.]

1798 RE   *The child's best companion, being a selection of spellings and lessons, adapted to improve the juvenal mind.* 16 leaves. (Melbourne UL).

[Anon.]

1677* S   *The child's Bible. Or, an introduction to the reading of the Bible. Being a collection of all the words that are found in the Old and New Testament . . . digested methodically under several heads, according to the different ways of spelling and pronouncing them. Together with a proposal of a more advantageous way of calling some of the letters, than hitherto hath been used.* (Yale UL). Alston, IV, 132, and Plate 20 for t.p. in full.   Pp. 49, 117; *35n., 49–50, 52.*

[Anon.]

[1856]* S   *The child's book to begin with; containing the alphabet and easy lessons in spelling and reading.* Carmarthen: William Spurrell. Pp. 32. (BL).   P. 68.

[Anon.]

[*c.* 1825?] RE
The child's easy primer: being the best introduction to reading and spelling. J. Catnach. T.p. illustrated in Leslie Shepard, *The history of street literature,* David and Charles, 1973, p. 153.

[Anon.]

1780 S   *The child's first book.* SPCK. Goldstrom, 1972b, p. 14.

[Anon.]

[*c.* 1840?]* S   *The child's first book.* Derby: T. Richardson. Pp 28. (Nottingham UL).

[Anon.]

[a. 1820] S   *The child's first book, Part I.* New edn, Rivington, 1820*; Part 2. 1820. (Leicester UL). Goldstrom, 1972a, p. 29, and 1972b, pp. 14–15, quotes and equates with SPCK volume in previous entry. There is no reference here to SPCK.

Many publishers produced small works with this title, usually undated.

[Anon.]

1855* S   *The child's first book and new pictorial primer.* H. Elliot. Pp. 36. (BL).

[Anon.]

1835 S   *The child's first book and Sunday School primer.* T. Hogg. Pp. 72. Chalmers, p. 123; anr edn 1838* (BL).

[Anon.]

1848 S   *The child's first book: containing the alphabet, words of two or three letters, and short sentences.* Glasgow. Chalmers, p. 123.

[Anon.]

1801* S   'The Child's First Book' improved, with a preface addressed to all affectionate mothers and teachers of children. For the author. Pp. x, 22. (BL); 2nd edn, Vernor and Hood, 1805, Chalmers, p. 123.   P. 97.

[Anon.]

[1860?] S   *The child's first book; or early instructor.* Woodbridge: Edward Pite. Pp. 72. (BL).

[Anon.]

[*c.* 1850?] RE   *The child's first book or easy lessons, etc.* Northampton: Taylor and Son. Pp. 69. (Bedford CHE).

[Anon.]

[a. 1820?] RE   *The child's first book: or, English primer; containing a quantity of spelling and reading lessons; to which are added several pieces of select poetry, the Church Catechism, &c.* Devonport: Samuel and John Keys. Advertised in *The true . . . history of Fair Rosamund* [*c.* 1820] (V&A).

[Anon.]

[a. 1825] S   *The child's first book, or, key to reading, adapted to the capacities of very young children, intended as an introduction to the Mentorian Primer.* 10th edn. Whittaker. Chalmers, p. 124. Cf. William Pinnock, *The Mentorian primer,* below.

[Anon.]

[1840?]* RE   *The child's first book; or, reading and spelling made easy.* W.S. Johnson. Pp. 12. (BL).

[Anon.]

[1823?] G   *The child's first . . . [to fifth] . . . grammar lessons . . . contracted into a table for the improvement of young children. Printed originally for the use of the Misses Wilmshurst's Seminary, Cromwell House, Malden.* Five parts. (BL).

[Anon.]

1854 RE   *The child's first lesson book, chiefly in words of one syllable.* D. Bogue. (V&A).

[Anon.]

1844* S   *The child's first noun book.* Seeley, Burnside and Seeley. (BL).

[Anon.]

[*c.* 1825?]* S   *The child's first spelling book or an easy introduction to reading.* Ipswich: J. Raw. Pp. 71. (Bedford CHE).

[Anon.]

[*c.* 1840] S   *The child's first step to learning.* Wood. Chalmers, p. 124, and Gumuchian, 105; anr edn (?) T. Goode, [*c.* 1850]*. Pp. 6 (BL); 22nd edn J.T. Wood, n.d. (Wandsworth PL).

[Anon.]

[*c.* 1840?]* S   *The child's first step up the ladder of learning.* Dean and Son (V&A).

[Anon.]

[*c.* 1805?]* S   *The child's friend; or, reading and spelling made completely easy, wherein the lessons are arranged in such order that the learner is led by simple and familiar words, to the more compound and difficult sentences; which is allowed by all teachers to be the most rational and complete mode of instruction.* Wellington and Ironbridge: F. Houlston. (Hull UL).

[Anon.]

1842 RE   *The child's guide to reading.* Edinburgh. (O).

[Anon.]

[*c.* 1850?]*   *Child's instructer (sic); or, an introduction to the spelling book; intended*

for the use of preparatory schools. Richardson. Pp. 70. (Nottingham UL).
[Anon.]

1797* RE   *The child's instructor: consisting of easy lessons for children on subjects which are familiar to them, in language adapted to their capacities. By a friend to little children.* Congleton: J. Dean. (Manchester PL). Alston, IV, 927 and Plate 102 for t.p.   P. 120.
[Anon.]

[a. 1828] RE   *The child's instructor; intended as a first book for children, with superior engravings. By a fellow of the Royal Society.* 4th edn Deal: T. Hayward, 1828 (Wandsworth PL); anr edn [*c.* 1840] Sotheby, Cat. 11 (1978), lot 106.
[Anon.]

1824* S   *The child's monitor; or select rules for spelling the English language: with a few simple questions in English grammar and arithmetic.* Ross: W. Farrer. Pp. 36. (BL; Glasgow UL).
[Anon.]

1742 S   *The child's new play-thing: being a spelling-book intended to make the learning to read, a diversion instead of a task. Consisting of . . . [stories etc.]. With a new invented alphabet, and a preface shewing the use of it. Designed for the use of schools, or for children before they go to school.* No copy; 2nd edn 1743* (BL; Wandsworth PL). British and American edns to 1819. Alston, IV, 551–60; NBL, 1946, no. 48; Thwaite, 1972, p. 43; Nila B. Smith, p. 28.   P. 162.
[Anon.]

1799* RE   *The child's new spelling primer; or, first book for children. To which is added the stories of Cinderella, and the Little Red Riding Hood.* Dublin: T. Wilkinson. (BL; Cambridge UL; NLI). Alston, IV, 943 and Plate 106 for t.p.
[Anon.]

[*c.* 1787] RE   *The child's own book. Containing the alphabet, and easy lessons, in verse and prose.* J. Marshall. Welch, 1972.
[Anon.]

[a. 1820] S   *The child's own spelling book containing a variety of instructive reading lessons.* Devonport: Samuel and John Keys. Price one penny. Advt *c.* 1820.
[Anon.]

1812* S   *The child's preceptor; or a short and easy guide to spelling and reading the English language; accompanied by a variety of instructive accounts, of pious, and virtuous young persons, formed as progressive lessons, and adapted to the capacities of children; to which is added a select Scripture pronunciation.* Bury: B. Crompton. (Glasgow UL). A pedagogical preface is signed 'B. Crompton'.
[Anon.]

[*c.* 1815?] RE   *The child's primer, or first book for children.* York: Kendrew (V&A; Melbourne UL); anr edn 1834, Chalmers, p. 125.
[Anon.]

1843* RE   *The Child's Reader, and Pleasure and Profit. By the author of Help to the Schoolmistress.* Darton and Clark. (BL). Two works, also published separately, each of 72 pp.   P. 241.
[Anon.]

1692* S   *The child's recreation, containing a necessary catechism . . . Also easie directions for speedy teaching children to spell, and read true English, &c.*

[colophon imprint] Will. Bonny for Tho. Howkins. (Columbia UL).

[Anon.]

[a. 1772] RE *The child's tutor; or, entertaining preceptor. To render his introduction into learning pleasing, instructive, and agreeable.* 3rd edn Newcastle: T. Saint. (Melbourne UL).

[Anon.]

1709 S *The child's tutor; or The Shorter Catechism . . . having before it all the words thereof, ranked in the most convenient order, as to the accent, sound of the vowels, and division of syllables.* Edinburgh: James Watson. No copy. Law, pp. 195–6.

[Anon.]

1781 RA *A choice collection of hymns, and moral songs; adapted to the capacities of young people, on the several duties and incidents of life . . . To which is added, specimens of divine poetry. By several authors.* Newcastle: T. Saint. Opie, 1973, no. 717; anr edn Hartford, Conn., 1801, Welch, 200.

[Anon.]

[a. 1852]* RA *Choice descriptive poetry: intended for the use of schools and families.* Whitaker. (BL, acquired 1852).

[Anon.]

1862* RA *Choice poems and lyrics.* Whitaker. Pp. 317. (BL). Not meant as a school text but 'to be placed in the hands of youth'.

CROWN, William 'Schoolmaster at Moulton, near Northampton'

[1788]* G *English grammar epitomised; or, a short, plain, easy compendium of English grammar, for the use of youth at schools.* Northampton: T. Dicey. (BL). Not in Alston. Pp. 178; *324*.

CHRISTIAN BROTHERS

1840a RS *The first book of reading lessons, in two parts.* 2nd edn Dublin, 1841 (BL); anr edn, Part 1, 1843 (St Mary's, Marino, Dublin); Part 2, 1848 (*ibid.*). Parts 2 and 3 are of the same date and in the same location. All were compiled mainly by Bro. Michael Paul Riordan. McDunphy, p. 133.

1841 RS *Third book of reading lessons.* Dublin, 1841 (O); anr edn 1843 (St Mary's, Marino, Dublin).

1840b RS *The literary class-book, or fourth series of select reading lessons, in prose and verse.* Dublin (St Mary's, Marino); 2nd edn 1841 (BL); 3rd edn 1846. Further edns and addns to 1887.

CHRISTIAN KNOWLEDGE SOCIETY see SOCIETY FOR PROMOTING CHRISTIAN KNOWLEDGE

CHRISTIE, James A. 'Headmaster, Duke of Bedford's School, Milton Abbot'

1849 S *The constructive etymological spelling-book; exhibiting . . . the etymology, and primary and present meanings, of above 8000 of the most useful English words . . . With numerous notes on the history and application of particular words* [etc.] (title from 10th edn) (BL); anr edn 1852 (BL); 10th edn 1866* (private colln); 11th edn 1872 (BL); 12th edn 1880 (BL).

CHRISTIE, William Dougal 1816–74

1871* RA *Dryden: Stanzas on the Death of Oliver Cromwell,* etc. Macmillan for Clarendon Press. (BL).

CHURCHILL, T.O.

1823* G *A new grammar of the English language; including the fundamental* *principles of etymology, syntax, and prosody . . . with notes and illustrations, critical and explanatory.* Pp. xii, 454. (BL).

CLAPHAM, Samuel 1755–1830
1810 G   *English grammar, taught by examples rather than by rules of syntax. DNB.*

[CLARE, William]
1690* G   *A compleat system of grammar English and Latin . . . in a method which renders it easie to all capacities, and by the use whereof the learner may attain to the perfect knowledge of the Latin tongue in less than one quarter of the time usually spent therein* [etc.]. (Cambridge UL); anr edn 1699* (BL); Scolar Press facsimile of 1690 edn, 1971*. *EGC*, p. 159.   P. *319n.*

CLARK, Edward
1680 S   *The protestant school-master. Containing plain and easie directions for spelling and reading English with all necessary rules for the true reading of the English tongue. Together with* [sectarian polemics]. (Bodley); 2nd edn 1682* (BL); 3rd edn (*c.* 1710?], Gumuchian, 107. Alston, IV, 138–40 and Plate 22 for t.p. of 1680 edn.   Pp. *55, 156.*

CLARK, Rev. T. see GALT, John; TABART, Benjamin

[CLARK, Thomas]
[1844] La   *An attempt at vocal English; that is, English spelled as spoken.* Aberdeen. (BL).

CLARK, William   'Conductor of an academy, Wisbech'
[a. 1835]a S   *The abcedarian's guide.* Noted on the t.p. of his English grammar, 1835 edn.
[a. 1835]b G   *A companion to [An English Grammar], or book of exercises.* Noted on the t.p. of his English grammar, 1835 edn.
1835* G   *An English grammar systematically arranged in a series of easy lessons.* Wisbech, (BL). GB gives a suspect date of 1810.   P. *352.*

CLARKE, Mrs
1824* RA   *Poems, moral and entertaining.* Northampton. Pp. 48. (BL). All are concerned with Adam and Eve and the Fall.

CLARKE, Hyde
1853 G   *A grammar of the English tongue, spoken and written; for self teaching and for schools.* (BL; Bristol PL); 2nd edn 1859* (Glasgow UL).   Pp. 352; *48, 52, 357, 363.*

CLARKE, John   1687–1734   'Master of the Publick Grammar School in Hull'
1720 Ed   *An essay upon the education of youth in grammar schools. In which the vulgar method of teaching is examined, and a new one proposed.* (BL); 2nd edn 1730* (London UL; BL). Alston, X, 162–5.   Pp. 201–2.
1731 Ed   *An essay upon study. Wherein directions are given for the due conduct thereof, and the collection of a library* [etc.]. (BL); 2nd edn 1737; Garland Press facsimile of 1731 edn, N.Y., 1969; Scolar Press facsimile of 1731 edn, 1971*. Alston, X, 173–5. A continuation of the previous entry.   Pp. 202, 279.

CLARKE, John   'Of Grantham in Lincolnshire'
[1772]* S   *The rational spelling-book, or, an easy method of initiating youth into the rudiments of the English tongue. Containing I. Orthography . . . II.* [English grammar] *III.* [English grammar in verse] *IV. Proper exercises and lessons, in prose and verse, fables, prayers, graces, sentences, &c.* (Yale UL); 14th edn Dublin, 1791* (BL). Alston, IV, 722–6, records nineteen edns in all to 1809

and reproduces t.p. of 1772, in Plate 77.   Pp. 102, 105–6, 107; *57, 103.*

CLARKE, Samuel

[a. 1855] G   *A poetical grammar of the English language, and an epitome of the art of rhetoric.* 2nd edn [1855] (BL). GB gives his first name as Robert, as does the Bodlian.

[Anon.]

1852* RA   *The class-book of poetry.* National Society; anr edn [1859] (BL).

[Anon.]

1831* RA   *The class reading book for schools, containing fables and true stories for children.* Pp. 48. For National Society, Roake and Varty. (BL).

[Anon.]

1814* Ex   *Classical English letter-writer: or, epistolary selections; designed to improve young persons in the art of letter-writing, and in the principles of virtue and piety. With introductory rules and observations . . . and biographical notices of the writers . . . By the author of Lessons for Young Persons in Humble Life.* York. (BL; Nottingham UL); 2nd edn York, 1821 (Holtom, Cat. 48, 1984).

[Anon.]

1808* RA   *Classical selections in verse.* Liverpool: James Smith. (BL).

CLEGHORN, William   'Teacher of English, Nicholson Square, Edinburgh'

1833*RE   *The Edinburgh child's guide,* Part I, Edinburgh: Oliver and Boyd. Pp. 12 (BL). Part 2, Edinburgh, 36 pp. (BL); Part 3, n.d. Pp. 36 (BL).

CLEMENT, Francis

[1576?] S   *The petie schole with an English orthographie, wherein by rules lately prescribed is taught a method to enable both a childe to reade perfectly within one moneth, & also the unperfect to write English aright,* 1587 (BL). The preface is dated 21 July 1576, and R.D. Pepper (p. xiv) refers to John Bagford's catalogue, Harl. MS 5899, fol. 56b, in which an edn of 1576 is recorded. Ed. R.D. Pepper, *Four Tudor books,* Scholars Facsimiles, Gainesville, 1966*; Scolar Press facsimile, 1967*. Alston, IV, 11.   Pp. 5, 73; *372.*

COAR, Thomas

1796* G   *A grammar of the English tongue. To which are added, exercises in bad English, to be corrected by the rules of syntax.* (BL). Alston, I, 495.

COBBETT, William   1763–1835

1818 G   *A grammar of the English language, in a series of letters. Intended for the use of schools and of young persons in general; but more especially for the use of soldiers, sailors, apprentices, and ploughboys.* New York; London, 1819 (BL); more than thirty edns to 1984, including 1836*. Ed. C.C. Nickerson and J.W. Osborne, Amsterdam: Rodopi, 1983* (the 1818 edn with the addns of 1819, 1820 and 1823); intro. Robert Burchfield, OUP, 1984* (the 1823 edn). Cobbett's grammar sold 13,000 copies in six months and a further 100,000 in the next fifteen years (E.P. Thompson, *The making of the English working class,* Penguin, 1980, p. 807, quoting M.L. Pearl). It should be remembered, however, that the merits of Cobbett's book have little to do with grammar.   P. 360.

1831* S   *A spelling book, with appropriate lessons in reading, and with a stepping stone to English grammar.* (BL); 2nd edn 1831, Chalmers, p. 125; 3rd edn 1832 (BL); 4th edn 1834.

COBBIN, Ingram   1777–1851   Secretary, British and Foreign School Society

1832 D   *The classical English vocabulary; containing a selection of words commonly used by the best writers . . . Intended as a supplement to The Grammatical and Pronouncing Spelling-Book.* (BL); anr edn 1834 (Harvard); anr edn 1859 (Boston PL).

[a. 1828]a G   *Elements of English grammar; being an improved edition of Grammar for Children.* 7th edn 1828 (BL); 20th edn [*c.* 1845] (Chicago UL); 33rd edn 1864 (BL).

1833 S   *Elements of spelling and reading, or a first book for children under six years of age.* (Harvard UL).

[a. 1828]b G   *Grammar for children.* From the t.p. of his *Elements*, above. 20th edn 1844, GB.

[a. 1830] S   *The grammatical and pronouncing spelling book on a new plan.* 2nd edn 1830 (Harvard UL); 8th edn 1838 (Chicago UL).

1831* RA   *The instructive reader, containing lessons on religion, morals, and general knowledge . . . With questions for examination, and elliptical recapitulations: designed to teach reading and to inform and develop the powers of the infant mind.* Westley and Davis. (BL); 6th edn 1852 (Harvard UL).   Pp. 240; 87.

COBBIN, J.

[1820?] G   *Lessons in grammar, designed more especially for the use of Sunday schools.* Nearly ready for publication in September 1819, *Gent. Mag.*, 89.ii (1819), 251.

COCKER, Edward   1631–1675/6   Writing-master

1696 S   (Cocker's) *Accomplish'd school-master: containing sure and easie directions for spelling, reading, and writing English . . . With divers tables of English words . . . both divided and whole, from one to six, seven and eight syllables . . . Likewise* [homophones, etc.]. (Yale UL); 18th edn 1748 (BL). Scolar Press facsimile of 1696 edn, 1967*. Alston, IV, 182–8 and Plate 36 for 1696 t.p.

1675* RA   (Cocker's) *Morals, or, the muses' spring-garden, adorned with many sententious disticks and poems in alphabetical order. Fitted for the use of all publick and private grammar and writing schools, for the scholars of the first to turn into Latin, and for those of the other to transcribe into all their various and curious hands.* Pp. ii, 68. (Nottingham UL); 2nd edn 1694, NBL, 1949, no. 311.   P. 157.

[COCKIN, William]   1736–1801   Writing-master

1775 P   *The art of delivering written language; or, an essay on reading. In which the subject is treated philosophically as well as with a view to practice.* (BL); Scolar Press facsimile 1969*. Alston, VI, 407.   Pp. 295–6.

COKE, Zachary

1654 Lo   *The art of logick; or the entire body of logick in English. Unfolding to the meanest capacity the way to dispute well, and to refute all fallacies whatsoever.* (BL); 2nd edn 1657 (Illinois UL). Scolar Press facsimile of 1654 edn, 1969*. Alston, VII, 51–2,   Pp. 147, 306.

[COLE, Lady (Marian)]

1844* RE   *The mother's primer. By Mrs Felix Summerly.* Pp. 28. (BL). Beautifully printed in red, blue and yellow, with a frontispiece by Mulready. Reprinted in 1971 as a gift book for the Friends of the Osborne and Lillian H. Smith Collections, Toronto.   P. *123.*

COLES, Elisha   1641/3 until after 1688   'School-master in Russel St, Covent Garden'

1674 S   *The compleat English schoolmaster. Or the most natural and easie method of spelling English. According to the present proper pronuntiation of the language in Oxford and London. Wherein children and foreigners shall have the whole body of English words in the plainest order digested and divided to their hands.* (O); anr edn 1692 (Yale); Scolar Press facsimile of 1674 edn, 1967*. In the preface Coles says he has been teaching for twelve years.   Pp. 37, 82–3, 90, 106; *50, 57, 70, 101, 156, 372.*

[1687?] S   *The pen's most easie and exact improvement, teaching to spell, read, and write, true English in a most compendious method . . By the author of Nolens, Volens.* Licensed November 1687; advertised in T. Osborne, 1688.

1675 G   *Syncrisis, or, the most natural and easie method of learning Latin: by comparing it with English* [etc.] (BL); 2nd edn 1677 (O); Scolar Press facsimile of 1677 edn, 1971*. A. Gabrielson, 'Elisha Coles's Syncrisis', *Englische Studien*, 70 (1936), 149–52; Foster Watson, 1903, p. 229.

1689* C   *The young schollar's best companion: or, an exact guide or directory for children and youth, from the ABC, to the Latin grammar, comprehending the whole body of English learning, in two parts* [etc.] *By E. Cole, a hearty lover of youth.* (BL); 2nd edn 1700 (BL); 3rd edn [1704] no copy. Alston, IV, 161–3 and Plate 28 for lengthy t.p. of 1689 edn.

Note Elisha Coles and his books, together with two relatives bearing the same name, Elisha, are discussed by Gerald Mander. 'The identity of Elisha Coles', *The Library*, 3rd series, 10 (January 1919), 34–5. Mander shows that *DNB* confuses Elisha Coles of London with his cousin Elisha Coles, Master of Erasmus Smyth's School, Galway.

[COLLARD, John]

1795 Lo   *An epitome of logic. In four parts. By N. Dralloc.* (Cambridge UL); 2nd edn as: *The essentials of logic: being a second edition of Dralloc's Epitome improved, comprising an universal system of practical reasoning* [etc.] *By John Collard,* 1796* (BL). Alston, VII, 265–6.

1799* Lo   *A praxis of logic for the use of schools.* (BL).

[Anon.]

1804 RA   *A collection of poetry, sacred and moral, for the use of schools.* Yarmouth. (O).

A collection of poetry for . . . elocution see NEWMAN, F.W.

[Anon.]

1772 RA   *A collection of visions and allegories: selected from the most eminent authors, for the improvement of the youth of both sexes.* (O).

COLLETT, John   Master of an academy at Bourton, Glos., then at Evesham

1805 P   *Sacred dramas intended for young persons.* Evesham (*NUC*).

COLLIER, Henry

1820 G   *An epitome of English grammar.* (BL).

COLLIER, R.   'Schoolmaster'

1807 P   *Effusions in verse: being a collection of addresses, tales, &c. Spoken for some years past at public academical recitations.* (BL: Bodley).

COLLIER, William Francis

1867 G   *First lessons in English grammar.* Edinburgh: Black. (BL); anr edn T. Laurie, [1876] (BL).

Bibliography 1

1866 G   *A grammar of the English language, with a sketch of its history* Edinburgh: T. Laurie. (BL; O).

1861* B   *A history of English literature, in a series of biographical sketches.* Nelson. (BL). Edns to 1919.   P. *219.*

COLLINS

[a. 1867] RS   *Progressive series* [of readers] Books 1–6. Advt.

COLLINS, Joshua   'Rector of Newport, and late Master of the Grammar School in that town' (*BL catalogue says the name is pseud.*)

1802 Ed   *An address to instructors and parents, on the right choice and use of books in every branch of education.* T. Reynolds (BL); 2nd edn as: *A practical guide to parents and guardians, in the right choice . . .* 1802*. Pp. viii, 148; 4th edn as: *A guide to parents and tutors . . .* T. Hamilton, 1805; rev. and enl. by Samuel Catlow as *A guide in the selection and use of elementary school-books.* 1818* (BL).   Pp. 128, 211–12.

COLLYER, John   Schoolmaster, Nottingham

[1729] S   *The English spelling book.* Title and date given on p. 1 of his *Grammar.* 5th edn 1737, *London Mag.,* 6 (1737), 648. No copy. Alston, IV, 420 (suppl. vol.) identifies the spelling-book with Collyer's *Reading made easy,* q.v.

1735* G   *The general principles of grammar; especially adapted to the English tongue. With a method of parsing and examination.* (BL). Alston, I, 72; Vorlat, 1975.   Pp. 321, 322, 323, 375.

[a. 1781] RE   *Reading made easy or, a preparative for the Testament and Bible. Beginning with easy lessons of words of one syllable, and going on by degrees to those of two, three, and the longest words. To which are added* [scripture histories and fables]. 22nd edn. Nottingham, 1781. Pp. 128. (Toronto PL); anr edn as (running title) *The new way to reading made easy* [*c.* 1780?]* lacks t.p. (Bedford CHE); anr edn 1801, NBL, 1949, no. 58. Alston, IV, 421 and Plate 51 for t.p. of 1781 edn.

COLQUHOUN, J. Stuart

1871 G   *A compendious grammar and philological handbook of the English language, for the use of schools and candidates for the army and civil service examinations.* Griffith and Farran. (BL).

[Anon.]

1688* S   *The compendious school-master: teaching the English-tongue after a more easie & demonstrable method than hath been hitherto published or taught. Wherein are contained I* [sounds of letters] *II* [spelling-lists and division of syllables] *. . . Together with significant comparisons, proverbs, sentences, poems, prayers, graces. By a lover of learning, and a hearty well-wisher to his beloved country.* (BL, shelf-mark 1568/3548) anr edn, as: *The English tutor, or a compendious . . .* 1701 (NYPL). Dobson, 1968, I, 374, gives date as 1687. Alston, IV, 158–9 and Plate 24 for t.p. of 1688 edn. The address to the reader, signed R.W., is about the author, not by him.   Pp. 77, 158; *157, 373.*

[Anon.]

[a. 1855] G   *A compendium of English grammar.* New edn. *The treasury of knowledge.* vol. III. (BL).

[Anon.]

[a. 1867]* La   *A compendium of etymology, comprising a selection of prefixes and* *affixes, and nearly five hundred words from the Saxon, Latin and Greek languages, with derivatives. Adapted for school classes and home lessons. By a teacher.* Sheffield: Pawson and Brailsford. (BL., acquired in 1867).

[Anon.]

[1703] S *The compleat English tutor, or the most exact school-master; teaching English more plain and easy than any other, in the truest method. I.* [Letters] *II. Directions for true spelling . . . III. How the letters are to be sounded . . . IV.* [Spelling-lists] *V-XV.* [Proper names, homophones, hard words, reading-passages, prayers, penmanship, etc.] *TC,* III, 349. No copy. Alston, IV, 214.

The compleat scholler see VERNON, John

[Anon.]

[1830?] G *The complete English grammar.* Penny National Library, vol. VII (BL).

[Anon.]

1755* Ex *The complete letter-writer.*

Note: The connections between works carrying this title are complicated, unresolved, and relevant here only because the books were used by young people, and often contained grammars. They were not designed as school-texts. Alston distinguishes two series: *The complete letter-writer, or new and polite English secretary . . .* from 1755, here called series A, and *The complete letter-writer, containing familiar letters . . .* from *c.* 1768? here called series B. Alston says that series B is 'based upon (and frequently confused with)' series A. The grammars in both series, however, are always similar and often identical; they may have a common origin. More substantial doubt is thrown on the separateness of the series by the fact that the title of III, 257, in series A, is the same as that of III, 285, in series B. The following have been consulted: 1755* (Hoxton PL), III, 244; 3rd edn 1756* (BL), III, 246; 4th edn 1757* (BL), III, 247; 12th edn 1768* (personal), III, 256; 13th edn 1770* (DLC), III, 257; anr edn N.Y., 1793* (Harvard), III, 285.

[Anon.]

1798* C *The complete young man's companion; or self instructor: being an introduction to all the various branches of useful learning and knowledge. Containing writing, grammar, arithmetic, geography, chronology, and miscellaneous articles . . . To which is added, the artist's assistant* [etc]. Manchester: Sowler and Russell. (Wigan PL). Alston, III, 423.   Pp. 77; *285.*

[Anon.]

1794* G *A comprehensive view of English grammar, for the use of schools.* W. Peacock and J. Scatcherd. Pp. 48. (Personal). Alston, I, 474a.

CONGREGATIONAL BOARD OF GENERAL EDUCATION see UNWIN, W.J., 1851b

CONNEL, Robert 'Teacher of English'

1831a* Ex *A catechism of English composition.* Edinburgh. (BL); 2nd edn 1839 (BL).

1831b* G *An improved system of English grammar, with copious exercises and explanatory observations.* Glasgow (BL); 2nd edn 1834, Wells, 1846; 4th edn 1843 (Wisconsin UL).

[a. 1853] RA *The young scholar's companion; or, a selection of reading lessons.* 11th edn Glasgow, 1853 (O).

CONNON, Charles Walker 'Schools of Greenwich Hospital'

1855* RA *The first four books of Milton's Paradise Lost; with copious notes, grammatical, classical, and critical. For the use of pupil teachers, training colleges, and the higher classes of schools.* Longman. (BL). Pp. 263; *262*.

1851* S *A first spelling book.* Edinburgh. (BL); 3rd edn 1863 (BL). P. 114.

1845* G *A system of English grammar; founded on the philosophy of language and the practice of the best authors. With copious exercises.* Edinburgh. (BL); 2nd edn 1852 (BL). P. *351*.

CONSTABLE

[1857?] RS *English reading books.* Books 1–6. Edinburgh. Advt.

[1857] RS *Advanced English reading book, literary and scientific.* Edinburgh; anr edn [1860]* (BL). P. 242.

CONSTABLE, T.

1857 G *A series of graduated exercises adapted to Morell's Grammar and Analysis.* Edinburgh: Constable. (BL).

[Anon.]

[1708] S *The consummate orthographist, or, youth's accomplisher, in right spelling and pointing, in writing. A manual aptly compos'd, and requisite for all reading, writing and grammar, scholars.* TC, III, 624. No copy. Alston, IV, 280.

[Anon.]

[1824]* B *Conversations on poetry: intended for the amusement and instruction of children. By the author of The Buxton Diamonds, &c.* William Darton. (Leicester UL; BL). P. 217.

[CONYBEARE, William John] 1815–57 Principal, Liverpool Collegiate Institution

1844* RA *English poetry. First book. To be learned by heart between the ages of eight and ten years. For use in the schools of the Collegiate Institution, Liverpool.* Liverpool: Wareing Webb. (BL); anr edn [1857] (BL); 6th edn [1869]. The preface is signed W.J.C.

COOK, Frederick Charles 1810–89 HMI

1849a* RA *First book of poetry for elementary schools.* Pp. vi, 102. (BL).

1849b* RA *Poetry for schools.* Pp. xii, 118. (BL). P. 221.

[COOK, J.] 'A father and a teacher'

1792* S *The Westminster spelling-book; or, child's first book . . . being the most natural, simple, and engaging introduction to spelling and reading, ever yet published . . . calculated so as to attract the attention, please the imagination, and engage the affection of children, while it cheats them into the path of learning. Volume I.* For the author. Pp. 146. (BL) P. 69.

1793* S *[Volume II.] . . . Principally intended for those who are somewhat advanced; but will serve also for initiation. Wherein words are divided as they are pronounced. The whole being new, rational and natural. To which is added a concise English grammar.* Pp. 168. (BL). Alston, IV, 891 and Plate 93 for t.p. of vol. I.

COOKE, Thomas

[1770?] Ex *The universal letter-writer; or, new art of polite correspondence. Containing . . . a new, plain and easy grammar of the English language.* (BL, shelf-mark 10920.aaa.24); anr edn [1775?]* (BL, shelf-mark 10920.bbb.14); anr edn 1788* (Bodley, shelf-mark Antiq.f.e.1788/1). Many edns and many uncertainties: different grammars are included in some edns. More than twenty edns to 1863. Alston, III, 289–96.

COOPER, Christopher *c.* 1655–98 'Master of the Grammar School, Bishop-Stortford'

1687* S *The English teacher, or the discovery of the art of teaching and learning the English tongue. Fitted for the use of schools, and necessary for all those that desire to read, write or speak our tongue with ease and understanding. In two parts. The first contains the principles. The second is for the practice of learners.* (O; Cambridge UL); anr edn 1688 (Harvard); as: *The compleat English teacher,* 1698, *TC,* III, 103, and advertised in George Fisher's *New spelling book,* 1700; ed. B. Sundby, Lund, 1953*; Scolar Press facsimile of 1687 edn, 1969. Alston, VI, 468–9. Cooper's book is based on his own *Grammatica linguae anglicanae,* 1685, but does not deal with accidence and syntax. It is praised by Dobson, 1968, I, 280–310. Padley, 1985. Pp. 37, 54, 73; *48, 50, 52, 53, 76, 81, 373.*

1685 G *Grammatica linguae anglicanae. Peregrinis eam addiscendi cupidis pernecessaria, nec non Anglis praecipue scholis, plurimum profitura.* (BL); anr edn 1685 (Trinity C, Dublin); ed. J.D. Jones, Halle, 1911*. Scolar Press facsimile of 1685 edn, 1968. Alston, I, 29–30; Vorlat, 1975.

COOTE, Charles 1761–1835

1788* G *Elements of the grammar of the English language. Written in a familiar style: to which is subjoined a history of the English language.* (BL; Glasgow UL); 2nd edn 1806 (O). Alston, I, 445.

COOTE, Edmund Master of the Grammar School, Bury St Edmunds

1596* S *The English schoole-maister, teaching all his scholers, of what age soever, the most easie, short, and perfect order of distinct reading, and true writing our English tongue that hath ever yet been knowne and published by any* [etc.] (BL). Alston, IV, 13–46, records edns up to the 54th 1737, and t.p. of 1596 edn in Plate 4. Ed. William Hart, unpublished doctoral thesis, U. of Michigan, 1963; Scolar Press facsimile of 1596 edn, 1968*. Pp. 16, 17, 76, 78, 90, 92, 131; *372.*

CORBET, James

1743* G *An introduction to the English grammar containing I. A great variety of monosyllables . . . II. Grammar in all its parts, to which are added large tables of words, from two to six and seven syllables. By James Corbet. Philologus.* Glasgow, 1743. (NLS; Glasgow UL). Alston, I, 90. P. 58.

CORBET, John

1784* G *A concise system of English grammar: designed for the use of schools, as well as private families.* Shrewsbury. Pp. 47. (BL); anr edn Madeley, 1785 (Guildhall L, London); 3rd edn Shrewsbury, 1788* (Shrewsbury PL, now lost?). Alston, I, 377–9. P. 342.

CORNER, Julia 1798–1875

1854* P *Little plays for little actors.* Two series. They include: *Whittington and his cat; Cinderella, or the little glass slipper,* etc. Also issued as *Little plays for little people.* (BL). P. *303.*

[*c.* 1840]* G *The play grammar, or, the elements of grammar, explained in easy* *games*. Thomas Dean. Pp. 109. (personal), NBL, 1949, no. 269; anr edn [1848] (BL); at least twenty-six edns to [1879?] (Melbourne UL).

[1857] G   *Round games and amusing exercises upon grammar. An addendum to Corner's Play Grammar*. (BL).

[CORNWALLIS, Caroline Frances]   1786–1858

1847 G   *General principles of grammar. (Small books on great subjects, no. 12)*. (O; BL); 2nd edn 1854 (BL).

CORNWELL, James   1812–1902   Principal, Borough Road Training College

[*c*. 1860] Ex   *A complete guide to English composition*. 49th edn 1904 (BL).

[1870]* RA   *Easy poetry. A first book of selected poems for schools and families*. (BL).

1844* Ex   *The young composer; or, progressive exercises in English composition. Part I. Comprising sentence-making, variety of expression, and figurative language, with appendices on the use of capitals and punctuation*. (BL); 17th edn 1855 (BL); 26th edn 1863 (BL). *Key*, 4th edn 1855 (BL). The preface says that Part II is soon to be published.

See also ALLEN, Alexander, and CORNWELL, James

CORRY, John

[*c*. 1820]* RA   *The beauties of Cowper; or, extracts from the work of that great poet; for the use of schools and the instruction and amusement of young persons of both sexes*. Rochdale: Joseph Littlewood. (BL).   P. *261*.

CORY, William Johnson, see JOHNSON, William

COTTLE, Joseph   1770–1853   Sometime teacher

1805 RA   *Selection of poems, designed chiefly for schools and young persons*. 2nd edn 1816; 3rd edn [1823]* (BL; Nottingham UL); 4th edn [1835?] (BL). Information from Dr Basil Cottle.

COTTON, Nathaniel   1705–88

1751* RA   *Visions in verse, for the entertainment and instruction of younger minds*. (BL); 3rd edn 1752 (BL); 6th edn 1760* (BL). At least twenty-five British and American edns to 1820. As: *The poetic monitor; or visions in verse: for the improvement of the young*, London: Edward Lacey [1848], Holtom, List 45, item 85.   Pp. 169; *167*.

COUTIE, George   'English master of Liverpool High School, Liverpool Institute'

1863* La   *Word expositor and spelling guide: a school manual, exhibiting the spelling, pronunciation, meaning, and derivation of all the important and peculiar words in the English language. With copious exercises for examination and dictation*. (BL; personal). Contains an interesting discussion of methods of teaching spelling, which could not be included in chapter 3, above.

COWPER, William   1731–1800   See CORRY, J., *c*. 1820; HALES, J.W., 1872; McLEOD, W., 1865; MASON, C.P., a. 1861

COX, Leonard   Master of Reading School

[1524?] B   *The arte or crafte of rhethoryke* (Cambridge UL; BL); anr edn 1532 (Bodley). Ed. F.I. Carpenter, Chicago, 1899, and reissued by Norwood Editions, Norwood Pa., [1975?]; English Experience facsimile of 1524 edn, Amsterdam, 1977*. Alston, VI, 6–7. The rhetoric is explicitly intended for 'the profyte of yonge studientes'.   Pp. 270–1.

CRABB, George   1778–1851   'Master of the Commercial & Literary Seminary, Walworth'

1801* Ed *The order and method of instructing children, with strictures on the modern system of education.* Pp. iv, 204. (BL). Pp. 211, 313.

1807* G *The preceptor and his pupils; or, dialogues, examinations, and exercises on grammar in general, and the English grammar in particular. For the use of schools and private students.* (BL; Hull UL).

1808* G *The preceptor and his pupils, part the second; containing the syntax of all languages, together with special rules, dialogues, examinations, and exercises on the English; to which are added a practical system of English composition, and a concise history of the formation of all languages.* (personal). *Key*: At p. 195 Crabb says, 'The tales to which these questions refer are to be found in the key.' Pp. 368, 369.

1810 La *The preceptor and his pupils; part the third; or, the most familiar synonyms in the English language critically and etymologically illustrated. Gent. Mag.,* 80 (November 1810), 455. Often issued as *English synonyms.*

CRAIK, George Lillie 1798–1866 Professor of English literature and history, Queen's College, Belfast.

1851 B *Outlines of the history of the English language for the use of junior classes in colleges and the higher classes in schools.* (BL); 3rd edn 1859 (Fulham PL); 5th edn 1864 (BL).

1844–5 B *Sketches of the history of literature and learning in England from the Norman conquest to the accession of Elizabeth. With specimens of the principal writers.* Continued in Series 2 to 1688; in series 3 to the present. 6 vols. Charles Knight (BL). As: *A compendious history of English literature, and of the English language,* 2 vols, 1861 (BL); 2nd edn 1864. Abridged as: *A manual of English literature, and of the history of the English language,* 1862 (BL) and many later edns. P. *219.*

CRAMPTON, T. Master of the Brentford Public School and TURNER, Thomas Master of the Redcross Street School, Bristol

1858* RE *The first English reading book; being a series of lessons on home, school, and things out of doors.* Pp. vi, 136. (BL; O).

CRANE, George Teacher

1843* G *The principles of language exemplified in a practical English grammar. With copious exercises. Designed as an introduction to the study of languages generally, for the use of schools, and self instruction.* (BL; O).

CRESSWICK, Mr English master, Prince of Wales Military Academy, Kensington

1789* RA *The female reader; or miscellaneous pieces in prose and verse; selected from the best writers, and disposed under proper heads; for the improvement of young women. By Mr Cresswick, teacher of elocution. To which is added a preface, containing some hints on female education.* J. Johnson. Pp. xx, 394. (Glasgow UL). *Mon. Rev.,* n.s. 3 (September 1790), 99; Hans, p. 115. Pp. 187; *186, 376.*

1792* RA *The lady's preceptor, or, a series of instructive and pleasing exercises in reading, for the particular use of females.* G.G.J. and J. Robinson. Pp. xii, 424. (BL). 2nd edn 1804* (BL). P. 193.

[CRISP, Stephen] 1628–92

1681* S *A new book for childern (sic) to learn in. With many wholsome meditations* *for them to consider. With directions for true spelling. And the ground of true reading and writing of true English. By S.C.* (BL); anr edn Newport, R.I. (Rhode Island Hist. Soc.). Alston, IV, 716 and Plate 74 for t.p. of 1769 edn. Alston does not record the 1681 edn.

CROCKER, Abraham   'Schoolmaster at Ilminster'

[1772]* G   *A practical introduction to English grammar and rhetoric.* Sherborne (O); anr edn London, 1775; anr edn Taunton, 1786 (Durham UL). Alston, I, 309–11.

CROFT, George   1747–1809   Master of Beverley Grammar School

1775 Ed   *General observations concerning education, applied to the author's method in particular.* Hull: J. Ferraby (BL typescript* from copy in Cambridge UL).   P. 206.

1784* Ed   *A plan of education delineated and vindicated: to which are added . . . a short dissertation upon the stated provision and reasonable expectations of publick teachers.* Wolverhampton: J. Smart (BL). Croft is now 'Master of Brewood-School'.

CROMBIE, Alexander   1762–1840   Master of an academy in Highgate

1802 G   *The etymology and syntax of the English language explained and illustrated.* (BL); 2nd edn as: *A treatise on the etymology and syntax of the English language.* 1809* (BL); at least seven further edns to 1865.

[CROSSE, Thomas]

[1686] S   *The experienc'd instructer, or a legacy to supply poor parents and their children to read distinctly, by the rule of spelling exactly. TC*, II, 170, no copy; 7th edn [1687], no copy. Alston, IV, 148–9.

CROSSLEY, John Thomas, see DUNN, Henry and CROSSLEY, J.T.

[CRUMPE, Thomas]

1712* S   *The anatomy of orthography: or, a practical introduction to the art of spelling and reading English, adapted to mean capacities. Composed for the use of English-schools, and humbly offered to the masters of charity-schools. By their loving brother, T.C. Φιλομαθ.* (BL). Alston, IV, 287, and Plate 40 for t.p.   Pp. 30, 97.

CUNDALL, Joseph see *Little Mary's spelling book.*

CURREY, George

1856* G   *An English grammar for the use of schools.* SPCK. (BL); anr edn [1863] (BL). The easier parts of the book were published separately as: *A grammar for beginners.*   Pp. *353, 368.*

CURRIE, James   Principal of the Church of Scotland Training College, Edinburgh

1866* S   (Chambers's) *Spelling book, with numerous exercises for dictation.* (BL).

1867* Ex   *English prose composition. A practical manual for use in schools.* Edinburgh. (BL).

[1870] G   *The practical school grammar.* Edinburgh. (BL).

[1866] G   *Rudimentary English grammar.* Edinburgh. (BL).

CURSON, Henry

1702* C   *The theory of sciences illustrated: or, the grounds and principles of the seven liberal arts . . . accurately demonstrated and reduced to practice. With variety of questions, problems and propositions both delightful and profitable.* (BL). Alston, III, 213.   Pp. 288; *277.*

CURTIS, John Charles   Principal, Borough Road Training College

1867* G   *Outlines of English grammar. For school and home use.* Simpkin Marshall. (BL; O).   Pp. *346n., 361.*

[1863]* RA   *The poetical reader, for school and home use.* Simpkin Marshall. (BL). Curtis compiled also *The new poetical reader,* 1872 (BL).

D., E.

1864* RA   *A book of juvenile poetry: containing historical, narrative, descriptive, and sacred pieces.* (BL).

D., T.

[1685] S   *The compleat English-man, or the London school; instructing children and elder persons speedily to spell, read and write, English; by teaching, I. To know vowels, consonants, and dipthongs. II. To divide words into syllables. III. Observations on most of the letters. IV. All English words divided into syllables.* [Also arithmetic; penmanship] Printed for T. Dawkes. *TC,* II, 128. No copy. Alston, IV, 146. It would seem possible that Dawkes was the author.

DAINES, Simon   'Schoolemaster of Hintlesham in Suffs.'

1640 S   *Orthoepia anglicana: or, the first principall part of the English grammar: teaching the art of right speaking and pronouncing English, with certaine exact rules of orthography, and rules of spelling or combining of syllables, and directions for keeping of stops or points between sentence and sentence.* (BL); ed. M. Rösler and R. Brotanek, Halle, 1908*; Scolar Press facsimile 1967. Alston, VI, 464 and Plate 7 for t.p. in full.   Pp. 33, 38, 51, 90–1, 156, 331; *52.*

DALE, Thomas   1797–1870   Professor of English language and literature, University College, London, 1828–30

1828* Ex   *An introductory lecture (to a course upon the principles and practice of English composition) delivered in the University of London.* Pp. 32. (BL).

DALGLEISH, Walter Scott

1863* Ex   *English composition in prose and verse, based on grammatical synthesis.* Edinburgh: James Gordon. (BL); 3rd edn 1864 (BL). In 6th edn, 1867, the book was divided into *Introductory textbook of English composition* and *Advanced textbook of English composition.* At least eleven edns in all to 1883. A *Key,* 1863 (BL) had at least four edns to 1872.

1865* G   *Grammatical analysis, with progressive exercises.* Edinburgh: Oliver and Boyd. (BL); 2nd edn 1865. At least nine edns in all to 1883. A *Key,* published in 1865, had at least seven edns to about 1870.   P. *370.*

1871 Ex   *Outlines of English composition, for elementary schools. With exercises.* Edinburgh. (BL); 2nd edn 1873. *Key,* 1871 (BL).

1867 G   *Outlines of English grammar and analysis, for elementary schools. With exercises.* Edinburgh (O); 2nd edn 1868; 3rd edn 1870 (BL). *Key* 1867 (BL).

1866* G   *A progressive English grammar. With exercises.* Edinburgh (BL); 2nd edn 1868 (BL); 3rd edn 1871 (BL); five further edns to 1898. *Key,* 1867 (BL).   Pp. *358, 368.*

1862* RA   *Shakespeare's Macbeth: adapted for educational purposes.* Edinburgh: J. Gordon (BL); 2nd edn, Nelson, 1864 (BL).

DALTON, John   1766–1844   Sometime teacher

1801* G   *Elements of English grammar: or a new system of grammatical instruction, for the use of schools and academies.* (Leeds UL); 2nd edn 1803* (BL).

[DANIEL, C.]

[1815]* *Daniel's first spelling book; consisting of words of one syllable, grammatically arranged. And designed to address the understandings of children.* Bradford: for C. Daniel. Pp. 18. (BL, who attribute to Daniel).

DARNELL, George 1798–1857 Schoolmaster in Islington

[a. 1855] G *Grammar made intelligible to children: being a series of short and simple rules, with ample explanations of every difficulty, and copious exercises for parsing.* Pp. 88. Stereotyped edn, Grant and Griffiths. (BL). Part 1 was issued separately as *An introduction to English Grammar* [1855?] (BL).

DARNELL, Thomas

1865 G *Parsing simplified. An introduction and companion to all grammars: consisting of short and easy rules, with parsing lessons to each, whereby very young students may . . . [understand] . . . the grammatical construction of the most complex sentences of our ordinary authors.* Griffith and Farran (BL); 4th edn [a. 1876]. Advt.

DAVIDSON, David

1815* G *An arrangement of English grammar; with critical remarks, and a collection of synonymes.* Edinburgh, (BL; Glasgow UL; Wisconsin UL).

1823 G *A syntactical English grammar, in which the rules of composition are briefly exemplified: the sentences are construed and parsed, and the whole is divided into short and easy lessons.* (Columbia UL).

DAVIDSON, Ellis A.

[1870] G *Our first grammar.* (O).

DAVIDSON, John Best

1839 G *The difficulties of English grammar removed; or English grammar simplified. Adapted for schools and self-instruction. To which is added a treatise on punctuation.* (title from 3rd edn). (O; BL); 3rd edn 1846* (Leeds UL; BL). P. 362.

[a. 1864] G *Punctuation made easy. For schools and self-instruction.* 'Tenth thousand'. 1864. (BL).

DAVIES, T. 'Schoolmaster'

[c. 1770?] S *The newest reading made quite easy: or, an introduction to reading the Holy Bible. Consisting of . . . lessons, so disposed, that the learner is led on with pleasure, step by step; from simple and easy, to compound and difficult words; which is allowed by all to be the most regular, speedy, and rational way of teaching.* (title from 28th edn). 28th edn 1787 (private colln); anr edn Gainsborough, 1794* (Nottingham UL); anr edn London, 1840* (BL); anr edn Derby, 1870* (private colln). A 53rd edn is in Preston PL. Alston, IV, 865–6 and Plate 87 for t.p. of 1787 edn. The author's name is sometimes given as DAVIE.

DAVIS, John

[a. 1864] G *Abridgment of Murray's English Grammar. Improved and illustrated, with copious explanatory observations . . . A new edition, thoroughly revised . . . by a member of the University,* 1864 (BL); anr edn Belfast, 1872* (personal).

1830* G *Murray's English Exercises, adapted to his English Grammar: consisting of excercises in parsing; instances of false orthography; . . . violations of the rules respecting perspicuous and accurate writing. Designed . . . for the use of schools. Enlarged by the Rev. John Davis, A.M.* Belfast (BL). *Key,* 1830 (BL). Pp. 308; *309, 367.*

[a. 1872] G   *Murray's first grammar for junior classes. By the Rev. John Davis.* Belfast: William Mullan. Advertised in 1872.

DAVIS, William

1869* RA   *The book of poetry for schools and families.* (BL).

1865* S   *The complete English spelling and dictation book, for home and school use; containing in carefully graduated spelling lessons, a systematic view of all the difficulties and irregularities of the English language, with copious dictation, transcription, and reading exercises.* (BL); rev edn 1871 (BL). Also issued in two parts: *The junior/senior English spelling . . .* [etc.]   P. 104.

1867 G   *Examples and exercises in English parsing, syntax, and the analysis of sentences.* Pp. 63. (BL; O).

DAWES, Richard   1793–1867

1851* RA   *Lessons and tales: a reading book for the use of children. Chiefly intended for the junior classes in elementary schools.* (BL).

1848 Ed   *Suggestive hints towards improved secular instruction, making it bear upon practical life. Intended for the use of schoolmasters and teachers in our elementary schools.* 3rd edn [1849]* (BL); 4th edn 1850, Goldstrom, 1972a, p. 210; anr edn 1853 (*LTM*, VII, 1954, item 150).   P. 25.

DAWNAY, William Henry, Viscount DOWNE

1857* G   *An elementary English grammar. By the Viscount Downe.* Pp. xii, 150. Longman. The preface is signed B.G. (BL; O).

DAWSON, Benjamin

[a. 1867] G   *Text book of English grammar, with exercises.* 2nd edn, Part 3, 1867 (O).

DAY, Angel

1586 Ex   *The English secretorie: wherein is contayned, a perfect method, for the inditing of all manner of epistles and familiar letters . . . Also, a declaration of all such tropes, figures or schemes, as either usually, or for ornament sake, are in this method required* [corrected and refined] *for young learners and practizers.* [title from] 2nd edn 1592* (BL). Ten edns in all to 1635. Scolar Press facsimile of 1586 edn, 1967. Title of 1586 edn in L.B. Wright, 1935, p. 140; title of 1599 edn in Howell, 1956, p. 330.

DEANE, John

[a. 1758] S   *The child's best guide: or, the easiest method of teaching to spell and read.* Gent. Mag., 28 (1758), 130.

DEARLE, Edward   'School-master, Golden-Lane'

1791* S   *A sure guide for all youth. Consisting of three parts: I. Seven gradations of spelling and reading. II. Of the creation, fall of man, and his recovery. III. Miscellaneous . . . Abstracted entirely from the holy scriptures of the Old and New Testaments.* (BL); 2nd edn 1792* (BL). A short grammar was added to the 2nd edn 'to gratify Friends'. Alston, IV, 881–2 and Plate 91 for t.p. of 1791 edn.   P. 98.

[Anon.]

1822* P   *Debate on the character of Julius Caesar. Written for the improvement of youth in the art of public speaking, and delivered in the Guildhall, Canterbury, by the young gentlemen of Mr Ambler's Academy, under the direction of Mr Dunnett, lecturer on oratory, public reader of poetry, and teacher of elocution.* Canterbury. Pp. 48. (BL). Cf below, DUNNETT, 1822.   P. 291.

[Anon.]

1813 G *The decoy; or, an agreeable method of teaching children the elementary parts of English grammar by conversations and familiar examples*, in: *A present for a little boy*. Welch, 1972; 2nd edn 1814* (DES), the title stopping at *grammar*; at least two British and two American further edns to 1823.

DEMAUS, Robert 1829?–1874 Master of the West End Academy, Aberdeen

1858 G *The analysis of sentences, with applications to parsing, punctuation, and composition*. Edinburgh, *DNB*; 4th edn 1871, *DNB*.

1859 RA *A class-book of English prose*. Edinburgh, *DNB*.

1866 RA *English literature and composition: a guide to candidates in those departments in the Indian Civil Service. With examination papers and specimen answers*. (BL).

1860* B *Introduction to the history of English literature*. Edinburgh (BL). P. *219*.

1857 RA *Selections from Paradise Lost, with notes*. Edinburgh, *DNB*; 2nd edn 1859, *DNB*.

DENHAM, Joshua Frederick 'Lecturer of St Bride's, Fleet Street'

1834* S *A spelling and reading book, upon new principles*. (BL); 3rd edn 1847 (BL, imperfect). Pp. 39; *30, 104, 123*.

DEVIS, Ellin Teacher at Campden House School, Kensington

1775* G *The accidence; or first rudiments of English grammar. Designed for the use of young ladies. With an appendix, containing an example of grammatical construction; maxims and reflections, by way of exercises for learners, and some occasional remarks and references. By a lady*. (Hull UL; BL); 3rd edn 1777* (BL); 5th edn 1786* (BL); anr edn [*c.* 1790]* (BL); 8th edn 1795* (BL); 9th edn 1797* (BL). At least eighteen edns to 1827. Recommended by Morrice, 1801, as 'Mrs Devis's English Grammar'. Alston, I, 320–8.

1778* La *The infant's miscellany: or easy lessons, extracted from different authors. On a new plan. Intended to facilitate the attainment of the English language to the youngest readers, by teaching them not only to read, but likewise to understand clearly what they read*. (BL). Published anonymously, but in her *Miscellaneous lessons*, p. iii, Ellin Devis says that she wrote 'about three years ago . . . the former edition, or rather a small volume designed for the same purpose' called *The infant's miscellany*.

1782* La *Miscellaneous lessons, designed for the use of young ladies. On a new plan*. (BL); 3rd edn 1794 (Illinois UL); 4th edn 1827 (Illinois UL). Alston, III, 355–6. Praised by Mrs Trimmer, *Guardian of Education*, 2 (1803), 489. P. *191*.

[Anon.]

1813 RE *Dialogues consisting of words of one syllable only; intended as a proper book to follow the Imperial Primer. By the author of . . . Summer Rambles*. Sotheby, HCI II, October 1974, lot 712; anr edn 1816* (BL; Nottingham UL).

[Anon.]

1826* S *Dictates; or, selections in prose and verse, for dictating as exercises in orthography*. Pp. vi, 40. (BL). P. 129.

[Anon.]

[a. 1833] P *Difficult pronunciation, with explanations of the words, by which an approved pronunciation of the most difficult English words in common use may be easily attained*. 5th edn 1833*, 48 pp. (BL).

[DILLON, Bartholomew]

1830* S   *A first book for infants; comprising, a novel division of the alphabet, with monosyllabic, and dissyllabic lessons on the creation.* Pp. 68. (BL; O); J.R. Brown, in the 1834 edn of his *Essay*, says that Dillon came from Wrexham.   Pp. 65–6.

DILWORTH, Thomas   'Schoolmaster in Wapping'

[1740] S   *A new guide to the English tongue: in five parts. Containing I.* [Spelling-lists and reading-passages] *II.* [Homophones] *III.* [English Grammar] *IV.* [Fables, etc.] *V.* [Prayers]. (title from 8th edn). The earliest complete copy is of the 13th edn, London, 1751, which is reproduced in facsimile by the Scolar Press, 1967*. Alston, IV, 423–548, lists 127 edns to 1800 in Britain and America and 21 dated edns after 1800; Plate 52 reproduces the t.p. of the 8th edn 1746. Dilworth's name was still being used in the middle of the nineteenth century: *Dilworth's new London spelling primer*, Norwich: Jarrolds, [c. 1850]* (BL).   Pp. 55, 99, 100–1, 104, 132, 161, 283.

[Anon.]

1813 RA   *Diurnal readings; being lessons for every day in the year: compiled from the most approved authorities, and calculated to combine entertainment with instruction.* Sherwood: Neely and Jones, 1813. Holtom, Spring 1979, item 821. Listed by Collins, (1802) 1818, among school readers.

DIXON, Henry   d. 1761   Master of St Alban's Charity School, Holborn

1728 S   *The English instructor; or, the art of spelling improved . . . In two parts. The first; containing monosyllables, expressing the most natural and easy things to the apprehensions of children . . . The second, being an instruction more particularly design'd for children of an higher class; such as . . . are capable of understanding and applying the rules there given. . . . Drawn up for the use of schools.* (Hull UL). Over seventy edns, including at least five American ones, to 1823. Scolar Press facsimile of 1728 edn, 1967*. Alston, IV, 324–35 and Plate 47 for t.p. of 1728 edn. M.G. Jones, 1938, pp. 106–9.   Pp. 102, 161; *52, 84.*

[DODSLEY, Robert]   1703–64

1748* C   *The preceptor: containing a general course of education . . . In twelve parts. I On reading, speaking, and writing letters . . . V On rhetoric and poetry . . . VII On logic.* 2 vols. (BL); 2nd edn 1754. Eleven further edns to 1796 are recorded in Alston, VII, 195–206. The preface is by Samuel Johnson; the logic is by DUNCAN, William, q.v.   Pp. 165; *164, 167.*

DOHERTY, Hugh

1841* G   *An introduction to English grammar, on universal principles.* (BL)   Pp. 363–4, 371.

DONATTI, Louis Anthony   'Professor of languages'

1839* G   *Elementary English reading book and grammar.* Pp. 36, iv. (Bodley, BL); 2nd edn 1839 (BL); 3rd edn 1842 (BL). Mainly, but not solely, for foreigners.   P. *346n.*

D'ORSEY, Alexander James Donald   'Master of the English department in the High School of Glasgow'

1842* G   *English grammar and composition. Part I. Orthography and etymology. Part II. Syntax and prosody,* 2 vols. Edinburgh: Chambers (BL); anr edn 1851, Schmitz, I, 200; anr edn 1873 (Wisconsin UL). A complete revision of the book was issued anonymously in 1853, under the same title, q.v.   Pp. 366; *378*.

[a. 1842] Ex   *Introduction to composition*. Noted in the preface to his *English grammar*, 1842.

1845* G   *Introduction to English grammar*. Edinburgh: Chambers. (BL).

[a. 1853] S   *Spelling by dictation: a series of progressive exercises in English orthography*. 6th edn, London and Glasgow, 1853* (BL); anr edn 1864 (private colln).   Pp. 129; *383*.

1861* Ed   *The study of the English language an essential part of a university course: an extension of a lecture delivered at the Royal Institution of Great Britain, February 1, 1861*. Cambridge. Pp. viii, 72. (BL). D'Orsey is now 'English lecturer at Corpus Christi College, Cambridge'.

[1876]* Ed   *'Thorough English'; or hints to teachers with regard to composition*. Simpkin Marshall. Pp. 16. Reprinted from *The Quarterly Journal of Education*. D'Orsey is now 'Lecturer in the Theological Department of King's College, London'.

DOUGALL, John   1760–1820

1810* C   *The modern preceptor; or, a general course of education; containing introductory treatises on language* [etc.]. 2 vols. (BL).

1815* C   *The young man's best companion and guide to useful knowledge*. Bungay. Pp. vii, 476; anr edn Bungay, 1821, Andrew Boyle, Cat. 824 (November 1971); anr edn (?) as: *The self-instructor: or young man's companion* Derby, 1842 (BL).

DOUGLAS, Archibald   'Schoolmaster in Stirling'

1770* S   *The English school reformed: or, an introduction to spelling and reading English. Wherein words of several syllables are so divided, that the sound of each syllable, when joined together, shall not only lead the scholar into the true pronunciation . . . but also greatly facilitate the labour of the teacher. Containing* [eight paragraphs]. *To which is added, a variety of divine songs and select fables.* Glasgow. (BL). Not in Alston. A note says that the book is meant for Scotland, and the Highlands, 'where many are taught to read English before they can speak it'.   Pp. 52; *45*.

DOUGLAS, James   'Lately head master, Great King Street School, Edinburgh'

[c. 1860?] G   *English grammar and analysis with a series of progressive exercises. For the use of schools*. 112th edn Edinburgh: Oliver and Boyd, 1891* (NLS).   P. *352*.

[c. 1850?] G   *An initiatory grammar for the use of junior pupils, intended as an introduction to the Principles of English Grammar*. 86th edn Edinburgh, 1867* (NLS); 109th edn 1871 (BL); anr edn 1874 (BL). The 43rd and 45th edns were advertised in 1863, the 56th in 1864, and the 65th in 1865.

[a. 1851] G   *Principles of English grammar*. 2nd edn Edinburgh and London, 1851* (BL); BL has 97th edn 1871; 98th 1872; 101st 1874.

1863–5* RS   *Progressive English reader*, Books 1–6. Edinburgh. (NLS lacks Book 1; BL); 11th edn 1873 (BL, Book 1 only is of 11th edn).

1861 RA   *Selections for recitation compiled for the use of elementary schools*. (dated from preface to 1st edn, in 5th edn). 5th edn Edinburgh, 1866* (NLS); anr edn 1869 (BL). A 3rd edn was advertised in 1863, a 4th in 1865.

1870 S   *Spelling and dictation exercises for the use of schools*. Edinburgh. (BL); 4th edn 1872 (BL).

DOWNE, Viscount see DAWNAY, William Henry

DRALLOC, N. see COLLARD, John

Dramatic dialogues see PILKINGTON, Mary

DRAPER, W.

1822* S   *The child's friend, being an entirely new and systematic arrangement of all the sounds, combinations of characters, and exceptions, in the English language.* (BL). Draper says he wrote the book at the age of seventy-seven.   P. *61*.

DRUMMOND, John   'Late teacher of English in Edinburgh'

1771 P   *The art of reading and speaking in public; being a collection for the use of schools and private perusal. Containing I. An introduction . . . II. Examples of speeches.* (title from 1780). Edinburgh (Yale UL); 2nd edn 1780* (Allegheny C, Meadville; NLS and BL have photographic copies).   Pp. 175; *287*.

1762* RA   *A collection of poems for reading and repetition. Selected from the most celebrated British poets.* Edinburgh. (NLS).   Pp. *173–4*.

1767* S   *A grammatical introduction to the modern pronunciation and spelling of the English tongue. For private perusal, and for public schools.* Edinburgh. (BL). Alston, IV, 709 and Plate 71 for t.p. Law, p. 198, with inexact title.   P. *35n*.

DRYDEN, John see CHRISTIE, W.D., 1871

[Anon.]

1819 RE   *The Dublin reading book.* Dublin. Goldstrom, 1972a, p. 56; anr edn Dublin, 1840 (BL). Originally published as wall-charts in 1813. Compiled for the Society for Promoting the Education of the Poor of Ireland.

[1819?] RE   *Questions on the Dublin reading book.* Dublin. Goldstrom, 1972a, p. 57. Compiled for the Society for Promoting the Education of the Poor of Ireland.

[Anon.]

1813 S   *The Dublin spelling book.* Dublin, for the Society for Promoting the Education of the Poor of Ireland. (Wall-charts), Goldstrom, 1972a, p. xi; 1819 (in book form); Dublin: P.D. Hardy, 1839 (BL); as: *A dictating spelling book, compiled for the Society for Promoting the Education of the Poor of Ireland* [c. 1840?]* (BFSS archives).

DULCKEN, Henry W.

[1860] RA   *Pearls from the poets. Specimens of the works of celebrated writers. Selected with biographical notes by H.W.D. With a preface by T. Dale.* (BL).

DUN, James

[a. 1766] S   *The best method of teaching to read and spell English, demonstrated: in eight parts . . . With an appendix, not in the former editions, containing some tables of monosyllables, placed in the best order for a child's first reading.* 4th edn Edinburgh, 1766*. (Glasgow UL). In the appendix Dun says that the book is not otherwise much changed from previous edns. Alston, IV, 708 and Plate 69 for t.p.   Pp. 93–4, 110–1, 116; *52*.

DUNCAN, Daniel   'Master of Islington School'

1731 G   *A new English grammar, wherein the grounds and nature of the eight parts of speech, and their construction is explain'd.* (Trinity C, Cambridge); Scolar Press facsimile 1967*. Alston, I, 61; Vorlat, 1975.   Pp. 333, 334.

DUNCAN, J.   Master of the Free Grammar School, Alton

[a. 1813]a S   *The English expositor; or explanatory spelling-book; containing an alphabetical collection of all the most useful . . . words in the English language,* *divided into syllables, and properly accented . . . Particularly calculated for teaching in classes.* (title from 19th edn). Advertised in 1813; 5th edn [*c.* 1824], Chalmers, p. 127; 19th edn [*c.* 1835?]* (private colln).

[a. 1813]b S   *First spelling book for children; containing a selection of monosyllables only, in natural and appropriate gradation, with a short, easy, and proper definition affixed to each word; intended as an introductory assistant to the English Expositor.* Advertisement in 1813; anr edn 1824, Chalmers, p. 131.

DUNCAN, William   1717–60   Professor of Philosophy, Aberdeen University
1748 Lo   *The elements of logick. In four books.* (BL). Alston, VII, 184–94, lists nineteen further edns to 1819. Scolar Press facsimile of 1748 edn, 1970*. The 'logick' was included in Dodsley's *Preceptor.*

DUNN, Henry
1837* Ed   *Popular education; or, the normal school manual: containing practical suggestions for daily and Sunday school teachers.* Pp. viii, 248. (BL); as: *The principles of teaching; or . . .,* 20th edn [*c.* 1860]* (BL). Quoted by Goldstrom, 1972a, *passim.*

DUNN, Henry, and   CROSSLEY, John Thomas
[*c.* 1839] RS   *Comprehensive primer, with simple exercises. Daily lesson books No. 1.* Goldstrom. 1972b, pp. 92–5, 110, 210. The books were accepted by the British and Foreign School Society in 1839, but had been published earlier.

[*c.* 1839?] RS   *Comprehensive spelling and reading book. Daily lesson books no. 2.*

[*c.* 1840]a RS   *Home and common things. Sixty-six lessons . . . in easy reading, comprising a considerable range of subjects and a large body of important facts.* Sequel to *Daily lesson books, no. 2.* Advt.

[*c.* 1840]b* RS   *Poetry and prose: with a series of lessons on the art of reading; being a supplement to Daily Lesson Book No. 3.* (BL).

[*c.* 1840]* RS   *Comprehensive class book. Daily lesson book No. 4.* (personal).

see BRITISH AND FOREIGN SCHOOL SOCIETY: *Revised lesson books.*

DUNNETT, Mr   Teacher of elocution
1822* RA   *The poetic reciter, or beauties of eminent poets, adapted for recitation in academies, selected and delivered by Mr Dunnett, lecturer in oratory, public reader of poetry, and teacher of elocution.* Canterbury: G. Wood. Pp. 48. (BL). Cf above, *Debate* . . . 1822.

DUNNOCK, Richard
1836* G   *An elementary grammar of the English language.* Pp. 22. Sheffield: Whitaker. (Sheffield PL).   P. *346n.*

DURY, John   1596–1680
[1649?] Ed   *The reformed school.* (Bodley). Issued with his *The reformed librarie-keeper* (1650) in 1651 (Bodley); ed H.M. Knox, Liverpool U. Press, 1958; Scolar Press facsimile of 1651 edn, 1972*. Alston, X, 49–50.

DYCHE, Thomas   Schoolmaster, Stratford-le-Bow
1723* S   *A dictionary of all the words commonly us'd in the English tongue; and of the most usual proper names; with accents directing to their true pronunciation.* (Bodley); 2nd edn, as *The spelling dictionary,* its usual name, 1725 (BL). Alston, IV, 311–16, lists eight edns in all to 1756, and Plate 43 gives t.p. of 1723 edn.   Pp. 50, 83–4, 95, 101, 104, 157; *50, 87.*

1707 S   *A guide to the English tongue. In two parts. The first proper for beginners . . .*

in which particular care is had to shew the accent for preventing of vicious pronunciation. The second, for such as are advanc'd to some ripeness of judgment, containing [sounds of letters; division of syllables; punctuation, etc.] (Christ Church, Oxford); 2nd edn 1710* (BL). Alston, IV, 223–79, records a 102nd edn in 1800 and many unnumbered edns to 1830. Scolar Press facsimile of 1707 edn, 1968*. For Jane Austen's possible use of Dyche's *Guide* see Margaret Weedon's letter in the *Times Literary Supplement*, 26 November 1982. The pronunciation of Dyche's name is indicated by the spelling DYTCHE, used in the *Crit. Rev.*, 23 (1811), 333 (Moon, 1976).

DYKE, Thomas 'Schoolmaster in London'

[1746?] S *Reading made perfectly easy; or, an introduction to the reading of the Holy Bible.* No copy. 24th edn, rev. D. Fenning, 1776* (Bedford CHE); 31st edn, London: W. Lane [*c.* 1780?]* (V&A, 60.Z.409). Alston, IV, 584–5 and 584a. Pp. *52, 57.*

EARLE, Margaret

1826* RE *The child's first lessons in spelling and reading.* (BL).

[Anon.]

[1859]* RE *Early lesson book. Part I.* Pp. 12. J. Mason. *Part II.* Pp. 24. (BL). The final note to Part I and the introduction to Part II are signed 'J.R.L., Wesleyan Normal Institution, Westminster.'

[Anon.]

1819 RE *An early stage on the road to learning; or, original lessons in words of one or two syllables only, adapted to the taste and capacity of little children.* Darton, Harvey and Darton (Melbourne UL); anr edn 1824, Chalmers, p. 128.

[EARNSHAW, Christopher]

1817* G *The grammatical remembrancer: a short but comprehensive English grammar for the use of young students in general . . . By the author of Orthoepy Simplified.* Huddersfield. (BL; Leeds UL). Pp. 351; *363.*

[1816?]* D *Orthoepy simplified: being a new and comprehensive explanatory pronouncing dictionary of the English language, selected from the works of Dr Johnson, Mr Walker, and others.* Leeds. (BL). No reference is made to possible use in school. Earnshaw's method of indicating pronunciation is repeated in his purely adult work *The pronouncing instructor: or general reader's assistant,* Leeds, 1818* (Glasgow UL).

[1815?]* RA *The wreath; or, miscellaneous poetical gleanings; including originals; from reliable sources.* Huddersfield. A secondary t.p. reads '. . . *gleanings, from various respectable sources.* Wakefield.' (BL).

An easy introduction to the English language see NEWBERY, John

[Anon.]

1845* S *An easy introduction to reading the English language. Designed for Sabbath-Day schools, in six parts . . . By a schoolmaster.* Wellington: Richard Corner. (BL). P. *123.*

[Anon.]

[*c.* 1830?]* RE *Easy lessons for young beginners.* Pictorial edn. Edinburgh: Jas Brydone. (Bedford CHE); anr edn (?) Ailoa [sic]: Stephen N. Morison, [*c.* 1830], Gumuchian, 2331. Pp. 60–1.

[Anon.]

1831 RE *Easy lessons; or, leading strings to knowledge.* Harris (Renier Colln, Bethnal Green Museum); 2nd edn [1838]; 3rd edn 1839; anr edn Grant and Griffith, 1848 (V&A). Moon, 229.

[Anon.]

[c. 1840?:* S *The easy monitor.* Derby: Mozley. Pp. 11. (Bedford CHE).

[Anon.]

1837* RA *Easy poetry for children.* John W. Parker. (BL).

[Anon.]

1865* RA *Easy poetry for children. A selection from the best authors.* (BL).

[Anon.]

[1868]* RA *Easy poetry lessons for children* [Book] A and [Book] B, each 14 unnumbered pp. Simpkin Marshall. (BL). Each price one penny.

[Anon.]

1864* RA *Easy rhymes and simple poems for young children. With illustrations.* Routledge. (BL).

[Anon.]

1825 RA *Easy rhymes for children from five to ten years of age. By a lady, author of Cato, or the Adventurers of a Dog.* J. Harris (V&A; Bedford CHE); anr edn 1828 (V&A); anr edn 1831* (BL).

[Anon.]

1794* G *An easy, short and systematical introduction to the English grammar. For the use of schools. By a school-master.* (unique copy in the colln of the late Professor T.W. Baldwin, Carbondale, Ill.). Alston, I, 475.

[Anon.]

1817* RE *Easy steps: intended for the use of young children, in and out of school, preparatory to their reading in classes. By the author of The Stranger's Offering, &c. Part the Second. Restricted (with a few exceptions) to words of two syllables.* Darton, Harvey and Darton. (BL).

[Anon.]

1864 RE *Easy steps to reading.* (Cambridge UL).

[Anon.]

1855* S *The easy way to teach children to spell and read.* Merthyr Tydfil: Rees Lewis. Pp. 12. (BL). Conspicuous for its beautiful type.

EATON, A. 'Teacher of languages'

1828* G *A reasoning grammar with additional employment of all the English monosyllable sounds, in the form of treatises, which are the commencement of an attempt to make a year's routine-study of language the study of a day.* (BL; O; Glasgow UL).

[ECCLES, Ellen Ann Shove]

1857 P *H.H.'s H book; shewing how he learned to aspirate his H's.* (BL); 3rd edn as: *Harry Hawkins's H book; shewing . . .* [etc.] 1869* (personal); anr edn [1879] (BL).

EDGEWORTH, Maria 1767–1849

1827 P *Little plays for children.* Vol. VII of *The parent's assistant.*

1801 RA *Moral tales,* 5 vols.; 2nd edn, 3 vols., 1802*. Pp. 208; *184.*

EDGEWORTH, Maria, and EDGEWORTH, Richard Lovell 1744–1817

1798* Ed *Practical education,* 2 vols. (Bristol UL); 2nd edn, 3 vols., 1801 (BL);

3rd edn as *Essays on practical education*, 2 vols, 1811 (BL); anr edn 1815. Alston, X, 231.   Pp. 36, 42, 52, 55, 209–10, 307; *184, 208, 383*.

1799* RE   *A rational primer. By the authors of Practical Education.* Bristol: Biggs and Cottle; London: J. Johnson. (London UL). Alston, VI, 514 and Plate 28 for a reproduction of pp. 2 and 5.   Pp. 36, 54, 122.

1816* RA   *Readings on poetry.* (BL); 2nd edn 1816. (BL).   Pp. 186, 208–9; *184*.

EDGEWORTH, Richard Lovell

1802* RA   *Poetry explained for the use of young people.* (BL).   Pp. 208–11; *184*.

1817* RA   *School lessons.* Two parts: pp. viii, 100; vi, 92. Dublin. (BL).   Pp. 211; 208.

[Anon.]

1750* RA   *The Edinburgh entertainer; containing historical and poetical collections. For the use of schools. Taken from the best authors.* Edinburgh. Pp. 355. (BL).   P. *172*.

EDMONDS, Mrs

1845 G   *Notes on English grammar, for juvenile pupils.* Hunter, 1848. No copy traced. 2nd edn 1847, Hunter 1848. No copy.

EDMONDS, George

[a. 1837] G   (*G.E.'s*) *Complete English grammar, with a supplemental grammar of etiquette.* 5th edn 1837*, 16 pp. (BL).

1837 G   *Three-halfpenny English grammar.* (O). Edmonds wrote also *The tri-national grammar* [1838?], largely a grammar of French, and *A universal alphabet, grammar and language* [1856] whose massive eccentricity cannot be described briefly; its intentions derive from Wilkins.

EDMUNDSON, Henry 1607–59 Master, Northleach Grammar School.

1655 La   ΣΥΝ ΘΕΩ. *Lingua linguarum. The naturall language of languages.* (O). Scolar Press facsimile, Menston, 1970*.   Pp. 117–9.

EDWARDES, Robert

[1591] S   *The Inglish Scholemaster.* No copy. *SR*, II, 572 and Alston, IV, 470.   P. *372*.

EDWARDS, J. (ed.)

1835 Ex   *A practical introduction to English composition: founded on Parker's Progressive Exercises, and comprising the whole substance of that valuable work.* (BL). *Progressive exercises in English composition*, by Richard Greene Parker, was published in Boston, Mass. in 1832.

EDWARDS, John 1637–1716

1714* C   *Some new discoveries of the uncertainty, deficiency, and corruptions of human knowledge and learning. With particular instances in grammar and the tongues, poetry* [etc.] (O; BL). Alston, III, 222.   P. 201.

EDWARDS, John

1850 La   *A history of the English language.* (Gleig's school series). (BL); anr edn 1858, *NUC*; anr edn 1859, *NUC*.

EDWARDS, Mrs M.C. 'Of Brentford Butts'

1796* G   *A short compendium of English grammar.* Brentford. Alston, I, 496.

EDWARDS, Oswald

1799 G   *A short and easy introduction to English grammar ... To which is annexed, an abstract of rhetoric.* Dublin. (private colln). Alston, I, 521a.

EDWARDS, Samuel   'Schoolmaster in Golden-Lane, Dublin'

1765* G   *An abstract of English grammar, including rhetoric and pronunciation.*
Dublin. (BL). Alston, I, 260.   Pp. 19–20, 100–1, 175–8, 288, 295, 332, 377;
346n., 383.

[*c.* 1735?] Ed   *Proposals for educating children, particularly those designed for trade,
in an English method.* [Dublin?]. Reprinted in his *Abstract of English grammar,*
1765* (previous entry), pp. v–viii.

EGELSHAM, Wells   d. 1786

1780* G   *A short sketch of English grammar. Intended for the use of such as study that
language only. Consisting of a few rules, abstracted chiefly from Johnson, Lowth,
Ash, &c.* Pp. iv, 32. (BL). Alston, I, 369. The work has caused difficulty: Watt
(*Bibliotheca Britannica*), GB, Allibone, Wells and Nichols (*Lit. Anecdotes*, II,
141) state incorrectly the title or the date, or both, and even Alston missed the
BL copy.   P. *318.*

[Anon.]

1825 Ex   *The elegant letter-writer; or, a selection of epistles, on the most familiar,
interesting, and instructive subjects which English literature affords.* Kerr and
Ashmead. Catalogue.

[Anon.]

[*a.* 1813] RA   *Elegant miscellaneous extracts, selected from Watts, Hervey, Newton,
Young, Blair, Sturm, &c. &c.* New edn Woodbridge, 1813*. (BL).

[Anon.]

1791* RA   *Elegant poems. Pope's Essay on Man, Universal Prayer, Blair's Grave,
Gray's Elegy, and The Fatal Sisters.* (BL); anr edn 1794, *NUC*; at least four
further edns to 1826 (BL). There is no indication of the intended readership,
but the choice of poems strongly implies a didactic purpose.

[Anon.]

1803 RA   *The elegant preceptor or an introduction to the knowledge of the world.* B.
Crosby. Gumuchian, 2370. Extracts from Johnson, Chesterfield, Addison and
others.

[Anon.]

1801* RA   *Elegant selections in prose and verse, from the most approved authors.*
Doncaster: W. Sheardon. (BL). The compiler hopes that the book will be used
'in the most respectable academies'.

[Anon.]

1814 RA   *Elegant selections, moral and entertaining, designed for youth.* R. Hawild.
Gumuchian, 2371.

[Anon.]

1854* La   *An elementary guide to the etymology of the English language. Compiled for
the use of schools.* Pp. 30. (BL).

[Anon.]

1841* C   *Elementary instruction for junior students, in a series of lessons. Selected and
arranged by a teacher of youth.* (BL).   P. 242.

[Anon.]

1785* G   *The elementary principles of English grammar, collected from various
authors; but chiefly from Dr Priestley, and printed for private use.* Bridport. (Yale
UL); anr edn, n.p., 1798* (Warrington PL). The dedication in 1785 is signed

M.A., but there is no reference to M.A. in 1798. Alston, I, 404–5.

[Anon.]

1843 G   *The elements of English grammar*. London: for Chester Diocesan Schools. Hunter, 1848.

ELEY, William   'Master of the Free Grammar School, Rolleston'

1824* S   *The English spelling book, arranged on a plan entirely new, by which an accurate pronunciation of the English language may be more easily acquired*. (NLS). An edn revised by William Birkin, as *The orthographical and etymological expositor*, was in preparation in 1838 (Birkin, 1838).

ELLIS, J.

1837 G   *An abridgment of Murray's English Grammar, in the way of question and answer, with . . . notes*. (BL); anr edn 1839 (BL); anr edn 1853 (BL).

ELLIS, James   'Late teacher of a private school in Norwich'

[a. 1719] S   *English orthography*. Known from the t.p. of the following entry. No copy. Alston, IV, 294.

1719 S   *The perfect school-master for the English tongue; or, reading made easy. Being a more plain, easy, regular, and speedy method, in bringing children to attain true spelling, and distinct reading, than had ever yet been extant . . . Corrected with additions, by William Motes, school-master of St Stephen's Parish, Norwich*. 1719* (Stockholm, Royal L). Alston, IV, 295.   Pp. 61, 104.

ELLIS, Sarah Stickney (formerly STICKNEY)

[a. 1831] RA   *The young ladies reader; or, extracts from modern authors, adapted for educational and family use. With an introductory chapter on reading aloud*. Advertised in 1831; anr edn 1845 (BL).

ELLIS, Tobias

[a. 1670] S   *The English school: containing, a catalogue of all the words in the Bible, beginning with one syllable, and proceeding by degrees to seven, divided and not divided; together with a brief and compleat table of the most usual and common English words . . . Fitted to the common use of English schools, being the first that ever came forth in this method*. (title from 1680 edn). No copies have survived of the edns before 1680, nor any record of the 1st. 5th edn 1680 (BL); other edns as *The royal catholick English school* or *The true royal English school* or *The true English school* to 1709. Scolar Press facsimile of 1680 edn, 1969*. Alston, IV, 65–75 and Plate 12 for t.p. of 1680.   Pp. 77n.; *26, 57*.

1684* S   *The poors English spelling-book, for his Majesties three kingdoms. Being a catalogue of all the words in the Bible, together with a praxis in prose and verse; and variety of pictures: all beginning with one syllable, and proceeding by degrees to eight, divided and not divided* [etc.]. Oxford. (DES). A simplified version of his *The English school*. Alston, IV, 144 and Plate 23 for t.p.

ELLISON, Seacome

1854* G   *A grammar of the English language for the use of schools and students: with copious examples and exercises*. Nathanial Cooke, Office of the National Illustrated Library. Pp. 103 and 12 pp. advts. (BL; O).   P. *361*.

ELPHINSTON, James   1721–1809   Master of a school in Kensington

1764* RA   *A collection of poems from the best authors, adapted to every age but peculiarly designed to form the taste of youth*. (BL; O).   P. *174*.

1765* G   *The principles of the English language digested: or English grammar reduced* *to analogy*, 2 vols. (Bristol UL). Abridged as: *The principles of the English language, digested for the use of schools*, 1766* (BL). Alston, I, 261–2.   Pp. 51, 334–5.

ELSTOB, Elizabeth   1683–1756   Sometime teacher

1715 La   *Rudiments of grammar for the English-Saxon tongue*, ed. C. Peake, Augustan Reprint Soc., Los Angeles, 1956*.   P. 377.

EMBLOW, William   'Member of the College of Preceptors'

1847* G   *An English school grammar*. Simpkin Marshall. 36 pp. (BL).

ENFIELD

[a. 1838] S   (Enfield's) *Progressive spelling book*. Advertised by Mozley in 1838 and by T. Tegg in 1842.

ENFIELD, William   1741–97   Lecturer in *Belles Lettres* at Warrington Academy

1818* Ed   *An essay on the cultivation of taste as a proper object of attention in the education of youth. By the Rev. William Enfield, LLD*. Newcastle. Pp. 16. (BL). A paper read at the Newcastle Literary and Philosophical Society in 1793.   P. 248.

1780* RA   *Exercises in elocution; selected from various authors, and arranged under proper heads: intended as a sequel to a work entitled The Speaker*. (BL); 3rd edn 1786, Hawkes, 1925; anr edn 1794, *DNB*; three further edns to 1812. Recommended by Morrice, 1801, p. 141, for ages eleven to fourteen.   P. *186*.

1774*RA   *The speaker: or, miscellaneous pieces, selected from the best English writers, and disposed under proper heads, with a view to facilitate the improvement of youth in reading and speaking. To which is prefixed an essay on elocution*. (BL etc.); anr edn 1782* (BL); anr edn 1799* (Wandsworth PL); anr edn 1829* (personal). About sixty edns to 1860. Alston, VI, 375–406.   Pp. 185–6, 210; *208*.

ENFIELD, William (not the author of *The speaker*)

1809* B   *A familiar treatise on rhetoric and belles lettres. By William Enfield, M.A., . . . assisted by eminent professional gentlemen*. Pp. 335. (BL). The author's name raises questions, if not suspicions.   P. *218*.

[Anon.]

1733* G   *The English accidence, being the grounds of our mother tongue: or, a plain and easy introduction to an English grammar . . . For the use of schools, by question and answer*. (Christ Church, Oxford). Alston, I, 64.   P. *322*.

[Anon.]

1853* Ex   *English grammar and composition. Chambers's educational course*. Edinburgh. (Cambridge UL; BL); anr edn 1857 (BL). A complete revision of Alexander D'Orsey's book of the same title.   Pp. 352, 355.

[Anon.]

[a. 1810] G   *English grammar epitomised, for the use of schools*. 3rd edn Halifax: J. Fawcett, Ewood Hall, 1810* (BL). See below, FAWCETT, John.

[Anon.]

1836 G   *An English grammar for the use of schools*. Dublin, for the Commissioners of National Education; anr edn 1838* (BL); a copy*, not of the 1838 edn, lacking t.p., is in Leeds UL (Museum of History of Education). Several edns to at least 1864.   P. 353.

[Anon.]

1810* G *English grammar, taught by examples, rather than by rules of syntax, &c.*
Darton, Harvey and Darton. (BL).   P. 350.

[Anon.]

[a. 1844] G *An English grammar, together with a first lesson in reading.* 2nd edn,
James Burns, 1844. Not traced. Listed by GB as 'not worth a pin'.

[Anon.]

[1809?] S *The English ladder; or a sure guide to the rudiments of English.* Cork.
(BL).

[Anon.]

[1686] S *English orthography, containing the art of writing right and spelling well;
with directions for reading English and writing letters to persons of all qualities.
Very necessary for young persons both men and women, especially who have not
learned the grammar.* Joseph Hindmarsh. *Huntington Lib. Quarterly,* 16 (1953),
422. Not in Alston.

[Anon.]

[*c.* 1840] G *English parsing made easy, in a progressive series of plain and familiar
examples . . . intended as a companion to Murray's abridgment of his grammar.*
Woodbridge. (Columbia UL).

[Anon.]

[*c.* 1820]* RE *The English primer, or, child's first book; in which are the most easy
reading and spelling lessons, adapted to promote the first rudiments of learning.*
Banbury: Rusher. (Nottingham UL; Bedford CHE).

[Anon.]

1844* RA *English prose; being extracts from the works of English prose writers, with
notes on their lives.* James Moore. Pp. xvi, 504. (BL). Written for 'the young',
but it would have been an expensive schoolbook.

[Anon.]

1706* G *The English scholar compleat: containing I. An English grammar . . .*
[derivatives from Latin; Latin tags; classical proper names] *VI. An English
rhetorick. VII.* [Greek roots and derivatives]. *Compos'd for the use of an English
school, at the Cock and Swan in Cannon-Street; and very useful for most people
under academics. With a letter in Latin to all Latin-masters, recommending it to
the use of several in their schools.* (BL). Alston, I, 39; Vorlat, 1975, p. 454, for title
in full.   P. 324.

[Anon.]

1844 G *English school grammar, with explanatory questions.* Hunter, 1848; anr edn
1853 (Hull UL).

[Anon.]

1826* S *An English spelling book.* Kilmarnock: J. Paterson. Pp. 75. (BL).

[Anon.]

[a. 1830]* S *The English spelling book improved: containing, in a progressive series, a
variety of tables of spelling, instructive lessons, and entertaining stories . . . To
which are added . . . a concise English grammar, &c. &c.* Banbury: Rusher.
(BL); 2nd edn [1830] (Leicester UL). Bodley attribute the authorship to John
Golby Rusher.

[Anon.]

1798* G   *English syntax rules, composed for the use of Sutton Academy, Nottinghamshire.* Mansfield: J. Drakard. Pp. 11 (Nottingham PL, mislaid since 1962). Alston, I, 514.

[Anon.]

1747* S   *The English tutor: in two parts. I. A spelling book, containing large tables of words from one to eight syllables . . . II. An English grammar, with notes; containing concise, but plain and comprehensive, rules, for speaking or writing English correctly: Free from all unnecessary difficulties; and the most useful rules distinguished, by the print, from the less useful* [etc.] (BL); 2nd edn, Part II only, 1760* (BL). Alston, I, 101–2.   P. 79.

[Anon.]

[1801?] D   *The English vocabulary, or spelling-book with the meaning annexed to each word. For the use of Ackworth School. To which is added a selection of moral and practical observations.* H. Thompson, *History of Ackworth School*, 1879, p. 166; 2nd edn 1806* (Friends House L); 8th edn 1819* (Friends House L); 19th edn 1841* (Friends House L); 21st edn [1843] (Leeds UL); at least two further unnumbered edns to 1889*. According to Thompson, *ibid.*, the book was compiled by 'Dr Binns, assisted by William Payne'. Alston, IV, 880, but see below, *A spelling book for . . . Ackworth School*, 1790.

[Anon.]

[a. 1867] La   *The English word book, Part I.* Nelson. Price threepence. Recommended by Edward Marks, 1867a, p. xiv, as the best and cheapest guide for teachers of derivation.

ENTICK, John   1703?–1773   Intermittent teacher

1765* D   *The new spelling dictionary, teaching to write and pronounce the English tongue with ease and propriety . . . For those that read Milton, Pope, Addison . . . and in particular to assist young people, artificers, tradesmen and foreigners, desirous to understand what they speak, read and write. To which is prefixed, a grammatical introduction to the English tongue.* (Linköpings Stiftsbiblioteket); 2nd edn 1766 (BL). At least sixty British edns, including revisions by W. Crakelt, Thomas Browne, John Robinson and others. Alston, V, 238–77.   P. 341.

1728* G   *Speculum Latinum: or, Latin made easy to scholars, by an English grammar only; neither tedious, nor obscure; composed on natural principles, . . . for the use and benefit of schools and families.* (O); Scolar Press facsimile 1967*. Alston, I, 60.   Pp. 318, 319n.

ERRINGTON, Prideaux

1723* RA   *Copies in verse, for the use of writing schools, and hymns for charity schools.* Newcastle-upon-Tyne (BL); as *New copies in verse . . .*, Newcastle-upon-Tyne, 1734* (BL).   P. 181.

[Anon.]

1800* G   *An essay towards an English grammar for Ackworth School.* York. (Cambridge UL, who attribute it to John Binns and Thomas Coar). Alston, I, 531.

[Anon.]

[1774]* RA   *Essays in prose and verse, partly collected, and partly original. For the* *improvement of younger minds.* (BL).   P. *192.*

[Anon.]

1808 G   *Essentials of English grammar for classical and French schools.* J. Hunter, 1848; 3rd edn 1821, GB. See below, *Lindley Murray examined,* 1809.

[Anon.]

1857 La   *Etymological exercises for elementary classes.* Constable. (BL).

[Anon.]

[a. 1845] La   *Etymological guide to the English language; being a collection, alphabetically arranged, of the principal roots* [etc.]. *By the compiler of the Edinburgh Sessional School Books.* 4th edn Edinburgh, 1845 (NLS); 5th edn 1850 (NLS); 6th edn 1857 (NLS).   P. *357.*

EVANS, John

1621 S   *The palace of profitable pleasure. Contayning and teaching with ease and delight, whatsoever is necessary to bee learned of an English scholler. Invented, taught, and experienced, by John Evans, Master of Artes.* (BL); Scolar Press facsimile 1967*. Alston, IV, 48 and Plate 5 for t.p.   Pp. 72, 125; *373.*

EVANS, John   1767–1827   Private teacher and 'Pastor of a congregation meeting in Worship Street, Islington'

[a. 1799] Ed   *An essay on the education of youth.* 2nd edn [1799]* (Dr Williams L). *Mon. Rev.,* 29 (April 1799), 435; Bryant, p. 108.

[a. 1794] RA   *Juvenile pieces, designed for the youth of both sexes.* 2nd edn [1794]* (BL); 4th edn 1804* (BL); 5th edn 1806 (BL); 6th edn 1818* (BL; Hull UL). Mostly youthful pieces by Evans himself.

1807a* RA   *The Parnassian garland, or, beauties of modern poetry . . . designed for the use of schools and the admirers of poetry in general.* Evans is here described as 'Master of a seminary for a limited number of pupils, Pullin's Row, Islington.' (BL).   P. 251.

1808* RA   *The poetic garland . . . Consisting of Porteus on Death, Blair's Grave, Gray's Church-Yard, Cunningham's Pile of Ruins, and Noyes's Distress. With biographical sketches and explanatory headlines.* Five parts, each with t.p. dated 1806. (BL).   P. 261.

1818 RA   *The progress of human life: Shakespeare's seven ages of man illustrated by a series of extracts . . . for schools and families* [with] *a brief memoir of Shakespeare.* Chiswick Press. (BL); 2nd edn 1823 (BL); anr edn 1820 (Nottingham UL); anr edn, as: *Shakespeare's Seven Ages of Man; or, the progress of human life . . .* 1834* (BL).

1807b* RA   *The prosaic garland . . . selected from the works of the distinguished writers of the present age. With introductory lines to each article. Designed for the use of schools.* (BL).

EVANS, Leslie Charles

[1868] G   *Parsing tables.* (O).

EVELYN, John   1620–1706

c. 1650* G   *The English grammar.* BL Additional MS 1590 ff. 94–8. Published as *John Evelyn's English grammar*: a transcript, with photographic reproduction of first and last pages, ed. Albert B. Cook III. Leeds Studies in English, n.s. XV, 1984*, 117–46.

EVES, Mrs   Crescent School, Birmingham

1800* G   *The grammatical play-thing, or, winter evening's recreation for young ladies from four to twelve years old.* Pp. xiii, 65. (Nottingham UL). Alston, I, 532.

EVES, Charles   'The Grammar School, 73 Myddleton St., Wilmington Sq., London'

1841* S   *The modern spelling book, and early educator; consisting of well-selected spelling, and improved reading lessons; to which are added very easy catechisms on natural history, astronomy, geography, &c. Expressly adapted to the capacities of young children.* (BL).

EVES, Charles, and   EVES, Georgiana

[a. 1852] S   *The derivative spelling book.* Tenth thousand. Simpkin Marshall, 1852* (BL; Hull UL). Georgiana Eves is here referred to as part-author of the preceding entry.   P. *357*.

EWING, Thomas   'Teacher of elocution and geography, 41 North Hanover St., Edinburgh'

[1819?] RA   *The English learner; or, a selection of lessons in prose and verse, adapted to the capacity of the younger classes of readers.* 2nd edn. Edinburgh: Oliver and Boyd, 1819* (BL). The preface is dated 1 March 1819.

[a. 1816] RA   *Principles of elocution: containing numerous rules, observations, and exercises, on pronunciation* [etc.]. *Also copious extracts in prose and poetry; calculated to assist the teacher, and to improve the pupil, in reading and recitation.* 2nd edn. Edinburgh, 1816*. Pp. 436. The preface is dated 14 November 1815. Ewing is here described as 'Teacher of English, Geography, and History'.   Pp. *287, 377*.

[a. 1819] P   *Rhetorical exercises.* T.p. of his *The English learner*, 1819.

[Anon.]

1804* G   *Examinations composed for the use of the pupils, at Ormskirk Classical and Commercial School. Vol. I. English Grammar.* A second t.p. reads: *Examinations adapted to L. Murray's Grammar and Exercises, Dr Crombie's Etymology and Syntax, and Irving's Elements of English Composition.* Ormskirk: T. Tasker. Pp. 182. (BL).   Pp. 254–5.

EXAMINATION PAPERS etc. (in chronological order)

1838*   London University matriculation (honours): *English composition* (BL 732.1.25).

1842*   London University matriculation (pass): *Grammatical structure of the English language.* (BL 732.g.31(1)).

1848*   British and Foreign School Society. General Examination for Schoolmasters: (i) *English language*; (ii) *English grammar* (BFSS archives).

1854*   British and Foreign School Society. The Normal College. Prospectus and prescribed texts: (i) *Grammar and English composition*: (ii) *Elocution. Readings in Prose and poetry.* (BFSS archives).

1856*   Royal Society of Arts. *The Examination Papers . . . containing the questions proposed to candidates . . . on the 10th, 11th, 12th and 13th of June, 1856.* Bell and Daldy, 1856. (RSA archives): *English literature*.

1857*   British and Foreign School Society. General Examination of Training Schools (Females): (i) *Grammar*; (ii) *English language.* (BFSS archives).

1857   `Oxford University Locals. Senior: (i) *Preliminary examination*; (ii) *English history and literature.* Junior: *Preliminary examination.*

1858*   Cambridge University Locals: (i) *English composition (junior)*; (ii) *Trench on the study of words (junior)*; (iii) *Analysis and parsing (senior)*; (iv) *English composition (senior)*, (BL 8369.e.2).

1858–82*   *The Oxford and Cambridge examiner. English grammar, parsing and analysis. Comprising the Oxford and Cambridge examination papers from 1858 to the present time.* Allman, [1883]. (BL 12983.aa.70).

1858*   Royal Society of Arts. Final Examination: *English literature.* (RSA Journal).

1859*   Do. *English literature.*

1860*   Do. *English literature.*

1862*   Cambridge University Locals (Junior): (i) *Rudiments of English grammar*; (ii) *Morell's grammar*; (iii) *English composition.* (BL 8369.e.2).

1869–80*   *London University matriculation papers in English, for twelve years, worked out in full as models.* By George B. Cox. Stewart's Educational Series I. London and Edinburgh, [1882]. (BL 12200.cc.5/20).

1874*   British and Foreign School Society. Final Examination (Senior): *Grammar.* (BFSS archives).

1876*   Oxford and Cambridge Schools Examination Board. Papers set in the examination for certificates, July 1876. (i) *English grammar and composition*; (ii) *Shakespeare: King Lear and The Tempest.* (BL 8367.cc.1).

[Anon.]

[a. 1813] S   *Exercises in false spelling; being a selection of pieces, from the most approved authors, in prose and verse. By a friend to youth.* 2nd edn, Newbury: W. Pinnock, [a. 1813]*. (Nottingham UL). Advertised in Pinnock's *Univ. Explan. Reader*, 1813. 5th edn, Whittaker, [*c.* 1820], Holtom, Cat., Winter 1980, 654.

[Anon.]

1787* G   *Exercises, instructive and entertaining, in false English.* Leeds: John Binns (BL); 2nd edn 1788 (BL); 6th edn 1797* (personal). At least twenty-one edns in all to 1841. Those not included by Alston, III, 378–80, include (all at Leeds) 5th (BL); 7th 1802 (Nottingham UL); 12th 1806 (Leeds PL); 13th 1809 (BL); 14th 1811 (private colln); 20th 1831 (Leeds PL). Kennedy, 5492, attributes to CARTER, John, of Leeds, q.v.   Pp. 326–7.

[Anon.]

1818* Ex   *Exercises of transposition to Walker's Themes and Essays, Part I.* Derby: H. Mozley, for the author. (BL). The exercises relate to John Walker's *The teacher's assistant in English composition*, 1801.   Pp. 285; 352.

[Anon.]

1756* C   *The expeditious instructor: or, reading, writing and arithmetick made plain and easy.* [Containing] *I. A succinct English grammar. II.* [homophones] . . . [Seventeen miscellaneous sections in all]. W. Reeve, for the author, Pp. 60. (BL).

[Anon.]

1704* S   *The expert orthographist: teaching to write true English exactly, by rule, and not by rote. According to the doctrine of sounds. And by such plain orthographical tables, as condescend to the meanest capacity. The like not extant before. For the use of such writing and charity-schools, which have not the benefit of the Latin tongue. By a schoolmaster, of above thirty years standing, in London. Persons of quality may be attended at their habitations; boarding-schools may be taught at convenient* times. . . . *Printed for, and sold by the author, at his house at the Blue-Spikes in Spread-Eagle-Court in Grays-Inn-Lane. Where it is also carefully taught.* Pp. xii, 112 (BL). Also issued as: *Right spelling very much improved. Teaching the speediest and surest way to write true English; by rule and not by rote . . . For the benefit of foreigners, and all such as desire to write true English with ease and certainty.* 1704* (BL). Alston, IV, 218–19 and Plate 38 for t.p. of *Right spelling*. Dobson, 1968, I, 358–65, had not seen a copy of *The expert orthographist*, but confirms the view put forward by K.L. Kern, 1913, that it is by the same author as *The writing scholar's companion*, 1695.   Pp. 127–8.

F., J.   'Schoolmaster
[a. 1806]a S   *The child's first book, or an easy and rational method of making children acquainted with the names and powers of letters and syllables.* 10th edn, Durham: G. Walker, 1811*. See the next entry.
[a. 1806]b S   *The child's second book, being a sequel to the first, part I consisting chiefly of words and spellings of one syllable. Part II advancing to words and spellings of two syllables. Drawn up for the use of Sunday Schools.* 2nd edn Penrith: J. Brown, 1806* (Nottingham UL).

FARNABY, Thomas   1575?–1647   Teacher
1648* B   *Troposchematologia: maximam partem ex indice rhetorico Farnabii deprompta, aditus insuper Anglicanis exemplis. In usum scholae regiae grammaticalis apud St Edmundi Burgum.* (BL). At least fifteen edns in all to 1767.   Pp. 145–6.

FARNELL, William Keeling   'Of Theatre Street House School, Norwich'
[1858]* G   *A practical English grammar and parsing expositor; containing clear definitions, concise rules* [etc.]. *Adapted to schools, private teachers, and self-instructors.* (BL).   Pp. 357; *346n.*

FARRAR, Frederic William *see* BOWEN, E.E.; HALES, J.W.; JOHNSON (CORY), W.

FARRO or FARROE, Daniel   Master of a boarding school in Red Lion Court, London
[1776?]* G   *The royal golden instructor for youth throughout the British dominions . . . being a copious abridgment of the Royal Universal British Grammar and Vocabulary . . . [etc.]. Both teacher and learner will discover inexpressible pleasure and utility.* [Bristol?] (BL; O). Alston, I, 148.   P. 76.
1754* G   *The royal universal British grammar and vocabulary. Being a digestion of the entire English language into its proper parts of speech . . . [etc.] Children may be taught the formation of more than ten thousand sentences, by marginal insertions, apposed to that part of speech term'd Qualities, which have not increased the volume two pages.* (BL); 2nd edn 1754* (BL); 3rd edn 1754 (Oslo UL). Alston, I, 145–7.   Pp. 333, 373; *76, 324.*

FAULKNER, W.   Headmaster, Queen Elizabeth's Grammar School, Worcester
[c. 1800] G   *Elements of grammar, or an introduction to the English language.* Thomas Martin, 1824, p. 271.

[Anon.]
[c. 1830?] RA   *The favourite reciter, containing a collection of pieces in prose and poetry suitable for recital in Sabbath schools.* Manchester. (Nottingham UL).
[FAWCETT, John]

1796* S *English exercises for the use of schools, in two parts: Part I. Exercises in orthography. Part II. Exercises in orthography and syntax. Printed at Brearley Hall, near Halifax.* (BL); 6th edn, Halifax: P.K. Holden, 1814* 'Sold also by J. Fawcett, Ewood-Hall, near Halifax.' (BL). *Mon. Rev.*, n.s. 21 (November 1796), 315. P. *326*. See above, *English grammar epitomised.*

[FELL, John] 1735–97 Sometime teacher

1784* G *An essay towards an English grammar. With a dissertation on the nature and peculiar use of certain hypothetical verbs.* (BL). Scolar Press facsimile 1967*. Alston, I, 204.

FELLOWS, John

[a. 1851] S *Gradational spelling book.* Simpkin. From Chalmers, p. 129.

[FELTON, Henry] 1679–1740

1713 B *Dissertation on reading the classics and forming a just style. Written in the year 1709.* Five edns to 1753. Scolar Press facsimile of 1713 edn, 1971*. Pp. 201, 280.

FENN, Lady (Eleanor) 1743–1813 Wrote anonymously or under names such as 'Mrs Lovechild' or 'Mrs Teachwell'

1785* S *The art of teaching in sport; designed as a prelude to a set of toys, for enabling ladies to instill the rudiments of spelling, reading, grammar, and arithmetic, under the idea of amusement.* (BL). Undated edns are widely recorded. Blackwell, Cat. A3, 1980, query the attribution to Lady Fenn, on grounds that are unconvincing. Alston, I, 366. P. 70.

[c. 1785] G *The child's grammar . . . containing a very plain and easy explanation of the several parts of speech; exemplified in the most familiar manner in sentences suited to the capacities of children: followed by parsing lessons, resolved into their elements . . . and also a second set of parsing lessons suited to a scholar more advanced in grammar; with directions for full examination.* Marshall. (title from 1799). The date conjecturally assigned to the 1st edn is from NBL, 1946, no. 115; anr edn Dublin, 1799* (Cambridge UL); at least forty edns to 1843, and a 50th edn is advertised in the 1876 edn of Morell's *Essentials.* Alston, I, 522–3; Moon, 1976, says that, by about 1830, 200,000 copies had been sold.

[1783]a* RE *Cobwebs to catch flies: or, dialogues in short sentences adapted to children from the age of three to eight years,* 2 vols. (BL; V&A); anr edn 1837* (private colln). Many undated edns, and many during 1820s and 1830s. BL has one edn of [1871]. NBL, 1949, attributes to Dorothy Kilner. Whalley, 1974, confirms the attribution to Lady Fenn and reproduces t.p. of 1st edn (p. 42).

1814* RE *Easy reading, adapted to the capacities of children, from five to seven years old . . . being a companion to, and intended to follow, the Little Vocabulary . . . By Mrs Lovechild.* (Nottingham UL).

[1783]b* RA *Fables in monosyllables, by Mrs Teachwell. To which are added morals, in dialogues, between a mother and children.* (BL; V&A); anr edn as: *Fables by Mrs Teachwell, in which the morals are drawn incidentally in various ways,* John Marshall [c. 1790]* (BL). The morals were also published separately as *Morals to a set of fables, by Mrs Teachwell . . . In two sets* [William's morals, George's morals] (V&A).

1784* C *The female guardian. Designed to correct some of the foibles incident to girls, and supply them with innocent amusement for their hours of leisure.* (BL), pp. 128,

iv. The work, in thirty-three issues with continuous page-numbers, is composed of reading and composition material. The author refers to herself throughout as Mrs Teachwell.   Pp. 207; *282, 184.*

[1799] G   *The friend of mothers: designed to assist them in their attempts to instil the rudiments of language and arithmetic, at an early age, and in a manner agreeable to their children.* Newbery. (private colln). Alston, I, 524; Roscoe, J116.

1797* S   *The infant's friend. Part I. A spelling book. By Mrs Lovechild. Part II. Reading lessons,* 2 vols. (BL). Alston, IV, 923 and Plate 99 for t.p. Roscoe, J117 and J118.   Pp. 99, 290.

[1826] S   *Infantine knowledge. A spelling book on a popular plan. By the author of The Child's Grammar.* From Moon, 1976; 2nd edn, ed. Rev. Thomas Smith [1828] (Worthing PL); 3rd edn by 1833; 4th edn by 1835; 5th edn 1837 (Preston PL); 6th edn 1837(?). The book is sometimes referred to as *Infantile knowledge*; Lady Fenn died in 1813, and there is uncertainty about authorship and dates.

[a. 1822] La   *The little vocabulary, by Mrs Lovechild.* 2nd edn, Darton, 1822. Chalmers, p. 130.

[c. 1790?] G   *The mother's grammar. Being a continuation of The Child's Grammar. With lessons for parsing. And a few already done as examples.* NBL, 1946, no. 116; anr edn [c. 1798?] (BL); anr edn [c. 1815?]* (Nottingham UL). Moon gives twenty edns in all to 1838. Alston, I, 518.

[c. 1820]* S   *Mrs Lovechild's golden present for all good little boys and girls.* York: Kendrew. 31 pp. (Bedford CHE; Hove PL). NBL, 1946, no. 19. An alphabet book for which Lady Fenn's pen-name has probably been borrowed.

1798a* G   *Parsing lessons for elder pupils: resolved into their elements, for the assistance of parents and teachers. By Mrs Lovechild.* (BL); 2nd edn 1803* (BL). Alston, I, 520; Roscoe, J142.

1798b* G   *Parsing lessons for young children: resolved into their elements, for the assistance of parents and teachers. By Mrs Lovechild.* (BL); anr edn [c. 1805], Moon, 270. Alston, I, 519; Roscoe, J123.

[1790?]* RA   *The rational dame; or, hints towards supplying prattle for children.* (BL); 4th edn [c. 1800] (BL; Wandsworth PL). BL has unnumbered edns of 1820 and 1825; Sotheby HIC, II (1974), lot 901, gives undated 5th edn. Quayle, 1983, gives [1783] as date of 1st edn.   P. *191.*

[1787]* S   *A spelling book, designed to render the acquisition of the rudiments of our native language easy and pleasant. Containing* [alphabets, monosyllables by sound, two-syllable words by accent; vocabs; reading-lessons] *To which is prefixed, The Child's Library; or, a catalogue of books, recommended to children from the age of three to twelve years. By Mrs Teachwell.* (BL); anr edn (?) as *A spelling book with easy lessons,* 1805, Moon, 273. NBL, 1946, no. 52; Osborne, p. 118; Alston, IV, 863 and Plate 84 for t.p.   P. 66.

[c. 1809] G   *Sportive exercises in grammar. By Mrs Lovechild.* Moon, 1023.

1809* G   *The teacher's assistant, in the art of teaching grammar in sport. Designed to render the subject familiar to children.* Harris. (BL). Cf. Lady Fenn's *The art of teaching in sport,* above.

FENN, John   'Fifty-eight years a schoolmaster', Woodbridge, Suffolk

1843* RA   *The school-master's legacy and family monitor: adapted to every age and station in life, inculcating the practice of religion and morality; dedicated to his late*

pupils. Woodbridge. (BL; Bristol UL). A book of maxims, which Fenn thinks
might be used as 'a school class book'.

FENNER, Dudley 1558?–1587

1584 Lo, B *The artes of logike and rethorike, plainelie set foorth in the Englishe
tounge, easie to be learned and practised.* (BL); ed. R.D. Pepper, *Four Tudor
Books*, Gainesville, 1966*. Howell, 1956, p. 219; Alston, VII, 17–18. Pp.
147–8.

FENNING, Daniel One-time schoolmaster of 'Bures in Suffolk'

1767* D *The new and complete spelling dictionary, and sure guide to the English
language . . . The whole principally designed for the use of schools.* (BL); 2nd edn
1773 (BL; Chicago UL). Alston, V, 278–9 and Plate 38a for t.p. of 1767 edn.

1771* G *A new grammar of the English language; or an easy introduction to the art of
speaking and writing English with propriety and correctness . . . Calculated for the
use, not only of schools, but of private gentlemen.* (BL); six numbered edns in all to
[1790?] and at least three further edns to 1800*. Scolar Press facsimile of 1771
edn, 1967*. Pp. 329–30; *163*.

1761* D *The royal English dictionary; or a treasury of the English language . . . To
which is prefixed a comprehensive grammar of the English tongue.* (BL). At least
five edns to 1775. Alston, V, 227–31.

1756* S *The universal spelling-book; or, a new and easy guide to the English
language.* [Part I. Spelling-lists and reading-passages. Part II. English
grammar. Part III. Vocabulary, by part of speech. Part IV. Miscellaneous
information]. (BL); 4th edn 1760* (BL); 10th edn 1767* (BL); 21st edn 1776*
(BL). Alston, IV, 630–73 and Plate 62 for 1756 t.p. Alston records eighty-four
edns to 1859, to which fifteen (and doubtless many more) can be added.
Johnson, p. 53, quotes much from an undated copy. He gives 1755 as date of
first publication, but without evidence. An edn of 1847*, published at London
by Richardson, is called *Wogan's improved universal spelling book*, but keeps
Fenning's name and contents (BL) Pp. 27, 102; *57*.

FENWICK, Elizabeth

1810 RE *Infantine stories; in words of one, two and three syllables.* (BL); anr edn
Boston, Mass. 1818, Welch, 404; anr edn [*c.* 1820], Sotheby, HIC, VI,
(October 1977), 2815. Osborne, p. 119; *NCBEL*, III, 1099.

1813 RE *Lessons for children; or, rudiments of good manners, morals and humanity.*
M.J. Godwin. Gumuchian, 2511, (V&A); anr edn 1820* (private colln); anr
edn 1828 (O). Specifically intended as a classbook. Selections, ed. E.V. Lucas,
were published in 1898.

[*c.* 1808] G *Rays from the rainbow. Being an easy method for perfecting children in
the first principles of grammar, without the smallest trouble to the instructor.*
Marshall, p. 476; 2nd edn 1812* (BL; Preston PL). Marshall, 1984, p. 275.

FENWICK, John

1811a Ex *English exercises for teaching grammatical composition.* Watt.

1811b RE? *English lessons.* Watt.

1811c G *New elementary grammnar of the English language.* Watt.

FERRIS, O. Allen

1862 La *Elementary lessons in English etymology, with copious exercises, Part I.*
London and Edinburgh. (BL).

[Anon.]

[1736] RE   *The first book for children: being an attempt to make the art of reading English, easy and pleasant, by the adapting the matter and manner of expression to the capacities of children.* Gent. Mag., 6 (March 1736), 172; 8th edn 1754* (DES). Alston, IV, 602.   P. 162.

[Anon.]

1855* RE   *The first book for children; designed for the use of schools.* Llanelly: Rees and Williams. (BL).

[Anon.]

[a. 1824] RE   *First book for children: or, reading made perfectly easy.* 69th edn, Derby: Mozley, 1824* (Nottingham UL).

[Anon.]

1836 RE   *First book for children, or reading made perfectly easy.* Leeds: J. Roberts. Sotheby, HIC, II, 936 (October 1974).

[Anon.]

[c. 1830?]* RE   *The first book or step to learning; containing short and easy lessons for children.* [second title:] *The English primer containing short and easy lessons for children.* Hereford: R. Elliott. (private colln).

[Anon.]

[a. 1850] G   *First elements of English grammar.* Edinburgh: Oliver and Boyd. 12 pp. Advertised in the *Sessional School Collection* and probably compiled for the Sessional School.

[Anon.]

1828* RE   *First guide to reading: or, an original reading made completely easy.* Wellington, Salop: Houston. (BL).

[Anon.]

[c. 1835] RE   *The first lesson book.* Webb, Millington. Gumuchian, 125.

[Anon.]

1843 RE   *The first phonic reading book.* Compiled with the approval of the Committee of Council on Education, reputedly by Kay-Shuttleworth. Quart. Rev., 74 (1844), 26–38; Goldstrom, 1972a (erroneously as 'First Phonetic Reader'), pp. 132, 217; OED s.v, phonic. Also *The second phonic reading book.*

[Anon.]

1808* RE   *The first reading and spelling book for the use of the Roman Catholic children instructed at the charity day-school of Bridzor* [Wilts.] Salisbury (BL); *A second reading book . . .* [etc.] 1809* (BL).

[Anon.]

1845 RA   *First school reader, comprising a selection of reading lessons, progressively arranged.* Souter. Chalmers, p. 157.

[Anon.]

[a. 1864] S   *The first spelling and reading book of easy lessons.* Halifax: W. Nicholson. Advertised in 1864.

[Anon.]

[c. 1835] RE   *The first step to learning; being an easy method of teaching children to read and spell.* Derby and London. Chalmers, p. 131.

[Anon.]

[c. 1820] RE   *The first step to learning: or, parents' best gift to their children;*

containing words from one to four syllables. To which are added easy reading, spelling, and fables, the whole of the Church Catechism, select poetry, &c. Price one penny. Devonport: Samuel and John Keys. Advt in their *The true . . . history of Fair Rosamund* (V&A).

[Anon.]

[*c.* 1855] G *First steps in grammar for very young children, in amusing lessons.* Darton and Co. Sotheby, HIC, II, 940 (October 1974).

[Anon.]

[*a.* 1854] RE *First steps in reading*, 3rd edn. Varty and Owen. Advt in 1854.

[Anon.]

[*c.* 1820]* RE *First steps in reading, in words of one syllable.* E. Wallis. (BL).

FISHER, Ann 1719–78 Married to Thomas Slack, of Newcastle

[1773?] D *An accurate new spelling dictionary, and expositor of the English language . . . To the whole is prefixed, a compendious, practical grammar of the English language* [etc.]. (title from 2nd edn); 2nd edn 1773* (Cambridge UL); 4th edn, Newcastle, 1781, no copy; 5th edn, mentioned in her *The new English tutor*, 1801, p. 48. Alston, V, 325, 327 and 325a. The publication details of this work seem to be particularly confused.

1770* G *A new English exercise book. Calculated to render the construction of the English tongue easy and familiar, independent of any other language. Laid down after the manner of Clarke's Examples for the Latin, and adapted to the rules of Fisher's Grammar.* Newcastle. (Hull UL; BL). Pp. 28 and 29 are reproduced in Gordon and Lawton, p. 80.

[1763?] S *The new English tutor: or, modern preceptor. Consisting of orthography . . . also, a practical abstract of English grammar* [etc.]. (title from 1774 edn). Newcastle. No copy. 3rd edn Newcastle, 1774* (Wisconsin UL); 11th edn Newcastle, 1801* (NLW). Alston, IV, 698–702, lists other edns to 1821* and reproduces in Plate 67 the t.p. of 3rd edn.   Pp. 84, 85; *54.*

[1745] G *A new grammar: being the most easy guide to speaking and writing the English language properly and correctly. Containing* [I. Orthography; II. Prosody; III. Etymology; IV. Syntax] *To which are added, exercises of bad English, in the manner of Clark and Bailey's Examples for the Latin . . . Designed for the use of schools, &c.* Newcastle upon Tyne. (title from 2nd edn). 2nd edn Newcastle, 1750* (BL); 3rd edn London, 1753* (BL); 4th edn Newcastle, 1754* (BL); 5th edn Newcastle, 1757* (BL). Alston, I, 109–40, lists thirty-five numbered and many unnumbered edns to 1811. From the 7th edn, 1762, the work was often known as *A practical new grammar.* Scolar Press facsimile of 1750 edn, 1968*.   Pp. 73, 128, 325–6; *283, 346n., 383.*

1756* RE *The pleasing instructor: or, entertaining moralist. Consisting of select essays, relations, visions and allegories . . . To which are prefixed, new thoughts on education. Designed for the use of schools, as well as the closet* [etc.]. (BL); 5th edn 1766* (BL). At least twenty-seven edns in all to about 1820.   Pp. 172–3. See below *The young scholar's delight,* 1770.

FISHER, Daniel Master of Cockermouth Grammar School

[*a.* 1750] S *The child's Christian education, or spelling and reading made easy.* 3rd edn [1750?] no copy; 5th edn 1754, no copy; 6th edn 1759* (BL). At least nineteen edns in all to 1821. Alston, IV, 588–92 and Plate 55 for advt t.p. of 5th edn.   Pp. 84, 161; *86.*

FISHER, George

[*c.* 1733]* C   *The instructor: or, young man's best companion: containing, spelling, reading, writing, and arithmetic* [etc.]. Pp. viii, 424. (BL). Alston, IV, 358–410, records seventy British and American edns to 1862, and there are others. The work was sometimes issued as *The American instructor* and is often attributed to Ann Fisher.

1700 *New spelling book*   see next entry

[1693] S   *Plurimum in minimo, or a new spelling book; being the most easy, speedy, and pleasant, way, to learn to read and write true English* [etc.]. No copy. As: *Fisher's new spelling book* . . . 1700* (Columbia UL), part of which is separately titled *The compleat school-master*; see below TRYON, Thomas, 1700. Alston, IV, 173–4.   Pp. 52, 58, 93, 99; *51, 64.*

FITCH, Joseph

[a. 1841] G   *A poetical grammar of the English language.* 2nd edn 1841 (O).

FLEMING, Caleb   1698–1779

[1765?] G   *Grammatical observations on the English language; drawn up particularly with a view to practice.* Alston, I, 263. No copy.

1748* Ed   *A modern plan: upon which the minds and manners of youth may be formed: or, a compendium of moral institutes made familiar.* (BL, shelf-mark T. 1614 (8).) Published anonymously. The dedication is signed 'Publicus', but in another copy (BL 699.h.13 (8)) it is signed 'Rusticus'.   P. 202.

FLETCHER, William   Master of Woodbridge Grammar School

[1837]* RA   *The child's handbook of a rational system of education. Rudiments of reading and thinking, Part I.* (BL).   Pp. 240–1; *383.*

1828a G   *The little grammarian; or, an easy guide to the parts of speech, and familiar illustrations of the leading rules of syntax: in a series of instructive and amusing tales.* (BL; Wandsworth PL); 2nd edn 1833* (some rearrangement of the title) (Leicester UL; ULIE). The 2nd edn was advertised by Grant and Griffiths in *Easy rhymes for children,* (1825) 1831. NBL, 1949, no. 267; Moon, 288.

1828b* RE   *The picturesque primer; or, useful matter made pleasing pastime for leisure hours.* (BL; V&A; Preston PL). Dated from preface. Anr edn 1837 (BL; Nottingham UL); anr edn [*c.* 1848] Chalmers, p. 131. NBL, 1949, no. 69. Moon, 289.

FLORIAN, Jolly B.   Master of an academy in Bath

1796* Ed   *An essay on an analytical course of studies, containing a complete system of human knowledge.* (BL). Mon. Rev., n.s. 20 (August 1796), 456–7. Hans, pp. 79–81.

FLOWER, Marmaduke, and   FLOWER, William Balmbro'

1844 G   *A practical English grammar, containing a complete new class of exercises . . . on a plan entirely new.* (Columbia UL).

FOGG, Peter Walkden

1792–6 G   *Elementa anglicana; or, the principles of English grammar displayed and exemplified . . . Vol. I Containing a copious collection of rules, examples, and exercises. Intended for the use of the pupil.* Stockport, 1792*. *Vol. II Containing a key . . . together with ample notes and dissertations, illustrating the various parts of this extensive subject.* Stockport, 1796*. (Stockport PL); Scolar Press facsimile of both volumes 1970*. Vol. II was also issued separately, 1796 (BL). Alston, I, 464.   Pp. 50, 86, 94, 294, 328, 340–1; *54, 342, 376.*

FOOT, William 'Master of the Academy, in Poland Street, Soho Square, London'

[a. 1747]* Ed *An essay on education: intended principally, to make the business of grammar-schools, of real service to such youth, as are not designed for the university. In a letter to Mr William Watts, Merchant, Master of the Academy, in Poland-Street, near Soho Square, London.* Bristol. (BL). *Gent. Mag.*, 17 (April 1747), 204. Hans, p. 86.   Pp. 202; *308.*

FORD, E.B.

1801* G *A short and easy introduction to English grammar.* Beverley. (DES).

FORDYCE, David 1711–51 Professor of Moral Philosophy, Aberdeen

1745–8 Ed *Dialogues concerning education,* 2 vols.

FORDYCE, David [Writing-master?]

[1792?]* Ex *The new and complete British letter-writer; or young secretary's instructor . . . with a concise and familiar English grammar* [etc.] (BL). Alston, III, 406.   P. *331.*

[FORRESTER, Alfred Henry, i.e. 'Alfred Crowquill'] 1804–72

1825 G *The holiday grammar, a Christmas present for the present Christmas, passing Murray, Dilworth, and all past grammarians in simplicity.* Sotheby, HIC, II (October 1974), lot 960.

[1842] G *The pictorial grammar.* (BL; Bodley; Preston PL); anr edn 1851* (Bedford CHE); anr edn [*c.* 1860] (Melbourne UL); anr edn 1873, Gumuchian, 1955; anr edn 1876 (Bedford CHE). According to Higson, contradicting *DNB,* the text was written by C.R. Forrester, Alfred's elder brother.

FOSTER, Edward Ward

1840 G *The elements of English grammar.* (BL; O).

[Anon.]

[*c.* 1790?]* RE *The foundation of all learning, or child's first book, by which a child will learn more in one month than by many others in twelve.* 5th edn Watts. [*c.* 1800] (BL). Cover title *The child's first book.* 6th edn Sotheby, HIC, II (October 1974), lot 978.

FOWLER, Thomas

[1590] RE *A most shorte, and profytable introductyon to learne to read wrytten and prynted hand with in a monethes space.* No copy. *SR* (A), II, 559.

FOX, Francis 1675–1738

[a. 1754] S *An introduction to spelling and reading. Containing lessons for children historical and practical; adorned with sculptures. Together with the chief rules for spelling, and dividing words into syllables.* (title from 7th edn). 7th edn 1754* (BL); at least twenty-two edns in all to 1815. Alston, IV, 603–9 and Plate 54 for t.p. of 1754 edn.

FOX, George 1624–91 and HOOKES, Ellis

1670 S *A primmer and catechism for children: or a plain and easie way for children to learn to spell and read perfectly in a little time.* (BL); as: *Instructions for right spelling, and plain directions for reading and writing true English. With several delightful things, very useful and necessary both for young and old to learn.* By *G.F. and E.H.* 1673* (BL); at least twelve further British and American edns to 1769. Scolar Press facsimile of 1673 edn, 1971*. Alston, IV, 76–89 and Plate 13 for 1670 t.p.   P. *157.*

[FOXTON, Thomas]

1728* RA *Moral songs composed for the use of children.* (BL); anr edn 1731,

NCBEL, II, 1018; 4th edn 1743, Sotheby, HIC, VI (October 1977), lot 2821a; in *A choice collection of hymns and moral songs*, Newcastle, 1781, Opie, 1973, no. 717. Facsimile of 1728 edn in Classics of Children's Literature, no. 4, Garland Publ. Co. Pp. 167–9.

FRANCIS, William   Teacher

1790* G   *A concise introduction to English grammar: compiled by William Francis, of Hook, for the use of his school.* Marlborough. (O). Alston, I, 450a.

[FRANK, Elizabeth]

1814* Ex   *Classical English letter-writer; or, epistolary selections . . . With introductory rules and observations on epistolary correspondence; and biographical notices of the writers . . . By the author of Lessons for Young Persons in Humble Life.* York: Thomas Wilson. Pp. xxiv, 368. (BL). Higson records an edn of 1811, but there is no indication that the 1814 edn is not the first.

1808* RA   *Lessons for young persons in humble life: calculated to promote their improvement in the art of reading; in virtue and piety; and, particularly, in the knowledge of the duties peculiar to their stations.* York. (BL).

FRAUNCE, Abraham   d. 1633

[1588] B   *The Arcadian rhetorike: or the praecepts of rhetorike made plaine by examples, Greeke, Latin, English, Italian, French, Spanish.* (O). ed. Ethel Seaton, Luttrell Society, no. 5, 1950*; Scolar Press facsimile 1969*. Alston, VI, 33.   P. *150*.

FRY, Alfred

1838 Ed   'The junior school of Bruce Castle, Tottenham', in: Central Society of Education, *Second publication of 1838*; reprinted Woburn Press, 1968*.   P. 308.

FRY, William   'Teacher of languages and mathematical sciences'

1784* D   *A new vocabulary of the most difficult words in the English language, teaching to pronounce them with ease and propriety.* (BL). Alston, V, 328 and Plate 49a for t.p.

FULTON, George   'Teacher of English' and master of a private school in Edinburgh

[a. 1823] D   *Johnson's dictionary of the English language in miniature. Improved and enlarged by George Fulton.* 3rd edn Edinburgh, 1823 (BL); 9th edn Edinburgh, 1830; anr edn Edinburgh, 1861 (BL).

1826* S   *A pronouncing vocabulary; with lessons in prose and verse, and a few grammatical exercises.* Edinburgh. (BL). In the preface Fulton says he has been teaching 'upwards of forty years'.   Pp. 241; *383*.

FULTON, George and KNIGHT, G.   'Teachers of English'

1802* D   *A general pronouncing and explanatory dictionary of the English language. To which is added, a complete vocabulary of Scripture proper names.* Edinburgh. (BL); 2nd edn 1807, Watt; as *A dictionary of the English language greatly improved*, 1833* (BL).

[1817] S   *The orthoepy of the English language simplified, unfolding that method of teaching it which has been long successfully practised in the school of Fulton and Knight, teachers of English.* Edinburgh, 1817*. (BL). Watt gives the date 1811, but there is no indication in the 1817 edn that it is not the first. The dedication is in the name of Fulton alone, and it is likely that he wrote the book. But the t.p.

shows that he wished Knight to be associated with it.   Pp. 36, 44, 60; *50*.

1800 S   *A pronouncing spelling book: with sacred extracts, in prose and verse, for reading and reciting.* Edinburgh: Peter Hill. (Glasgow UL); anr edn 1813, Watt; 6th edn 1817* (BL); anr edn 1835.   P. 107.

FURSMAN, J.

[1820?]* S   *Reading and spelling made easy, containing nearly two hundred progressive lessons of reading and spelling arranged for every day of the week and month, Church catechism, etc.* (Devonport printed) 72 pp. (BL).

G., J.   Of the Literary and Commercial Seminary, Bristol

1796* G   *An easy introduction to the English language.* Bristol: for the author. (Bristol PL). Alston, I, 497.   Pp. 341; *330*.

G., J.

1694* S   *A play-book for children, to allure them to read assoon as they can speak plain. Composed of small pages, on purpose not to tire children, and printed with a fair and pleasant letter.* (Bodley). Alston, IV, 175; Carpenter and Prichard, 1984.   P. 158.

GALL, James

[a. 1832] Ed   *Key to the one book for teaching children to read. With an introductory essay on the fundamental principles of education.* Edinburgh. 2nd edn 1832* (BL; Hull UL). The one book is the Bible.   Pp. 65, 240; *30, 44–5*.

1840 Ed   *A practical enquiry into the philosophy of education.* Edinburgh. (BL; Reading UL).

[GALT, John]   1779–1839

[a. 1821?] RE   (Clark's) *English primer, or, child's first book.* Chalmers, p. 133. Galt wrote textbooks under the name Rev. T. Clark.

1821 RA   *The national reader; consisting of easy lessons in morals, history . . . and general knowledge. By the Rev. T. Clark.* (dated from preface). New edn, J. Souter [1822?] (BL); anr edn, n.d.* (Nottingham UL); anr edn 1833 (Chalmers, p. 133).   P. 243.

GARDINER, Jane   Of Elsham Hall [School], Beverley

1799* G   *The young ladies' English grammar; adapted to the different classes of learners. With an appendix, or abbreviation of the grammar.* York (BL); 2nd edn London, 1808 (BL); 3rd edn 1809 (BL). Alston, I, 525.   Pp. 334; *325*.

GARTLY, G.   'Teacher of English grammar, &c., Glasgow'

[1831]* G   *Murray's grammar and exercises abridged, comprising the substance of his large grammar and exercises. With additional notes and illustrations.* (Leeds UL). The preface is dated 14 February 1831. Anr edn 1859 (BL).

GAULTIER, L.E.C.   1746?–1818

1800–1* G   *A method of making abridgments; or, easy and certain rules for analysing authors.* [Part I. Explanations and rules; Part II. Application of the rules] (BL). *Mon. Rev.*, 32, n.s. (September 1800), 102; Moon 1976. Cf. his *Méthode pour analyser la pensée sans déranger l'ordre des mots qui l'expriment*, 2nd edn Paris, 1806* (Manchester UL).   Pp. 336–7.

GAWTHROP, Hugh   'Teacher of elocution at the Birkenhead Mechanics Institute'

1847* RA   *The elocutionary reader; or, rhetorical class book; adapted to the use of schools.* (BL); anr edn rev. J. Davenport, 1862 (BL).

GEDDES, A.

1783 G   *A new English grammar.* Newcastle. No copy. Alston, I, 376a.

[Anon.]

1846* RA   *The gem book of poesie; to aid in the development of the religious and moral feelings and affections. By the author of The Ancient Poets and Poetry of England.* (BL; Fulham PL). The compiler may be William Martin.   P. 222.

General principles of grammar see CORNWALLIS, Caroline Frances

[Anon.]

1784 P   *A general view of English pronunciation. To which are added, easy lessons for the use of the English class.* Edinburgh. (Nottingham UL); Scolar Press facsimile 1968*. Alston, VI, 501.   P. *44.*

GENTLEMAN, Francis   1728–84

1772* RA   *The new pleasing instructor: or, entertaining moralist. By Mr Gentleman.* York, (BL). Attributed by BL to Robert Gentleman. Alston, VI, 370.

1771 P   *The orator: or, English assistant. Being an essay on reading and declamation.* Edinburgh (Bodley). Prefixed also to his *The new pleasing instructor,* York, 1772. Alston, VI, 369–71; *NCBEL,* II, 834.

GENTLEMAN, Robert   1746–95   Sometime master of a boarding school in Shrewsbury

1788 C   *The young English scholar's pocket companion. In six parts. Selected from the best writers, divided into short lessons, and adapted to the capacities of children. Part I. A compendious English grammar* [history; geography; chronology; arithmetic; coinage]. Kidderminster (private colln); 2nd edn 1797* (BL). Alston, III, 385–6.

GIBBONS, Thomas   1720–85   Tutor, Mile End Academy

1767 B   *Rhetoric; or, a view of its principal tropes and figures, in their origin and powers: with a variety of rules to escape errors and blemishes.* (BL); Scolar Press facsimile 1969*. Alston, VI, 222.   Pp. *166, 279.*

[GIGNOUX, John]

1757* S   *The child's best instructor in spelling and reading. Wherein words of several syllables are so divided, that the sound of each syllable, when joined together, shall lead the scholar into the true and correct pronunciation* [etc.]. (BL); at least nine British edns in all to 1788. The book is often attributed to John Entick, whose grammar was included in the 4th edn (not recorded by Alston), advertised in Ash's *Grammatical institutes,* 1763 edn. Alston, IV, 675–82 and Plate 62 for facsimile of the very full t.p.

1759* Ex   *Epistolary correspondence made pleasant and familiar: calculated chiefly for the improvement of youth. Containing sixty letters in the English and French languages . . . The French translations by Philip Bellie, Master of the Ladies French Boarding School, in Cheney-Walk, Chelsea.* Pp. viii, xviii, 292. (BL). In the preface Gignoux says that most such books are for adults, but this one is for young people 'absent from their Parents, Relations, &c., either at School, or elsewhere'.

GILDON, Charles   1665–1724

1718* B, RA   *The complete art of poetry. In six parts.* 2 vols. (BL); Garland Press facsimile, N.Y., 1969. The first five parts, comprising vol. I, are critical; the sixth, comprising vol. II, is an anthology of short pieces.   Pp. 179; 180–1.

1711* G   *A grammar of the English tongue, with notes, giving the grounds and reason of grammar in general . . . Adapted to the use of . . . the schools.* (BL; Bodley, etc.); 2nd edn as: *. . . in general. To which are now added, the arts of poetry, rhetoric, logic, &c. Making a compleat system of an English education.* 1712* (BL); 3rd edn 1714* (BL). Eight edns in all to 1782. Scolar Press facsimile of 1711 edn, 1967. Alston, I, 42–51; Vorlat, 1975. Published anonymously and in the past often attributed to Sir Richard Steele and to John Brightland.   Pp. 27, 200–1, 343; *46, 50, 51, 163, 342, 376.*

GILES, James   'Master of the Free School, Gravesend'

1803* G   *English parsing: comprising the rules of syntax, exemplified by appropriate lessons under each rule . . . For the use of schools, private teachers, and elder students.* Gravesend. (BL). 2nd edn 1810; 3rd edn advertised in 1819; 9th edn 1834 (Wisconsin UL); anr edn Woking, 1854 (BL); 15th edn London, [*c.* 1855]* (Leeds UL); 17th edn advertised in 1859. The book appeared sometimes under the title *Parsing lessons . . . Gent. Mag.,* 78 (April 1808), 334.   P. *324.*

GILES, John Allen   1808–84   Sometime teacher

[a. 1852] G   *English grammar in question and answer.* 2nd edn 1852. (BL).

1839 G   *An enlarged edition of Murray's abridged English Grammar.* Harvey and Darton. (BL).

GILES, T.A.

1836 RA   *Class-book of general information on Bible history, heathen mythology, history, geography, grammar* [etc.]. W. Pickering. (Bedford CHE).

[a. 1858] G   *Elements of English grammar, for the use of schools.* 2nd edn 1838. (Columbia UL).

GILFILLAN, George   1813–78

1851* RA   *The book of British poesy, ancient and modern; being select extracts from our best poets, arranged in chronological order. With an essay on British poetry.* (BL).

GILL, Alexander   1567–1635   'High Master, St Paul's School, London'

1619* La   *Logonomia anglica qua gentis sermo facilius addiscitur.* (BL, etc.); 2nd edn 1621* (BL, etc.). Scolar Press facsimile of 1621 edn, 1969*. Facsimile of 1619 edn, ed. with notes, etc. by Bror Danielson and Arvid Gabrielson and translation by R.C. Alston, Stockholm Studies in English XXVI, 2 vols., Stockholm, 1972*.   Pp. 29, 48, 62, 142; *342, 363. For 1621 edn see pp. 41, 50.*

GILL, George

[*c.* 1866?] RS   (Gill's) *Illustrated series of reading books.* Books 2 and 3 (O).

[*c.* 1865?] RS   *The illustrated series of technical reading books.* Standard 1, Liverpool, [P1871] (O); Standard 2, London, [*c.* 1865] (O).

GILL, J.W.   'First-class certificated master'

[1854]* G   *First steps in English grammar. Compiled for the purpose of enabling teachers to put into the hands of their pupils a book containing only such parts as should be committed to memory.* 32 pp. (BL).   P. *347.*

GILLEADE, G.   'Westwood House Academy, St Ives'

1816* G   *A compendious English grammar, in twenty-eight praxes or lessons, comprising above one thousand six hundred examples, at full length.* Pp. viii, 208. Spalding: T. Albin. (BL).   P. *350.*

GILMOUR, J.

1840 RE *Gradual primer, or teaching and learning made easy*. Greenock. (O).

[Anon.]

[a. 1834] Ed *The Glasgow infant school magazine*, 2nd edn 1834*. Twelve nos., each of 24 pp., continuous page-nos. Passages for reading, with questions and answers. (Private colln).

GLEIG, George Robert 1796–1888 'Inspector General of military education'

[a. 1853] G *An explanatory English grammar*. Gleig's School Series. Longman. (BL).

[a. 1863] RE *First school book to teach reading and writing*. Gleig's School Series. Longman. (BL). Followed by *Second school book* (BL).

[c. 1850] La *History of the English language*. Gleig's School Series. (BL). P. 358.

GODSKIRK, Ro., and HUME, James

[a. 1745] S *The Edinburgh new method in three parts* [I monosyllables; II pronunciation, division of syllables; III kinds of words] *To all which is added, some rules of spelling. For the use of schools*. 4th edn, Edinburgh, 1745*. (BL). Law, p. 150, refers to an edn of 1750 which includes 'of teaching English' in the title.

[GODWIN, Mary Jane]

1809 P *Dramas for children. Imitated from the French of L.F. Jauffret, by the author of Tabart's Popular Tales*. (BL); 2nd edn 1817. Peter H. Marshall, *William Godwin*, Yale, 1984, p. 437.

GODWIN, William 1756–1836

[1805]* RA *Fables ancient and modern. Adapted for the use of children from three to eight years of age. By Edward Baldwin, esq*. 2 vols. (BL). At least ten British edns in all to 1824 and at least eight American edns to 1818. Marshall, *ibid.*, pp. 267–8. P. 290.

1818* Ed *Letter to a young American: on the course of studies it might be most advantageous for him to pursue*. Pp. 15 (BL). P. 248.

1810 G *A new guide to the English tongue*. First prefixed to the 2nd edn of W.F. Mylius' *The Christ's Hospital dictionary of the English tongue*, which Godwin had revised as *Mylius' school dictionary*, 1809. Issued together with Hazlitt's *A new and improved grammar of the English language*, 1810* (BL). The combined Hazlitt/Godwin volume was abbreviated and added to by Godwin as: *Outlines of English grammar, partly abridged from Hazlitt's New and Improved Grammar of the English Tongue*, 1810. Keynes, 1932; Marshall, 1984.

[Anon.]

1788 RE *The golden primer; or, an easy and entertaining guide to the art of reading*. Gainsborough: Mozley. Chalmers, p. 133, from Gumuchian, no. 135.

GOLDSMITH, J. see PHILLIPS, Sir Richard

GOLDSMITH, Oliver 1730?–1774

1767a* RA *The beauties of English poesy*. 2 vols. (BL). The preface and notes are printed in the *Collected works*, ed. Arthur Friedman, Oxford, 1966, vol. V. Pp. 179; 180. See also p. 280.

1759* Ed *The Bee, no. 6*. 'On education'. In *Collected works*, ed. Arthur Friedman, Oxford, 1966, I, 455–66. P. 204.

1767b* RA *Poems for young ladies. In three parts. Devotional, moral and entertaining.* 2 vols. The compiler is anonymous. (BL); new edn 'By Dr Goldsmith', 1770* (BL); anr edn 1785 (BL). P. 180.

[1872] RA (Goldsmith) *The Deserted Village, etc. with notes and analysis.* Edinburgh: Laurie. (BL).

[1870]* RA *Goldsmith's Traveller, Deserted Village, and The Hermit. With life and glossary.* Chambers' English classics for use in school. (BL).

1865* RA *Goldsmith's Traveller, with explanatory notes, exercises in the analysis of sentences, and a life of the poet.* Longman. ('Oxford Local Examinations'). (BL).

GOLDSMITH see also HALES, J.W., 1874; McLEOD, W., 1858; MASON, C.P., 1865.

[GOOD, Thomas] 1609–78 Master of Balliol College, Oxford

1677 Lo *A brief English tract of logick.* [Oxford]. (Bodley); Scolar Press facsimile 1967*. Alston, VII, 66.

[Anon.]

[*c.* 1850] RE *The good child's new primer, in easy lessons.* Yorkshire J.S. Publishing and Stationery Co. 8 pp. (Wandsworth PL).

[Anon.]

[*c.* 1850]* RE *The good child's reading and spelling book.* (BL, t.p. clipped).

GOODWIN, Thomas

1855 G *The student's practical grammar of the English language, together with a commentary on the first book of Milton's Paradise Lost.* (BL; O).

GORDON, James Publisher

[*c.* 1850?] RA *Advanced reading book, literary and scientific*; 3rd edn Edinburgh [a. 1862] advt. In use by the Society of the Holy Child Jesus *c.* 1850.

[a. 1862] RS *First [to sixth] English reading book.* Edinburgh. Advt.

GORDON, William 'Teacher of the mathematics'

1755 C *Every young man's companion: containing directions for spelling, reading, and writing English* [etc.] (Patent Office, London); 4th edn 1765* (BL), containing a rhetoric among its twenty four numbered components. Six edns in all to 1777. Alston, IV, 624–9 and Plate 61 for t.p. of 1755 edn. Pp. 164; 79.

GOUGH, James b. 1712 and GOUGH, John 1721–91 Teachers

1754* G *A practical grammar of the English tongue ... In five parts. I.* [Orthography] *II. Analogy, which treats of the several parts of speech. III. Etymology, or the derivation of words ... IV.* [Syntax] *V.* [Prosody]. *For the use of schools. First compiled by James Gough, of Mountmelick. Revised ... by John Gough, of Cole Alley, Dublin.* Dublin: Isaac Jackson. (BL). At least eight edns to 1801. The 2nd and subsequent edns contained a dictionary, separately titled and perhaps separately issued as *A new compendious expositor of English words.* Scolar Press facsimile of 1754 edn, 1967*. Alston, I, 144a, 193–6. Pp. 178, 331; *321, 346n.*

[GRACE, John Austin]

1850a S *An introduction to the school expositor.* Dublin: Powell (St Mary's Merino, Dublin). Published for the Christian Brothers.

1850b S *The school expositor.* Dublin: Powell (St Mary's, Merino, Dublin); anr edn, Gill (NLI). A spelling-book compiled for the Christian Brothers. McDunphy, 1976.

[Anon.]

[a. 1839] RE   *The graded primer.* 10th edn. Simpkin Marshall. Chalmers, p. 122.

[Anon.]

1852 G   *Graduated grammar. (National education, or, illustrated two-penny school books).* The Bodleian copy has been missing since 1883.

GRAHAM, George Frederick

1842* Ex   *English; or, the art of composition explained in a series of instructions and examples.* (BL); 2nd edn 1844 (BL).   Pp. 281, 312.

1862* G   *English grammar practice; or, exercises on the etymology, syntax, and prosody of the English language.* (BL).   Pp. 353; *87, 368.*

1847* Ṣ   *English spelling; with rules and exercises. Intended as a class-book for schools, or for home teaching.* (BL).   P. 129.

1857* Ex   *English style; or, a course of instruction for the attainment of a good style of writing. With an historical sketch of the English language . . . Intended for the higher classes in schools and colleges.* Pp. xvi, 372 (BL); 3rd edn 1869 (BL).   Pp. 310; *281, 314.*

1846 La   *English synonymes classified and explained: with practical exercises.* (BL); 2nd edn 1853 (BL); 3rd 1858 (BL).

1843* G   *Helps to English grammar; or, easy exercises for young children.* (BL); anr edn 1851 (Leeds UL); anr edn 1855 (Wisconsin UL).   P. 367.

1845 Ed   'On English grammars', *Classical Museum,* 2 (1845), 404–11.

1852* RA   *Studies from the English poets: a reading book for the higher classes in schools.* (BL).   P. 257.

GRAHAM, William   Of Cupar Academy, Fife, and subsequently of the Scottish Institution for the Education of Young Ladies

1836 La   *Exercises in etymology.* Edinburgh: Chambers (BL); 2nd edn [1855] (Birmingham UL; BL); rev. edn as: *Exercises on . . .* 1870* (Leicester UL).   P. *357.*

1829* La   *Exercises on the derivation of the English language; to which is added, in a series of extracts, the history of language; and a view of its general principles, as pointed out by the etymologies of various tongues; intended for the use of the higher classes in English schools.* Cupar: R. Tullis. (N.E. Fife District L, Cupar). Doughty, no. 70.   P. 357.

[a. 1837] P   *Principles of elocution, in which the subjects of articulation, inflexion, modulation, and the measure of speech, are familiarly explained; to which is added a selection of pieces in the various styles of reading, recitation, oratory, &c.* 2nd edn Edinburgh, 1837* (BL); anr edn Edinburgh, 1855 (BL).

[Anon.]

1829* Ed   'Grammar – English grammar', *The Schoolmaster,* 1, no. 18 (5 September 1829), 185–8.

[Anon.]

[a. 1854] G   *Grammar explained in verse.* Advertised for one farthing by Varty and Owen, in GILL, J.W., 1854 (above).

[Anon.]

1842* G   *Grammar lessons by a lady. Designed as a supplement to Mary's Grammar.* John Rodwell. The preface is signed M., but the writer is not Mrs Marcet. (personal).

[Anon.]

1837* G *A grammar of the English language: suited to the capacities of children.* Bicester: J. Smith. 78 pp. (O). P. *346n.*

[Anon.]

1815* G *Grammatical errors, which occur in conversation and writing, pointed out and corrected, by a simple and familiar method agreeably to the rules of Murray's Grammar.* 38 pp. (BL).

[Anon.]

1796 B *Grammatical figures and a system of rhetoric.* No copy. Alston, VI, 263.

[Anon.]

1802 G *A grammatical game in rhyme. By a lady.* NBL, 1946, no. 117; NBL, 1949, no. 266; Gumuchian, 3275; illustrated in Sotheby HIC, VI (October 1977*), Plate 71.

[Anon.]

[a. 1870] RE *Grammatical primer.* Chambers's minor educational series. Advt.

[Anon.]

[c. 1840] S *The grammatical spelling book.* Referred to in the preface of Green's *Universal primer,* (1780?) *c.* 1840, as 'lately appeared'. The spelling-lists are arranged by part of speech.

[Anon.]

[c. 1830]* RE *The grandfather's pet; or, reading made easy: . . . For the use of schools.* Ryle and Paul. 18 pp. (private colln).

[Anon.]

[c. 1840] S *Grandmamma Easy's pretty poetical spelling book, about trees, fruit and flowers.* Dean. Chalmers, p. 134.

GRANT, John

1813 G *A grammar of the English language: containing a complete summary of its rules, with an elucidation of the general principles of elegant and correct diction, accompanied with critical and explanatory notes, questions for examination, and appropriate exercises.* Anr edn [*c.* 1824]* (Leeds UL). The preface is dated 8 January 1813, and a second t.p., dated 1813, is bound up with the Leeds copy. *Gent. Mag.,* 85.i (April 1815), 345, notices *An abridgment . . . for the use of junior classes.*

[a. 1824] G *A guide to the exercises* [in his grammar], *with notes and explanations. Intended chiefly for private learners.* Advertisement in his grammar, *c.* 1824.

GRANVILLE, George

[a. 1827] G *Imperial school grammar.* T.p. of the *Key* (next entry).

1827* G *A key to the orthographical lessons, and parsing exercises, contained in Part I. of The Imperial School Grammar: executed according to the new and improved system of parsing, by formulae, in a series of six classes, as therein proposed.* (BL).

GRAY, James 'Master of the English school at Peebles'

[a. 1794] S *A concise spelling book for the use of children. In three parts.* [I. and II.: spelling-lists; reading-passages] *III. Some observations on the principles of the English language* [final -e; contractions; homophones]. 7th edn Edinburgh, 1794* (BL); 11th edn 1804 (Peebles PL); 14th edn 1809* (NLS); 29th edn rev. Alex. Barrie, 1824 (NLS); 40th edn 1834 (Columbia UL, N.Y.). Alston, IV, 911 and Plate 96 for t.p. of 1794 edn.

GRAYSTON, John, and BIRKBY, Thomas Simpson
1865 RS   *The [first . . .] third reading book.* (O).

GREAVES, Paul
1594 G   *Grammatica anglicana, praecipue quatenus a Latina differt, ad unicam P. Rami methodum concinnata . . . Authore Paulo Greaves.* Cambridge. (Cambridge UL; BL); ed. O. Funke, Vienna, 1938*. Scolar Press facsimile 1969*. Alston, I, 2, for refs. Vorlat, 1975.   P. 55.

GREEN, J.   'Master of the academy in Denmark Street [Bristol]'
1771* S   *A grammatical spelling-book: wherein, after a new, concise, and rational method, are exhibited, first, the most common words; and secondly, the most difficult words in the English language. To which is added, mnemonics, or the art of memory.* (BL; Cambridge UL). Alston, IV, 718 and Plate 72 for t.p.

[1780?] RE   *Universal primer; or child's first book.* 88 pp. Darton and Clark. [*c.* 1840]* (V&A). The preface shows that the author is the same as J. Green in the preceding entry, and a reference to Mrs Barbauld suggests a date after 1778.   P. 60.

GREEN, Matthias
1837* G   *An English grammar.* Birmingham printed. (BL); anr edn 1866 (BL); anr edn 1868 (Bodley).

GREEN, Robert   Master of an academy in Durham
1779* G   *A short abstract of English grammar, calculated for the introduction of young people of both sexes, into that very necessary, but ('till of late) much neglected part of education.* Newcastle. (BL). Alston, I, 365a.

GREEN, Thomas
1765* D   *The royal spelling dictionary of the English language . . . for the instruction of our youth of both sexes* [etc.] (BL); 2nd edn 1775* (BL). The grammar in the 1st edn does not contain even the parts of speech, and is shortened still further in the 2nd edn. Alston, IV, 704–5 and Plate 68 for 1765 t.p.

GREENWOOD, James   d. 1737   Sur-Master, St Paul's School, London
1711* G   *An essay towards a practical English grammar, describing the genius and nature of the English tongue: giving likewise a rational and plain account of grammar in general, with a familiar explanation of its terms.* (BL); 2nd edn 1722* (BL); 3rd edn 1729* (BL); 5th edn 1753* (BL). Scolar Press facsimile of 1711 edn, 1968*. Alston, I, 52–6; Vorlat, 1975.   Pp. 95, 120, 322, 340; *333, 342.*

1737* G   *The royal English grammar, containing what is necessary to the knowledge of the English tongue. Laid down in a plain and familiar way. For the use of young gentlemen and ladys.* (Columbia UL). Nine edns in all to 1780. Alston, I, 76–84. Vorlat, 1975.

1717* Ra   *The virgin muse. Being a collection of poems from our most celebrated English poets. Designed for the use of young gentlemen and ladies, at schools . . . With notes, and a large index, explaining the difficult places, and all the hard words.* (BL); 2nd edn 1722* (BL); 3rd edn 1731, *NCBEL,* II, 360, where it is also said that *The virgin muse* is included in *The young clerk's assistant* [1733].   Pp. 171–2; 180–1.

GREGORY, George   1754–1808
[*c.* 1802?] G   *A grammar of the English language.* Advertised in David Irving, 1801, as 'speedily will be published' by R. Phillips.

1808* B *Letters on literature, taste, and composition, addressed to his son.* 2 vols. (Glasgow, Mitchell L). P. *215.*

GREIG, John

[*c.* 1824] C *The expeditious self-instructor; containing the elements of reading, grammar, writing* [etc.]. Chalmers, pp. 20, 134.

GRIMWADE, J.G.W.

1822* S *The first principles of reading, made easy to the meanest capacity. Printed for, and sold by the author:* Hadleigh. (Glasgow UL; BL).

GROOMBRIDGE, H. 'Lecturer on elocution, Geography, &c.'

1797* G *The rudiments of the English tongue; or, a plain and easy introduction to English grammar: wherein the principles of the language are methodically digested. To which is added, an essay on elocution.* Bath. (Bristol PL). Alston, I, 504.

[Anon.]

1862 B *Guide to English literature . . . arranged in simple language in the form of question and answer.* Bookseller's catalogue, 1961. P. *219.*

[Anon.]

[1703?] RE *A guide to true English, by the help of which children may be taught in a short time, both to master their reading . . . and afterwards to write true English . . . Composed for the use of a reading school, at the Cock and Swan in Cannonstreet.* [London?]. No copy. From Alston, IV, 215.

[Anon.]

[1697] S *A guide to true spelling; in two parts. The first shewing the letters, fitted with names to express their proper sounds . . . The second containing their various uses, their change of and losing their sounds, and dividing of words into syllables. With seven tables.* [1. homophones; 2. homographs] *3. Of words of the same characters; but of different spellings and significations.* [4. words of same spelling, different quantity and meaning; 5. of same spelling, different accent and meaning; 6. of same sound and spelling, different meaning; 7. same sound and meaning, different spelling]. *TC,* III, 8. No copy. Alston, IV, 190.

GUY, John

[*c.* 1830] RE (Guy's) *British primer, or, reading made easy.* Simpkin Marshall. Gumuchian, 138.

1854* S *The etymological and analytical spelling book and expositor. Adapted for the use of schools and private families.* (BL).

[a. 1854] G *Lindley Murray simplified; or English grammar adapted for the use of junior classes and private families.* 19th edn 1854 (BL).

[a. 1860] S *The London spelling book.* Advertised in his *Stepping stone,* 27th edn.

1796* RA *Miscellaneous selections: or, the rudiments of useful knowledge . . . Designed for senior scholars in schools, and for young persons in general. Compiled by J. Guy, Master of the Literary and Commercial Seminary, Bristol. Author of an English Grammar,* 2 vols. Bristol. (BL). The author may not be John Guy, or the same John Guy; all the Guys wrote English grammars.

[1854] G *The mother's own catechism of grammar.* (BL).

[1840?] G *Stepping-stone to grammar, for the use of schools and private families.* (dated from preface). 20th edn [1854] (BL); 27th edn [*c.* 1860]* (Leeds UL).

GUY, John, and KENNY, William Stopford

[1846]* S *The new universal spelling book, being an easy introduction to the English* *language*. Allman (private colln); anr edn [1854] (BL). The preface, signed by Kenny, is dated 1846: the original spelling-book, by Guy, has been enlarged with better reading-lessons.

GUY, Joseph (the elder)

1811 RA   *The British reader, being a sequel to the Spelling Book*. From Watt, *Bibliotheca Britannica*, 1824, s.v. 'Spelling book'.

1839 G   (Guy's) *First English grammar, for the junior classes in schools*. (BL).

1831 Ex   (Guy's) *Juvenile letter writer; being model letters for the use of schools and families. Intended to assist children and youth, in their first attempts at epistolary correspondence*. (BL); anr edn 1851, bookseller's catalogue; 5th edn 1865 (BL).

1826 S   (Guy's) *New British expositor; or, a sequel to his New British Spelling Book*. (BL); anr edn as: *J.G's school expositor; or learner's new spelling assistant*. 1856 (BL).

[a. 1819a] RE   (Guy's) *New British primer for children of an early age, to precede the New British Spelling Book*. Advertised in 1819.

[a. 1819b] RA   (Guy's) *New British reader; or, sequel to his New British Spelling Book*. 3rd edn advertised a. 1819; 8th edn 1835* (BL).

[a. 1810] S   (Guy's) *New British spelling book, or an easy introduction to spelling and reading, in seven parts*. 2nd edn 1810* (Hull UL); anr edn lacking t.p., frontispiece dated 1829, preface dated 1816 (Bedford CHE); 19th edn advertised in 1819; 35th edn 1832, Chalmers, p. 134; 37th edn 1834 (Nottingham UL); anr edn [1859] (BL); 61st edn 1842 (BL); anr edn 1864 (BL).

GUY, Joseph (junior)   'Master of the academy, 38 Foley St, Cavendish Square' 1813 G   *An English school grammar* (Wisconsin UL); 4th edn, 1816, Baldwin and Cradock (Wandsworth PL); 5th edn 1819* (Hull UL).   Pp. 282; *239*.

1849* RA   (Guy's) *Learner's poetic task book; being a choice selection of pieces, chiefly from the modern British poets; suitable to be committed to memory*. (BL).

1829 G   (Guy's) *New exercises in English syntax*. (BL).

1818* RA   *New exercises in orthography; containing selections from the most admired authors, in prose and verse*. 105 pp. (BL; Leicester UL); 14th edn 1847 (Melbourne UL).

1852* RA   (Guy's) *New speaker: containing choice selections of poetry and prose . . . intended to furnish youth, in schools and families, with a class-book*. (BL).

[1820?]* Ex   *Outlines in narrative, regular subjects, English themes and essays; adapted to Walker's system of easy rules for writing exercises*.   36pp. (BL).

1851* G   (Joseph Guy's) *Preparatory English grammar, for very young children; containing the essentials of the study proper to be first known by them*. 60 pp. (BL).

1850* S   (Guy's) *Royal Victoria spelling book for very young children, arranged upon a novel plan, and suited to the capacities of the dullest learners*. (BL).

H., C.W.

1841 G   *The principles of English grammar applied to the interpretation of scripture*. Romsey. (O; BL).

H., R.

1851 G   *A common sense grammar of the English language*. (BL); anr edn Dublin, 1851* (BL; O)   P. 348.

H., T. 'Teacher of a private school'

1667* RA *A guide for the childe and youth, in two parts: the first, for children, containing plain and pleasant directions to read English; . . . The second, for youth. Teaching to write, cast accompts, and read more perfectly.* (Keele UL); three further edns to 1799 in Alston, IV, 318–20 and 61a. Sotheby, HIC, III (1975), no. 118, records an edn of 1723. BL have an imperfect copy, lacking t.p. (shelf-mark CH.730/2) catalogued as a separate work.   P. 157.

H.H.'s H book see ECCLES, Ellen Ann Shove

[HACK, Maria] 1777–1844

1812 G *First lessons in English grammar, with questions and exercises, adapted to the capacities of children, from six to twelve years old; designed as an introduction to the abridgment of Murray's Grammar.* Chichester. *DNB*, advertisement in Rippingham, 1813; anr edn London, 1815, Gumuchian, 5207; anr edn 1848 (Columbia UL).

HALES, John Wesley 1836–1914 'Lecturer in English literature and classical composition at King's College School, London

1872* RA *Cowper: First and fourth books of The Task. With notes.* Seeley. (BL).   Pp. 265–6; *383*.

1874* RA *Goldsmith: The Traveller . . . and The Deserted Village . . . with notes philological and explanatory.* Macmillan. (BL).

1872 RA *Longer English poems with notes, philological and explanatory, and an introduction on the teaching of English. Chiefly for use in schools.* (BL); 3rd edn 1874* (Ulster, New UL). The introduction, 'Suggestions on the teaching of English', was written in 1869.

1867* Ed 'The teaching of English' in *Essays on a liberal education*, ed. F.W. Farrar, pp. 293–312.

HALEY, William

1792 RE *The young Christian instructed in reading and in the principles of religion.* Compiled for the use of Sunday Schools. Dublin: W. Sleator. (NLI).

HALL

1833 G (Hall's) *Lessons on the analogy and syntax of the English language.* Madden/Skeat.

HALL, Clara

[c. 1830a]* RA *The poetic garland: a collection of pleasing pieces, for the instruction and amusement of youth.* (BL).   P. 56.

[c. 1830b]* RA *The poetic primer: a circlet of little rhymes for little readers.* (BL).

[c. 1830c]* RA *Rhymes and reason: or, mirth and morality for the young: a selection of poetic pieces, chiefly humourous* (BL, incomplete?).

HALL, Henry

1838 G *Evening amusements in English grammar.* Souter. 3 vols., with two packs of cards. Bookseller's catalogue, 1953.

HALL, James 'Teacher of the English language, Cupar, Fife'

1789* G *English grammar: or, an essay towards speaking and writing the English language grammatically and inditing elegantly.* Cupar: for the author. Pp. viii, 239 and twelve pages of subscribers ('encouragers'). (NLS).   P. 376.

HALL, Maria

1851* S *Guide to English orthography, in which the words containing difficulties are classed and arranged, and the rules of orthography illustrated by numerous* *examples. Written for the use of children.* (BL).

HALLIFAX, Charles

[a. 1754] Ex   *Familiar letters on various subjects of business and amusement.* 2nd edn
1754. A grammar was added to the 5th London edn, [1765?]* (BL). Alston, III,
276.

HAMILTON, R.

[1806?] G   *Lowth's Introduction to English Grammar simplified.* Aberdeen (Aberdeen UL, PL). Alston, I, 256n.

HAMMOND, Samuel   'Master of the Earl of Cardigan's Free-School, Dean,
Northamptonshire'

1744* RE   *The young English scholar's guide. Containing* [twelve numbered
sections, including] *IV. Above three hundred choice morals . . . having no words
of more than two syllables; and those parted into syllables by the rules of spelling*
[biblical passages; spelling-rules; homophones]. (BL). Alston, IV, 560a and
Plate 54 for t.p. in full.

HAMMOND, Samuel   'Schoolmaster in Nottingham

[1750?]* S   *A new introduction to learning: or, a sure guide to the English
pronunciation and orthography: in plain prose for the ease, and familiar verse for
the pleasure, as well as profit, of the learner . . . By which all who can read may
learn, without a teacher, to speak and write English as correctly as they that have
had a liberal education.* [etc.] Nottingham. (BL; Nottingham PL); anr edn as *A
guide to the English pronunciation . . .* 1755 (Yale). Two of the three copies that
Alston records as in Nottingham PL are of the 4th and 5th edns, but undated.
Alston, VI, 477–8 and Plates 13 and 14 for t.p. and pp. 24–5.   P. 109.

[Anon.]

1842 G   *Handbook of English grammar.* Dublin: Machen. Hunter, 1848.

HARLAND, S.   'School-Master in Norwich'

[a. 1714] S   *The English spelling-book revis'd; with alterations and additions. In two
parts. Part I. Collected and digested for the weak apprehensions of children in their
first steps to learning. Part II. Aims at a farther help, when their capacities are
grown stronger. And may be of use to older people.* (title from 3rd edn). 2nd edn
[1714], no copy; 3rd edn Norwich, 1719* (BL). Alston, IV, 291–2 and Plate 41
for t.p.   Pp. 84, 159; 46.

HARLAND, W.   Of Cloughton.

1828* RE   *The child's assistant: or, a most easy introduction to reading the English
language.* Scarborough: Ainsworth. (BL).

HARPER, T.

[1810?]* S   *The Christian teacher.* (BL, lacks t.p.); 3rd edn [1826?] (BL).

[HARRIS, Benjamin]

[c. 1710?]* RE   *The new English tutor enlarg'd, for the more easie attaining the true
reading of English.* (BL, unique copy, t.p. cropped). Alston, IV, 137. Harris'
works raise complex problems; see refs. in Alston, and Ford, 1897.   P. *161*.

1679* S   *The Protestant tutor. Instructing children to spel and read English, and
grounding them in the true Protestant religion.* (BL); as *The Protestant tutor,
instructing youth and others, in the compleat method of spelling, reading, and
writing, true English,* 1716* (BL). Alston, IV, 133–7 and Plate 21 for t.p. of 1679
edn. The t.p. of an edn of 1713, not recorded by Alston, is photographed in

Marjorie Reeves' *Sheep bell and ploughshare*, Moonraker Press, 1978. The Garland Press Classics of Children's Literature, no. 3, purports to contain the 1679 edn, but the advertised title is that of 1716.   P. *156*.

HARRIS, James   Teacher
1830 G   *The verbs of the English language explained, in which the words commonly called auxiliaries are traced to their respective etymons.* (Glasgow UL; BL).

HARRIS, James   'Head Master, Cathedral Grammar School, Chester'
1862* G   *Easy exercises in English grammar and composition.* (BL); 2nd edn 1865 (BL; O).   P. *353*.

HARRISON, Matthew
1848 La   *The rise, progress and present structure of the English language.* (BL); 1st American edn Philadelphia, 1850, GB.

HARRISON, Ralph   1748–1810   Master of a school in Manchester
1777* G   *Institutes of English grammar: comprising, I. The different kinds, relations, and changes of words. II. Syntax . . . With exercises of true and false construction. Adapted to the use of schools.* Manchester. (BL); 9th edn 1805*. At least nine British edns to 1805 and fifteen American edns, as *Rudiments of . . .*, to 1812. Scolar Press facsimile of 1777 edn, 1967. Alston, I, 331–43.

HARRISON, William   'School-master, Bradford'
[a. 1834] G   *Lines on English grammar, descriptive of the different parts of speech . . . to which are appended prose definitions of their technicalities: accompanied with tables for etymological parsing.* 3rd edn Bradford and London, 1834* (BL). Preface dated December 1834, from Bradford. Perhaps the same author as the following.   P. *346n*.

HARRISON, William
1853 RE   *The infantile class book; or, easy reading, adapted for classes.* Bingley: J. Harrison. NBL, 1946, no. 80.

HARROLD, E.
[a. 1787] G   *A short introduction to English grammar: adapted to the use of schools. With an appendix, containing I. The grammatical figures, and examples of the ellipsis. II. [Transposition]. III. [Derivation]. IV. Examples of grammatical analysis. V. Ungrammatical English, to be corrected by way of exercise. VI. Miscellaneous exercises.* 3rd edn Birmingham, 1787* (Birmingham PL). 5th edn 1798*. At least six edns in all, copies of which are in Birmingham PL. Alston, I, 435–8.   P. *324*. See below, anon. Work of same title.

HART, John
1570* S   *A methode or comfortable beginning for all unlearned, whereby they may bee taught to read English, in a very short time, with pleasure: so profitable as straunge, put in light, by I.H. Chester Heralt.* (Folger; BL); ed. Bror Danielsson, *John Hart's works on English orthography and pronunciation*, 2 vols., Stockholm, 1955*, 1963. Alston, VI, 520.   Pp. 29, 31, 37.

1551 La   *The opening of the unreasonable writing of our inglish toung: wherin is shewid what necessarili is to be left, and what folowed for the perfect writing thereof.* BM: MS Royal 17.C.VII; ed. Bror Danielsson, 1963* (see previous entry).   P. 343.

1569* La   *An orthographie, conteyning the due order and reason, howe to write or paint thimage (sic) of mannes voice, most like to the life or nature. Composed by*

I.H. Chester Heralt. (BL); ed. Bror Danielsson, 1963* (see entry above for 1570); facsimile edn, English Experience, Amsterdam, 1968; Scolar Press facsimile 1969*. Alston, VI, 519, for refs.   Pp. 27, 36, 63; *29, 48, 51, 52, 62.*

HARTLEY, A.M.   'Teacher of elocution'

1846* RA   *The academic speaker: a system of elocution designed for schools and self-instruction, embracing a series of lessons in the art, and a copious selection of extracts from the best authors* [with notes]. Glasgow. (BL). His *Juvenile sketch book*, Glasgow, 1838, is a miscellany intended as a reward book.   P. *288.*

[a. 1854] RA   *The oratorical class book: with the principles of elocution simplified and illustrated . . . Intended for the use of public and private seminaries.* (title from 15th edn). 15th edn Glasgow, 1854*. (BL).

HARTLEY, Cecil

[a. 1820] P   *Principles of elocution, or, the art of speaking in public facilitated.* 2nd edn 1820. (BL).

1822* B   *Principles of English poetry familiarized: including the rules necessary for the construction of English verse, and the different species of poetry* [twenty-six kinds enumerated]. *Illustrated by numerous examples from antient and modern poets.* (BL).   P. *218.*

1818 Ex   *Principles of punctuation: or the art of pointing familiarized, and illustrated by passages from the best writers . . . Composed for the use of seminaries of education.* (BL). Gent. Mag., 89.i (1819), 628.

HARVEY, J.

1841 G   *Abridgment of Murray's English Grammar. Improved: with an enlarged appendix.* (Ipswich printed). (BL; Bodley).

1821* G   *Key to the parsing exercises, contained in Lindley Murray's Grammatical Exercises and in his Abridgment of English Grammar . . . with notes.* Halesworth: T. Tippell (BL); 2nd edn 1829 (BL).

HARVEY, Jane

[a. 1820] RA   *Poems, original and moral, for the use of children.* 3rd edn Derby, [1820]* (BL).   P. 213.

1818 RA   *Sacred hymns for the use of children; being particularly adapted for Sunday schools. By a lady.* Derby. (BL); 2nd edn [1820?] (BL).   P. 213.

HASTIE, Thomas   'Schoolmaster, Newcastle'

[c. 1780?] S   *The only method to make reading easy, or, child's best instructor; containing* [Picture alphabet; sentences, fables, poems; church catechism]. (title from 1839 edn). NBL, 1946, no. 76, suggests [c. 1775], Chalmers, p. 135, gives the Newcastle printer as Angus [c. 1780]; 73rd edn Newcastle: Charnley, 1839* (BL; Newcastle UL; Liverpool UL; Bedford CHE; Hove PL). Not in Alston.   Pp. 105–6.

HAWKINS, John   'School-master at St George's Church, Southwark'

1692 S   *The English school-master compleated: containing several tables of common English words, from one, to six, seven, and eight syllables, both whole and divided . . .* [prayers; rules for behaviour] *Also, brief and easy rules for the true and exact spelling, reading, and writing of English according to the present pronunciation thereof in both universities, and City of London. To which is added* [arithmetic etc.]. (title from 2nd edn). (BL, incomplete); 2nd edn 1694* (BL). Three further edns to 1705. Alston, IV, 167–71 and Plate 28 for 1692 t.p. in full.   Pp. 113, 127; *157, 372.*

HAWLEY, John Hugh
1869 G   *A first book of English grammar*, [Leamington] (O).
HAYWARD, Thomas   b. 1561?   Teacher
[after 1625]* S   *The English institutions*. BM: MS Sloane 2609, fols. 1–91. The work, which is unfinished, deals mostly with the letters, slightly with syllables. Dobson, 1968, pp. 321–4. Salmon, 1958.   Pp. 37, 54, 90.
HAYWARD, Thomas   d. 1779?
1738* RA   *The British muse, or, a collection of thoughts moral, natural, and sublime, of our English poets: who flourished in the sixteenth and seventeenth centuries*. 3 vols. (BL); anr edn as: *The quintessence of English poetry*, 3 vols., 1740 (BL). Contains a review of previous collections.   Pp. 171, 275.
HAYWOOD, J.   Teacher
1800* G   *A short introduction to the English tongue in two parts. Wherein declension and government are concisely explained, and simplified to the capacities of children; with notes, &c.* Sheffield: J. Montgomery (Sheffield PL); 2nd edn Sheffield, 1805* (Sheffield PL). Alston, I, 536.
HAZLITT, William   1778–30
1829 G   'English grammar', in *The Atlas*, 15 March. Reprinted in *Collected works*, ed. A.R. Waller and A. Glover, 1902–6, vol. XII, in *Complete works*, ed. P.P. Howe, 1930–4, vol. XX; in W.F. Bolton, *The English language* vol. I, CUP, 1966*.
1810 G   *A new improved grammar of the English tongue: for the use of schools. In which the genius of our speech is especially attended to, and the discoveries of Mr Horne Tooke and other modern writers on the formation of language are, for the first time, incorporated . . . To which is added, A New Guide to the English Tongue, in a letter to Mr W.F. Mylius . . . By Edward Baldwin, Esq.* M.J. Godwin. (BL). Reprinted in *Complete works*, ed. P.P. Howe, 1931*, II, 1–110. See above, GODWIN, William.   P. 87.
[Anon.]
1854 G   *The heart's ease, or grammar in verse, for very young children.* (O).
HEAVEN, George
1830* RE   (Souter's) *Progressive primer. A first book for children; arranged on a simple and pleasing plan, calculated to lead them, by easy gradations, to the acquirement of the first principles of the English language.* John Souter. (BL).
HEBERDEN, William   1767–1845
1818* Ed   *On education. A dialogue, after the manner of Cicero's philosophical disquisitions.* (BL).
HELME, Elizabeth
1816* RE   *A preparatory exercise on the road leading to the land of learning, by easy paths and short stages. In progressive lessons of increasing syllables.* Brentford. (BL; Glasgow UL).
[Anon.]
1770* Ex   *A help to elocution and eloquence. Containing three essays. I. On reading and declamation, wherein the principles of both are laid down . . . II. On the marks and characters of the different passions and affections of the mind. III. On composition, tending to explain and illustrate the beauties of fine writing, and the principles on which they depend . . . To which is added, a very large collection of examples, in prose and verse . . . for the exercise of the scholar in reading and*

declaiming. For the use of schools. (BL); anr edn 1780 (BL). Alston, VI, 366. [Anon.]

[a. 1850] S *Helps to the orthography of the English language.* 3rd edn Edinburgh: Oliver and Boyd, 35 pp. Advertised in the *Sessional School collection*, 1850, and probably written for the school.

HENSON, John 'Head-Master of the Free Grammar School, Nottingham'

[*c.* 1756?]* G *A compendium of English grammar, containing chiefly the two parts, etymology and syntax. In which the rules and examples . . . will give* [children] *a sufficient knowledge of grammar in general, whereby they may be prepared for learning the Latin, French, or any other language, without burden to the memory.* Nottingham. (Nottingham UL; Nottingham PL). Alston, I, 198, who dates [1760?].   Pp. 318, 333.

HERRIES, John 'Lecturer in the Old Jewry, London'

1773 P *The elements of speech.* (BL); Scolar Press facsimile 1968*. Alston, VI, 373; Cohen, 1977, p. 107.

HEWES, John

1624* G *A perfect survey of the English tongue, taken according to the use and analogie of the Latine. And serveth for the more plaine exposition of the grammaticall rules and precepts collected by Lillie, and for the more certaine translation of the English tongue into Latine. Together with sundry good demonstrations, by way of sentences in either tongue.* (O); 2nd edn as: *A survey of . . .,* 1632* (O); Scolar Press facsimile of 1624 edn, 1972. Alston, III, 139–40.   P. *319n.*

HEWETSON, Isaac

[1800]* S *Reading made easy; or, a step in the ladder to learning: whereby, the young student is led gradually on, from the easiest words, to those of two and three syllables.* Penrith. (Friends House L). Alston, IV, 955 and Plate 110 for t.p.

HEWLETT, Esther

[a. 1826] RA *The new speaker; or selections from the most esteemed authors, in prose and verse.* 2nd edn 1826* (BL); 3rd edn 1834 (Bedford CHE).   P. *237.*

1821* RA *The young reviewers; or, the poems dissected.* William Darton. Published anonymously. (V&A; Hove PL; Bedford CHE).   Pp. 215–16.

HEWLETT, John 1762–1844 Master of Shacklewell School, Surrey

[1786] S *An introduction to reading and spelling. Written on a new plan, in two parts, for the use of schools. Part I.* [spelling, reading-lessons] *Part II.* [grammar; rules for reading]. (title from 4th edn). No copy; 2nd edn 1787, no copy; 4th edn 1798* (Nottingham UL); 5th edn advertised in 1816; 7th edn 1807* (BL); anr edn 1816* (BL). Alston, IV, 857–9 and Plate 85 for t.p. of 4th edn.   P. *185.*

HEYCOCK, C. see BULLEN, H.St.J.

[Anon.]

1860* S (Heydon's) *First spelling book for children. Being an easy introduction to spelling.* Simpkin Marshall. (BL).

HEYWOOD, John Publisher

1871–3 RS *The Manchester readers. Books 1–9.* Manchester. (Preston PL; BL); new edn, three parts [1875] (BL).

HIGGINSON, Edward Teacher

1864* G *An English grammar specially intended for classical schools and private students.* (BL; O)   Pp. *358, 369.*

HIGGINSON, T.E.

1803 G *English grammar, with a praxis perfectly elucidating each chapter, and an appendix for more advanced students. Designed for the use of schools.* Dublin. (Columbia UL).

HILEY, Richard

1848a G *The child's first English grammar.* (BL).

1863* Ex *English composition, argumentative and general . . . in a graduated series of practical lessons and exercises, intended for the upper classes in schools . . . and forming Part Third of Progressive English Composition.* (BL).

1832* G *A grammar of the English language; together with the principles of eloquence and rhetoric.* (BL); 2nd edn as: *A treatise on English grammar, style and poetry,* 1835 (Leeds PL). At least fourteen edns in all to 1863. P. *368.*

1831 G *(Hiley's) grammar abridged.* (BL). At least fourteen edns to 1863.

[*c.* 1846] G *Questions and exercises adapted to Hiley's English Grammar, Style, and Poetry.* 10th edn [a. 1863]; 12th edn 1867 (BL). A *Key* was published in 1846 (BL).

[a. 1843] Ex *An introduction to English composition, consisting of six courses of exercises, progressively arranged, and adapted both to classical and English schools.* 3rd edn 1843* (BL).

1848b* Ex *Practical English composition; part one, or junior series, consisting of four courses of exercises, progressively arranged, and divided into appropriate lessons.* (BL). P. 283.

1852* Ex *Practical English composition; part two . . . Forming an introduction to argumentative composition.* (BL); 2nd edn 1853. Seven edns in all by the 1860s. A *Key* to Part 1 was published in 1855, to Part 2 in 1859 (BL).

HILL, E.D.

1864 G *An elementary grammar of the English language.* Printed in Gloucester. (O).

HILL, Elizabeth

1796* RA *The poetical monitor: consisting of pieces select and original for the improvement of the young in virtue and piety: intended to succeed Dr Watts' Divine and Moral Songs. Published for the benefit of the Shakespear's Walk Female Charity School, St George in the East.* (BL); 2nd edn 1798 (BL). At least eleven edns in all to 1831. Longman, p. 182 gives the attribution to Elizabeth Hill. P. *198.*

[a. 1815] RA *A sequel to The Poetical Monitor, consisting of pieces, select and original, adapted to improve the minds and manners of young persons.* 2nd edn 1815* (BL). P. 220.

HILL, John

1687* Ex *The young secretary's guide; or a speedy help to learning . . . containing the true method of writing letters upon any subject . . .* [etc.] (BL). Twenty-seven edns in all to 1764. John Hill is sometimes identified, or confused, with Thomas Hill; see Nash, p. 23.

HILL, William Of Huddersfield

1833* G *Fifteen lessons on the analogy and syntax of the English language.* Huddersfield. (BL). P. 348.

[a. 1839] G *The grammatical textbook, for the use of schools.* 2nd edn Leeds, 1839* (Leeds PL; photocopy in ULIE).

[between 1833 and 1839] G *Progressive exercises*. Mentioned in the preface to his *The grammatical textbook*, 2nd edn, as being for use with his *Fifteen lessons* and his *Rational school grammar*.

[between 1833 and 1839] G *The rational school grammar*. Advertised in his *The grammatical textbook*, 2nd edn. A fifth edn is listed by HUNTER, John 1848.

HILL, William Of Manchester

1847* S *The educational monitor: a new system which will enable the student to fix knowledge rapidly in the mind*. Whittaker (BL); 2nd edn as: *The educational monitor, Part I. Spelling lessons; to which are added reading lessons* [etc.] 1848* (BL); 5th edn as: *The memory of language and rhyming mnemonical expositor*, 1852* (BL). The title was changed because people thought *The educational monitor* was a magazine.   Pp. 63–4; 60.

[1865]* S *How to teach the alphabet in a few hours*. Manchester: Heywood. (BL).   P. 63.

1852 *The memory of language* see above *The educational monitor*.

[HINCHCLIFFE, Joseph] 1781–1854 Master of Horton House Academy, Bradford

1826* S *Dictates; or, selections in prose and verse, for dictating as exercises in orthography*. Pp. vi, 40. (BL). See the next item.

1830 S *Dictates; or, selections in prose and verse, for dictating as exercises in orthography. In six parts, each forming an annual course*. Pp. 244, Bradford printed (Bradford PL); 2nd edn 1838. See William Scruton, 'Joseph Hinchcliffe, schoolmaster', *Bradford Antiquary*, 2 (1895), 180–4, where the title of this work is given as *The dictate book, or select pieces for . . .*, and the number of pages as xiv, 274. Information from Bradford City Library. The 1830 form of the book, much enlarged from 1826, was published in Hinchcliffe's name.

1829* RA *The juvenile speaker; or, selections for reading or recitation, with introductory remarks on elocution, and plates, exhibiting attitudes of gesture, and examples of inflection*, Part 1. Pp. xxi, 254. Bradford printed. (BL); Part 2. Pp. xliii, 274, noted in *Bradford antiquary* (see previous entry); 2nd edn 1838; 3rd edn 1840 (*ibid.*).

HINDMARSH, John Hall Joint Master, Perth Academy, 1825–40

1828 P *The juvenile elocutionist. Comprised in a series of exercises in prose and verse; to which are prefixed an outline of the science of elocution, and to each lesson a pronouncing and explanatory vocabulary, according to Mr Walker's system*. (title from 2nd edn). Edinburgh. 2nd edn, Edinburgh 1833 (Perth and Kinross PL).

[a. 1833] P *Rhetorical dialogues*. Advertised in 2nd edn of his *The juvenile elocutionist*. This may be the work for which, under the title *The modern rhetorical beauties of the English language*, he was seeking subscriptions some time after 1831 (Edward Smart, *History of Perth Academy*, 1932, p. 140.)

[a. 1824] RA *The rhetorical reader; consisting of choice specimens in oratorical composition, in prose and verse: to which are prefixed, Mr Walker's rules on elocution*. 2nd edn Edinburgh, 1824 (Perth and Kinross PL); 3rd edn 1835; 4th edn London, 1845* (BL); 5th edn 1862.

HINE, J. 'Teacher'

1831* RA *Selections from the poems of William Wordsworth, Esq., chiefly for the use of schools and young persons*. Pp. xvi, 366. (BL); anr edn 1834. R. Batt, 1836, preface; *Quart. Rev.*, 74 (June 1844), 25.   Pp. 261–2.

HODGES, Richard 'Schoolmaster in Southwark'

1644 S   *The English primrose: far surpassing others of this kinde, that ever grew in any English garden: by the ful sight whereof, there wil manifestly appear, the easiest and speediest-way, both for the true spelling and reading of English, as also for the true-writing thereof: that ever was publickly known to this day.* (BL); Scolar Press facsimile 1969*. Alston, VI, 533. Dobson, 1968, I, 165–86.   Pp. 35, 78, 104; *48, 50, 52, 106, 372.*

[1644?] P   *Most plain and familiar examples (taken out of the English Primrose) shewing the great uncertaintie of the sounds of the vowels, and forces of the consonants, whereby the English-tongue is exprest: & how to know them with certaintie.* Dobson, 1968, I, 166, says this is a distinct pamphlet, bound with the BL copy of *The English primrose.* It is reproduced without comment in the Scolar Press facsimile*.

1653 S   *Most plain directions for true-writing: in particular for such English words as are alike in sound, and unlike both in their signification and writing: and of such words whose sounds are so neer alike, that they are oftentimes taken one for another* [etc.] (Christ Church, Oxford); Scolar Press facsimile 1968*. A revised version of his *Plainest directions,* 1649. Alston, VI, 577.

1649 S   *The plainest directions for the true-writing of English . . . especially of such words whose sounds are altogether alike, and their signification altogether unlike. And of such whose sounds are so near alike, that they are oftentimes taken one for another.* (BL). A revised form of his *A special help,* 1643, and itself revised in his *Most plain directions,* 1653. Alston, VI, 576.

1643* S   *A special help to orthographie: or, the true-writing of English. Consisting of such words as are alike in sound, and unlike both in their signification and writing: as also, of such words which are so neer alike in sound, that they are sometimes taken one for another.* 27 pp. (BL); facsimile edn Ann Arbor, 1932. Alston, VI, 575 and Plate 55 for t.p.

HODGSON, Isaac 'Master of the Grammar School, Southampton'

1770* G   *A practical English grammar, for the use of schools and private gentlemen and ladies, with exercises of false orthography and syntax at large.* (BL); new edn 1783; 5th edn 1787* (BL); anr edn 1796 is recorded by Allibone, *A critical dictionary of English literature,* Philadelphia, 1882. Alston, I, 289–91.

HODGSON, Solomon

1799 RA   *The hive of ancient and modern literature; a collection of essays, narratives, allegories and instructive compositions.* Newcastle, *NCBEL,* II, 426; anr edn [1800?] *NCBEL,* II, 428; 3rd edn 1806* (BL); 4th edn 1812 (BL). The preface is addressed to 'judicious teachers'.   P. *195.*

HODGSON, William Ballantyne   1815–80

1868* Ed   *Exaggerated estimates of reading and writing, as a means of education.* 16 pp. (BL).   P. 62.

HODSON, Thomas

1800* C   *The accomplished tutor; or, complete system of liberal education: containing the most improved theory and practice of the following subjects: I. English grammar and elocution . . .* [etc.] 2 vols. (BL); 2nd edn 1802* (BL: Nottingham UL); 3rd edn 1806* (BL). Alston, III, 432.

HOFLAND, Barbara (formerly HOOLE)   1770–1844   Sometime teacher

1810* P   *Little dramas for young people, on subjects taken from English history:*
    intended to promote among the rising generation an early love of virtue and their
    country. By Mrs B. Hoole. (BL). The preface, from 'Boarding school,
    Harrogate', is dated 20 October 1809. Gumuchian, 3075.   P. *302.*

HOLLAND, John   1766–1826

1804 RA   *Definitions, maxims, proverbs, and precepts on grammar . . .* [etc.] *proposed*
    for copies in penmanship, and for exercises in grammar and composition.
    Manchester (Bolton PL); 2nd edn Bolton, 1804* (BL).   P. 223.

1813 G   *English grammar.* Recorded in *Bibliographica Boltoniensis,* 1913. Not
    traced.

HOLLAND, John, and HOLLAND, Thomas   Of Bolton in the Moors

[a. 1798] RA   *Exercises for the memory and understanding, consisting of select pieces of*
    prose and verse. 3rd edn Manchester, 1798* (BL) 519 pp.; 4th edn Bolton,
    1805* (BL; Bolton PL; Manchester PL), 432 pp.   Pp. 207–8.

HOLLIDAY, John

[a. 1750] S   *The modern English spelling-book.* Noted in *Gent. Mag.,* 20 (August
    1750), 384.

HOLMES, John   b. 1702   Master of Holt Grammar School, Norfolk

1739* B   *The art of rhetoric made easy: or, the elements of oratory briefly stated, and*
    fitted for the practice of the studious youth of Great-Britain and Ireland: In two
    books. (BL). Book 2, which has a separate t.p. and pagination, is dated 1738.
    2nd edn 1755* (BL); eight further British edns, usually with John Stirling's *A*
    system of rhetoric, to 1820. Alston, VI, 167–9; Howell, 1971, pp. 125 f.   Pp.
    163–4, 280, 309; *278.*

HOLYOAKE, George Jacob   1817–1906

1848* G   *A bill for the better security of grammar. December 1848. Parliamentary*
    grammar class. City of London Mechanics' Institute, Gould Square, Crutched
    Friars. G.J. Holyoake Speaker. 19 pp. Lithographed copy of MS. (BL shelf-
    mark 1865.c.1).

1846 G   *The hand-book of grammar.* (BL).

[a. 1847] G   *Practical grammar: intended for those who have little time for study.* 5th
    edn 1847 (BL); 8th edn 1870 (BL).

[Anon.]

1852 G   *The home grammar.* (BL).

HOME, Henry, Lord Kames   1696–1782

1762 B   *Elements of criticism.* 3 vols. Edinburgh. 6th edn 1785; 7th edn 1788*.
    Many edns to 1883. Facsimile of 1785 edn, Garland Press: N.Y., 1969. Alston,
    VI, 209–18; *NCBEL,* II, 2066.

HOOLE, Charles   1610–67   Master of Rotherham Grammar School, etc.

1660 Ed   *A new discovery of the old art of teaching schoole, in four small treatises.*
    (BL); ed. E.T. Campagnac, Liverpool, 1913; Scolar Press facsimile 1969*.
    Foster Watson, 1903; P.J. Wallis, 1954. The four treatises, each with a separate
    t.p. dated 1659, are: I. *The petty schoole. Shewing a way to teach little children to*
    read English with delight and profit, (especially) according to the New Primar. II.
    The usher's duty, or a plat-forme of teaching Lillie's grammar. III. *The master's*
    method, or the exercising of scholars in grammars, authors, and exercises: Greek,
    Latine, and Hebrew. IV. *Scholastick discipline: or, the way of ordering a*

grammar-school [etc.] No. I occupies pp. 1–41; numbering starts again with II and is continuous through to the end of IV (pp. 1–209). Pp. 59, 113, 144, 277, 320; *60, 68, 119, 120–1, 135, 140, 152–3, 309n., 372, 379, 383.*

[*c.* 1650] S *A plain and easy primer for children, both the pictures of beasts and birds for each letter in the alphabet for their easie remembrance and delight in learning.* (BL, t.p. only). Freeman, p. 19. Hoole describes the primer in *The petty schoole*, pp. 9, 13–23.

HOOPS, James 1707–85 'Schoolmaster in Berwick'

1774* D *A new vocabulary for the instruction of youth.* Edinburgh. 200 pp. (Mrs J.D. Cowe, Berwick). The grammar occupies pp. 1–44. Alston, III, 519 and Plates 48 and 49 for t.p. and first page of vocabulary.

HOPE, A. 'Teacher of English'

1806 G *A compendious grammar of the English language.* Carlisle. (BL); 2nd edn 1814 (Michigan UL); 3rd edn Annan, 1823* (BL). P. 370.

HOPKINS, Henry 'Conductor of a school at Birmingham'

1837* S *Exercises in orthography and composition.* Pp. vi, 228. (BL). The exercises in composition were issued separately a. 1844 and had at least sixteen edns; the remaining *Exercises in orthography on an improved plan* had edns in 1845 (BL) and *c.* 1850* (Hull UL; private colln). A *Key* to both sets of exercises had a 2nd edn in 1844 (BL) and at least five further edns to 1877. P. 129.

HORNE, Thomas 1610–54 Teacher

1641 B Χειραγωγία *sive manuductio in aedem Palladis. Qua utilissima methodus authores bonos legendi indigitatur* (title from 1687) (O); anr edn 1687* (BL). Pp. 102–10 contain examples in English. Howell, 1956, p. 339. P. 145.

1651* B *Rhetoricae compendium, Latino-Anglice.* (Queens' C. Cambridge, photocopy in BL). 39 pp., of which 17 are 'A short epitome of rhetorick'. Alston, VI, 72; Howell, 1956, pp. 273, 339. P. 145.

HORNSEY, John d. 1820 'Schoolmaster, Scarborough'

1806 S *The child's monitor; or parental instruction; in five parts: containing a great variety of progressive lessons, (interspersed with moral and religious reflections) adapted to the comprehension of children; and calculated to instruct them in reading, in the use of stops, in spelling, and in dividing words into proper syllables* [etc.] (title from 2nd edn) York, from bookseller's catalogue; 2nd edn 1809*253 pp. (Leicester UL); 3rd edn advertised in 1813; anr edn 1819 (private colln); 5th edn advertised in 1818; anr edn [*c.* 1824] Chalmers, p. 136; 7th edn 1826, and 9th edn, 1832, both in York Minster L. P. 87.

[1818] S *English exercises, orthographical & grammatical, in two parts: being a selection of choice pieces, in prose and verse . . . Designed to improve the juvenile mind in spelling and grammar.* (dated from preface); 2nd edn York, 1824* (private colln); 3rd edn 1828. All the pieces are in 'false' spelling. Pp. 355; *327.*

1807 S *The first guide to reading; or book of monosyllables; being an introduction to The Child's Monitor.* (title from 3rd edn). Chalmers, p. 136, as *The book of monosyllables*; 3rd edn York, 1815* (personal); 4th edn advertised in 1818. P. 17.

[1811?] C *The new young man's companion; or, the youth's guide to general knowledge: designed chiefly for the benefit of private persons . . . yet particularly useful in schools*. Notice in *Gent. Mag.*, 81 (December 1811), 555. The work contains spelling, grammar, logic, rhetoric, letter-writing, etc.

[a. 1810] S   *The pronouncing expositor; or, a new spelling book: in which the divisible words are divided agreeably to the plan recommended by Dr Lowth and Dr Ash, pronounced and explained, chiefly after the manner of Walker, Browne, Jones &c.* (title from edn a. 1875, Leeds UL). Hornsey's preface says the 1st edn was reviewed in the *Anti-Jacobin Review* for February 1810. A 3rd edn is advertised in his *First guide*, 1815; 7th edn [c. 1824], Chalmers, p. 136; 8th edn advertised in 1818; 11th edn 1829 (York Minster L); 18th edn 1840 (catalogue); 19th edn 1842 (York Minster L).

1793* G   *A short English grammar in two parts: simplified to the capacities of children: with notes, and a great variety of exercises* [etc.] York. (BL). At least six edns in all to 1816, and an abridgment, 2nd edn 1818 (BL). Alston, I, 468–9.   P. 324.

HORSFALL, William

1852 G   *The Horsfallian system of teaching English grammar*. Glasgow (O).

HORT, William Jillard

1822a* RA   *The English reading book in prose: adapted to domestic and school education*. (Nottingham UL). Vol. IV of Hort's Easy Course of Domestic Education.

1822b* RA   *The English reading book, in verse: adapted* [as above]. (BL). Vol. V, as above.

1822c* D   *An English school dictionary of select words, with their meanings affixed, intended to be committed to memory, as well as for reference*. (BL). Vol. IX, as above.

1822d* G   *Exercises for the illustration and enforcement of the rules of the English grammar: equally adapted to domestic and to school education*. (BL). Vol. VII, as above. The *Key* to the exercises is vol. VIII (BL).

1822e* RE   *A first spelling book; intended to lead the pupil, by an easy and gradual method, to a correct pronunciation and accentuation of the English language. Adapted* . . . [as above]. (BL). Vol. II, as above.

1822f* G   *An introduction to English grammar: equally adapted* . . . [as above] (BL). Vol. VI, as above.

1822 g* RA   *Introductory English reading book, intended to give easy lessons in reading; to convey useful information; to inculcate good principles*. (Nottingham UL; BL). Vol. III, as above.

[Anon.]   'A school-master of London'

[1683] S   *Hortus anglicanus. A new garden of English words; beginning with a choice and methodical collection of all monosyllables turned into English metre, and proceeding to those of two, three, or four, syllables* . . . *Useful not only for English school-masters in teaching children to spell and read; but may be serviceable to elder learners, and to strangers*. No copy. *TC*, II, 33 (June 1683). Alston, IV, 143.   P. 372.

HOSKINS, John   1566–1638

[c. 1600?] B   *Directions for speech and style*. BL: MS Harley 4604. Ed. Hoyt H. Hudson, Princeton U.P., 1935*; in Louise Brown Osborn, *The Life, letters and writings of John Hoskyns*, New Haven, 1935. Howell, 1956, p. 330.   Pp. 150–1; 274.

HOUGHTON, John 'Master of a private grammar-school, Namptwich, Cheshire'
1766* G *A new introduction to English grammar: in the simplest and easiest method possible.* (Harvard). Alston, I, 278. Pp. 166–7, 332; *173.*

HOUSTON, William 'Professor of elocution'
[a. 1826a] S (Houston's) *English spelling-book, classed and arranged upon a system entirely new and original, intended as an easy, progressive and expeditious introduction to the English language.* Stereotype edn 1826* (Glasgow UL). P. 69.
[a. 1826b] [Primer: an introduction to his spelling-book]. Advertised in the *English spelling book.*
[a. 1827?] D (Houston's] *Spelling assistant: or, epitome of modern dictionaries.* 7th edn [*c.* 1827] (Melbourne UL).

HOWARD, Mrs
[1856]* RA *Poetry for home and day schools.* (BL).
[*c.* 1856]* RE *Reading lessons for home and day schools.* (BL).
[Anon.]
[*c.* 1830] RE *Howe's primer, or the child's first book.* Derby: W. Bemrose. Chalmers, p. 136.

HUGHES, E. 'C.M., British teacher'
[1869a]* Ex *A series of composition exercises for the use of elementary schools.* Cardigan: J.R. James [for] Dyfed Association of British Teachers. (BL).
[1869b] G *Some of the peculiarities of English grammar; being a collection from various sources, of exceptions to rules.* Cardigan. (BL). With the preceding, part of The Cambrian Educational Course. P. 354.

HUGHES, Edward 'Head Master of the Royal Naval Lower School, Greenwich'
1855 RS *Reading lessons,* Books 1–4. (BL).
1851* RA *Select English poetry, with prose introductions, notes, and questions; to which is added an etymological appendix of Greek, Latin and Saxon roots. For the use of schools.* (BL); as: *Select specimens of English poetry . . .,* 5th edn 1856 (BL). Pp. 253, 257, 259.
1853 RA *Select specimens of English prose.* (BL).

HUME, Alexander Rector, Edinburgh High School 1596–1606
[*c.* 1617] G *Of the orthographie and congruitie of the Britan tongue.* First printed in EETS No. 5, 1865*. Pp. *41, 50, 51, 344.*

HUNT, L.H. 'Master of the Classical & Commercial School, Charles St., Westminster'
[1823?]* G *A syntax of the English language; with new and copious examples, from some of our best authors in verse and prose* [with parsing lessons] *so arranged, that the particular points of each rule may frequently occur in a single extract. For the use of higher classes in schools, as well as for the enquiring amongst other classes.* Saffron Walden. (BL; Hull UL).

HUNT, Thomas 1611–82 'School-Master at St Dunstan's in the East'
1661 S *Libellus orthographicus: or, the diligent school-boy's directory. Being certain plain and profitable dialogue-wise-placed rules and directions, for the better understanding of (especially) the English orthography.* (BL). Scolar Press facsimile 1968*. NBL, 1949, no. 253; Dobson, 1968, p. 338; Alston, IV, 61 and Plate 10 for t.p. Pp. 27, 80.

HUNTER, John Principal of Uxbridge School

1862a* B   *Examination questions on the first two books of Milton's Paradise Lost, and on Shakspeare's Merchant of Venice. Preceded by a copious variety of critical observations on Paradise Lost.* (BL).

1845 G   *Exercises in English parsing.* (BL); anr edn 1848 (BL); 4th edn 1849 (BL).

1860a* Ex   *An introduction to the writing of precis or digests, as applicable to narratives of facts or historical events, correspondence, official documents, and general compositions . . . Adapted for use in schools . . . and specially designed . . . for the Civil Service Examinations.* (BL); 4th edn 1864; anr edn [1882] (BL). A *Key* was also published in 1860.

1860b* RA   (Samuel Johnson) *Rasselas, a tale* [with] *a life of Dr Johnson.* (BL).

1853 G   *Manual of English grammar.* (BL).

1860c RA   (Milton) *The first book of Milton's Paradise Lost: with a prose translation or paraphrase, the parsing of the more difficult words, specimens of analysis, and numerous illustrative notes.* 2nd edn 1861* (BL).

1862b* RA   (Milton) *The second book of Milton's Paradise Lost . . .* [as for Book 1] (BL). Books 3, 4 and 5 were separately published in 1873. An edn of *Samson Agonistes,* with *Lycidas,* was published in 1870, and of *L'Allegro* and *Il Penseroso* in 1864.   P. 263.

1858* G   *Paraphrasing and analysis of sentences, simplified for the use of schools; and forming a manual of instruction and exercise for normal students, pupil teachers, &c.* Pp. iv, 68. (BL). A *Key* was published in 1860 (BL).

1861a Ex   *A school manual of letter-writing . . . with observations and exercises on epistolary composition.* (BL).

1861b* RA   *Shakspeare's comedy of The Merchant of Venice: with introductory remarks; copious interpretation of the text; and numerous critical and grammatical notes. Adapted for scholastic or private study, and for those qualifying for university and government examinations.* (BL).

1860d* RA   *Shakspeare's Henry the Eighth: with introductory remarks; copious interpretation of the text; critical, historical, and grammatical notes; specimens of parsing, analysis, examination questions, etc. and a life of Cardinal Wolsey.* (BL); new edn 1872* (BL).

1861c* RA   *Shakspeare's tragedy of Julius Caesar: with . . .* [as for *Merchant of Venice*] *. . . numerous extracts from the history on which the play is founded.* Hunter edited most of Shakespeare's plays as examination texts.

1870 RA   *Spenser's Faerie Queene, Book I, Cantos 1–6. With notes* [etc.] (BL).

1848* G   *Textbook of English grammar; a treatise on the etymology and syntax of the English language: including exercises in parsing, punctuation, and the correction of improper diction; an etymological vocabulary of grammatical terms; and a copious list of the principal works on English grammar. For the use of students in training colleges, and the upper classes in national and other elementary schools.* Pp. xx, 190. (BL); new edn 1859, Schmitz, Suppl. 2, p. 62.   P. 371.

HUNTLEY, Thomas

1793* G   *A short system of English grammar.* Cirencester. Alston, I, 470 (Woodbrooke College).   P. 334.

HUTCHINSON, James

1851 S   *The first book, for the use of schools and private families.* (dated from preface); 15th edn 1860* (NLS; O). A simplified version of his *The modern spelling book.*

[a. 1853] G   *The juvenile grammar, for the use of schools and private families.* 6th edn
    1853 (Pennsylvania UL); 9th edn 1854* (V&A); 59th edn 1881 (Columbia
    UL). An abridgement of his *The practical English grammar.*

[a. 1860] S   *The juvenile spelling assistant, for the use of schools and private families.*
    41st edn 1860* (NLS); 63rd edn 1865 (Bedford CHE); 112th edn 1897 (Boston
    PL).

1852 S   *The modern spelling book, for the use of schools and private families.* (dated
    from preface). 21st edn 1859* (NLS).   P. 69.

1850 G   *The practical English grammar, for the use of schools and private families.*
    (dated from preface). 9th edn 1854 (Columbia UL); 16th edn 1859* (NLS; O).
    A *Key* was advertised in 1854.

HUTHERSALL, John

[a. 1814] G   *A compendious system of practical English grammar; in which nothing is
    introduced, but what is absolutely necessary* [etc.] 4th edn 1814 (Columbia UL).

[Anon.]

[1845]* RE   *The illuminated London primer.* 16 pp. (BL).   Pp. 59, 100.

[Anon.]

[a. 1850] RA   *The illustrated London instructor: being a companion to the Reading
    Book.* Illustrated London News. 3rd edn 1850, Holtom catalogue, Summer
    1979, item 547.

[Anon.]

1850 RA   *The illustrated London reading book.* Illustrated London News. Black-
    well, Cat. A80, 1985; 2nd edn 1850* (Wandsworth PL); 3rd edn 1851 (O).

[Anon.]

1849 S   *The illustrated London spelling book.* Illustrated London News. Chalmers,
    p. 137; anr edn [*c.* 1850]* (private colln). anr edn 1851 (O).

[Anon.]

[1853]* RE   *Illustrated spelling and reading book,* pp. viii, 136, Cassell. (BL).

[Anon.]

[*c.* 1834] RE   (Windett's] *Imperial primer.* Chalmers, p. 163. Not traced.

[Anon.]

[*c.* 1845?]* RE   *Imperial primer, or mother's assistant.* C. South. (BL).

[Anon.]

[a. 1785] S   *The imperial spelling book.* Recommended by Lady Fenn in *The art of
    teaching in sport,* 1785, p. 25.

[Anon.]

[a. 1820] S   *The improved child's instructor, intended as a first and easy introduction
    to spelling and reading.* Devonport: Samuel and John Keys. Advertisement in
    The true and interesting history of Fair Rosamund, c. 1820 (V&A).

[Anon.]

[*c.* 1845?] S   *The improved reading and spelling made easy, being an easy introduction
    to the various English spelling books.* Dublin: C.M. Warren. (NLI).

[Anon.]

[*c.* 1835?] RE   *The improved reading made easy, containing spelling tables of two,
    three, four, five, six, seven and eight letters and from one to five syllables. With
    correspondent reading lessons to which are added select pieces for the amusement
    and instruction of the young mind.* 8th edn Hereford: T. Davies and Son, 71 pp.
    (Bedford CHE).

[Anon.]

[1861]* RE   *The improved reading made easy or first book for children. By Isaac Watts, D.D.* J. Bysh. (BL). Chalmers, p. 162, records a *Reading made easy*, 1810, also attributed to Watts.

[Anon.]

[1856]* S   *Improved royal primer. Being an easy introduction to spelling & reading, intended as a first book for children*, John Pryse: Great Oak St., Llanidloes and Next Door to Post Office, Rhayader. 14 pp. (BL).

[Anon.]

[*c.* 1850?] RE   *Improved royal primer, containing easy lessons.* Dublin: C.M. Warren. (NLI).

[Anon.]

[1851] RE   *The indestructible primer.* (BL).

[Anon.]

[*c.* 1850] RE   *The indestructible reading book*, Addey, Chalmers, p. 137; anr edn (?) W. Kent [*c.* 1860]. Gumuchian, 3133.

[Anon.]

[*a.* 1853]   *The indestructible spelling book*, 16 pp. Addey and Co. Holtom, Cat. 1980, item 622.

[Anon.]

[1870] RE   (J.H's) *Infant school primer*, 2 parts. Manchester: J. Heywood. (BL).

[Anon.]

1825* RE   *Infant stories: intended to convince little girls that to be good is to be happy. In words not exceeding two syllables.* Harvey and Darton. Pp. 108 (Glasgow UL).

[Anon.]

1861 RE   *The infantile instructor; or child's first lesson.* (BL).

[Anon.]

1827 RE   *The infant's companion, intended as a first book for the instruction of children.* Deal. (BL).

[Anon.]

1819 RE   *The infant's friend, or easy reading lessons for young children. Revised and arranged by a lady.* J. Harris (BL); anr edn 1820, Moon, 395; anr edn 1822 (Wandsworth PL); anr edn 1824 (V&A); anr edn 1850, Sotheby, HIC, III (1975), no. 1341. Whalley, p. 34. Chalmers, p. 130, attributes it to Lady Fenn, whose spelling-book had the same title.

[Anon.]

1822 G   *The infant's grammar, or a pic-nic party of the parts of speech.* Osborne, II, 715; anr edn 1824 (Bedford CHE; Preston PL); anr edn [*c.* 1825] (V&A); undated edns at Moon, 396; Scolar Press facsimile of 1824 edn, 1977*.

[Anon.]

[*a.* 1855] RE   *The infant's help to reading.* 4th edn [1855]*. (BL). Nine sheets 17 ins. by 13.75 ins., printed both sides.

[Anon.]

[1846?] RE   *The infant's illuminated primer.* (BL).

[Anon.]

[1800?] S   *The infant's letter box.* (BL).

[Anon.]

[*c.* 1800]* S   *The infant's library*, John Marshall. 16 vols. Vol. I contains an illustrated alphabet; vol. II syllables and short words. (V&A). Various volumes, variously dated, in Preston PL, Nottingham UL, and elsewhere.

[Anon.]

[*c.* 1830] RE   *The infant's primer*, E. Marshall. Chalmers, p. 137; 7th edn Derby, 1841, Sotheby, HIC, VI (April 1977), no. 2849.

[Anon.]

1864 RE   *The infant-school first 'standard' reading book. By two certificated masters.* (O).

[INGLIS, Robert]

[1862]* RA   *Gleanings from the English poets. Chaucer to Tennyson, with biographical notices of the authors.* Edinburgh. (BL); anr edn 1881 (BL).

INNES, Henry   'Teacher of elocution'

[a. 1835] S   *The British child's spelling book, on a plain, pleasing, progressive system; for the use of children of the various Christian denominations. Containing* [I. Spelling-lists; II. Lessons in natural history; III. Fables and tales; IV. Poetry; V. Geography; VI. Elocution; VII. Catechism]. 3rd edn John Limbird, 1835*. (BL).   P. 99.

1835 RA   *The British youth's reader.* John Limbird. (BL).

1834* RA   *The rhetorical class book: or, the principles and practice of elocution defined and illustrated upon a new . . . system. Being an exposition of the organs and the operations of speech; with selections from popular writers* [etc.] John Limbird. (BL).   P. *288*.

[Anon.]

[*c.* 1790]* S   *Instruction and amusement united; or, reading made easy. Calculated to teach children, by leading them on by degrees, the easiest and most speedy method of spelling and reading . . . For the use of schools.* Huddersfield: J. Brook. 108 pp. (Preston PL, incomplete).   P. *383*.

[Anon.]

1728* S   *Instructions for beginners. Containing a short, easy, and natural method, for teaching children to spell and read.* For the author. 32 pp. (O).   Pp. 51, 116; *161*.

[Anon.]

[a. 1831] RA   *Instructive extracts.* Edinburgh: Oliver and Boyd. Compiled for the Edinburgh Sessional School and advertised in the *Sessional School collection*, 1850; introduced into Ackworth School in 1831 (Thompson, 1879, p. 193).

[Anon.]

1798* S   *The instructor: or an introduction to reading and spelling the English language. By the author of The Elementary Principles* [of English grammar]. Glasgow. (BL). Alston, IV, 932 and Plate 101 for t.p.

[Anon.]

1845 Ex   *Introduction to English composition; consisting of simple instructions in the art of forming sentences, for children from eight to ten years old.* Edinburgh: Chambers. (NLS).

[Anon.]

1854 G   *Introduction to English grammar.* Edinburgh. Chambers' Educational Course. (O).

[Anon.]

[a. 1796] RA   *An introduction to reading: or a collection of essays, tales, poems, moral* sentences, &c. intended as an introduction, or companion to The Speaker. Compiled by the publisher. Sael. Mon. Rev., n.s. 19 (April 1796), 449, notices vol. II favourably. Chalmers, p. 156, lists 'Sael's Introduction to Reading', 2 vols., W. Walker.

[Anon.]

1824 S   *An introduction to spelling.* Morpeth: Markham. Chalmers, p. 138.

[Anon.]

1837 RA   *An introduction to the art of reading, with suitable accent and intonation.* For the Commissioners of National Education in Ireland: Dublin, Akenson, p. 231; 2nd edn Dublin, 1844 (BL); 3rd edn 1850 (BL); 4th edn 1869* (personal).

IRELAND, COMMISSIONERS OF NATIONAL EDUCATION (after 1831)

1831 RS   *First book of lessons.* Dublin. Akenson, p. 231; anr edn Dublin, 1835* (BL); other Dublin edns in 1836 (BL) and 1847 (NLI). The text is mostly by James Carlile. Revised, mainly by William McCready, as: *First reading book*, Dublin, 1865 (NLI); anr edn Glasgow, 1869 (BL).

1834 RS   *Second book of lessons.* Dublin. (Cambridge UL; O); anr edn 1836* (BL); new edn, n.d. (NLI); new edn 1852 (BL); anr edn 1855 (BL). Revised as: *Second reading book*, 1865.

1836 RS   *Sequel no. 1 to Second Book of Lessons.* Dublin. (BL); new edn 1853 (BL); anr edn 1857* (private colln). The preface says that although this is the second sequel to the second book it may be called Sequel no. 1.

1835 RS   *Third book of lessons.* Dublin. (BL; O); anr edn 1835* (BL); anr edn 1836 (BL; NLI); rev. Richard Whately, 1846 (BL; NLI); further edns to at least 1863. The original text was mostly by William McDermott. Revised, mainly by William McCready, as: *Third reading book*, Dublin, 1867 (NLI), and later edns to 1874 (Leeds UL) and 1876 (NLI).

1846 RS   *Supplement* [to the third book?]. Dublin. Akenson, p. 231 (NLI); anr edn 1847 (NLI); anr edn 1862 (NLI). The text mainly by Richard Whately.

[1834?] RS   *Fourth book of lessons.* Dublin (BL; NLI); anr edn 1835* (BL). Further edns to at least 1868*. The text mainly by James Carlile. Revised, mainly by William McCready, as: *Fourth reading book*, Dublin 1867 (NLI) and edns to 1888.

1853 RS   *Supplement to the fourth book of lessons.* Dublin (BL); anr edn 1859 (Cambridge UL).

1835* RS   *Fifth book of lessons.* Dublin (BL); anr edn 1836 (NLI; O); further edns in 1846 (NLI); 1847 (NLI); 1852 (BL); London: Routledge 1863* (private colln); anr edn Dublin, 1865 (BL). Text by James Carlile and Alexander McArthur. Revised as: *Fifth reading book*, Dublin, 1868 (NLI).

see also *Agricultural class book,*   1848
        Biographical sketches of . . . British poets,   1849
        An English grammar for the use of schools,   1836
        Introduction to the art of reading,   1837
        Poetic selections,   1869
        A reading book for the use of female schools,   1838
        Sacred poetry,   1835
        Selections from the British poets,   1821

IRELAND, J.   'Master of a grammar school, North Shields'

1784* RA   *Beauties in prose and verse: or, the new . . . collection, selected from the most eminent English authors. To which is added, a practical English grammar.* Newcastle: T. Angus. (Newcastle on Tyne PL). Alston, III, 371.

IREMONGER, Frederic

1818* Ed   *Dr Bell's system of instruction broken into short questions and answers for the use of masters and teachers in the national schools.* (BL); new edn 1825* (Leicester UL); anr edn 1836 (BL). Substantial quotations in Goldstrom, 1972b, pp. 55–9.   P. 65.

[Anon.]

1740 S   *The Irish spelling-book; or, instruction for the reading of English, fitted for the youth of Ireland.* Dublin. (BL; Jena UL); as *A new English grammar*, 1743; Scolar Press facsimile of 1740 edn, 1969*. Alston, IV, 422 and 422a, and Plate 53 for the full title.   Pp. 19, 85, 91–2, 106-7, 109–10; *35n., 52, 104, 326.*

IRVINE, William Balfour   'Teacher of English, Dundee'

[a. 1870] G   *The parts of speech: an easy grammar for beginners.* 2nd edn Edinburgh, 1870; 10th edn 1876; anr edn London, 1883 (BL). A sequel, *An English grammar*, had a 2nd edn in 1875.

IRVING, Christopher   Holyrood House Academy, Southampton

[1821?]* G   *A catechism of English grammar; carefully compiled from the best authors: with numerous exercises. For the use of schools.* (BL; Nottingham UL). *Gent. Mag.*, 92 (February 1822), 157.

IRVING, David   1778–1860

1801* Ex   *The elements of English composition. Containing practical instructions for writing the English language with perspicuity and elegance; and designed . . . to succeed to the study of English grammar, and of the Latin and Greek classics.* (BL); at least eleven edns in all to 1841. See below, PHILLIPS, Sir Richard, *Five hundred questions.*   Pp. 255, 305.

ISBISTER, Alexander Kennedy   1822–83   Teacher

1865 G   *The elements of English grammar and analysis.* 2 Parts. (BL).

1867 RE   *First steps in reading and learning on the system of word-building.* (BL).

1870 RA   *The illustrated public school speaker.* (BL).

1870 P   *Lessons on elocution and good reading for girls based on grammatical analysis.* (BL).

1865 La   *Outlines of the English language.* (BL).

1869 RE   *The word builder: an easy introduction to reading, spelling, and writing.* (BL).

J., J. see *Prittle prattle*

JACKSON, Isaac

1793* S   *The true reading made easy, compiled by Isaac Jackson (Bookseller) or the method, of teaching young children at first, to spell and read English, made perfectly easy and regular. In two parts. Containing I.* [Alphabets; spelling-lists; one-syllable lessons] *II.* [Lists to six syllables, accented, divided; lessons; punctuation; spelling-rules]. *Designed, for the use of children in Free-Schools and others, as the most proper book for beginners.* Dublin: Robert Jackson. 107 pp. (BL). Not in Alston.

JACKSON, J.

[a. 1753] S   *Orthographia; or, the new English instructor. In two parts. Part I containing* [Spelling-lists to six syllables; lessons; Watts' Directions for Reading; proper names; homophones; words whose meaning is changed with the addition of -e final] *Part II A compendious English grammar* [etc.] 2nd edn. Advertised in 1753. No copy. Alston, IV, 593 and Plate 55 for title-page advertisement.

JACKSON, Robert J.

1868 G   *A grammar without rules, or useful synonyms exemplified.* Bristol. (O).

JACOB, Joseph

[1701] RE   *The scripture instructor, or an essay, consisting of seven parts, viz. Letters, syllables, reading, catechism, history, poetry, calendar. Composed chiefly for the use of children.* No copy. *TC*, III, 276. Alston, IV, 208.

JAMES, J.H.

1847* G   *The elements of grammar, according to Dr Becker's system, displayed by the structure of the English tongue; arranged as a practice for translation into foreign languages.* (BL).   P. 370.

1848* G   *Primary instruction in English grammar, systematically developed according to modern views.* (BL; O).

JAMES, S.

1810 S   *Dilworth improved, or a new guide to the English tongue.* Whittingham. Chalmers, p. 138.

JAMES, Samuel Benjamin

[1870] G   (Murby's) *Penny grammar for parish schools.* (BL).

JAMESON, Anna Brownell   1794–1860

[a. 1814] D   *A first or mother's dictionary for children; containing upwards of three thousand eight hundred words . . . simply and familiarly explained, and interspersed throughout with occasional remarks: the whole adapted to the capacities of younger pupils.* Gent. Mag., 84 (1814), ii, 660; 2nd edn 1824, Chalmers, p. 138; anr edn [1825?]* (BL); 4th edn [c. 1840] Chalmers, p. 138.   P. 355.

JAMIESON, Alexander

1819a* Lo   *A grammar of logic and intellectual philosophy, on didactic principles; for the use of schools and private instruction.* (BL; Nottingham UL); 6th edn New Haven, 1837 (BL).

1818a* B   *A grammar of rhetoric and polite literature; comprehending the principles of language and style, the elements of taste and criticism: with rules for the study of composition and eloquence . . . for the use of schools, or private instruction.* (BL); anr edn New Haven, 1821 (Wisconsin UL); 2nd edn London, 1823 (BL); New Haven edns to 1849, Hess. Gent. Mag., 89 (1819), i, 627.   Pp. 217; *383*.

1818b* B   *The rhetorical examiner, comprehending questions and exercises on The Grammar of Rhetoric and Polite Literature; for the use of schools and private students.* (BL). Gent. Mag., 69 (1819), i, 59.   P. 217.

[c. 1819] B   *The rhetorician's assistant.* Gent. Mag., 69 (1819), i, 59.

1819b* B   *The young logician's companion; comprising questions and exercises on The Grammar of Logic and Intellectual Philosophy.* (BL; Hammersmith PL).

JAMIESON, P.

[c. 1820?]* RA   *Juvenile library, or school class book; consisting of reading lessons in those branches of knowledge most necessary to be known.* (Nottingham UL).   P. 242.

JARDINE, George 1742–1827 Professor of logic and rhetoric, Glasgow University

1818 Lo *Outlines of philosophical education, illustrated by the method of teaching the logic class in the University of Glasgow.* Glasgow. (Glasgow UL); 2nd edn Glasgow, 1825* (BL); Jamieson, 1819a, p. 138; C.J. Wright, 1979.   P. 314.

[JOEL, Thomas] Teacher

1770* G *An easy introduction to the English grammar. Composed for the conveniency of children under seven years of age.* Chichester: 'For the use of Mr T. Joel's school'. (BL); anr edn London, 1775 (NYc). Alston, I, 292–3.

JOHNS, Bennett George

1841* RA *The book of poetry.* James Burns. (BL); 2nd edn 1847 (BL). Published anonymously.

1846* S *Easy dictation lessons, in prose and verse.* (BL).

[c. 1860?] RA *The first book of poetry.* 11th edn 1884 (BL).

1845* Ed *Hints to teachers of the children of the poor.* (BL). Johns is 'Normal Master, St Mark's College, Chelsea'

[c. 1860a] RA *The poetical school-book for junior classes,* vol. III of Darton's School Library (BL). Johns is 'Headmaster of the Grammar School, Dulwich College'.

[c. 1860b[RA *The prose reading book for junior classes,* vol. IV of Darton's School Library. (BL).

1848 G *Short and simple grammar lessons.* J. Hunter, 1848.

JOHNSON, Charles

1767 Ex *The complete art of writing letters . . . To which is prefixed, a compendious and useful grammar of the English language.* Gabrielson, p. 142, from bookseller's catalogue of 1914; 5th edn 1770; 6th edn as *The complete art of writing letters,* 1779* (Stockholm, Royal L). The grammar is at pp. 1–20. Alston, III, 297–8.

JOHNSON, Cuthbert William 1799–1878

1846* S *The English rural spelling book, with easy and progressive lessons; intended as an introduction to the English language; and to the first principles of the practical and scientific cultivation of the soil.* (BL).   Pp. 241–2.

JOHNSON, E.

1830* Ex *Essays on interesting and useful subjects; with a few remarks on English composition; designed to assist youth in the style and arrangement of themes.* Pp. vii, 247. (BL; O).   Pp. 309–10.

JOHNSON, Ralph 'Schoolmaster'

1665 C *The scholars guide from the accidence to the university. Or, short, plain, and easie rules for performing all manner of exercise in the grammar school, viz. rules for spelling, orthography, pointing, construing, parsing . . . variation, amplification, allusion, imitation, observation, moving-passion. As also rules for making colloquys, essays, fables, characters, themes, epistles, orations, declamations . . . Together with rules for translation* [etc.] (O; BL); at least five edns in all to 1699; Scolar Press facsimile of 1665 edn, 1971*. Alston, VI, 92a–92d.   P. 144.

JOHNSON, S

1758* Ex *A compleat introduction to the art of writing letters . . . To which is prefixed, a short but useful grammar of the English language.* (BL); 2nd edn 1760 (O). Alston, III, 267–8, calls him Samuel, but Hill and Powell, *Boswell's life of*

Johnson, v, 553, refer to him by the initial only.

JOHNSON, Samuel   Of London. 1709–84

1755* G   *A grammar of the English tongue*. Prefixed to his Dictionary. Alston V, 177–218a.   Pp. 58, 73, 167; *50, 51, 324.*

JOHNSON, Samuel   Of Halifax

1864 S   (Johnson's) *New illustrated spelling and reading book containing easy gradations and simple lessons for children learning to read*. Halifax: William Nicholson. (Bedford CHE).

JOHNSON, Thomas

[1590] S   *The pathwaye to readinge; or, the neweste spelling A, B. C; conteyninge a most shorte, easie, and profitable way of teaching to spell and reade.* No copy. Alston, IV, 12. F. Watson, 1909, p. 533; Hazlitt, 1888, p. 212.

JOHNSON, William (later William Johnson CORY)   1823–92   Teacher

1867* Ed   *On the education of the reasoning faculties*, in F.W. Farrar, *Essays on a liberal education*, pp. 313–63.   Pp. 310–11.

JOHNSTON, Robert   'Teacher, of Swords Endowed School'

1869* Ex   *Civil Service precis, containing full instructions as to indexing and precis-writing.* (BL); 6th edn 1877 (BL).

1868 S   *The Civil Service spelling book.* (BL); 10th edn 1878 (BL).

1871 Ex   *English composition and essay-writing, intended chiefly for the use of students preparing for competitive examinations; with specimens of essays written by successful candidates.* (BL); 2nd edn 1874 (Hull UL).

JOHNSTON, William

1800* RA   *A new introduction to Enfield's Speaker; or, a collection of easy lessons.* (BL).

1764* D   *A pronouncing and spelling dictionary: wherein, by a new and sufficient method, the proper sounds of English words are exactly ascertained.* (BL); 2nd edn 1772* (O); 3rd edn [1795?] (Alston). Scolar Press facsimile of 1764 edn*, Menston, 1968.   Pp. 42; *54, 84.*

1772* G   *A short grammar of the English language* (O). Issued both as a separate work and as part of the 2nd edn of his dictionary, above.

[JOHNSTONE, Christian Isobel]

1828* RA   *Diversions of Hollycot, or the mother's art of thinking.* Edinburgh. (BL).

1842* RA   *Rational reading lessons; or, entertaining intellectual exercises for children.* Edinburgh. (BL).

JOHNSTONE, William   Master of an academy at Stanmore

1818* Ed   *Results of experience in the practice of instruction, or hints for the improvement of the art of tuition as it regards the middling and higher classes of society, with a view to the general attainment of an enlarged or encyclopediac course of liberal education during the years usually spent at school, being an elucidation of the basis of the system pursued at Stanmore Academy.* (BL). *Gent. Mag.,* 90.i (March 1820), 244; Bryant, p. 107.   Pp. 261, 355.

JONES, E.   'Teacher of the classics & geography, at Mr Booth's Academy, Bromley'

[1770] S   *The Oxford spelling-book; or, the complete English tutor . . . Consisting of I. [Reading-lessons, one-syllable words] by which means . . . the head and heart are equally improved. This is certainly much better adapted to answer the purpose of education, than a string of unconnected words without meaning, which, being void of entertainment, it is with difficulty that the scholar can confine his attention to them. II.*]Moral songs, from Watts, simplified]. *III.* [Proverbs]. *IV–XVI.* [Spelling-lists, fables, tales]. *XVII.* [Geography]. *XVIII–XXI.* [Homophones etc.]. *XXII–XXVI.* [Capitals, abbreviations, spelling-rules, punctuation, pronunciation]. Unique copy formerly in possession of S. Roscoe. Alston, IV, 717 and Plate 75 for t.p. NBL, 1949, no. 143.

JONES, John 1645–1709

1701 S *Practical phonography: or, the new art of rightly speling and writing words by the sound thereof. And of rightly sounding and reading words by the sight thereof. Applied to the English tongue.* (BL; London UL); as *The new art of spelling . . . Design'd chiefly for persons of maturity,* 1704; anr edn 1705; ed. E. Ekwall, Halle, 1907*; Scolar Press facsimile of 1701 edn, 1969*. A prospectus for the work, *Phono-graphy,* 1698, is in BL. Alston, VI, 471–2.   Pp. 55–6, 79.

JONES, John 'Writing-Master and Accomptant, in Small-Street, Bristol'

[a. 1740] G *A step towards an English education: in two essays on the excellency of geography. For the improvement of youth . . . Second edition . . . Together with an essay on the great usefulness of an English grammar; to the youth of both sexes, at the writing-school. With an abstract of a letter, by the Reverend J. Watts, D.D.* 2nd edn Bristol, 1740* (Bristol UL). Alston, III, 233.   Pp. 114, 317.

JONES, John (junior) Teacher

[1775] S *The English orthographist.* No copy. Advt. in *Bristol Journal,* 4 February 1775 and 11 February 1775 (information from Jonathan Barry).

JONES, Joseph

[1852] G *A concise sketch of English grammar.* Derby. (O).

JONSON, Ben 1572–1637

1640 G *The English grammar. Made by Ben. Johnson. For the benefit of all strangers, out of his observation of the English language now spoken, and in use.* In vol. II of his *Works,* 1640. Originally written, probably in a fuller form, before 1623. Ed. C.H. Herford, Percy and Evelyn Simpson, *Works,* vol. III (text) 1947*, and vol. XI (commentary) 1952*, where earlier edns are discussed. Scolar Press facsimile of 1640 edn, 1972*. Alston, I, 8–12; Vorlat, 1975.   P. 97.

JOWSEY, Richard

1836 G *A supplement to Murray's abridgment of English grammar, chiefly selected from Murray's larger grammar, with an exemplification of syntactical parsing.* Sheffield. (Sheffield PL).

[Anon.]

1862* RA *The junior reader. No. 2. Progressive English reading books.* Pp. viii, 284. Nelson's School Series. (BL).

[Anon.]

[1857] G *The junior school English grammar: adapted to The Elements of English Grammar. With copious exercises in parsing and false syntax.* (NLS; BL); anr edn [1858] (O).

[Anon.]

[1822]* P *Juvenile drama, adapted to Hodgson's theatrical characters and scenes of the same,* 2 vols. (BL); in eighteen parts (each part a play) [1825?] (BL). The 1822 volumes contain thirty plays, but it is very doubtful that 'Life in Paris' or

'Mary the Maid of the Inn' would be considered educational, even when supported by 'Ivanhoe' and 'Guy Mannering'.

[Anon.]

1841* P *The juvenile elocutionist; or, Murray's introduction revised: designed to improve the junior classes of learners in the art of reading and correct delivery.* Belfast: Joseph Smyth. (Private colln). The work is meant to follow on from *The juvenile preceptor*, which is unidentified; it is not likely to be George Nicholson's four-volume work, q.v.

[Anon.]

[*c.* 1830] RE (Harrison's) *Juvenile instructor, or first book for children.* Devizes: J. Harrison. Chalmers, p. 135.

[Anon.]

[a. 1833] RA *The juvenile manual of interesting, instructive, and serious reading, selected and original.* Second edn Edinburgh. (BL).

[Anon.]

1810* RA *The juvenile reader: a collection of lessons selected from the most approved authors; being intended to follow the reading-made-easy, or spelling-book, and form an easy introduction to the larger and more difficult selections. For the use of schools.* Doncaster: Thomas and Hunsley. (BL).

[Anon.]

1830* RE *The juvenile reader's assistant, containing observations on the rudiments of good reading, chiefly selected from Walker's Rhetorical Grammar, with two tables to accompany, used in the Misses Wilmshurst's Seminary, Cromwell House, Maldon. An appendix is added, which gives directions for teaching children to read, beginning at the early age of three years.* Maldon: P.H. Youngman. 54 pp. (Glasgow UL; BL). See below, Miss WILMSHURST.   P. 214.

[Anon.]

1799 RE *Juvenile stories and dialogues, composed chiefly of words of two syllables, for the use of schools and young readers.* Vernor and Hood. Chalmers, p. 139; anr edn, E. Newbery, 1801 (Leicester UL; Wandsworth PL). Roscoe, J202(2).

K., A.

1827* RA *Poetic gleanings, from modern writers, with some original pieces. By a governess.* (BL).; 2nd edn 1834 (BL).

K., P.

[1707?]* Ex *The scholar's instructor, in a familiar way of speaking, whereby the young beginner may speedily attain the knowledge of the English, Latin and Greek tongues; gathered for the use and delight of masters and scholars.* (BL). Alston, III, 214.   Pp. 304, 309.

KAVANAGH, Maurice D.

1859 G *A new English grammar: calculated to perfect students in the knowledge of grammar, parsing, derivation, and the principles of composition.* Catholic Publishing and Bookselling Co. (BL; O).   P. *352.*

KAY, R. 'Writing-Master & teacher of English grammar, Newcastle'

1801* S *The new preceptor; or, young lady's and gentleman's true instructor in the rudiments of the English tongue. Containing rules for pronunciation, with lessons from one to two or more syllables to elucidate them.* Newcastle: M. Angus. (BL: V&A; Nottingham UL; Bedford CHE). Diack, p. 26, repeated by Chalmers, p. 139.   Pp. 45; *50, 52, 60.*

KAY-SHUTTLEWORTH, Sir James see *First phonic reading book*

KEACH, Benjamin 1640–1704

[a. 1705?]* RE *The child's delight: or instructions for children.* 3rd edn 83 pp. (BL). Alston, III, 501.

[a. 1693] S *Instructions for youth, or the child and youth's delight; teaching an easy way to spell and read true English,* 2nd edn [1693]. No copy. Anr edn, as: *Instructions for children,* N.Y., 1695; as: . . . *for children,* 4th edn 1696, W. Sloane, no. 214 (NY.c); as: . . . *for children,* 25th edn 1738* (Glasgow UL), Other edns to 1763 in Alston, III, 489–97. NBL, 1946, no. 45, gives the author's name as REACH, in an undated edn of *Instructions for children.* P. 156.

KEANE, Augustus Henry

1860 La *Handbook of the history of the English language, for the use of schools and colleges.* (BL); anr edn 1875 (BL).

[Anon.]

[a. 1846] S (Keble's) *First British spelling book intended as a guide to a correct knowledge of the English language.* (title from 9th edn.) 3rd edn 1846 (preface); 9th edn [*c.* 1855?]* (Nottingham UL).

[Anon.]

[*c.* 1850] S (Keble's) *Second British spelling book,* Margate. Chalmers, p. 139.

[Anon.]

[*c.* 1845] RE (Keble's) *New primer; or reading made easy.* Margate. NBL, 1946, no. 78; anr edn [*c.* 1870], Sotheby, Cat. 11 (1976–7) no. 43.

KEMPE, William Master of Plymouth School

1588 Ed *The education of children in learning: declared by the dignitie, utilitie, and method thereof. Meete to be knowne, and practised aswell of parents as schoolemaisters.* Facsimile ed. R.D. Pepper, in *Four Tudor books on education,* Gainesville, 1966*. Quoted by Howell, 1956, pp. 259–61 (on logic and rhetoric), by Baldwin, 1944, II, 253–4, 305 (for themes). A photograph of the 1588 t.p. is reproduced in Craig Thompson, 1958, p. 42. Pp. 116; *143.*

[KENNETT, White] 1660–1728

[1708?] RE *The Christian scholar: in rules and directions for children and youth sent to English schools. More especially design'd for the poor boys, taught and cloathed by charity, in the parish of St Botolph, Aldgate.* (title from 5th edn) *DNB*; 5th edn 1710* (BL). At least twenty-three edns to 1836. P. 72.

KENNION, Charlotte

1842* G *The etymology and syntax of Murray's English Grammar systematically arranged; and containing much additional matter, with copious exercises and directions for parsing.* (BL; O).

1853 RE *Juvenile reading book.* (BL).

KENNY, William David Teacher

1858* G *An English grammar; adapted to the comprehension of young persons, with syntactical observations for more advanced students, orthographical exercises . . . and questions for examination.* (BL). P. 360.

1839 S *Grammatical spelling assistant.* (BL).

1849 RE *Progressive reading book.* (BL).

KENRICK, William 1725?–1779

1773* B *A rhetorical grammar of the English language. Wherein the elements of* *speech in general, and those of the English tongue in particular, are analyzed; and the rudiments of articulation, pronunciation, and prosody intelligibly displayed.* (title from 1784 edn). Prefixed to his *New dictionary*, 1773, and published separately in 1784* (Glasgow UL); Scolar Press facsimile of 1784 edn, 1972*. Alston, V, 283; VI, 497–8.   Pp. 85, 283n.: *287*.

KER, Patrick

[1686] S   *Grammatista, or the young grammarian; being a short spelling book, very useful for children and those of riper years; containing, 1. The alphabet. 2. Words from one to nine syllables. 3. A description of every letter. 4.* [Abbreviations] *5.* [Synonyms] *6. Poems in English and Latin for copies. 7–14.* [Miscellaneous]. No copy. *TC*, II, 180 (December 1686). Alston, IV, 150.

KERR

[*c.* 1756?] [A spelling-book]. The SPCK in Scotland sent three dozen of 'Kerr's Spelling Book' to the Orphan Hospital in 1756 (Law, p. 46), and in 1758 they sent two hundred copies of the first page of the spelling-book to a charity school recently opened in Edinburgh (Law, p. 37). In 1759 the Society gave forty copies of the first sheet of the book to its own new charity schools in Edinburgh (Law, p. 55). Dr Law has so far been unable to trace a copy of the spelling-book.

KERR, P.   Teacher

[1809?] S   *Exercises in spelling*. No copy. Attributed by Sheriff Aeneas G. Mackay, in an appendix to his *History of Fife and Kinross*, 1896, to the printing house of R. and G.S. Tullis, Cupar. (Doughty, no. 122).

[Anon.]

1788* G   *A key to spelling, and an introduction to the English grammar. Designed for the use of charity and Sunday schools.* Privately printed. (BL). Alston, I, 446.

[Anon.]

1825* S   *A key to spelling; in which the powers of the letters are arranged on so simple and uniform a system, as to render instruction in reading easy, expeditious, and complete.* (BL).   P. 97.

[KEYS, Adam]   'Plumb's House Academy, Whiston'

1831* RE   *The excitement: or, a collection of amusing and instructive lessons; . . . Adapted to the self-corrective method of teaching to read, explained in the preface by a teacher and friend to youth.* Prescot: A.T. Ducker. (BL; NLS). The work recorded by Chalmers, p. 139, is not by Keys, but is a juvenile annual (information from NLS).   P. 239.

[a. 1824] RE   *The rhyming primer; or, introduction to the spelling book.* 4th edn Derby: H. Mozley, 1824* (BL). Keys is here described as 'Schoolmaster, Prescot'.   Pp. 103; *383*.

KIGAN, John

1825* G   *A practical English grammar, agreeably to the new system. Adapted to the use of schools, and private students; containing copious examples of wrong choice of words, under etymology: and wrong arrangement of them under syntax. With a key . . . and questions . . . to be answered by the pupil.* Belfast: Simms and M'Intyre (O).

1823* G   *Remarks on the practice of grammarians; with an attempt to discover the principles of a new system of English grammar.* Belfast. (O; BL; Glasgow UL).   P. 363.

KILDARE PLACE SOCIETY see SOCIETY FOR THE EDUCATION OF THE POOR OF IRELAND

KILHAM, Hannah (formerly SPURR) 1774–1832

1818a* S   *First lessons in spelling: consisting chiefly of words of common occurrence. To which are added, a few lessons of religious instruction, proposed to be committed to memory.* Darton and Harvey. (Friends House L).   Pp. *61, 346n.*

1818b* G   *Lessons on language; or, an easy introduction to the nine parts of speech.* Darton and Harvey. (Friends House L).

KING, George

[a. 1854] G   *A new and comprehensive grammar of the English language.* 3rd edn Coventry, 1854. (O).

KING, Walter William

[a. 1856] G   *Grammar at sight, a chart and key to the English language, including rules for the composition of verse and prose, illustrations of the figures of speech, and a few useful hints on oratory.* 2nd edn 1856 (BL).

1841 G   *A grammatical chart; or a key to English grammar.* (BL; O).

KIRKBY, John   1705–54

1746* G   *A new English grammar, or, guide to the English tongue, with notes . . . To which is added a brief Latin grammar upon the same foundation.* (Leicester UL); Scolar Press facsimile 1971*. Alston, I, 100. Gibbon, *Autobiography* (World's Classics edn, pp. 22–4).   Pp. *93, 325.*

KIRKUS, William

1863 G   *English grammar: for the use of the junior classes in schools.* (O).

KITSON, Roger   'Writing Master'

1798* G   *A short introduction to English grammar, with orthographical exercises,* Norwich: Stevenson and Matchett. (BL). GB records 'Roger Kilson, E.G., England, 1807'. Alston, I, 515.

KNIGHT, Anne

1846 RA   *School room lyrics.* Darton and Clarke. J. Smith, II, 70–1; anr edn 1850* (Friends House L); anr edn [1859?] (Hull UL); anr edn [1864] (BL).

KNOWLES, James   1759–1840   Teacher

1829* P   *Orthoepy and elocution; or, the first part of a philosophical and practical grammar of the English language, for the use of teachers, academies, and public speakers. By James Knowles, teacher of reading, elocution, grammar, and composition.* Glasgow. (BL).   P. *287.* See also pp. 377–8.

KNOWLES, James Sheridan   1784–1862

[a. 1823] RA   *The elocutionist, a collection of pieces in prose and verse, peculiarly adapted to display the art of reading, in the most comprehensive sense of the term.* (title from 7th edn). 3rd edn Belfast, 1823 *DNB*; 7th edn Belfast, 1831* (BL). At least twenty-eight edns in all to 1883.   P. *377.*

KNOWLES, John

1785* G   *The principles of English grammar: with exercises of false construction. Adapted to the use of schools, and private tutors.* Liverpool (Liverpool UL); 4th edn London, 1796* (BL). Six edns in all to 1805. Alston, I, 417–21.

KNOX, Vicesimus   1752–1821   Headmaster of Tonbridge

1790 RA   *Elegant epistles: being a copious collection of familiar and amusing letters,* *selected for the improvement of young persons, and for general entertainment*. (title from 1807 edn) (BL); edns in 1791, 1794, 1803, 1807* (BL) and five further edns to 1822. For an abridgment see his *Models of letters*.   For all Knox's works see pp. 188–90, and also pp. 136, 195.

[1783] RA   *Elegant extracts; or, useful and entertaining passages in prose selected for the improvement of scholars at classical schools in the art of speaking, in reading, thinking, composing*. (title from c. 1790; date of 1st edn from *DNB*) anr edn 1784 (BL); anr edn c. 1790* (BL, shelf-mark 830.k.32); at least twelve other British and two American edns to 1824. For an abridgment see his *The prose epitome*.

[c. 1784[* RA   *Elegant extracts; or useful and entertaining pieces of poetry, selected for the improvement of youth, in speaking, reading, thinking, composing; and in the conduct of life*. (BL). Twelve British and four American edns to 1826. For an abridgment see his *The poetical epitome*.

1778–9* Ed   *Essays, moral and literary*, 2 vols. (BL). Many edns to 1827; facsimile of 1779 edn, Garland Press, N.Y., 1972. Alston, III, 323–37. Essay 72 is 'On the best method of exciting literary genius in boys who possess it'.

1781* Ed   *Liberal education: or, a practical treatise on the methods of acquiring useful and polite learning*. (BL). Eleven British edns to 1795. Alston, X, 280–91.

1794 RA   *Models of letters, for the use of schools and private students. Being an epitome of the . . . volume, entitled, Elegant Epistles*. (BL).

1791a* RA   *The poetical epitome; or, elegant extracts abridged from the larger volume*. (Nottingham UL); anr edn 1807* (Leeds UL).

1791b RA   *The prose epitome; or, elegant extracts abridged from the larger volume*. (Glasgow UL).

L., J.R. see *Early lesson book* [1859]

[LAMB, Charles and Mary]

1809 RH   *Poetry for children, entirely original*. 2 vols. *The works of Charles Lamb*, ed. W. Macdonald, 1903*, vol. VIII. 1st American edn 1812; many modern edns. Rosenbach, 462; Thwaite, 1972, pp. 90, 132–3. See below, MYLIUS, W.F., 1809b.

1807* RH   *Tales from Shakespear designed for the use of young persons*, 2 vols. 1st American edn 1813, Welch, 744; many later British edns.

LAMBERT, Thomas   'School-master'

1786 S   *An easy introduction to reading the English language*, Leeds. (BL, lost); anr edn 1803* (BL). Alston, IV, 860. BL used to have a copy of the 1786 edn; their copy of the 1803 edn is perished and much of the t.p. is crumbling. The book seems to have contained only sentences comprising words of up to three letters.

LAMONT, Mrs

1832 RE   *The teacher's treasure, and dunce's delight; to be used immediately after the alphabet. Being a simple and expeditious method of teaching to read*, Belfast. (BL); 2nd edn London, 1834* (BL).

LANCASTER, Joseph   1778–1838

[1807?] S   *New invented spelling book*. NBL, 1949, no. 60g, records 'two pages from Lancaster's New Invented Spelling Book', without date or provenance. Watt, *Bibliotheca Britannica*, 1824 s.v. 'Spelling Book', gives 1808; David Salmon, 1912, p. 432, says he has not seen a copy but thinks it was first published in 1807. Chalmers, p. 140, gives '*A spelling book*: Harvey, c. 1840' but it is not clear whether this is a title or a description, and there is no source or location. No copy is known to BFSS Archives.

LANE, A. 'Late Master of the Free-School of Leominster in Herefordshire, now teacher of a private school at Mile-end-green near Stepney'

1700* G   *A key to the art of letters: or, English a learned language . . . being an essay to enable both foreigners, and the English youth of either sex, to speak and write the English tongue well and learnedly . . . With a preface shewing the necessity of a vernacular grammar.* (BL; personal); anr edn 1705 (O); 2nd edn 1706 (Oxford U. Press). Scolar Press facsimile of 1700 edn, 1969. Padley, pp. 181–90, 378– 81.   Pp. 320–1, 334; *28, 48, 50, 346n.*

LANE, Moses   'Schoolmaster in London'

1681* S   *The Protestant school: or, a method, containing several forms of prayer, psalms, lessons . . . also a catalogue of all the English words, beginning with one syllable, and proceeding by degrees to eight, divided and not divided; the readiest way for teaching children and elder persons to spell, pronounce, read and write true English . . . Fitted to the common use of all English schools; having a thousand words more than any yet extant.* (BL); anr edn 1698 (Folger). Alston, IV, 141–3 and Plate 21 for long t.p. in full.

LARKIN, Joseph

[after 1859] G   *A grammar for the people. Three parts.* Manchester. (O).

LATHAM, Robert Gordon   1812–88. Professor of English language and literature, University College, London

1843 G   *An elementary English grammar* (BL; O); 2nd edn 1847 (Wisconsin UL); 5th edn 1850 (Cape Town, S.A. L); at least six other edns to 1875. For Latham generally, see Quirk, chap. 5.

1862 La   *Elements of comparative philology* (BL).

1849a* G   *The elements of English grammar, for the use of ladies schools.* (BL); rev. F.J. Child, Cambridge, Mass., 1852. GB.   P. *358.*

[a. 1861] G   *An English grammar for classical schools.* 3rd edn 1861* (BL).   P. *358.*

1841* G   *The English language.* (BL); 2nd edn 1848 (BL); 3rd edn 1850 (BL); 4th edn 1855 (BL); 5th edn 1862 (BL).   Pp. 87–8; *358.*

1876* G   *Essential rules and principles for the study of English grammar.* (BL).

1847 Lo   *First outlines of logic applied to grammar and etymology.* DNB.

1850* G   *A grammar of the English language, for the use of commercial schools.* (BL).

1851*   *A handbook of the English language, for the use of students in the universities and higher classes of schools.* (BL); 2nd edn 1855 (BL); 3rd edn 1858 (BL). At least six further edns to 1878.   P. *358.*

1849b* La   *History and etymology of the English language, for the use of classical schools.* (BL); 2nd edn rev. 1854 (BL).

1854 Ed   *On the importance of the study of language as a branch of education for all.* (BL; Nottingham UL). Reprinted in his *Essays, chiefly philological,* 1860.

LATHAM, Robert Gordon, and   MABERLY, Mary Caroline

1861 G   *A smaller English grammar for the use of schools.* (BL). 2nd edn 1861 (BL).

LAURIE   publisher

1864 RS   *First class readers. Parts 1 & 2.* (BL).

[a. 1870] RS   (Laurie's) *technical series of reading books. Designed and edited by J.*

Stuart Laurie. Books 1–6, new edn [1870]* (BL, Book 2 only).

LAURIE, James Stuart   1837–1904   Inspector of schools, till 1863

[1868]* G   *English grammar simplified*. (BL). 6th edn 1877.   P. *361*.

1862* RS   *First steps to reading: being an introduction to the graduated series of English reading books*. (BL).   Pp. 36, 124, 353.

[1866]* S   *Manual of English spelling, containing all the difficulties of spelling, in a series of systematically graduated lessons, with numerous practical exercises*. (BL).

See also below, LONGMAN (Publisher), 1863, for work by Laurie

LAURIE, William S.   'Warehousemen & Clerks' Schools, Manchester'

1869* G   *The grammar of words. A handbook for elementary classes*. (BL).

LAWRIE, Andrew   Master of the parochial school of St Cuthbert's, Nicolson Street, Edinburgh

1779* C   *The Merchant Maiden Hospital Magazine*. Edinburgh. Pp. 64. (Edinburgh PL). The book is not part of a series. It includes spelling, reading aloud and grammar. Law, pp. 131, 201, attributes it to James Lawrie, but the dedication is signed by Andrew Lawrie. Alston, III, 347.   Pp. 296; *35, 52*.

LAWSON, John   1712–59   Lecturer in oratory, Trinity College, Dublin

1758 B   *Lectures concerning oratory*. Dublin (BL). Two further edns to 1760; Scolar Press facsimile of 1758 edn, 1969*. Alston, VI, 203–6.   Pp. 282; *165–6*.

LAWSON, R.

[a. 1860?] G   *English grammar*. Advt *c*. 1860.

LEAN, William Scarnell   'Principal of the Flounders Institute, Ackworth'

1874* Ed   *Familiar notes on modes of teaching English*. 27 pp. (BL; DES). Contains a list of books for English teaching.

[Anon.]

[1858]* RE   *Learning to read: the first book for children*. 64 pp. Jarrold. (BL). New edn as *Learning to read: with easy lessons in script* [a. 1866]. Three grades, pp. 32, 64, 84. Running title *The child's first book*. (BL).

[LEIGH, Percival]   1813–89

1840* G   *The comic English grammar*. (O; BL). New edn 1851. Later edns in 1903 and 1907.

LEINSTEIN, Madame

[*c*. 1820]a S   *Punctuation in verse; or, the good child's book of stops*. Dean and Munday. NBL, 1946, no. 118. Osborne, II, 719; Gumuchian, no. 3710; variously dated.

[*c*. 1820]b G   *The rudiments of grammar, in verse; or, a party to the fair*. Dean and Munday. NBL, 1946, no. 119; Gumuchian, no. 3711. Variously dated.

LEITCH, Neil   Teacher

[a. 1843] RS   *The instructive reader: consisting of lessons in science, religion and morality*. 2nd edn Glasgow, 1843 (BL); anr edn 1852* (BL). A sequel to his *The juvenile reader*.

1839 RS   *The juvenile reader; consisting of religious, moral, and intellectual instruction; exercises in spelling, explanation, and derivation; and an appendix containing select pieces for recitation; the principal prefixes, affixes, and roots of the English language*. (title from 1843 edn) Glasgow, Chalmers, p. 140; anr edn [1843?]* (Glasgow, Mitchell L); anr edn [1852] (BL). Ellis, pp. 9–10.

1825 RS *The monitorial class books; being an easy introduction to English reading.* 3 parts. Glasgow: Collins. Chalmers, p. 140. Part 1, 25th edn 1848, Part 2, 35th edn 1852, Part 3, 21st edn 1852 (all in BL).

1836 RS *Practical and economical readers,* Glasgow: Collins. Chalmers, p. 140.

[*c.* 1830] S *The young scholar's spelling book.* Chalmers, p. 140. Anr edn Glasgow, [1852] (BL).

LEMOINE, Henry 1756–1812 Sometime teacher

[1797]* B *The art of speaking; upon an entire new plan. And in which the operations and emotions of the mind are particularly considered. The whole illustrated by a numerous selection of examples, ancient and modern, in prose and verse.* (BL). Alston, VI, 431.

LENNIE, William 1779–1852 'Teacher of English & Geography, Edinburgh'

[*c.* 1820] S *The child's ABC, being Part II of An easy Introduction to The Child's Ladder.* Referred to by Meston, 1823, p. 177. Stereotype edn Edinburgh, 1842* (preface dated 1834). P. *44.*

[a. 1823] RE *The child's ladder.* A reading book-referred to by Meston, 1823, p. 177.

[a. 1842] S *An easy introduction to The Child's Ladder.* Listed on the t.p. of his *The Child's ABC.*

[a. 1829] RA *Sequel to The Child's Ladder, containing extracts from the scriptures, with tales and poems, carefully adapted to the capacities of children.* 12th edn Edinburgh, 1829, Holtom, List 45; 21st edn Edinburgh, 1851 (NYc, N.Y.).

1810 G *The principles of English grammar briefly defined, and neatly arranged . . .* [etc.] Edinburgh. NBL, 1949, no. 266a; 7th(?) edn 1821 (O); 9th edn 1824* (NLS); at least ninety-four edns in all to 1894.

[a. 1816] G *A key to Lennie's Principles of English Grammar, containing an enlarged account of the author's method of teaching grammar, intended for ladies, junior teachers, private students, and others.* (title from 6th edn). 2nd edn Edinburgh, 1816 (BL); 5th edn 1822 (BL); 6th edn 1824* (Leicester UL; NLS); 13th edn 1843* (personal); at least three further edns to 1894. See BIDLAKE, J.P., 1863. Pp. 350; *383.*

LENOIR, P.V.

1800* S *The logographical-emblematical English spelling book; or, a method of teaching children to read. Being founded upon an entirely new principle, by which any infant, four or five years old, and of ever so slow an apprehension, will, with the greatest ease to himself, and teachers acquire, in a few months, the utmost steadiness and fluency in reading, and be enabled to make his way, at first sight, through any book that may be put in his hands. To which are added instructions to enable any persons to put this method in practice; as likewise four copper-plates, exhibiting the emblems upon which this system is founded.* (Bristol UL; BL); anr edn 1818* (BL); 6th edn 1826 (BL); 8th edn 1839 (Cambridge UL). In the preface to his *French pronunciation . . . made easy,* 1799, Lenoir says that his English method has been in his mind for four years and its publication is dependent on the success of the French volume. Pp. 39, 69; *122.*

[Anon.]

[*c.* 1825] RE *A little reading book for young children.* SPCK. Chalmers, p. 158.

[Anon.]
[*c.* 1865] RE   *Lesson book of common things.* Chambers. Advt.
[Anon.]
[*a.* 1827] RE   *Lessons extracted from The Teacher's Assistant. By Mrs Trimmer.*
Advt by Rivington a. 1827; new edn 1836*, 72 pp. (BL).
[Anon.]
1713* S   *Lessons for children, historical and practical; to which are added, some*
prayers and the chief rules for spelling and dividing words into syllables . . . Drawn
up for the use of a charity-school in the country. (BL); 4th edn 1725 (Hull UL);
5th edn 1734 (BL). Alston, IV, 288–90 and Plate 40 for 1713 t.p.   P. 201.
[Anon.]
1831* RE   *Lessons from the psalms, in monosyllables.* Rivington. (BL).
[Anon.]
1842 RA   *Lessons in reading for children in families and schools, with questions on the*
principal subjects. Religious Tract Society. Date from Chalmers, p. 140; BL
and Nottingham UL have undated edns.
[Anon.]
[*a.* 1823] RA   *Lessons, intended for introduction into schools and cottages: consisting of*
descriptive hymns, selected from A Manual of Sacred Poetry, for the Use of Public
and Private Charities. 2nd edn Birmingham, 1823, Goldstrom, 1972a, p. 214.
LEVER, Ralph   d. 1585
1573 Lo   *The arte of reason, rightly termed, Witcraft, teaching a perfect way to argue*
and dispute. (BL); Scolar Press facsimile 1972*. Alston, VII, 9.   P. *343*.
LEWIS, Mark   Sometime teacher
[1670?]a* G   *An apologie for a grammar printed about twenty years since, by M.*
Lewis and reprinted for the use of a private school at Tottenham High Cross. Part
of his [*Institutio*] 1670, beginning at p. 31, but it sounds as if it had been
separately issued at some time. Padley, 1985.
[1670?]b* Ed   *An essay to facilitate the education of youth, by bringing down the*
rudiments of grammar to the sense of seeing. (BL, lacking t.p.). anr edn, title
continuing: . . . *seeing, which ought to be improved by syncrisis. Fitted to*
children's capacities, for the learning, especially of the English, Latin and Greek
tongues: but may be as a general grammar, and a foundation to any tongue: in three
parts, an accidence, a middle-grammar, and a critical or idiomatical grammar.
1674* (O). For the difficulties concerning this work see *EGC*, p. 570. Alston,
X, 82. Padley, 1985.   Pp. 322, 334; *319n., 333n.*
[1670?]c* G   [*Institutio?*] *grammaticae puerilis: or the rudiments of the Latin and*
Greek tongues. Fitted to children's capacities, as an introduction to larger
grammars. (BL; Cambridge UL. T.p. of both copies cropped). The title is
often quoted as *Rudimenta* . . . but the Cambridge copy makes *Institutio* seem
more probable. The Cambridge copy reads *Introdu-duction*, at a line break.
The 1st edn of Wing (L1843) had given the title as *Grammaticae pueriles*
[1670?]; the 2nd edn (L1842A) gives *Institutio grammaticae pueriles*, which is
difficult Latin, and a date, 1661, without any location. An edn of 1671 is
recorded in the Folger Library. See *EGC*, p. 570; Padley, pp. 176 f.   P. *319*.
[1675]a *A model for a school*   Authorship uncertain: see below, by title.
[1675]b* Ex   *Plain, and short rules for pointing periods and reading sentences*

grammatically, with the great use of them. (BL, lacks t.p.; Huntington L). P. 331.

1675* G *Vestibulum technicum: or, an artificial vestibulum. Wherein, the sense of Janua Linguarum is contained, and most of the leading words chapter by chapter, are compiled into plain, and short sentences, fit for the initiation of children* [etc.]. (BL); edn rev. by Seth Boncle, 'School-master of the . . . Company of Mercers', 1682* (Nottingham UL). Lewis' long and important preface is omitted from the rev. edn.

Mark Lewis' educational work (and the copies in which it survives) needs, and would repay, thorough examination. It is referred to by J.B., 1680, p. 37; Samuel Shaw, *Grammatica Anglo-Romana*, 1687, preface; Francis Brokesby, 1701, chap. 4; Joshua Oldfield, 1707, p. 394; Solomon Lowe, *A grammar of the Latin tongue*, 1726, pp. vi, 1, and in his *The occasional critique*, no. IV, 1736. See also *EGC passim* and Cohen, 1977, 28–30.

LEWIS, William Greatheed

[1821]* G *A grammar of the English language, in which the genius of the English tongue is consulted, and all imitations of the Greek and Latin grammars are discarded . . . intended for the use of schools and young persons in general. To which is added, a brief view of the discoveries of Mr Horne Tooke.* (dated from preface) (BL). P. 360.

[Anon.]

[a. 1788] G *Lilly's accidence improved: or, a complete introduction in English prose to the several parts of Latin grammar: together with an abstract of English grammar, and a system of rhetoric illustrated by examples of classic authority.* (title from 1793 edn). 7th edn, 1788, Kennedy, 5922, as *Lilly's accidence enlarged*; new edn W. Lowndes, 1793* (NYc). *Mon. Rev.*, 80 (February 1789), 184. Not in Alston.

LEWIS, Henry

1866 G *The English language: its grammar and history, together with a treatise on English composition.* (O); 3rd edn 1872 (O); 4th edn 1873 (private colln).

[Anon.]

1809 G *Lindley Murray examined; or an address to classical, French and English teachers, in which several absurdities, contradictions and grammatical errors in his grammar are pointed out. By an Oxonian.* Oxford. (O). Hunter, 1848, says the author wrote also *Essentials of English grammar*, 1808, q. v.

LINDSAY, John 'Late Fellow of Dulwich College'

1842* G *English grammar for the use of national and other elementary schools.* Rivington. Pp. 88. (BL; O). Dedicated to Alexander Wilson, Master of the National Society's Central School at Westminster.

[LING, Nicholas (ed.)]

1597* RA *Politeuphuia. Wit's commonwealth.* (BL); anr edn 1598 (BL); twenty-six further edns to 1699; edns 'for the use of schools' in 1699 (BL) and 1722 (BL).

LINNINGTON, R.T.

1833* RA *The rhetorical speaker; and poetical class book. Comprising preliminary observations on the structure of language, an analysis of poetry, directions for the modulation of the voice, the delineation of the passions, &c. Together with a . . .*

selection of pieces . . . for recitation and reading, with copious instructions for their delivery. (BL).   Pp. 288–9; *220.*

1837* RA   *The scientific reader and practical elocutionist; containing original readings in the sciences . . . A new collection of modern poetry, orations, and dramatic scenes; accompanied by an introduction to the practice of elocution, versification, &c. Together with a copious glossary of scientific terms, and a series of five hundred questions . . . Intended as a companion to The Rhetorical Speaker.* (BL).   P. 242.

[Anon.]

1846 G   *The little linguist; or, a complete guide to English philology, comprising a grammar in miniature, with all the rules of syntax; verbal distinctions, &c., and numerous English examples. The whole designed to promote a habit of perspicuity in speaking and writing the language.* George Nodes. Cover title: *Maunder's little treasury. Linguist.* (Wandsworth PL).   P. *357.*

[Anon.]

[*c.* 1850]* S   *Little Mary's spelling book.* W. Kent (BL). The preface is signed J.C., probably for Joseph Cundall, although some volumes in the Little Mary series have been attributed to Julia Corner. Eighteen volumes in the series, with some duplication, are in BL (shelf-mark 1607/4261).   P. *129.*

[Anon.]

1742 RA   *Little master's miscellany: or, divine and moral essays in prose and verse; adapted to the capacities, and design'd for the improvement of the youth of both sexes. Containing, dialogues on the following subjects . . .* [nine topics] . . . *to which is added select fables, moral songs and useful maxims.* (title from 2nd edn; date of 1st edn from Sotheby's catalogue, 2 June 1982, item 119). 2nd edn Birmingham, 1748* (BL); 3rd edn Birmingham, 1750, Quayle, pp. 21–2; 5th edn Birmingham, 1765 (BL).   P. 179.

[Anon.]

[*c.* 1830?]* RE   *The little primer.* No imprint. (Bedford CHE). Alphabet, syllables and one-syllable words.

[Anon.]

[1856] RE   *The little primer.* Nelson. Late edn [1886]* (BL).

[Anon.]

[*c.* 1855?]* RE   *The little primer.* J.L. Marks (Bedford CHE). One folded sheet of eight pages; alphabet and syllables only, no words.

[Anon.]

[1780?]* S   *The little spelling book, or child's best instructor, being a pleasant introduction to spelling and reading.* Bath: Steart and Pyrry. (BL).

[Anon.]

1798 S   *The little teacher, for reading and spelling well. By a parent.* (Toronto PL); anr edn 1814, Sotheby, HIC, IV, 1976, no. 1607; American edns from 1802. *Mon. Rev.* n.s. 28 (March 1799), 335. Alston, IV, 934 and Plate 104 for facsimile t.p.

LLOYD, Miss E.

[*a.* 1813] G   *Grammatical dialogues for children.* 2nd edn 1813, T. Martin, 1824, p. 77; anr edn 1814, Watt.

LLOYD, Richard

1652 G   *An English grammar.* No copy known. Alston, I, 13.

1654* S   *The schoole-masters auxiliaries, to remove the barbarians siege from Athens; advanced under two guides. The first, leading by rule and reason to read and write English dexterously. The second, asserting the Latine tongue in prose and verse, to its just inlargement, splendor, and elegancy.* (BL); anr edn 1659 (BL). Both edns include a reissue of Lloyd's Latin grammar of 1653. Alston, VI, 465–6; Watson, 1908, pp. 183–4.   Pp. 18, 41, 63; *50, 52, 383.*

LLOYD, W.F.

1848 RE   *Help for infants in spelling, reading and thinking.* Hamilton. (BL).

LOCKE, John   1632–1704   Sometime teacher

1693 Ed   *Some thoughts concerning education,* ed. James L. Axtell from 5th edn, 1705, Cambridge, 1968*; Scolar Press facsimile of 1693 edn, 1970*. For bibliographical information see Axtell's checklist.

LODWICK, Francis   1619–94

1686 Ed   *A second essay concerning the universal primer.* In *Philosophical Transactions 16,* no. 182, pp. 134–7; facsimile reprint in Salmon, 1972*, pp. 243–6.   Pp. 121; 345.

[Anon.]

1774* Lo   *Logic. By question and answer. For the use of Portsea-Academy.* Portsmouth: R. Carr. (O). Alston, VII, 250.

[Anon.]

[1731]* Ex   *The London medley; containing the exercises spoken by several young noblemen and gentlemen, at the annual meeting of the Westminster scholars, on the 28th January, 1730/31, at Westminster School.* (BL). Pp. 30. At p. 14 there is a line marking 'the end of the exercises.' The remaining poems seem to be adult.

[Anon.]

[1711] S   *The London new method and art of teaching children to spell and read distinctly and perfectly. By learning them to know the letters in the several usual prints, the true sounds of dipthongs, then syllables of 2, 3, 4, 5, 6, 7, 8, 9 letters, all the rules of spelling . . . So as the child may immediately pass from learning this book to read the Bible in less than twelve months time, without the help of any other book.* (title from 1723 edn). No copy; anr edn 1714, no copy; anr edn 1723* (BL); anr edn [1725?] (BL). The preface to 1723 edn is signed 'Is. C.' Alston, IV, 285–6.   P. *161.*

LONGMAN, Publisher

1862   *First steps to reading* . . . see LAURIE, J.S.

1866 RS   *Graduated series of reading lesson books, adapted to the six standards of the revised code, Books 1–6.* A revision by J.D. Morell of J.S. Laurie's revision of 1863. Goldstrom, 1972a, pp. 167, 212.

1859–61 RS   *Graduated series of reading lesson books, Books 1–5.* Goldstrom, 1972a, pp. 167, 212. Books 1–3, 5 (O). Abridged edn 1866 (O).

1863* RS   *Standard series of elementary reading books, Books 1–6* (BL; O), anr edn 1866 (BL). A revision by J.S. Laurie of the *Graduated series.* Goldstrom, 1972a, pp. 167, 212.

See also BILTON, Charles, [a. 1868], *The first* [etc.] *reading book*

LONGMAN, Joseph 'Writing master at Child-Okeford, Blandford'

1786* RA *Sentences, divine, moral, and historical; in prose and verse; with copies for the alphabet. Designed for the conduct of human life, and particularly for the improvement of youth, in good sense, and correct English.* Salisbury: E. Easton, Pp. vi, 360. (BL).   P. 181.

LORD, Walter John

1832* G *A new arrangement of the English grammar, adapted to the junior classes. In which the expressions, definitions and rules by Lindley Murray, are attempted to be simplified and rendered more easy of acquirement and retention.* Trowbridge, 56 pp. (BL; O).

LORDAN, J.

1827* S *The new London pronouncing spelling book and key of English sounds . . . on a system recommended by Sheridan, Walker, the Edgeworths, &c. Part I.* Pp. 106. (BL).   Pp. 57, 68; *44*.

LOUGHTON, William 'School-master, Kensington'

1734* G *A practical grammar of the English tongue: or, a rational and easy introduction to speaking and writing English correctly and properly . . . free from the hard and unnecessary terms of the Latin rudiments . . . Designed for the use of schools: and tho' calculated chiefly for such as require only an English education, may yet be a useful foundation to those who are design'd for higher studies.* (BL); 2nd edn 1735* (BL); 4th edn 1740* (BL); 5th edn 1744* (BL). For other edns to 1755 see Alston, I, 65–71. See also John Bancks, *The progress of language, a poetical essay to Mr William Loughton . . . on his Practical Grammar of the English Tongue,* in *Miscellaneous Works,* 1738, vol. II (*Gent. Mag.,* 9 (1739), 655); FOX, Francis, a. 1754, preface; Nichols, *Lit. Anec.,* II, 46, 115; *EGC*; Vorlat, 1975.   P. *346n.*

LOWE, Edward Clarke 'Headmaster, St John's School, Hurstpierpoint'

1866* C *An English primer: compiled under the supervision of E.C. Lowe.* Brighton. Includes religious instruction, arithmetic, Euclid, history, geography. Pp. 131–60 on 'The Mother Tongue'. Described by the compiler as 'a dry text book' to be 'well learned by heart' on the assumption that 'the oral teaching of an animated master' will 'quicken its facts'. 2nd edn Brighton, 1868* (BL).

1868* RA *The young Englishman's first poetry book.* Brighton. (BL).   P. 222.

LOWE, Solomon Master of an academy at Brook Green, Hammersmith

1755* S *The critical spelling-book. An introduction to reading and writing readily and correctly . . . Designd-for a standard of the language: and contriv'd by a proper gradation of instructions, disposd in a picturesque manner, for the easy and expeditious attaining-to a rational knowledge of it.* (BL); 2nd edn 1770* (BL); Scolar Press facsimile Leeds, 1967*.   Pp. 85, 97–8; *51, 103, 113*.

1737a* G *English grammar reformd into a small and easy method for the readier learning and better understanding of the English tongue by way of introduction to other languages.* 8 pp. (Edinburgh UL); Scolar Press facsimile in his *Four tracts on grammar,* 1971*. Alston, I, 85.

1737b* B *Rhetoric delineated in a small compass and easy method for the readier learning and better understanding the beauty and energy of discourse whether written or spoken.* 4 pp. (Edinburgh UL). Alston VI, 165.   Pp. *163, 346n.*

LOWRES, Jacob 'Certificated master'

1862* G *Companion to English grammar, being a guide to analysis of sentences,* *paraphrasing, higher order of parsing, punctuation, composition or style, figurative language. With numerous exercises for pupils. For the use of schools.* (BL).   P. *368*.

1863* G   *Grammar of English grammars; or advanced manual of English grammar and language, critically and historically considered . . . With exercises.* (BL; O). The book contains a chronological list of about 250 English grammars from the sixteenth to the nineteenth century.

1852* S   *The spelling and dictation lesson book; or, an easy way of learning to spell well, with examples of different ways of teaching this art: to which are added . . .* [anecdotes, etc.] *. . . arranged alphabetically for headlines in copy-books.* (BL).   P. *129*.

[a.1851] G   *A system of English parsing and derivation, with the rudiments of English grammar . . . For the use of schools,* 2nd edn 1851* (BL); anr edn 1864 (BL).

[LOWTH, Robert]   1710–87

1762* G   *A short introduction to English grammar: with critical notes.* (BL); 2nd edn 1763 (O). At least forty British and ten American edns to 1838. Scolar Press facsimile of 1762, 1969*.   Pp. 85, 94, 328, 331–2, 334; *3*.

LUDLOW, George   'Master of the Reading and Writing School, Christ's Hospital, Hertford'

1836* RA   *The class reading book: adapted for schools, and particularly designed to furnish youth with practical information on a variety of interesting subjects.* J.W. Parker for SPCK (BL); 3rd edn 1840 (Leeds UL).

LYDAL, Thomas   'Schoolmaster in Canterbury'

[1701] S   *The expert English school-master; being an exact and easie method of teaching to spell, read, and write, after the plainest manner; containing many tables of most common words and proper names . . . both whole and divided, for the ease of the learner; who, after he is instructed herein, will be capable of reading the Bible. Also* [homophones; difficult pronunciation; proverbs; accounts; penmanship] *With poems, moral instructions* [etc.]. *TC*, III, 276, November 1701, no copy; 2nd edn 1703, *TC*, III, 379, no copy. Alston, IV, 209–10.   P. *372*.

LYE, Thomas   1621–84   Headmaster, Bury St Edmunds School, 1647

1671 S   *The child's delight.* (Harvard: Bristol UL microfilm). Scolar Press facsimile 1968*. NBL, 1949, no. 254. Alston, I, 28. Pp. 69–162 are an English grammar. Alston comments that the NBL date, 1684, is probably an error, but the title as quoted in the NBL catalogue, *The child's delight together with an English grammar,* is not that of 1671 and may well point to a later edn. Recommended by J.B., 1680, p. 37.   Pp. 96; *50, 52, 69, 76, 121*.

1673 S   *Reading and spelling English made easie. Wherein all the words of our English Bible are set down in an alphabetical order and divided into their distinct syllabls. Together with the grounds of the English tongue laid in verse, wherein are couch't many moral precepts . . . Tolle, lege.* (Yale). 2nd edn as: *A new spelling book: or, reading and spelling English made easie. Wherein . . .* 1677 (BL); 3rd edn [1682], no copy: 5th edn 1696. Scolar Press facsimile of 1677 edn, 1969*. Alston, IV, 90–3 and Plate 14 for 1677 t.p. Watson, 1903, p. 228; Dobson, 1968, p. 354; Cohen, 1977, p. 146.   Pp. 19, 73, 116.

LYELL, James

1804* G   *The rudiments of the English tongue; or, a plain and easy introduction to English grammar; wherein the principles of the language are methodically digested,* *with useful notes and observations, explaining the terms of grammar, and farther improving its rules.* Arbroath: J. Findlay. (Glasgow UL, incomplete copy, pp. iv, 24).

LYNCH, Patrick 1754–1818 Teacher

1796* G *The pentaglot preceptor; or elementary institutes of the English, Latin, Greek, Hebrew, and Irish languages. Vol. I. containing a complete grammar of the English tongue. For the use of schools.* Carrick: John Stacy. (BL). Pp. i–xi contain 'A review of the most celebrated English grammars hitherto published', dated in the BL copy 1 May 1802, although the t.p. carries the date 1796. 2nd edn as: *A plain, easy and comprehensive grammar of the English tongue,* Carrick, 1805 (BL). Dowling, p. 140; Alston, I, 498a. P. 342.

LYON, Charles Jobson

1832* G *Analysis of the seven parts of speech of the English language, with a view to fix their character, and furnish simple rules for ascertaining them; as also to elucidate and facilitate the method of parsing.* Edinburgh. (BL; O). P. 360.

M. see *Grammar lessons,* 1842.

[M., I.]

1831a RA *Selections from the poems of Robert Southey, Esq.* Moxon. (BL). Intended for school use.

1831b* RA *Selections from the prose works of Robert Southey . . . chiefly for the use of schools and young persons.* Moxon. (BL); anr edn 1832 (BL); anr edn as: *The beauties of the prose works of . . .,* 1833* (Leicester UL).

[1831?] RA *Selections from the poems of William Wordsworth, Esq. Chiefly for the use of schools and young persons.* Moxon. Advt in selection of Southey's prose, above.

M., T. 'A private tutor'

1774* G *The grammarian's vade-mecum, or pocket companion; containing the general terms of grammar in the French and English languages: disposed in alphabetical order.* (BL.) Alston, III, 520. Pp. 183, 341–2; *324.*

M'CARTNEY, William

1791* La *An illustration of a design for teaching the English language, in three parts: 1. The grammar, idioms, and other peculiarities. 2. Readiness in the command of a pure extemporary phraseology. 3. Ease and accuracy in the practice of writing,* Edinburgh. (NLS). Alston, III, 399.

1792* La *A specimen of the method of teaching the English language, on the principles stated in his pamphlet,* Edinburgh. An attempt to be more specific than he had been in the previous work. (Glasgow UL). Pp. 281, 315.

MACCREA, John

[c. 1840] S *Pronouncing spelling book.* No copy traced. Chalmers, p. 142.

M'CULLOCH, John Murray Headmaster, Circus Place Sch, Edinburgh

1827* RA *A course of elementary reading in science and literature . . . to which is added, a copious list of the Latin and Greek primitives . . . For the use of Circus Place School,* Edinburgh (BL); 19th edn 1850* (BL). Fifty-three edns to 1882. P. 242.

1837a* RS *A first reading book for the use of schools, containing the alphabet and progressive lessons on the long and short sounds of the vowels,* Edinburgh. (BL). Forty-nine edns to 1895. Pp. 39–40, 68; *30.*

1837b*RS *A second reading book for the use of schools; containing progressive lessons on the pronunciation of double consonants and diphthongs, and on the middle and broad sound of the vowels*, Edinburgh. (BL). At least thirty-three edns to 1862.

1837c* RS *A third reading book for the use of schools; containing simple pieces in prose and verse, with exercises on the more difficult words and sounds occurring in them*, Edinburgh. (BL). At least twenty-eight edns to 1858.

1858* RS *A fourth reading book for the use of schools; to which is added a synopsis of English spelling*, Edinburgh (BL); 5th edn 1861.

1834* G *A manual of English grammar, philosophical and practical; with exercises; adapted to the analytical mode of tuition*, Edinburgh (BL); 6th edn 1839* (ULIE). At least twenty-four edns to 1873. See below, *Prefixes and affixes*, a. 1836.   P. 285.

[*c.* 1837] S *A manual of English pronunciation and spelling*. Advertised in 1837 as 'in the press'.

1831* RA *A series of lessons, in prose and verse, progressively arranged; intended as an introduction to A Course of Elementary Reading*, Edinburgh. (BL). 5th edn rev 1836*. Fifty-eight edns to 1882.   Pp. 251–2.

McDOWALL, William

1850 RA *Rhetorical readings for school*. Edinburgh. (BL).

M'GAVIN, William

[1862]* RA *A poetical book; selected for the use of the junior classes in schools*, Glasgow (BL). Another edn 1879.

MacGOWAN, James 'Master of the preparatory and finishing classical and commercial academy, Hope Street, Liverpool'

1823* La *Nature's first English lessons, taken down from life. In two parts. Part I.* (BL). Includes a verbatim chronological record of the words spoken by Susan between the ages of ten and thirty months.

1817* G *A practical English grammar, in which the syntax is greatly simplified.* [With exercises], Edinburgh (NLS). 3rd edn London, 1825 (NYct); 4th edn London, 1836 (Columbia UL). MacGowan here describes himself as 'teacher of languages in Edinburgh'.

MacILMAIN, Roland

1574 Lo *The logike of the moste excellent philosopher P. Ramus martyr, newly translated, and in divers places corrected, after the mynde of the author.* (BL); Scolar Press facsimile 1966*.   Pp. 146–7.

[McILQUHAM, William] d. 1803 or 1804 Teacher

1781* G *A comprehensive grammar: in which the principles of the English language are methodically digested into plain, and easy rules. With notes, and observations, explaining the terms of grammar, and improving its use.* Glasgow. (Glasgow PL); 3rd edn 1789* (Glasgow PL); 5th edn 1797* (BL); 6th edn 1802* (Glasgow PL). Alston, I, 370–3; Scotland, I, 111.   P. *342.*

MacINTOSH, Daniel

1852 G *Elements of English grammar*. Edinburgh. (BL; O).

MacINTOSH, Duncan

1797* G *A plain, rational essay on English grammar: the main object of which is to point out a plain, rational and permanent standard of pronunciation. To which is given, a Gamut or Key . . . pointing out the quantity and quality of every syllable* *and word, according to the present mode among polite scholars*, Boston, Mass. (BL); London, 1808* (as *A plain, rational, and patriotic essay on* . . . (BL); Scolar Press facsimile of 1797 edn, 1969*. Alston, VI, 511.

McLACHLAN, John   HM Dr Bell's School Edinburgh
[a. 1863*] G   *A first grammar*, Edinburgh. (BL).

McLAREN, James   'Teacher of English'
1820* RA   *A collection from the most approved English authors, in prose and verse; for the use of schools and private classes*. Dundee. (Hull UL).

McLEOD, Walter   'Headmaster, The Model School, Royal Military Asylum, Chelsea'
1850a G   *An explanatory English grammar for beginners*. (BL).
1865* RA   *The first book of Cowper's Task, the Sofa: with explanatory notes, exercises in the analysis of sentences, and a life of the poet*. Longman. (BL).
1849a* RA   *The first poetical reading book. Compiled for the use of families and schools*. (BL).   P. 253.
1850b* RA   *The second poetical reading book*. (BL).
1848* RE   *A first reading book. For the use of families and schools*. (BL).   P. 65.
1849b RE   *The second reading book*. (BL).
1858 RA   *Goldsmith's Deserted Village, with remarks on the analysis of sentences, exercises in parsing, notes* . . . *and a life of the poet*. (BL); 2nd edn 1858 (BL).
1850c RE   *My first school book to teach me reading and writing*. Gleig (NLS); anr edn 1853* (BL). The sequel, *My second school book* . . . was advertised in 1853.   P. 120.
1871 RA   *The Prologue to Chaucer's Canterbury Tales*. (BL).
1863* RA   *Thomson's Spring: with a life of the poet, notes critical, explanatory, and grammatical, and remarks on the analysis of sentences, with illustrative examples. For the use of schools*. (BL).   Pp. 262–3.

MacMULLEN, James Alexander
1860 G   *A manual of English grammar*. (O).

MacNAB, Henry Grey   1761–1823
1818* Ed   *Analysis and analogy recommended as the means of rendering experience and observation useful in education*. Paris. (BL).   P. 248.
[c. 1786a]   *The director, in teaching English*. Announced on the t.p. of his *A plan of reform* as shortly to be published. Not known.
1785 P   *Heads of a course of elocution. With exercises; partly from manuscripts*. Glasgow. (Glasgow PL). Gaskell, 677.
1786a* Ed   *A plan of reform, in the mode of instruction, at present practised in English schools. Also, a proposal for the improvement of public speaking*. Glasgow. (BL). Gaskell, 680.
[c. 1786b]   *The reader and speaker*. Announced on the t.p. of his *A plan of reform* as shortly to be published. Not known.
1786b P   *A synopsis of a course of elocution*. Glasgow. (Glasgow UL). Gaskell, 680A; Alston, VI, 422.

MacQUEEN, John   St Bees School
[1869]* G   *Easy exercises in English*. (BL).   Pp. *352, 353*.
1861 G   *Easy lessons in English grammar, for home study*. Whitehaven, Crosthwaite and Co. (once in Carlisle PL).

Magazine see W., G.

MAITTAIRE, Michael 1668–1747 Second Master, Westminster School

1712* G *The English grammar: or, an essay on the art of grammar, applied to and exemplified in the English tongue.* Scolar Press Facsimile 1967*. Alston, I, 57. Vorlat, 1975. Pp. 28; *50, 279.*

[Anon.]

1829 RE *Mamma's lessons for her little boys and girls. By the author of Transformation of a Beech Tree. First part. A series of reading lessons in words of three or four letters. Second part. Chiefly in monosyllables.* (title from 1833). (Bedford CHE); 4th edn 1833* (Nottingham UL); at least eleven edns in all to 1852. Moon, 515.

[Anon.]

1835 RE *Mamma's little child's first step to learning.* The Nursery Library, Hamilton Adams. (BL).

[Anon.]

[1870?] RE *Mamma's little primer.* (BL).

[Anon.]

[*c.* 1860?]* RE *Mamma's pretty primer for a good child.* Simpkin Marshall for Thomas Albin. (Bedford CHE),

MANGIN, Edward 1772–1852

1808* B *An essay on light reading, as it may be supposed to influence moral conduct and literary taste.* (BL). P. 247.

MANNEVILLE, William Teacher

1851* G *English grammar simplified. Designed for the use of schools and self-tuition.* (BL). Pp. *357, 361, 362.*

MANSON, David 1726–92 Teacher

1764 RE *Directions to play the literary cards: invented for the improvement of children in learning and morals . . . till they become proficients in spelling, reading* [etc.] [Belfast?]. (Hull UL).

[*c.* 1757] S *A new primer: or, child's best guide,* Belfast (no copy); Dublin, 1838* (V&A); Dublin, 1839* (V&A). Many edns as *Primer* or *Spelling book* to 1845; advertised in the 1872 edn of John Davis, 1864. Alston, IV, 683–9; Heartman, no. 104.

MANSON, George HM General Assembly's Normal Sch Edinburgh

1846* La *The pupil's guide to English etymology,* Edinburgh. (BL). P. *357.*

MANSON, John Teacher

[1867]* RE *Progressive lessons in reading for beginners,* Glasgow. (BL; O). *Sequel,* n.d., and *Second book* [1867] (O).

[MANT, Elizabeth] d. 1849

1814* RE *The parent's poetical anthology: being a selection of English poems, primarily designed to assist in forming the taste and the sentiments of young readers.* (BL); 3rd edn 1832, Gumuchian, 3941; 5th edn 1849 (Nottingham UL). P. 220.

[Anon.]

1856* G *Manual of the analysis of language.* Pp. viii, 24 (BL). P. *363.*

[Anon.]

1802 P *The manual of orthoepy: being an attempt, on a new plan, to render a right* *pronunciation of words attainable at first sight. LTM*, no. 24 (1960); anr edn 1832* (BL; Glasgow UL).

1762* D *A new pocket dictionary; or English expositor . . . and a plan for the improvement of children in virtue and learning, without the use of the rod. With the present state and practice of the play-school in Belfast.* Belfast. (Nottingham UL); as *Manson's pronouncing dictionary* [etc.], rev. John Davis. Belfast, 1823 (BL). Alston, V, 231a.

[Anon.]

[a. 1823] RA *A manual of sacred poetry, for the use of public and private charities.* See above *Lessons intended for introduction into schools . . .* a. 1823.

Manual of the system of teaching reading see BRITISH AND FOREIGN SCHOOL SOCIETY

[Anon.]

[1869] La *A manual of words curiously derived, for the use of students of the English language. By a teacher.* Cardigan. Cambrian Educational Course. (BL).

[Anon.]

1724* La *The many advantages of a good language to any nation: with an examination of the present state of our own: As also, an essay towards correcting some things that are wrong with it.* (O; BL); Scolar Press facsimile 1969; Garland Press facsimile N.Y, 1969*. Often attributed to Thomas Wilson, 1663–1755, Bishop of Sodor and Man; *DNB* attributes to Francis Hutchinson, 1660–1739, Bishop of Down and Connor. The preface refers throughout to the authors as 'we'. Alston, VI, 538.

MARCET, Jane 1769–1858

1844* La *Conversations on language, for children.* (BL; O).

1842 G *The game of grammar.* Cards and counters. (BL).

1835* G *Mary's grammar.* (BL); 2nd edn 1836 (Osborne, 722); 3rd edn 1838 (V&A); 4th edn 1840, Gumuchian, 3946; 5th edn 1841 (Liverpool UL); 7th edn 1843, GB; anr edn 1851 (BL); anr edn 1865* (personal); anr edn 1870 (Wisconsin UL); anr edn 1902 (personal). P. 361.

1845a* RE *The mother's first book; containing Reading-made-easy, and The Spelling Book. In two parts.* (BL).

1845b G *Willy's grammar, interspersed with stories for the use of children.* (BL; O); 3rd edn 1850 (Leicester UL).

MARKHAM, William

[a. 1738] G *A general introduction to trade and business . . . Part I. The principles of grammar explain'd; whereby the reading and writing of true English are render'd very easy.* Advertised in and mentioned in the preface to his *An Introduction*, 1728.

[1728] S *An introduction to spelling and reading English.* (No copy). 5th edn 1738*. (BL). Many edns to 1885. Alston, IV, 336–43. P. 161.

MARKS, Edward N.

[1870a]* RE *Cousin Charley's step by step to learning. With the hide and seek alphabet.* (BL).

[1866]* RE *The ear and the eye; or, a new way to try. A picture primer in rhyme,* Edinburgh. (BL). Pp. 68; 123.

[a. 1867] S *Handbook of English spelling and pronunciation, with dictation, and other exercises.* A prospectus and specimen pages were advertised in his *The royal road,* 1867.

[1870b] RE   *The one syllable alphabet of nouns, in rhyme.* (BL).

[1867a]* S   *The royal road to spelling and reading. An illustrated spelling book, in which all the peculiarities of English spelling and pronunciation are explained on the 'step by step' principle.* (BL).

[1867b]   *The way to learn by sound and sight; how to spell and read and write.* (BL).

[1865]* RE   *Words to spell and read as well.* (BL).

MARSH, Thomas

1862 G   *Grammar of the English language, inculcating its history and development, with all the latest improvements; particularly adapted for schools.* (printed in Jersey). (O).

MARSHALL, Charles

[a. 1780] S   *An introduction to the English tongue; designed for a spelling book.* 5th edn [1780?]* (BL); 6th edn (1790?]* (BL); 7th edn (Northampton PL). Alston, IV, 773–5. A grammar was added to the 6th edn.

MARTIN, Benjamin   1704–82   Teacher and instrument-maker

1737* C   *Bibliotheca technologica, or a philological library of literary arts and sciences.* Four edns to 1776. Alston, III, 224–7.   P. *163.*

1748* La   *Institutions of language; containing a physico-grammatical essay on the propriety and rationale of the English language.* Scolar Press facsimile 1970. Alston, I, 103. The essay was included in Martin's dictionary, *Lingua britannica reformata,* 1749, but not in its 2nd edition, 1754.   P. *342.*

1754* C   *An introduction to the English language and learning. In three parts. Part I. A spelling-book of the arts and sciences* . . . [grammar, rhetoric, logic, poetry and eighteen others]. *Part II. The rudiments of English grammar, with the rules of orthography, construction, emphasis, and a just elocution. Part III. Lessons on all the above-mentioned sciences* . . . *With a preface, shewing, that nothing short of the method here taken can be sufficient for a plan of genuine English education.* (O; BL photocopy). 2nd edn 1756* (BL photocopy); 3rd edn 1766 (BL photocopy). Alston, I, 149–51.   Pp. 107, 203, 373; 102.

[MARTIN, John]

1798* P   *Thoughts on elocution.* (BL). Alston, VI, 432.   P. 286.

MARTIN, Thomas

1824* G   *A philological grammar of the English language; in a series of lessons; containing many original* . . . *observations on the nature and construction of language; on the comparative merits of more than one hundred treatises of English grammar; on the various new and popular modes of teaching; on the necessity of examining the principles of grammars and grammarians.* Pp. xii, 401 and list of subscribers. (BL). The address to subscribers is dated December 1823, from Birmingham.

MARTIN, William   1801–67   Sometime teacher

1863 G   *First English course, based upon the analysis of sentences; comprising the structure and history of the English language.* (BL; O).

[a. 1856] RA   *Instructive lessons in reading and thinking; being the useful knowledge lessons of the Intellectual Reading Book; for the use of national, infants', and other schools.* New edn 1856* (BL).

1851a La   *The intellectual expositor and vocabulary; comprising tables of prefixes, affixes, and primitive roots.* (BL). 3rd edn [1865?].

1852* G   *The intellectual grammar; comprising orthography, etymology, syntax, and prosody; the principles of articulation, spelling, and pronunciation; with definitions, examples, exercises, illustrations, model lessons, hints to the teacher and pupil, upwards of a thousand interrogations on the text, and numerous explanatory and suggestive notes, with an elementary course of juvenile composition.* (BL).   Pp. 65–6, 352, 365; *30, 62–3, 353.*

1851b RE   *Intellectual primer.* (O); 2nd edn 1835* (BL).   Pp. *54, 123.*

1851c* RE   *Intellectual reading book.* (BL); 2nd edn [1854] (BL).   P. 242.

1851d* S   *Intellectual spelling book of pronunciation.* (BL); 4th edn [1860].

[1838]* RA   *The moral and intellectual school book, containing instructions for reading and speaking, lessons on religion, morality, science . . . with copious extracts from the modern poets.* (BL).

[a. 1853] RA   *School poetry. Vol. I. The poetry of faith, hope and charity. Vol. II. The poetry of nature.* Advertised in 1853.

See also *The ancient poets and poetry of England,* and *The gem book of poesie.*

MASON, Charles Peter   Teacher

1858* G   *English grammar, including the principles of grammatical analysis.* (BL). At least thirty-nine edns to 1898.   P. *357. See also p. 370.*

1872a G   *First notions of grammar for young learners.* (BL; NLS). At least nineteen edns to 1899.

1861 G   *First steps in English grammar for junior classes.* (BL; NLS).

1865* RA   *(Goldsmith) The Deserted Village. With notes on the grammatical analysis of sentences, and a brief sketch of the life of Goldsmith.* (BL).

1872b G   *Outlines of English grammar for the use of junior classes.* (BL; NLS). At least twenty edns to 1897.

[a. 1861] RA   *(Cowper's) The Task, Book I* and *Book II.* Advertised in 1861.

MASON, John   Master of a school in Camberwell

1648 P   *Princeps rhetoricus, or Πιλομαχία. The combat of caps.* (BL). A detailed account and interpretation of a play in English, much interspersed with Latin, about the proceedings following on the loss of a schoolboy's cap. There is quotation from the play but not a full text. See Northup, 1912*.

[MASON, John]   1706–63

1748 P   *An essay on elocution. Intended chiefly for the assistance of those who instruct others in the art of reading.* Five edns to 1787. Included in his *Essays,* 1761*. Scolar Press facsimile 1968. Alston, VI, 322–7.

1749a B   *An essay on the power and harmony of prosaic numbers: being a sequel to one on the power of numbers.* Reprinted in his *Essays,* 1761*. Scolar Press facsimile 1967. Alston, VI, 454.

1749b B   *An essay on the power of numbers, and the principles of harmony in poetical compositions.* Reprinted in his *Essays,* 1761*. Scolar Press facsimile 1967*. Garland Press facsimile N.Y., 1969. Alston, VI, 453.

1761* B   *Essays on poetical and prosaic numbers, and elocution,* 2nd edn. (Nottingham UL). The three essays of 1748 and 1749, of which it was treated as a 2nd edition. Alston, VI, 327.

MASON, Arthur   'Teacher of languages in Edinburgh'; retired in 1779 [a. 1764] RA   *A collection of English prose and verse for the use of schools.* 4th edn Edinburgh, 1764* (NLS); Air (*sic*), 1796* (BL).   Pp. 175–6.

[a. 1757] S   *An English spelling book, for the use of schools . . . with a preface, concerning the method of teaching to read and spell English, particularly adapted to this book,* 2nd edn Edinburgh, 1757 (Gumuchian, 5244); 3rd edn Edinburgh, 1761* (BL). About nineteen edns to 1819. Alston, IV, 691–4; Law, pp. 150–3.

MATHER, William   Teacher

1681* S   *A very useful manual, or the young man's companion, containing plain and easy directions for spelling, reading and writing English* [etc.]. (BL); 2nd, and subsequent, edns as *The young man's companion,* 1685 (Friends House L); at least twenty-four edns to 1775; reprinted N.Y., 1939. Alston, III, 178–99.

MATHESON, John   The Royal School, Margaret St, Cavendish Square, London

1819* G   *The theory and practice of English grammar: adapted to the new modes of instruction, in which every rule and observation in syntax is elucidated by various examples; also, remarks on punctuation, prosody, rhetoric and composition.* (BL); 2nd edn 1821 (BL).

MATTHEWS, George

[a. 1866] S   *Easy lessons on spelling, reading, writing, tables & arithmetic.* Rev. edn, sixth thousand, 1866* (BL).

MAUNDER, Samuel   1785–1849   Brother-in-law and partner of William Pinnock

[1825]   *The little lexicon; or multum in parvo of the English language.* (BL). At least five edns to *c.* 1845.

[a. 1849] G   *The miniature English grammar.* Reprinted in his *The treasury of knowledge.*

1830 C   *The treasury of knowledge, and library of reference, 2 parts.* (BL); 21st edn, 1854*, contains an English grammar.

1844* RE   *The universal class-book: a new series of reading lessons . . . for every day in the year.* (BL); 3rd edn 1847 (BL).

[MAURICE, Mary Atkinson]

1829* RA   *Aids to development; or, mental and moral instruction exemplified in conversations between a mother and her children,* 2 vols. (Leeds UL); 2nd edn rev. 1832 (BL); 3rd edn 1836 (Holtom, 1979 Cat., item 528).   Pp. 256, 259.

MAVOR, William Fordyce   1758–1837   Sometime teacher

1798a RA   *The British Nepos; or youth's mirror: being select lives of illustrious Britons . . . Written purposely for the use of schools.* (NUC); as: *The British Nepos; or mirror of youth* [etc.] 2nd edn 1800* (Nottingham UL); many edns to 1838.   P. *192.*

[1801?] S   *The English spelling book, accompanied by a progressive series of easy and familiar lessons* (title from 1807). (Illinois UL), Sotheby HIC, IV, 1976, item 1680; 48th edn 1807* (DES); 446th edn 1840* (personal). Higson, p. 40, queries a 1st edn *c.* 1780, but this is unlikely. The uncertainty is whether the 1st edn was 1801 or 1802 (the date of the engraved frontispiece); Cf. Blackwell, Cat. A80, 1985, item 667. At least 469 numbered edns to 1866 and many others under various titles to *c.* 1902. Chalmers, pp. 19, 63–9, 144.   P. 261.

1805 RH   *A father's gift to his children.* An enlarged edn of *The juvenile olio* and *The youth's miscellany.*   P. *191.*

[*c*. 1860?]   (Mavor's) *First book for children; intended as an introduction to a correct knowledge of the English language.* (Yale); Chalmers, p. 144.

[1850?]* S   (Mavor's) *First spelling book*, J.T. Wood (BL 12981.ccc.16((8)).

[a. 1871] RE   (Mavor's) *Second spelling and reading book*, Milner. Bookseller's catalogue, 1980.

[1854]* S   (Mavor's) *Introductory lessons in spelling and reading*, T. Goode, 24 pp. (BL 12985.a.83(5)).

1796* RH   *The juvenile olio; or mental medley: consisting of original essays, moral and literary; tales, fables, reflections, &c. Intended to correct the judgment, to improve the taste, to please the fancy, and to humanize the mind . . . Written by a father, chiefly for the use of his children.* (BL; V&A).   P. *191*.

[*c* 1850]* S   (Mavor's) *New London spelling book*, G. Ingram (BL 12981.ccc.16(7)). Gumuchian, 5416, records an edn by John Rosewarne, London and Belper, [*c*. 1845].

1801a* RA   *The new speaker; or, English class-book . . . To which are prefixed, a short system of rhetoric; and an essay on enunciation . . . For the use of schools.* (BL); 3rd edn 1807* (DES). Chalmers, p. 144, records 2nd edn 1803; 4th 1811 (O). The rhetoric is from Blair.

1801b RH   *The nursery garland; being a selection of short poems, adapted to very early youth* (dated from preface, reprinted); 2nd edn 1806* (BL); 3rd edn 1809 (Reading UL); as: *The garland: a selection . . .* 1812 (BL).   P. *191*.

[a. 1855] RE   (Mavor's) *Universal primer*, W.S. Johnson. Advt. in 1855.

1798b RH   *The youth's miscellany, or a father's gift to his children.* (*NCBEL*, II, 1028).   P. *191*.

MAVOR, William Fordyce, and   PRATT, Samuel Jackson

1801* RA   *Classical English poetry, for the use of schools.* (BL); at least fourteen edns to 1834. Pratt's name was dropped by 1823 at the latest.   Pp. 193; *184, 195n.*

MAXWELL, Caroline

1828* P   *The juvenile edition of Shakespeare; adapted to the capacities of youth.* Pp. viii, 360. (BL; Nottingham UL).

MAYHEW, Henry   1812–87

[1847]* S   *The Prince of Wales's library: No. 1, The Primer.* (BL). *DNB* says it was published in 1844. The series was not continued.

1842* Ed   *What to teach and how to teach it, Part I.* (BL); anr edn 1844.

MAYNE, J.L.

1799* G   *A compendious English grammar, with ungrammatical exercises, to be corrected according to rule: also exercises in false English*, Birmingham. (Birmingham PL). Alston, I, 526.   P. 333.

MAYO, Elizabeth   1793–1865

1830* Ex   *Lessons on objects, as given in a Pestalozzian school.* (BL); Preface by Charles Mayo. At least sixteen edns to 1859.   Pp. 355–6.

1838* RA   *A selection of hymns and poetry for the use of infant schools and nurseries . . . Prepared at the request of the committee of the Home and Colonial Infant School Society.*

MEIKLEJOHN, John Miller Dow   1836–1902   School and university teacher

1862–6 G   *An easy English grammar for beginners, being a plain doctrine of words and sentences. 4 Parts*, Manchester. (BL; O).

1870* Ed   *The fundamental error in the Revised Code, with special reference to the problem of teaching to read.* (BL.)   Pp. 103, 124, 126.

1879* Ed   *The problem of learning to read, restated and attempted to be solved. With suggestions for methods and plans.* Pp. 75. (BL).   P. *132.*

See also SONNENSCHEIN, Adolf, and MEIKLEJOHN. Most of Meiklejohn's grammatical works were published after 1880.

MEILAN, Mark Anthony   *c.* 1743– after 1816   'Private teacher of the English language'

[1771?]* G   *A grammar of the English language. Intended for the use of young gentlemen and ladies passed (sic) the first principles of letters.* (Royal Library, Stockholm). Alston, I, 304.   P. 79.

1803* G   *An introduction to the English language; with an appendix, containing five hundred violations of grammar, extracted from many of our best writers, and here corrected: to which are added, instances of false figures, and other anomalies of style; with reasonings on them.* 2 vols. (BL). A different work from the preceding.   P. *351.*

MENDENHALL, W   'Writing-Master, &c Bath'

1813* G   *The classification of words; or, the English youth's first step in the study of language; but more particularly in the grammar of his own,* Bath. (Glasgow UL); Philadelphia, 1814 (Yale).

[Anon.]

1797 RH   *Mental amusement: consisting of moral essays, allegories, and tales interspersed with poetical pieces, by different writers . . . calculated for the use of private families and schools.* London, G. Sael. (Bookseller's catalogue, July 1961); 2nd edn as *Mental amusement; or, the juvenile moralist . . .* [1798]* (BL).   P. 191.

[Anon.]

1821* RE   *The Mentorian primer; or, Pinnock's second book for children at an early age,* W. Pinnock, Mentorian Press. 72 pp. (Nottingham UL).

MERCAT, John

[a. 1622] S   *A plaine method for speedy learning to reade.* No copy. Described by Brinsley, 1622, p. 59, as 'a little Briefe, of a sheet of paper'. Brinsley calls the author Merest; the form Mercat is given by Herford and Simpson, *Ben Jonson,* II, 419.

Merchant Maiden Hospital Magazine see LAWRIE, Andrew.

MERCY, Blanch

1799* G   *A short introduction to English grammar. In two separate volumes. Volume the first – or scholar's book, contains* [parts of speech, parsing]. *Volume the second – or instructress's book, contains the manner of exercising and interrogating the scholars throughout their lessons and exercises, &c.* Both volumes of the 1st edn were published at London; a copy of vol. I is in Columbia UL, New York, but no copy has been traced of vol. II. Both volumes of the 2nd edn were published in Carlisle, vol. I in 1800 (Nottingham UL) and vol. II in 1801* (NYc).   Pp. 284, 321, 339.

MERES, Francis   1565–1647   Sometime teacher

1598* RA   *Palladis tamia. Wits treasury. Being the second part of Wits Commonwealth.* (BL). Another edn as *Wits commonwealth. The second part. A treasurie of divine, morall, and phylosophicall similies, and sentences, generally usefull. But* *more particularly published, for the use of schools*, 1634* (BL); as *Witts academy, chiefly for young schollers*, 1636 (BL). Facsimile of 1598 edn, intro. Don Cameron Allen, N.Y., 1938*   Pp. 140–1.

MEREST, John, see MERCAT, John

MERRICK, Harriot

1820 G   *An easy introduction to English grammar, for children under eight years*. J. Hunter, 1848.

MERRIMAN, Thomas   'Schoolmaster in Reading'

1750* G   *A compendious English grammar: wherein are comprised all the chief principles, and necessary rules of that art. For the use and improvement of all those who are designed only for an English education*, Reading. (BL). Alston, I, 141.   P. *283*.

[MESTON, W.]

1823* Ed   *A practical essay on the manner of studying and teaching in Scotland: or a guide to students at the university, to parish schoolmasters, and family tutors. In two parts*, Edinburgh. (BL).   Pp. 44, 61–2, 281–2, 307–8.

METCALFE, Lister   'Curate at Middleham, in the county of York'

[a. 1771] G   *The rudiments of the English tongue; or, the principles of English grammar, methodically digested into plain rules, and adapted to the capacities of children: after the plan of Mr Ruddiman's Latin Rudiments*, 2nd edn, Newcastle, 1771* (BL); 3rd edn Newcastle, 1777* (BL). Alston, I, 288 records a work of the same title, Newcastle, 1769, but this might also be the 1st edn of James Murray's *Rudiments*, [a. 1771], q.v. below. The grammar in Metcalfe's 3rd edn is different from that in his 2nd. Murray considered that Metcalfe had appropriated his (Murray's) grammar and altered its categories: 'Mr Metcalf, in his Edition of these Rudiments, has made so free as to alter the Terms which were used to express some of the Heads of Grammar contained therein. . .This is an unfair Way of publishing the Works of others, thus to alter the very Sense of the Author without his Consent' (Murray, preface).   P. 282.

MIEGE, Guy   1644–1718?   Sometime teacher

1688* G   *The English grammar; or, the grounds, and genius of the English tongue.* (Cambridge UL). Alston records an anonymous pirated edn as *A compleat guide to the English tongue* [1689?] of which BL has a copy dated [1722?]*. The 2nd edn, 1691* (O), retains the original title. Alston, I, 31–3.

MILLAR, James

1855 G   *Outlines of English grammar*. Edinburgh. (O).

[MILLARD, John]

1812 P   *The new art of memory, founded upon the principles taught by M. Gregor von Feinagle: and applied to Chronology, History, Geography, Languages, Systematic Tables, Poetry, Prose, and Arithmetic*. 2nd edn 1813; 3rd edn 1813* (Leeds UL). The first two edns are dated by their prefaces, reprinted in the 3rd edn.   P. 260.

MILLARD, John   'Professor of elocution'

1869 P   *A grammar of elocution*. (BL). 2nd edn 1882. (BL).

MILLEN, John   'Teacher of English, George Square, Glasgow'

1846* G   *An initiatory grammar of the English language*. Edinburgh. (BL); advertised by Oliver and Boyd in 1871.

MILLER, The Misses

1830 G   *The Brighton English grammar.* (BL; O).

MILLIGAN, George

1831* G   *A catechism of English grammar; with select exercises.* Edinburgh. (BL);
2nd edn 1839 (Michigan UL).

MILLIGAN, John

1852 G   *Exposition of the grammatical structure of the English language. Being an
attempt to furnish an improved method of teaching grammar.* Belfast (O); anr edn
Edinburgh, 1854 (O).

[MILNER, John]

1736 B   *Rhetoric; or the principles of oratory delineated . . . now made public as a
testimony of respect to the British youth.* (BL). Alston, VI, 164.

MILNS, William   Master, City Commercial School

[a. 1794] G   [An English grammar] In his *The Well-bred Scholar*, 1794, p. 3, Milns
refers to an English grammar that he wrote and, apparently, published. It
seems (p. 21) to have been a catechetical form of Lowth's grammar.   Pp.
207, 281, 304, 307, 321.

1794* Ed   *The well-bred scholar, or practical essays on the best methods of improving
the taste, and assisting the exertions of youth in their literary pursuits,* 560 pp.
(BL). Alston, III, 410–11.

MILTON, John see J. BUCHANAN, J., 1773: CONNON, C.M., 1855; DEMAUS, R.,
1857; HUNTER, J., 1860c, 1862a, 1862b; MONFRIES, A., 1867; WALKER, J.,
1786; WESLEY, J., 1763.

[Anon.]

1813 G   *A miscellaneous selection of ungrammatical sentences from various authors:
in order to exercise the ingenuity of young persons in applying the rules of English
grammar.* Eighty-nine manuscript pages of quotations, dated 14 April 1813.
Holtom, List 40, item 754.

[Anon.]

1671 Ed   *A model for a school for the better education of youth.* (Illinois UL);
[1675?]* (BL). Authorship uncertain. The dedication is signed A.B., taken by
Lawson and Silver, p. 221, and by Cohen, 1977, to be A. Banister, whose
academy in Chancery Lane the pamphlet advertises. But the model relates also
to the school at Tottenham whose proprietor was Arthur Brett (*DNB*). Mark
Lewis taught there and his work is commended in the pamphlet, which BL,
Wing and Alston (X, 83) attribute to him.   Pp. 298–9.

[Anon.]

1793* BH   *Modern beauties in prose and verse . . . designed for general entertainment; and calculated for the improvement and amusement of youth.* Darlington.
(BL).   P. *191.*

[MOGRIDGE, George]   1787–1854

[a. 1854] RE   *The new illustrated primer. By Old Humphrey. Revised by T.B.S.*
S.W. Partridge, [1870] (Hull UL).

MONFRIES, Alexander

1867 RA   *An introduction to the study of Milton.* (BL).

MONGAN, Roscoe

1864* G   *The practical English grammar; comprising also an analysis of sentences;*

composition, &c. (Glasgow UL; BL). An abridgment was published in the same year. (BL).   Pp. 283; *310, 369.*

1861 S   *The practical spelling book, pronouncing, explanatory, and derivative, with useful annotations from the works of Latham, Trench, Richardson, Worcester, &c.* 2nd edn 1862* (BL); 3rd edn 1864 (BL). At least sixteen edns in all to 1879. The 1st edn is dated by its preface, reprinted in the 2nd edn.   P. *84.*

MONTEITH, R.

1704* S   *The true and genuine art, of exact pointing; as also what concerns the distinction of syllables; the marking of capitals; and italick, or different character: to be used, in prints and manuscripts, as well Latine, as English.* Edinburgh. (Glasgow UL).   P. *330.*

MOODY, T.

[1857] G   *A catechism of English grammar, on an entirely new and improved principle.* (Printed in South Petherton). (O).

MOORE, J.S.   'Master of the Brewers' Company's School'

1838* S   *A new spelling book of the English language.* (BL).

MOORE, John Hamilton

[a. 1784] RA   *The young gentleman and lady's monitor, and English teacher's assistant; being a collection of select pieces from our best modern writers: calculated to eradicate vulgar prejudices and rusticity of manners; improve the understanding; rectify the will; purify the passions; direct the minds of youth to the pursuit of proper objects; and to facilitate their reading, writing, and speaking the English language, with elegance and propriety . . . Divided into small portions for the ease of reading in classes.* 4th edn 1784* (BL); 5th edn 1787 (Liverpool UL); 6th edn 1791 (BL); American edns from 1792 to 1809. Belok, p. 57.   Pp. 193; *192.*

MOORE, Thomas

1810 S   *Orthography and pronunciation.* 176 pp. GB.

[Anon.]

[*c.* 1865] RA   *Moral class book.* Chambers. Advt.

[Anon.]

[*c.* 1840] RA   *The moral and intellectual school-book.* 348 pp. Darton and Clark. Holtom, Cat. 1980, item 598.

[Anon.]

1758* RA   *The moral miscellany: or, a collection of select pieces, in prose and verse, for the instruction and entertainment of youth.* (BL); 2nd edn 1765* (BL). At least six edns in all to 1787. The preface makes it clear that the book was intended for school use.   P. *173.*

[Anon.]

[1819?]* RA   *The moral poetical miscellany; being a collection of short poems, peculiarly adapted to impress on the youthful mind the most exalted sentiments of religion and virtue.* (BL 11601.bb.15). The author's pedagogical intention is shown by the vocabulary preceding each poem.   P. *221.*

MORE, Hannah   1745–83

1782 P   *Sacred dramas; chiefly intended for young persons: the subjects taken from the Bible.* (BL); anr edn Chiswick Press, 1818* (personal). At least twenty-five edns to 1855.   P. *303.*

1799 Ed   *Strictures on the modern system of female education.* 5th edn Dublin, 1800*. Many edns, British and American, to 1858. Alston, X, 334–45.   P. 194.

MORELL, John Daniel   1816–91   Inspector of schools

[1852]* G   *The analysis of sentences explained and systematised, after the plan of Becker's German grammar.* (BL). At least nine edns to 1858.   Pp. *370–1*.

[a. 1872] S   *A complete manual of spelling on the principle of contrast and comparison.* Fifteenth thousand, 1872. (BL).

[1854]* G   *The essentials of English grammar.* (BL). Edns to *c.* 1891. First published in two parts: I, 18 pp., price twopence; II, 27 pp., price threepence.

1871 G   *The first step in grammar.* (BL).

1866* RS   *Graduated series of reading lesson books, 1–6.* See above, Longman, publisher.

1857a G   *A grammar of the English language, together with an exposition of the analysis of sentences.* Edinburgh, 1860 (Cape Town, S.A. Library); London, 1865* (private colln); rev. by P.A. Barnett as *The new Morell,* 1893 (BL); by A.G. Palmer as *Morell's grammar simplified,* [1873] (BL).   P. 81.

1855 Lo   *A handbook of logic for the use of schools and teachers.* (BL); 2nd edn 1857 (BL)

[1872?] Ex   *A practical introduction to English composition on a new plan. With 300 exercises.* (BL); anr edn [*c.* 1880] (Hull UL).

[1874]* RE   *Reading teaching itself by means of a self-consistent notation on the principle of contrast, with five hundred rhymes.* (O).   Pp. 126–7.

1857b* G   *A series of graduated exercises, adapted to Morell's Grammar and Analysis* (private colln); anr edn Edinburgh, 1860 (Cape Town, S.A. Library). A *Key* by W.B. Morgan was published in 1870.

MORELL, John Daniel, and   IHNE, Wilhelm

1857 RA   *A poetical reading book, with aids for grammatical analysis, paragraphing, and criticism.* Edinburgh. *DNB*; anr edn 1860.

MORRICE, David   Teacher

1801* Ed   *The art of teaching, or communicating instruction, examined, methodized, and facilitated; as well as applied to all the branches of scholastic education.* (BL; Nottingham UL). The preface summarises Morrice's career and teaching-posts. The sequel, *Mentor,* 1801*, is concerned with the student's conduct and with his study of mathematics.   Pp. 194; *128*.

MORRIS, Richard   1833–94   Teacher

1867 RA   *Chaucer: Prologue; Knight's Tale; Nonnes Prestes Tale.* Oxford: Clarendon Press (BL).

MORTIMER, F.L., see BEVAN, Favell Lee

MOSCRIP, John   Teacher, 'of the free English reading school, Berwick-upon-Tweed'

1790* S   *The easy instructor: or, the only method to make the orthography and pronunciation of the English language easy . . . For the use of schools,* Berwick. (BL). Alston, IV, 879.   Pp. 60; *35n*.

[Anon.]

[*c.* 1820] RH   *The mother's book of poetry . . . for the use of schools and young minds.*

Advertised, in an undated edn published by Hamilton, Adams, of Mrs Barbauld's *More instructive lessons*, as being 'uniform with Pinnock's *Catechisms*'.

[Anon.]

1821 RE *Mrs Sherwood's primer; or first book for children*, Wellington: F. Houlston. It is not yet known how far, if at all, Mrs Sherwood is the author. Heartman, 1935, p. 119; Morgan, 1977.

MULCASTER, Richard 1532?–1611 High Master, St Paul's School

1582 S *The first part of the Elementarie which entreateth chefelie of the right writing of our English tung.* Ed. E.T. Campagnac, Oxford, 1925*; Scolar Press facsimile 1970*. Alston, VI, 462.   Pp. 372; *115*.

1581 Ed *Positions wherein those primitive circumstances be examined, which are necessarie for the training up of children.* Ed. R.H. Quick, 1888*; facsimile edn, English Experience, Amsterdam, 1971; ed. R.L. deMolen (text slightly abbreviated), N.Y., 1973. Alston, X, 18–19.   Pp. 16, 30; *115*.

[MULLION, Mary]

1820* P *New sacred dramas for young persons.* (BL; Glasgow UL).

[MUNDAY, Anthony] 1553–1633

1600 RA *Bel-vedere: or the garden of the muses.* Anr edn as: *The garden of the muses*, 1610; anr edn, as *Bodenham's Belvedere*, from 1600 edn, Spenser Society, 1875*.   P. *171*.

MUNDAY, Francis 'Schoolmaster in Sarum'

[a. 1721] S *The way to reading made easy and delightful: in two parts.* A spelling-book by Mr Munday is referred to by Isaac Watts in the preface to his *The art of reading*, 1721, and in an advertisement in John Clarke's *An introduction to the making of Latin* in the same year. Munday's spelling-book is listed by L. Howell, *History of the Holy Gospel*, 1729 (Longman, p. 263), and Part I of it is included in the composite *Watts's compleat spelling-book*, Dublin, 1737, q.v. under Watts, 1721. Not in Alston.

MURBY, Thomas Publisher

1868–70* RS *Excelsior readers for all classes of elementary schools, Books 1–6.* Edited by Francis Young. (BL).

[c. 1845] RS *Standard series of elementary reading books*: Book 5, *Poetry and Adventure*, by J.S. Laurie, was published in a 6th edn by Murby in 1845. It is not clear whether this series is related to the series of the same name edited by J.S. Laurie and issued by Longman in 1863.

MURRAY, Alexander Teacher

1785 G *An easy grammar for the use of schools. In three parts. I.* [parts of speech]. *II. Additional remarks . . . III. Exercises of bad English.* Newcastle (no copy); 2nd edn, London and Berwick, 1787* (BL); 3rd edn, London, 1793 (no copy); 4th edn, 1804 (*Gent. Mag.*, 75 (January 1805), 59); 5th edn Berwick, 1806. Alston, I, 422–4.   P. 343.

1778 S *A spelling book on a new plan*, Newcastle. No copy. Alston, IV, 769.

MURRAY, Gerald

1847 G *The reformed grammar; or philosophical test of English composition.* (BL; O); Abridged by the author, 1849 (BL).

MURRAY, James 1732–82

[a. 1771] G *The rudiments of the English tongue: or, the principles of English grammar, methodically digested into plain rules, adapted to the use of schools. To which is subjoined, grammatical exercises upon the parts of speech, and the whole of English syntax, on a plan entirely new.* 2nd edn, Newcastle, 1771* (Nottingham UL). Alston, I, 304a and Supplement p. 7; Higson, 1967, p. 41. The anonymous work of 1769, of the same title and also published in Newcastle, recorded at Alston, I, 288, may be the 1st edn either of James Murray's grammar or of that by Lister Metcalfe, q.v.   P. 338.

MURRAY, L. [pseud.?]

[1814?] C *The young man's best companion, and book of general knowledge, containing English grammar* [etc.] By L. Murray, F.A.S., preface dated 7 July 1814, from edn published by Thomas Kelly, 1824 (Nottingham UL) and 1828* (private coll.). There were many works with this title, as in BL catalogue under MAN.

MURRAY, Lindley 1745–1826

1797a* G *An abridgment of L. Murray's English Grammar, with an appendix, containing an exemplification of the parts of speech, and exercises in syntax, designed for the use of the younger class of learners.* York. (BL); 3rd edn York, 1799* (Leeds UL). Alston, I, 505–10, records edns to 1877 (including 166 American edns after 1800) the latest numbered edn being the 133rd of 1864. *DNB* says there were more than 120 edns of 10,000 copies each, and Altick, p. 389, says 1 million copies were sold by about 1826. T. Martin, 1824, p. 270, says that the abridgment 'passes through three editions annually'. For other British abridgments of Murray's grammar see ELLIS, J., 1837; HARVEY, J., 1841; SMITH, W.B. 1860. American abridgments are listed in NUC.   P. *324. See also pp. 198, 350, 360, 366 for Murray generally.*

1797b* G *English exercises, adapted to the grammar lately published by L. Murray; consisting of exemplifications of the parts of speech; instances of false orthography; violations of the rules of syntax; defects in punctuation; and violations of the rules respecting perspicuity and accuracy. Designed for the benefit of private learners, as well as for the use of schools.* York. (BL); 27th edn York, 1820* (Leeds UL); anr edn London, 1863* (Leeds UL). Alston, III, 416–21, records edns to 1864, the latest numbered edn being the 52nd, of 1848. Both Alston and NUC list over seventy American edns, continuing into the 1880s. For the *Key*, 1797, see below.   Pp. 329; *326.*

1795* G *English grammar, adapted to the different classes of learners, with an appendix, containing rules, and observations for promoting perspicuity in speaking and writing.* York (BL; Leeds UL); 2nd edn York, 1796* (Leeds UL); 3rd edn York, 1797* (Leeds UL); 8th edn York, 1802* (BL); 28th edn York, 1816* (Leeds UL). Alston, I, 480–9, records British edns to 1871; NUC gives over 140 American edns to 1896. *CBEL*, II, 932, estimates that there were 200 edns, world-wide, before 1850.   P. *87.*

1808 G *An English grammar: comprehending the principles and rules of the language, illustrated by appropriate exercises, and a key to the exercises,* 2 vols., York (BL; Leeds UL); 2nd edn, York, 1809* (BL); eight edns to 1853. A combination of the *English grammar* of 1795, the *English exercises* of 1797 and the *Key to the exercises*, 1797. Alston records the edns without distinguishing them from those of the grammar alone (Alston, I, 100–1).

1799* RA   *The English reader: or, pieces in prose and poetry, selected from the best writers. Designed to assist young persons to read with propriety and effect; to improve their language and sentiments; and to inculcate some of the most important principles of piety and virtue. With a few preliminary observations on the principles of good reading*, York. (Leeds UL). At least 25 British edns to 1845 and over 350 American ones to 1860 (*NUC*).   P. *183*.

1804* S   *An English spelling book; with reading lessons adapted to the capacities of children: in three parts, calculated to advance the learners by natural and easy gradations; and to teach orthography and pronunciation together*, York. (BL.) At least fifty-one British edns to 1854; thirteen American ones to 1829.   P. 103.

[a. 1805]   *A first book for children*, York. 13th edn, York, 1818* (Nottingham UL); 17th edn, York, 1825 (BL); unnumbered edn, 1846 (Wisconsin UL); '150th thousand', 1859 (*DNB*). American edns: 3rd edn N.Y., 1805: 5th edn Philadelphia, 1818 (NUC).

1801* RA   *Introduction to the English Reader; or, a selection of pieces in prose and poetry; calculated to improve the younger class of learners, in reading; and to imbue their minds with the love of virtue. With rules and observations for assisting children to read with propriety.* York (BL); 22nd York, 1825* (BL). 31 numbered British edns to 1836, and unnumbered ones in 1841, 1843 and 1865. 107 American edns to 1880 (NUC).   Pp. *183, 195*.

1797c G   *Key to the exercises adapted to L. Murray's English Grammar. By the author of the exercises.* [York] (BL); 18th edn York, 1827* (Leeds UL); 23rd edn York, 1837* (personal). About thirty British edns to 1855 and twenty-seven American ones to 1854 (NUC). Often reprinted with the *Exercises*.

1800* RA   *Sequel to the English Reader; or, elegant selections in prose and poetry. Designed to improve the highest class of learners in reading; to establish a taste for just and accurate composition; and to promote the interests of piety and virtue.* York (Leeds UL); 2nd edn York, 1805 (Leeds UL); 3rd edn York, 1808 (BL). At least eight British edns in all to 1843 and thirty-eight American ones to 1848.   Pp. 193; *183*.

MURRY, Ann

1778* S   *Mentoria: or, the young ladies instructor, in familiar conversations on moral and entertaining subjects*, (BL). Dialogue 2 is 'On Orthography, and the Practical Use of Grammar'. Twelve edns to 1823. Alston, III, 338–44. *The Sequel to Mentoria* was first published in 1799.

[Anon.]

1794* Ex   *Musae Berkhamstedienses: or poetical prolusions by some young gentlemen of Berkhamsted School.* Berkhamsted. (BL); 2nd edn as *Poetical prolusions in the English and Latin languages by some . . .*, Berkhamsted, 1799* (BL).   Pp. 291–3.

[Anon.]

[1750?] RE   *A museum for young gentlemen and ladies; or, a private tutor for little masters and misses. Containing . . . Directions for reading with elegance and propriety* [eleven further sections], (Bishop Lonsdale College, Derby); 4th edn

1763* (BL); 15th edn [1796?]* (Nottingham UL); seventeen edns to 1806, and another, by Pickering and Chatto in 1932 (*NCBEL*, II, 413). Thwaite, 1966, p. 163. Roscoe, J253.

[Anon.]

[*c.* 1850] S *My first lesson book to teach me spelling and reading*, Keble. Chalmers, p. 146.

[Anon.]

[*c.* 1870?] RA *My poetry book*, Religious Tract Society. (Wandsworth PL).

MYLIUS, William Frederick Teacher at Christ's Hospital

1809a D *The Christ's Hospital dictionary of the English tongue*, M.J. Godwin: 2nd edn as: *Mylius's school dictionary*, M.J. Godwin, 1809, revised by William Godwin and with his own grammar added, *A new guide to the English tongue*, q.v. 9th edn 1819* (BL). Marshall, p. 279, says the dictionary had sold 25,000 copies by 1819.

[1809?] RA *The first book of poetry for the use of schools. Intended as reading lessons for the younger classes.* There is uncertainty about the date of the first edn: Gumuchian, 3596, gives 1811; NBL 1973, no. 758, gives 1810; Marshall, pp. 279, 452 gives 1809. No copy earlier than 1811* (BL) has been traced. The authorship is also in doubt. Marshall offers evidence for thinking that the book is 'probably Godwin's work'. The anthology contains a number of pieces attributed to 'Mrs Leicester' (i.e. Charles and Mary Lamb, from their *Poetry for children*, 1809). Commentators vary in the number of poems that they say Mylius took from the Lambs: they consult varying edns of both works; they do not distinguish between pieces and complete poems, nor between Mylius's three anthologies. The edn of 1811 contains twenty-seven pieces from 'Mrs Leicester'. Anr edn 1820* (BL); 10th edn 1828 (BL). A 12th edn, revised by W. Routledge, 1847* (personal), is virtually a new selection, reducing the number of poems by the Lambs to three.

1809b RA *The junior class book: or reading lessons for every day in the year . . . For the use of schools*, M.J. Godwin. This work is said on the t.p. of Mylius' *The poetical class-book*, 1810, to be already published, and is therefore not the work referred to in the preface: a similar collection in the press, for junior pupils. The latter must be his *The poetical class-book*, 1810, q.v. Marshall, p. 279, argues that *The junior class book* is largely Godwin's work.

1810* RA *The poetical class-book; or, reading lessons for every day in the year, selected from the most popular English poets, ancient and modern. For the use of schools.* (BL); 2nd edn 1814; 7th edn 1835. Marshall, pp. 288, 452, argues that the work is William Godwin's.

MYLNE, Andrew 1775?–1856

[a. 1818] G *An epitome of English grammar, with a variety of exercises for the use of schools.* 5th edn Edinburgh, 1818* (NLS); 7th edn Edinburgh, 1820 (NYct); 11th edn Edinburgh, 1832, GB; 12th edn 1837, Hunter, 1848; anr edn New York, 1854.

N., J. [probably John Needham Minister of Callowhill Street Church, Bristol]

1765* RA *Select lessons in prose and verse, from various authors, designed for the improvement of youth. To which are added a few original pieces.* Bristol (BL); 2nd edn Bristol, 1774* (BL); 5th edn Bristol, 1793* (personal); at least eleven edns in all to 1807. The compiler's identity was suggested to me by Jonathan Barry.   P. 175.

N., J.

[*c.* 1800] RH   *The half-holiday task book; or mirror of the mind: consisting of numerous stories and interesting tales, in prose and verse; calculated to enlighten the minds, and improve the hearts of young children of either sex.* (V&A).

N., J.

[*c.* 1835?]* RH   *Blossoms of peace: a series of tales and narratives, in prose and verse; designed as easy lessons for young persons of either sex.* (BL). Estimates of the book's date vary from 1825 to 1840.

NARES, Robert   1753–1829   Sometime teacher

1784* P   *Elements of orthoepy: containing a distinct view of the whole analogy of the English language; so far as it relates to pronunciation, accent, and quantity.* (BL); as *General rules for the pronunciation of the English language,* 1792 (BL); Scolar Press facsimile of 1784 edn, 1968*. Alston, VI, 499–500.

NASMITH, Mrs

[1856] G   (Mrs Nasmith's) *Map of English grammar.* Kingsland. (O).

NATIONAL SOCIETY FOR PROMOTING THE EDUCATION OF THE POOR IN THE PRINCIPLES OF THE ESTABLISHED CHURCH

1812–14 RS   *Central school books.* Goldstrom, 1972a, pp. xi, 16; anr edn 1836* (BL, 863.i.22).

1867–8* RS   *National reading books, Books 1–6* (BL). Goldstrom, 1972a, pp. 172, 215.

[1868] RS   *National reading books: religious series, Books 1–3* (BL).

1852* RS   *Reading for national schools, Books 1–2.* (BL, 12985.aa.33 (7) and (8)).

See also *The practical manual . . .,* 1833

NEALE, Jane K.

1866 RA   *Tales for village schools. Amusing and instructive.* (BL).

NEEDES, Richard

1812 G   *Examples of parsing, for children. Intended as an introduction to the parsing of those parts of sentences, &c given in Mr Murray's small grammar as parsing exercises.* (BL).

[Anon.]

1711 La   *The needful attempt, to make language and divinity plain and easie.* (Bath UL); Scolar Press facsimile 1969*. Alston, VI, 537; Abercrombie, 1965a, pp. 57–60; Cohen, 1977, p. 49. Orthographical reform; the author's main recommendations are given in Latin also.   Pp. 29–30, 42; *61.*

NEIL, Samuel   1825–1901   Teacher

1857 Ex   *Composition and elocution; or, hints on how to speak and how to write: designed as a manual for self-instruction. DNB;* 2nd edn 1857* (BL).

1854* Ex   *The elements of rhetoric; a manual of the laws of taste, including the theory and practice of composition.* (BL).

1873 P   *Julius Caesar, with introduction and notes.* Collins School and College Classics. (BL).

1867* RA   *Pope's Essay on Criticism with notes critical, explanatory, illustrative, and grammatical, &c. Specially prepared for the use of students.* [Series title] University B.A. examination. (BL).

[a. 1859] Ex *The young debater.* 2nd edn 1859 (BL); anr edn 1863 *DNB*.

NELSON, T.   Publisher

1858 RS   *Reading lessons.* no. 5 (O).

NELSON, W.L.   St Stephen's School, Edinburgh

[c. 1840] RS   *Scriptural educational course*, 1–4. *The primer*, [1870] (BL); *First reading book*, Edinburgh, 1851 (BL); *Second reading book*, 3rd edn Edinburgh, 1846 (BL); *Third reading book*, 4th edn Edinburgh, 1852. (BL).

NESBIT, Anthony   1778–1859   Master of an academy in Kennington

1817 G   *An introduction to English parsing, adapted to Murray's Grammar and Exercises.* (BL); 2nd edn York, 1823 (Columbia UL).

NESBIT, Anthony, NESBIT, J.C., and NESBIT, E.P.

1846 Ed   *Prospectus of the classical, commercial and scientific academy . . . of Kennington Lane.* Lambeth, 1846 (BL).

[Anon.]

[c. 1800]* RE   *New and improved child's first book; or an introduction to reading. For schools.* London: Simpkin Marshall, and Dudley: J. Rann. Pp. 84 (BL). This is the cover title of an edn of *Reading made completely easy, or an introduction to reading the Holy Bible.* Cf. DYKE, 1746; PALEY, 1790; and *The new readng made easy* [a. 1790].

[Anon.]

1771* G, D   *A new and improved spelling dictionary of the English language; teaching to write as well as to spell correctly . . . To which is added . . . a compendious English grammar.* (BL; Glasgow UL). Alston, IV, 719.

[Anon.]

[c. 1840?] RE   *A new and much improved reading made easy. Being an easy and expeditious method of initiating children into the knowledge of the English language.* Stereotype edn, Dublin. (Iowa UL).

[Anon.]

1837 RE   *A new and pleasing introduction to reading: designed to conduct the youthful mind into a progressive acquaintance with the knowledge of letters, the sound of syllables, and the use of words*, Bocking: J.F. Shearcroft. (Chalmers, p. 146).

[Anon.]

[a. 1762] Ex   *The new art of letter-writing, divided into two parts* [1. Directions; 2. Model letters] *By a gentleman of fortune for his own amusement and the instruction of his children*, 2nd edn 1762 (BL 1607/1585) 3rd edn 1763 (Duke UL).

[Anon.]

[1786?] P   *The new art of speaking, or, a complete modern system of rhetoric, elocution and oratory.* (BL). Alston, VI, 420a; Wardle, p. 172.

A new book of spelling with syllables see *An alphabet and plaine pathewaie*

[Anon.]

[a. 1808] RA   *A new collection, in prose and verse, for the use of schools.* 22nd edn Glasgow, 1808 (NLS).

[Anon.]

1785 Ex   *The new complete letter-writer: or, the art of correspondence. Containing letters on the most important subjects* [etc.] . . . *To which are added, the principles of politeness* [etc.] . . . *and a copious English spelling dictionary*, Glasgow (Lib.

Co., Philadelphia); Glasgow, 1788* (Glasgow, Mitchell L.)

[Anon.]   'By a school-master in the country'

1736* G   *A new English accidence, by way of short question and answer, built upon the plan of the Latin grammar, so far as it agrees with, and is consistent with the nature and genius of the English tongue. Designed for the use and benefit, and adapted to the capacity of young lads at the English school. In order to teach them the grounds of their mother tongue, and fit them for the more easy and expeditious attaining the grammar of the Latin, and any other language.* (O). Alston, I, 75; *EGC*; Vorlat, 1975.

[Anon.]

1855* RE   *The new English primer, or youth's instructor, being the second book for children, consisting of progressive lessons for youth.* Merthyr-Tyddfil: R. Lewis. (BL).

[Anon.]

1846* S   *The new English spelling book, designed to teach orthography and orthoepy: with a critical analysis of the language, and a classification of its elements. On a new plan.* (BL; Harvard).

[Anon.]

[*c.* 1820]* RE   *A new first book* [*on an easy plan*, Glasgow: John Hadden] (NLS 2/724(7), lacks t.p.); anr edn Glasgow, John Hadden [1860] (BL).

[Anon.]

[*c.* 1820]* RE   *A new second book, on an easy plan.* Glasgow: John Hadden (NLS 2/724 (8)).

[Anon.]

[*c.* 1825?] RE   *New improved young child's tutor*, Derby, T. Richardson. Pp. 12. (Bedford CHE).

[Anon.]

1791 RA   *A new introduction to reading; or a collection of easy lessons, arranged on a new plan. Designed for the use of schools.* Mon. Rev., n.s. 9 (November 1792), 328; 2nd edn [1793] Alston, IV, 903, from *British Critic*, 4 (1794), 195. Illinois UL has an edn of 1795. The publisher's dedication to a 3rd edn, not traced, is reprinted in the 4th edn 1797* (London printed, Baltimore reprinted) in Bordeaux Municipal Library, Alston, IV, 924. An edn of 1804* (BL; Yale) not mentioned by Alston, is a 'third edition enlarged'. All these edns need to be looked into. Alston treats the 1797 edn as a separate work by William Enfield because it professes to be 'designed as an introduction to *The Speaker*'. But publishers often tried to link their works to Enfield's famous collection, and the differences between 1797 and 1804 are compatible with the revision implied by the title of 1804. A further complication is that the 1797 edn reprints the preface of the 2nd edn, in which it is explained that that edn is a simplified form of the 1st.

[Anon.]

1843 RE   *New juvenile reader.* Derby: T. Richardson. Chalmers, p. 154.

[Anon.]

[1832?]* RE   *The new London primer*, Orlando Hodgson, 14 pp. (BL 12981.a.41(1); V&A); anr edn [1854] (BL).

[Anon.]

[1854]* RE   *New London primer, being an easy introduction to the various English* *spelling books*, T. Goode (BL 12985.aa.32(1)); 1855* (BL); n.d. (BL; Wandsworth PL).

[Anon.]

[*c.* 1800] RE *The new London reading made completely easy, or an introduction to reading the Holy Bible*, London, T. Evans (NBL, 1946, no. 51).

[Anon.]

[*c.* 1820] RE *The new London reading made easy, or the child's own book, to which is added select pieces of poetry and the church catechism*, new edn. (Preston PL).

[Anon.]

1771* S *A new lottery book of birds and beasts, for children to learn their letters by as soon as they can speak*. Newcastle (V&A; BL; Nottingham UL).

[Anon.]

1819* RE *A new lottery book, on a plan entirely new. Designed to allure little ones into a knowledge of their letters &c by way of diversion*. Edinburgh (V&A 60.T.156). Whalley, p. 33.   P. 71.

[Anon.]

1789 RA *The new mentor; being a miscellaneous selection, in prose and verse, from the most celebrated authors; calculated to form the taste, and improve the mind, of the rising generation. Highly proper for the use of public seminaries, and adapted to the youth of both sexes*. (*Mon. Rev.*, n.s. 111 (November 1790), 338); 1810 (Chicago UL).

[Anon.]

[1859]* RE *New model primer*, T. Goode (BL 12983.a.68(8)).

[Anon.]

1749 S *A new playbook for children, or an easy and natural introduction to the art of reading*. T. Harris. Chalmers, p. 148.

[Anon.]

[1859]* RE *New preparatory primer*. T. Goode. (BL).

[Anon.]

[*c.* 1853?]* RE *New primer*, T. Goode. 6 pp. (BL 12981.ccc.16(9); O.

[Anon.]

[*a.* 1838]* RE *The new primer; consisting of easy lessons in reading and spelling. To which is added suitable prayers, &c. &c.*, Shrewsbury: Tibnam. (Bedford CHE). Inscription date 6 May 1838.

[Anon.]

[1859]* RE *New primer for a good child*, T. Goode. 24 pp. (BL 12983.a.68 (10)).

[Anon.]

[1830?] RE *New primer for the use of young children*, Derby: T. Richardson. Tuer, p. 476; [*c.* 1845]* (V&A 60.R. Box XII). Chalmers, p. 154, gives *c.* 1825. Undated edns in Nottingham UL and Bedford CHE.

[Anon.]

[*c.* 1845?] RE *The new primer, in words of one syllable*, Derby: J. and C. Mozley. (V&A 60.R.Box II). NBL, 1949, No. 155.

[Anon.]

1830* RE *The new primer or first book for children*, Ellesmere: T. Thompson, 35 pp. (Bedford CHE).

[Anon.]

[1860?]* RE   *A new primer; or, infant's easy book*, for the booksellers, 16 pp. (BL 12981.a.41(5)).

[Anon.]

[a. 1835] RE   *The new primer, or ladder to learning. Consisting of words of two letters to easy reading lessons (sic)*, London: John Limbird. Advt. in Innes, a. 1835.

[Anon.]

[1693] RE   *A new primer, or, the child's recreacon, teaching an easy and speedy way to spell and reade English, with a short & plaine catechisme and godly prayers and graces.* No copy. *SE*(E), 12 March 1693. Not in Alston.

[Anon.]

[c. 1820]* RE   *New reading made easy.* Derby: T. Richardson (BL; V&A).

[Anon.]

[c. 1825?] RE   *New reading made easy, consisting of a variety of useful lessons.* Alnwick: W. Davidson. (Nottingham UL; Wandsworth PL).

[Anon.]

[c. 1820] Re   *A new reading made easy: containing a great variety of easy spelling and reading lessons.* Devonport: Samuel and John Keys (advt.).

[Anon.]

[a. 1790] RE   *The new reading made easy; or an introduction to the reading of the Holy Bible*, new edn. H. Goldney (Stafford PL); Lincoln: W. Brooke, 1803, Sotheby HIC, IV (October 1976), lot 1860; Alston, IV, 875.

[Anon.]

[1861]* RE   *The new royal primer*, J. Bysh, 24 pp. (BL 12983.a.66).

[Anon.]

1835* RE   *The new royal spelling primer*, Derby: T. Richardson. (BL 12835.aa.80; Bedford CHE). Chalmers, p. 153, says Thomas Richardson was himself the author.

[Anon.]

1820 P   *New sacred dramas for young persons.* Longman. Modelled on Hannah More's *Sacred dramas.* Bookseller's catalogue.

[Anon.]

1796 RE   *A new sequel to Mrs Barbauld's Lessons, adapted to children from four to seven years old. By the compiler of An Easy Introduction to Reading, &c.* (title from 4th edn) Nottingham: Sutton, Chalmers, p. 148; 2nd edn London: G. Sael, 1796, Chalmers; 4th edn, G. Sael, 1797* (Cambridge UL).

[Anon.]

[c. 1830?]* RE   *New Tom Thumb, consisting of a series of easy and useful lessons adapted expressly for schools.* Newcastle: T. Simpson and Sons, 8 pp (Nottingham UL).

[Anon.]

[c. 1799]* RE   *The new universal primer, or, an easy book suited to the tender capacities of children. Authorised by His Majesty King George*, Derby: J. Drewry. (DES). Undated edns in Bedford CHE; Nottingham UL; BL (12805.a.36; Ch.800/75). Chalmers, p. 148.

NEWBERY, John   1713–67   Possibly the author of some of the following:

1745–8   *The circle of the sciences; or the compendious library.* The series originally comprised seven numbered volumes, published in 1745–6: a spelling-book; a grammar; a dictionary; penmanship; arithmetic; rhetoric; poetry. In 1748 three volumes were added: logic; geography; chronology; but, presumably to keep the volumes to the liberal number seven, the volume on penmanship was excluded from, and the spelling-book and the dictionary were made introductory to, the series. The order of the volumes in 1748 was: grammar; arithmetic; rhetoric; poetry; logic; geography; chronology. Volumes on criticism, history and philosophy were announced but not, Roscoe thinks, published. *See* p. 383, *above.*

[1745?] S   *The royal battledore; or first book for children to learn their letters and figures.* Advert., Thwaite, 1966, p. 160; as: *The royal battledore: being the first introductory part of The Circle of the Sciences,* n.d. Roscoe, J21(3A); anr edn [*c.* 1780] Roscoe, J21(4) (O).

[1745?] S   *An easy introduction to the English language: or, a pretty entertaining spelling-book for little masters and misses.* Advt., Thwaite, 1966, p. 161, Roscoe, J70; as: *The infant tutor: or, an easy spelling-book for . . .* Advt., Thwaite, 1966, p. 169; 6th edn 1763* (BL). Edns to 1783.

1745* G   *An easy introduction to the English language; or, a compendious grammar for the use of young gentlemen, ladies, foreigners. Being the second volume of The Circle of the Sciences.* (BL); as: *Grammar made familiar and easy . . . being the first volume of The Circle of the Sciences,* 2nd edn 1748*; six further edns, variously numbered, to 1787, Roscoe, J64. In 1776* the grammar was issued together with the rhetoric as: *Grammar and rhetorick, being the first and third volumes of The Circle of the Sciences*; the 1776 volume contains also a second English grammar, intended particularly as a preparation for Latin. Alston, I, 91–9; Roscoe, J65.   P. *319.*

Spelling dictionaries: the complexities of publication can be followed only by close reference to Roscoe, 1973, who gives locations. He distinguishes three similar dictionaries: I. *An easy spelling dictionary,* 1745, continued as *A spelling dictionary* from 1748 to 1786, Roscoe, J71. J268. II. *A new spelling dictionary,* [a. 1780], Roscoe, J263A. III. *Newbery's new spelling dictionary,* 1788 and 1792, Roscoe, J265.

I. 1745 D, G   *An easy spelling dictionary of the English language, on a new plan . . . being the third volume of The Circle of the Sciences.* Editions consulted: Dublin, 1753*; 5th edn 1755*; 6th edn 1757*; 11th edn 1766*; 12th edn Dublin, 1769*. An English grammar was introduced into the 1755 edn. For the 11th edn see below.

II. [a. 1780]* D   *A new spelling dictionary of the English language . . . to which is prefixed, a short English grammar.* (BL 12981.de.10). Roscoe, J263A; Alston, IV, 576. The so-called English grammar is quite different from that in 1755, above: it contains letters, punctuation, division of syllables, quantity and accent, but nothing on parts of speech or syntax.

III. 1788* D   *Newbery's new spelling dictionary of the English language.* Roscoe, J265, Alston, IV, 578. Roscoe does not record any grammar, but a copy in BL (12984.a.59) reads '. . . to which is prefixed, a new and concise introduction to English grammar'. This grammar differs substantially from those mentioned above in that it gives nine parts of speech rather than four, but it too has no syntax.

The grammars published by Newbery have received attention, although not from

Roscoe, because Newbery is recorded, in December 1766, as having paid Goldsmith five guineas for 'writing an English grammar' (Balderston, p. 32) and it is tempting, especially for booksellers, to attribute one of these grammars to Goldsmith. Contrary, however, to the tradition noted by Alston, IV, 571, and followed by Blackwell (Cat. A1115, 1978, p. 19) the grammar in the 1766 edn of the spelling-dictionary of 1745 is not a new one. It is the same in substance (four parts of speech, especially) as the grammar in the 1755 edn and as the one in *The pocket dictionary*, 1753. Apart from the grammar in *Newbery's new spelling dictionary* (above), 1788, and from the grammar for Latin in the combined grammar and rhetoric of 1776 (Roscoe, J65, Alston, I, 97) the variations in wording, arrangement and subsidiary contents such as punctuation amongst these grammars are not sufficient to make a 'new' grammar in the sense usually attributed to Newbery's payment. But Goldsmith may very well have rearranged and superficially revised existing material.

1748 Lo   *Logic made familiar and easy to young gentlemen and ladies. To which is added a compendious system of metaphysics, or ontology. Being the fifth volume of The Circle of the Sciences.* (BL); 2nd edn 1755; 3rd edn 1769* (BL). At least three other edns to 1789, Roscoe, J66. Combined with *The art of poetry* in one volume as: *Logic, ontology, and the art of poetry*, 1776. Alston, VII, 225–31; Roscoe, J67.   P. 313.

1746* B   *The art of rhetorick laid down in an easy and entertaining manner, and illustrated with several beautiful orations from Demosthenes, Cicero, Sallust, Homer, Shakespear, Milton, &c. Being the sixth volume of The Circle of the Sciences.* (BL); as: *Rhetoric made familiar and easy to young gentlemen and ladies, with* . . . 2nd edn 1748* (BL); 3rd edn 1769* (BL). Four other edns to 1789. Alston, VI, 182–8; Roscoe, J69.   P. *164.*

1746* RA   *The art of poetry made easy, and embellish'd with great variety of the most shining epigrams, epitaphs, songs, odes, pastorals, &c. from the best authors. Being the seventh volume of The Circle of the Sciences.* (BL). As: *Poetry made familiar and easy to young gentlemen and ladies* . . . *Being the fourth volume of The Circle of the Sciences.* 2nd edn 1748* (BL); 3rd edn 1769* (BL). Two further edns to 1788, Roscoe, J68. See the anon. *The art of poetry*, 1762.   Pp. 164–5, 181.

1756 Ex   *Letters on the most common, as well as important, occasions of life, by* [fourteen named writers] . . . *with* . . . *a dissertation on the epistolary style* . . . *For the use of young gentlemen and ladies.* (BL); at least nine edns to 1788. Roscoe, J266.

[1744?] RH   *A little pretty pocket-book, intended for the instruction and amusement of little Master Tommy and pretty Miss Polly* . . . *To which is added, a little song-book, being a new attempt to teach children the use of the English alphabet, by way of diversion.* No copy. 10th edn 1760 (BL, incomplete); 1767 (BL); edns to 1787. Facsimile of 1787 edn, Worcester, Mass., ed. F.G. Melcher, N.Y., 1944; facsimile of 1767 edn, ed. M.F. Thwaite, OUP, 1966*. Roscoe, J225; Rosenbach, 120; Darton, chap. 1.

1753* D   *A pocket dictionary or complete English expositor* . . . *to which is prefix'd an introduction containing an history of the English language, with a compendious grammar.* (BL); 2nd edn 1758* (BL); 3rd edn 1765* (BL); 4th edn 1779. Starnes and Noyes, 1946, chap. 20; Alston, VI, 165–8; Roscoe, J295.   P. *342.*

NEWBERY, Thomas

1563 RH   *A booke in Englysh metre, of the great marchaunt man called Dives Pragmaticus, very preaty for children to rede: whereby they may the better, and more readyer, rede and wryte wares and implementes, in this world contayned* (Manchester, John Rylands L.); John Rylands Facsimiles no 2, Manchester, 1910*. L.B. Wright, 1935, p. 367.   Pp. 138–9.

[NEWMAN, F.W.]

1850 RA   *A collection of poetry for the practice of elocution.* (O).

NEWTON, John   1622–78

1677* C   *The English Academy: or, a brief introduction to the seven liberal arts . . . Chiefly intended for the instruction of young scholars, who are acquainted with no other than their native language.* (BL); 2nd edn 1693* (BL; Hull UL). Alston, III, 176–7.   Pp. 322; 57.

1671a* Lo   *An introduction to the art of logick: composed for the use of English schools, and all such who having no opportunity of being instructed in the Latine tongue, do however desire to be instructed in this liberal science.* (BL); 2nd edn 1678 (O). Alston, VII, 63–4; Howell, 1956, p. 316.   Pp. 143, 148.

1671b* B   *An introduction to the art of rhetorick. Composed for the benefit of young schollars and others, who have not opportunity of being instructed in the Latine tongue; and is very helpful to understand the figurative expressions in the holy Scriptures.* (O) Alston, VI, 93; Howell, 1956, p. 271.   Pp. 140, 142, 153, 155–6; *372.*

1668* Ed   *The scale of interest, or the use of decimal fractions, and the table of logarithmes.* (BL). The lengthy preface discusses Newton's views on education in grammar and English schools.

[1669]* G   *School pastime for young children: or the rudiments of grammar, in an easie and delightful method, for teaching of children to read English distinctly, and write it truly. In which, by way of preface, a new method is propounded, for the fitting of children first for trades, and then for the Latin, and other languages.* (BL). Alston I, 27 = IV, 64. Vorlat, 1975.   Pp. 35, 143; *50, 121, 372.*

NIBLETT, Alfred Newson

1861 G   *English class handy-book: comprising the outlines of English grammar.* (O).

NICHOLSON, George   1760–1825

1803–7 C   *The juvenile preceptor; or a course of moral and scientific instruction,* 4 vols. Ludlow:–

vol. I   1803 RE   *Spelling and reading lessons not exceeding one syllable* (BL); 2nd edn 1805* (BL; O).   Pp. 120; *43.*

vol. II   1803* RA   *Spelling lessons from two to seven syllables, with appropriate moral tales, and poems.* (BL).

vol. III   Not traced.

vol. IV   [a. 1807] D   *A spelling and pronouncing dictionary; arranged in four parts, according to the number of syllables*; 2nd edn 1807* (BL).

NICHOLSON, J[ames]   Teacher ('Mathematician')

[1793]* G   *The rudiments or first principles of English grammar,* Newcastle (O); 2nd edn Newcastle, 1802 (Newcastle PL). Alston, I, 471 and Supplement, where he gives Nicholson's first name as James; Tyler, I, 73, calls him Joseph.

NICHOLSON, William

1864* G   *The grammar of the English language made easy: with numerous practical* *exercises in . . . derivation; comprising Anglo-Saxon, or English, Latin, and Greek affixes, and prefixes, and very comprehensive lists . . . amounting to nearly 10,000 words.* Halifax: W. Nicholson. (BL; O). Pp. 357, 368.

1843 G *The young man's self-teaching grammar of the English language.* (BL).

NIGHTINGALE, Joseph 1775–1824 Sometime teacher

1822 G *The lady's grammar; or, an easy and familiar introduction to the English tongue.*

NIXON, H.

1826 G *The English parser, being a complete and original system of English parsing, with examples and models.* (BL; Columbia UL).

1833 G *A new and comprehensive English grammar* (GB; not BL, NUC)

NIXON, William

1781 B *Prosody made easy,* Cork (BL); Philadelphia, 1786 (BL).

NORWOOD, Mr Included among the list of authors of English grammars in J. Jones' *A step towards an English education,* 2nd edn 1740, p. 22. No grammar yet traced.

[Anon.]

[1845?] G *Notes on English grammar for the use of juvenile pupils* (BL; O).

[Anon.]

1820 S, RE *The Nottingham new reading made easy: or, first book for children; containing the most plain and easy lessons in reading and spelling,* Nottingham. Chalmers, p. 148.

[Anon.]

1824* G *Observations on grammar, &c. for the use of the grammar school, Leeds,* Leeds: Robinson and Hernaman. (Leeds City L.) P. *363.*

[Anon.]

1813* Ed *Observations on works of fiction in general, and particularly those for childhood and adolescence.* (BL). Pp. 247–8.

ODELL, J.

1806 La *An essay on the elements, accents and prosody of the English language, intended to have been printed as an introduction to Mr Boucher's supplement to Dr Johnston's Dictionary.* (BL).

[Anon.]

1734* Ed *Of education.* (BL). Rothblatt, p. 153; Alston, X, 196. P. 305.

OGILVIE, John 1733–1813

1774* Ex *Philosophical and critical observations on the nature, characters and various species of composition,* 2 vols. (BL). Facsimile reprint, Garland Press, N.Y. Alston, VI, 231. P. 305.

OLDFIELD, Joshua 1656–1729 Teacher

1707* Ed *An essay towards the improvement of reason; in the pursuit of learning, and conduct of life.* (BL; O). Alston, III, 796; Bryant, p. 107. Pp. 278; *148.*

OLIPHANT, R.

1781* G *A compendium of English grammar drawn up for the use of the young ladies at the boarding school,* Newcastle upon Tyne. (Newcastle PL). Alston, I, 374.

OLIVER, Samuel

1825* G *A general, critical grammar of the Inglish language; on a system novel, and extensive: exhibiting investigations of the analogies of language, written, and* *spoken, discussions on the authorities of grammarians, and a general grammatical criticism of the learned and the modern languages in comparative illustration of the Inglish tongue: to which is prefixt a discourse on the study of languages in polite education. For the author, Baldwin, Cradock & Joy.* (BL; O).   Pp. 90: *368.*

OLLEY, J.B.

1827 G   *The root of grammar correctly taught in one month, particularly recommended for the nursery, preparatory schools and parents.* (*CBEL*, 3, 135).

OLLYFFE, Thomas   Writing-master

1719* RA   *Miscellaneous sentences in prose and verse, collected from many eminent authors, and digested into alphabetical order, for the use of schools.* (BL).   P. 181.

[Anon.]

[a. 1779] RE   *The only reading made easy; or, child's best instructor: containing emblematic cuts for the alphabet, select scripture and moral sentences, instructive fables, and edifying pieces of poetry. Methodically digested into lessons from one to seven syllables, properly divided, and calculated after the manner prescribed by Mr Locke, to gain the attention of children.* Advertisement in Robert Green, 1779.

[Anon.]

1779* G   *The only true guide to English grammar; displaying the genuine structure and peculiar idiom of the English language; adapted to the capacities of children, and such as are only English scholars* [etc.], Dumfries. Alston, I, 365, records a MS attribution, on the only known copy (Philadelphia Library Co) to John M. Ray.   P. *324.*

[Anon.]

1798* RA   *The oratorical instructor; being a collection of pieces for the use of those desirous to attain eloquence.* (BL). Alston, VI, 434.

[Anon.]

[c. 1825] RE   *The original reading made easy improved,* Beilby & Knotts. Chalmers, p. 149.

[Anon.]

[a. 1765] S   *Orthography new modelled; or Dixwell's new method of spelling.* Dixwell. *Gent. Mag.*, 35 (January 1765), 48. Not traced.

OSBORN, T.   'Schoolmaster'

1688 S   *A rational way of teaching. Whereby children, and others, may be instructed in true reading, pronouncing and writing of the English tongue* [etc.] (Hamburg UL); Scolar Press facsimile 1969*. Dobson, I, 374; Alston, IV, 155 and Plate 26 for t.p.; C. Johnson, (1904) 1963, p. 21, reproduces frontispiece. Presumably by the same author as the following.   Pp. 109, 373.

OSBORN, Thomas   'Minister of the gospel and teacher of a private school in Hatton Garden'

[1694] S   *The grounds of reading, writing, and pronouncing, of the English tongue laid down in a new and easie method.* No copy, *TC*, II, 513; anr edn [1701] no copy, *TC*, III, 262. Alston, IV, 176–7.

OSWALD, John   1804–67

1833 D   *An etymological dictionary of the English language . . . adapted to the modern system of tuition.* Edinburgh: A. and C. Black; anr edn 1834; 7th edn 1847 (BL).

[a. 1842] La   *An etymological manual of the English language.* 8th edn Edinburgh, 1842 (BL); 10th edn 1843 (BL); 12th edn 1846 (BL).

[a. 1850] La   *The etymological primer . . . of the English language, Part II.* 6th edn Edinburgh, 1850 (BL).

[a. 1839] G   *Outlines of English grammar.* 5th edn Edinburgh, 1839, Hunter 1848; 6th edn 1849 (BL).

[Anon.]

1845 G   *Outline of English grammar,* B. Steill, Royal Pictorial Toy Books. Osborne, 1975, p. 140; Sotheby, HIC, 6 (1977), lot 2866.

[Anon.]

[a. 1857] G   *Outline of English grammar,* Sunday School Union. (Leicester UL).

[Anon.]

1791* G   *Outlines of English grammar. For the use of children: intended as an introduction to performances upon a more extended scale.* Worcester. (Cambridge UL.) Alston, I, 457.

[OWEN, Edward]

1777* G   *A short system of English grammar, with a copious collection of exercises to explain the rules of orthography, syntax and punctuation,* Warrington. (Warrington PL). Alston, I, 344.   Pp. 122; *283.*

OWEN, John

1652 RE   *The primer, or an easie way to teach children the true reading of English, with a necessary catechisme to instruct youth in the grounds of Christian religion.* (BL).

OWEN, John   'Master of a school in Hemsted, Herts.'

1732 S   *The youth's instructor in the English tongue: or, a spelling-book . . . to which is added, a compendious grammar of the English tongue. First designed for the author's own scholars.* (Sion college); 2nd edn 1738; 3rd edn Philadelphia, 1753; Scolar Press facsimile of 1732 edn, 1967*. Alston, IV, 357a and b.; Cohen, 1977, pp. 68–9.   Pp. 79; *51, 323.*

[Anon.]

1867 RE   *Oxford reading book for little children, Parts 1 & 2.* Oxford. (O).

P[ACKWOOD], J[osiah]

1816 G   *Introductory English exercises arranged under the rules of syntax in Murray's abridgement.* Rugeley. (BL).

PALAIRET, John   1697–1774   Teacher (*DNB*)

[a. 1746] S   *A new English spelling book,* 2nd edn [1746]. No copy. Alston, IV, 583. Solomon Lowe, 1755, p. 9, dismisses the book as more than usually superficial.

PALEY, William   1743–1805

1790* S   *The young Christian instructed in reading and in the principles of religion. Compiled for the use of the Sunday schools in Carlisle.* (BL). Much of the book is taken verbatim from Joseph Robertson's *An introduction to the study of polite literature,* 1782. Paley was accused of plagiarism, which he admitted and defended (Nichols, *Lit. Anecdotes,* III, 502; *Gent. Mag.,* 62 (1792), 322, 324, 408; *DNB*). Chalmers, p. 149, says Paley's book was issued also as *Reading made completely easy; or, a necessary introduction to reading the Bible,* but the latter is by Thomas Dyke, q.v. Nevertheless at least one of the undated edns listed by Chalmers, about 1855, carries Paley's name. Its contents do not closely resemble either Paley's 1790 work or Dyke's (as revised by Fenning); they do resemble an anonymous work in V&A, attributed there to Dyke and here given under his name.   P. 84.

PALGRAVE, Francis Turner   1824–97

1875* RA   *The children's treasury of English song* (BL); 2nd edn as: . . . *of lyrical song,*' 1876; later edns as: . . . *of lyrical poetry.*   P. 222.

1861* RA   *The golden treasury of the best songs and lyrical poems in the English language* (BL); revised impression 1861*; 2nd edn 1891; Second series 1896. Many edns.

Palladis Tamia, see MERES, Francis

PALMER, A.G.

[1869] G   *A catechism of Morell's grammar* (BL).

[1873] G   *Morell's grammar simplified* (BL).

[PALMER, Charlotte]   Teacher

1797* Ed   *Letters on several subjects, from a preceptress to her pupils who have left school* (BL). Parts are reprinted in her *Roots of Knowledge,* q.v.

1811* G   *Roots of knowledge; or, foundational lessons on English grammar: occasionally interspersed with letters on various subjects. Designed for the use of young ladies from sixteen to twenty years of age* (Glasgow UL), 36 pp., but apparently to be continued in fortnightly 'numbers'. The work is erratic and disturbed, with little reference to English grammar.

PAPE, Daniel   Of Morpeth, later Vicar of Penn, Staffs

1790* G   *A key to English grammar, by which it has been proved, by experience, that a boy, with a tolerable capacity, and of ten years of age only, may, in a few months, be taught to write the English language properly and correctly, though totally unacquainted with the Latin and Greek languages.* Newcastle (BL); as: *A compendious English grammar,* London, 1806 (Stafford PL). Alston, I, 451, calls the 1806 edn a reprint, but it contains 166 pages against the 48 of the 1790 edn.   P. 328.

[Anon.]

[1795?]* Ex   *A paraphrase on the Rev. Dr Watts's celebrated distich, on the study of languages. Addressed to the young gentlemen of the English Grammar School. By one of their school-fellows.* (BL, shelf-mark 11632.c.59(2)). Lacks t.p. and any indication of its origin.

PARDON, William

[1746] S   *Spelling new modelled; or, the natural and easy way to spell and read English.* No copy. Solomon Lowe, 1755, says the book is embarrassing and useless.

[Anon.]

1804* RE   *The parlour teacher,* 30 pp. (Bedford CHE).

[PARSONS, John]

[c. 1780]* S   *The first book for English schools; or the rational schoolmaster's first assistant: being a new method to avoid perplexity to the scholar, and a great deal of unnecessary trouble to the teacher,* Nottingham. (BL). The attribution is from a MS note in the BL copy, which says Parsons, rector of Wilford, near Nottingham, had a thousand copies of the book printed at his own expense for the poor. A printed note at the end says the price of sixpence cannot be reduced, and that another sixpenny book, from three to eight syllables, is being printed. Alston, IV, 772 gives t.p. in full.

[Anon.]

1850 RE   *The patent indestructible primer.* (BL 12982.a.67)

[Anon.]

1822 G   *The path of learning strewed with roses,* Published by John Marshall in imitation of the following item. Opie, 1980, intro. and p. 124.

[Anon.]

1820 G   *The paths of learning strewed with flowers: or English grammar illustrated.* (BL; Bedford CHE; Preston PL; Melbourne UL); reprinted in Opie, 1980*. Published by John Harris, a delightful and famous work.

PATMORE, Coventry   1823–96

1862* RA   *The child's garland from the best poets.* (BL; Glasgow UL); other edns in 1873, 1883, 1895.   P. 213.

PAYNE, Joseph   1808–76   Teacher

1830* Ed   *A compendious exposition of the principles and practice of Professor Jacotot's celebrated system of education.* (BL).   P. *125n.*

1839* RA   *Select poetry for children: with brief explanatory notes. Arranged for the use of schools and families.* (BL). At least eighteen edns to 1874.

1845 RA   *Studies in English poetry: with short biographical sketches, notes explanatory and critical. Intended as a text-book for the higher classes in schools, and as an introduction to the study of English literature* (title from 1859). New edn 1848 (Hull UL); 3rd edn 1856 (BL); 4th edn 1859* (BL); 8th edn 1881 (BL).

1868* RA   *Studies in English prose . . . together with a sketch of the history of the English language . . . intended as a textbook for schools and colleges.* (BL); 2nd edn 1881. (BL).

PEACHAM, Henry   1546–1634

1577 B   *The garden of eloquence conteyning the figures of grammer and rhetorick, from whence maye bee gathered all manner of flowers, coulors, ornaments, exornations, formes and fashions of speech.* (BL; O); rev. edn 1593 (BL); facsimile of 1593, intro. W.G. Crane, Gainesville, 1954; facsimile of 1577, Scolar Press, 1971*. Alston, VI, 21–2.   Pp. 150, 283.

[PEACOCK, Thomas Love]   1785–1866

1814 G   *Sir Hornbook; or, Childe Launcelot's expedition. A grammatico-allegorical ballad.* 2nd edn 1815; 3rd edn 1815; five further edns to 1855; in *The works of Thomas Love Peacock*, ed. H.F.B. Brett-Smith and C.E. Jones, vol. VI, 1927*, pp. 261–6.

PELHAM   One of Sir Richard Phillips' pen-names was M. Pelham; he also used Margaret Pelham, Mary Pelham, Miss or Mrs Pelham. Dorothy Kilner wrote for children under the initials M.P., said by Harvey Darton (1958, p. 164) to be derived from Maryland Point, the village where she lived. But later, at her publisher's request to name herself, she used the names M. Pelham (*NCBEL*, II, 1024) or Mary Pelham (*OCCL*, s.v. *Kilner*). Some confusion has been caused.

PEMBERTON, Robert

1857 Ed   *The infant drama: a model of the true method of teaching all languages.*

London: Infant Euphonic Institution, 1857. (BL).

1851 G   *The natural method of teaching the elements of grammar, for the nursery and infant schools.* (O).

PENGELLEY, Edward

1840* G   *The elements of English grammar illustrating its four divisions; with an appendix, or exercises on its various rules.* (BL).

PENNIE, J.F.

1822* RA   *The harp of Parnassus: a new selection of classical English poetry . . . Designed for schools and young readers in general.* (BL).

PERCIVAL, Thomas   1740–1804

1775 RH   *A father's instructions to his children: consisting of tales, fables and reflections, designed to promote the love of virtue, a taste for knowledge, and an early acquaintance with the works of nature.* (title from 1781); 5th edn 1781* (BL); at least thirteen edns in all to 1806.   P. 311.

PERKES, J.

[1688] S   *The art of spelling; containing, 1. An ABC for children, consisting of alphabets and syllables; with short rules and examples of dividing words. 2. Rules for the true spelling, reading, and writing, of English; by way of question and answer. 3. Two tables of the most usual words, whose spelling or sense may be mistaken . . .* By J.P., M.A.   TC, II, 239. No copy; 2nd edn [1701] no copy; 5th edn [c. 1730?] no copy. Alston, IV, 156–57a. John Hawkins, (1692) 1694, quotes in his preface what 'Mr Perkes saith in his Preface to the Art of Spelling'.

PERRY, James   'Principal of the Perryian Schools'

1829* RA   *The middle stage of reading, orthography, & composition, according to the 'Perryian Principia, and Course of Education' . . . Volume 2D of the Perryian Course of Education.* (private colln).

1828* C   *The Perryian principia and course of education.* For the author. Two columns to the page: xlviii cols., 602 cols., 18 unnumbered pages of index. (BL).

PERRY, William   Master of the Academy at Kelso, then at Edinburgh

1774* C   *The man of business and gentleman's assistant . . . together with an essay on English grammar*, Edinburgh. (NLS); 3rd edn, Edinburgh, 1777 (BL) omits the grammar. The book is mainly concerned with arithmetic and book-keeping. Alston, III, 315–16; Law, p. 200.

1776a* S   *The only sure guide to the English tongue; or, a new pronouncing spelling-book . . . Designed for the use of schools, and private families. To which is added, a comprehensive grammar of the English language*, Edinburgh. (BL); Alston, IV, 734–58, lists fifty-six further edns, British and American, to 1835, and reproduces the t.p. of 1776 edn. C. Johnson, pp. 206–9; Law, pp. 153–4, rather overestimates the originality of Perry's book.   Pp. 47, 50, 51; 54.

1776b* RA   *The orator; being a collection of pieces in prose and verse, selected from the best English writers, both ancient and modern; intended to facilitate the advancement of youth in reading and speaking. To which is added an appendix* [of homophones], *Edinburgh.* (BL); anr edn 1777. Alston, VI, 580–1.

1808* P   *Philosophy for youth: or, scientific tutor: being the young natural and experimental philosopher's useful companion . . . To which is prefixed exercises in* *elocution.* (BL). The first part is drawn mostly from his *The orator*; the second part explains mechanics, hydrostatics and pneumatics; the third part is a dictionary of scientific and other terms.

1775* D   *The royal standard English dictionary . . . To which is prefixed a comprehensive grammar of the English language, Edinburgh.* At least twenty-one other edns, British and American, to 1813. The grammar is very much the same as those in his previous works of 1774 and 1776.

[Anon.]

[1859]* RE   *Peter Easy's exciting, amusing, and easy method of teaching children to read.* [Sheerness?] (BL). The book consists of a printed label, an advertisement leaflet and cardboard letters stuck onto pages. There is no indication of how it is to be used.

PHILIPPS, Jenkin Thomas   d. 1755   Teacher

1721 Ed   *A compendious way of teaching the learned languages, and some of the liberal sciences at the same time; us'd formerly by Tanaquil Faber* [etc.] (BL); 2nd edn as: *A compendious way of teaching ancient and modern languages,* 1723* (BL); 3rd edn 1728; 4th edn 1750; Scolar Press facsimile 1972. Recommended by Chapman, (1773) 1792, p. 104.

1726 G   *An essay towards an universal and rational grammar; together with rules for learning Latin, in English verse. Formerly composed by Mr Shirley.* (BL); 2nd edn as *A rational grammar; with easy rules in English to learn Latin,* 1731* (BL); 3rd edn 1741*; Scolar Press facsimile of 1726 edn, 1971*, in which the book is assigned to Shirley.

PHILLIPS, John

1847 G   *The popular class room grammar: for the grammatical class of the People's Institute, Rochdale.* Rochdale. J. Hunter, 1848.

PHILLIPS, Sir Richard   1767–1840   Sometime teacher

Phillips wrote, compiled, or took credit for, textbooks under a variety of names: S. BARROW; David BLAIR, J. GOLDSMITH; Mary or Margaret PELHAM; C.C. CLARKE; James ADAIR. They are listed here under his own name.   *See above,* pp. 238–9.

1806 RA   *The class book: or, three hundred and sixty-five reading lessons, adapted to the use of schools; for every day in the year. Selected . . . by the Rev. David Blair.* (BL) (title from 4th edn); 4th edn 1808* (private colln). At least seventeen edns in all to 1835, and an edn in Paris, 1858 (BL).

[a. 1830] S   *A familiar vocabulary or spelling book, of such terms of science, and technical words of art, as occur in elementary books and in the school studies of youth.* By David Blair. 2nd edn [1830]*. (BL). The running title throughout is 'A popular vocabulary'.

1810 S   *The first step to knowledge; being an easy introduction to the various English spelling books. By the Rev. J. Goldsmith,* Darton. Chalmers, p. 150; anr edn 1813, Chalmers; new edn, n.d.* (Hull UL).

[1824]* G   *Five hundred questions and exercises on Murray's English Grammar, and Abridgment; also on Irving's Elements of English Composition . . . By James Adair.* (Nottingham UL); another edn 1826* (BL).   Pp. *255, 352.*

1824* Ed   *Illustrations of the interrogative system of education. By Sir Richard Phillips.* (BL 816.1.47(60)). A defensive puff for his own books and for the system of asking questions without providing the answers.

1835 Ed *A letter to the schoolmasters and governesses of England and Wales on the new theories of education.* (DES).

[1805?] RE *The London primer; or, a first book for children at a very early age* (title from 1809) *Edinburgh Rev.*, April 1805; 40th edn 1807 (DES); 40th edn 1809 (Leeds UL; Chalmers, p. 149); [*c.* 1820?]* (BL 12981.a.41(4)); 250th edn [1850?] (BL 12835.aa.14). The book appears sometimes as by M. Pelham, but it is likely that several different works are concealed behind this obvious and successful title.

[1811]b* Ex *Models of juvenile letters on familiar subjects in English, French and Italian, with topics for the exercises of students and observations relative to commercial letters. By the Rev. David Blair.* (BL); new edn 1821; reissue 1831. Recommended in *The Juvenile Reader's Assistant,* 1830, which was not published by Phillips.

[a. 1809] G *A practical grammar of the English language, accompanied by numerous exercises . . . By the Rev. David Blair.* 4th edn 1809 (BL; Glasgow UL). At least eighteen edns to 1871.

[a. 1813] RA *Reading exercises for the use of schools, on a new and improved plan; being a sequel to Mavor's Spelling-Book . . . By the Rev. David Blair.* Advertised in Rippingham, 1813; new edn (preface 1817) n.d.* (Leeds UL); anr edn 1820 (BL). Chalmers, p. 150, gives other undated edns. P. *239.*

[*c.* 1815?]* RA *The second step to knowledge, or, flowers and fruits. By the Rev. J. Goldsmith* (private colln.); [*c.* 1840?] (BL). A prose and verse collection, including a sketch of grammar.

1811a* RA *Six hundred questions and exercises, intended to perfect young persons in Blair's Universal Preceptor* (BL); anr edn as . . . *intended as exercises in conformity with the genuine interrogative system,* Whittaker, [1837, preface] (BL).

1811c* C *The universal preceptor; being a general grammar of arts, sciences and useful knowledge. By the Rev. David Blair.* (personal); 2nd edn 1811 (Hull UL; BL); 7th edn 1814* (Nottingham UL); 21st edn 1828* (personal); many edns, to 79th [1858] (BL). The book was used in Killingworth Colliery Schools in 1842 (Gordon and Lawton, p. 140). P. *358.*

[Anon.]
1843* S *The phonetic spelling book, exhibiting all the monosyllables of the English language, under a fourfold arrangement,* Bath (BL).

[Anon.]
1844 G *Pictorial grammar for children.* B. Steill. (BL).

[Anon.]
[*c.* 1850?]* S *The pictorial primer: or, reading made easy.* W.S. Johnson. (private colln]; anr edn [1858] (BL).

[Anon.]
[*c.* 1850] S *The pictorial spelling-book, accompanied by a progressive series of easy and familiar lessons.* Sotheby, Cat. April 21–2, 1977, lot 2017.

[Anon.]
[a. 1855]* RE *The pictorial spelling book; or, lessons on facts and objects.* Advt. in 1855; new edn, Hall and Virtue, 1859* (BL).

[Anon.]
1824* RE *The picturesque primer, or first steps up the ladder of learning,* John

Harris. (V&A); anr edn 1834, Chalmers, p. 151. Seventy-two pictures, each with a rhyming couplet.

[PILKINGTON, Mary]   1766–1839   Sometime governess

1792* RH   *Dramatic dialogues, for the use of young persons. By the author of The Blind Child.* E. Newbery, 2 vols. (BL; vol. I only); Gumuchian, 4569; Roscoe, J290; Rosenbach, 239, lists contents of 1798 Boston edn, but follows Darton in attributing to Elizabeth Pinchard.   P. *302.*

PILLANS, James   1778–1864   Rector, Edinburgh High School; Professor of Humanity, University of Edinburgh

1856* Ed   *Contributions to the cause of education,* Edinburgh. (BL; BFSS). Includes his *Letters;* next item.

1827–8* Ed   *Letters on the principles of elementary teaching, chiefly in reference to the parochial schools of Scotland: Letter I,* Edinburgh, 1827; *Letter II,* Edinburgh, 1828. (BFSS).   P. *62.*

PINCHARD, Elizabeth see PILKINGTON, Mary

PINDER, William   'Master of the Foxdale Mines National School'

1856* G   *First steps in English grammar, for little children.* (BL; O).

PINNOCK, George

1854–60 G   *English grammar,* in *First steps to knowledge series,* Allman. (BL); 1878 (Columbia UL).

1856 La   *The new London expositor: being a collection of the most useful derivative words in the English language.* (BL).

PINNOCK, William   1782–1843   Sometime teacher

[1820?] RA   *A catechism of poetry, explanatory of its nature, origin, and properties; with select examples . . . the whole calculated to improve and assist youth in poetical recitation and composition,* Pinnock and Maunder, Mentorian Press, n.d. (engraved t.p. Geo. B. Whittaker, 1822)*, (Nottingham UL); Harvard and Illinois UL have edn of [1820?]. 3rd edn [1822?] (BL); 4th edn 1827 (Boston PL).   P. *218.*

[a. 1820] G   *A catechism of the principles of English grammar, to which are added . . . some easy parsing lessons . . . By a friend of youth.* 3rd edn [1820?] Newbury (BL); 4th edn, Newbury, [1821?] (BL). At least twenty-five edns to 1834, often as *A catechism of English grammar.*

[a. 1822] B   *A catechism of rhetoric, written in an easy and familiar style, intended for young people, and adapted to the use of schools and private teaching,* 3rd edn 1822* (BL); 4th edn 1827 (BL). Attacked in *Quart. Rev.,* 74 (June 1844), 15.

1829 G   *A comprehensive grammnar of the English language, with exercises written in a familiar style; accompanied with questions for examination, and notes critical and explanatory. Intended for the use of schools, and for private tuition.* Poole and Edwards (NYct); anr edn 1830* (BL); 4th edn 1838 (NYct). The 1807 edn of Hewlett's *An introduction to reading and spelling* carries an advt by Simpkin, Marshall for 'Pinnock's grammar of the English language, 6th edn with questions and exercises'. It is not clear what work this can be.

[a. 1813]a S   *Elements of punctuation, with notes critical and explanatory: comprising exercises for the use of senior pupils.* Advertised in his *Universal explanatory reader,* 1813, and referred to by Parker and Fox, 1840 (USA) p. 116. A Key to the exercises was also published.

[a. 1831]a G   *English grammar made easy, for the use of young children*, W. Sell. Advertised in Pinnock's *First steps*, 1831a.

[c. 1815] S   *Exercises in false spelling. Being a selection of pieces from the most approved authors, in prose and verse.* 5th edn, Whittaker, [c. 1820], 139 pp. Catalogue.

1811a S   *Exercises to the Elements of Punctuation, accompanied with notes critical and explanatory.* Alton (BL); 2nd edn Newbury [1812?] (BL); (Newcastle UL).

The explanatory English spelling book see his *The universal explanatory spelling book.*

[a. 1813]b RS   *The first reader, containing little explanatory lessons.* Advt in his *Universal explanatory English reader*, a. 1813; perhaps an issue of *An introduction to the Universal Explanatory Reader.*

1831a* RE   *The first step to knowledge made easy, intended as a preparatory reader, for the use of young children . . . In two parts*, W. Sell. (private colln). 240 pp., with a separate t.p. for Part 2 at p. 125.

1831b* RE   *The second step . . .* [as above] 208 pp., with a separate t.p. for Part 2 at p. 109.

[a. 1831]b G   (Pinnock's) *Improved edition of Murray's abridged English grammar, with numerous exercises, questions for examination, and explanatory notes*, W. Sell. Advertised in his *First step . . .* 1831.

1810a S   *Introduction to the Explanatory Spelling Book*, Alton. Chalmers, p. 151; 8th edn [c. 1824] (*ibid.*).

[a. 1810] RS   *An introduction to the Universal Explanatory Reader, calculated for children from five years old to nine.* 2nd edn Alton, 1810; 8th edn 1820 (N.Y., Washington Sq. L); 11th edn, . . . *designed for junior classes in schools and private tuition; and forming a sequel to The Juvenile Reader*, 1833 (Leicester UL).

[a. 1813]c RS   *The juvenile reader, being a sequel to the First Reader . . . for children from four to seven years old.* Advt in his *Universal explanatory reader*, 1813; anr edn . . . *being a sequel to the Mentorian Primer* [c. 1824], Chalmers, p. 151; 11th edn 1822 (Ohio, Cleveland PL).

1811b* S   *A key to the Elements of Punctuation, accompanied with notes critical and explanatory, for the use of young men and senior classes in schools.* Alton (BL); 2nd edn Newbury, [1812?] (BL).

[c. 1824] RS   *The Mentorian primer; or, Pinnock's second book for children at an early age.* Whittaker. Chalmers, p. 151. See above, *The child's first book, or, key to reading.*

[1813]d RS   *The universal explanatory English reader, calculated to assist both teacher and pupil: consisting of selections in prose and poetry, on interesting and improving subjects.* Newbury: Mentorian Press, S. Maunder, [1813] (Austin, Texas UL); new edn, Winchester, 1813* (BL); 5th edn, London, 1821 (BL); 6th edn, as: *Pinnock's explanatory English reader and universal class book*, 1827* (BL); 7th edn, do., 1832 (Hull UL); 8th edn 1841* (Holtom, List 50; 1985).   Pp. 255–6; *251.*

1810b S   *The universal explanatory spelling book, (on an improved plan), calculated to assist British youth in attaining their mother tongue with ease.* (title from 1811) Alton, Chalmers, p. 151; Alton, 1811* (BL). Many edns, often as *The* *explanatory English spelling book*, to 31st edn, 1842 (Harvard).

PINNOCK, William Henry   1813–85

1837 G   *An elementary English grammar, upon an entirely new principle.* Effingham
    Wilson. (BL).

PITMAN, John Rogers   1782–1861

1822* P   *The school Shakspeare; or, plays and scenes from Shakspeare, illustrated for
    the use of schools, with glossarial notes, selected from the best annotators.* Pp. xxiv,
    596. (BL); anr edn 1834 (BL).

A plain, practical English grammar see *The schoolboy's short English grammar.*

[Anon.]

[1850?] RE   *Plain words for those who can read but little.* (BL).

[Anon.]

1812* G   *The plainest and most necessary principles of English grammar . . .
    calculated for the instruction of young children: and printed for the use of Bridport
    Grammar School.* Dorchester. (BL).   P. *347.*

PLATTS, John   1775–1837

1825 D   *A dictionary of English synonymes, for the use of schools.* (BL).

1823* RA   *The female monitor, or ladies class book, being a new selection of three
    hundred and sixty-five reading lessons,* Derby: H. Mozley. (BL).   P. *223.*

1821* RA   *The literary and scientific class book; consisting of three hundred and
    sixty-five reading lessons, adapted to the use of schools of both sexes, for every day
    in the year. With one thousand questions for examination.* (BL); selections ed.
    L.W. Leonard, 1826 (BL).   P. *242.*

1822* RA   *The new juvenile reader, for the use of schools and private teachers; being a
    sequel to Bigland's, Vyse's, Fenning's and Markham's spelling books,* Derby.
    (BL); 4th edn [*c.* 1835] Chalmers, p. 151.

[Anon.]

[1598] RE   *A playne and ready forme to teach children to reade in a short tyme.* No
    copy. *SR*(A), III, 116.

[Anon.]

1863 RH   *Playtime with the poets: a selection of the best English poetry for the use of
    children. By a lady.* (BL).

[Anon.]

[1825] RE   *The pleasing instructor,* Knight and Bagster (Preston, Harris L.)
    Collins, (1802) 1818, p. 40, says a work of this title preceded Enfield, i.e. *c.*
    1774, but he is probably referring to Ann Fisher, 1756.

[Anon.]

[a. 1818] RA   *The pleasing preceptor,* 2 vols. (BL).

[Anon.]

[1831]* RA   *Poems for youth, on sacred subjects. By the author of Verses for Children,
    Botanical Multiplication Tables, &c. &c.* (BL; NLS).

[Anon.]

[1760?]* RA   *Poems, moral and divine. Collected from the best authors; principally
    intended to instil good impressions into youth. And worthy the perusal of all those,
    who have a love to virtue, and taste for poetry.* (BL).   P. *180.*

[Anon. ed]

[*c.* 1835]* RE   *The poems of Thomas Gray and Robert Blair, arranged for the use of
    young people,* Edward Lacey (Durham UL).

[Anon. ed.]

[1820?]* RA   *Poems, religious, moral and instructive, for the young*, Watchet: T. Whitehorn (BL).

[Anon.]

1818 RA   *Poems, selected from the works of approved authors*, Dublin. Welch, no. 1034; anr edn Dublin, 1822* (BL); anr edn Dublin, 1825 (BL). No authors' names or sources are given, nor is there any preface; but the poems suggest young readers, if not an explicitly pedagogic purpose.

[Anon.]

1845* RA   *The poetic manual, for the use of schools. Written by a brother and a sister.* (BL).

[Anon.]

1869 RA   *Poetic selections for the use of . . . advanced pupils of national schools.* For the Irish Commissioners of National Education, Dublin: Thom. (NLI).

[Anon.]

1766* Ex   *Poetical blossoms: or, the sports of genius. Being a collection of poems upon several subjects. By the young gentlemen of Mr Rule's Academy at Islington.* (BL). Hans, p. 92.

[Anon.]

1803 RA   *The poetical fabulator, or beauties in verse, selected from the most eminent authors.* York: T. Wilson and R. Spence. Gumuchian, 4588; anr edn York, 1810* (BL).

[Anon.]

1823* RA   *Poetical gems; a collection of pieces, from the most admired authors, to commit to memory. Selected by a father and mother.* (O). Moon, 668.

[Anon.]

1827 RA   *The poetical ladder; or a selection of poetry, arranged gradationally, to suit the capacities of children from four to ten years of age. By a lady.* Birmingham. N. Russell, *A bibliography of William Cowper*, 1963, p. 157. Not traced.

[Anon.]

1762* RA   *The poetical miscellany; consisting of select pieces from the works of* [twelve poets]. *For the use of schools.* (BL); 2nd edn 1769, *NCBEL*, II, 390; 3rd edn 1778* (BL); 4th edn 1789* (BL).   P. 174.

[Anon.]

[a. 1824] RA   *The poetical piece-book: a collection of sacred and moral poetry, for the use of schools*, 5th edn Yarmouth and London, 1824 (St Louis UL); Manchester: W. Willis, 1846 (NYPL).

[Anon.]

1777* RA   *The poetical preceptor; or, a collection of select pieces of poetry; extracted from the works of the most eminent English poets . . . and calculated for the use, not only of schools, but of private gentlemen.* (BL; Glasgow UL); 3rd edn 1785 (*LTM*, Cat. 28 (1963), item 249); 5th edn 1796 (BL); 6th edn 1806* (BL). A sequel to *The polite preceptor*, 1776.   P. *191*.

[Anon.]

[a. 1831] RA   *The poetical primer.* Quoted in M'Culloch, 1831, p. 101.

[Anon.]

[a. 1836] RA   *Poetical selections for the use of young people*, 2nd edn 1836* (BL). Preface written from Nottingham.

[Anon.]

[*c.* 1820] RA   *The poetical task-book; consisting of original pieces . . . designed for the use of schools, and of young persons generally.* Gumuchian, 4589 (*NUC*).

[Anon.]

1856 RA   *A poetry book for national schools.* (NLS; BL); new edn 1857* (Nottingham UL); as *A poetry book for schools,* 1864* (Fulham PL); 1866 (Wandsworth PL).

[Anon.]

1870 RA   *Poetry for beginners. A selection of short and easy poems for reading and recitation in schools and families. . . . Dr Cornwell's Series.* (NLS).

[Anon.]

1823* RH   *Poetry without fiction: for children, between the ages of three and seven; with the conversations of a mother with her children, intended to make the latter comprehend what they learn, and to convey such instruction as may arise out of each subject. By a mother.* (Liverpool UL).   P. 216.

[Anon.]

1761 RA   *The polite instructor; or youth's museum. Consisting of moral essays, tales . . . and allegories . . . With an introduction, containing rules for reading . . . To which is added, a collection of letters.* (BL); Alston, VI, 333.

[Anon.]

1774* RA   *The polite preceptor; or, improving moralist. Consisting of a choice collection of relations, visions, allegories, and moral essays, selected from the most eminent English authors . . . designed for the use of schools.* (BL).   P. *191.*

[Anon.]

1776 RA   *The polite preceptor: or, a collection of entertaining and instructive essays; selected from the best English writers . . . with a view to inspire into the minds of youth the love of virtue, and the principles of true taste and just reasoning. LTM,* Cat. 16 (1956), item 57; 5th edn 1795* (BL).   P. *191.*

Politeuphuia: Wits Commonwealth see LING, Nicholas

POLLARD, William   1828–93   Teacher

1865 RA   *The Ackworth reading book, being selections from the best English authors, in prose and poetry: designed as a reading book for senior classes; and compiled for the use of Ackworth School.* (BL); 2nd edn 1866* (Leeds UL). The poetry section was published as *The Ackworth poetical reader,* 1872*, and the whole reading-book, the prose sections enlarged, was reissued as *Choice readings in English literature, prose and poetry* in 1873*.   P. 254.

POOLE, Joshua   d. before 1657   Teacher

1646* G   *The English accidence: or, a short, plaine, and easie way, for the more speedy attaining to the Latine tongue, by the help of the English.* (O); 1655* (BL); as: *The youth's guide: or English accidence,* 1662 (BL)*; 1670* (BL); Scolar Press facsimile of 1646 edn, 1967*. P. Wallis, *N&Q,* September 1954; *EGC, passim.* Vorlat, 1975.

1657 Ex   *The English Parnassus: or, a helpe to English poesie. Containing a collection of all rhyming monosyllables, the choicest epithets, and phrases: with some general forms upon all occasions, subjects, and theams, alphabetically digested. Together with a short institution to English poesie, by way of preface,* Pp. xxx, 646, misnumbered from p. 288) (BL; Glasgow UL); 1677; 1678; Scolar Press facsimile of 1657 edn, 1972*. Alston, VI, 552–4. Published posthumously. Pp. 151–3; 274–5.

1663 B *Practical rhetorick. Or, certain little sentences varied according to the rules prescribed by Erasmus, in his most excellent book De Copia Verborum & Rerum. Wherein children may be exercised, when they first begin to translate Latin.* (Dr Williams L); Scolar Press facsimile 1972*. Alston, VI, 92. Published posthumously. In the preface to *The English Parnassus* the rhetoric is said to be 'already in the *Printers* hands,' but it took six years to appear.   P. 275.

[Anon.]

[a. 1790] RE   *The poor child's friend, or familiar lessons adapted to the capacities of all ranks of children,* 2nd edn York, 1790* (BL).

[Anon.]

[a. 1789] RE   *The poor girl's primer.* Used in the Sheffield Girls Charity School, 1789. M.G. Jones, 1938, p. 77n.

POPE, Alexander   1688–1744

Anonymous editions: *The Universal Prayer* was regularly included in school anthologies, and it seems probable that eighteenth-century editions of the *Essay on Man,* with which the *Universal Prayer* had been associated by Pope, carried the title of the latter in order to attract school custom:

1792* RA   *The Universal Prayer.* Perth: R. Morrison (BL).

1795* RA   *The Universal Prayer.* Newcastle on Tyne: S. Hodgson. (BL).

1796* RA   *The Universal Prayer.* Darton and Harvey. (BL).

1871 RA   *Pope's Essay on Criticism. With notes.* 'Chambers's English Classics for use in schools'. (BL).

See also AIKIN, J., 1796; NEIL, S., 1866; PATTISON, M., 1869, WALKER, J., 1786.

[Anon.]

1827 G   *Popular errors in English grammar, particularly in pronunciation, familiarly pointed out,* Wilson. NBL, 1946, no. 123.

PORTERFIELD, James   'Schoolmaster in Edinburgh'

1694* S   *A choice jewel for children, or, a firm and easie foundation, laid for reading of the sacred scriptures; with the Shorter Catechism . . . in syllables, whereby such may attain to true spelling, and the ready reading of the catechism, and scripture, or any Latine or English book, comprehended in few lessons, never extant before,* Edinburgh. (Aberdeen UL). Alston, IV, 178.   Pp. 67, 107.

1695 S   *Edinburgh's English school-master, containing in XXXVI lessons all the words of the Old and New Testament with the catechism, and instructions therewith. Being the easiest way to spell and read either English or Latine, that ever was publickly known to this day. Examined by the colledges of Edinburgh and Glasgow,* Edinburgh. (Glasgow PL); As: . . . *or, magnum in parvo, containing in few lessons an easy way to spell, or read* . . . 3rd edn, Edinburgh, 1711* (BL). Alston, IV, 180–1.   Pp. 67; 372.

[Anon.]

1688* S   *A posing-book for scholars in short questions and answers. Containing a mixture of several things not commonly known among the meaner sort; and yet of great usefulness for all to understand that are willing to be scholars. Being only a rude essay, by a lover of learning, who intends (God permitting, and the inhabitants* *of England accepting) not only to make this more compleat, but also to prepare by degrees such helps for learning so far as concerns English, that none shall have cause more to complain for want of it: but the slothful, and wilfully ignorant.* 20 pp. (BL).

POSTLETHWAITE, Richard

1795* G *The grammatical art improved: in which the errors of grammarians and lexicographers are exposed.* (BL). Alston, I, 492.

A practical essay on the manner of studying . . . in Scotland, see MESTON, W.

[Anon.]

[1717] S *A practical guide to the English tongue; or, a new and familiar method of teaching children to spell and read in a little time.* No copy. Alston, IV, 293.

[Anon.]

1833* Ed *The practical manual of the Madras or National system of education as practised at the Society's central schools, London.* (BL). A letter of commendation to the author from Andrew Bell is addressed to 'Mr H.'. Pp. 21–2; 65.

[Anon.]

[1866]* Ex *Practical textbook of English composition*, Edinburgh, T. Laurie. Constable's Educational Series. (NLS).

[Anon.]

1816* Ed *A practical treatise on day-schools; exhibiting their defects, and suggesting hints for their improvement, with simple and rational plans of teaching the usual branches of education, and a table for the arrangement of business . . . to which are added, tables, showing the proficiency that children are capable of making according to the age at which they commence their studies, and the length of time they are likely to continue them . . . By a schoolmaster.* (BL). Pp. 61, 214, 347–8.

[PRAT, Joseph]

1622* S *The order of orthographie: or, sixty six rules shortly directing to the true writing, speaking, and pronouncing the English tongue.* (Boston: Mass. Hist. Soc.). Alston, IV, 49.

[Anon.]

[a. 1836] G *Prefixes and affixes of the English language, with examples. To be committed to memory. Extracted chiefly from Mr M'Culloch's Manual of English Grammar*, Edinburgh. Advertised by Oliver and Boyd, price twopence.

[Anon.]

1801 RE *The present; or, lessons of instruction for the use of young persons.* Huddersfield. (V&A).

A president for young pen-men see R., M.

PRESTON, Henry Writing-master

[1674?] S *Brief directions for true-spelling. Being an abbreviat of the most usefull rules, conducible to the promoting that excellent knowledge of writing true English, much wanted by many, especially such as never well understood the Latin-tongue.* (Huntington L); anr edn [1674?] no copy; anr edn [1685] no copy; Scolar Press facsimile of Huntington Library copy, 1968*. Alston, IV, 95–7 and Plate 15 for t.p. Pp. 74, 108; 50, 52, 55.

[Anon.]

[1580] S *A pretie schole of spellinge and writinge Englishe.* No copy. SR(A), II, 375.

[Anon.]

[*c.* 1744] RH   *A pretty book for children; or, an easy guide to the English tongue. Perfectly well adapted to their tender capacities, and answers the end of a child's guide, spelling-book, and history-book all in one.* No copy until 5th edn, London, 1751. More than ten edns in all to 1789. Roscoe, J307.

[Anon.]

[*c.* 1760] RH   *A pretty play-thing for children of all denominations: containing I. The alphabet in verse, for the use of little children. II. An alphabet in prose, interspersed with proper lessons in life, for the use of great children. III. The sound of the letters explained by visible objects, delineated on copper plates. IV. The Cuz's Chorus, set to music. To be sung by children, in order to teach them to join their letters into syllables, and pronounce them properly.* Undated edns at St Bride Institute, London: Pierpont Morgan L; O; and, not recorded by Roscoe, BL(Ch 790/102(2))*; Roscoe, J309.   P. 71.

[PRICE, Owen]   d. 1671   Master, Magdalen College School

1668* S   *English orthographie or the art of right spelling, reading, pronouncing, and writing all sorts of English words. Wherein such, as one can possibly mistake, are digested in an alphabetical order, under their several, short, yet plain rules* [etc.] Oxford. Anr edn as: *English orthographie: teaching, I. The letters of every sort of print. II. All syllables made of letters . . .* Oxford. (BL); Scolar Press facsimile of 1668 edn, 1972*. Alston, IV, 62–3; Dobson, 1968 I, 339f.   Pp. 49, 75.

1665* S   *The vocal organ, or a new art of teaching the English orthographie, . . . whereby any outlandish or meer English man, woman, or child, may speedily attain to the exact spelling, reading, writing, or pronouncing of any word in the English tongue, without the advantage of its fountains, the Greek, and Latine. Compiled by O.P. Master of Arts, and Professor of the art of pedagogie.* Oxford. (BL). Scolar Press facsimile 1970*. Alston, VI, 467; Dobson, 1968, I, 339f.   Pp. 18–19, 51, 109; *50, 53, 54.*

PRIESTLEY, Joseph   1733–1804   Teacher

1777 B   *A course of lectures on oratory and criticism.* (BL); Anr edn Dublin, 1781; Facsimile reprints of 1777 edn: (i) V.M. Bevilacqua and R. Murphy, Southern Illinois UP, Carbondale [1965]; (ii) Garland Press, N.Y. (iii) Scolar Press, 1968*. Alston, VI, 234–5.   Pp. 206–7.

1761* G   *The rudiments of English grammar; adapted to the use of schools. With observations on style.* (BL); enl. edn 1768* (BL); 3rd edn 1772* (BL); Scolar Press facsimile of 1761 edn, 1969*. Other edns to 1798, and reprinted in *Works*, 1826 and 1833. Alston, I, 199–207.   Pp. 311; *172, 173, 283.*

[Anon.]

[1780?]* RE   [*A primer, or reading-book for children*] (BL c.40.a.78). The work lacks title-page or running title.   P. 52.

[Anon.]

1781 RE   *The primmer, corrected and improved,* Greenock; W. McAlpine. Chalmers, p. 152, source not stated.

[Anon.]

1786* RE   *The primmer, or first part of the new method of teaching to read the English tongue, suited to the weak capacities of children. For the use of schools.* Glasgow; J. and M. Robertson. (Glasgow UL).   Pp. 64, 72.

[Anon.]

[n.d.] RE   *The Prince of Wales primer*, Ottley: William Walker, 10 pp. (Melbourne UL).

[Anon.]

[n.d.] RE   *(Rosewarne's) new and improved Prince of Wales' primer, or, ladder to learning.* Belper: John Rosewarne, 8 pp. (Wandsworth PL).

[Anon.]

[a. 1840] G   *The principles of English grammar; with the rules of syntax exemplified* [etc.], Edinburgh: Scottish School Book Association. 4th edn Edinburgh, 1840, Hunter 1848; anr edn 1841 (BL); anr edn 1847, Hunter 1848.

[Anon.]

1855* RE   *The principles of English reading. By the author of one of the grammars recommended by the Committee of Council on Education*: Glasgow: George Cameron [and others], 36 pp. (BL).   P. 55.

[Anon.]

1752* G   *Prittle prattle. Or, a familiar discourse on the persons I, thou, he or she. We, ye or you, and they. Designed for the use and benefit of the youth of the people called Quakers, who have not had the opportunity of learning a grammar. By a lover of truth.* For the author. (Woodbrooke; Friends House). The Woodbrooke copy has a manuscript attribution to 'J.J.' Alston, I, 142.

[Anon.]

1834 G   *Progressive exercises; or easy steps to the knowledge of grammar. By the author of Flora's Offering to the Young.* (BL T. 1532 (6)).

[Anon.]

[a. 1810] S   *The progressive spelling book, commencing with words of two letters, and proceeding gradually to those of seven syllables*: 2nd edn, Stourport: G. Nicholson [1810]*. (BL). Cf. George Nicholson's *Juvenile preceptor*.   P. 43.

[Anon.]

1708* Ed   *A proposal for teaching poor children to read*, etc. An unnumbered leaf following p. 44 of the 2nd edn of Joseph Downing's *A new catalogue of books and small tracts against vice and immorality*, (BL 1477.aa.2(2)). The proposal is not in the 1st edn, 1707, of the catalogue. Pinchbeck and Hewitt, I, 290.

Proposals for the amendment of school-instruction see BUTLER, J.

[Anon.]

1828* RE   *The proton, or child's manual for reading English*: Rivington. (BL T.1215(6)).   P. 60.

PRYDE, David   HM Edinburgh Merchant Company's Educational Institution for young ladies

1862* B   *Biographical outlines of English literature. For the use of schools.* Edinburgh. (BL; NLS).   P. 219.

1871* Ex   *Studies in composition. A textbook for advanced classes.* Edinburgh. (BL; NLS).

PULLEN, P.H.   Teacher

1820* Ed   *The mother's book; exemplifying Pestalozzi's plan of awakening the understanding of children in language, drawing, geometry, geography, and numbers.* (BL); 2nd edn 1822 (Boyle, Cat. 865 (1978), item 340). The work includes grammar, composition and rhetoric. The preface indicates that the author was a man.   Pp. 55, 368; *309*.

[Anon.]

1824 S   *Punctuation personified: or pointing made easy. By Mr Stops*: J. Harris. (BL); 1826 (Bedford CHE); Scolar Press facsimile of 1824 edn, 1978*; Opie, 1980, pp. 54–7, with some omissions. Moon, 829; Rosenbach, 764; Osborne, II, 734.

[Anon.]

[a. 1799] C   *The pupil's friend; or repetition book. Selected from the best modern authors, and designed for the use of schools and academies, and especially the naval and military academy at Gosport, Hants. Part I.* [spelling, grammar]. *Part II.* [arithmetic]. *Part III.* [collects, catechism]. 3rd edn Gosport, 1799* (BL). Alston, I, 528.   P. 339.

PUTSEY, W.   Master of the Classical and Mathematical School, Pickering

[a. 1818] RE   *The child's companion*. In the preface to his *The juvenile class-book*, 1818, Putsey says this was a first book for children written 'some time ago'. No copy.

1818* RE   *The juvenile class-book; or, sequel to the Child's Companion . . . adapted to the capacities of children who have made some progress in reading*. (BL).   P. *128*.

1821* G   *A practical English grammar . . . with an appendix containing a variety of exercises in orthography, syntax, parsing, and punctuation. Accompanied also by a grammatical retrospect, or questions for a thorough examination of the pupil in every department of grammar*. (BL); 2nd edn 1829 (Columbia UL).   P. *346n*.

[PUTTENHAM, George]   *c.* 1529–90

1589 B   *The arte of English poesie. Contrived into three bookes: the first of poets and poesie, the second of proportion, the third of ornament*. (O); ed. E. Arber, Birmingham, 1869; ed. Gladys D. Willcock and Alice Walker, Cambridge, 1936*; Scolar Press facsimile 1968. Alston, VI, 34.   Pp. 139, 333.

PYCROFT, James   1813–95

1844* B   *A course of English reading, adapted to every taste and capacity, with anecdotes of men of genius*. (BL); 2nd edn 1850* (BL); 3rd edn 1854 (BL); 4th edn 1861 (BL).   P. 215.

[*c.* 1844] RA   *Rational reading lessons, and key*. Chalmers, p. 152.

Quarterly Review, 71 (1843), 54–83*: 'Books for children'.   Pp. 249–50

Quarterly Review, 74 (1844), 1–26*: 'Children's books'.

[Anon.]

1814 RE   *Questions adapted to lessons extracted from The Teacher's Assistant. By Mrs Trimmer. Designed for the use of the National Society's Central and other schools*. (BL); new edn 1836*, 48 pp. (BL).   P. 256.

R., J.

[1705] B   *Rules for rhetorick, translated for the younger scholars in Bury School. TC*, III, 468. No copy.

R., J.W.

1839* G   *An epitome of English grammar . . . with questions for examination at the end of each division; and an appendix, containing exercises in parsing: designed for the younger classes of learners*. (BL; O).   P. 347.

R., M.

1615 Ex   *A president for young pen-men. Or the letter-writer. Containing letters of sundry sortes, with their severall answers . . . For the instruction of those that can write, but have not the guift of enditing.* Wright, (1935) 1958, p. 145.

R., S.

[a. 1860] RA   *School-room lyrics.* Noted on the t.p. of the same author's *School-room poetry.*

1860* RA   *School-room poetry* (printed in Ipswich) (BL).

R., T.

[1700?] S   *Rudimenta anglicana, or brief rules for reading and writing true English; together with the church catechism.* No copy. Alston, IV, 207.

RAE, George

1844 G   *First lessons in English grammar.* (BL).

[RAIKES, Robert?]

[a. 1786?] S   *The Sunday School scholar's companion.* The preface to the 2nd edn of *The Salisbury spelling-book* (August 1786) refers to a spelling-book 'by Mr Raikes' and classes it amongst those which 'contain too many figurative and oriental expressions; too many other words remote from common use'; no title is given. Chalmers, p. 153, gives the above title and the date 1794, without any indication of his source. Raikes is more likely to have been the printer than the author: he printed Ussher's grammar and spelling-book of 1794 and his grammar of 1785; but neither of these was intended for Sunday schools.

RAINE, Matthew   'Master of the Free Grammar School at Hartforth'

1771* G   *English rudiments; or, an easy introduction to English grammar for the use of schools*: Darlington. (ULIE; BL); 2nd edn Darlington, 1776* (BL). The book is followed by separately numbered pages, 3–48, of *English exercises: or a collection of English examples adapted to the rules of the English Rudiments.* Alston, I, 307–8.   Pp. 332, 540; *338.*

RAINOLDE, Richard   *c.* 1530–1606

1563 B   *A booke called The Foundation of Rhetorike, because all other partes of rhetorike are grounded thereupon, every parte sette forthe in an oracion upon questions.* (Cambridge UL); ed. Francis R. Johnson (Scholars' Facsimiles and Reprints), N.Y., 1945; facsimile edn English Experience, Amsterdam, 1969; Scolar Press facsimile 1972*. Alston, VI, 18. Howell, 1956, pp. 140–2.   P. *154.*

RAMSAY, Andrew Michael (Chevalier Ramsay)   1686–1743

1732 Ed   *A plan of education for a young prince.* (BL); 3rd edn Glasgow, 1741* (Leicester UL; Glasgow UL); reprinted in D. Burgess, 1759.

[Anon.]

1804 RE   *The rational primer*: Darton and Harvey. Sotheby, April 1977, lot 2149; 1816, Sotheby, April 1977, lot 2150; NBL, 1946, no. 63. Not an edn of Edgeworth, 1799.

RAWLINSON, William Wyndham   Of Keynsham Academy

1815 G   *Practical English grammar.* Recorded by T. Martin, 1824, p. 84.

[Anon.]

1799* RA   *The reader, or reciter: by the assistance of which any person may teach himself to read or recite English prose with the utmost elegance and effect. To which* *are added, instructions for reading plays. On a plan never before attempted.* Cadell and Davies. (BL).

[Anon.]

1857* RE *Reading analysed: being a series of lessons for teaching reading. Equally suitable for the instruction of children and adults; with elementary reading lessons, graduated on a new principle*: Oscar F. Owers, 101 Edgeware Road. Printed by M. Snell, 5a Newcastle Place, Edgeware Road, Paddington. (BL 12983.b.19). P. 98.

[Anon.]

[1698] S *Reading and spelling made more easie; with variety of pictures to please and delight the child.* T. Parkhurst. *TC*, III, 86. Not in Alston.

[Anon.]

1838 RA *A reading book for the use of female schools.* For the Commissioners of National Education, Dublin. Akenson, p. 231; anr edn Dublin, 1845 (NLI); anr edn 1846 (NLI); anr edn 1847 (NLI); anr edn 1850* (BL); further edns to 1862. P. 242.

[Anon.]

1830 RE *Reading easy; or the child's stepstone to learning*: Northampton. (O).

[Anon.]

[a. 1786] RE [*Reading made compleatly easy*] T. Lowndes, 94 pp. No t.p.; dated by inscription. (Bedford CHE).

[Anon.]

1806 RE *Reading made completely easy ... For the use of schools. Being an improvement of Dyke, Weald, etc.* Crosby. NBL, 1946, No. 59.

[Anon.]

[c. 1870] RE *Reading made completely easy (Harris's first book)*: Otley, J.S. Publishing Co. Ellis, 1971.

Reading made completely easy see also DYKE, [1746?], and PALEY, 1790.

[Anon.]

[c. 1830] RE *Reading made easy*, Derby: Richardson. Advt. in *New primer*, Richardson, [1830?].

[Anon.]

1856* Ed *Reading made easy by means of the phonetic alphabet*, Bath and London: Isaac Pitman, 16 pp. (BL 12991.f.6). A pamphlet, quoting from articles in *The Phonetic Journal* during previous six years.

[Anon.]

[1854]* RE *Reading made easy for juvenile learners*, T. Goode (BL; V&A).

[Anon.]

1811 RE *Reading made easy; in a regular and speedy method of teaching young children to spell and read English*, Dublin: Fox. (Leicester UL; DES).

[Anon.]

[a. 1835] RE *Reading made easy; in a variety of useful lessons*, Berwick, 4th edn. 1835* (BL). P. 131.

[Anon.]

1869 RE *Reading made easy in spite of the alphabet.* Diack, p. 32.

[Anon.]

[a. 1838]* RE *Reading made easy, or an introduction to reading and spelling,*

consisting of suitable lessons, catechisms, prayers etc. For the use of schools in general, Shrewsbury: Tibnam. Cover title: *The new primer; consisting of easy lessons in reading and spelling*. Inscription date 6 May 1838. (Bedford CHE).
[Anon.]

1821* RE *Reading made most easy; consisting of a variety of useful lessons*, Workington: R. Moody. (BL). Pp. 37, 60; 64.
Reading made most easy see also RUSHER, William
[Anon.]

1784* RE *Reading made quite easy and diverting. Containing symbolical cuts for the alphabet; tables of words of one, two, three and four syllables, with easy lessons from the scriptures . . . instructive fables and edifying pieces of poetry, with songs, moral and divine, from I. Watts. Methodically digested; and calculated after the manner prescribed by the great Mr Locke, to gain the attention of children, who being cozened or cheated into a love of learning by the humour of the narration, are almost insensibly led on to read the longest words with ease and pleasure. New edn . . . By Tom Thumb, a lover of children, W. Wield, and others.* (BL 1478.c.17); anr edn 1789, NBL, 1973, no. 22. Cf. WEALD, 1746, below.
Reading without tears see BEVAN, Favell Lee
[Anon.]

[1865]* RA *Readings in English poetry. A collection of specimens from our best poets . . . chronologically arranged, with biographical notices and explanatory notes*: Chambers. (BL).

[Anon.]

[a. 1844] RA *Readings in English prose. A collection of specimens from our best prose writers from A.D. 1558 to 1860 . . . With biographical notices and explanatory notes and an introduction containing specimens from English writers . . . to 1558.* (Title from 1865); what seems to be the same book was noticed in *Quart. Rev.*, 74 (June 1844), 25 as 'Readings in English Prose from Lord Bacon downwards'; anr edn [1865]* (BL).
[Anon.]

[a. 1845] RA *Readings in English prose literature*: J.W. Parker, 3rd edn (from advt).
[Anon.]

1833* RA *Readings in poetry; a selection from the best English poets, from Spenser to the present time; and specimens of several American poets of deserved reputation. To which is prefixed a brief survey of the history of English poetry*: J.W. Parker, for SPCK (BL); a 5th edn was advertised in 1845. Pp. 237–8.
[Anon.]

1764* G *A real English grammar; in which the nature of the several parts of speech, and of their dependence on each other, is set forth in a plain and familiar manner fitted for the use of boys*, Dublin. (Columbia UL). Alston, I, 258. Pp. 334, 335.
[Anon.]

1711* Ed *Reasons for an English education, by teaching the youth of both sexes the arts of grammar, rhetoric, poetry, and logic. In their own mother-tongue.* Pp. 6. (BL). Sometimes reprinted in the 1712 edn of Gildon's *A grammar of the English tongue*, 1711, q.v. Alston, X, 154, attributes to John Brightland, but there seems to be no firm evidence.

REID, Alexander 1802–60 Headmaster, Edinburgh Institution

1844 D *A dictionary of the English language, containing the pronunciation, etymology, and explanation of all words authorized by eminent writers. To which are added a vocabulary of the roots of English words and an accented list of proper names.* (BL). Eighteen edns to 1864. The 19th edn was issued also in a cheap form, five shillings, for schools.

1839 Ex *Rudiments of English composition; designed as a practical introduction to correctness and perspicuity in writing, and to the study of criticism: with copious exercises. For the use of schools,* Edinburgh. (BL); 17th edn 1869*; 18th edn 1872. A *Key* was published in 1843. Pp. 282; *309.*

1837* G *Rudiments of English grammar,* Edinburgh (BL); 2nd edn London, 1839, GB; 11th edn Edinburgh, 1854 (Hull UL). At least twenty-three edns in all to 1874. P. *364.*

REID, Hugo Principal, People's College, Nottingham

1850* G *Outlines of English grammar; with a series of instructive extracts, for lessons in reading and grammatical exercises,* Nottingham: W. Taylor. (Nottingham UL). P. *346n.*

REID, John 1764/5–1830

1829* G *An outline of English grammar; with explanatory notes and orthographical exercises. For the use of schools,* Glasgow (Mitchell L); anr edn, Glasgow, 1830 (Columbia UL). P. *358.*

[Anon.]

1776* G *Remarks on the English tongue, for the instruction of youth,* Eton. (BL); anr edn 1779. Alston, I, 329–30.

REVIS, B.

1856 G *English grammar in metre.* (O).

REYNOLDS, George

[1813]* Ed *The Madras school grammar; or, the new system reduced to questions and answers. Designed for the use of higher classes, to qualify the scholars therein for competent teachers. Chiefly arranged from the Rev. Dr Bell's instructions.* (BL). A manual of pedagogy, not a grammar of English.

RHODES, Benjamin

1795* G *A concise English grammar, rendered easy to every capacity, so that (without any other help) a person may acquire the knowledge of the English language. To perfect the learner, there are many exercises of good and bad English, annexed to every rule of syntax; also, punctuation, and a help to reading, speaking, and composing; with many examples of composition, on interesting subjects, expressive of the true sublime; extracted from the best English authors. To which are added, a short compendium of logic and rhetoric, and a sketch of the constitution of England,* Birmingham. (O; BL). Alston, I, 493.

[Anon.]

[a. 1820] S *The rhyming and pronouncing primer; or, child's first book, on a new plan: in which the spelling lessons are systematically arranged, and the accurate pronunciation of every word is rendered easy . . . For the use of schools and families*: J. Souter. 3rd edn [1820?]* (BL). P. *62.*

[Anon.]

[1841] RE *The rhyming primer, or child's delight,* Glasgow. (BL).

RIACH, Alexander

[1772] G *Rudiments of the English tongue . . . on the plan of Mr Ruddiman's Rudiments of the Latin Tongue*, Edinburgh. No copy. Alston, I, 314.

RICE, John

1765*P *An introduction to the art of reading with energy and propriety.* (BL); Scolar Press facsimile 1969*. Alston, IV, 365; Cohen, 1977, *passim*.   Pp. 306–7.

1773*Ed *A lecture on the importance and necessity of rendering the English language a peculiar branch of female education.* (BL). Alston, X, 263.   P. 290.

RICE, M.

1835* Ex *An initiatory step to English composition, or grammatical analysis facilitated, by means of an expository theory, accompanied by suitable exercises, with difficult modes of construction explained.* (BL).   Pp. 370; *367*.

RICHARDS, W.   'Accomptant'

1743*C *The young man's new companion, or youth's general director, containing . . . a compendious English grammar.* (Edinburgh, Institute of Chartered Accountants). Alston, III, 236.

RICHARDS, W.   'Master of the Academy in Shadwell'

[c. 1781]* Ed *Youth's general instructor: or, a short and easy introduction to the arts and sciences. Part the first. Containing I. A short essay on the important advantages of a well-conducted education. II. A plan for a regular progress in learning.* (BL). Alston, X, 292.   P. 207.

RICHARDS, W.F.

1854 Ed *Manual of method for the use of teachers in elementary schools.* (BL; Cambridge UL); 2nd edn 1856 (BL).

RICHARDS, William

1680 Ex *The English orator, or rhetorical descants by way of declamations upon some notable themes both historical and philosophical. In two parts.* [title from *TC*]. (H. Huntington L) Wing, 1375A.

RICHARDSON, Alexander

1629 Lo *The logicians school-master: or, a comment upon Ramus logick . . . Whereunto are added, his Prelections on Ramus his Grammer; Talaeus his Rhetorick.* (title from 1657 edn.) (Dr Williams L): 2nd edn 1657* (BL). Alston, VII, 42–3. Howell, 1956, pp. 209f.

Right spelling very much improved see *The expert orthographist*

Riley's emblems see WYNNE, J.H.

RIPPINGHAM, John   'Lecturer upon eloquence at the Surrey Institution'

1813* P *The art of extempore public speaking, including a course of discipline for obtaining the faculties of discrimination, arrangement, and oral discussion; designed for the use of schools and self-instruction.* (private colln); 2nd edn 1814* (BL).

[1811?] Ex *Rules for English composition, and particularly for themes: designed for the use of schools, and in aid of self-instruction.* 3rd edn 1816* (dedication dated 1811) (BL); Poughkeepsie, 1816 (from 2nd London edn) (BL); 6th edn London, 1833 (BL).   Pp. 314; *313*.

[RITSON, Anne]

1811* P *Classical enigmas, adapted to every month in the year, composed from the English and Roman histories, heathen mythology, and names of famous writers;*

meant to amuse youths of all ages, and at the same time exert their memories. (BL); new edn 1815 (BL).

1813 P   *Exercises for the memory: an entire new set of improving enigmas, being the forty English and twelve Welch counties, in verse; including upwards of three hundred different events and anecdotes, selected from the Grecian, Roman and English histories, mythology, poetical and dramatic authors, also the most public buildings and places in and about London and Westminster.* (Liverpool UL); 2nd edn 1814* and 1818 (BL).

1821 RA   *The monthly monitor: consisting of easy reading lessons; or, short stories, adapted to every season of the year.* (BL).

[Anon.]

[*c.* 1844] RE   *The road to learning: or, original lessons, in words of one or two syllables, for little children,* Harvey and Darton. Chalmers, p. 154.

[Anon.]

[*c.* 1825] RE   *The road to learning strewed with flowers, or the child's first book,* Dean and Munday. (Bedford CHE).

[ROBERTS, G.]

[*a.* 1825] Lo   *A catechism of logic,* Pinnock, 6th edn (BL). An undated 3rd edn is also in BL.

[ROBERTS, M.]

1867 RS   *The Oxford reading book,* Parts 1 and 2 (O).

ROBERTS, William   'Teacher of elocution, Edinburgh'

1828* P   *A catechism of elocution, or the elements of practical rhetoric, in the form of a dialogue: illustrated by numerous exercises; with select and appropriate pieces in prose and verse. Intended for the use of schools, private-teachers, and students in general,* Edinburgh. (Glasgow PL).

ROBERTSON, George   'Schoolmaster between the two North-Doors of Paul's, in the new Buildings'

1651* S   *Learning's foundation firmly laid, in a short method of teaching to read English . . . Whereby any one of discretion may be brought to read the Bible truly in the space of a month, though he never knew letter before* [etc.] (BL); anr edn 1676* (Stockholm, Royal L); 4th edn [1703?] no copy. Watson, 1908, p. 184; Cohen, 1977, p. 146; Alston, IV, 54–6, and Plate 8 for t.p.   Pp. 81–2, 112; *106.*

ROBERTSON, George   'Master of the Free School, Kilworth Beauchamp'

1676* S   *English orthographie: or, certaine sure rules teaching to write true English.* (Stockholm, Royal L). Alston, IV, 129.   P. 27.

ROBERTSON, J.

1869 G   *Murby's English grammar and analysis taught simultaneously.* (O).

ROBERTSON, James   'School-master in Glasgow'

1722* S   *The ladies help to spelling,* Glasgow. (O), Alston, IV, 310.

[ROBERTSON, Joseph]   1726–1802

1785* Ex   *An essay on punctuation.* (BL); 2nd edn 1786 (BL). Five British edns in all to 1808 and American edns, including abridgments, to 1806. Scolar Press facsimile of 1785 edn, 1969*. Alston, III, 573–80.   Pp. 295; *188.*

1799* P   *An essay on the nature of the English verse, with directions for reading poetry.* (BL). Alston, VI, 461.

1782 P   *An introduction to the study of polite literature.* 2nd edn 1785; 3rd edn 1799;

4th edn 1808* (BL). The running title throughout the book is 'On Pronunciation'.

ROBINSON, Mr, and ROE, Mr

Hoole, 1660, refers to 'Mr Roe' and 'Mr Robinson' as teachers of reading whose textbooks were in print (*Petty school*, pp. 12–13) and he refers later (p. 19) to 'Mr R.', who taught reading without spelling, but he does not mention any textbook by him. John Newton, 1669, in what reads like an independent reference, commends the teaching of 'Mr Roe' and 'Mr Robinson' but does not mention their books (b2 verso). Thomas Lye, 1671, lists 'Mr Row' amongst those from whose work (including by implication their books) he has benefited. Campagnac, in his edition of Hoole, suggests that Robinson may be Hugh Robinson, headmaster of Winchester, 1613–27, but Dobson, 1968, I, 201, argues against this and suggests Robert Robinson, author of *The art of pronunciation*, 1617. It does not necessarily follow that Hoole's 'Mr R.' is either Robinson or Roe; he might be George Robertson, of London (above, 1651) who did teach reading without spelling.

ROBINSON, H.G.   Principal of the Diocesan Training College, York

1863* RA   *The first book of The Excursion, by William Wordsworth. The Wanderer. With notes to aid in grammatical analysis and paraphrasing.* Edinburgh and London. (BL); 2nd edn 1864 (BL).

1860* Ed   'On the use of English classical literature in the work of education'. *Macmillan's Magazine*, no. 12 (October 1860), 425–34. Kearney, 1980.   P. 250.

ROBINSON, Hugh

1867 RA   *The literary reader: prose authors.* Nelson. Catalogue.

ROBINSON, John   'Master of Arundel St. Seminary, Strand, London'

1800a* S   *The art of teaching the orthography, accent and pronunciation of the English language by imitation. Containing a great diversity of illustrative remarks: with prefatory observations on syllabication, or, the division of words into syllables; in which that system, as taught by the ancient, and some modern grammarians, is proved to be founded on erroneous principles, which entirely defeat their own object.* (Hull UL). Alston, VI, 515.   Pp. 86; *35n*.

1800b S   *The new English spelling book; or, a key to the spelling, accentuation, and pronunciation of the English language: carefully selected from the best dictionaries . . . accompanied by progressive lessons in reading . . . to which is prefixed an essay on accent, double accent, and syllabication.* (title from 5th edn); 2nd edn 1800; 5th edn 1819* (BL); 7th edn 1826 (BL). Alston, IV, 960.   P. 86.

1804* S   *The proper names of the Bible, New Testament, and Apocrypha: divided and accented, with other facilities for their pronunciation, agreeably to the best usage, and to English analogy. To which is added a selection of . . . scriptural pieces, calculated to instruct youth in the art of reading with propriety; and at the same time to inculcate the principles of morality and religion: in which it has been attempted to shew the learner the emphatic words in every sentence.* (BL).

ROBINSON, Robert   Inspector of National Schools, Ireland

1863* Ed   *A manual of method and organisation. Adapted to the primary schools of Great Britain, Ireland, and the colonies.* (BL); 2nd edn 1867; 3rd edn 1869; anr edn 1882.   Pp. 108, 296–7, 347, 353; *109, 365, 383*.

ROBINSON, William L.

[1876?] RE   *A phonic reading book*, Manchester. 2nd edn 1876 (BL).

1876* Ed   *Phonic reading and how to teach it. Being the introduction to the 'Phonic Reading Book'*, Manchester. (BL).   Pp. 40, 69.

1862* RE   *The pronouncing reading book, for children from five to ten years of age, on a new plan . . . with an introduction to the art of reading.* (BL).   Pp. 95–6; 48.

1868* S   *The Wakefield spelling book, Parts 3 and 4.* (BL). Parts 1 and 2, originally published, it seems, after Parts 3 and 4, were for junior classes. (BL).   Pp. *54, 87.*

RODGERS, James   'Master of the Infants School, Cheltenham'

[c. 1825]* Ed   *A practical treatise on infant education; being an entire plan for organising and conducting infant schools.* (BL); anr edn 1836 (Gloucester County L).   P. 71.

ROE, Mr see ROBINSON, Mr

ROE, Richard Baillie

1801 B   *The elements of English metre, both in prose and verse.* (BL).

1829* S   *An English spelling-book, containing all the common words in the language. To which is prefixed an introduction, in three parts, exhibiting I. The sounds of the letters. II. The quantities of the syllables. III. A rhythmical classification of words,* Dublin. (BL).   Pp. 107–8, 126.

ROGERS, Henry   1806–77   'Professor of the English language & literature, University College, London'

1838* G   *A general introduction to a course of lectures on English grammar and composition.* (BL).   Pp. 363, 365.

ROLLIN, Charles   1661–1741

1734* B   *The method of teaching and studying the belles lettres, or an introduction to languages, poetry, rhetoric, history . . . &c. With reflections on taste; and instructions with regard to the eloquence of the pulpit, the bar and the stage . . . Designed more particularly for students in the universities.* (Translated from *De la manière d'enseigner et d'étudier les belles-lettres, par raport à l'esprit et au coeur,* 1726–8.) Many edns to 1810. Alston, X, 181–95.   Pp. *163, 180, 184.*

RONKSLEY, William   'Sometime teacher of a grammar school'

1712* RE   *The child's weeks-work: or, a little book, so nicely suited to the genius and capacity of a little child, both for matter and method, that it will infallibly allure and lead him on into a way of reading with all the ease and expedition that can be desired.* (BL). Sloane, 256; Johnson, p. 47; *OCCL*, p. 460.   Pp. 161–2.

[1699] RE   *Reading made more easie, or a necessary preparation for the psalter; compos'd for the little ones, with variety of pictures for their ease and delight.* No copy. *TC*, III (May 1699).

[ROOME, Thomas]   Teacher

1812* G   *A companion to English grammar, or familiar exercises, adapted to the capacities of children, and designed as an introduction to the study of the English language.* Nottingham. (Nottingham UL).   Pp. *81, 351.*

[ROSCOE, William, and others]

1820* RA   *Poems for youth. By a family circle, Part I.* (BL); Part II was published in 1821* (BL).

ROSS, Thomas

[1797] S   *A spelling book,* Edinburgh. No copy. Alston, IV, 928.

ROSS, William

1842* La   *An elementary etymological manual of the English language for the use of* *schools. To which is prefixed, practical observations on teaching etymology.* (BL).

ROSS, William Stewart 1844–1906 Sometime teacher

[1870] G *A practical textbook of grammatical analysis,* Edinburgh. (BL).

[1869]* P *A system of elocution, based upon grammatical analysis, with copious extracts for practice, for the use of schools,* Edinburgh. (Leeds UL); new edn London, [1878] (BL). P. *220.*

ROTHWELL, J[ames] 'Master of the Free School, Blacrod'

1787* G *A comprehensive grammar of the English language, for the use of youth,* Warrington. (Wigan PL); 2nd edn London, 1797* (Wigan PL). Alston, I, 439–40. P. *328.*

ROUSSEAU, S.

1813 Ex *Rules for punctuation; or, an attempt to facilitate the art of pointing a written composition, on the principles of grammar and reason.* (BL). Advertised in 1816 as *Punctuation, or . . . for the use of schools.*

ROWBOTHAM, J.

1839* S *A new derivative spelling-book, in which not only the origin of each word is given from the Greek . . . and other languages; but also their present acceptation, with the parts of speech accurately distinguished, and the syllables accented agreeably to the most correct pronunciation.* (BL); anr edn 1855 (BL); anr edn 1858 (BL). BL catalogue gives Rowbotham's first name as John; Chalmers, p. 154, gives it as James.

ROWDEN, Frances Arabella

1820* B *Biographical sketches of the most distinguished writers of ancient and modern times . . . Intended for the use of schools and private education.* (Bookseller). P. *219.*

ROWE, Harry

1797* RA *Macbeth: a tragedy. Written by William Shakespeare. With notes by Harry Rowe.* York: for the annotator, Wilson, Spence and Mawman. Pp. 88 (BL); 2nd edn 1799 (BL). Prepared for Rowe's puppet company.

ROWTON, Frederic

1846 Ex *The debater: a new theory of the art of speaking; being a series of complete debates, and questions for discussion; with references to the best sources of information on each particular topic.* (BL); 2nd edn 1850* (personal). Not known to me at the time chapter 6 was written.

[Anon.]

[*c.* 1850]* RE *The royal Albert improved primer, being a first book for children,* S. Marks and Sons. (V&A).

[Anon.]

[*c.* 1746?] S *The royal guide; or, an easy introduction to reading English . . . Most humbly inscribed to His Royal Highness Prince Edward,* E. Newbery. (Title from edn [*c.* 1770]). (V&A); Whalley, p. 139; [*c.* 1768?] (Bath PL); [*c.* 1770?]* (V&A 60.Z.414). Alston, IV, 711–12; Roscoe, J323, describes the incomplete or undated condition of all known copies.

[Anon.]

[*c.* 1830] RE *The royal London primer: or, reading made easy,* Johnson. No copy. Anr edn Ryle and Co. [*c.* 1850]* (Bedford CHE).

[Anon.]

[*c.* 1820]?* RE   *The royal penny reading easy*, Wellingborough, W. Bellamy. (Bedford CHE).

[Anon.]

[1746?] RE   *The royal primer; or an easy and pleasant guide to the art of reading*, J. Newbery. Sotheby sale notice in *TLS*, 11 November 1977, records a copy inscribed 1746. Roscoe, J324, records no edn earlier than a possible 1751, and describes some of the uncertainties surrounding this book. Undated edns before 1800 are in BL (C.27.a.41; 905.a.8(1)) and in V&A (60.Z.416)*. American edns from 1768 to 1796 are listed in Heartman, 1935. British edns after 1800 include London, 1804, F.C. Morgan, 244; 1831, Sotheby, 21 April 1977, lot 2242; Dublin, 1813 (Huntington L); Dublin, 1818* (BL); London [1854?], [1858] and [1870?] (BL).

[Anon.]

[*c.* 1829] RE   *The royal primer, improved*, Banbury: J.G. Rusher. Chalmers, p. 155.

[Anon.]

[1827] RE   *The royal primer; or, high road to learning*, Harris. No copy; anr edn 1831, no copy; anr edn [*c.* 1835]* (V&A). Moon, 733.

[Anon.]

[1748?] S   *The royal spelling book and grammar.* No copy. Alston, IV, 587.

ROZZELL, William

1795 G   *A poetical introduction to English grammar, designed for the purpose of assisting the memories of youth.* No copy. Alston, I, 494.

RUDD, Sayer   d. 1757   'Master of the Academy at Deale, in Kent'

1755 La   Πρόδρομος: *or, observations on the English letters. Being an attempt to reform our alphabet, and regulate our manner of speling.* (O); Scolar Press facsimile 1967*. Alston, VI, 480.   Pp. 28, 38–9.

[Anon.]

1795* G   *Rudiments of constructive etymology and syntax.* (BL); 2nd edn 1797 (BL). Alston I, 490–1.   P. *324.*

[Anon.]

1788* G   *Rudiments of English grammar; for the use of young beginners*, Falmouth. (BL). Alston, I, 448.

[Anon.]

[*c.* 1746]   *The rudiments of English learning*: Cooper. *Gent. Mag.*, 16 (June 1746), 332. Cf. Alston, IV, 582. No copy.

[Anon.]

[1854] G   *The rugged path made smooth; or, grammar illustrated in scriptural truths. By a lady.* (BL).

RUSHER, William   1759–1849   Master of the charity school, Banbury

[1767?] S   *Reading made most easy.* No copy. No datable copy of an early edn seems to have survived. An undated Banbury edn is in V&A; 150th edn, Banbury, [*c.* 1815?], in Blackwell's catalogue A.18 (1981); 220th edn, Banbury, [*c.* 1830]* (BL); anr edn Newcastle, 1831 (Wandsworth PL); 405th edn, Newcastle, [*c.* 1835] (BL); anr edn, Woodbridge, [*c.* 1845] (BL); 459th edn (O). The conjectural dates and professed edn numbers are inconsistent with each other, and the latter may often be publishers' puff by implication. Only inspection would show how far books carrying this title have any relation to Rusher's original; until some copy approaching that original is discovered, discussion is very speculative. Alston, IV, 870, and Supplement, p. 34.

RUSHTON, William

1869 G   *Rules and cautions in English grammar, founded on the analysis of sentences.* (BL; O).

RUSSEL, William P.

1804 La   *A challenge to all England, or an elegant specimen of the verbotomical spelling-book, or improved vocabulary of the English language.* (BL).

1805* La   *Verbotomy; or, the anatomy of words; shewing their component parts: being an elegant specimen of what may be accomplished in the arrangement of language . . . [By] W.P. Russel, verbotomist; or word-dissector . . . Sold by the author, wherever his habitation may happen to be. At present it is no. 23, Maiden-Lane, Covent Garden.* Russel hopes the book will be used in schools.

RUSSELL, John   1787–1863   'Late headmaster of Charterhouse School'

1833* G   *English grammar.* (BL); nine further edns to 1842.

RUSSELL, John

[1868] S   *Guide to the difficulties of English spelling.* Murby. (BL).

[1870] La   *(Murby's) Handbook of English etymology, with exercises and suggestions for teachers.* T. Murby. (BL).

S., N.

[1677] S   *The English tutor, or the plain path-way to the English tongue. Being a most plain and familiar method for the teaching of children to spell and read English exactly; both in whole words, and also divided . . . prepar'd and methodized for the use and benefit of English schools.* (title from 1716 edn). No copies of any edn before the 7th, 1716* (BL, missing last leaf). Alston, IV, 130–1, and Supplement p. 27, where he suggests Nathaniel Strong as the author, but evidence is lacking.   Pp. 91, 106; 57.

S., R.

1672* Ex   *Ludus ludi literarii: or, schoolboys' exercises and divertisements. In XLVII speeches; some of them Latine, but most English; spoken (and prepared to be spoken) in a private school about London, at several breakings up, in the year 1671.* (BL).   P. 277.

SABINE, H.

1802 G   *English grammar.* Allibone. No copy.

1813 S   *An invaluable discovery in writing, by which the most imperfect . . . hands are reformed . . . to which is added an easy . . . mode of spelling.* (BL).

[Anon.]

1835* RA   *Sacred poetry adapted to the understanding of children and youth.* For the Commissioners of National Education in Ireland. Dublin. Compiled by James Carlile. (BL); anr edn 1837, Akenson, pp. 231, 240; BL has edns 1845, 1850, 1854; anr edn 1855 (NLI).   P. 221.

SADLER, Percy

1853 G   *The stepping stone to English grammar. Containing several hundred questions and answers.* (BL; O); new edn 1867 (Wisconsin UL).

ST QUENTIN, Dominique

1812* G   *The first rudiments of general grammar, applicable to all languages. Comprised in twelve elementary lessons. Particularly calculated for the instruction of children, and adapted to the Abbé Gaultier's method of teaching with analytical tables.* (private collection; Columbia UL). The book is to be used with a board and counters.   P. *363*.

[Anon.]

[1786] S   *The Salisbury spelling-book, for the use of Sunday schools; with historical and moral extracts from the New Testament, and prayers for children of different ages at the Sunday schools,* [Salisbury]. No copy; 2nd edn Salisbury, 1786* (BL). Alston, IV, 855–6 gives 12th edn Salisbury, 1809 (Leicester UL), to which can be added anr edn, Salisbury: J. Easton, 1813 (DES).

SALMON, Nicholas

1798* G   *The first principles of English grammar, methodically exhibited and explained, upon a plan entirely new, tending to render the knowledge of them useful in the study of other languages.* (BL). Alston, I, 516.

SAMPSON, George

1790 G   *An essay towards the ascertaining of English grammar,* Londonderry. No copy known. Alston, I, 452.

SAXON, Samuel   Teacher

[a. 1737] S   *The English schollar's assistant: or, the rudiments of the English tongue. In four parts.* I.[Letters]; II.[Syllables]; III.[Words]; IV.[Sentences] . . . *And for a further assistance to teachers the interrogatories are annex'd under each head to examine children by.* No copy of 1st edn. 2nd edn, Reading, 1737*; Scolar Press facsimile 1971. Vorlat, 1975.

SAYER, Thomas   Lilling Academy, near York

1860* Ed   *Fireside remarks on education.* (O). Pp. 50–4 contain a highpitched attack on novel-reading.

The school expositor see GRACE, John Austin

[Anon.]

[a. 1702] S   *The school of vertue: being a useful book to teach children to spell.* Advertised in P.K., *c.* 1700, and in *A little book for little children,* 1702.

[Anon.]

1863 G   *The schoolboy's short English grammar, on an original plan; being a collection of short definitions, designed to be committed to memory,* Manchester. (BL; O). As: *A plain, practical English grammar, on an original plan, being a collection of short definitions . . . with examples and exercises. By two schoolmasters.* Manchester, [1871] (BL; NLS).

[Anon.]

1855 La   *The schoolmaster at home. Errors in speaking and writing corrected; a few words on the letters H and R; with familiar synonymes, and words of similar sound distinguished.* (BL); anr edn N.Y., 1857 (BL).

SCOFFIN, William   Teacher

[1690] S   *A help to true spelling and reading, or a very easie method for the teaching rightly to spell, and exactly to read, English* [etc.]. No copy. 2nd edn as: *A help . . . method for the teaching children, or elder persons, rightly to spell . . .* [as above], 1705* (Toronto PL). Alston, IV, 164–5.   Pp. 60, 156.

SCOTT, A.

1820* G *Grammar of the English language; being the precursor of a series of grammars.* Stockdale. (BL). The projected grammars are of foreign languages.   P. *364.*

1822* RE *The rational primer, or introduction to the pronouncing books, in which by means of the first or name sounds of letters, their union in simple words and the combination of these in little stories, the first notion of the use of language, as well as the fundamental knowledge of letters, and their imitation in writing, may be communicated to children; the methods of Bell, Pestalozzi, &c being also employed. With important directions to teachers.* Stockdale. Pp. 235. (BL).   P. *65.*

SCOTT, John 'Schoolmaster at South Shields'

1771 S *The schoolboy's sure guide; or spelling and reading made agreeable and easy. Wherein the pronunciation and spelling of the English language are reduced to a few general heads . . . To which are added, several lessons, moral and religious.* (title from 1774; no copy of 1771 edn); anr edn Edinburgh, 1774* (BL); anr edn Dundee, 1797, Kennedy, 7849. Alston, IV, 720–1 and Plate 76 for t.p. of 1774 edn.   P. *126.*

SCOTT, Walter 'Master of the Grammar School, Bourn, Lincs.'

[1855] G *The parts of speech: an introduction to English grammar, in verse; with questions.* (BL).

SCOTT, William   Teacher

1793a RA *Beauties of eminent writers, selected and arranged for the instruction of youth in the proper reading and reciting of the English language . . . To which is added, a concise system of English grammar, with exercises in orthography . . . For the use of schools and private classes,* Edinburgh, 2 vols. (Leeds UL); 2nd edn 1795* (NLS); 3rd edn 1797* (BL, vol. II of 2nd edn); 4th edn 1799 (NLS); 8th edn 1806/7 (NLS); anr edn London, 1826 (BL).

1809 G *A concise system of English grammar* see his *Principles of English grammar.*

1807* P *Elements of elocution: consisting of rules, observations, and concise exercises, methodically arranged as an assistant to teachers; and particularly calculated for the improvement of youth, in the reading and speaking of the English language,* Edinburgh. (Glasgow PL).

1776 S *An introduction to reading and spelling.* No copy; 7th edn Edinburgh, 1796* (NLS). Alston, IV, 759–64, lists other edns to 1803, to which add Edinburgh, 1820 (Edinburgh PL).   Pp. *26, 45, 50, 52.*

1779* RA *Lessons in elocution; or, miscellaneous pieces in prose and verse, selected from the best authors, for the perusal of persons of taste, and the improvement of youth in reading and speaking,* Edinburgh (BL); 3rd edn, 'greatly altered' and containing an English grammar, 1789* (Oslo UL); 11th edn Edinburgh, 1797 (Sotheby, Cat. 13, April 1979); 12th edn Edinburgh, 1799* (BL); 15th edn Edinburgh, 1801 (O); at least forty-six American edns 1788–1850. Gumuchian, 5267; Nietz, 1961, p. 62; Belok, p. 103; Carpenter, 1963, p. 170.

1777a D *A new spelling, pronouncing, and explanatory dictionary of the English language . . . to which is prefixed an introductory essay, in three parts. I. [Pronunciation]. II. [Elocution]. III. [English grammar].* No copy; Edinburgh,

1786* (Lund UL); anr edn Edinburgh, 1802* (NLS); other edns to 1815 in Alston, V, 307–10, to which add Edinburgh, 1798 (Edinburgh PL). The grammar is the same as that in his *Lessons in elocution*, 1789 edn. Law, p. 155.

1777b G *Principles of English grammar*, Edinburgh. No copy; presumably the same as his *A concise system of English grammar*, Edinburgh, 1809 (Edinburgh PL). It is likely that the *Principles* are the same as the grammar, with that title, in the 1789 edn of *Lessons in elocution* and as the one, called *Elements of English grammar*, in the *Dictionary* (above). GB adds to the uncertainty by giving just 'Grammar, 1797'.

1793b* G *A short system of English grammar, with examples of improper and inelegant constructions and Scotticisms; selected chiefly from Lowth's Introduction to English Grammar, of which it may be considered an abridgment. To which are added, exercises in English pronunciation and orthography*, Edinburgh, 38 pp. (NLS). Alston, I, 472.

Note: Scott's designation of himself varies. In the 1786 edn of the dictionary and in 1807 he is 'Teacher of Elocution and Geography'. In the 1789 edn of *Lessons in elocution* he is 'Teacher of English, Writing, and Accounts'. In 1793 (*Beauties*) he is 'Teacher of the English language and Geography' or, in the grammar, just 'Teacher of the English language'. Biographical outline in Law, pp. 155–6.

SCOTTISH SCHOOL BOOK ASSOCIATION

[1845]a RS *The child's first book. No. 1. The primer*. Edinburgh. (BL).

[1845]b RS *The child's first book. No. 2. Second lessons*. Edinburgh (BL).

[1845]c* RS *The child's first book. No. 3. Third lessons*. (BL; O; NLS). P. 88.

[a. 1847] RS *Manual of English pronunciation, or sequel to Third Lessons*. Advertised in 1847.

1847* RS *The child's first book. No. 4. Readings in prose and verse*. Edinburgh (BL; O); anr edn Glasgow, 1868 (NLS).

1840* RS *First collection of instructive extracts*. Edinburgh (NLS).

1841* RS *Second collection of instructive extracts*. Edinburgh (NLS).

1867 RS *Progressive series: my fourth book*. Glasgow (NLS). *My fifth* and *My sixth* books followed.

[a. 1867] RS *Progressive lessons in reading, with aids in composition, and explanatory notes and questions on each lesson. To which is added a list of prefixes . . . and . . . primitives*. Stereotyped edn Glasgow, 1867* (NLS; O).

1863 RS *The advanced reader. Lessons in literature and science*. Glasgow. (O); anr edn 1867 (NLS).

See also *Principles of English grammar*, [a. 1840]

The young child's grammar, 1846

SCRAGGS, George Glyn Master of a boarding school at Buckingham

1802* Ex *English composition, in a method entirely new, with various short contrasted examples, from celebrated writers, the whole adapted to common capacities, and designed as an easy help to form a good style, and to acquire a taste for the works of the best authors. To which are added, an essay on the advantages of understanding composition, and a list of select books for English readers with remarks*. (BL; Hull UL; Leicester UL). Pp. 281, 285.

[a. 1802] RA *Instructive selections, or the beauties of sentiment, being striking extracts from near 150 of the best authors, ancient and modern, in prose and poetry, on subjects religious, moral, literary and entertaining.* A 2nd edn dated 1802 is advertised in his *English composition.* No copy.

[Anon.]

[a. 1813] S *The scripture spelling book.* An introduction to *The Christian child's reader.* Advertised by Pinnock in 1813.

SEALLY, John 1747?–1795 Teacher

[1773?]* B *Belles lettres for the ladies: or, a new and easy introduction to polite literature. Comprehending not only the elements of oratory, but a summary account of the lives and characters of the most illustrious writers . . . and also, the beauties of composition; with examples in every species of style.* (2 vols.) (O). Alston, VI, 229. P. *184.*

[a. 1787] *The complete young man's companion.* A 2nd edn was advertised in Mary Weightman's *The juvenile speaker,* 1787a.

1767 S *The universal tutor: or, new English spelling book and expositor.* No copy. Alston, IV, 710.

SEARCH, Edward see TUCKER, Abraham.

SEARLE, Thomas

1822 G *An English grammar in verse, with examples selected from scripture,* Chipping Norton. (O; BL).

1828 Ex *The English letter-writer,* Dresden. (BL).

[Anon.]

[1704] S *The second book for children, or the compleat schoolmaster. In two parts. I. Easie and plain directions for spelling, reading, and writing, true English, according to the most accurate method. With divers tables, wherein the most common English words, and proper names used in scripture, are divided into syllables . . . II. The grounds and principles of religion* [etc.]. No copy. *TC,* III, 414. Alston, IV, 220.

[Anon.]

[1856]* RE *The second class book,* Llanelly: Rees and Thomas. 24 pp. (BL).

[Anon.]

1803* Ex *The secretary, and complete letter writer . . . to which is added . . . an introduction to English grammar,* Birmingham. (BL).

[SEDGER, John] Teacher

1798 G *The structure of the English language; exhibiting an easy and familiar method of acquiring a grammatical knowledge of its constituent parts.* (BL). Scolar Press facsimile 1970*. Alston, I, 517. Pp. 339; *323.*

SEELEY, Sir John Robert 1834–95 Professor of Modern History, Cambridge, and sometime teacher in school

1868 Ed *English in schools,* in *Macmillan's Magazine,* November. Reprinted in his *Lectures and essays,* 1870; rev. edn ed. M. Seeley, 1895*.

[Anon.]

[1855]* RA *Select poetry for children. A book for school and home use.* (BL; NLS).

[Anon.]

[a. 1870] RA *Select poetry for standard five.* Chambers. (Advt).

[Anon.]

[1838] RA *A selection of hymns and poetry, for the use of infant and juvenile schools and families. In five parts. Prepared at the request of the committee of the Home and Colonial Juvenile School Society.* 2nd edn 1840; 3rd edn 1846* (BL); 6th edn 1857 (BL). The prefaces to the 1st and 2nd edns, reprinted in the 3rd, are dated 1838 and 1840.

[Anon.]

1861* RA   *A selection of poetry for the use of schools. Part 1,* York: T. Brady. (BL).

[Anon.]

1812* RA   *A selection from the Spectator, printed for the use of Charter-House School.* (BL); 2nd edn 1827, *NCBEL,* III, 1103. Plain text, without introduction.

[Anon.]

1821–2 RA   *Selections from the British poets . . . with introductions.* Dublin. 2 vols. For the Commissioners of National Education in Ireland. (NLI).   P. 254.

1849 RA   *Selections from the British poets chronologically arranged from Chaucer to the present time.* Akenson, p. 231; anr edn, 2 vols. Dublin, 1851–2* (BL); anr edn 1855 (BL); anr edn 1856 (Leeds UL, vol. II only). A revision of the previous work, taken over from their predecessors by the 1831 Commissioners.

[Anon.]

1862* RA   *Selections of poetry for reading and study.* (BL).   P. *221.*

[Anon.]

1807* G   *The self-instructor, or young man's best companion; being an introduction to all the various branches of useful knowledge: containing writing, grammar* [etc.], Liverpool. (BL); anr edn Liverpool, [1813] (Hull UL); anr edn Liverpool, [1815] (BL).

[Anon.]   'By a teacher'

1845* C   *The self-instructor's assistant in the study of the common subjects taught in English schools, and also in classics and mathematics,* (Torquay printed) (BL).

[SERGEANT, John]   1622–1707

1657 B   *The mysterie of rhetorique unvail'd, wherein above 130 the tropes and figures are severally derived from the Greek into English, together with lively definitions and variety of Latin, English, scriptural examples . . . Eminently delightful and profitable for young scholars . . . enabling them to discern and imitate the elegancy in any author they read. By John Smith, Gent.* (BL). Ten edns in all to 1721; abridged edn 1739; Scolar Press facsimile 1969*. Alston, VI, 80–7. 'John Smith' is one of several pseudonyms that Sergeant is said to have used.   P. 151.

[Anon.]

[a. 1850] RA   *The Sessional School collection; consisting of religious and moral instruction; a selection of fables; descriptions of animals, places, manners &c.* 12th edn Edinburgh: Oliver and Boyd, 1850* (personal).

[Anon.]

[a. 1850] RE   *The Sessional School first book.* Edinburgh: Oliver and Boyd. Advertised in the *Sessional school collection,* 1850.

[Anon.]

[a. 1850] RE   *The Sessional School second book.* 14th edn advertised as above.

SEWELL, Elizabeth Missing   1815–1906   Teacher

1861 S   *Dictation exercises.* Second edn 1862* (BL); 2nd series 1865* (BL).   Pp. 129–30.

1872 G   *Grammar made easy.* (BL).

SEWELL, William   'Schoolmaster'

1789* G   *English grammar methodized, in a concise and comprehensive treatise. Compiled for the use of schools.* Bristol: J. Norton. (Chicago PL; NYct). Alston, I, 449a.   Pp. 94, 292–3, 339; *283, 376.*

SHAKESPEARE, William

Anonymous edition:

1859* P   *Hamlet . . . with notes, glossarial, grammatical, and explanatory.* Routledge. (BL). The cover is headed 'Middle Class Examination'.

Editions and collections by named editors, see:

EVANS, J., 1818

HUNTER, J., 1860–2

MAXWELL, C., 1828

NEIL, S., 1873

PITMAN, J.R., 1822

ROWE, H., 1797

SHORTER, T., 1865

SMART, B.H., 1839

SHARP, John   'Teacher of the Free English School, Berwick upon Tweed'

1781* S   *A most easy guide to reading and spelling English, for the use of schools. In two parts . . . with a preface comprehending the substance of the book in a more orderly and particular manner,* Berwick. (BL). Alston, IV, 776 and Plate 82 for t.p.   P. 105.

SHARP, Ralph

1819* B   *The flowers of rhetoric, the graces of eloquence, and the charms of oratory; depicted by men celebrated for their taste, genius, diction, and erudition: particularly by* [thirty-six names, from Homer to Curran]. (BL).

SHATFORD, W.   'Schoolmaster, Kettering'

1834* G   *An English grammar, adapted to the younger classes of learners.* (BL).   P. *346n.*

SHAW, John   'Headmaster of the Free Grammar School, Rochdale'

1778* G   *A methodical English grammar: containing rules and directions for speaking and writing the English language with propriety: illustrated by a variety of examples and exercises. For the use of schools.* (BL); 4th edn 1793*. Alston, I, 353–5.   Pp. 338–9, 343; *383.*

SHAW, Samuel   1635–96   Master of the Grammar School, Ashby-de-la-Zouch

1678–9* P   *Words made visible: or, grammar and rhetorick accommodated to the lives and manners of men.* 2 parts. (BL); anr edn, as: *Minerva's triumph,* 1680; anr edn 1681; Scolar Press facsimile of 1678–9 edn, 1972*.   P. *297.*

SHAW, Thomas Budge   1813–62   Professor of English literature, St Petersburg

1848 B   *Outlines of English literature. DNB.* 2nd edn 1849* (BL); as *The Student's manual of English literature,* ed. W. Smith, 1864, 1868; as *A complete manual of English literature,* N.Y., 1867. Carpenter, p. 164; Applebee, p. 10.   P. *219.*

1864* RA   *The student's specimens of English literature,* ed. with additions by W. Smith. (BL). The preface does not make it clear whether the publication is posthumous or whether there was an earlier edn.

SHELLEY, Edward

[a. 1847] G   *The people's grammar; or English grammar without difficulties for the million.* 2nd edn Huddersfield, 1847 (O).

SHELLEY, George   1666?–1736?   Writing-master, Christ's Hospital

1712* RA   *Sentences and maxims divine, moral, and historical, in prose and verse. Design'd for the conduct and instruction of human life; and particularly for the improvement of youth in good sence and correct English. The whole containing a select and curious collection of copies of all sorts.* (BL); 3rd edn 1761 (BL).   P. 181.

SHEPHERD, W.,   JOYCE, J. and   CARPENTER, Lant

1815* Ed   *Systematic education: or elementary instruction in the various departments of literature and science; with practical rules for studying each branch of useful knowledge,* Liverpool, 2 vols. (BL); 2nd edn London, 1817; 3rd edn 1822.   P. *358*.

SHERIDAN, Thomas   1687–1738   Teacher

1714* G   *An easy introduction of grammar in English. For the understanding of the Latin tongue. Compil'd not only for the ease and encouragement of youth, but also for their moral improvement; having the syntaxis examples gather'd from the choicest pieces of the best authors,* Dublin. (BL). See next item.

[1714?]* RA   *A method to improve the fancy. In which is a choice collection of images and descriptions (sic). With various figurative beauties, gather'd from the best Latin and English poets, both ancient and modern,* Dublin. Pp. 253–336 of his *An easy introduction* . . ., but with a separate t.p.

SHERIDAN, Thomas (the younger)   1719–88

1756 Ed   *British education: or, the sources of the disorders of Great Britain. Being an essay towards proving, that the immorality, ignorance, and false taste, which so generally prevail, are the* . . . *consequences of the present defective system of education. With an attempt to shew, that a revival of the art of speaking, and the study of our own language, might contribute* . . . *to the cure of those evils* [etc]. (BL); 2nd edn Dublin, 1757; anr edn London, 1769; Garland Press facsimile of 1756 edn, N.Y. Scolar Press facsimile of 1756 edn, 1971*. For Sheridan's educational influence see especially W. Benzie, *The Dublin Orator,* U. of Leeds School of English, 1972, not, regrettably, used in the present study.

1762 P   *A course of lectures on elocution: together with two dissertations on language.* (BL). British edns to 1798, American to 1803. Scolar Press facsimile of 1762, 1968*. Alston, VI, 355–63.   Pp. 294, 295; *203, 286*.

1759 P   *A discourse* . . . *introductory to his course of lectures on elocution and the English language.* (BL); 2nd edn 1764 (O); reprinted in his *A course of lectures,* 1762*, Alston, VI, 331–2.

1761 La   *A dissertation on the causes of the difficulties which occur, in learning the English tongue, with a scheme for publishing an English grammar and dictionary.* (BL); anr edn 1762; anr edn 1764; included in his *A course of lectures,* 1762*; Scolar Press facsimile of 1761 edn, 1967. Alston, VI, 483–5, 355 note.

1786 P   *Elements of English: being a new method of teaching the whole art of reading, both with regard to punctuation and spelling.* Part 1. (Edinburgh UL); anr edn Dublin, 1789; Scolar Press facsimile of 1786 edn, 1968*. Alston, VI, 503–5.   Pp. 43–4, 62; *48, 50, 51, 52, 286*.

1775 P   *Lectures on the art of reading. In two parts. Containing Part I. The art of reading prose. II. The art of reading verse.* 2 vols. (title from 1781 edn). (O; BL); 2nd edn, 1781* (BL). Seven further edns to 1805. Alston, VI, 408–15.

1781 P   *A rhetorical grammar of the English language. Calculated solely for the purpose of teaching propriety of pronunciation, and justness of delivery,* Dublin (O; Cambridge UL). Printed also in his *A general dictionary,* 1780. Scolar Press facsimile 1969*. Alston, VI, 494–6; Cohen, 1977, pp. 108–9.   Pp. 294; *43, 54.*

[Anon.]

1796* P   *Sheridan and Henderson's practical method of reading and reciting English poetry, elucidated by a variety of examples taken from some of our most popular poets, and the manner pointed out in which they were read or recited by the above gentlemen: intended for the improvement of youth, and as a necessary introduction to Dr Enfield's Speaker.* (Nottingham UL; BL); Dublin, 1797. Alston, VI, 426–7. Recommended by Morrice, 1801, for ages eleven to fourteen.   Pp. 187–8; *186.*

SHERRY, Richard   d. after 1555   Master of Magdalen College School, Oxford

1555 B   *A treatise of the figures of grammar and rhetorike, profitable for al that be studious of eloquence, and in especiall for suche as in grammer scholes doe reade moste eloquente poetes and oratours.* (Cambridge UL; Lambeth Palace). Alston, VI, 9; Howell 1956, p. 132. A substantial revision of the following work.

[1550] B   *A treatise of schemes and tropes very profytable for the better understanding of good authors, gathered out of the best grammarians and oratours.* (BL); Scholars' Facsimiles, Gainesville, Florida, 1961*. Alston, VI, 8; Howell, 1956, p. 125.   Pp. 149–50, 271.

SHIRLEY, James, see PHILIPPS, Jenkin Thomas

[Anon.]

1786* G   *A short and easy introduction to English grammar . . . first drawn up for the use of Miss Davies's boarding-school, Tryon's Place, Hackney.* (Boston, Mass., PL); Alston, I, 433.   P. 94.

[Anon.]

1800* G   *Short and easy rules for attaining a knowledge of English grammar. To which are added a few letters for the formation of juvenile correspondence.* (Leicester UL); anr edn 1801 (Nottingham UL). Edns to 1813. Alston, I, 535.

[Anon.]

1794* G   *A short English grammar, designed principally for children.* (Aberdeen UL; NLS). Alston, I, 476.   P. 322.

[Anon.]

1793* G   *A short grammatical introduction to the English tongue,* Sheffield. (O). Alston, I, 467, suggests an attribution to J. Hayward (above) but the categories in the two grammars differ substantially.

[Anon.]   'Schoolmaster'

[1693] S   *A short introduction into orthography, or the method of true spelling; published for the common good; but especially for the use of a private grammar and writing school in White-cross Street.* By Richard ——. No copy. *TC,* II, 460 (May 1693). Alston, IV, 172.

[Anon.]

1782 G   *A short introduction to English grammar, adapted to the use of schools, with an appendix; containing, 1. Grammatical figures, and examples of the ellipsis. 2. Observations upon transposition with examples. 3. Observations upon the derivation of words. 4. Examples of grammatical analysis.* Alston, I, 376, suggests that this may be the 1st edn of Harrold (a. 1787) above. The resemblance in titles is so close that this seems probable.

[Anon.]

1793* G   *A short introduction to grammar*, Stockton upon Tees. Alston, I, 467a.

[Anon.]

[1851]* RA   *Short poems and hymns for children to commit to memory.* (BL).

[Anon.]

1853* S   *A short spelling course for the lowest classes in schools.* (BL).

SHORTER, Thomas

1861a* RA   *A book of English poetry, for the school, the fireside, and the country ramble.* (BL).

1862 RA   *A book of English prose. Selected chiefly from recent and living authors.* (BL).

1861b* RA   *Poetry for school and home, from the best authors.* (BL); new edn, 1894.

1865* P   *Shakespeare, for schools and families. Being a selection and abridgment of the principal plays.* Pp. vi, 640. (BL).

SHOVELLER, John   'King's House Academy, near Portsmouth'

1815* Ed   *An essay on the most effectual methods of advancing youth in scholastic education, containing an outline of the course of studies . . . at King's House Academy.* Portsea. (BL); 2nd edn as *Scholastic education; or, a synopsis of the studies recommended to employ the time, and engage the attention of youth; a suggestion of the most efficient methods of tuition and a notice of the authors which may be advantageously used in a scholastic course.* Portsmouth. (BL).   P. 214.

[Anon.]

[*c.* 1815]* RE   *The silver primer; or, first book for children.* York. (V&A). Chalmers, p. 156, gives edns in 1820 and 1834; NBL, 1973, no. 62; Whalley, p. 140; Gumuchian, no. 211.

SIMMONITE, William Joseph

1843* G   *Juvenile grammar of the English language, being an abridgment of the Practical Self-Teaching Grammar; comprising orthography, etymology, syntax, and prosody, with exercises and illustrations; also an introductory system of composition, for the use of schools,* Sheffield: J.H. Greaves. (Sheffield PL; BL).

1841* G   *The practical self-teaching grammar of the English language: comprising orthography, etymology, syntax, & prosody, with copious exercises and practical illustrations. Also, style, rhetoric, and a complete system of composition . . . for the use of schools, local preachers, and young men,* Sheffield and London. (Sheffield PL; BL; O).

[Anon.]

1836 RE   *Simple lessons in reading.* Orr. Chalmers, p. 123. A work with same title was advertised by Chambers in 1845.

[SIMPSON, E.C.]   Teacher

1838* RA   *Rhymes for the young. Written for use in the author's own school.* (BL).

SIMPSON, George   'A master in Bristol Grammar School'

1858* Ex   *Elliptical English. A course of practical exercises in composition. With a key. Two parts.* (BL).   P. 354.

SIMPSON, Robert
[a. 1831] RE   *A primer, for the use of Sunday schools*, SPCK. New edn 1831. (BL).
SINNETT, John Taylor   'English tutor to Armand Carrel, the Junius of France'
1848 G   *The plain and easy English grammar for the industrious classes*, from Lowres, 1863; anr edn 1853* (BL). The grammar was advertised in November 1846, according to Q.D. Leavis, *Fiction and the reading public*, 1932, p. 176.   Pp. 286–7.
SKILLERN, Richard Solloway   1774–1836   Master, Crypt School, Gloucester
1802 G   *A new system of English grammar; or, English so illustrated, as to facilitate the acquisition of other languages, whether ancient or modern. With an appendix, containing a complete system of parsing*. Gloucester (title from 1808 edn), Austin, p. 116. 2nd edn, Gloucester, 1808* (BL). P.H. Fisher, *N&Q*, 7 January 1854.
SLACK, Mrs Ann see FISHER, Ann
SLATER, Eliza
1830 G   *One hundred and ten aphorisms in general and English grammar*. (BL; O). [Anon.]
[a. 1845] G   *A slight sketch of English grammar*. Advertised, price sixpence by Richardson of Derby, *c*. 1845. [Anon.]
[a. 1856] S   *The small preceptor; or, a new set of lessons for children*, Glasgow, new edn 1856* (BL); anr edn [1883] (BL).
SMALLFIELD, George
1838 Ex   *Principles of punctuation*. Privately printed. 70 pp. (BL).
SMART, Benjamin Humphrey   *c*. 1786–1872   Private teacher of elocution
1841* G   *The accidence and principles of English grammar*. (BL); Skeat, 1886, records an edn of 1847. Smart's grammatical writings were advertised in various combinations. His work generally is for adults but often has a (hopeful) eye on school use.
1812* P   *A grammar of English sounds, or the first step in elocution; intended also as a second spelling-book: for the use of schools. To which is prefixed an introductory essay, comprising directions for applying the work to training youth, systematically, in a nervous and graceful articulation; teaching orthography* [etc.] (BL). An abbreviation of his *A practical grammar of English pronunciation*.   Pp. 88; 287.
1847* G   *Grammar on its true basis. A manual of grammar, containing examination questions, exercises in orthography, etymology, syntax, prosody . . . auxiliary to the Accidence and Principles of English Grammar*. (BL). A key was published separately in the same year (BL).   P. 360.
1858* G   *An introduction to Grammar on its True Basis, with relation to logic and rhetoric; submitted to teachers as well as learners*. (BL).
1849* Lo   *A manual of logic: being one of two sequels to Grammar on its True Basis*. (BL).
1848* B   *A manual of rhetoric, with exercises for the improvement of style or diction, subjects for narratives, familiar letters, school orations, etc*. (BL).
1831* La   *An outline of sematology; or, an essay towards establishing a new theory of grammar, logic, and rhetoric*. (BL; O).   Pp. 360, 364.

1810 P   *A practical grammar of English pronunciation on plain and recognised principles . . . together with directions to persons who stammer . . . comprehending some new ideas relative to English prosody.* Dated in the preface to his *Theory of elocution.*   P. *287.*

1823* Lo   *Practical logic: or hints to young theme-writers.* (BL).   P. *310.*

1820* P   *The practice of elocution, or a short course of exercises for acquiring the several requisites of a good delivery, arranged to correspond with The Theory of Elocution.* (BL); 3rd edn 1832* (BL); 4th edn 1842; 5th edn 1845; 6th edn 1851. Used by Samuel Worcester in Massachusetts, 1841.

1811 G   *Rudiments of English grammar elucidated, or a guide to parsing: containing a view of grammatical distinctions upon rational principles* [etc.] Advt in his *Grammar of English sounds*; DNB.

1837* La   *Sequel to Sematology. An attempt to clear the way for the regeneration of metaphysics* [etc.]. (BL).

1839* P   *Shakespearian readings: selected and adapted for young persons and others. First series, illustrative of English and Roman history.* (BL); anr edn 1842 (BL).

1819* P   *The theory of elocution, exhibited in connexion with a new philosophical account of the nature of instituted language.* (BL).

1855* La   *Thought and language: an essay having in view the revival, correction, and exclusive establishment of Locke's philosophy.* (BL).

SMART, Martin

1813* RA   *The female class-book; or, three hundred and sixty-five reading lessons, adapted to the use of schools, for every day in the year . . . selected principally from female writers, or on subjects of female education and manners.* (BL).   P. *223.*

SMETHAM, Thomas   Master of an academy at Southgate

1774* G   *The practical grammar; or, an easy way to understand English . . . To which is added, a poetical epitome of grammar, for the help of the memory, with a supplement, containing examples of bad English to be turned into good . . . and a short English grammar, upon the plan of the Latin.* (BL). Alston, I, 317–19.   Pp. 380–1; *319, 346.*

SMITH, Adam   1723–90

1762–3 B   *Lectures on rhetoric and belles lettres.* Students' notes recorded in 1762–3. Ed. John M. Lothian, Nelson, 1963*; ed. J.C. Bryce, vol. IV of the *Glasgow edition of the works and correspondence of Adam Smith*, Oxford, Clarendon Press, 1983*.   Pp. 279; *163.*

SMITH, Charles John   'Late curate, St Paul's, Knightsbridge'

1846* G   *A manual of English grammar; adapted to the use of classical, and the upper classes in parochial schools.* (BL; O).

SMITH, Charles William   'Professor of elocution'

1860* P   *Dramatic scenes from standard authors. For private representation and schools.* (BL).

[1847] P   *Hints on elocution, comprising observations on the improvement and management of the voice . . . selected from Austin, Blair, Burgh* [et al.] (BL). At least five edns to 1868.

SMITH, Charlotte   1749–1806

1804* RH   *Conversations introducing poetry: chiefly on subjects of natural history. For the use of children and young persons,* 2 vols. (BL); anr edn 1815. NBL, 1973, no. 730; anr edn 1819 (BL); in one volume 1863 (BL).   Pp. 213–14.

SMITH, Harriet

1848 G   *English grammar simplified*. Bath. (BL; O).

SMITH, James   'Master of the Public Grammar School at Holt'

[a. 1778] G   *A compendium of English grammar . . . with an appendix, containing general directions for reading . . . to which are added, English exercises, for the use of schools. The whole designed principally for children before they enter upon Latin grammar; and for such as have not the advantage of a classical education*, Norwich, 3rd edn, 1778* (Gresham Sch L); Alston, I, 349–52, gives three further edns to 1794.

SMITH, James   Master of the English School, St Andrews

[a. 1812] S   *English spelling book*. No copy. Mentioned on the t.p. of 1812 edn of his *The reader and speaker*.

1805 RA   *The reader and speaker, or English class-book for the use of* schools, Cupar: R. Tullis. No copy. Doughty no. 11. 3rd edn as *The reader and speaker, or, English class-book, containing, 1. Lessons moral and instructive. 2. Lessons narrative and pathetic. 3. Characters and epistles. 4. Poetry. 5.Miscellaneous pieces. 6. Dramatic pieces. 7. Speeches and soliloquies. 8. Concise passages which exemplify the modulation and management of the voice in reading and speaking. To which is added, an epitome of English grammar*, Cupar, 1812* (N.E. Fife District Library, Cupar), Doughty, no. 27; 4th edn Cupar, 1823 (St Andrews UL), Doughty, no. 59.

SMITH, John, see SERGEANT, John

SMITH, John   1767–1821   Private teacher, of Timberhill, Norwich

[1825?]* G   *Exercises in false English; distinctive, instructive, and entertaining*. Norwich. (BL).   P. 327.

[a. 1816] G   *A grammar of the English language, upon improved principles, as defined in the preface*. 2nd edn Norwich, 1816 (BL; Glasgow UL; Wisconsin UL); 3rd edn Norwich, [c. 1820]* (BL).   P. 95.

1812 G?   *Introduction to a practical knowledge of the English language*, Norwich. No copy. Watt; Allibone.

[c. 1820]* G   *A key to the false exercises, under the syntax rules, in the third edition of A Grammar of the English Language . . . containing also general specimens of parsing. With an appendix*, Norwich. (BL).

SMITH, John   'Lecturer on early education [and] on Smith & Dolier's plans of instruction'

[c. 1831] La   *A key to pleasant exercises in reading, parsing, and mental arithmetic*. [8th edn] Liverpool, printed 1840*. Pp. 140. In the preface Smith says he has revised his work seven times and that it has had seven editions in a little more than nine years. It is a book of independent exercises, not a book of solutions to another work; an expanded form of the following work.   P. 123.

[1830]* Ed   *A key to reading, designed to assist parents and teachers to superintend lessons for youth . . . To which are added, an imaginary grammatical picture, an introduction to mental arithmetic, and a sketch of mnemonics*. Liverpool. (BL); 2nd edn [1830] (BL; Glasgow UL).   Pp. 256–7, 356.

1834* La   *Lessons on words and objects, with easy and amusing experiments for the parlour or school*. (Liverpool printed). (BL); anr edn 1840, Chalmers, p. 157.

SMITH, Peter 'Teacher of English composition, &c'

1826* G *An analytical system of English grammar., . . . illustrated by appropriate rules, examples and exercises . . . adapted to the use of public schools and private seminaries,* Edinburgh. (BL). An abridgment of the grammatical part of his *A practical guide.*

1824* G *A practical guide to the composition and application of the English language; or, a compendious system of English grammar, literary criticism, and practical logic,* Edinburgh. (BL; Glasgow UL; Wisconsin UL).

SMITH, Thomas 'Schoolmaster'

a. 1764 S *An easy spelling book for children: beginning with short lessons in words of one syllable . . . To which are added, several scripture histories, and select fables, adorned with neat cuts, for the entertainment of children. The sixth edition: with . . . additions and alterations, by the Rev. Mr John Parsons, late Rector of Wilford,* Nottingham: S. Creswell, 1764* (ULIE, incomplete). Alston, IV, 877 and Supplement, records 16th edn, Derby, and 19th edn, Nottingham, 1816* (Nottingham County L, incomplete copy).   P. *161.*

SMITH, Thomas

1832 G *Smith's edition of Lindley Murray's grammar.* So described by GB.

SMITH, Thomas Buckley 'Principal of the People's College, Nottingham'

[1861]* RA *Choice specimens of English and American poetry, with an appendix of essentials for elocutionary practice. For the use of schools and private families.* (BL).   P. *238.*

[1860] RA *Masterpieces of literature, in prose and poetry.* (BL); anr edn [1861] (BL).

[1858]a* S *The national illustrated reading and spelling book for the young.* (BL).   Pp. 40; *123.*

[1858]b RA *The pupil's manual of choice readings, No. 2 of A New Series of English Manuals.* Piper, Stephenson and Spence. (BL).

[a. 1861] Ex *The pupil's manual of composition* (advt 1861).

1858–9 S *The pupil's manual of spelling.* 2 parts. (BL).

SMITH, W.B. 'Headmaster, City of London Freemen's Orphan School'

[1860]* G *Abridgment of Murray's English Grammar, with an appendix. Designed for the younger classes of learners.* (BL).

SMITH, William 'Teacher', Edinburgh

1822 RE *First lessons in teaching a child to read and spell English on a plain and easy (learned) method,* Edinburgh: J. Glass (BL); 2nd edn with improvements, 1823* (BL).

[SNELL, George]

1649* Ed *The right teaching of useful knowledg, to fit scholars for som honest profession; shewing so much skil as anie man needeth (that is not a teacher) in all knowledges, in one schole, in a shorter time in a more plain waie, and for much less expens than ever hath been used since of old the arts were so taught in the Greek and Romane empire.* (BL). Alston, X, 47.   Pp. 119–20, 374.

SOCIETY FOR THE EDUCATION OF THE POOR OF IRELAND (Kildare Place Society)

See *The Dublin reading book,* 1819
       Questions on the Dublin reading book, [1819?]
       The Dublin spelling book, 1819

SOCIETY FOR THE PROMOTION OF CHRISTIAN KNOWLEDGE
1831* RS   *The first miscellaneous reading book for the use of schools.* (BL). The society was here called the Christian Knowledge Society.
1835–7 RS   *The instructor,* 1–7. Goldstrom, 1972a, p. 101n.
1838 RS   (Graded readers) 1–4. No copies. Goldstrom, *ibid.*
1851 RS   *First reading book.* (BL).
1854a* RS   *Second reading book.* (BL).
1854b* RS   *Third reading book.* (BL; Fulham PL).
1857 RS   *Supplement to the Third Reading Book.* Advt.
1854c RS   *Fourth reading book.* (Fulham PL); anr edn 1856 (BL).
[1844?] RS   *Reading books,* 1–2. Chalmers, p. 158.
See also *A little reading book* [*c.* 1825].

SONNENSCHEIN, Adolf and   MEIKLEJOHN, John Miller Dow
1869* RE   *The English method of teaching to read. I. The nursery book. II. The first course. III. The second course. IV. Third & fourth courses.* (BL). Diack, pp. 139f; Mathews, p. 154.   P. 130.

SOUTHEY, Robert see M., I., 1831.

SPALDING, William   1809–59   Professor of logic & rhetoric, Aberdeen
1853 B   *The history of English literature, with an outline of the origin and growth of the English language,* Edinburgh. (BL). At least fourteen edns to 1883.   P. *219.*

[Anon.]
[*a.* 1846] RA   *Specimens of English poetry. For the use of Charterhouse School.* 8th edn 1846 (Charterhouse Sch L); 11th edn 1855 (Leicester UL); anr edn 1867* (BL); anr edn 1883 (BL).

[Anon.]
[*a.* 1864] RE   *The speedy teacher, or child's gradual primer.* Advertised by W. Nicholson of Halifax in 1864.

[Anon.]
1856 S   *Spelling and dictation,* 3 parts. Nelson. (BL).

[Anon.]
[1864]* S   *A spelling and dictation class book. With etymological exercises,* Edinburgh, Constable's Educational Series. (Glasgow UL; O).   P. *130.*

[Anon.]
[*c.* 1790?]* S   [Spelling-book], Halesworth: W. Harper. Incomplete, runs from p. 7 to p. 66 (privately owned).

[Anon.]
[*c.* 1815?]* S   [Spelling-book]. Lacks t.p. (BL shelf-mark T.975* (8)).

[Anon.]
[1684] S   *A spelling book for children, after a new and more accurate method than any yet extant.* TC, II, 87 (1684). No copy. Alston, IV, 145.

[Anon.]
1707* S   *A spelling-book for children, with a short catechism.* (BL). Alston, IV, 222.

[Anon.]
1790* S   *A spelling book for the use of Ackworth School.* (Friends House L). Alston, IV, 880 and Plate 91. Alston says that this is an earlier edn of *The English Vocabulary.* [1801?], but the two works are quite different.

[Anon.]

1804* S *A spelling-book, or introduction to knowledge; intended for the use of Sunday-Schools.* (Glasgow UL).

[Anon.]

1813* S *A spelling book, or introduction to reading; compiled at the request of the Sunday School Union,* 2 parts. (Glasgow UL).

[Anon.]

1796* S *A spelling-book; upon a new plan,* Edinburgh, SPCK. (Mitchell L, Glasgow). Alston, IV, 914.   P. 76.

[Anon.]

1835* S *Spelling exercises, for the use of schools,* Berwick. (BL; O).

[Anon.]

[*c.* 1797?]* S *Spelling lessons.* (BL). Alston, IV, 925 and Plate 101 for t.p.   P. *107.*

[Anon.]

1825* S *Spelling, questions, and stories for infant schools, and nurseries,* 4 parts, Exeter. (BL).   Pp. 239–40.

SPENCE, Thomas 1750–1814 'Teacher of English in Newcastle'

1775* D *The grand repository of the English language,* Newcastle upon Tyne. (Boston, Mass., PL); Scolar Press facsimile 1969*. Alston, V, 304 and Plate 45. The dictionary contains an English grammar.

1782* RE *The real reading-made-easy: or, foreigners' and grown persons' pleasing instructor to reading English,* Newcastle upon Tyne (Newcastle PL). Alston, VI, 541–2. Published anonymously and printed in reformed spelling.   P. 47.

SPENCER, Thomas

1628 Lo *The art of logick, delivered in the precepts of Aristotle and Ramus* [etc.]. (BL); as *Logicke unfolded: or, the body of logicke in English,* 1656 (BL); Scolar Press facsimile of 1628 edn, 1970*. Alston, VII, 40–1.

SPROSON, Philip

1740* RE *The art of reading: or, the English tongue made familiar and easy to the meanest capacity. Containing* ... [etc.] (Edinburgh UL; BL); anr edn 1752 (no copy). Alston, IV, 549–50. The long title is reproduced in Alston's Plate 53.   Pp. 84–5, 101; *51, 121.*

STACKHOUSE, Thomas 1677–1752 Sometime teacher

1731* La *Reflections on the nature and property of languages in general, and on the advantages, defects, and manner of improving the English tongue in particular.* (BL). Scolar Press facsimile 1968*. Alston, III, 805.   P. 202.

STACKHOUSE, Thomas 1756–1836 (nephew of the preceding)

1800a* Ex *A new essay on punctuation: being an attempt to reduce the practice of pointing to the government of distinct and explicit rules, by which every point may be accounted for after the manner of parsing.* (BL). Alston, III, 582.

1800b Ex *An appendix and key to Stackhouse's essay on punctuation. By the author of the essay.* (BL). Alston, III, 583.

[Anon.]

1866 RA *The standard poetry book. Selected from the best authors.* Routledge. (BL).

STAPLETON, George

1797* G   *The road to knowledge; or, young man & woman's best friend: being a plan of general instruction as far as relates to the useful pursuits and purposes of life.* (BL). Alston, III, 422.

STEEL, David

1786* Ex   *Elements of punctuation: containing remarks on an Essay on Punctuation; and critical observations on some passages in Milton.* (BL). Alston, III, 581. The essay is by Joseph Robertson.

[STEELE, Joshua]   1700–91

1775 P   *An essay towards establishing the melody and measure of speech to be expressed and perpetuated by certain symbols.* (BL); 2nd edn, as *Prosodia rationalis: or, an essay . . . by peculiar symbols,* 1779 (BL); Scolar Press facsimile of 1775 edn, 1969. Alston, VI, 492–3; B.H. Smart, 1812, pp. 147–8; Abercrombie, 1965c, chap. 5; Quirk, p. 95.

[Anon.]

1831 RE   *Stepping stones for tottering feet, or reading lessons adapted to Mrs Williams' syllabic method.* Chalmers, p. 158. The reference is presumably to Honoria Williams, 1817.

STEVENS, Edward Thomas, and   HOLE, Charles   Teachers

1866* RS   *The advanced lesson book: consisting of reading lessons in history, geography, literature, and science.* (BL). A continuation of their *Grade lesson books.*

1866–8* RS   *The complete reader. Being a carefully graduated system of teaching to read and spell . . . Especially designed for upper and middle-class schools: I The primary reader; II The intermediate reader; III The exemplar of style; IV The senior class reader.* (BL).

[1867] RE   *First lessons in reading* (24 sheets). (BL).

1864 RE   *The grade lesson book primer. For the use of infant classes.* (BL).

1863–4* RS   *The grade lesson books, in six standards. Especially adapted to meet the requirements of the 'revised code'.* (BL).

1872 RS   *Useful knowledge reading books, adapted to the use of board schools.* Standards 1–6. (BL).

STEWART, William   'Teacher of English, Geography and History, Perth'

1849* G   *A grammar of the English language,* Edinburgh. (BL).   P. *377.*

a. 1849 RE   *The orthoepic primer.* Noted on the t.p. of his grammar.

STIRLING, John   Master of St Andrews School, Holborn

[1730?] S?   *A new method of teaching or acquiring the English tongue.* No copy. Alston, I, 60a.

1735 G̀   *A short view of English grammar . . . Containing . . .* [twelve paragraphs]. *For the use of schools.* (Hull UL); 2nd edn 1740* (BL). Alston, I, 73–4. Vorlat, 1975.   Pp. 318–19.

1733* B   *A system of rhetoric . . . for the use of schools.* (O); 3rd edn 1740* (BL). Many edns, often including Holmes' *Art of rhetoric.* In addition to those recorded by Alston, VI, 146–61, BL has London edns of 1817, 1820, 1822, 1827. Howell, 1971, p. 137n, records a Dublin edn of 1864. Scolar Press facsimile of 1733 edn, 1968*.   P. *163.*

STIRLING, Walter

a. 1814a RA   *The poetical moralist, consisting of selections and extracts from the most eminent authors, for the use of young persons,* 3rd edn Winchester, 1814* (BL).   P. 222.

a. 1814b RA   *The prose moralist, consisting of a selection of pieces in prose, from the most eminent English writers, intended for youth,* Winchester: James Robbins. No copy. Advertised in *The poetical moralist.*

STODART, M.A.

1839* B   *Hints on reading: addressed to a young lady.* (BL).   Pp. 248–9.

STORMONTH, James

1861 G   *The school grammar. Combined throughout with aids to composition.* Edinburgh. (O).

STORY, Joshua

1778* G   *An introduction to English grammar,* Newcastle (BL); 2nd edn (a rhetoric added) 1781; 3rd edn 1783*. Five edns in all to 1793. Alston, I, 356–9.   Pp. 339; *330.*

STRETCH, L.M.   'Master of the Academy, Meastham'

1770* RA   *The beauties of history, or pictures of virtue and vice, drawn from real life. Designed for the instruction and entertainment of youth.* 2 vols. (BL). At least fourteen edns to 1833.

STRONG, Nathaniel   'Schoolmaster in London'

[1674] S   *England's perfect schoolmaster, or most plain and easie rules for writing and spelling true English.* No copy; 2nd edn 1676 (O); 3rd edn 1681* (BL). At least eleven British and American edns in all to 1710. Alston, IV, 101–9; Johnson, 22–4; Gabrielson, 1929, 138.   P. *106.*

STUBBS, R.   'Grammar Master'

1777* G   *Rules and exercises on English grammar: for the use of Monmouth-Boarding School,* Hereford. (Guildhall L). Alston, I, 347a.

SULLIVAN, Robert   1800–68   Inspector of schools

[a. 1843] G   *An attempt to simplify English grammar; with observations on the method of teaching it.* 2nd edn Dublin, 1843, J. Hunter, 1848; 3rd edn Dublin, 1844 (NUC); 4th edn 1847, Hunter; 12th edn 1849 (once reported in Oxford Institute of Education L); 57th edn Dublin, 1864* (Glasgow UL); 85th edn Dublin, 1869* (Cambridge UL); edns of 1916 and 1921 (BL). An advt in 85th edn says that in 1868 there were in circulation in Britain and the colonies 239,236 copies of Sullivan's textbooks.

[a. 1868?] G   *First English grammar.* (BL has Dublin edns of 1876, 1916 and 1920.) Sullivan died in 1868.

1850* RA   *The literary class book; or, readings in English literature: to which is prefixed an introductory treatise on the art of reading and the principles of elocution,* Dublin (BL; O); at least nineteen edns to 1890.   Pp. 220, 383.

1831 La   *A manual of etymology,* Dublin. In 1833 it was enlarged as *The dictionary of derivations;* reissued under its original title by 1860* (BL; O).

[1842] S   *The spelling-book superseded; or, a new and easy method of teaching the spelling, meaning, pronunciation, and etymology of all the difficult words in the English language; with exercises on verbal distinctions.* 4th edn Dublin, 1842 (O); 29th edn Dublin, 1853* (BL); 123rd edn Dublin, 1868* (Fulham PL); further edns to 1920.   P. *129.*

[Anon.]

[*c*. 1800] RE   *The Sunday school reading primer*, Derby: Richardson (BL copy
destroyed in the war; Bedford CHE, n.d.); anr edn [*c*. 1845?] (Preston PL).
Chalmers, p. 154.

[Anon.]

[*c*. 1830]* S   *The Sunday school spelling book* (BL copy, T.13.2299 (5), lacks t.p.).
82 pp.

SUNDAY SCHOOL UNION

[1830] RS   *Reading books* [1–5?]. *Part 1* (Nottingham UL); *The Sunday School
reader*, 1858*: 'an intermediate class-book between the Third Book . . . and
the Sunday Reading Book'. (BL).   P. 261.

See also *The Sunday School spelling book* [*c*. 1830]

[Anon.]

[1822]* RA   *A supplement to Dr Watts's Divine Songs . . . selected from various
authors; and especially intended for the use of Sunday schools*, 54 pp. (BL T973*
(4); Bedford CHE).

SUTCLIFFE, Joseph

1815* G   *A grammar of the English language. To which is added, a series of classical
examples of the structure of sentences, and three important systems of the time of
verbs.* (BL); 2nd edn 1821* (BL). J. Hunter, 1848, describes the 2nd edn as
'recomposed and made a new work'. Wells, 1846 (USA), gives 1815 as 2nd edn;
Wisconsin UL gives 2nd edn as 1818. *Gent. Mag.*, 85.i (April 1815),
614.   Pp. 357; *88*.

[Anon.]

[1869]* RE   *The syllabic reading book. A course of progressive lessons for simplifying
the work of learning to read*: two parts (BL).   Pp. *39, 123*.

SYMES, Christopher

[1681?]*   *Nature and art teaching to read English within one, two, or three moneths at
most.* (A single printed sheet, BL Harley 5949/343). Alston, IV, 140b.   P.
76.

SYMONS, Jelinger Cookson   1809–60   Inspector of schools

1852 Ed   *School economy: a practical book on the best modes of establishing and
teaching schools, and of making them thoroughly useful to the working classes by
means of moral and industrial training.* Reprinted, Woburn Press, 1971*.   P.
40.

TABART, Benjamin

1818 S   *The national spelling-book, or, a sure guide to English spelling and
pronunciation, arranged on such a plan as cannot fail to remove the difficulties and
facilitate general improvement in the English language.* (title from revised edn).
Gent. Mag., 88.i (1818), 616; new edn rev T. Clark [*c*. 1820]* (Hammersmith
PL; BL).

TALBOT, James

1707 Ed   *The Christian school-master; or, the duty of those who are employed in the
public instruction of children: especially in charity schools.* (BL; Leeds UL); anr
edn 1811 (BL); anr edn 1817* (BFSS). M.G. Jones, 1938, pp. 76f. NBL, 1949,
no. 486.   P. 113.

TAPNER, John   'Schoolmaster at Boxgrove, in Sussex'

[1780]* RA   *A new collection of fables in verse. Intended to implant prudential, benign and beneficent sentiments in the heart; and bend the mind to the practice of social virtues, and Christian graces.* (BL). The date is Arnold Muirhead's, *LTM*, no. 19, November 1957; the BL date is [1770?].

[1761]* RA   *The school-master's repository: or, youth's moral preceptor. Containing, a select store of curious sentences and maxims, in prose and verse. Together with the greatest variety of copies in single and double-line pieces, hitherto published. Designed more particularly for the use of schools.* (BL).   P. 182.

TAYLOR, Mrs

1791* G   *An easy introduction to general knowledge and liberal education; for the use of the young ladies, at Strangeways Hall, Manchester,* Warrington. (BL; Warrington PL); 2nd edn 1799. Alston, III, 400–1.

[TAYLOR, Ann and Jane]   1782–1866; 1783–1824

1808? RH   *Hymns for infant minds.* The date 1808, though given by *NCBEL* and Thwaite, 1972, is suspect; *OCCL* follows *DNB* and Darton, 1982, in preferring 1810. At least fifty-two separate edns to 1877* in Britain, and at least thirty-five in America to 1820 (Welch, 1972).

1808* RH   *Limed twigs, to catch young birds.* (BL); 2nd edn 1811; 3rd edn 1815* (BL); edns to 1881.

1804–5 RH   *Original poems for infant minds,* 2 vols. There were other contributors. Very many edns, including 30th, 1875*, well into the twentieth century. Facsimile of 1804–5 edn in Classics of Children's Literature, no. 17, Garland Publ. Co.   P. 352.

TAYLOR, Charles James Fox

1853 RE   *The typographical pronouncing system of reading, upon a new and original plan.* Book 1 (O).

TAYLOR, J.   'Headmaster of the Academy, Dronfield, Chesterfield'

1804* G   *A system of English grammar, upon a plan entirely new; intended as a means of facilitating the progress both of public and private education,* Sheffield: J. Montgomery. (BL; Sheffield PL; Glasgow UL).

TEGG, Thomas   1776–1845

[a. 1839] S   *The first book for children, designed for the use of schools, containing easy and progressive lessons of reading and spelling adapted to the infant mind and by their arrangement calculated to insure improvement,* 70 pp. (Bedford CHE). The preface to the Bedford copy, 1839*, says there were 'numerous' previous edns.

TELFAIR, Cortes   'Curer of impediments in speech'

1775* S   *The town and country spelling-book; in four parts. I.* [Single words and short sentences; syllables divided] *II.* [Single words; syllables undivided] *III.* [Reading-lessons, undivided] *IV.* [Pronunciation]. *With an appendix, containing observations on accent, emphasis, pauses, &c.,* Edinburgh. (BL). Law, pp. 149, 200; Alston, IV, 728, reproduces the t.p. in full.

[THACKERAY, Thomas]

1847* RA   *Florilegium poeticum anglicanum: or, selections from English poetry, for the use of classical schools.* (BL); 2nd edn 1852* (BL).

THACKWRAY, Mrs   Of Beckford House Boarding School, Walworth

[a. 1813] G   *A grammatical catechism, in two parts, with notes. For the use of schools; exhibiting a compendium of grammar, in question and answer, designed for the purpose of examination in that study.* 2nd edn 1813* (Nottingham UL). Pp. 346, 357.

THAMAR, Mrs

1823* RE *The Sunday School primer; or, child's first book, being an introduction to reading the Holy Bible.* (BL).

[Anon.]

[*c.* 1790?]* P *The theatre of youth; being a selection of pleasing dramas, for the improvement of young persons,* Huddersfield: Brook and Lancashire, n.d. 61 pp. (Bedford CHE). P. *302.*

THELWALL, John 1764–1834 Sometime teacher of elocution and master of a boarding school

1805* P *Mr Thelwall's introductory discourse on the nature and objects of elocutionary science; and the studies and accomplishments connected with the cultivation of the faculty of oral expression: with outlines of a course of lectures on the science and practice of elocution,* Pontefract. (BL). This is a fuller version of the discourse printed in the same year in his *The trident of Albion, an epic effusion.*

1802* P *Selections, &c., for Mr Thelwall's lectures on the science and practice of elocution,* York. (BL); as *Selections and original articles, for . . .,* Birmingham, 1806 (BL, with author's additions); as *Selections for the illustration of a course of instructions on the rhythmus and utterance of the English language,* London, 1812* (BL).

1810* P *The vestibule of eloquence . . . original articles, oratorical and poetical, intended as exercises in recitation.* (BL).

THELWALL, S.M.

1859*RE *The syllabic primer and reading book, based on the principle that the sound of letters is determined by their position in a syllable or word. With an explanation of the method of teaching.* (BL). P. 40.

[Anon.]

1689 S *Thesaurium trilingue publicum: being an introduction to English, Latin, and Greek. In two parts. The first, teaching orthography, and the exactest way of pointing yet extant: also two lessons for every day in the week for children, and an alphabetical table of most primitive words, both grammatically and truly divided; with* [homophones]. *The second, containing a method* [for Greek]. (Shrewsbury Sch L); Scolar Press facsimile 1970*. Alston, IV, 160. Pp. 83, 157; *51, 373.*

THOMAS, L[ambrocke]

1654 S *Milke for children, or a plaine and easie method teaching to read and write; together with briefe instructions for all sorts of people. Also an appendix of prayer.* (Harvard).

[Anon.]

1803 RE *Thomas Lovechild's only method to make reading easy, or, little masters' and misses' best instructor,* York: Wilson. Chalmers, p. 161.

THOMPSON, J.

1831* G *Notes of syntax, adapted to Murray's English Exercises. Designed for the younger classes of learners.* (BL).

THOMPSON, J.B.

1858* G *A concise grammar of the English language, for the use of beginners.* 64 pp. (BL; O). P. 364.

[THOMPSON, William]   Schoolmaster in Nottingham

1711* S   *The child's guide to the English tongue: or, a new spelling-book; containing short and easie directions for spelling, reading, pointing, and pronouncing of English.* (Friends House L; BL); anr edn Boston, Mass., 1716 (no copy). Alston, IV, 283–4, reproduces t.p. in full).   P. 3.

THOMSON, Andrew Mitchell   1779–1831   Sometime teacher

1823* RA   *A collection, in prose and verse, for the use of schools,* Edinburgh. (BL). Diack, pp. 16–17.

[c. 1825?] RS   *Lessons for schools,* Parts 1–4. M'Culloch, 1827, p. iv; Chalmers, p. 30, from 1847 list by Committee of Council.   P. 60.

THOMSON, James   1700–48   see MCLEOD, W., 1863

THRING, Edward   1821–87   Headmaster of Uppingham

1852* G   *The child's grammar: being the substance of The Elements of Grammar taught in English; adapted for the use of junior classes.* (BL).

1851* G   *The elements of grammar taught in English; with questions.* (BL); 3rd edn 1860 (BL); at least three further edns to 1885.

1868a* G   *Exercises in grammatical analysis,* Oxford. (BL; Wisconsin UL).

1868b* G   *On the principles of grammar,* Oxford. (BL).

TICKEN, William   Writing-master

1806 G   *A practical English grammar for the use of students preparing for the Royal Military College.* (Columbia UL). *Edin. Rev.,* 9 (1806), list of new publications, July–October.

TILLEARD, James   'Corresponding Secretary of the Association'

1855* G   *A lecture on the method of teaching grammar. Delivered before the United Association of Schoolmasters, at the first annual meeting.* 16 pp. (BL).   P. 370.

1859 Ed   'On elementary school books', in *Trans. Nat. Assoc. for the Promotion of Social Science* (1859), 387–96. Reprinted as *On elementary school books,* 1860* (BL). Goldstrom, 1972a, 198–9.

TOBITT, R.

1825 G   *Grammatical institutes, or the principles and rules of English grammar. Abridged and versified for the use of schools and young persons,* J. Souter. (U. California, Berkeley).

TODD

[a. 1782] S   *A new and complete spelling book.* Advertised by H. Turpin and J. Fielding in the 3rd edn, 1782, of *The young moralist.*

TODD, James

1748* RA   *The school-boy and young gentleman's assistant, being a plan of education: containing the sentiments of the best authors under these following heads, viz. Health, Manners, Religion and Learning* [etc.]. The dedication is signed 'Ja. Todd, B.D.' (BL). Alston, X, 210.   Pp. 63, 203.

TODD, William   'Schoolmaster in London'

1764* RE   *The youth's guide and instructor to virtue and religion . . . Containing 1. The alphabet with spelling regularly proceeding from one syllable to six, with lessons . . . 2. The duty of parents . . . 3. The threats of vengeance pronounced against all disobedient children.* 108 pp. (Bedford CHE).

[Anon.]

1843* S   *Tom Thumb's alphabet, or reading made easy,* Ipswich: J. Page (BL); anr edn [c. 1850] (V&A). NBL, 1973, no. 617; Whalley, p. 139.

[Anon.]

1747 S   *Tom Thumb's play-book to teach children their letters as soon as they can speak, or easy lessons for children and beginners: being a new and pleasant method to allure little ones into the first principles of learning.* (title from 1771; Rosenbach, 72). First published in 1747 (NBL, 1973, no. 610). Many British and American edns till the middle of the nineteenth century, mostly undated, e.g. Alnwick, [*c.* 1840] (V&A). See: Rosenbach; Osborne, II, 742; Welch, 1972; Chalmers, p. 160; Sotheby, HIC VI, 2515.

TOMKINS, Thomas   1743–1816   Writing-master

[a. 1785] RA   *Poems on various subjects: selected to enforce the practice of virtue, and with a view to comprise in one volume the beauties of English poetry.* 3rd edn 1785* (BL); BL has edns of 1800, 1811, 1819, 1823; *DNB* gives only 1807.   P. *192.*

1806* RA   *Rays of genius collected to enlighten the rising generation,* 2 vols. (BL).

TONKIS, Thomas   Fellow of Trinity College, Cambridge.

1613* G *De analogia anglicani sermonis liber grammaticus.* (BL, MS Reg. F. xviii) Dobson, I, 313f.   P. 318.

TOP, Alexander

1603* La   *The olive leafe: or, universall abce. Wherein is set foorth the creation, descent, and authoritie of letters: together with th'estimation, profit, affinitie or declination of them: for the familiar use of all studentes, teachers, and learners of what chirography soever, most necessarie. By two tables, newly and briefly composed characteristicall and syllabicall.* (O; BL); Scolar Press facsimile 1971. Alston, III, 760; Salmon, 1962, pp. 349f.   Pp. 48–9; *51.*

TORKINGTON, Robert

1806* S   *The Christian child's spelling-book . . . to which are added, scriptural tables, and hymns, from Dr Watts.* (DES); 2nd edn 1809 (BL).   P. 94.

TOWNSHEND, John Haynes

[1854]* RA   *Miscellanies in prose and verse, for the perusal of youth.* (BL). The pieces are all by Townshend himself.

[Anon.]

[*c.* 1855] G   *The toy grammar; or, learning without labour*; Dean's sixpenny coloured toy books. (V&A).

TRAPP, Joseph   1679–1747

1742 B   *Lectures on poetry read in the schools of natural philosophy at Oxford . . . . Translated from the Latin, with additional notes.* (BL); Scolar Press facsimile 1973; facsimile in series *Anglistica & Americana,* Hildesheim, Georg Olms Verlag, 1969*. The lectures were first published as *Praelectiones poeticae* in 3 vols. at Oxford, 1711, 1715, 1719. The translation and notes were by William Bowyer and William Clarke.   Pp. 162–3.

TRAYS, Henry

1855 G   *English grammar.* (O).

[Anon.]   Teacher

1680* Ex   *A treatise of stops, points, or pauses, and of notes which are used in writing and in print; . . . Composed for the authors use, who is a hearty wel-willer to (and accordingly hath endeavoured the promoting of) the attainments of children, and others, in the tru spelling, and exact reading of English . . . Printed for the authors use in his school.* (O; BL). Scolar Press facsimile 1968. Alston, III, 569.   Pp. *330, 331.*

TRENCH, Richard Chenevix 1807–86

1868* RA   *A household book of English poetry, selected and arranged with notes.* (BL). At least four edns to 1888.

1855 La   *English past and present.* Lectures given to King's College School, London, in 1854. 4th edn 1859*. Many edns into the twentieth century.

1851 La   *On the study of words.* Based on lectures given to the Diocesan Training School, Winchester. 6th edn 1855*. Many edns into the twentieth century.

[TRENOW, F.J.C.]   Of Dorchester Academy

[1819?] G   *The pupil's assistant, consisting of grammatical questions, with an example to each rule, of the exercises in false syntax, corrected and parsed at length, with observations; taken from the abridgment of Murray's English Grammar.* 4th edn Dorchester, n.d.* The preface is signed and dated 1819. (BL).

TRIMMER, Sarah 1741–1810

[a. 1798] S   *The charity school spelling book. Part I. Containing the alphabet, spelling lessons, and short stories of good and bad girls, in words of one syllable only.* (title from 5th edn); 4th edn 1798, Chalmers, p. 161; 5th edn 1799* (BL); 6th edn 1800 (Hull UL; Birmingham UL); 7th edn 1802, NBL, 1949, no. 150; 9th edn 1805 (DES); 10th edn 1807 (Reading UL). Alston, IV, 937–8. According to Higson, 1967, originally published as *The little spelling book,* 1786, q.v., but there is little resemblance between the books.

[a. 1794] S   *The charity school spelling book. Part II. Containing words divided into syllables, lessons with scripture names, &c.* 2nd edn 1794* (Nottingham UL); 4th edn 1798* (BL); 5th edn 1800 (Hull UL); new edn 1818 (BFSS). Alston, IV, 936–8).

1786* RE   *Easy lessons for young children.* (Bedford CHE; Glasgow UL); 3rd edn 1792* (Leicester UL); 6th edn 1807, Chalmers, p. 161; 11th edn Paris, 1859 (BL).

1802–6* Ed   *The guardian of education, a periodical work; consisting of a practical essay on Christian education . . . extracts from sermons and other books relating to religious education; and a copious examination of modern systems of education, children's books, and books for young persons,* 5 vols. (BL).

[a. 1786] S   *The little spelling book for young children,* 2nd edn 1786* (Glasgow UL); 7th edn 1800* (DES). Alston, IV, 861–2. See above, *The Charity school spelling book, Part I.*   P. 200.

TRINDER, William Martin

1781* G   *An essay on the English grammar,* (Columbia UL). Alston, I, 375.

[Anon.]

1696* G   *The true method of learning the Latin tongue by the English, and of obtaining the more perfect knowledge of the English by the Latin; containing a grammar for both the languages.* (BL); Scolar Press facsimile 1971*.

TRUSLER, John 1735–1820

[1790?]* G   *An English accidence; or, abstract of grammar; for the use of those who, without making grammar a study, wish to speak and write correctly. With rules for reading prose and verse.* (BL; DES). Alston, I, 450b.

1790 RA   *Proverbs exemplified, and illustrated by pictures from real life, teaching morality and a knowledge of the world.* (V&A); as *Proverbs in verse, or moral instruction conveyed in pictures, for the use of schools . . . To which are prefixed rules for reading verse,* [after 1814], Blackwell, Cat. A3 (March 1980).

TRYON, Thomas 1634–1703

1700* S *The compleat school-master: or, child's instructor: being a new method of teaching children at three years old to read and write English, also to understand Latin or French in 12 months time as well as he can understand English. Found out by Tho. Tryon. With divers other useful things, by G.F.* (Columbia U, N.Y.). The Columbia copy occupies pp. 89–142 of George Fisher's *New spelling book*, 1700, which is presumed to be an edn of his *Plurimum in uno* [1693], of which no copy exists. P. 89 is a separate t.p., as given here; pp. 91–6 are an abbreviated version of parts of *A new method*, the rest being a compendium. *TC*, III, 187 and 217; Alston, IV, 174, 200–2.

1695* Ed *A new method of educating children: or, rules and directions for the well ordering and governing them, during their younger years.* (BL; Reading UL). NBL, 1949, no. 29; Alston, X, 139.   P. 115.

TUCKER, Abraham 1705–74

1773* La *Vocal sounds. By Edward Search.* (BL); Scolar Press facsimile 1969*. Abercrombie, 1965b, 61–8; Alston, VI, 490.   Pp. 47, 306.

TUCKEY, Mary Ann

1829* G *Assisting questions on English grammar, with answers; comprising an explanation of etymology, and the rules of syntax.* (BL).   P. 370.

TUITE, Thomas

1726 S *The Oxford spelling-book; being a complete introduction to English orthography . . . In four parts. I. Of letters . . . II. Of syllables . . . III. Of words . . . IV. Of sentences.* (BL); Scolar Press facsimile 1967*. Alston, IV, 323 and Plate 46 for t.p. in facsimile.   Pp. 46, 103–4, 108, 122; *48, 50*.

TURNBULL, George

1742* Ed *Observations upon liberal education in all its branches* [etc.]. (BL; Leicester UL). Alston, X, 201.   P. 291.

TURNER, C. Brandon

1840 G *A new English grammar.* (O). A much revised edn of Goold Brown's *The institutes of English grammar*, first published in New York in 1823. Turner's book was usually treated, as by Bain, 1863, as a new work.

TURNER, Daniel 1710–98 Baptist minister and private tutor, Abingdon

1739* G *An abstract of English grammar and rhetoric: containing the chief principles and rules of both arts, necessary to the writing the language correctly and handsomely . . . Designed to introduce the English scholar to a just notion of the propriety, and beauty, of his mother tongue.* (BL); anr edn Dublin, 1741. Alston, I, 87–8.   Pp. *163, 323*.

1771* B *An introduction to rhetoric; containing all the principal tropes and figures, in English verse . . . For the use of schools,* Abingdon. Pp. viii, 24. (O). Alston, VI, 228.   P. *163*.

TURNER, H.H.

1874 RA *Wordsworth. Excursion, Book I. Introduction and notes by H.H. Turner.* Rivington. English school classics. (BL).

TURNER, John

1843 G *The intellectual English grammar,* Brighton. No copy.

TURNER, William 1658–1726 'Master of the Free School, Stamford'

1710a S *The art of spelling and reading English, with proper and useful lessons for children, prayers, psalms, hymns, &c. For the use of English schools. Dedicated to* *the Honourable Society for Propagating Christian Knowledge.* (Oxford, Christ Church; Stockholm UL); 2nd edn 1718* (BL). Garbrielson, 158–60; Alston, IV, 281–2 and Plate 39 for t.p. of 1710 edn. Vorlat, 1975.   P. *161.*

1710b* G   *A short grammar for the English tongue: for the use of English schools. Dedicated to the Honourable Society for Propagating Christian Knowledge.* (BL); anr edn, anon., 1716 (NLS). Gabrielson, 140–1; Alston, I, 40–1.

[Anon.]

1772* Ex   *The tutor; or epistolary guide . . . To which are prefixed, a new introduction to English grammar, and a complete spelling dictionary.* (Harvard UL). Alston, IV, 727 and Plate 78 for t.p.; Roscoe, J365(1).

[Anon.]

[1815]* RA   *Twenty-six poetical extracts, selected from celebrated authors, and printed from copper plates engraved expressly for the work, each embellished with a beautiful vignette, illustrative of the subject,* R. Miller. Issued also on 'large cards'. (Bedford CHE).

[Anon.]

1869* RA   *Typical selections from the best English authors, with introductory notices.* Oxford (BL); 2nd edn enl., 2 vols, as: *. . . best English writers,* preface signed E.E.S., 1876* (BL).

[Anon.]

1835* G   *Universal grammar illustrated: with observations upon the construction of the English language.* Whittaker. (BL).   Pp. 362–3.

[Anon.]

[c. 1850] RE   (Marks's) *Universal primer, and preparatory spelling book. Consisting of progressive lessons, being a first book for children.* Advt c. 1850; NBL, 1949, no. 157.

[Anon.]

[1859]* RE   *The universal primer containing a variety of reading and spelling for the use of children.* W.S. Fortey. (BL).

[Anon.]

1833* RE   *The universal primer, for children: being an easy introduction to spelling and reading, adapted to the capacities of the youngest learners.* Harvey and Darton, 72pp. (private colln).

[Anon.]

[1858]* RE   *The universal primer, illustrated.* T. Goode. (BL).

[Anon.]

[c. 1785] RE   *The universal primer; or a new and easy guide to the art of spelling and reading.* Marshall. NBL, 1949, no. 145.

[Anon.]

[c. 1820] RE   *The universal primer, or, child's guide to learning.* Devonport: Samuel and John Keys. Advt c. 1820.

[Anon.]

[c. 1845] RE   *The universal primer, or reading made easy,* W.S. Johnson. Chalmers, p. 161. Cf. Mavor, [a. 1855], above.

[Anon.]

[c. 1810] RE   *The universal primer; or, child's first lesson.* Congleton: Dean. NBL, 1949, no. 61; 10th edn n.d. (Bedford CHE).

The universal spelling book see FENNING, 1756

[*c.* 1820] S   *The universal spelling book: or, a new and easy guide to the English language*, Devonport: Samuel and John Keys. Advt *c.* 1820.

UNWIN, William Jordan   Principal of Homerton College

[1862] G   *English grammar.* (BL).

1861 RE   *The infant school reader.* (BL).

1851a Ed   *Reading in primary schools, with directions for using the normal chart of the English language.* (BL).

[1859]a S   *Spelling and pronunciation. An accompaniment to the normal chart of the elementary sounds of the English language.* (BL); anr edn 1862 (BL).

1851b RS   *The training school readers*: Approved by Congregational Board of General Education. Goldstrom, 1972a, pp. 114, 219; Book 1, Divisions 1 and 2, n.d.* (personal); Book 2, Division 1 [1853] (BL); anr edn 1862 (BL).

[1859]b RE   *Writing-reading method; the child's first book.* (BL).

URMSTON, John   'Schoolmaster at Kensington'

[1700] S   *The London spelling-book: being a most easie and regular method of teaching to spell, read, and write, true English*, No copy. *TC*, III, 200. 4th edn as: . . . . *a more easie method* [etc.] 1710* (BL); 9th edn 1722. Alston, IV, 203–6 and Plate 37 for t.p. of 4th edn. Two illustrations are reproduced by Johnson, pp. 48–9.   Pp. 16–17, 90, 279, 375.

[Anon.]

1858* G   *The useful English grammar.* 48 pp. (BL; O).

USSHER, George Neville

1785* G   *The elements of English grammar, methodically arranged for the use of those who study English grammatically without a previous knowledge of the learned languages*, Glocester: R. Raikes. (O); 2nd edn (a rhetoric added) 1786* (BL); at least four further British edns to 1806 and five American edns to 1804. Scolar Press facsimile of 1785 edn, 1967*. Alston, I, 426–32.   P. 321.

USSHER, M.

1794* G   *A pronouncing grammar and spelling book*, Gloucester: R. Raikes (BL). Not in Alston.

VALPY, Richard   1754–1836   Headmaster, Reading School

1825* P   *The Critic; or, a tragedy rehearsed: altered from Sheridan; as it was performed at the triennial visitation of Reading School, in October, 1824.* (BL).

1800* P   *King John, an historical tragedy, altered from Shakespeare, as it was acted at Reading School, for the subscription to the naval pillar, to be erected in honor of the naval victories of the present war.* Reading. (BL).

1802* P   *The merchant of Venice, a comedy, altered from Shakespeare, as it was acted at Reading School, in October 1802*, Reading. (BL).

1804* P   *Poems, odes, prologues, and epilogues, spoken on public occasions at Reading School.* (BL). The pieces were written by adults, performed by boys, and collected by Richard Valpy. Nichols, *Literary anecdotes*, IX, 758.   Pp. 301–2.

1795 P   *The roses, or King Henry VI, for the benefit of the fund for the cheap repository for moral and religious tracts.* (BL); 2nd edn as: . . . *Sixth. An historical tragedy. Represented at Reading School, October 15th, 16th, and 17th, 1795. Compiled principally from Shakespeare*, 1810*. (BL).

[VAUGHAN, Catherine Maria]

[1866]a* RS   *An advanced reading book*, SPCK. 368 pp. (BL).

[1866]b* RS   *An advanced reading book for girls*, SPCK. 191 pp. (BL).

1866* RA   *Words from the poets. Selected for the use of parochial schools and libraries.* (BL).

VAUGHAN, William   1577–1641

1600* RA   *The golden-grove, moralized in three books: a worke very necessary for all such, as would know how to governe themselves, their houses, or their countrey.* (O); 2nd edn 1608, *DNB*. Brinsley, 1612, p. 183; Hoole, 1660, p. 182; Howell, 1956, p. 391; Charlton, p. 122.   Pp. 273; *140*.

VERE, Thomas

[1734] S   *Orthography; or a key to the English tongue.* No copy. Alston, IV, 419.

[VERNON, John]

1666 Ed   *The compleat scholler: or, a relation of the life, and latter-end especially, of Caleb Vernon; who dyed in the Lord on the 29th of the ninth month, 1665. Aged twelve years and six months.* (BL); 2nd edn 1666* (BL).   Pp. 308–9.

VICKERS, John

1866 G   *A new course of practical grammar.* (O).

[Anon.]

[*c.* 1840] RE   *The Victoria primer or first book for children*, York: James Kendrew. Sotheby, HIC, I, July 1974, lot 446.

[Anon.]

[*c.* 1850] RE   *The Victoria primer, or reading made easy, containing a variety of easy lessons in reading and spelling*, W.S. Johnson. Sotheby, HIC, VI, October 1977, lot 2612.

[Anon.]

1847 La   *A vocabulary designed for the use of preparatory schools, on the Pestalozzian system.* Stamford. (O).

[Anon.]

1818* G   *Voyage to Locuta; a fragment: with etchings, and notes of illustration. Dedicated to Theresa Tidy, author of the Eighteen Maxims of Neatness and Order. By Lemuel Gulliver, jun.* J. Hatchard, pp. viii, 47. (BL).

VYSE, Charles   'Master of the Academy, West Ham Abbey'

1776* S   *The new London spelling-book. Or the young gentleman and lady's guide to the English tongue. In five parts. I* [Spelling-lists]. *II* [Homophones]. *III* [Grammar; punctuation; rules for reading]. *IV* [Reading-lessons]. *V* [Behaviour]. (Yale UL). Alston, IV, 765–8, gives edns to 1843, to which the following may be added, including those given without locations by Chalmers, p. 162: 1781, Chalmers; 1791 and 1793 (BL); 1805 (BL); 1807 (DES); 1809 (BL); 1813 (BL); 1824, Derby, Chalmers; [*c.* 1840]* (BL); 1843, Derby (Melbourne UL); [*c.* 1850]* (BL). Alston, Plate 77, reproduces the 1776 t.p., and Chalmers, pp. 18, 57–62, reproduces pages of text from various edns. The copyright of the spelling-book was sold *c.* 1800 for £2500, with an annuity of fifty guineas to Vyse (Mumby, 1930, p. 263, 1974, p. 195).   Pp. 333; *57*.

W., G.

1703 La   *Magazine, or, animadversions on the English spelling; observing the contradictions of the English letters warring themselves against themselves.* (Bath UL); ed. D. Abercrombie, Augustan Reprint Soc., Los Angeles, 1958; Scolar Press facsimile 1968*. Alston, VI, 535. Abercrombie, 1965a, pp. 54–7.   Pp. 42, 49–50.

W., N.

1641* S *A most easie way to attaine to the true reading of English, with short rules for the teacher. By N.W. Gent.* (BL). Alston, IV, 51 and Plate 8 for t.p. The BL copy is incomplete, comprising t.p. and one leaf only.

W., T.

[1702 or later]* S *A little book for little children: wherein are set down, in a plain and pleasant way, directions for spelling, and other remarkable matters. Adorn'd with cuts. By T.W.* 16 pp. (BL). The date is derived from the frontispiece of Queen Anne. I agree with Darton, p. 59, that this book is by a different author from Thomas White, whose work of the same title had a 12th edn in 1702 and was first published in 1674 (Sloane, 1955) or earlier (see below). T.W.'s is a spelling-book, lighthearted and secular in tone; White's is not a spelling-book; its emphasis is on the grimmer aspects of religion and on the deaths of 'holy children'. Thwaite, 1972, gives date for T.W. as *c.* 1712; *OCCL* says 'variously dated at 1702 & 1712'. Not in Alston.   P. 158.

WADDELL, James   'English teacher, Princes Street'

1799* Ex *A selection of exercises, for facilitating the improvement of youth: in a thorough knowledge of the orthography and syntax of the English language. To which is added* [punctuation; letter-writing; commercial forms] Glasgow, pp. xvi, 372. (Glasgow PL) Alston, III, 430–1.   Pp. 282–3, 333–4, 339.

WALKER, Donald

1836* S *Reading and writing, or improved spelling book, conformably with Walker's Principles of Pronunciation, and with the views of Sheridan, Edgeworth, Bell, &c, as well as with other methods, by which the earliest education is divested of its irrational, arbitrary, and repulsive character, and habits of wrong pronunciation are from the first rendered impossible.* Pp. xxxviii, 308. (BL); Devonport, 1842 (BL). Walker wrote also *British manly exercises*, 1834.   Pp. *30, 43, 50.*

WALKER, John   1732–1807

1789 RA *The academic speaker, or a selection of parliamentary debates, orations, odes, scenes, and speeches, from the best writers, proper to be read and recited by youth at school. To which is prefixed elements of gesture . . . explained and illustrated by plates.* (title from 4th edn). (O); 2nd edn 1791; 3rd edn 1797; 4th edn 1800/1801* (BL; ULIE). At least five further edns to 1823.   Pp. 287–8, 300–1; *185, 376.* See also pp. *185–6.*

1791 *A critical pronouncing dictionary of the English language.* (BL). Many edns to 1873. Scolar Press facsimile of 1791 edn, 1968*.   Pp. 80–1; *48, 287.*

1781* P *Elements of elocution. Being the substance of a course of lectures on the art of reading; delivered at several colleges in the university of Oxford,* 2 vols. (BL); 2nd edn 1799; 3rd edn 1806* (BL). At least eight further British edns to 1838. Scolar Press facsimile 1969*. Alston, VI, 416–17.   Pp. 186, 295; *184, 287.*

1786 RA *English classics abridged; being select works of Addison, Pope, and Milton, adapted to the perusal of youth, of both sexes, at school. To which are prefixed observations on the several authors, addressed to parents and preceptors.* (title from 2nd edn). 2nd edn 1807* (BL).   Pp. 198–9.

English themes and essays   see his *The teacher's assistant,* below

1777* P *Exercises for improvement in elocution; being select extracts from the best authors, for the use of those who study the art of reading and speaking in public.* (BL).   P. 187.

1783* P *Hints for improvement in the art of reading.* (BL). Alston, VI, 418.

1787* P *The melody of speaking delineated; or, elocution taught like music, by visible signs, adapted to the tones, inflexions, and variations of voice in reading and speaking; with directions for modulation, and expressing the passions. Exemplified by select passages from the best authors.* (BL); Scolar Press facsimile 1970*. Alston, VI, 421, with illustrative page in Plate 2.

1805* G *Outlines of English grammar; calculated for the use of both sexes at school: in which the practical rules of the language are clearly and distinctly laid down, and the speculative difficulties as much as possible avoided.* (BL); anr edn 1810 (Skeat).

1785 P *A rhetorical grammar, or course of lessons in elocution.* (BL). Seven British and two American edns to 1823. Scolar Press facsimile 1971*. Alston, VI, 419–20. P. *350.*

1801 Ex *The teacher's assistant in English composition; or, easy rules for writing themes and composing exercises, on subjects proper for the improvement of youth of both sexes at school.* (title from 2nd edn). (Hull UL); 2nd edn 1802* (BL); as: *English themes and essays; or, the teacher's assistant in composition; being a system of easy rules for writing exercises, illustrated by examples, adapted to the use of both sexes, at school: to which are added, hints for correcting and improving juvenile composition,* 1805* (Leicester UL); as *The teacher's assistant,* Carlisle, 1808 (DLC); as *English themes,* 3rd edn 1807 (private colln); 7th edn 1827* (personal); 8th edn 1832 (Hull UL); 10th edn 1842, *DNB;* 11th edn 1853, *DNB.* See above *Exercises of transposition,* 1818. Pp. 311, 313–4, 315; *309.*

WALKER, Obadiah 1616–99 Master of University College, Oxford

1673 Ed *Of education especially of young gentlemen. In two parts.* Oxford. Six edns in all to 1699. Scolar Press facsimile 1970*. Pp. 113, 276–7, 299.

1659* B *Some instructions concerning the art of oratory. Collected for the use of a friend [,] a young student.* (BL); 2nd edn Oxford, 1682. Howell, 1956, pp. 324f; Alston, VI, 89–90. Pp. 275–6; *283.*

WALKER, William 1623–84 Headmaster, Grantham Grammar School

1669 Ed *Some improvements to the art of teaching, especially in the first grounding of a scholar in grammar learning. Shewing a short, sure, and easie way to bring a scholar to variety and elegancy in writing Latine. Written for the help and ease of all ushers of schools, and country school-masters, and for the use and profit of all younger scholars.* (London UL); 2nd edn 1676 (O); at least nine edns in all to 1730; Scolar Press facsimile of 1669 edn, 1972*. Hindle, *N&Q,* 166 (1934), 182. P. *140.*

WALL, Charles

[a. 1851] S *Grammatical spelling book.* Chalmers, p. 162.

WALL, George 'Teacher of reading, elocution, geography, &c.'

1810–12* C *The Hibernian preceptor, comprising the elements of simple spelling . . . and a series of reading lessons interspers'd thro' the spelling tables . . . also an introduction to English grammar . . . with a selection of pieces taken from the best authors.* 2 vols. Vol. I, Parsonstown, 1810; Vol. II, Dublin, 1812. (BL). Pp. 114, 355.

WALLIS, John 1616–1703

1653* G *Grammatica linguae anglicanae,* Oxford. (BL; O); 2nd edn Oxford, 1664* (some addns); 4th edn Oxford, 1674* (many addns, including a praxis on the

Lord's Prayer, etc.); 5th edn Oxford, 1699 (the definitive edn, with many addns). For details of these and other edns see J.A. Kemp, *John Wallis's Grammar of the English Language*, Longman, 1972*, a new edn based on the 6th edn, 1765, with translation and commentary, but omitting the chapters on etymology and poetry, and the praxis. For locations see Alston, I, 14–24. Scolar Press facsimile of 1653 edn, 1969*. Vorlat, 1975.   Pp. 81; *53, 323, 342, 344.*

WARD, H. 'Schoolmaster, Whitehaven'

1789 RA *The academic reader. Containing miscellanies in prose and verse, selected from the most elegant writers in the English language. Intended to assist in acquiring the happy talent of graceful reading,* Whitehaven. No copy. One was said to be in Carlisle PL, but is not now there.

1777* G *A short, but clear system of English grammar, with exercises of bad English, designed for the use of schools, and for those gentlemen and ladies who may want the assistance of a master . . . With an appendix, containing* [parsing; instructions for reading and speaking; pronouncing dictionary]. Whitehaven. (Carlisle PL). P. *346n.*

WARD, John   1679?–1758   Master of a school in Moorfields; Professor of Rhetoric, Gresham College

1758* G *Four essays upon the English language: namely, I. Observations on the orthography. II. Rules for the division of syllables. III. The use of the articles. IV. The formation of the verbs, and their analogy with the Latin.* (BL); Scolar Press facsimile 1967*. Alston, I, 152.

1759* B *A system of oratory, delivered in a course of lectures publicly read at Gresham College,* 2 vols. (BL). Alston, VI, 207.   Pp. *279, 287.*

WARD, William   'Schoolmaster at Hinkley, Leicestershire'

1762* S *The scripture spelling book; or, an assistant to families and school-boys, in reading the New and Old Testament. Being a new attempt, and upon a plan quite different from all other spelling-books: containing* [scriptural spelling-lists; introduction to reading and spelling; punctuation, etc.]. Coventry. (BL); anr edn 1786 (O). Alston, IV, 695–6 and Plate 65 for t.p. in full.

WARD, William   Master of Beverley Grammar School

1765* G *An essay on grammar, as it may be applied to the English language. In two treatises. The one speculative, being an attempt to investigate proper principles. The other practical, containing definitions and rules deduced from the principles, and illustrated by a variety of examples from the most approved writers.* (BL); reissued in 1778, 1779, 1788. Scolar Press facsimile 1969*. Alston, I, 264–7; *EGC, passim.*   Pp. *334, 336.*

1767* G *A grammar of the English language, in two treatises. The first, containing rules for every part of its construction; with a praxis both of true and false English, shewing how the rules are to be applied in resolving the true, and in rectifying the false. The second, shewing the nature of the several parts of speech, and the reasons of every part of construction.* York. (BL). Part 1 is an abridgment of Part 2 of the *Essay*. Part 2 is an abridgment of Part 1 of the *Essay*. A 3rd edn was published at Northampton in 1771* (Aberdeen UL). It is not clear whether the issue of [1766?] – the following entry – is counted as the 1st edn; whether there was an unrecorded edn of the 1767 volume before 1771; or whether the *Essay* is regarded as the 1st edn, and the edns of 1767 and 1771, simplified but (unlike the 1766 edn) still related to the whole of the *Essay*, as the 2nd and 3rd. Alston, I, 269–70.   P. 204.

[1766?] G *A practical grammar of the English language.* York. (Wisconsin UL). An abridgment of the practical treatise in the *Essay*, 1765, and presumably a separate issue of Part I of the 1767 edn. Alston, I, 268.

[WARDEN, John], the elder 'Teacher of English'

1737 RA *A collection from the Spectator, Tatler, Guardian, Mr Pope, Mr Dryden, from Mr Rollin's Method of Teaching and Studying the Belles Lettres, and his Universal History. For the benefit of English schools,* Edinburgh. (Glasgow UL); anr edn Newcastle upon Tyne, 1752 (Hull UL; Nottingham UL); anr edn Newcastle, 1761* (BL); anr edn Edinburgh, 1765 (BL).   Pp. *172, 376*.

WARDEN, John, the younger 'Teacher of English in Edinburgh'

1753* S *A spelling-book: wherein the pronunciation and spelling of the English tongue are reduced to a very few principles or general heads. With a preface . . . offering some hints concerning a method of teaching. For the use of English schools,* Edinburgh. (NLS); 3rd edn [1761], no copy; anr edn Newcastle, 1773, no copy; anr edn Newcastle, 1812 (Newcastle PL). Alston, IV, 599–601 and Plate 57 for t.p. of 1753 edn.   Pp. 31, 58, 67, 101, 125–6, 375; *84, 375*.

WARREN, Elizabeth

1850 G *Aunt Jane's grammar. Question and answer, for the use of schools and families.* (O).

[Anon.]

1859–64 RS (Watson's) *First . . . fifth book of reading:– First book of reading, embracing the alphabet and easy exercises on the long and short vowel sounds,* Glasgow: Watson, 1859* (NLS; O). *Second book of reading, embracing progressive exercises on the pronunciation of double consonants and diphthongs, and on the most common vowel sounds,* 1859* (NLS; O). *Third book. . .* 1859 (O); *Fourth book . . .* 2nd edn 1864 (O); *Fifth book . . .* 1864 (O).   Pp. 63, 66.

WATTS, Isaac 1674–1748

1721* P *The art of reading and writing English: or, the chief principles and rules of pronouncing our mother-tongue, both in prose and verse; with a variety of instructions for true spelling.* (BL); 4th edn 1734*; as: *Watts's compleat spelling-book,* Dublin, 1737*. At least twenty edns in all to 1813. Scolar Press facsimile of 1721 edn, 1972*. Alston, IV, 296–309.   Pp. 27, 91, 109, 293f.

1753 Ed *A discourse on the education of children and youth,* in *The posthumous works,* ed. D. Jennings and P. Doddridge; included with *The improvement of the mind,* 1798*.   P. 300.

1715 RA *Divine songs attempted in easy language for the use of children.* (Dr Williams' L); anr edn 1773* (BL). Very many British and American edns until early twentieth century; Pafford, 1971, starting from the figures given by Wilbur Macey Stone, estimates about 700. Pafford includes facsimiles of edns of 1715* and *c.* 1840*. Facsimile of 1715 edn in Classics of Children's Literature, no. 4, Garland Publ. Co.   P. *168*.

1706* RA *Horae lyricae. Poems chiefly of the lyric kind. In two books. I. Songs, &c. sacred to devotion. II. Odes, elegys, &c. to virtue, loyalty and friendship.* (BL); 2nd edn 1709 (BL); 3rd edn 1715* (BL). Many edns to 1854.   Pp. 167–8.

1741 Ed *The improvement of the mind; or a supplement to The Art of Logic.* (BL);

2nd edn 1743 (BL); anr edn 1798* (personal). Many edns to 1868.

1725* Lo   *Logick: or, the right use of reason in the enquiry after truth, with a variety
of rules to guard against error, in the affairs of religion and human life, as well as in
the sciences.* (BL); 4th edn 1731* (BL). First American edn 1789. At least fifty
edns in all to 1855. Alston, VII, 148–78; Howell, 1971, pp. 333–44.   P. *313*.

WATTS, Thomas   The Academy, Little Tower Street

[a. 1716] C   *An essay on the proper method for forming the man of business: in a letter,
&c.* 2nd edn 1716 (BL); 4th edn 1722* (BL). Edited by Arthur H. Cole, Boston,
[1946] (BL).

[Anon.]

[c. 1780] RE   *The way to reading made easy or the child's first book, consisting of
scripture sentences, and other pieces, disposed in such order as to instruct the young
learners in their faith and duty, at the same time that they are led on, with pleasure,
step by step, from simple and easy, to compound and difficult words, which is
acknowledged by all, to be the most speedy and rational way of teaching. For the use
of schools. A new edition. To which are now added, Hymns by Mrs Barbauld,
Lessons by Dr Mavor, and the most important truths and duties of Christianity
stated by Archdeacon Paley.* (title from 1811 edn) (Liverpool UL); anr edn
Birmingham: Knott and Lloyd, 1811* (Nottingham UL); anr edn 1815 (BL).
Chalmers, p. 162, from Gumuchian, 202.

WEALD, William

[1746] S   *Reading made easy.* No copy. As: *Weald's lessons improved; or the royal
universal reading made easy, in three parts. I. A collection of verses and tables of
one syllable only. II. Verses and tables of two syllables. III. A dialogue between a
father and his child; the church catechism; divine songs; short prayers, &c.... for
teaching the first rudiments of reading and spelling,* Scarbro.: T. Storry, 1847*
(BL). Commended, as 'Mr Weald (in his Reading made easy)', by Lowe, 1755,
p. 17. Alston, IV, 586, discusses the frequency of editions and the lack of copies
and of information. Cf. *Reading made quite easy*, 1784, above.

WEBSTER, J.B.

[a. 1800]* RA   *The domestic instructor. Selected principally from celebrated authors,
with original pieces . . . Adapted for private families and public schools.* 354 pp.
(V&A). Inscription date 23 December 1800.   P. 192.

WEEDON, T.

1848* G   *A practical grammar of the English language.* (BL; Wisconsin UL).

[WEIGHTMAN, Mary]

1787a* RA   *The juvenile speaker: or dialogues, and miscellaneous pieces in prose and
verse: for the instruction of youth, in the art of reading.* (BL; Nottingham UL);
4th edn 1806 (BL). Recommended by Morrice, 1801, p. 140, for ages eight to
eleven.   P. 187.

1787b* RA   *The polite reasoner: in letters addressed to a young lady, at a boarding
school in Hoddesdon, Hartfordshire.* (BL).

WELLS, Samuel   'Writing master in Cheltenham'

1760* G   *The construction of the English language; or, a short, easy, and
comprehensive, grammar, for the use of English schools. To which are added, some
easy lessons upon familiar subjects adapted to the capacities of children,* n.p.
(Cheltenham PL). Alston, I, 197.

WEMYSS, Thomas   'Teacher of an academy near York'

1808* RA   *Poetry for children, consisting of selections of eight lines only. Compiled from seventy of the most esteemed ancient and modern poets.* (Liverpool UL).   P. 251.

WERENFELS, Samuel

1744* P   *The usefulness of dramatic interludes, in the education of youth: an oration spoke before the masters and scholars of the University of Basil, by Mr Werenfels. Translated from the Latin by Mr Duncombe.* (BL). NBL, 1949, no. 40.   P. 300.

WESLEY, John   1703–91

1750 Lo   *A compendium of logick*, Bristol. (O); 2nd edn 1756* (BL); 3rd edn [*c.* 1790?] (BL). Occasional edns to 1836. Alston, VII, 240–2.

1770* RA   *An extract from Dr Young's Night Thoughts on life, death, and immortality*, Bristol, 241 pp. (BL).

[1763] RA   *An extract from Milton's Paradise Lost with notes*, 2nd edn 1791* (BL). The preface to the 1st edn is dated 1 January 1763. Altick, p. 36.   Pp. 198–9.

1748* G   *A short English grammar*, Bristol. 12 pp. (private colln; NUC); 2nd edn Bristol, 1761*; 3rd edn London, 1778. Alston, I, 104–6.

WEST, Thomas   'Late Master of the English Free School, Dedham'

[a. 1819] S   *The English pronouncing spelling book . . . a first book for children.* Advertised in *A practical treatise*, 1819, published by Darton, Harvey and Darton.

WHARTON, Jeremiah

1654* G   *The English grammar: or, the institution of letters, syllables, and words in the English tongue . . . More especially profitable for scholars immediately before their entrance into the rudiments of the Latine tongue.* (O; Cambridge UL); as: *A new English grammar*, 1655* (BL). Scolar Press facsimile of 1654 edn, 1970*. Dobson, 1968, I, 337–8; Alston, I, 25–6. Vorlat, 1975.   P. 324.

WHATELY, Richard   1787–1863

1828 B   *Elements of rhetoric; comprising an analysis of the laws of moral evidence and of persuasion, with rules for argumentative composition and elocution* (title from 6th edn). 5th edn 1836 (BL); 6th edn 1841* (Bristol UL); American edns to 1869; ed. Douglas Ehringer, Carbondale, [1963].   Pp. 218, 308.

WHITE, John   'Master of a boarding school in Butterly, near Tiverton'

1701* S   *The country-man's conductor. In reading and writing true English, containing such rules as the author, by near forty years practice in teaching, hath found necessary and useful to that end. Printed chiefly for the use of the author's own school . . . To which are added, some examples of the English of our honourable ancestors, and also of our western dialect*, Exeter. (BL); 2nd edn as *The conductor in spelling, reading & writing, true English . . .* Exeter, 1712* (BL) (text unchanged). Alston, IV, 211–12 and Plate 37 for t.p. in full.   P. 342.

WHITE, John   'Teacher of elocution, grammar, &c., Aberdeen'

1826* RA   *The elementary elocutionist: a selection of pieces in prose and verse, to exemplify the art of reading; accompanied with exercises and notes, and preceded by an introduction, containing a new view of the cause of inflection; from which Mr Walker's system of rules is shown to be erroneous*, Aberdeen. 312 pp. (BL).

1830–1 RS   *The first . . . third book for children:– First book* [not traced]; *Second book*, Edinburgh, [1830?] (O); *Third book*, Edinburgh, 1831 (O).

WHITE, John   'Teacher of English, Geography and History, Edinburgh'

[1850]* G   *A system of English grammar; with numerous exercises progressively arranged. For the use of schools and private students.* Edinburgh (NLS; O). White published textbooks in other subjects between 1830 and 1845.

WHITE, Thomas

[1674] RE   *A little book for little children: wherein are set down several directions for little children and several remarkable stories both ancient and modern of little children. Divers whereof are of those lately deceased. By Thomas White, minister of the gospel.* Sloane, 1955. Title from 12th edn, 1702* (BL). Thwaite, 1972. See above, T.W., 1702.

WHITWORTH, T.   'Professor of the Greek, Latin, and English classics, composition, elocution &c.'

1819* G   *A complete parsing grammar; or, a practical key to the grammatical construction of the English language. For the use of families, private teachers, public academies, and senior as well as junior students.* (BL).

WICKS, John Harris   'Master of the boarding school, Englefield House, Egham'

1817   *The remembrancer, containing a selection of questions in . . . arithmetic and English grammar.* (BL).

WILBY, F.

1844 S   *The infant school spelling-book and pictorial dictionary.* Darton and Clark. Osborne, II, 747; Chalmers, p. 163.

[Anon.]

[*c.* 1825] RA   *The wild garland, a collection of infantile poems with pleasing exercises,* William Darton. Sotheby, HIC, VI, 1977, Lot 2675.

WILKINS, James   'Licensed teacher'

1818* G   *Grammatical questions, with notes, adapted to Lindley Murray's Abridgment of English Grammar. With an appendix; containing observations on the sounds of letters; rules for spelling and dividing words into syllables; exercises; and directions for scanning and reading English verse.* Stamford: John Drakard. 88 pp. (BL).   P. *352.*

WILLIAMS, Alexander   'Master of the Academy, Lambeth

[a. 1814]a RE   *Exercises in reading, being a collection of lessons, designed as a sequel to the Improved Universal Spelling Book.* Advt in 1814 by the publisher James Robbins of Winchester.

[a. 1816] S   *Fenning's Universal Spelling Book, revised, improved, and greatly enlarged; or, an easy introduction to the English language, containing . . .* [an English grammar different from those in other edns of Fenning]. 8th edn Winchester, 1816* (O).

[a. 1814]b RE   *Royal English primer, or first book for children of an early age.* Advt in 1814 by the publisher James Robbins of Winchester.

WILLIAMS, David   1738–1816

1774* Ed   *A treatise on education. In which the general method pursued in the public institutions of Europe, and particularly in those of England . . . are considered; and a more practicable and useful one proposed.* (BL).   Pp. 280–1.

WILLIAMS, David   Teacher

1818* G   *The catechism of English grammar: containing the principles of the* *language, and rules and directions for speaking and writing it with propriety and accuracy. With a variety of exercises . . . To which is subjoined, a copious list of solecisms, or vulgar and erroneous modes of expression.* (BL).

1850* Ex *Composition, literary and rhetorical, simplified.* (BL). P. 305.

[a. 1813] G *Grammatical questions: or English grammar taught rationally, not by rote.* Advt in 1813 by Sherwood, Gilbert and Piper.

WILLIAMS, Henry W.

1830* Ex *The principles of English composition; or a concise development of the leading principles to be regarded, in order to the attainment of a correct and elegant English style. Designed, in particular, for the use of schools.* (O). The preface is dated from Bristol, October 1830.

WILLIAMS, Honoria

1821* G *Conversations on English grammar, in a series of familiar and entertaining dialogues between a mother and her daughters . . . with a number of appropriate questions following each conversation. Adapted to the use of establishments for young ladies, as well as to private tuition, and to preparatory schools for young gentlemen.* (BL); 2nd edn 1825 (BL); 3rd edn 1826 (Wisconsin UL). Pp. 40; 106, 122–3.

[1871:* RE *A first reading book: to be used next after the tablets, in Mrs Williams' syllabic method of teaching to read,* Whittaker. (BL). Preface dated May 1871; the attribution to Honoria Williams is by BL.

1817* Ed *A summary method of teaching children to read; upon the principle originally discovered by the Sieur Berthaud, considerably improved; with an entirely new arrangement, calculated to adapt it to the English language.* With nine copper plates. (BL); anr edn 1819, Chalmers, p. 163; as *Syllabic spelling; or, a summary method . . .* 1820 (BL); 4th edn 1829* (BL); 5th edn 1830 (Leicester UL); 6th edn, rev. Lady Leighton, 1858 (BL).

NBL, 1949, no. 150a, and others give Mrs Williams' names as Helen Maria. The *DNB* entry for Helen Maria Williams does not refer to these books, which are not ones she is likely to have written.

WILLIAMS, Jeremiah 'Schoolmaster in London'

[a. 1784?] S *The newest reading made completely easy: or, an introduction to reading the Holy Bible.* 36th edn, n.d. Coventry (Roscoe). Alston, IV, 876, and Suppl., p. 34. The estimated date is Alston's.

]WILLIAMS, John] Vicar of Catherington

[a. 1752] Ed *Education of children and young students in all its branches, with a short catalogue of the best books in polite learning and the sciences.* 2nd edn 1752*, 44 pp. (BL; O, with author's (?) MS emendation to '3rd' edn). Pp. 178, 203, 290, 344–5; *383*.

[a. 1780]* G *The first principles of English grammar, in verse, for the use of young people. By J.W.* n.d., n.p. (O; BL). The work is dedicated to James Harris (d. 1780) and refers to Lowth's grammar (1762).

1760* Lo *The young mathematician's logic, upon the plan of Dean Aldrich's celebrated Aristotle's Logic, and serving to explain the same. To which is annexed, critical remarks upon grammar in general.* (O). Alston, VII, 247.

WILLIAMS, William

[1760?] S *A new English spelling book and expositor: a more plain and easy method of teaching children and adults to spell, read, write and understand the English tongue*. No copy. Advertised in Felix Farley's *Bristol Journal*, 12 January 1760, as being 'in the press'. Information from Jonathan Barry.

WILLIAMS, William Claude

1851 G   *A plain English grammar, for the use of North London Collegiate School.* (O).

WILLMOTT, Robert Aris   1809–63

1859 RA   *Wordsworth: poems, selected and edited. DNB*; anr edn 1865 (BL).

[WILMSHURST, Miss]   Of 'The Miss Wilmshursts' Seminary, Cromwell House, Maldon'

1833* G   *The first part of the progressive parsing lessons; or, an introduction to Murray's grammar.* Maldon: P.H. Youngman. Pp. 102 with six-page list of books and materials used in the seminary. (O). Probably first issued before 1833: the preface says that a new edn of Part 2 is being prepared. Cf. *The child's first . . . grammar lessons*, above.

1803–8 S   *The pronouncing spelling book; containing a number of rules for spelling, exemplified by spelling lessons, placed progressively according to their difficulty; and divided agreeably to the recommendation of Dr Lowth.* Part 1, 1803; Part 2, 1808 (Watt, *Bibliotheca Britannica; Gent. Mag.*, 78.i (April 1808), 333). Watt gives the author as 'Mrs Wilmot', the *Gent. Mag.* as 'Wilmhurst', Sarah Trimmer as 'Mrs Wilmshurst' (*Guardian of Education*, 2, 114). See above, *The juvenile reader's assistant*, 1830.

WILSON, Mrs   'Of Poplar'

1803* C   *A brief compendium of juvenile instruction, or a progressive inlet to useful knowledge.* (BL). Chap. 1 is an English grammar; later chapters include 'An epitome of iconology'.

WILSON, Alexander   'Principal, National Society Training Institute, London'

1853* G   *Abstract of the Manual of English Grammar for the use of pupils in elementary schools*, National Society. 24 pp. (BL); new edn as *Abstract of English grammar*, [1862]*, 24 pp. (BL).

[a. 1842] G   *Outlines of English grammar, compiled for the use of National and other schools*, 2nd edn 1842* (O; BL); anr edn 1844 (Nottingham UL); anr edn 1845, Hunter 1848.   Pp. *346n.*, *357*.

1842* La   *Outlines of etymology, compiled for the use of National and other schools.* 16 pp. (BL).

WILSON, George   'Teacher at an academy in London'

[1756?] C   *The youth's pocket companion: or, universal preceptor. Containing what is absolutely necessary for every young man to know and practise, under the following heads, viz. A plain and easy grammar of the English language . . . [etc.]* (title from 1759 edn) (Nottingham UL); 2nd edn 1759* (Leicester UL); anr edn 1777. Alston, III, 264–6.   P. 325.

WILSON, J.

[a. 1822] RA   *The youth's reader; or, second book for children*, 2nd edn Nottingham, 1822* (BL; Nottingham UL); 3rd edn 1826* (BL).

WILSON, John   'Teacher of elocution, South Bridge, Edinburgh'

1798* P   *Principles of elocution, and suitable exercises; or, elegant extracts, in prose and verse . . . intermixed with remarks on the various kinds of composition, and rules for reading and reciting them.* Edinburgh. (BL). Alston, VI, 433.

WILSON, John

1844 Ex   *A treatise of grammatical punctuation.* Manchester. (BL); as *A treatise on English punctuation*, Boston, Mass., 1850, GB; 6th edn Boston, 1856 (BL).

WILSON, M.

1855 G   *Complete English grammar.* LOWRES, 1863.

WILSON, Mark

1862 RE   *The first reading book.* (BL; O).

WILSON, Richard   Of Grantham Grammar School

1845* G   *Interrogative English grammar.* Grantham. (O; BL).   P. *346n.*

WILSON, Thomas   1525?–1581

1553 B   *The arte of rhetorique, for the use of all suche as are studious of eloquence, sette forth in English.* (BL). Seven further edns to 1585; ed. G.H. Mair (1560 and 1585 texts) Oxford, 1909*; intro. R.H. Bowers, Scholars Facsimile (1553 text), Gainesville, 1962; facsimile edn of 1553 text, Theatrum Orbis Terrarum, Amsterdam, 1969*; ed. T.J. Derrick, Garland Press, N.Y., 1982. Alston, VI, 10–17.   Pp. 153–4, 272.

1551 Lo   *The rule of reason, conteinyng the arte of logique, set forth in Englishe.* (BL); 1553* (BL). Seven edns in all to 1580. Facsimile of 1551 edn, Theatrum Orbis Terrarum, Amsterdam, 1970*; ed. Richard S. Sprague, Northridge, Ca., 1972.   P. 146.

[WINFIELD, G.W.]   Master of St Martin's School, Adelaide St, Strand

[1846]* S   *Spelling lessons to be learnt at home. Intended for the use of National schools.* (BL); 3rd edn 1847 (BL).

WINKS, Joseph Foulkes   Sometime teacher

[1834]* RA   *The British school book, for reading and recitation; being selections of prose and poetry, from the most approved standard writers of Great Britain, Ireland and America.* Leicester. (BL; Leicester UL). The pieces in the earlier volume are all included in this, with seventy additional ones. This volume is dated by its preface.

[1830?]* RA   *Choice pieces, from British and American authors. Designed for the young, and adapted for reading and recitation in schools and families.* London and Leicester. (BL).   P. *237.*

[1848]* S   (Winks') *Spelling and reading book for sabbath and day schools, containing progressive lessons, easy reading, and select passages from the holy scriptures; also spelling words of six letters, to four syllables, scripture names accented and explained, with explanations of religious words.* Leicester. (BL).   P. 68.

[Anon.]

1785 RA   *Wisdom in miniature: or, the young gentleman and lady's pleasing instructor: being a collection of sentences, divine, moral, and historical. Collected from the writings of many ingenious and learned authors, both antient and modern. Intended not only for the use of schools, but as a pocket companion for the youth of both sexes. By the editor of The School and Family Testament.* Coventry (NUC); 2nd edn Coventry, 1787* (BL). In all at least eleven British and twenty-four American edns, under varying titles. Gumuchian, 5848 and 5849; Rosenbach, 202 etc.   P. 192.

WISE, Thomas   'Accomptant'

1754* C   *The newest young man's companion, containing, a compendious English* *grammar* . . . [Penmanship; Letter-writing; Commercial forms; Arithmetic; Book-keeping; Geography; Oil-painting; Fireworks] *and an English spelling dictionary. The whole calculated to qualify persons for business, without a master, and illustrated with a map of the world.* Berwick (Edinburgh UL); 2nd edn 1755 (Columbia UL); 3rd edn 1758*. Eleven edns in all to 1778, and a thirteenth edn seen with a torn t.p. Alston, IV, 615–21 and Plate 60 for t.p. of 1754 in facsimile.

WISE, T[homas]   'Schoolmaster'

[1790?]* S   *Reading made easy, and best guide to spelling: containing, lessons for spelling and reading, on moral and religious subjects, from words of one syllable to those of six or eight syllables: in which are interspersed passages from the sacred scriptures, so as to render it a proper introduction to the reading of the Holy Bible* . . . *Designed for the use of schools.* (BL). Alston, IV, 878 and Plate 90 for t.p. in facsimile.

WISEMAN, Charles

1764* G   *A complete English grammar on a new plan. For the use of foreigners, and such natives as would acquire a scientifical knowledge of their own tongue. In two parts. Containing.* . . . [I. Pronunciation. II. Parts of speech] *The whole interspersed with several short praxes and remarks at the end of every part of speech. To which are added, similar comparisons of the Old English, Scotch, and Welsh tongues, with the modern English* . . . [etc.]. (BL; Leicester UL). Preface by Goldsmith. Alston, I, 257.   Pp. 342; *318.*

[WISEMAN, Thomas John]

1846* G   *A school grammar of the English language. By the Christian Brothers.* Dublin: William Powell. (O).   Pp. 360; *352.*

[WITHERS, Philip]

[1789?] La   *Aristarchus, or the principles of composition. Containing a methodical arrangement of the improprieties frequent in writing and conversation. With select rules for attaining to purity and elegance of expression.* (title from 2nd edn) (BL); 2nd edn [1790?]* (Bristol UL; BL); anr edn 1822 (BL). Alston, III, 396–7.   P. *328.*

Wit's Academy see MERES, 1598
Wit's Commonwealth see MERES, 1598 and LING, 1597
Wit's Treasury see MERES, 1598

WOOD, Helen

1827 G   *The grammatical reading class book, or, easy introduction to English grammar, in entertaining conversations between a lady and her daughters: in which the parts of speech are familiarly explained, and the rules of grammar introduced and illustrated in a pleasing manner* . . . *Intended for the use of schools and families.* (GB); 3rd edn 1828* (private colln); 6th edn 1841 (GB); 10th edn 1865 (Wisconsin UL).

WOOD, J.

[a. 1845] P   *A grammar of elocution.* Mentioned in the 1845 edn of J.H. Hindmarsh's *The rhetorical reader.*

WOOD, James

1777* G   *Grammatical institutions; or a practical English grammar.* Newcastle-upon-Tyne. (Newcastle PL). Alston, I, 347.   P. *282.*

WOOD, John

1828 Ed   *Account of the Edinburgh sessional school, and the other parochial institutions for education established in that city in the year 1812; with strictures on education in general.* (title from 2nd edn). 2nd edn Edinburgh, 1829* (BL). At least five edns in all to 1840. The date for the 1st edn is that given by Jill E. Gray, introduction to Sarah Fielding's *The governess*, OUP, 1968, p. 53.   Pp. 364; 76.

1839 G   *First elements of English grammar.* Edinburgh. Hunter, 1848.

WOOD, Samuel

[a. 1833] P   *A grammar of elocution: in which the five accidents of speech are explained and illustrated.* 2nd edn 1833* (BL).

WOODWARD, Robert William

[a. 1830] S   *New English spelling book, on an improved plan.* 10th edn, J. Fairbairn, [c. 1830]. Chalmers, p. 163.

WOOLGAR, William 'Accomptant'

1761 C   *Youth's faithful monitor: or, the young man's best companion. Containing a compendious English grammar.* (title from 3rd edn). No copy. 3rd edn 1766* (BL); 5th edn 1770 (BL).

[Anon.] 'Schoolmaster'

1854* RE   *The word-making primer, designed for use in elementary schools. By a schoolmaster.* (BL).   P. 132.

WORDSWORTH, William   1770–1850

Anonymous editions:

1859* RA   *The Excursion. Book I. The Wanderer.* SPCK. Pp. 32. (BL). Plain text, no introduction.

1873 RA   *The Excursion. Book I. The Wanderer.* 'Chambers's English Classics for use in schools'. (BL).

[1874] RA   *The Excursion. Book I. The Wanderer.* Collins' School Classics. (BL).

[1873] RA   *Wordsworth's Excursion: The Wanderer* [and Longfellow's] *The Wreck of the Hesperus.* (BL).

1862 RA   *Wordsworth's poems for the young.* 92 pp., illustrated. Alexander Strachan. Catalogue.

See also   M., I., a. 1831
              BROMBY, C.H., 1864
              HINE, J., 1831
              ROBINSON, H.G., 1863
              TURNER, H.H., 1874
              WILLMOTT, R.A., 1865

WOTTON, Antony   1561?–1626   and   WOTTON, Samuel   1600–1680/1

1626* Lo   *The art of logick. Gathered out of Aristotle, and set in due forme, according to his instructions, by Peter Ramus . . . Published for the instruction of the unlearned.* (BL). Howell, 1956, p. 232.   P. 148.

WOTTON, Henry

1753* Ed   *An essay on the education of children, in the first rudiments of learning. Together with a narration of what knowledge, William Wotton, a child of six years of age, had attained unto, upon the improvement of those rudiments, in the Latin,*

Greek, and Hebrew tongues. (BL). Written in 1673. *DNB* s.v. William Wotton. Alston, X, 214.   Pp. 77; 59.

[Anon.]

1828 RA   *The wreath, a selection of poems, chiefly designed for young persons.* Dublin: W. Espy. Blackwell, Cat. A1113, 1978.

WRIGHT, George

[a. 1782] RA   *The young moralist, consisting of allegories and entertaining essays, in prose and verse . . . chiefly designed to implant the principles of virtue and morality in the minds of young gentlemen and ladies.* (title from 3rd edn) 1782* (BL); 4th edn 1792 (V&A); 5th edn 1819 (BL; V&A).   Pp. 191–2.

WRIGHT, George   'Teacher of English and the Mathematics'

1794* G   *The principles of grammar, or youth's English directory.* Sunderland. (BL). Alston, I, 477.   P. 94.

WRIGHT, James   'Public and private lecturer on English elocution'

1814* P   *The school orator; or, exercises in elocution theoretically arranged: from which, aided by short practical rules to be committed to memory, and repeated after the manner of reciting the rules in the Latin syntax, students may learn to articulate every word with propriety . . . [etc.]* (BL); 2nd edn 1818, Boyle, Cat. 824, 1972; 3rd edn 1823* (personal); 5th edn 1833 (BL).   Pp. 289; 220.

[between 1814 and 1818] P   *The philosophy of elocution elucidated and exemplified.* An advertisement in the 2nd edn, 1818, of his *The school orator* says that *The philosophy of elocution* was published since the 1st edn, 1814, of *The school orator.* James Knowles, 1829, p. 225, refers to it scornfully.

WRIGHT, Thomas   Master of South Town Seminary, Great Yarmouth

[c. 1795?]a* G   *An English grammar,* n.d., n.p. The only copy of the work, 70 pp. is as part of a composite volume, including arithmetical tables and an address on filial obedience, for use in Wright's school (Great Yarmouth PL). The grammar was advertised in Wright's *Miscellany,* q.v., as 'The elements of English grammar'. Alston, I, 534.

[c. 1795?]b S   *An English spelling-book on a new plan.* [Great Yarmouth?]. No copy. Advertised in his *Miscellany.* Alston, IV, 910a (Suppl., p. 34).

[c. 1795]* C   *A miscellany, for young persons.* Great Yarmouth. (BL; O). Alston, III, 413. Pp. 51–105 contain 'a poetical epitome of grammar' and sections on syntax and usage.

[Anon.]

1695 S   *The writing scholar's companion: or, infallible rules for writing true English with ease and certainty: drawn from the grounds and reasons of the English tongue . . . Composed for the benefit of all such as are industriously ambitious of so commendable an ornament, as writing true English is generally esteemed. Recommended especially to the youth of both sexes, and to be taught in schools.* (BL). Ed. E. Ekwall, Halle, 1911*. Dobson, 1968, pp. 358f; Alston, IV, 179 and Plate 32 for t.p. See above, *The expert orthographist,* 1704.   Pp. 27, 45–6, 74, 93; 43, 88.

[WYNNE, John Huddlestone]   1743–88

1772* RA   *Choice emblems, natural, historical, fabulous, moral and divine, for the improvement and pastime of youth.* (BL). At least eleven British and eleven American edns to 1815. 'For the use of schools' added to the title by the 7th edn,

1793. The 3rd and 4th edns, 1779 and 1781, were entitled *Riley's emblems*. Roscoe, J389.

WYNNE, Richard 1719–99

1775* G *A universal grammar, for the use of those who are unacquainted with the learned languages, and are desirous of speaking and writing English, or any other modern language, with accuracy and precision.* (BL). Alston, I, 328a. *P. 341.*

YATES, M.T.

[a. 1871] G *Grammar made easy, in rhyme.* Manchester: John Heywood. Price one penny. Advt in 1871.

YEOMANS, John 'Schoolmaster in Five Fields Row, Chelsea'

1759* Ed *The abecedarian, or, philosophic comment upon the English alphabet. Setting forth the absurdities in the present custom of spelling . . . with . . . a syllableium, or universal reading table, for beginners, calculated after the present use, for the way of all schools throughout the kingdom.* (BL). Alston, VI, 482 and Plate 15 for t.p. Pp. 46–7, 115; *51.*

YOUNG, Edward 'Schoolmaster in London'

[1675] S *The compleat English scholar, in spelling, reading, and writing: containing plain and easie directions for spelling, and reading English, according to the present pronunciation . . . [etc.] (title from 12th edn). 18th edn [1710]* (BL). Forty-one edns to 1752. Alston, IV, 110–28 and Plate 18 for t.p. of 12th edn, 1696. Dobson, 1968, pp. 350–3. Pp. 35; *50, 373.*

YOUNG, Henry Of Spalding, Lincolnshire

1832* G *The youth's memoriter, and English exercise book . . . comprising in one volume all that is necessary for an English scholar to commit to memory, and all the exercises usually put into his hands.* (BL). P. 347.

[Anon.]

1846* G *The young child's grammar.* Edinburgh: Scottish School Book Association. (BL). An introduction to the SSBA's *Principles of English grammar.*

[Anon.]

[a. 1854] Ex *The young composer; or, progressive exercises in English composition.* British and Foreign School Society syllabus, 1854 (BFSS Archives).

[Anon.]

1808 RA *The young gentleman and lady's instructor; or new reader and speaker: being a collection of pieces in poetry and prose, designed as a pleasing and useful companion to young persons in general.* Holtom, List 52, 1984; 2nd edn Lewes: J. Baxter. (Preston, Harris PL). Cover title: *The instructor, or pleasing companion for youth.*

[Anon.]

[a. 1800] RA *The young gentleman and lady's poetical preceptor . . . Calculated to form the taste to classic elegance; and, while it delights the fancy, to improve the morals, and to harmonize the heart.* 2nd edn Coventry: N. Merridew, 1807* (private colln). The 1st edn was dedicated to Cowper, in his lifetime; Cowper died 25 April 1800. The 1st edn had notes, omitted in the 2nd.

[Anon.]

1814* C *The young man's companion, or youth's instructor; being a guide to various branches of useful knowledge.* Oxford. 862 pp. (private colln); new edn, 'to which is prefixed an introductory address on the advantages of education', Oxford,

1825 (Reading UL). Contents include grammar and penmanship.

Young Mathematician's Logic see WILLIAMS, John, 1760

[Anon.]

1804* RA   *The young reader's instructor, being a collection of lessons, in prose and verse, intended for the lower classes in schools, with an introduction, comprising easy lessons for children.* Doncaster: D. Boys. (BL).

[Anon.]

1770 RA   *The young scholar's delight. Being the most easy introduction to learning and science.* Newcastle. (Durham UL). Attributed to Ann Fisher by Alston in the introductory note to the Scolar Press edn of her *A new grammar*.

[Anon.]

1779* RE   *The young scholar's pocket companion: being an easy introduction to the art of reading. In three parts. Containing I. The first principles of pronunciation. II. The Assembly's shorter catechism, divided into lessons . . . III. Easy lessons in prose and verse.* Glasgow: J. and J. Robertson and J. Duncan. (V&A). Alston, IV, 770.

[Anon.]

1752* RA   *The young student's assistant; or, literary entertainer: containing, select essays in prose and verse, on the interesting and important consequences of a virtuous, or a misguided education* [by Rollin, Fénelon *et al.*] J. Fuller. (BL).   P. 180.

[Anon.]

[1871]* G   *The young student's English grammar for schools.* Manchester: Heywood. (NLS).   P. 351.

[Anon.]

1825 RA   *The youth's best friend; or reading no longer a task.* Deal: Hayward. NBL, 1949, no. 158; anr edn 1829 (V&A).

[Anon.]

[a. 1829] RA   *Youth's guide, adapted to the use of schools, by a gentleman. Containing a variety of original reading and spelling lessons.* 2nd edn Deal: Hayward, 1829. NBL, 1946, no. 72; Sotheby, HIC, VI (1977), 2741. Sotheby's catalogue does not record the words 'by a gentleman'.

[Anon.]

1792 RA   *The youth's instructor. Prose and verse. Consisting of moral stories and fables . . . For schools and families.* Dublin. (NUC).

[Anon.]

1847* RA   *The youth's poetical instructor, or useful lessons in poetry; being a selection of moral, entertaining, and religious pieces.* (BL); Part 2, Belfast, 1851 (BL).   P. 238.

British ABCs and alphabet books consulted

Hornbooks, battledores, ABCs and alphabet books The hornbook (a wooden bat onto which was fastened a piece of vellum or paper, covered with horn as a protection) displayed the alphabet in upper and lower case, a few syllables, the numerals, and often doctrinal matter such as the Lord's Prayer and the Creed. The many variations are described in Tuer, 1897. The wooden bat was later replaced by one made of cardboard, called a battledore, on which the letters were printed. In the middle of the eighteenth century the bat-shaped battledore was replaced by a small piece of folded cardboard carrying, often, several alphabets and more doctrinal matter and retaining the name battledore. The first ABCs contained, in booklet form, the same matter as the hornbook, with additions; some were so much enlarged that they became spelling-books. The alphabet book was, and still is, a special form of ABC: secular, with very varied pictures and reading-matter attached to each letter. There are collections of battledores in the British Library; the University of Leeds Museum of the History of Education; Bedford College of Higher Education; Wandsworth Public Library; Harris Public Library, Preston, and elsewhere. Many are listed, without locations, in Chalmers, 1976.

There is a large literature about, and many collections of, ABCs. The few that have been consulted are listed below. As only two or three of them are by named authors the anonymity of the others is not stated in each entry.

[c. 1538?]   *The ABC both in Latyn and Englysshe* (BL); facsimile reprint ed. E.S. Shuckburgh from the copy in Emmanuel C, Cambridge, 1889*. Butterworth, 1953. In the original *ABC* is printed *BAC*.

[1545]*   *The A.B.C. set forthe by the Kynges maiestie and his clergye, and commaunded to be taught through out all his realme.* (BL). Butterworth, 1949 and 1953.

1698   *The ABC with the catechism* (BL); anr edn 1719*.

[c. 1542]   *The abc with the pater noster ave | credo | and X commaundementes in Englysshe.* (Illinois UL). Butterworth, 1949 and 1953.

1714*   *The ABC with the shorter catechism.* Edinburgh. (BL).

1972*   *100 nineteenth-century rhyming alphabets in English. From the library of Ruth M. Baldwin.* Carbondale: S. Illinois University Press.

1824   *Aldiborontiphoskyphorniostikos*: reprinted by Opie, 1980*. Thwaite, 1972.

[1852]*   *Alphabet of nouns; or, good child's ABC (Aunt Busy-Bee's series)* (V&A). Whalley, 1974.

1776*   *The careless child's alphabet, designed to fix the learner's attention to the shape of the letters.* Northampton. Sotheby, HIC, June 1982, lot 26.

[1884]   CRAWHALL, Joseph: *Old Aunt Elspa's ABC.* Scolar Press facsimile reprint 1978*.

[1830?]   *The galloping guide to the ABC, or the child's agreeable introduction to a knowledge of the gentlemen of the alphabet.* Banbury. (V&A; BL); facsimile Stockham, 1974*. Whalley, 1974.

[*c.* 1820?]   *The golden pippen.* Facsimile in Stockham, 1980*.

[*c.* 1791]   *History of an apple pie, written by Z.* Reproduced in Opie, 1980*.

1820   *The hobby-horse, or the high road to learning* ('A was an Archer . . '); reproduced in Opie, 1980*.

[*c.* 1830?]*   *The illustrated ABC, or the child's first step to learning.* Sudbury: H.M. Ives. (Nottingham UL).

[1850?]*   *The illustrated alphabet.* (BL).

[*c.* 1826]   *The life and death of Apple Pie.* Scolar Press facsimile, London, 1978*.

1811*   *A new and entertaining alphabet for young children, where some instruction may be gained, and much amusement.* W. Darton. (Nottingham UL).

1864*   *New royal ABC and spelling book (Cousin Honeycomb's series).* Dean and Son. (V&A).

1819   *Nursery novelties* ('Oh dear, says little Allspice A'). J. Harris. Reproduced in Opie, 1974*.

[*c.* 1818]   *The picture alphabet.* Reproduced in Stockham, 1974*.

1809* R[ANSOME], R.   *The assembled alphabet; or, acceptance of A's invitation.* (Bedford CHE)

[1818] R[ANSOME], R.:   *The invited alphabet; or, address of A to B, containing his friendly proposal for the amusement and instruction of good children.* B. Tabart, 1809* (Nottingham UL); reproduced in *100 nineteenth century rhyming alphabets,* above.

1830   *The picture alphabet, for the instruction and amusement of boys and girls.* Otley: W. Walker. Reproduced in Stockham, 1974*.

[*c.* 1850]*   (Wood's) *Pretty alphabet for children.* T. Wood. (BL).

[*c.* 1800?]   *The silver penny, for the amusement and instruction of good children.* York: J. Kendrew. Reproduced in Stockham, 1974*. Whalley, 1974, p. 27; Rosenbach, 354.

American texts consulted

This list is confined to the short titles of works within the period that have been consulted. The 754 volumes of the *National Union Catalogue* make it unnecessary to provide more detailed information. As the place of publication is normally in America the occasional exceptions are recorded as, for example, 'London, England'.

ADAMS, Daniel
1803a* *The thorough scholar; or, the nature of language with the reasons, principles and rules of English grammar.* Boston. (BL).   P. 251
1803b *The understanding reader: or, knowledge before oratory. Being a new selection of lessons . . . I In reading. II In the definition of words. III In spelling.* 3rd edn Leominster, Mass., 1805*. (BL).   P. 250.

ALDEN, Abner
1797 *An introduction to reading and spelling. Being the first part of A Columbian Exercise.* Boston. 7th edn 1816* (BL, vol. II only) Alston, IV, 918–20.
1802 *The reader . . . Being a third part of A Columbian Exercise.* 5th edn Boston, 1822* (BL).   P. 246.

ALEXANDER, Caleb
1793* *Grammatical elements, or, a comprehensive theory of English grammar. Intended for the use of children of both sexes.* Boston (AAS). Alston, I, 473.
1792 *A grammatical system of the English language.* 6th edn Boston, 1801*. (BL). Alston, I, 458–62.
1797a* *The young gentlemen and ladies' instructor . . . designed as a reading book for the use of schools and academies.* Boston (Harvard UL).   P. 193.
1797b* *The young ladies and gentlemen's spelling book.* Providence, R.I. (Rhode Island Hist. Soc.). Alston, IV, 921–2.   Pp. 52, 54.

ALGER, Israel
1824* *The English reader: or, pieces in prose and poetry, selected . . . by Lindley Murray . . . to which . . . is scrupulously applied, Mr Walker's pronunciation of the classical proper names.* Boston. (BL). Alger treated all three of Murray's readers in this way.

ALLISON, Burgiss
1815* *The American standard of orthography and pronunciation, and an improved dictionary of the English language, abridged for the use of schools.* Burlington. (BL).

[Anon.]
1809* *The American poetical miscellany.* Philadelphia. (BL).   P. 245.

[Anon.]

1809* *The American prose miscellany*. Philadelphia. (BL). This and the preceding item were intended as school books and 'for more mature age'. They claim to contain a 'greater proportion of *American* productions' than can be found in any similar work. P. *245*.

[BABCOCK, Elisha]

1798* *The child's spelling book: calculated to render reading completely easy to little children; to impress upon their minds the importance of religion, and the advantages of good manners*. Hartford. (Yale UL). Alston, IV, 930–1. P. *52*.

BALCH, William Stevens

1839* *A grammar of the English language, explained according to the principles of truth and common sense, and adapted to the capacities of all who think. Designed for the use of schools*. Boston (BL). P. 350.

1829* *Inductive grammar. By an instructer*. Windsor, Vermont and Boston (DLC).

BARNARD, Frederick Augustus Porter

1836* *Analytic grammar, with symbolic illustrations*. N.Y. (BL). The elaborate, coherent but impractical symbolism is derived from the teaching of the deaf and dumb.

BARRETT, John

[1818] *A grammar of the English language: containing a variety of critical remarks, the principal part of which are original*. 2nd edn Boston, 1819* (BL).

BARRETT, Solomon

1845 *The principles of grammar*. Rev. edn Albany, 1849* (BL).

1837* *The principles of language: containing a full grammatical analysis of English poetry, confirmed by syllogistical reasoning and logical induction*. Albany. (BL). The work does not live up to its title.

BENEZET, Anthony

1776 *The Pennsylvania spelling book*. 6th edn Dublin, 1800* (BL, imperfect). Alston, IV, 729–33, and Plate 79 for title in full.

BETHUNE, Joanna

1830* *The infant school grammar, consisting of elementary lessons in the analytical method, illustrated by sensible objects and actions*. N.Y. (BL). The analytical method is parsing.

BINGHAM, Caleb

1794 *The American preceptor; being a new selection of lessons for reading and speaking*. 4th edn Boston, 1797* (BL). Pp. 193; *195*.

1792* *The child's companion; being a concise spelling-book*. Boston (AAS). Alston, IV, 885–90, and Plate 92 for title in full.

1797* *The Columbian orator: containing a variety of pieces; together with rules; calculated to improve youth and others in the ornamental and useful art of eloquence*. Boston (BL); 2nd edn Boston, 1799* (BL). P. *195*.

BLAKE, John Lauris

[1832] *The first reader; a class-book for schools*. Concord. (BL).

1832* *The high school reader . . . Consisting of extracts in prose and poetry*. Boston. (BL).

BOYD, James Robert
1844   *Elements of rhetoric and literary criticism . . . For the use of common schools and academies.* N.Y. 5th edn N.Y., 1846* (BL).

BRACE, Joab
1839*   *The principles of English grammar . . . Arranged on the principles of Lennie's Grammar.* Philadelphia. (BL).

BROWN, Goold
[1821?]   *The child's first book: being a new primer, for the use of families and schools.* 6th edn N.Y., 1827* (DLC).   Pp. 103, 114; *98.*

1850*   *The grammar of English grammars, with an introduction historical and critical.* Boston (BL); 10th edn N.Y., 1875* (BL). Pp. xx, 1102.   Pp. 45, 368; *52, 351.*

1823   *The institutes of English grammar . . . Designed for the use of schools.* N.Y.; anr edn N.Y., 1845* (BL).

BROWN, James
1836*   *An appeal from the British system of English grammar to common sense. Designed to aid the introduction of the American system of English syntax.* Philadelphia. (Boston PL).   P. 361.

1839*   *An English syntascope, developing the constructive principles of the English phrenod, or language, and impressing them on the memory by pictorial, and scenical demonstration.* Philadelphia. (Boston PL).   P. 362.

1840*   *An exegesis of English syntax, designed to enable teachers, pupils, and others to comprehend fully, the present popular system of English grammar, as presented by Murray, and simplified by later writers.* Philadelphia. (BL). In spite of its title the book is hostile to Murray and advocates 'the American system'.

BULLIONS, Peter
1844   *Practical lessons in English grammar and composition.* N.Y., 1853* (BL).

[BUMSTEAD, Josiah Freeman]
1841   *Spelling and thinking combined; or, the spelling-book made a medium of thought.* Boston. Anr edn 1846* (BL)   P. 124.

BURR, Jonathan
1797*   *A compendium of English grammar, for the use of schools, and private instructers. To which are annexed, exercises, corresponding to the grammar.* Boston. (BL). Alston, I, 502.

CAREY, Mathew
1800   *The school of wisdom: or American monitor.* Philadelphia. (NYPL).   Pp. *193, 195.*

CARROL, James
1795   *The American criterion of the English language: containing the elements of pronunciation . . . For the use of English schools and foreigners.* New London. Scolar Press facsimile, Menston, 1970*. Alston, VI, 508.   Pp. 55; *52.*

CARSON, James
1794*   *A practical grammar of the English tongue. Containing all that is necessary to be committed to memory . . . Composed chiefly for the benefit of his own school.* Philadelphia. (NYc). Alston, I, 474.

CHAMBERS, Joseph G.

1812*   *Elements of orthography: or, an attempt to form a complete system of letters.*
        Zanesville. (BL).

CHESSMAN, Daniel

[a. 1821]   *A compendium of English grammar; comprising all that is necessary to be
            committed to memory by students: abridged from Lindley Murray's excellent
            treatise.* 3rd edn Hallowell, Me., 1821* (BL).

[Anon.]

1802   *The child's first book; being an easy introduction to spelling and reading.*
       Boston; anr edn Boston, 1816* (BL).

[Anon.]

1800*   *The child's first primer; or, a new and easy guide to the invaluable science of
        ABC.* Philadelphia. (Yale). Heartman, 1935, no. 38.

CLARK, Stephen W.

1847   *A practical grammar . . . illustrated by a complete series of diagrams.* 6th edn
       N.Y., 1854* (BL). The diagrams illustrate sentence analysis.

CLEVELAND, Charles Dexter

1849   *A compendium of English literature, chronologically arranged, from Sir John
       Mandeville to William Cowper.* Philadelphia, 1850* (BL).

COBB, Enos

1820   *A self-explaining grammar of the English language, for the use of schools and
       academies.* 2nd edn Boston, 1821* (BL).   Pp. 349–50.

COCHRAN, Peter

1802*   *The Columbian grammar; or, a concise view of the English language.* Boston.
        (BL).

COLBURN, Warren

1832   *First lessons in reading and grammar, for the use of schools; chiefly from the
       works of Miss Edgeworth.* Boston. Anr edn 1836* (BL).   Pp. 257; 246.

COBB, Lyman

1835*   *The North American reader.* N.Y. (NUC).   P. 246.

1831   *Second lessons . . .* [as above]. Anr edn Boston, 1844* (BL). *Third lessons*
       (1832) Boston, 1838* (BL). *Fourth lessons* (1833) Boston, 1838* (BL).

COMLY, John

1803   *English grammar made easy to the teacher and pupil. Principally compiled for
       the use of West-town boarding school, Pennsylvania.* Dated from preface. 5th edn
       Philadelphia, 1812* (Friends House L).

COOK, Amos Jones

1812   *The student's companion: containing a variety of poetry and prose . . . To which
       are added miscellaneous matters, particularly designed to improve youth in reading
       and parsing the English language.* 2nd edn Concord, 1825* (BL).

CUMMINGS, Jacob Abbot

1819   *The pronouncing spelling book adapted to Walker's Critical Pronouncing
       Dictionary.* Anr edn, 'revised from the 4th edn', Concord, 1840* (BL). Nietz,
       1961, p. 22, reproduces pages showing phonetic diacritical marks. Nietz, and
       also Monaghan, 1983, call him CUMMINS.

CURTIS, Abel

1779   *A compend of English grammar: being an attempt to point out the fundamental
       principles of the English language.* 4th edn 1785* (NYct). Alston, I, 360–4.

DANA, Joseph

1792* *A new American selection of lessons in reading and speaking . . . For the use of schools.* Boston. (BL). Expresses an obligation to Knox's *Elegant extracts.* P. *195.*

DEARBORN, Benjamin

1795* *The Columbian grammar; or, an essay for reducing a grammatical knowledge of the English language to a degree of simplicity, which will render it easy.* Boston. (BL). Intended for those not learning Latin. Pp. 340; *285.*

EDWARDS, Bela Bates

1832 *The eclectic reader, designed for schools and academies.* Boston. Anr edn Boston, 1835* (BL). Out of thirty-seven named authors eleven are American.

ELMORE, D.W.

1830* *English grammar, or a natural analysis . . . of the English language.* Troy, N.Y. (BL). He proposes three primary parts of speech: noun, relative word and particle, but loses his way among their subdivisions. P. *363.*

EMERSON, Benjamin D.

1833 *The first class reader: a selection for exercises in reading, from standard British and American authors . . . For the use of schools in the United States.* Windsor. Anr edn Boston, 1835* (privately owned).

ENGLAND, John

[a. 1823] *Reading book, containing useful and pleasing lessons, with an abridgement of a considerable portion of sacred history.* 3rd edn London (England), 1823* (BL). England was Roman Catholic Bishop of Charleston, S. Carolina.

[Anon.]

[*c.* 1750]* *An English grammar, wrote in a plain familiar manner, adapted to the youth of both sexes.* St John's, Antigua. (O). Alston, I, 108. P. 280.

FELCH, Walton

1821* *A concise grammar of the English language; adapted to the memory, and designed as an improvement upon . . . Murray and others.* Southbridge, Mass. (BL).

[Anon.]

1850 [in special type] *First phonetic reader. First edition.* 4th edn Boston, 1852* (BL). Based on the system of Pitman and Ellis, 1847. Attributed to Elias Longley.

FOSDICK, David

1838* 'On elocution', in *The introductory discourse, and the lectures delivered before the American Institute of Instruction . . . August 1837.* Boston, 1838. (BL).

FOWLE, William Bentley

1842 *The common school speller.* Boston. 30th edn [cover title gives 35th] Boston, 1845* (BL). The edn numbers probably continue from his *Improved guide,* below.

1829 *The improved guide to English spelling; in which, by the aid of a simple, yet particular, classification, the use of all figures and marks to indicate the pronunciation is rendered unnecessary.* Boston. Anr edn Boston, 1840* (BL).

1824* *The rational guide to reading and orthography: being an attempt to improve the arrangement of words in English spelling books.* Boston. (BL).

1827* *The true English grammar: being an attempt to form a grammar of the English* *language, not modelled upon those of the Latin and Greek, and other foreign languages*, Part 1. Boston (BL). Part 2 was published in 1829 (BL).

FOWLER, William Chauncy

1850* *English grammar. The English language, in its elements and forms: with a history of its origin and development.* N.Y. (BL). A monumental work of 688 pp.

FRANKLIN, Benjamin

1751 Ed *Idea of the English school, sketch'd out for the consideration of the trustees of the Philadelphia Academy.* In *Benjamin Franklin on education*, ed. John Hardin Best, NYct, 1962*.

1749 Ed *Proposals relating to the education of youth in Pennsylvania. Ibid.*

FRASER, Donald

1794* *The Columbian monitor*, N.Y. (Harvard UL). Alston, IV, 409. A miscellany containing dialogues, letters, grammar, rules for behaviour.

FRAZEE, Bradford

1844* *An improved grammar of the English language, on the inductive system: with which elementary and progressive lessons in composition are combined.* Philadelphia. (BL).   P. *366.*

FREEMAN, Samuel

1790 *The Columbian primer, or the school mistresses guide to children, in their first steps to learning.* Boston. (Boston PL). Heartman, 1935, no. 44.   P. *122.*

FROST, John

1829* *Elements of English grammar, with progressive exercises in parsing.* Boston. (BL).

[1828] *Five hundred progressive exercises in parsing. Adapted to Murray's and other approved treatises of English grammar.* 2nd edn Boston, 1828* (BL).

GALLAUDET, Thomas Hopkins

1830 *The child's picture defining and reading book.* Hartford; 3rd edn 1833* (BL); anr edn Glasgow, 1834* (BL).   P. *123.*

GOLDSBURY, John

1846* *A brief review of four different theories of English grammar, opposed to that of Murray.* (New Theories of Grammar). Boston. (BL). The grammarians discussed are James Brown, William S. Balch, Oliver B. Peirce and Smith B. Goodenow.

GOODENOW, Smith Bartlett

[a. 1843] *An essay on English grammar; designed as an introduction to the New England Grammar.* 2nd edn Boston, 1843* (BL).

1839 *New England grammar. A systematic textbook of English grammar, on the eclectic plan.* Portland. 2nd edn Boston, 1843* (BL).   P. 366.

GREEN, Richard W.

1829 *Inductive exercises in English grammar: designed to give young pupils a knowledge of the first principles of language . . . The whole intended to inculcate habits of thinking, reasoning, and expressing thought.* N.Y. 5th edn Philadelphia, [1831]* (BL).   Pp. 43, 366.

GREENE, Samuel Stillman

1854 *The elements of English grammar; so arranged as to combine the analytical and synthetical methods.* Philadelphia. Anr edn Philadelphia, 1858* (BL).   P. 367.

1867   *A grammar of the English language.* Philadelphia. Anr edn Philadelphia, 1870* (BL).   P. 349.

GROUT, Jonathan

1799*   *The young child's accidence: being a small spelling book for little children: containing a selection of words in modern use.* (AAS). Alston, IV, 947 and Plate 98, for t.p. in full.

GURNEY, David

1801   *The Columbian accidence; or, a brief introduction to the English language.* Boston; 2nd edn Boston, 1808* (BL).

HALE, Enoch

1799*   *A spelling book; or the first part of a grammar of the English language, as written and spoken in the United States.* Northampton (AAS). Alston, IV, 948 and Plate 107 for t.p.   P. 47.

HALLOCK, Edward J.

1842*   *A grammar of the English language: for the use of common schools, academies and seminaries.* N.Y. (BL).   Pp. 368, 369.

HAZEN, Edward

1829   *The speller and definer . . . designed to answer the purposes of a spelling book, and to supersede the necessity of the use of a dictionary as a class-book.* N.Y.; anr edn Philadelphia, 1845* (BL).

HEATON, Benjamin

1799*   *The Columbian spelling-book.* Wrentham, Mass. (NYct). Alston, IV, 949 and 949a, and Plate 108 for t.p.

HUBBARD, John

1804   *The American reader: containing a selection of narration, harangues, addresses, orations, dialogues, odes, hymns, poems, &c.* Walpole, N.H. 5th edn Walpole, 1811* (BL).

[HUTCHINS, Joseph]

1788*   *An abstract of the first principles of English grammar; compiled for the use of a private school.* Philadelphia. (AAS). Alston, I, 441, 455–6.

[JOHNSON, Samuel]

1765*   *The first easy rudiments of grammar applied to the English tongue . . . By one who is extremely desirous to promote good literature in America, and especially a right English education.* N.Y. (NYct). Alston, I, 259 and Supplement.   P. *113*.

JONES, Hugh

1724   *An accidence to the English tongue.* London (England); Scolar Press facsimile, Menston, 1967*. Alston, I, 59.

KEAGY, John Miller

1826   *The Pestalozzian primer, or, first steps in teaching children the art of reading and thinking.* Harrisburg, Pa. Cited by Mathews, 1966.   P. 123.

KNEELAND, Abner

1802*   *The American definition spelling book . . . Upon a plan agreeable to Mr Noah Webster's easy standard.* Keene, N.H. (BL); anr edn Concord, 1814* (personal).   Pp. 95; *48*.

1807*   *A brief sketch of a new system of orthography.* Walpole, N.H. (BL).

1832*   *Key to the New System of Orthography.* Boston. (BL).   Pp. 47–8; *50*.

LEE, Thomas J.
1821   *A spelling-book* (dated from preface); anr edn Boston, 1830* (BL). Edns to 1844.

[LOWELL, Anna Cabot (Jackson)]
1843   *Poetry for home and school. First and second parts*. Boston; 2nd edn (in one volume) Boston, 1846* (BL).

MCGUFFEY, William Holmes
1836   *The eclectic reader: consisting of progressive lessons in reading and spelling.* Cincinnati. Varying volumes in various series. Of the 1836 series in six books Applebee says its use was 'virtually universal for the next fifty years'. See Stanley W. Lindberg, *The annotated McGuffey, selections from the McGuffey Eclectic Readers, 1836–1920*, 1976*; McGuffey's *Fifth eclectic reader*, rev. 1879 edn, foreword by H.S. Commager, New American Library, 1962*.   P. *247*.

MANN, Horace
1839   *Second annual report to the Massachusetts Board of Education* (covering the year 1838); facsimile, Horace Mann League and National Education Association, Boston 1948*.   Pp. 117, 123.

MERRIAM, George
1828   *The American reader: containing extracts suited to excite a love of science and literature, to refine the taste, and to improve the moral character*. Boston; 2nd edn Brookfield, 1829* (BL).   P. 246.
1833*   *The easy primer*. Boston. (DLC) 1st edn anonymous.

MILLER, Alexander
1795*   *A concise grammar of the English language, with an appendix chiefly extracted from Dr Lowth's critical notes*. N.Y. (DLC). An attempt to break away from Latin models.   Pp. 334; *321*.

[Anon.]
1787   *Miscellanies, moral and instructive, in prose and verse . . . for the use of schools*. Philadelphia and London (BL). Anr edn Dublin (printed in Philadelphia), 1789* (BL). The compiler was a lady.

MORGAN, Jonathan
1814*   *Elements of English grammar*. Hallowell, Me. (BL). Praises the 'neglected Webster'.

MORLEY, Charles
1838*   *A practical guide to composition, with progressive exercises in prose and poetry*. Hartford. (Michigan UL).   Pp. 312; *354*.

[Anon.]
[1822]   *The national primer . . . in which words are arranged according to their vowel sounds*. York, Pa. Anr edn Baltimore, 1823* (DLC). Heartman, 1935, no. 103.

[Anon.]
[1690?]   *The New England primer*. Boston. Facsimile of 1727 edn in P.L. Ford, 1897*; anr edn Newburyport, [1800?]* (BL). See also Heartman, 1922; Rosenbach, (1933) 1971; Nila Banton Smith, (1934) 1965.   Pp. *3, 26, 57*.

NEWMAN, Samuel Phillips
1831*   *A practical method of teaching rhetoric*. American Institute of Instruction, *Introductory Discourse*: Boston (BL).
1827   *A practical system of rhetoric; or the principles and rules of style, inferred from*

examples of writing. Portland. Anr edn, rev. from 5th American edn, London (England), 1837* (BL).

OLNEY, Jesse

1833* *The easy reader . . . designed to aid in thinking, spelling, defining, and correct reading.* New Haven (DLC).

PARKER, Richard Greene

1838* *Lecture on the teaching of composition in schools.* American Institute of Instruction, Boston. (BL).   P. 312.

1839* *Lecture on the teaching of English grammar.* American Institute of Instruction. Boston. (BL).   Pp. 353; *361.*

1832 *Progressive exercises in English composition.* Boston. Anr edn Boston, 1834* (BL); anr edn Boston, 1836* (personal).   Pp. 286; *309.*

1835 *Progressive exercises in rhetorical reading. Particularly designed to familiarize the younger classes with the pauses and other marks in general use.* Boston. (BL); anr edn London (England), 1836* (BL).

PARKER, Richard Greene, and FOX, Charles

1835 *Progressive exercises in English grammar. Part I. Containing the principles of analysis, or English parsing.* Boston. 10th edn (8th edn on cover) 1843* (BL).

1835 [as preceding] *Part II. Containing the principles of the synthesis or construction of the English language.* Boston. 4th edn (on cover 3rd edn 1835) Boston, 1839*. (BL).

1840 [as above] *Part III. Containing the rules of orthography and punctuation, the principles of etymology, and the prosody of the English language* [also elementary rhetoric and logic]. Boston. (BL).

PARKHURST, John Luke

1820 *A systematic introduction to English grammar.* Concord. 2nd edn Concord, 1824* (BL).   P. *353.*

PARSONS, John Usher

1836* *The analytical spelling book. By an analytical teacher.* Portland. (DLC). The 1st edn was published anonymously.   P. 119n.

1837* *The analytical system of teaching orthography.* Boston. (Boston PL).   P. *119n.*

PASTORIUS, Francis Daniel

[1698]* *A new primmer or methodical directions to attain the true spelling, reading & writing of English . . . By F.D.P.* N.Y. (Friends House, London). Alston, IV, 191 and Plate 34 for t.p.   P. 83.

[PEABODY, Nathaniel]

1830* *First lessons in grammar on the plan of Pestalozzi.* Boston. (BL).

PEIRCE, John

1782* *The new American spelling-book . . . Containing* [Dilworth's tables and an English grammar]. Philadelphia. (NYct).   P. 102.

PICKBURN, John

1759 *The moral instructor; or, a collection of sentences from the best authors, disposed in easy lessons for children.* 7th edn Boston, 1805* (cover title gives 7th edn Louth, 1828) (BL).

PICKET, Albert

1812 *The juvenile instructor, or, natural grammar and reader.* N.Y. Anr edn as: *The juvenile instructor, containing a new method of analytical and synthetical parsing . . . by means of a vinculum or chain.* N.Y., 1815* (NYPL).

1804* *The union spelling book: combining the scheme of pronunciation, accentuation, and orthography of Walker, with the easy reading lessons of Mavor and Murray. The arrangement of the spelling part being entirely new.* N.Y. (Princeton UL).   Pp. 87, 105.

PICKET, Albert, and PICKET, John W.

[a. 1847] *The analyzer and expositor; containing exercises in English etymology, definition, and reading.* Cincinnati. Rev. edn Cincinnati, 1847* (DLC). The Pickets produced at least nineteen textbooks, mostly linguistic. What is largely the same material was worked into various sequences during a period of forty years.

PIERPONT, John

1823 *The American first class book; or exercises in reading and recitation.* Boston. 26th edn N.Y., [1835?]* (BL). Carpenter, 1963, says that Pierpont was stressing American authors in order to cut out Lindley Murray (p. 70); Nila B. Smith, 1965, p. 64; Reeder, 1900, pp. 45–6; Nietz, 1961, pp. 67–9.

1828 *Introduction to the National Reader . . . designed to fill the same place in the common schools of the United States, that is held by Murray's Introduction, and the compilations of Guy, Mylius and Pinnock.* Boston. Anr edn Boston, 1833* (personal).

1827 *The national reader: a selection of exercises in reading and speaking, designed to fill the same place in the schools of the United States, that is held in Great Britain by the compilations of Murray, Scott, Enfield, Mylius, Thompson, Ewing, and others.* Boston. Anr edn re-edited by E.H. Barker, London (England), 1829* (Glasgow UL).   Pp. 245; 249.

1830 *The young reader: to go with the spelling book.* Boston. 15th edn Boston, 1839* (BL).

PIKE, James

1808* *The Columbian orthographer; or, first book for children.* Boston. (personal); anr edn Boston, 1814 (BL).   Pp. 114; 54.

1810 *An English spelling book; or, an introduction to the art of reading.* Boston. 3rd edn Boston, 1822* (BL).

PORTER, Ebenezer

1831* *The rhetorical reader. Consisting of instructions for regulating the voice, with a rhetorical notation . . . Designed for the use of academies and schools.* Andover. (BL).

POWERS, Daniel

1845* *A grammar on a new system.* West Brookfield, Mass. (BL). The new system is to rely on reading and not on parsing.   P. 351.

[Anon.]

1799* *Practical exercises in grammar, punctuation and rhetoric.* Exeter (Huntington L). Alston, III, 428.   Pp. 284–5.

PRENTISS, Thomas Mellen

1799* *The Maine spelling book.* Leominster. (NYPL).

[Anon.]

1830 *The progressive reader; or juvenile monitor.* Concord. Anr edn Concord 1837* (BL).

QUIN, Edward C.
1824   *The La Fayette primer, and New Jersey instructor, No. 1.* Caldwell, N.J. (DLC).   P. 67.
REED, Abner
1800   *The first step to learning; or, little child's spelling and reading book.* East Windsor. 2nd edn East Windsor, 1800* (BL).   P. 60.
RICHARDSON, Joseph
1810*   *The American reader: a selection of lessons . . . wholly from American authors.* Boston (BL).   P. 246.
1811*   *The young ladies' selection of elegant extracts from the writings of illustrious females: and some of the best authors of the other sex.* Boston (BL).
[RICKARD, Truman and ORCUTT, Hiram]
1847   *Class book of prose and poetry; consisting of selections from the best English and American authors . . . Designed as exercises in parsing.* Boston. 2nd edn Boston, 1850* (BL). Carpenter, 1963, pp. 162–3.
ROSS, Robert
[1785]*   *The new American spelling book; or a complete primer.* New Haven. (AAS). Alston, IV, 853.   Pp. 85–6, 114; *26, 52, 57.*
1784   *A new primer, or little boy and girl's spelling-book.* Bennington. Anr edn Boston, 1788* (Boston PL). BL has a fragmentary copy, lacking t.p. (shelf-mark 1568/4053).   P. 73.
S., G.
1793   *A new introduction to reading: or, a collection of easy lessons . . . Designed as an introduction to the Speaker.* Philadelphia. 5th edn Philadelphia, 1796* (NYPL). Alston, IV, 905–8.
SANBORN, Dyer H.
1836   *Analytical grammar of the English language, embracing the inductive and productive methods of teaching.* Concord. 2nd edn Concord, 1840* (BL).   Pp. 350, 366.
SANDERS, Charles Walton
[1845?]*   *Primary education; as connected with the use of Sanders' series of school books.* Pp. 12. N.Y. (BL).
1838   *Sanders' spelling book . . . Designed to teach a system of orthography and orthoepy in accordance with that of Dr Webster.* N.Y. Anr edn Andover, 1839* (BL).
SHERMAN, John
1826*   *The philosophy of language illustrated: an entirely new system of grammar; wholly divested of scholastic rubbish, of traditionary falsehood, and absurdity.* Trenton Falls (Boston PL).   Pp. 362, 364.
[Anon.]
1818*   *A short but comprehensive grammar. Designed for the use of schools, By a teacher of youth.* Salem. (BL).
SIGOURNEY, Lydia Huntley
1839*   *The boy's reading book; in prose and poetry, for schools.* N.Y. (Glasgow UL).
[c. 1837]   *The girl's reading book; in prose and poetry, for schools.* N.Y. 9th edn N.Y., 1839* (Glasgow UL).
SMITH, Roswell Chamberlain
1831   *English grammar on the productive system: a method of instruction recently*

adopted in Germany and Switzerland, in the place of the inductive system. *Designed for schools*. Boston. Anr edn Boston, 1832* (personal).

[Anon.]

1769*   *The spelling-book and child's plaything. Calculated for the instruction and amusement of children*. New London. (AAS). Alston, IV, 715 and Plate 73 for t.p.

STANIFORD, Daniel

1800   *The art of reading . . . exemplified by a variety of selected and original pieces.* Boston; 11th edn Boston, 1816* (BL).

1797   *A short but comprehensive grammar . . . To which is added an appendix, comprehending a list of vulgarisms and improprieties.* Boston; 4th edn Boston, 1807* (Wisconsin UL). P. 330.

STERLING, William A.

1796*   *The child's instructor: being an easy introduction to the orthography of the Columbian language.* Fairhaven, Vt. (Vermont Hist. Soc.).

STRONG, Titus

[a. 1821]   *The young scholar's manual, or companion to the spelling book, consisting of easy lessons.* 2nd edn Greenfield, 1821; 8th edn Greenfield, 1830* (BL).   P. *51.*

[THOMAS, Isaiah]

1785*   *The new American spelling book . . . To which is added an . . . English grammar . . . The whole . . . rendering the use of a primer unnecessary.* Worcester. (Harvard UL). Alston, IV, 852.   Pp. *52, 57.*

TICKNOR, Almon

[1849]*   *The Columbian spelling-book.* Pottsville, Pa. (BL).   P. 114.

TOWER, David Bates

1846*   *The gradual speller and complete enunciator; showing the orthography and orthoepy of all words in common use.* N.Y. (BL).   Pp. 103, 117; *104–5, 129.*

TOWN, Salem

1837   (Town's) *Spelling book, in which children, from the alphabet, are taught the formation, spelling and meaning of words at the same time.* Albany. Anr edn, as: *Town's speller and definer, revised and enlarged*, Portland, 1853* (private colln).   Pp. *48, 51–2.*

WATERMAN, Foster

1793*   *The child's instructor, being an original spelling book . . . Principally designed for the use of schools.* 2 vols. Boston. (Harvard UL). Alston, IV, 909 and Plate 112 for t.p.   Pp. 47, 87.

WEBSTER, Noah

1789   *Dissertations on the English language.* Boston. Facsimile edn Scolar Press, Menston, 1967*. Alston, III, 395.   Pp. 51; *376.*

1831*   *The elementary primer.* N.Y. (BL).

[1783]   *A grammatical institute, of the English language . . . designed for the use of English schools in America. Part I.* Hartford. Scolar Press facsimile, Menston, 1968*. At least 220 further edns to 1843. Alston, IV, 784–847 and Plate 78 for t.p.   Pp. 102; *52.*

1784   [as above] . . . *Part II. Containing a plain and comprehensive grammar . . . with an analytical dissertation, in which the various uses of the auxiliary signs are . . . explained: and an essay towards investigating the rules of English verse.*

Hartford. Scolar Press facsimile, Menston, 1968* Alston, I, 381–403,   Pp. 325; *283, 341.*

1785*   [as above] . . . *Part III. Containing the necessary rules of reading and speaking, and a variety of essays, dialogues, &c.* Hartford. (BL). 3rd edn as: *An American selection of lessons in reading and speaking,* Philadelphia, 1787* (BL). Monaghan, 1983, pp. 103, 295; Johnson, (1904) 1963, pp. 266–9 (quots.).   Pp. 245; *193, 195.*

1790a*   *The little reader's assistant; containing I. A number of stories . . . II. Rudiments of English grammar. III. A federal catechism . . . IV. General principles of government and commerce.* Hartford (NYPL). Much interesting quotation in Johnson, 1963.

1790b*   *Rudiments of English grammar, being an introduction to the second part of the Grammatical Institute.* Hartford. (BL). Included within *The little reader's assistant* (above) as Part II. Alston, I, 76 and nos. 453–4 and 454a–454e in Supplementary volume, p. 9.

[1830?]   *Series of books for systematic instruction in the English language.* New Haven. Pp. 16. A pamphlet describing and advocating Webster's schoolbooks. Monaghan, 1983, pp. 155, 267.

WEED, Enos

[1797]*   *The American orthographer . . . Book I. The bibliographical spelling book. Book II. The geographical spelling book. Book III* [a spelling-book in reformed orthography]. Danbury, for the author, who describes himself as 'Physician and surgeon in difficult cases'. The date 1797 derives from the author's note *To the public* and is accepted by Alston and Rosenbach; the John Carter Brown Library copy carries a MS date of 1798. Weed seems to use 'bibliographical' to mean 'pertaining to the Bible'. Alston, IV, 941, gives title incorrectly as *The American orthography.*

WELLS, W.H. (1846)   *Wells's school grammar.* Andover, Mass. Pp. v–viii contain a list of grammars.

WILLARD, Samuel

1828*   *General class-book, or interesting lessons in prose and verse . . . combined with an epitome of English orthography and pronunciation.* Greenfield, Mass. (BL).

WOODBRIDGE, William

1800a*   *A plain and concise grammar of the English language; containing large exercises of parsing and incorrect English.* Middleton, Conn. (NYPL). Alston, I, 533.   P. 328.

1800b*   *The plain spelling book, and easy guide to reading . . . With easy lessons in reading both prose and poetry.* Middletown, Conn. (NYPL). Alston, IV, 962 and Plate 108 for t.p.   Pp. *45, 52.*

WORCESTER, Noah

[a. 1798]   *The natural teacher: or, the best spelling book for little children.* 2nd edn Concord, 1798* (NYPL). Alston, IV, 940 and Plate 105 for t.p.

WORCESTER, S.T.

1831*   *Sequel to the spelling book.* Boston. (BL).

WORCESTER, Samuel

1841   *An introduction to the third book for reading and spelling.* Boston. Anr edn Boston, 1846* (BL).

[c. 1830]   *A third book for reading and spelling.* Boston; 107th edn Boston, 1847*

(BL). BL has also the 20th edn, 1839.   P. 246.

1834   *A fourth book of lessons for reading; with rules and instructions.* Boston. Anr edn Boston, 1844* (BL).

1829*   *(Worcester's) Spelling-book. A spelling-book for the United States of America.* Boston and N.Y. (BL).   *See above, p. 122.*

WRIFFORD, Allison

1835*   *A brief developement of the great secret of giving and receiving instruction and maintaining school government . . . By an experienced teacher.* Concord. (BL). The BL copy has a MS attribution to Allison Wrifford, which is rejected by *NUC.*

1834*   *The intellectual and rhetorical reader; containing the true method of teaching the art of reading, and also a brief developement of the elements of elocution.* Concord (BL). *NUC* attributes this work to Anson Wrifford.   P. 296.

[Anon.]

1792*   *The young gentlemen and ladies' accidence: or, a compendious American grammar of the English tongue. Plain and easy.* Worcester. (NYct).

The reader plays such a prominent part in the teaching of English in America (more prominent than in Britain) that it may be useful to supplement this list with the names of other authors within the period who wrote series of readers, details of which can be found in the *National Union Catalogue*:

Jacob Abbot	Lucius Osgood
Oliver Angell	Samuel Putnam
Lyman Cobb	William Russell
William Darby	William D. Swann
Samuel G. Goodrich	William Swinton
George S. Hillard	J. Madison Watson
Henry Mandeville	Marcius Willson

Modern works consulted

AARSLEFF, Hans (1983) *The study of language in England, 1780–1860*. U. of Minnesota Press. First published in 1967.

ABERCROMBIE, David (1965a) 'Forgotten phoneticians', in his *Studies in phonetics and linguistics*. First published in the *Transactions of the Philological Society*, 1948.

(1958) Introduction to G.W., *Magazine*, 1703. Augustan Reprint Society, no. 7, Los Angeles.

(1965b) 'What is a letter?', in his *Studies in phonetics and linguistics*. First published in *Lingua*, 2 (1949), 54–63.

(1965c) 'Steele, Monboddo and Garrick', in his *Studies in phonetics and linguistics*.

AKENSON, Donald H. (1970) *The Irish education experiment. The national system of education in the nineteenth century*. Routledge.

ALSTON, R.C. (1965–) *A bibliography of the English language from the invention of printing to the year 1800*. Vol. I 'English grammars [etc.]', Leeds, 1965; vol. IV 'Spelling books', Bradford, 1967; vol. V 'The English dictionary', Leeds, 1966; vol. VI 'Rhetoric [etc.]', Bradford, 1969; vol. VII 'Logic [etc]', Bradford, 1967; vol. X 'Education and language teaching', Leeds, 1972; *Supplement*, Leeds, 1973.

ALTICK, Richard D. (1963) *The English common reader: a social history of the mass reading public, 1800–1900*. Chicago. First published in 1957.

APPLEBEE, Arthur N. (1974) *Tradition and reform in the teaching of English: a history*. Urbana. Ill. National Council of Teachers of English.

ARMYTAGE, W.H.G. (1961) 'Foster Watson, 1860–1929'. *British Journal of Educational Studies*, 10, 5–18.

ATKINSON, Norman (1969) *Irish education: a history of educational institutions*. Dublin: Allen Figgis.

AUSTIN, Roland (1939) *The Crypt School, Gloucester, 1539–1939*. Gloucester.

BALDERSTON, K.C. (1926) *A census of the manuscripts of Oliver Goldsmith*. N.Y.

BALDWIN, Thomas Whitfield (1943) *William Shakspere's petty school*. Urbana: U. of Illinois Press.

(1944) *William Shakspere's small Latin and less Greek*. 2 vols. Urbana: U. of Illinois Press.

BALMUTH, Miriam (1982) *The roots of phonics: a historical introduction*. N.Y.: McGraw Hill.

BARBOUR, F.A. (1896) 'History of English grammar teaching'. *Educational Review*, N.Y., 12, 487–507.

(1902) *The teaching of English grammar: history and method*. Boston, Mass.

BELOK, Michael V. (1973) *Forming the American minds: early school books and their compilers, 1783–1837*. Moti Katra: Satish Book Enterprises.

BEYER, Arno (1981) *Deutsche Einflüsse auf die englische Sprachwissenschaft im 19. Jahrhundert.* Goppingen.

BOLGAR, R.R. (1983) 'The teaching of letter-writing in the sixteenth century'. *Hist. Edn.*, 12, 245–53.

BROOKS, Greg, and PUGH, A.K. (eds.) (1984) *Studies in the history of reading.* Centre for the Teaching of Reading, U. of Reading School of Education, with United Kingdom Reading Association.

BROWN, J. Howard (1933) *Elizabethan schooldays.* Oxford: Blackwell.

BRYANT, Margaret (1972) 'Topographical resources: private and secondary education in Middlesex from the sixteenth to the twentieth century', in T.G. Cook (ed.), *Local studies and the history of education.* Methuen.

BURTON, Edward (1834) *Three primers put forth in the reign of Henry VIII.* Oxford. 2nd edn 1848.

BUTLER, Vera M. (1969) *Education as revealed by New England newspapers prior to 1800.* N.Y., Arno Press.

BUTTERWORTH, Charles C. (1953) *The English primers, 1529–1545: their publication and connection with the English Bible and the reformation in England.* Philadelphia: U. of Pennsylvania Press.

(1949) 'Early primers for the use of children'. *Papers of the Bibliographical Society of America*, 43, 374–82.

CARPENTER, Charles (1963) *History of American school-books.* Philadelphia: U. of Pennsylvania Press

CARPENTER, Humphrey and PRITCHARD, Mari (1984) *The Oxford companion to children's literature.* O.U.P. Cited as *OCCL.*

CHALMERS, George S. (1976) *Reading easy, 1800–50.* London: Broadsheet King.

CHARLTON, Kenneth (1965) *Education in renaissance England.* Routledge.

COGGIN, Philip A. (1956) *Drama and education: an historical survey from ancient Greece to the present day.* Thames and Hudson

COHEN, Murray (1977) *Sensible words. Linguistic practice in England, 1640–1785.* Baltimore: Johns Hopkins Press.

COHEN, Sol (1974) *Education in the United States: a documentary history.* 5 vols. N.Y., Random House.

COMMAGER, Henry Steele (1962) Preface to the reprint of the 1879 edn of McGuffey's *Fifth eclectic reader.* N.Y., New American Library.

COOK, Albert B. (1984) 'John Evelyn's English Grammar'. *Leeds Studies English.* n.s. 15, 117–46.

CREMIN, Lawrence A. (1970) *American education: the colonial experience 1783.* N.Y., Harper and Row.

CRESSY, David (1975) *Education in Tudor and Stuart England.* Edward A.

(1976) 'Educational opportunity in Tudor and Stuart England'. *Hist. .dn Quarterly*, 16, 301–20.

(1980) *Literacy and the social order: reading and writing in Tudor and Stuart England.* C.U.P.

DANIELSON, Bror (1960) 'A note on Edmund Coote. Prolegomena for a critical edition of Coote's *English School-Master, 1596'. Studia Neophilogica*, 32, 228–40.

DARTON, F.J. Harvey (1982) *Children's books in England.* 3rd edn rev. Brian Alderson. Cambridge U. Press. First published in 1932; 2nd edn 1958.

DAVIES, Frank (1973) *Teaching reading in early England.* Pitman.

D.E.S. (1975) Department of Education and Science: *A language for life* (the Bullock Report). HMSO.

(1984) Department of Education and Science: *English from 5 to 15.* HMSO.

DEVERELL, Arthur Frederick (1963) *Canadian bibliography of reading and literary instruction, English, 1760–1959.* Vancouver: Copp Clark Publ. Co.

DIACK, Hunter (1965) *In spite of the alphabet.* Chatto and Windus.

DOBSON, E.J. (1968) *English pronunciation, 1500–1700.* 2 vols. 2nd edn. O.U.P. First published in 1957.

DOBSON, Lance (1981) 'Literacy and the development of the teaching of English', in *Language in use*, Part 2, Educational Studies. Open University.

DOUGHTY, D.W. (1967) *The Tullis Press, Cupar, 1803–1849.* Dundee: Abertay Hist. Soc., Publication no. 12.

DOWLING, P.J. (1968) *The hedge-schools of Ireland.* Cork.

ELLIS, Alec (1971) *Books in Victorian elementary schools*, Library Association Pamphlet 34.

ELSON, Ruth Miller (1964) *Guardians of tradition: American schoolbooks of the nineteenth century.* Lincoln: Nebraska U. Press.

EVANS, Charles (1903–55) *American bibliography*, 1639–1800. 13 vols. Chicago. *Supplements* by Ralph R. Shaw and Richard Shoemaker, for 1801–19, 21 vols., N.Y., 1958–65; by Roger P. Bristol, Bibliographical Society of America, Charlottesville, 1970.

FORD, Paul Leicester (1897) *The New England Primer: a history of its origin . . . with a reprint of the unique copy of the earliest known edition (1727).* Reprinted N.Y., Teachers College Columbia University, 1962.

FREEMAN, R.B. (1976) 'Children's natural history books before Queen Victoria'. Hist. Edn Soc. *Bulletin*, 17, 7–21 and 18, 6–34.

FRIES, Charles Carpenter (1963) *Linguistics and reading.* N.Y.

GABRIELSON, Arvid (1929) 'Professor Kennedy's bibliography of writings on the English language. A review with a list of additions and corrections'. *Studia Neophilologica*, 2, 117–68.

GASKELL, Philip (1964) *A bibliography of the Foulis Press.* Hart Davis.

GILMORE, William J. (1982) 'Elementary literacy on the eve of the industrial revolution: trends in rural New England, 1760–1830'. *Proceedings of the American Antiquarian Society*, 92, 86–171.

GOLDSTROM, J.M. (1972b) *Education: elementary education, 1780–1900.* Newton Abbot: David and Charles.

(1972a) *The social content of education, 1808–70. A study of the working-class school reader in England and Ireland.* Irish U. Press.

GORDON, Peter, and LAWTON, Denis (1978) *Curriculum change in the nineteenth and twentieth centuries.* Hodder and Stoughton.

GOSDEN, P.H.J.H. (1969) *How they were taught. An anthology of contemporary accounts of learning and teaching in England, 1800–1950.* Blackwell.

GUMUCHIAN, K.A. (1967) *Les Livres de l'enfance du XVe au XIXe siècle*, ed. Paul Garault. Reprint by the Holland Press of the two-volume edition first published at Paris by Gumuchian et Cie.

HANS, Nicholas (1951) *New trends in education in the eighteenth century.* Routledge.

HARPER, G.H. (1980) 'Textbooks: an underused source'. Hist. Edn. Soc. *Bulletin*, 25, 30–40.

HAWKES, A.J. (1925) *Lancashire printed books.* Wigan.

HAZLITT, W.C. (1888) *Schools, school-books and schoolmasters.*

HEAL, Ambrose (1962) *The English writing-masters and their copy-books, 1570–1800.* Hildesheim: Olms. Originally published in 1931.

HEARTMAN, Charles Frederick (1935) *American primers, Indian primers, Royal primers. And thirty-seven other types of non-New England primers issued prior to 1830. A bibliographical checklist.* Highland Park, N.J. (BL).

(1922) *The New England Primer issued prior to 1830. A bibliographical checklist.* N.Y. First published in 1915.

HESS, Glenn Carson (1949) *An analysis of early American rhetoric and composition textbooks from 1784–1870.* EdD dissertation, U. Pittsburgh.

HIGSON, C.W.J. (1967–76) *Sources for the history of education.* Library Association.

HODGES, Richard E. (1977) 'In Adam's fall: a brief history of spelling instruction in the United States'. In ROBINSON (1977), below, pp. 1–16.

HOWATT, A.P.R. (1984) *A history of English language teaching.* O.U.P.

HOWELL, Wilbur Samuel (1971) *Eighteenth century British logic and rhetoric.* Princeton U. Press.

(1956) *Logic and rhetoric in England, 1500–1700.* N.Y.

HUEY, Edmund Burke (1928) *The psychology and pedagogy of reading; with a review of the history of reading and writing and of methods, texts and hygiene in reading.* N.Y. First published at N.Y. in 1908; reprinted M.I.T., Cambridge, Mass., 1968.

JOHNSON, Clifton (1963) *Old-time schools and school-books.* N.Y. Dover. First published at N.Y. in 1904.

JONES, David (1980) *Toy with the idea. Teaching toys from the collections of the Norfolk Museums Service.* [Norwich].

JONES, E. Aldred (1934) 'Newcome's Academy and its plays'. *The Library*, 4th series, 4, 339–47.

JONES, M.G. (1938) *The charity school movement.* C.U.P. Reprinted, Cass, 1964.

KEARNEY, Anthony (1980) 'J.W. Hales and the teaching of English literature, 1860–1900', in Hist. Edn Soc. *Bulletin*, 26, 42–6.

KENNEDY, A.G. (1927) *Bibliography of writings on the English language.* Cambridge, Mass.

KEYNES, Geoffrey (1932) 'Hazlitt's grammar abridged'. *The Library*, 4th series, 13, 97–9.

LANCASHIRE, Ian (1984) *Dramatic texts and records of Britain: a chronological topography to 1558.* C.U.P.

LAW, Alexander (1965) *Education in Edinburgh in the eighteenth century.* London U. Press.

LAWSON, John, and SILVER, Harold (1973) *A social history of education in England.* Methuen.

LINDBERG, Stanley W. (1976) *The annotated McGuffey. Selections from the McGuffey Eclectic Readers*. N.Y., Van Nostrand Reinhold.

LIVERMORE, George (1849) *The origin, history and character of the New England Primer*. Cambridge, Mass. Reprinted 1915.

LONGMAN, Charles James (1936) *The house of Longman, 1724–1800*. Ed. J.E. Chandler. Longman.

MCDUNPHY, T.A. (1976) 'Christian Brothers in print'. *Christian Brothers Educational Record*, 129–46.

MCKERROW, R.B. (1910) 'Some notes on the letters *i, j, u* and *v* in sixteenth century printing'. *The Library*, 3rd series, 1, 239–59.

MCMURTRY, Jo (1985) *English language, English literature. The creation of an academic discipline*. Hamden, Conn., Archon Books.

MARSHALL, Peter H. (1984) *William Godwin*. Yale U. Press.

MATHEWS, Mitford M. (1966) *Teaching to read historically considered*. Chicago U. Press.

MATHIESON, Margaret (1975) *The preachers of culture*. Allen and Unwin.

(1976) 'Persistence and change in the claims for English in schools'. *Edl Studies*, 2, 217–26.

MICHAEL, Ian (1984) 'Early evidence for whole word methods', in BROOKS and PUGH, above, pp. 56–64.

(1970) *English grammatical categories and the tradition to 1800*. C.U.P.

(1979) 'The historical study of English as a subject: a preliminary enquiry into some questions of method'. *Hist. Edn*, 8, 193–206.

(1985) 'Prosing, transposition and other linguistic exercises'. *Histoire, épistémologie, langage*, 7, 2, 71–85.

(1986) 'Seventeenth century teachers' views on reading and spelling'. Second Colloquium on the History of Reading, *Proceedings*, ed. Nigel Hall, Greg Brooks and A.K. Pugh (forthcoming).

MONAGHAN, E. Jennifer (1980) *Noah Webster's speller, 1783–1843: causes of its success as reading test*. PhD dissertation, Yeshida U.

(1983) *A common heritage: Noah Webster's Blueback Speller*. Hamden, Conn., Archon Books.

MOON, Marjorie (1976) *John Harris's books for youth, 1801–1843. A check list*. Cambridge: Five Owls Press. *Supplement*, 1983.

MORGAN, F.C. (1977) *Books published before 1830. Exhibited at Malvern Public Library in 1911*. 2nd impression. Hereford.

MOTTER, T.H.V. (1929) *The school drama in England*. Longman.

MUMBY, Frank A. (1930) *Publishing and bookselling*. 5th edn rev. with addns by Ian Norrie, 1974.

NASH, Ray (1959) *American writing masters and copybooks. History and bibliography through colonial times*. Colonial Soc. of Massachusetts. Boston.

NATIONAL BOOK LEAGUE (1946) *Children's books of yesterday*. Catalogue of an exhibition arranged by Percy Muir.

(1949) *The English at school*. Catalogue of an exhibition arranged by Arnold Muirhead.

(1973) *Three centuries of nursery rhymes and poetry for children*. Catalogue of an exhibition presented by Iona and Peter Opie.

NELSON, William (1952) 'The teaching of English in Tudor grammar schools'. *Studies in Philology*, 69, 119–43.

NEUBURG, Victor E. (1968) *The penny histories: a study of chapbooks for young readers over two centuries.* O.U.P. Includes facsimiles of seven chap-books.

(1977) *Popular literature: a history and guide.* Penguin.

NEWBOLT REPORT, (1921, presented 1919) *The teaching of English in England.* HMSO.

NICHOLS, John (1812–15) *Literary anecdotes of the eighteenth century,* 9 vols.

NIETZ, John A. (1961) *Old textbooks.* Pittsburgh: Pennsylvania U. Press.

(1953) 'Significance of research in old textbooks'. *Hist. Edn J.*, 4, 146–8.

NORTHUP, Clarke S. (1912) 'On a school play of 1648'. *Englische Studien*, 45, 154–60.

O'DAY, Rosemary (1982) *Education and society, 1500–1800.* Longman.

ONG, Walter J. (1958) *Ramus, method, and the decay of dialogue: from the art of discourse to the art of reason.* Cambridge, Mass., Harvard U. Press.

OPIE, Iona and Peter (1980) *A nursery companion.* O.U.P.

(1973) *The Oxford book of children's verse.* O.U.P.

O'RAIFEARTAIGH, T. (1950) 'What was an English school?' Royal Soc. of Antiquaries of Ireland: *Journal*, 80, 129–45.

OSBORNE, Edgar (1958; 1975) *The Osborne collection of early children's books, 1566–1910*, ed. Judith St John. 2 vols. Toronto Public Libraries.

PADLEY, G.A. (1985) *Grammatical theory in western Europe, 1500–1700. The trends in vernacular grammar, I.* C.U.P.

PAFFORD, J.H.P. (1971) Isaac Watts' Divine Songs . . . facsimile reproductions of the first edition of 1715 and an illustrated edition of c. 1840, with an introduction and bibliography. O.U.P.

PALMER, D.J. (1965) *The rise of English studies: an account of the study of English language and literature from its origins to the making of the Oxford English School.* O.U.P.

PEPPER, R.D. (1966) *Four Tudor books on education . . . facsimile reproductions, with an introduction.* Gainesville: Scholars facsimiles and reprints. The books are Plutarch (tr. Elyot), *The education . . . of children*; Clement, *The petie schole*; Fenner, Ramus' logic and rhetoric; Kempe, *The education of children.*

PINCHBECK, Ivy, and HEWITT, Margaret (1969–73) *Children in English society from Tudor times to the eighteenth century.* 2 vols. Routledge.

POLLOCK, Linda A. (1983) *Forgotten children: parent–child relations from 1500 to 1900.* C.U.P.

POTTER, Stephen (1937) *The muse in chains: a study in education.* Cape.

QUAYLE, Eric (1983) *Early children's books: a collector's guide.* David and Charles.

QUIRK, Randolph (1974) 'The study of the mother tongue', in his *The linguist and the English language*, E. Arnold. A lecture delivered in 1961.

REEDER, Rudolph R. (1900) *The historical development of school readers and of method in teaching reading.* N.Y.

ROACH, J. (1971) *Public examinations in England, 1850–1900.* C.U.P.

ROBINSON, H. Alan (ed.) (1977) *Reading and writing instruction in the United States.* Newark, Del. International Reading Association.

ROSCOE, Sydney (1973) *John Newbery and his successors, 1740–1814.* Five Owls Press.

ROSENBACH, A.S.W. (1971) *Early American children's books.* N.Y. Dover. First published in 1933.

ROTHBLATT, Sheldon (1976) *Tradition and change in English liberal culture.* Faber.

SALMON, David (1912) 'Lancaster's writings, continued'. *Educational Record,* June 1912.

SALMON, Vivian (1962) 'Early seventeenth-century punctuation as a guide to sentence structure'. *Rev. Engl. Studies,* 13, 347–60. Reprinted in her *The study of language in seventeenth century England.* Amsterdam: Benjamins, 1979.

(1975) 'John Brinsley: seventeenth century pioneer in applied linguistics'. *Historiographia Linguistica,* 2, 175–89. Reprinted as above.

(1961) 'Joseph Webbe: some seventeenth century views on language-teaching and the nature of meaning'. *Bibliothèque d'humanisme et renaissance,* 23, 324–40. Reprinted as above.

(1958) 'Thomas Hayward, grammarian'. *Neophilologus,* 43, 64–74.

(1972) *The works of Francis Lodwick: a study of his writings in the intellectual context of the seventeenth century.* Longman. Includes facsimile texts.

SCHEURWEGHS, G., and VORLAT, Emma (1959) 'Problems of the history of English grammar'. *English Studies,* 60, 135–43.

SCHMITZ, Bernhard (1876) *Encyclopädie des philologischen Studiums der neuern Sprachen.* 2nd edn. 4 vols. Leipzig.

SCOTLAND, James (1969) *The history of Scottish education.* U. London Press.

SIMON, Joan (1979 'Private classical schools in eighteenth century England: a critique of Hans'. *Hist. Edn.,* 8, 179–91.

SIZER, Theo R. (1964) *The age of the academies.* N.Y., Columbia U. Teachers College.

SKEAT, Walter W. (1896) 'English grammars', in his *Student's pastime,* 1896, pp. 241–51. First published in *N&Q* 6 (1888) from lists compiled by Sir Frederick Madden from booksellers' catalogues.

SLOANE, William (1955) *Children's books in England and America in the seventeenth century.* N.Y.

SMART, Edward (1932) *History of Perth Academy.* Perth: Milne, Tannahil and Methven.

SMITH, Alan (1975) 'Endowed schools in the diocese of Lichfield and Coventry, 1660–99'. *Hist. Edn.,* 4, 5–20.

(1976) 'Private schools and schoolmasters in the diocese of Lichfield and Coventry in the seventeenth century'. *Hist. Edn.,* 5, 117–26.

SMITH, Joseph (1867) *A descriptive catalogue of Friends' books.* A supplement was issued in 1893.

SMITH, Nila Banton (1934) *American reading instruction.* N.Y.; rev. edn Newark, Del., 1965.

SOMMERVILLE, C. John (1983) 'The distinction between indoctrination and education in England, 1549–1719'. *J. Hist. Ideas,* 44, 387–406.

SOTHEBY AND CO. (1974–7) Catalogues of a 'Highly important collection of children's books', six parts. Cited as HIC, I, etc.

SPUFFORD, Margaret (1981) *Small books and pleasant histories: popular fiction and its readership in seventeenth century England.* Methuen.

STARNES, D.T., and NOYES, Gertrude E. (1946) *The English dictionary from*

Cawdrey to Johnson, 1604–1755. U. North Carolina Press.

STATIONERS COMPANY (1875–94) *A transcript of the registers of the Company of Stationers of London, 1554–1640,* 5 vols. Ed. Edward Arber. Cited as *SR*(A).

STATIONERS COMPANY (1913) *A transcript of the registers of the Company of Stationers, 1640–1708,* 3 vols. Ed. G.E.B. Eyre. Cited as *SR*(E).

STEWART, W.A.C., and McCANN, W.P. (1967–8) *Educational innovators.* 2 vols. Macmillan. Vol. I covers 1750–1880.

STOCKHAM, Peter (1974) *Chapbook ABCs.* N.Y., Dover. Includes five facsimile reprints.

TAYLOR, W.L. (1953) 'Cloze procedure: a new tool for measuring readability'. *Journalism Quarterly,* 30, 415–33.

TEAFORD, John (1970) 'The transformation of Massachusetts education, 1670–1780'. *Hist. Edn. Quarterly* (Fall), 287–307.

The Term Catalogues (1903–6) Ed. Edward Arber. 3 vols. They cover the years 1668–1709. Cited as *TC.*

THOMPSON, Craig R. (1958) *The Schools in Tudor England.* Charlottesville: U. Virginia Press for Folger Shakespeare L. Reprinted in Louis B. Wright and V.A. La Mar, *Life and Letters in Tudor and Stuart England,* Cornell and Oxford, 1963.

THOMPSON, Henry (1879) *A history of Ackworth School during its first hundred years.*

THWAITE, Mary Florence (1972) *From primer to pleasure in reading: an introduction to the history of children's books in England . . . to 1900.* 2nd edn. Library Association. First published in 1963.

(1966) *John Newbery: A Little Pretty Pocket-Book.* Introduction to a facsimile of the 1767 edn. O.U.P.

TOMSON, Richard S. (1971) 'The English grammar school curriculum in the eighteenth century: a reappraisal.' *British J. Edl Studies,* 19, 32–9.

TREMAINE, Marie (1952) *A bibliography of Canadian imprints, 1751–1800.* Toronto U. Press.

TROUSDALE, Marion (1982) *Shakespeare and the rhetoricians.* Scolar Press.

TUCK, J.P. (1956) 'The beginning of English studies in the sixteenth century'. (Durham) *Research Review,* no. 7, 65–73.

TUCKER, Alan (1973) *Reading games, some Victorian examples with an essay on the teaching of reading.* Wymondham: Brewhouse Press Broadsheets no. 11.

TUER, Andrew White (1897) *History of the hornbook.* Leadenhall Press, 2 vols. 2nd edn. First published in 1896. 2nd edn reprinted, Amsterdam: Emmering, 1971; reprinted N.Y., Arno Press, 1 vol., 1979.

TYLER, Priscilla (1954) 'Grammars of the English language to 1850: with special emphasis on school grammars used in America'. Western Reserve U., (PhD dissertation).

VICKERS, Brian (1970) *Classical rhetoric in English poetry.* Macmillan.

VORLAT, Emma (1975) *The development of English grammatical theory, 1586–1737.* Louvain U. Press.

(1964) 'Progress in English grammar, 1585–1735', 4 vols. (mimeo). Luxembourg: Peiffer.

WALLIS, P.J. (1954) 'Joshua Poole, schoolmaster'. *N&Q,* 386–7.

WARDLE, David (1971) *Education and society in nineteenth century Nottingham.* C.U.P.

WATSON, Foster (1899) 'The acting of plays by schoolboys'. *Gent. Mag.*, 286, 274–84.

(1909) *The beginnings of the teaching of modern subjects in English.* Pitman; reprinted, S.R. Publishers, East Ardsley, 1971.

(1903) 'The curriculum and textbooks of English schools in the first half of the seventeenth century'. *Trans. Bibliog. Soc.*, 6, 159–267.

(1908) *The English grammar schools to 1660: their curriculum and practice.* C.U.P.; reprinted, Cass, 1968.

WATT, R. (1824) *Bibliotheca Britannica*, 4 vols. Edinburgh.

WEBSTER, Charles (1970) *Samuel Hartlib and the advancement of learning.* C.U.P.

(1975) 'The curriculum of the grammar schools and universities 1500–1600: a critical review of the literature'. *Hist. Edn.*, 4, 51–68.

WELCH, d'Alte A. (1972) *A bibliography of American children's books printed prior to 1821.* Worcester, Mass., American Antiquarian Society and Barre Publishers.

WELSH, Charles (1885) *A bookseller of the last century* [viz. John Newbery].

WHALLEY, Joyce I. (1974) *Cobwebs to catch flies: illustrated books for the nursery and schoolroom, 1700–1900.* Elek.

WRIGHT, C.J. (1979) 'Academics and their aims: English and Scottish approaches to university education in the nineteenth century'. *Hist. Edn.*, 8, 91–7.

WRIGHT, Louis B. (1935) *Middle-class culture in Elizabethan England.* Chapel Hill, N.C.; reissued Cornell U. Press, 1958.

INDEX